CONGRATULATIONS!

As a student purchasing Stock and Watson's *Introduction to Econometrics*, you are entitled to a prepaid subscription to premium services on our Companion Website at www.aw.com/stock_watson.

Be sure to visit the Website for data sets, projects, tutorials, quizzes, and more!

The duration of your subscription is 6 months.

To activate your prepaid subscription:

1. Launch your Web browser and go to the Companion Website at www.aw.com/stock_watson.
2. Click on Register/Log In.
3. Follow the instructions on the screen to register yourself as a new user. Your pre-assigned Access Code is located below:

ACCESS CODE:

WSSWIE-GRILL-GAPPY-ZONED-HIJAZ-POSSE

4. During registration, you will choose a personal Login Name and Password for use in logging into the Companion Website.
5. Once your personal Login Name and Password are confirmed, you can begin using the Companion Website.

This Access code can be used only once to establish a subscription. This subscription is not transferable.

If you did not purchase a new textbook, this Access Code may not be valid!

Introduction to Econometrics

The Addison–Wesley Series in Economics

Introduction to Econometrics

James H. Stock
HARVARD UNIVERSITY

Mark W. Watson
PRINCETON UNIVERSITY

Addison
Wesley

Boston   San Francisco   New York
London   Toronto   Sydney   Tokyo   Madrid
Mexico City   Munich   Paris   Cape Town   Hong Kong   Montreal

Editor-in-Chief: Denise Clinton
Executive Development Manager: Sylvia Mallory
Development Editor: Jane Tufts
Managing Editor: James Rigney
Production Supervisor: Katherine Watson
Design Manager: Regina Kolenda
Text Design: Electronic Publishing Services Inc., N.Y.C., and Regina Kolenda
Project Management, Art Studio, and Elecronic Composition: Electronic Publishing Services
    Inc., N.Y.C.
Cover Designer: Regina Kolenda
Supplements Editor: Andrea Basso
Senior Media Producer: Melissa Honig
Senior Manufacturing Buyer: Hugh Crawford
Manufacturing Coordinator: Caroline Fell
Marketing Manager: Adrienne D'Ambrosio

Printed in the United States of America.

Library of Congress Cataloging-in-Publication Data
Stock, James H.
Introduction to econometrics / James H. Stock, Mark W. Watson.
    p. cm.
Includes index.
ISBN 0-201-71595-3
  1. Econometrics. I. Watson, Mark W. II. Title
HB139 .S765 2003
330'.01'5195—dc21

                                                    2002071217

ISBN 0-201-71595-3

10 9 8 7 6 5 4   —CRW—05 04 03

Brief Contents

Contents

Key Concepts

PART THREE   Further Topics in Regression Analysis   269

PART FOUR   Regression Analysis of Economic Time Series Data   425

PART FIVE   The Econometric Theory of Regression Analysis   571

General Interest Boxes

Preface

Econometrics can be a fun course for both teacher and student. The real world of economics, business, and government is a complicated and messy place, full of competing ideas and questions that demand answers. Is it more effective to tackle drunk driving by passing tough laws or by increasing the tax on alcohol? Can you make money in the stock market by buying when prices are historically low, relative to earnings, or should you just sit tight as the random walk theory of stock prices suggests? Can we improve elementary education by reducing class sizes, or should we simply have our children listen to Mozart for ten minutes a day? Econometrics helps us to sort out sound ideas from crazy ones and to find quantitative answers to important quantitative questions. Econometrics opens a window on our complicated world that lets us see the relationships on which people, businesses, and governments base their decisions.

This textbook is designed for a first course in undergraduate econometrics. It is our experience that to make econometrics relevant in an introductory course, interesting applications must motivate the theory and the theory must match the applications. This simple principle represents a significant departure from the older generation of econometrics books, in which theoretical models and assumptions do not match the applications. It is no wonder that some students question the relevance of econometrics after they spend much of their time learning assumptions that they subsequently realize are unrealistic, so that they must then learn "solutions" to "problems" that arise when the applications do not match the assumptions. We believe that it is far better to motivate the need for tools with a concrete application, and then to provide a few simple assumptions that match the application. Because the theory is immediately relevant to the applications, this approach can make econometrics come alive.

Features of This Book

This textbook differs from others in three main ways. First, we integrate real-world questions and data into the development of the theory, and we take seriously the substantive findings of the resulting empirical analysis. Second, our choice of topics reflects modern theory and practice. Third, we provide theory and assumptions that match the applications. Our aim is to teach students to become sophisticated consumers of econometrics and to do so at a level of mathematics appropriate for an introductory course.

Real-world Questions and Data

We organize each methodological topic around an important real-world question that demands a specific numerical answer. For example, we teach single-variable regression, multiple regression, and functional form analysis in the context of estimating the effect of school inputs on school outputs. (Do smaller elementary school class sizes produce higher test scores?) We teach panel data methods in the context of analyzing the effect of drunk driving laws on traffic fatalities. We use possible racial discrimination in the market for home loans as the empirical application for teaching regression with a binary dependent variable (logit and probit). We teach instrumental variable estimation in the context of estimating the demand elasticity for cigarettes. Although these examples involve economic reasoning, all can be understood with only a single introductory course in economics, and many can be understood without any previous economics coursework. Thus the instructor can focus on teaching econometrics, not microeconomics or macroeconomics.

We treat all our empirical applications seriously and in a way that shows students how they can learn from data but at the same time be self-critical and aware of the limitations of empirical analyses. Through each application, we teach students to explore alternative specifications and thereby to assess whether their substantive findings are robust. The questions asked in the empirical applications are important, and we provide serious and, we think, credible answers. We encourage students and instructors to disagree, however, and invite them to reanalyze the data, which are provided on the textbook's companion Web site (**www.aw.com/stock_watson**).

Contemporary Choice of Topics

Econometrics has come a long way in the past two decades. The topics we cover reflect the best of contemporary applied econometrics. One can only do so much in an introductory course, so we focus on procedures and tests that are commonly used in practice. For example:

- *Instrumental variables regression*. We present instrumental variables regression as a general method for handling correlation between the error term and a regressor, which can arise for many reasons, including simultaneous causality. The two assumptions for a valid instrument—exogeneity and relevance—

are given equal billing. We follow that presentation with an extended discussion of where instruments come from, and with tests of overidentifying restrictions and diagnostics for weak instruments—and we explain what to do if these diagnostics suggest problems.

- *Program evaluation.* An increasing number of econometric studies analyze either randomized controlled experiments or quasi-experiments, also known as natural experiments. We address these topics, often collectively referred to as program evaluation, in Chapter 11. We present this research strategy as an alternative approach to the problems of omitted variables, simultaneous causality, and selection, and we assess both the strengths and the weaknesses of studies using experimental or quasi-experimental data.

- *Forecasting.* The chapter on forecasting (Chapter 12) considers univariate (autoregressive) and multivariate forecasts using time series regression, not large simultaneous equation structural models. We focus on simple and reliable tools, such as autoregressions and model selection via an information criterion, that work well in practice. This chapter also features a practically oriented treatment of stochastic trends (unit roots), unit root tests, tests for structural breaks (at known and unknown dates), and pseudo out-of-sample forecasting, all in the context of developing stable and reliable time series forecasting models.

- *Time series regression.* We make a clear distinction between two very different applications of time series regression: forecasting and estimation of dynamic causal effects. The chapter on causal inference using time series data (Chapter 13) pays careful attention to when different estimation methods, including generalized least squares, will or will not lead to valid causal inferences, and when it is advisable to estimate dynamic regressions using OLS with heteroskedasticity- and autocorrelation-consistent standard errors.

Theory That Matches Applications

Although econometric tools are best motivated by empirical applications, students need to learn enough econometric theory to understand the strengths and limitations of those tools. We provide a modern treatment in which the fit between theory and applications is as tight as possible, while keeping the mathematics at a level that requires only algebra.

Modern empirical applications share some common characteristics: the data sets typically are large (hundreds of observations, often more); regressors are not fixed over repeated samples but rather are collected by random sampling (or some other mechanism that makes them random); the data are not normally distributed; and there is no a priori reason to think that the errors are homoskedastic (although often there are reasons to think that they are heteroskedastic).

These observations lead to important differences between the theoretical development in this textbook and other textbooks.

- *Large-sample approach.* Because data sets are large, from the outset we use large-sample normal approximations to sampling distributions for hypothesis testing and confidence intervals. Our experience is that it takes less time to teach the rudiments of large-sample approximations than to teach the Student t and exact F distributions, degrees-of-freedom corrections, and so forth. This large-sample approach also saves students the frustration of discovering that, because of nonnormal errors, the exact distribution theory they just mastered is irrelevant. Once taught in the context of the sample mean, the large-sample approach to hypothesis testing and confidence intervals carries directly through multiple regression analysis, logit and probit, instrumental variables estimation, and time series methods.

- *Random sampling.* Because regressors are rarely fixed in econometric applications, from the outset we treat data on all variables (dependent and independent) as the result of random sampling. This assumption matches our initial applications to cross-sectional data; it extends readily to panel and time series data; and because of our large-sample approach, it poses no additional conceptual or mathematical difficulties.

- *Heteroskedasticity.* Applied econometricians routinely use heteroskedasticity-robust standard errors to eliminate worries about whether heteroskedasticity is present or not. In this book, we move beyond treating heteroskedasticity as an exception or a "problem" to be "solved"; instead, we allow for heteroskedasticity from the outset and simply use heteroskedasticity-robust standard errors. We present homoskedasticity as a special case that provides a theoretical motivation for OLS.

Skilled Producers, Sophisticated Consumers

We hope that students using this book will become sophisticated consumers of empirical analysis. To do so, they must learn not only how to use the tools of regression analysis, but also how to assess the validity of empirical analyses presented to them.

Our approach to teaching how to assess an empirical study is threefold. First, immediately after introducing the main tools of regression analysis, we devote

Chapter 7 to the threats to internal and external validity of an empirical study. This chapter discusses data problems and issues of generalizing findings to other settings. It also examines the main threats to regression analysis, including omitted variables, functional form misspecification, errors-in-variables, selection, and simultaneity—and ways to recognize these threats in practice.

Second, we apply these methods for assessing empirical studies to the empirical analysis of the ongoing examples in the book. We do so by considering alternative specifications and by systematically addressing the various threats to validity of the analyses presented in the book.

Third, to become sophisticated consumers, students need firsthand experience as producers. Active learning beats passive learning, and econometrics is an ideal course for active learning. For this reason, the textbook Web site features data sets, software, and suggestions for empirical exercises of differing scopes.

Approach to Mathematics and Level of Rigor

Our aim is for students to develop a sophisticated understanding of the tools of modern regression analysis, whether the course is taught at a "high" or a "low" level of mathematics. Parts I-IV of the text (which cover the substantive material) are accessible to students with only precalculus mathematics. Parts I-IV have fewer equations, and more applications, than many introductory econometrics books, and far fewer equations than books aimed at mathematical sections of undergraduate courses. But more equations do not imply a more sophisticated treatment. In our experience, a more mathematical treatment does not lead to a deeper understanding for most students.

This said, different students learn differently, and for the mathematically well-prepared students, learning can be enhanced by a more explicitly mathematical treatment. Part V therefore contains an introduction to econometric theory that is appropriate for students with a stronger mathematical background. We believe that, when the mathematical chapters in Part V are used in conjunction with the material in Parts I-IV, this book is suitable for advanced undergraduate or master's level econometrics courses.

Contents and Organization

There are five parts to the textbook. This textbook assumes that the student has had a course in probability and statistics, although we review that material in Part I. We cover the core material of regression analysis in Part II. Parts III, IV, and V present additional topics that build on the core treatment in Part II.

Part I

Chapter 1 introduces econometrics and stresses the importance of providing quantitative answers to quantitative questions. It discusses the concept of causality in statistical studies and surveys the different types of data encountered in econometrics. Material from probability and statistics is reviewed in Chapters 2 and 3, respectively; whether these chapters are taught in a given course, or simply provided as a reference, depends on the background of the students.

Part II

Chapter 4 introduces regression with a single regressor and ordinary least squares (OLS). In Chapter 5, students learn how they can address omitted variable bias using multiple regression, thereby estimating the effect of one independent variable while holding other independent variables constant. In Chapter 6, the methods of multiple regression are extended to models with nonlinear population regression functions that are linear in the parameters (so that they can be estimated by OLS). In Chapter 7, students step back and learn how to identify the strengths and limitations of regression studies, seeing in the process how to apply the concepts of internal and external validity.

Part III

Part III presents extensions of regression methods. In Chapter 8, students learn how to use panel data to control for unobserved variables that are constant over time. Chapter 9 covers regression with a binary dependent variable. Chapter 10 shows how instrumental variables regression can be used to address a variety of problems that produce correlation between the error term and the regressor, and examines how one might find and evaluate valid instruments. Chapter 11 introduces students to the analysis of data from experiments and quasi-, or natural, experiments, topics often referred to as "program evaluation."

Part IV

Part IV takes up regression with time series data. Chapter 12 focuses on forecasting and introduces various modern tools for analyzing time series regressions such as unit root tests and tests for stability. Chapter 13 discusses the use of time series data to estimate causal relations. Chapter 14 presents some more advanced tools for time series analysis, including models of conditional heteroskedasticity.

Part V

Part V is an introduction to econometric theory. This part is more than an appendix that fills in mathematical details omitted from the text. Rather, it is a self-contained treatment of the econometric theory of estimation and inference in the linear regression model. Chapter 15 develops the theory of regression analysis for a single regressor; the exposition does not use matrix algebra, although it does demand a higher level of mathematical sophistication than the rest of the text. Chapter 16 presents and studies the multiple regression model in matrix form.

Prerequisites Within the Book

Because different instructors like to emphasize different material, we wrote this book with diverse teaching preferences in mind. To the maximum extent possible, the chapters in Parts III, IV, and V are "stand-alone" in the sense that they do not require first teaching all the preceding chapters. The specific prerequisites for each chapter are described in Table I. Although we have found that the sequence of topics adopted in the textbook works well in our own courses, the chapters are written in a way that allows instructors to present topics in a different order if they so desire.

TABLE I   Guide to Prerequisites for Special-Topic Chapters in Parts Three–Five

Chapter	Prerequisite parts or chapters							
	Part I	Part II	8.1, 8.2	10.1, 10.2	12.1-12.4	12.5-12.8	13	15
8	▨	▨						
9	▨	▨						
10.1, 10.2	▨	▨						
10.3–10.6	▨	▨	▨	▨				
11	▨	▨	▨	▨				
12	▨	▨						
13	▨	▨			▨			
14	▨	▨			▨	▨	▨	
15	▨	▨						
16	▨	▨						▨

This table shows the minimum prerequisites needed to cover the material in a given chapter. For example, estimation of dynamic causal effects (Chapter 13) first requires Part One (as needed, depending on student preparation), Part Two, and Sections 12.1-12.4.

Sample Courses

Several different types of courses can be taught using this book.

Standard Introductory Econometrics

This course introduces econometrics (Chapter 1) and reviews probability and statistics as needed (Chapters 2 and 3). It then moves on to regression with a single regressor, multiple regression, the basics of functional form analysis, and the evaluation of regression studies (all of Part II). The course proceeds to cover regression with panel data (Chapter 8), regression with a limited dependent variable (Chapter 9), and/or instrumental variables regression (Chapter 10), as time permits. The course concludes with experiments and quasi-experiments in Chapter 11, topics that provide an opportunity to return to the questions of estimating causal effects raised at the beginning of the semester and to recapitulate core regression methods. *Prerequisites: algebra and introductory statistics.*

Introductory Econometrics with Time Series and Forecasting Applications

Like the standard introductory course, this course covers all of Part I (as needed) and all of Part II. Optionally, the course next provides a brief introduction to panel data (Sections 8.1 and 8.2) and takes up instrumental variables regression (Chapter 10, or just Sections 10.1 and 10.2). The course then proceeds to Part IV, covering forecasting (Chapter 12) and estimation of dynamic causal effects (Chapter 13). If time permits, the course can include some advanced topics in time series analysis such as conditional heteroskedasticity (Section 14.5). *Prerequisites: algebra and introductory statistics.*

Applied Time Series Analysis and Forecasting

This book also can be used for a short course on applied time series and forecasting, for which a course on regression analysis is a prerequisite. Some time is spent reviewing the tools of basic regression analysis in Part II, depending on student preparation. The course then moves directly to Part IV and works through forecasting (Chapter 12), estimation of dynamic causal effects (Chapter 13), and advanced topics in time series analysis (Chapter 14), including vector autoregressions and conditional heteroskedasticity. An important component of this course would be hands-on forecasting exercises, available to instructors on the book's accompanying Web site. *Prerequisites: algebra and basic introductory econometrics or the equivalent.*

Introduction to Econometric Theory

This book is also suitable for an advanced undergraduate course in which the students have a strong mathematical preparation, or for a master's level course in econometrics. The course briefly reviews the theory of statistics and probability as necessary (Part I). The course introduces regression analysis using the non-mathematical, applications-based treatment of Part II. This introduction is followed by the theoretical development in Chapters 15 and 16. The course then takes up regression with a limited dependent variable (Chapter 9) and maximum likelihood estimation (Appendix 9.2). Next, the course optionally turns to instrumental variables regression (Chapter 10), time series methods (Chapter 12), and/or the estimation of causal effects using time series data and generalized least squares (Chapter 13 and Section 16.6). *Prerequisites: calculus and introductory statistics. Chapter 16 assumes some previous exposure to matrix algebra.*

Pedagogical Features

The textbook has a variety of pedagogical features aimed at helping students to understand, to retain, and to apply the essential ideas. *Chapter introductions* provide a real-world grounding and motivation, as well as a brief road map highlighting the sequence of the discussion. *Key terms* are boldfaced and defined in context throughout each chapter, and *Key Concept boxes* at regular intervals recap the central ideas. *General interest boxes* provide interesting excursions into related topics and highlight real-world studies that use the methods or concepts being discussed in the text. A numbered *Summary* concluding each chapter serves as a helpful framework for reviewing the main points of coverage. The questions in the *Review the Concepts* section check students' understanding of the core content, and *Exercises* give more intensive practice working with the concepts and techniques introduced in the chapter. At the end of the textbook, the *References* section lists sources for further reading, the *Appendix* provides statistical tables, and a *Glossary* conveniently defines all the key terms in the book.

Supplements to Accompany the Textbook

An array of supplementary resources for instructors and students is available to adopters of *Introduction to Econometrics*. The *Solutions Manual,* by Jiangfeng Zhang of the University of California, Berkeley, provides worked solutions to all the end-of-chapter exercises. For instructors, a *Test Bank,* by Manfred W. Keil of

Claremont McKenna College, offers a rich supply of test problems and questions of various types. The Test Bank is available on the *Instructor's Resource CD*, which also contains PowerPoint slides of the text figures, tables, and Key Concepts; and the complete Solutions Manual.

In addition, a companion Web site, found at **www.aw.com/stock_watson**, provides a wide range of additional resources for students and faculty. These include data sets for all the text examples, suggested empirical exercises, ideas for student projects, sample solutions to the text's end-of-chapter exercises, student practice quizzes, PowerPoint slides, EViews and STATA tutorials for students, and an Excel add-in for OLS regressions. And for instructors interested in course management, we offer CourseCompass, an interactive online learning environment powered by Blackboard. Contact your Addison-Wesley representative for details.

Acknowledgments

A great many people contributed to this project. Our biggest debts of gratitude are to our colleagues at Harvard and Princeton who used early drafts of this book in their classrooms. At Harvard's Kennedy School of Government, Suzanne Cooper provided invaluable suggestions and detailed comments on multiple drafts. As a co-teacher with one of the authors (Stock), she also helped to vet much of the material in this book while it was being developed for a required course for master's students at the Kennedy School. We are also indebted to two other Kennedy School colleagues, Alberto Abadie and Sue Dynarski, for their patient explanations of quasi-experiments and the field of program evaluation and for their detailed comments on early drafts of the text. At Princeton, Eli Tamer taught from an early draft and also provided helpful comments on the penultimate draft of the book.

We also owe much to many of our friends and colleagues in econometrics who spent time talking with us about the substance of this book and who collectively made so many helpful suggestions. Bruce Hansen (University of Wisconsin, Madison) and Bo Honore (Princeton) provided helpful feedback on very early outlines and preliminary versions of the core material in Part II. Joshua Angrist (MIT) and Guido Imbens (University of California, Berkeley) provided thoughtful suggestions about our treatment of materials on program evaluation. Our presentation of the material on time series has benefited from discussions with Yacine Ait-Sahalia (Princeton), Graham Elliott (University of California, San Diego), Andrew Harvey (Cambridge University), and Christopher Sims (Princeton). Finally, many people made helpful suggestions on parts of the manuscript close to their area of expertise: Don Andrews (Yale), John Bound (University of Michigan), Gregory

Chow (Princeton), Thomas Downes (Tufts), David Drukker (Stata, Corp.), Jean Baldwin Grossman (Princeton), Eric Hanushek (the Hoover Institution), James Heckman (University of Chicago), Han Hong (Princeton), Caroline Hoxby (Harvard), Alan Krueger (Princeton), Steven Levitt (University of Chicago), Richard Light (Harvard), David Neumark (Michigan State University), Joseph Newhouse (Harvard), Pierre Perron (Boston University), Kenneth Warner (University of Michigan), and Richard Zeckhauser (Harvard).

Many people were very generous in providing us with data. The California test score data were constructed with the assistance of Les Axelrod of the Standards and Assessments Division, California Department of Education. We are grateful to Charlie DePascale, Student Assessment Services, Massachusetts Department of Education, for his help with aspects of the Massachusetts test score data set. Christopher Ruhm (University of North Carolina, Greensboro) graciously provided us with his data set on drunk driving laws and traffic fatalities. The research department at the Federal Reserve Bank of Boston deserves thanks for putting together their data on racial discrimination in mortgage lending; we particularly thank Geoffrey Tootell for providing us with the updated version of the data set we use in Chapter 9, and Lynn Browne for explaining its policy context. We thank Jonathan Gruber (MIT) for sharing his data on cigarette sales, which we analyze in Chapter 10, and Alan Krueger (Princeton) for his help with the Tennessee STAR data that we analyze in Chapter 11.

We are also grateful for the many constructive, detailed, and thoughtful comments we received from those who reviewed various drafts for Addison-Wesley:

Michael Abbott, Queen's University, Canada

Richard J. Agnello, University of Delaware

Clopper Almon, University of Maryland

Joshua Angrist, Massachusetts Institute of Technology

Swarnjit S. Arora, University of Wisconsin, Milwaukee

Christopher F. Baum, Boston College

McKinley L. Blackburn, University of South Carolina

Alok Bohara, University of New Mexico

Chi-Young Choi, University of New Hampshire

Dennis Coates, University of Maryland, Baltimore County

Tim Conley, Graduate School of Business, University of Chicago

Douglas Dalenberg, University of Montana

Antony Davies, Duquesne University

Joanne M. Doyle, James Madison University

David Eaton, Murray State University

Adrian R. Fleissig, California State University, Fullerton

Rae Jean B. Goodman, United States Naval Academy

Bruce E. Hansen, University of Wisconsin, Madison

Peter Reinhard Hansen, Brown University

Ian T. Henry, University of Melbourne, Australia

Marc Henry, Columbia University

William Horrace, University of Arizona

Òscar Jordà, University of California, Davis

Frederick L. Joutz, The George Washington University

Elia Kacapyr, Ithaca College

Manfred W. Keil, Claremont McKenna College

Eugene Kroch, Villanova University

Gary Krueger, Macalester College

Kajal Lahiri, State University of New York, Albany

Daniel Lee, Shippensburg University

Tung Liu, Ball State University

Ken Matwiczak, LBJ School of Public Affairs, University of Texas, Austin

KimMarie McGoldrick, University of Richmond

Robert McNown, University of Colorado, Boulder

H. Naci Mocan, University of Colorado, Denver

Mototsugu Shintani, Vanderbilt University

Mico Mrkaic, Duke University

Serena Ng, Johns Hopkins University

Jan Ondrich, Syracuse University

Pierre Perron, Boston University

Robert Phillips, The George Washington University

Simran Sahi, University of Minnesota

Sunil Sapra, California State University, Los Angeles

Frank Schorfheide, University of Pennsylvania

Leslie S. Stratton, Virginia Commonwealth University

Jane Sung, Truman State University

Christopher Taber, Northwestern University

Petra Todd, University of Pennsylvania

John Veitch, University of San Francisco

Edward J. Vytlacil, Stanford University

M. Daniel Westbrook, Georgetown University

Tiemen Woutersen, University of Western Ontario

Phanindra V. Wunnava, Middlebury College

Zhenhui Xu, Georgia College and State University

Yong Yin, State University of New York, Buffalo

Jiangfeng Zhang, University of California, Berkeley

John Xu Zheng, University of Texas, Austin

We thank several people for carefully checking the page proof for errors. Kerry Griffin and Yair Listokin read the entire manuscript, and Andrew Fraker, Ori Heffetz, Amber Henry, Hong Li, Alessandro Tarozzi, and Matt Watson worked through several chapters.

We have benefited from the help of an exceptional development editor, Jane Tufts, whose creativity, hard work, and attention to detail have improved the book in many ways, large and small. Addison-Wesley provided us with first-rate support, starting with our excellent editor, Sylvia Mallory, and extending through the entire publishing team. Jane and Sylvia patiently taught us a lot about writing, organization, and presentation, and their efforts are evident on every page of this book. We also extend our thanks to the rest of the superb Addison-Wesley team, who helped us through every step of the intricate process of publishing this book: Adrienne D'Ambrosio (marketing manager), Melissa Honig (senior media producer), Regina Kolenda (senior designer), Katherine Watson (production supervisor), and especially Denise Clinton (editor-in-chief).

Above all, we are indebted to our families for their endurance throughout this project. Writing this book took a long time—for them, the project must have seemed endless. They more than anyone bore the burden of this commitment, and for their help and support we are deeply grateful.

PART ONE | # Introduction and Review

CHAPTER 1

Economic Questions and Data

A sk a half dozen econometricians what econometrics is and you could get a half dozen different answers. One might tell you that econometrics is the science of testing economic theories. A second might tell you that econometrics is the set of tools used for forecasting future values of economic variables, such as a firm's sales, the overall growth of the economy, or stock prices. Another might say that econometrics is the process of fitting mathematical economic models to real-world data. A fourth might tell you that it is the art and science of using historical data to make numerical, or quantitative, policy recommendations in government and business.

In fact, all these answers are right. At a broad level, econometrics is the science and art of using economic theory and statistical techniques to analyze economic data. Econometric methods are used in many branches of economics, including finance, labor economics, macroeconomics, microeconomics, marketing, and economic policy. Econometric methods are also commonly used in other social sciences, including political science and sociology.

This book introduces you to the core set of methods used by econometricians. We will use these methods to answer a variety of specific, quantitative questions taken from the world of business and government policy. This chapter poses four of those questions and discusses, in general terms, the econometric approach to answering them. The chapter concludes with a survey of the main types of data available to econometricians for answering these and other quantitative economic questions.

1.1   Economic Questions We Examine

Many decisions in economics, business, and government hinge on understanding relationships among variables in the world around us. These decisions require quantitative answers to quantitative questions.

This book examines several quantitative questions taken from current issues in economics. Four of these questions concern education policy, racial bias in mortgage lending, cigarette consumption, and macroeconomic forecasting.

Question #1: Does Reducing Class Size Improve Elementary School Education?

Proposals for reform of the U.S. public education system generate heated debate. Many of the proposals concern the youngest students, those in elementary schools. Elementary school education has various objectives, such as developing social skills, but for many parents and educators the most important objective is basic academic learning: reading, writing, and basic mathematics. One prominent proposal for improving basic learning is to reduce class sizes at elementary schools. With fewer students in the classroom, the argument goes, each student gets more of the teacher's attention, there are fewer class disruptions, learning is enhanced, and grades improve.

But what, precisely, is the effect on elementary school education of reducing class size? Reducing class size costs money: it requires hiring more teachers and, if the school is already at capacity, building more classrooms. A decision maker contemplating hiring more teachers must weigh these costs against the benefits. To weigh costs and benefits, however, the decision maker must have a precise quantitative understanding of the likely benefits. Is the beneficial effect on basic learning of smaller classes large or small? Is it possible that smaller class size actually has no effect on basic learning?

Although common sense and everyday experience may suggest that more learning occurs when there are fewer students, common sense cannot provide a quantitative answer to the question of what exactly is the effect on basic learning of reducing class size. To provide such an answer, we must examine empirical evidence—that is, evidence based on data—relating class size to basic learning in elementary schools.

In this book, we examine the relationship between class size and basic learning using data gathered from 420 California school districts in 1998. In the California data, students in districts with small class sizes tend to perform better on standardized tests than students in districts with larger classes. While this fact is consistent with the idea that smaller classes produce better test scores, it might simply reflect many other advantages that students in districts with small classes have over their counterparts in districts with large classes. For example, districts with small class sizes tend to have wealthier residents than districts with large classes, so students in small-class districts could have more opportunities for learning outside the classroom. It could be these extra learning opportunities that lead to higher test scores, not smaller class sizes. In Part II, we use multiple regression analysis to isolate the effect of changes in class size from changes in other factors, such as the economic background of the students.

Question #2: Is There Racial Discrimination in the Market for Home Loans?

Most people buy their homes with the help of a mortgage, a large loan secured by the value of the home. By law, U.S. lending institutions cannot take race into account when deciding to grant or deny a request for a mortgage: applicants who are identical in all ways but their race should be equally likely to have their mortgage applications approved. In theory, then, there should be no racial bias in mortgage lending.

In contrast to this theoretical conclusion, researchers at the Federal Reserve Bank of Boston found (using data from the early 1990s) that 28% of black applicants are denied mortgages, while only 9% of white applicants are denied. Do these data indicate that, in practice, there is racial bias in mortgage lending? If so, how large is it?

The fact that more black than white applicants are denied in the Boston Fed data does not by itself provide evidence of discrimination by mortgage lenders, because the black and white applicants differ in many ways other than their race. Before concluding that there is bias in the mortgage market, these data must be examined more closely to see if there is a difference in the probability of being denied for *otherwise identical* applicants and, if so, whether this difference is large or small. To do so, in Chapter 9 we introduce econometric methods that make it possible to quantify the effect of race on chance of obtaining a mortgage, *holding constant* other applicant characteristics, notably their ability to repay the loan.

Question #3: How Much Do Cigarette Taxes Reduce Smoking?

Cigarette smoking is a major public health concern worldwide. Many of the costs of smoking, such as the medical expenses of caring for those made sick by smoking and the less quantifiable costs to nonsmokers who prefer not to breathe secondhand cigarette smoke, are borne by other members of society. Because these costs are borne by people other than the smoker, there is a role for government intervention in reducing cigarette consumption. One of the most flexible tools for cutting consumption is to increase taxes on cigarettes.

Basic economics says that if cigarette prices go up, consumption will go down. But by how much? If the sales price goes up by 1%, by what percentage will the quantity of cigarettes sold decrease? The percentage change in the quantity demanded resulting from a 1% increase in price is the *price elasticity of demand*. If we want to reduce smoking by a certain amount, say 20%, by raising taxes, then we need to know the price elasticity to calculate the price increase necessary to achieve this reduction in consumption. But what is the price elasticity of demand for cigarettes?

Although economic theory provides us with the concepts that help us answer this question, it does not tell us the numerical value of the price elasticity of demand. To learn the elasticity we must examine empirical evidence about the behavior of smokers and potential smokers; in other words, we need to analyze data on cigarette consumption and prices.

The data we examine are cigarette sales, prices, taxes, and personal income for U.S. states in the 1980s and 1990s. In these data, states with low taxes, and thus low cigarette prices, have high smoking rates, and states with high prices have low smoking rates. However, the analysis of these data is complicated because causality runs both ways: low taxes lead to high demand, but if there are many smokers in the state then local politicians might try to keep cigarette taxes low to satisfy their smoking constituents. In Chapter 10 we study methods for handling this "simultaneous causality" and use those methods to estimate the price elasticity of cigarette demand.

Question #4: What Will the Rate of Inflation Be Next Year?

It seems that people always want a sneak preview of the future. What will sales be next year at a firm considering investing in new equipment? Will the stock market go up next month and, if so, by how much? Will city tax receipts next year cover planned expenditures on city services? Will your microeconomics exam next week focus on externalities or monopolies? Will Saturday be a nice day to go to the beach?

One aspect of the future in which macroeconomists and financial economists are particularly interested is the rate of overall price inflation during the next year. A financial professional might advise a client whether to make a loan or to take one out at a given rate of interest, depending on her best guess of the rate of inflation over the coming year. Economists at central banks like the Federal Reserve Board in Washington, D.C., and the European Central Bank in Frankfurt, Germany, are responsible for keeping the rate of price inflation under control, so their decisions about how to set interest rates rely on the outlook for inflation over the next year. If they think the rate of inflation will increase by a percentage point, then they might increase interest rates by more than that to slow down an economy that, in their view, risks overheating. If they guess wrong, they risk causing either an unnecessary recession or an undesirable jump in the rate of inflation.

Professional economists who rely on precise numerical forecasts use econometric models to make those forecasts. A forecaster's job is to predict the future using the past, and econometricians do this by using economic theory and statistical techniques to quantify relationships in historical data.

The data we use to forecast inflation are the rates of inflation and unemployment in the United States. An important empirical relationship in macroeconomic data is the "Phillips curve," in which a currently low value of the unemployment rate is associated with an increase in the rate of inflation over the next year. One of the inflation forecasts we develop and evaluate in Chapter 12 is based on the Phillips curve.

Quantitative Questions, Quantitative Answers

Each of these four questions requires a numerical answer. Economic theory provides clues about that answer—cigarette consumption ought to go down when the price goes up—but the actual value of the number must be learned empirically, that is, by analyzing data. Because we use data to answer quantitative questions, our answers always have some uncertainty: a different set of data would produce a different numerical answer. Therefore, the conceptual framework for the analysis needs to provide both a numerical answer to the question and a measure of how precise the answer is.

The conceptual framework used in this book is the multiple regression model, the mainstay of econometrics. This model, introduced in Part II, provides a mathematical way to quantify how a change in one variable affects another variable, holding other things constant. For example, what effect does a change in class size have on test scores, *holding constant* student characteristics (such as family income) that a school district administrator cannot control? What effect does your race have on your chances of having a mortgage application granted, *holding constant* other factors such as your ability to repay the loan? What effect does a 1% increase in the price of cigarettes have on cigarette consumption, *holding constant* the income of smokers and potential smokers? The multiple regression model and its extensions provide a framework for answering these questions using data and for quantifying the uncertainty associated with those answers.

1.2   **Causal Effects and Idealized Experiments**

Like many questions encountered in econometrics, the first three questions in Section 1.1 concern causal relationships among variables. In common usage, an action is said to cause an outcome if the outcome is the direct result, or consequence, of that action. Touching a hot stove causes you to get burned; drinking water causes you to be less thirsty; putting air in your tires causes them to inflate; putting fertilizer on your tomato plants causes them to produce more tomatoes. Causality means that a specific action (applying fertilizer) leads to a specific, measurable consequence (more tomatoes).

Estimation of Causal Effects

How best might we measure the causal effect on tomato yield (measured in kilograms) of applying a certain amount of fertilizer, say 100 grams of fertilizer per square meter?

One way to measure this causal effect is to conduct an experiment. In that experiment, a horticultural researcher plants many plots of tomatoes. Each plot is tended identically, with one exception: some plots get 100 grams of fertilizer per square meter, while the rest get none. Moreover, whether a plot is fertilized or not is determined randomly by a computer, ensuring that any other differences between the plots are unrelated to whether they receive fertilizer. At the end of the growing season, the horticulturalist weighs the harvest from each plot. The difference between the average yield per square meter of the treated and untreated plots is the effect on tomato production of the fertilizer treatment.

This is an example of a **randomized controlled experiment**. It is controlled in the sense that there are both a **control group** that receives no treatment (no fertilizer) and a **treatment group** that receives the treatment (100 g/m^2 of fertilizer). It is randomized in the sense that the treatment is assigned randomly. This random assignment eliminates the possibility of a systematic relationship between, for example, how sunny the plot is and whether it receives fertilizer, so that the only systematic difference between the treatment and control groups is the treatment. If this experiment is properly implemented on a large enough scale, then it will yield an estimate of the causal effect on the outcome of interest (tomato production) of the treatment (applying 100 g/m^2 of fertilizer).

In this book, the **causal effect** is defined to be the effect on an outcome of a given action or treatment, as measured in an ideal randomized controlled experiment. In such an experiment, the only systematic reason for differences in outcomes between the treatment and control groups is the treatment itself.

It is possible to imagine an ideal randomized controlled experiment to answer each of the first three questions in Section 1.1. For example, to study class size one can imagine randomly assigning "treatments" of different class sizes to different groups of students. If the experiment is designed and executed so that the only systematic difference between the groups of students is their class size, then in theory this experiment would estimate the effect on test scores of reducing class size, holding all else constant.

The concept of an ideal randomized controlled experiment is useful because it gives a definition of a causal effect. In practice, however, it is not possible to perform ideal experiments. In fact, experiments are rare in econometrics because often they are unethical, impossible to execute satisfactorily, or prohibitively expensive. The concept of the ideal randomized controlled experiment does, however, provide a theoretical benchmark for an econometric analysis of causal effects using actual data.

Forecasting and Causality

Although the first three questions in Section 1.1 concern causal effects, the fourth—forecasting inflation—does not. You do not need to know a causal relationship to make a good forecast. A good way to "forecast" if it is raining is to observe whether pedestrians are using umbrellas, but the act of using an umbrella does not cause it to rain.

Even though forecasting need not involve causal relationships, macroeconomic theory suggests patterns and relationships that might be useful for forecasting inflation. As we see in Chapter 12, multiple regression analysis allows us to quantify historical relationships suggested by economic theory, to check whether those relationships have been stable over time, to make quantitative forecasts about the future, and to assess the accuracy of those forecasts.

1.3 Data: Sources and Types

In econometrics, data come from one of two sources: experiments or nonexperimental observations of the world. This book examines both experimental and nonexperimental data sets.

Experimental versus Observational Data

Experimental data come from experiments designed to evaluate a treatment or policy or to investigate a causal effect. For example, the state of Tennessee financed a large randomized controlled experiment examining class size in the 1980s. In that experiment, which we examine in Chapter 11, thousands of students were randomly assigned to classes of different sizes for several years and were given annual standardized tests.

The Tennessee class size experiment cost millions of dollars and required the ongoing cooperation of many administrators, parents, and teachers over several years. Because real-world experiments with human subjects are difficult to administer and to control, they have flaws relative to ideal randomized controlled experiments. Moreover, in some circumstances experiments are not only expensive and difficult to administer but also unethical. (Would it be ethical to offer randomly selected teenagers inexpensive cigarettes to see how many they buy?) Because of these financial, practical, and ethical problems, experiments in economics are rare. Instead, most economic data are obtained by observing real-world behavior.

Data obtained by observing actual behavior outside an experimental setting are called **observational data**. Observational data are collected using surveys, such as a telephone survey of consumers, and administrative records, such as historical records on mortgage applications maintained by lending institutions.

Observational data pose major challenges to econometric attempts to estimate causal effects, and the tools of econometrics tackle these challenges. In the real world, levels of "treatment" (the amount of fertilizer in the tomato example, the student-teacher ratio in the class size example) are not assigned at random, so it is difficult to sort out the effect of the "treatment" from other relevant factors. Much of econometrics, and much of this book, is devoted to methods for meeting the challenges encountered when real-world data are used to estimate causal effects.

Whether the data are experimental or observational, data sets come in three main types: cross-sectional data, time series data, and panel data. In this book you will encounter all three types.

Cross-Sectional Data

Data on different entities—workers, consumers, firms, governmental units, and so forth—for a single time period are called **cross-sectional data**. For example, the data on test scores in California school districts are cross sectional. Those data are for 420 entities (school districts) for a single time period (1998). In general, the number of entities on which we have observations is denoted by n, so for example in the California data set $n = 420$.

The California test score data set contains measurements of several different variables for each district. Some of these data are tabulated in Table 1.1. Each row lists data for a different district. For example, the average test score for the first district ("district #1") is 690.8; this is the average of the math and science test scores for all fifth graders in that district in 1998 on a standardized test (the Stanford Achievement Test). The average student-teacher ratio in that district is 17.89, that is, the number of students in district #1, divided by the number of classroom teachers in district #1, is 17.89. Average expenditure per pupil in district #1 is $6,385. The percent of students in that district still learning English—that is, the percent of students for whom English is a second language and who are not yet proficient in English—is 0%.

The remaining rows present data for other districts. The order of the rows is arbitrary, and the number of the district, which is called the **observation number,** is an arbitrarily assigned number that organizes the data. As you can see in the table, all the variables listed vary considerably.

With cross-sectional data, we can learn about relationships among variables by studying differences across people, firms, or other economic entities during a single time period.

TABLE 1.1   Selected Observations on Test Scores and Other Variables for California School Districts in 1998

Observation (district) number	District average test score (fifth grade)	Student-teacher ratio	Expenditure per pupil ($)	% of students learning English
1	690.8	17.89	$6,385	0.0%
2	661.2	21.52	5,099	4.6
3	643.6	18.70	5,502	30.0
4	647.7	17.36	7,102	0.0
5	640.8	18.67	5,236	13.9
⋮	⋮	⋮	⋮	⋮
418	645.0	21.89	4,403	24.3
419	672.2	20.20	4,776	3.0
420	655.8	19.04	5,993	5.0

Note: The California test score data set is described in Appendix 4.1.

Time Series Data

Time series data are data for a single entity (person, firm, country) collected at multiple time periods. Our data set on the rates of inflation and unemployment in the United States is an example of a time series data set. The data set contains observations on two variables (the rates of inflation and unemployment) for a single entity (the United States) for 167 time periods. Each time period in this data set is a quarter of a year (the first quarter is January, February, and March; the second quarter is April, May, and June; and so forth). The observations in this data set begin in the second quarter of 1959, which is denoted 1959:II, and end in the fourth quarter of 2000 (2000:IV). The number of observations (that is, time periods) in a time series data set is denoted by T. Because there are 167 quarters from 1959:II to 2000:IV, this data set contains $T = 167$ observations.

Some observations in this data set are listed in Table 1.2. The data in each row correspond to a different time period (year and quarter). In the second quarter of 1959, for example, the rate of price inflation was 0.7% per year at an annual rate. In other words, if inflation had continued for 12 months at its rate during the second quarter of 1959, the overall price level (as measured by the Consumer Price Index, CPI) would have increased by 0.7%. In the second quarter of 1959, the rate of unemployment was 5.1%, that is, 5.1% of the labor force reported that they did not have

TABLE 1.2   Selected Observations on the Rates of Consumer Price Index (CPI) Inflation and Unemployment in the United States: Quarterly Data, 1959–2000.

Obervation number	Date (Year:quarter)	CPI inflation rate (% per year at an annual rate)	Unemployment rate (%)
1	1959:II	0.7%	5.1%
2	1959:III	2.1	5.3
3	1959:IV	2.4	5.6
4	1960:I	0.4	5.1
5	1960:II	2.4	5.2
⋮	⋮	⋮	⋮
165	2000:II	3.0	4.0
166	2000:III	3.5	4.0
167	2000:IV	2.8	4.0

Note: The U.S. inflation and unemployment data set is described in Appendix 12.1.

a job but were looking for work. In the third quarter of 1959, the rate of CPI inflation was 2.1%, and the rate of unemployment was 5.3%.

By tracking a single entity over time, time series data can be used to study the evolution of variables over time and to forecast future values of those variables.

Panel Data

Panel data, also called **longitudinal data**, are data for multiple entities in which each entity is observed at two or more time periods. Our data on cigarette consumption and prices are an example of a panel data set, and selected variables and observations in that data set are listed in Table 1.3. The number of entities in a panel data set is denoted by n, and the number of time periods is denoted by T. In the cigarette data set, we have observations on $n = 48$ continental U.S. states (entities) for $T = 11$ years (time periods) from 1985 to 1995. Thus there is a total of $n \times T = 48 \times 11 = 528$ observations.

TABLE 1.3   Selected Observations on Cigarette Sales, Prices, and Taxes, by State and Year for U.S. States, 1985–1995

Observation number	State	Year	Cigarette sales (packs per capita)	Average price per pack (including taxes)	Total taxes (cigarette excise tax + sales tax)
1	Alabama	1985	116.5	$1.022	$0.333
2	Arkansas	1985	128.5	1.015	0.370
3	Arizona	1985	104.5	1.086	0.362
⋮	⋮	⋮	⋮	⋮	⋮
47	West Virginia	1985	112.8	1.089	0.382
48	Wyoming	1985	129.4	0.935	0.240
49	Alabama	1986	117.2	1.080	0.334
⋮	⋮	⋮	⋮	⋮	⋮
96	Wyoming	1986	127.8	1.007	0.240
97	Alabama	1987	115.8	1.135	0.335
⋮	⋮	⋮	⋮	⋮	⋮
528	Wyoming	1995	112.2	1.585	0.360

Note: The cigarette consumption data set is described in Appendix 10.1.

Cross-Sectional, Time Series, and Panel Data

Key Concept 1.1

- Cross-sectional data consist of multiple entities observed at a single time period.
- Time series data consist of a single entity observed at multiple time periods.
- Panel data (also known as longitudinal data) consist of multiple entities, where each entity is observed at two or more time periods.

Some data from the cigarette consumption data set are listed in Table 1.3. The first block of 48 observations lists the data for each state in 1985, organized alphabetically from Alabama to Wyoming. The next block of 48 observations lists the data for 1986, and so forth, through 1995. For example, in 1985, cigarette sales in Arkansas were 128.5 packs per capita (the total number of packs of cigarettes sold in Arkansas in 1985 divided by the total population of Arkansas in 1985 equals 128.5). The average price of a pack of cigarettes in Arkansas in 1985, including tax, was $1.015, of which 37¢ went to federal, state, and local taxes.

Panel data can be used to learn about economic relationships from the experiences of the many different entities in the data set and from the evolution over time of the variables for each entity.

The definitions of cross-sectional data, time series data, and panel data are summarized in Key Concept 1.1.

Summary

1. Many decisions in business and economics require quantitative estimates of how a change in one variable affects another variable.
2. Conceptually, the way to estimate a causal effect is in an ideal randomized controlled experiment, but performing such experiments in economic applications is usually unethical, impractical, or too expensive.
3. Econometrics provides tools for estimating causal effects using either observational (nonexperimental) data or data from real-world, imperfect experiments.

4. Cross-sectional data are gathered by observing multiple entities at a single point in time; time series data are gathered by observing a single entity at multiple points in time; and panel data are gathered by observing multiple entities, each of which is observed at multiple points in time.

Key Terms

randomized controlled experiment (8)

control group (8)

treatment group (8)

causal effect (8)

experimental data (10)

observational data (10)

cross-sectional data (10)

observation number (11)

time series data (12)

panel data (13)

longitudinal data (13)

Review the Concepts

1.1 Design a hypothetical ideal randomized controlled experiment to study the effect of hours spent studying on performance on microeconomics exams. Suggest some impediments to implementing this experiment in practice.

1.2 Design a hypothetical ideal randomized controlled experiment to study the effect on highway traffic deaths of wearing seat belts. Suggest some impediments to implementing this experiment in practice.

1.3 You are asked to study the relationship between hours spent on employee training (measured in hours per worker per week) in a manufacturing plant and the productivity of its workers (output per worker per hour). Describe:

a. an ideal randomized controlled experiment to measure this causal effect;

b. an observational cross-sectional data set with which you could study this effect;

c. an observational time series data set for studying this effect; and

d. an observational panel data set for studying this effect.

CHAPTER 2

Review of Probability

This chapter reviews the core ideas of the theory of probability that are needed to understand regression analysis and econometrics. We assume that you have taken an introductory course in probability and statistics. If your knowledge of probability is stale, you should refresh it by reading this chapter. If you feel confident with the material, you still should skim the chapter and the terms and concepts at the end to make sure you are familiar with the ideas and notation.

Most aspects of the world around us have an element of randomness. The theory of probability provides mathematical tools for quantifying and describing this randomness. Section 2.1 reviews probability distributions for a single random variable, and Section 2.2 covers the mathematical expectation, mean, and variance of a single random variable. Most of the interesting problems in economics involve more than one variable, and Section 2.3 introduces the basic elements of probability theory for two random variables. Section 2.4 discusses three special probability distributions that play a central role in statistics and econometrics: the normal, chi-squared, and $F_{m,\infty}$ distributions.

The final two sections of this chapter focus on a specific source of randomness of central importance in econometrics: the randomness that arises by randomly drawing a sample of data from a larger population. For example, suppose you survey ten recent college graduates selected at random, record (or "observe") their earnings, and compute the average earnings using these ten data points (or "observations"). Because you chose the sample at random, you could have chosen ten different graduates by pure random chance; had you done so, you would have observed ten different earnings and you would have computed a different sample average. Because the average earnings vary from one randomly chosen sample to the next, the sample average is itself a random variable. Therefore, the sample average has a probability distribution, referred to as its sampling distribution because this distribution describes the different possible values of the sample average that might have occurred had a different sample been drawn.

Section 2.5 discusses random sampling and the sampling distribution of the sample average. This sampling distribution is, in general, complicated. When the sample size is sufficiently large, however, the sampling distribution of the sample average is approximately normal, a result known as the central limit theorem, which is discussed in Section 2.6.

2.1 Random Variables and Probability Distributions

Probabilities, the Sample Space, and Random Variables

Probabilities and outcomes. The gender of the next new person you meet, your grade on an exam, and the number of times your computer will crash while you are writing a term paper all have an element of chance or randomness. In each of these examples, there is something not yet known that is eventually revealed.

The mutually exclusive potential results of a random process are called the **outcomes**. For example, your computer might never crash, it might crash once, it might crash twice, and so on. Only one of these outcomes will actually occur (the outcomes are mutually exclusive), and the outcomes need not be equally likely.

The **probability** of an outcome is the proportion of the time that the outcome occurs in the long run. If the probability of your computer not crashing while you are writing a term paper is 80%, then over the course of writing many term papers, you will complete 80% without a crash.

The sample space and events. The set of all possible outcomes is called the **sample space**. An **event** is a subset of the sample space, that is, an event is a set of one or more outcomes. The event "my computer will crash no more than once" is the set consisting of two outcomes: "no crashes" and "one crash."

Random variables.   A random variable is a numerical summary of a random outcome. The number of times your computer crashes while you are writing a term paper is random and takes on a numerical value, so it is a random variable.

Some random variables are discrete and some are continuous. As their names suggest, a **discrete random variable** takes on only a discrete set of values, like 0, 1, 2, . . . , whereas a **continuous random variable** takes on a continuum of possible values.

Probability Distribution of a Discrete Random Variable

Probability distribution.   The **probability distribution** of a discrete random variable is the list of all possible values of the variable and the probability that each value will occur. These probabilities sum to one.

For example, let M be the number of times your computer crashes while you are writing a term paper. The probability distribution of the random variable M is the list of probabilities of each possible outcome: the probability that $M = 0$, denoted $\Pr(M = 0)$, is the probability of no computer crashes; $\Pr(M = 1)$ is the probability of a single computer crash; and so forth. An example of a probability distribution for M is given in the second row of Table 2.1; in this distribution, if your computer crashes four times, you will quit and write the paper by hand. According to this distribution, the probability of no crashes is 80%; the probability of one crash is 10%; and the probability of two, three, or four crashes is, respectively, 6%, 3%, and 1%. These probabilities sum to 100%. This probability distribution is plotted in Figure 2.1.

Probabilities of events.   The probability of an event can be computed from the probability distribution. For example, the probability of the event of one or two crashes is the sum of the probabilities of the constituent outcomes. That is, $\Pr(M = 1 \text{ or } M = 2) = \Pr(M = 1) + \Pr(M = 2) = 0.10 + 0.06 = 0.16$, or 16%.

Cumulative probability distribution.   The **cumulative probability distribution** is the probability that the random variable is less than or equal to a particular

TABLE 2.1 Probability of Your Computer Crashing *M* Times					
	Outcome (number of crashes)				
	0	1	2	3	4
Probability distribution	0.80	0.10	0.06	0.03	0.01
Cumulative probability distribution	0.80	0.90	0.96	0.99	1.00

FIGURE 2.1 **Probability Distribution of the Number of Computer Crashes**

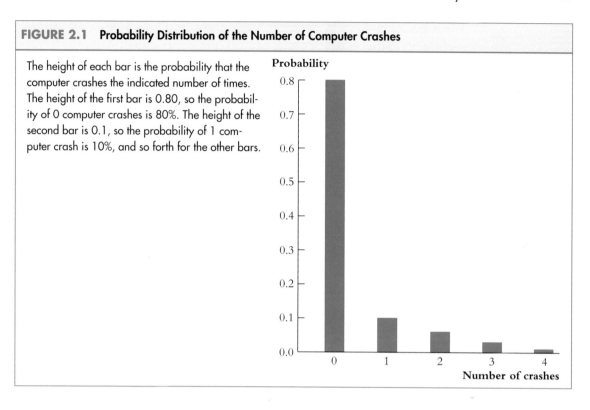

The height of each bar is the probability that the computer crashes the indicated number of times. The height of the first bar is 0.80, so the probability of 0 computer crashes is 80%. The height of the second bar is 0.1, so the probability of 1 computer crash is 10%, and so forth for the other bars.

---

value. The last row of Table 2.1 gives the cumulative probability distribution of the random variable M. For example, the probability of at most one crash, $\Pr(M \le 1)$, is 90%, which is the sum of the probabilities of no crashes (80%) and of one crash (10%).

A cumulative probability distribution is also referred to as a **cumulative distribution function**, a **c.d.f.**, or a **cumulative distribution**.

The Bernoulli distribution. An important special case of a discrete random variable is when the random variable is binary, that is, the outcomes are 0 or 1. A binary random variable is called a **Bernoulli random variable** (in honor of the seventeenth-century Swiss mathematician and scientist Jacob Bernoulli), and its probability distribution is called the **Bernoulli distribution**.

For example, let G be the gender of the next new person you meet, where $G = 0$ indicates that the person is male and $G = 1$ indicates that she is female. The outcomes of G and their probabilities thus are

$$G = \begin{cases} 1 \text{ with probability } p \\ 0 \text{ with probability } 1 - p, \end{cases} \tag{2.1}$$

where p is the probability of the next new person you meet being a woman. The probability distribution in Equation (2.1) is the Bernoulli distribution.

Probability Distribution of a Continuous Random Variable

Cumulative probability distribution.   The cumulative probability distribution for a continuous variable is defined just as it is for a discrete random variable. That is, the cumulative probability distribution of a continuous random variable is the probability that the random variable is less than or equal to a particular value.

For example, consider a student who drives from home to school. This student's commuting time can take on a continuum of values and, because it depends on random factors such as the weather and traffic conditions, it is natural to treat it as a continuous random variable. Figure 2.2a plots a hypothetical cumulative distribution of commuting times. For example, the probability that the commute takes less than 15 minutes is 20% and the probability that it takes less than 20 minutes is 78%.

Probability density function.   Because a continuous random variable can take on a continuum of possible values, the probability distribution used for discrete variables, which lists the probability of each possible value of the random variable, is not suitable for continuous variables. Instead, the probability is summarized by the **probability density function**. The area under the probability density function between any two points is the probability that the random variable falls between those two points. A probability density function is also called a **p.d.f.**, a **density function**, or simply a **density**.

Figure 2.2b plots the probability density function of commuting times corresponding to the cumulative distribution in Figure 2.2a. The probability that the commute takes between 15 and 20 minutes is given by the area under the p.d.f. between 15 minutes and 20 minutes, which is 0.58, or 58%. Equivalently, this probability can be seen on the cumulative distribution in Figure 2.2a as the difference between the probability that the commute is less than 20 minutes (78%) and the probability that it is less than 15 minutes (20%). Thus, the probability density function and the cumulative probability distribution show the same information in different formats.

2.2   Expected Values, Mean, and Variance

The Expected Value of a Random Variable

Expected value.   The **expected value** of a random variable Y, denoted $E(Y)$, is the long-run average value of the random variable over many repeated trials or

FIGURE 2.2   **Cumulative Distribution and Probability Density Functions of Commuting Time**

(a) Cumulative distribution function of commuting time

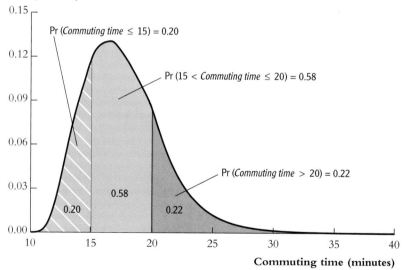

(b) Probability density function of commuting time

Figure 2.2a shows the cumulative probability distribution (or c.d.f.) of commuting times. The probability that a commuting time is less than 15 minutes is 0.20 (or 20%), and the probability it is less than 20 minutes is 0.78 (78%). Figure 2.2b shows the probability density function (or p.d.f.) of commuting times. Probabilities are given by areas under the p.d.f. The probability that a commuting time is between 15 and 20 minutes is 0.58 (58%), and is given by the area under the curve between 15 and 20 minutes.

occurrences. The expected value of a discrete random variable is computed as a weighted average of the possible outcomes of that random variable, where the weights are the probabilities of that outcome. The expected value of Y is also called the **expectation** of Y or the **mean** of Y and is denoted by μ_Y.

For example, suppose you loan a friend $100 at 10% interest. If the loan is repaid you get $110 (the principal of $100 plus interest of $10), but there is a risk of 1% that your friend will default and you will get nothing at all. Thus, the amount you are repaid is a random variable that equals $110 with probability 0.99 and equals $0 with probability 0.01. Over many such loans, 99% of the time you would be paid back $110, but 1% of the time you would get nothing, so on average you would be repaid $110 × 0.99 + $0 × 0.01 = $108.90. Thus the expected value of your repayment (or the "mean repayment") is $108.90.

As a second example, consider the number of computer crashes M with the probability distribution given in Table 2.1. The expected value of M is the average number of crashes over many term papers, weighted by the frequency with which a crash of a given size occurs. Accordingly,

$$E(M) = 0 \times 0.80 + 1 \times 0.10 + 2 \times 0.06 + 3 \times 0.03 + 4 \times 0.01 = 0.35. \qquad (2.2)$$

That is, the expected number of computer crashes while writing a term paper is 0.35. Of course, the actual number of crashes must always be an integer; it makes no sense to say that the computer crashed 0.35 times while writing a particular term paper! Rather, the calculation in Equation (2.2) means that the average number of crashes over many such term papers is 0.35.

The formula for the expected value of a discrete random variable Y that can take on k different values is given as Key Concept 2.1.

Expected value of a Bernoulli random variable.   An important special case of the general formula in Key Concept 2.1 is the mean of a Bernoulli random variable. Let G be the Bernoulli random variable with the probability distribution in Equation (2.1). The expected value of G is

$$E(G) = 1 \times p + 0 \times (1 - p) = p. \qquad (2.3)$$

Thus the expected value of a Bernoulli random variable is p, the probability that it takes on the value "1."

Expected value of a continuous random variable.   The expected value of a continuous random variable is also the probability-weighted average of the pos-

Expected Value and the Mean

Suppose the random variable Y takes on k possible values, $y_1, \ldots, y_k$, where y_1 denotes the first value, y_2 denotes the second value, etc., and that the probability that Y takes on y_1 is p_1, the probability that Y takes on y_2 is p_2, and so forth. The expected value of Y, denoted $E(Y)$, is

$$E(Y) = y_1 p_1 + y_2 p_2 + \cdots + y_k p_k = \sum_{i=1}^{k} y_i p_i, \qquad (2.4)$$

where the notation "$\sum_{i=1}^{k} y_i p_i$" means "the sum of $y_i p_i$ for i running from 1 to k." The expected value of Y is also called the mean of Y or the expectation of Y and is denoted μ_Y.

Key Concept 2.1

sible outcomes of the random variable. Because a continuous random variable can take on a continuum of possible values, the formal mathematical definition of its expectation involves calculus and its definition is given in Appendix 15.1.

Variance, Standard Deviation, and Moments

The variance and standard deviation measure the dispersion or the "spread" of a probability distribution. The **variance** of a random variable Y, denoted $\text{var}(Y)$, is the expected value of the square of the deviation of Y from its mean, that is, $\text{var}(Y) = E[(Y - \mu_Y)^2]$.

Because the variance involves the square of Y, the units of the variance are the units of the square of Y, which makes the variance awkward to interpret. It is therefore common to measure the spread by the **standard deviation**, which is the square root of the variance and is denoted σ_Y. The standard deviation has the same units as Y. These definitions are summarized in Key Concept 2.2.

For example, the variance of the number of computer crashes M is the probability-weighted average of the squared difference between M and its mean, 0.35:

$$\text{var}(M) = (0 - 0.35)^2 \times 0.80 + (1 - 0.35)^2 \times 0.10 + (2 - 0.35)^2 \times 0.06$$
$$+ (3 - 0.35)^2 \times 0.03 + (4 - 0.35)^2 \times 0.01 = 0.6475. \qquad (2.5)$$

The standard deviation of M is the square root of the variance, so $\sigma_M = \sqrt{0.6475} \cong 0.80$.

Variance and Standard Deviation

The variance of the discrete random variable Y, denoted σ_Y^2, is

$$\sigma_Y^2 = \text{var}(Y) = E[(Y - \mu_Y)^2] = \sum_{i=1}^{k} (y_i - \mu_Y)^2 p_i. \tag{2.6}$$

The standard deviation of Y is σ_Y, the square root of the variance. The units of the standard deviation are the same as the units of Y.

Variance of a Bernoulli random variable.   The mean of the Bernoulli random variable G with probability distribution in Equation (2.1) is $\mu_G = p$ (Equation (2.3)) so its variance is

$$\text{var}(G) = \sigma_G^2 = (0 - p)^2 \times (1 - p) + (1 - p)^2 \times p = p(1 - p). \tag{2.7}$$

Thus the standard deviation of a Bernoulli random variable is $\sigma_G = \sqrt{p(1 - p)}$.

Moments.   The mean of Y, $E(Y)$, is also called the first moment of Y, and the expected value of the square of Y, $E(Y^2)$, is also called the second moment of Y. In general, the expected value of Y^r is called the rth **moment** of the random variable Y. That is, the rth moment of Y is $E(Y^r)$.

Just as the mean is a measure of the center of a distribution and the standard deviation is a measure of its spread, moments with $r > 2$ measure other aspects of the shape of a distribution. In this book, higher moments of distributions (moments with $r > 2$) are mainly used in the mathematical assumptions and derivations that underlie statistical and econometric procedures.

Mean and Variance of a Linear Function of a Random Variable

This section discusses random variables (say X and Y) that are related by a linear function. For example, consider an income tax scheme under which a worker is taxed at a rate of 20% on his or her earnings and then given a (tax-free) grant of $2,000. Under this tax scheme, after-tax earnings Y are related to pre-tax earnings X by the equation

$$Y = 2,000 + 0.8X. \tag{2.8}$$

That is, after-tax earnings Y is 80% of pre-tax earnings X, plus $2,000.

Suppose an individual's pre-tax earnings next year are a random variable with mean μ_X and variance σ_X^2. Because pre-tax earnings are random, so are after-tax earnings. What are the mean and standard deviations of her after-tax earnings under this tax? After taxes, her earnings are 80% of the original pre-tax earnings, plus $2,000. Thus the expected value of her after-tax earnings is

$$E(Y) = \mu_Y = 2{,}000 + 0.8\mu_X. \tag{2.9}$$

The variance of after-tax earnings is the expected value of $(Y - \mu_Y)^2$. Because $Y = 2{,}000 + 0.8X$, $Y - \mu_Y = 2{,}000 + 0.8X - (2{,}000 + 0.8\mu_X) = 0.8(X - \mu_X)$. Thus, $E[(Y - \mu_Y)^2] = E\{[0.8(X - \mu_X)]^2\} = 0.64E[(X - \mu_X)^2]$. It follows that $\mathrm{var}(Y) = 0.64\mathrm{var}(X)$, so, taking the square root of the variance, the standard deviation of Y is

$$\sigma_Y = 0.8\sigma_X. \tag{2.10}$$

That is, the standard deviation of the distribution of her after-tax earnings is 80% of the standard deviation of the distribution of pre-tax earnings.

This analysis can be generalized so that Y depends on X with an intercept a (instead of $2,000) and a slope b (instead of 0.8), so that

$$Y = a + bX. \tag{2.11}$$

Then the mean and variance of Y are

$$\mu_Y = a + b\mu_X \text{ and} \tag{2.12}$$

$$\sigma_Y^2 = b^2\sigma_X^2, \tag{2.13}$$

and the standard deviation of Y is $\sigma_Y = b\sigma_X$. The expressions in Equations (2.9) and (2.10) are applications of the more general formulas in Equations (2.12) and (2.13) with $a = 2{,}000$ and $b = 0.8$.

2.3   Two Random Variables

Most of the interesting questions in economics involve two or more variables. Are college graduates more likely to have a job than nongraduates? How does the distribution of income for women compare to that for men? These questions concern the distribution of two random variables, considered together (education and employment status in the first example, income and gender in the second).

Answering such questions requires an understanding of the concepts of joint, marginal, and conditional probability distributions.

Joint and Marginal Distributions

Joint distribution.   The **joint probability distribution** of two discrete random variables, say X and Y, is the probability that the random variables simultaneously take on certain values, say x and y. The probabilities of all possible (x, y) combinations sum to one. The joint probability distribution can be written as the function $\Pr(X = x, Y = y)$.

For example, weather conditions—whether or not it is raining—affect the commuting time of the student commuter in Section 2.1. Let Y be a binary random variable that equals one if the commute is short (less than 20 minutes) and equals zero otherwise, and let X be a binary random variable that equals zero if it is raining and one if not. Between these two random variables, there are four possible outcomes: it rains and the commute is long ($X = 0$, $Y = 0$); rain and short commute ($X = 0$, $Y = 1$); no rain and long commute ($X = 1$, $Y = 0$); and no rain and short commute ($X = 1$, $Y = 1$). The joint probability distribution is the frequency with which each of these four outcomes occurs over many repeated commutes.

An example of a joint distribution of these two variables is given in Table 2.2. According to this distribution, over many commutes, 15% of the days have rain and a long commute ($X = 0$, $Y = 0$), that is, the probability of a long, rainy commute is 15%, or $\Pr(X = 0, Y = 0) = 0.15$. Also, $\Pr(X = 0, Y = 1) = 0.15$, $\Pr(X = 1, Y = 0) = 0.07$, and $\Pr(X = 1, Y = 1) = 0.63$. These four possible outcomes are mutually exclusive and constitute the sample space so the four probabilities sum to one.

Marginal probability distribution.   The **marginal probability distribution** of a random variable Y is just another name for its probability distribution. This term is used to distinguish the distribution of Y alone (the marginal distribution) from the joint distribution of Y and another random variable.

TABLE 2.2   Joint Distribution of Weather Conditions and Commuting Times

	Rain ($X = 0$)	No Rain ($X = 1$)	**Total**
Long Commute ($Y = 0$)	0.15	0.07	0.22
Short Commute ($Y = 1$)	0.15	0.63	0.78
Total	0.30	0.70	1.00

The marginal distribution of Y can be computed from the joint distribution of X and Y by adding up the probabilities of all possible outcomes for which Y takes on a specified value. If X can take on l different values $x_1, \ldots, x_l$, then the marginal probability that Y takes on the value y is

$$\Pr(Y = y) = \sum_{i=1}^{l} \Pr(X = x_i, \ Y = y). \tag{2.14}$$

For example, in Table 2.2, the probability of a long rainy commute is 15% and the probability of a long commute with no rain is 7%, so the probability of a long commute (rainy or not) is 22%. The marginal distribution of commuting times is given in the final column of Table 2.2. Similarly, the marginal probability that it will rain is 30%, as shown in the final row of Table 2.2.

Conditional Distributions

Conditional distribution. The distribution of a random variable Y conditional on another random variable X taking on a specific value is called the **conditional distribution of Y given X**. The conditional probability that Y takes on the value y when X takes on the value x is written $\Pr(Y = y | X = x)$.

For example, what is the probability of a long commute $(Y = 0)$ if you know it is raining $(X = 0)$? From Table 2.2, the joint probability of a rainy short commute is 15% and the joint probability of a rainy long commute is 15%, so if it is raining a long commute and a short commute are equally likely. Thus, the probability of a long commute $(Y = 0)$, conditional on it being rainy $(X = 0)$, is 50%, or $\Pr(Y = 0 | X = 0) = 0.50$. Equivalently, the marginal probability of rain is 30%; that is, over many commutes it rains 30% of the time. Of this 30% of commutes, 50% of the time the commute is long $(0.15/0.30)$.

In general, the conditional distribution of Y given $X = x$ is

$$\Pr(Y = y | X = x) = \frac{\Pr(X = x, \ Y = y)}{\Pr(X = x)}. \tag{2.15}$$

For example, the conditional probability of a long commute given that it is rainy is $\Pr(Y = 0 | X = 0) = \Pr(X = 0, \ Y = 0)/\Pr(X = 0) = 0.15/0.30 = 0.50$.

As a second example, consider a modification of the crashing computer example. Suppose you use a computer in the library to type your term paper and the librarian randomly assigns you a computer from those available, half of which are new and half of which are old. Because you are randomly assigned to a computer, the age of the computer you use, $A\ (= 1$ if the computer is new, $= 0$ if it is old), is a random variable. Suppose the joint distribution of the random variables M and A is given in

Part A of Table 2.3. Then the conditional distribution of computer crashes, given the age of the computer, is given in Part B of the table. For example, the joint probability $M = 0$ and $A = 0$ is 0.35; because half the computers are old, the conditional probability of no crashes, given that you are using an old computer, is $\Pr(M = 0 | A = 0) = \Pr(M = 0, A = 0)/\Pr(A = 0) = 0.35/0.50 = 0.70$, or 70%. In contrast, the conditional probability of no crashes given that you are assigned a new computer is 90%. According to the conditional distributions in Part B of Table 2.3, the newer computers are less likely to crash than the old ones; for example, the probability of three crashes is 5% with an old computer but 1% with a new computer.

Conditional expectation. The **conditional expectation of Y given X**, also called the **conditional mean of Y given X**, is the mean of the conditional distribution of Y given X. That is, the conditional expectation is the expected value of Y, computed using the conditional distribution of Y given X. If Y takes on k values $y_1, \ldots, y_k$, then the conditional mean of Y given $X = x$ is

$$E(Y|X = x) = \sum_{i=1}^{k} y_i \Pr(Y = y_i | X = x). \qquad (2.16)$$

For example, based on the conditional distributions in Table 2.3, the expected number of computer crashes, given that the computer is old, is $E(M|A = 0) = 0 \times 0.70 + 1 \times 0.13 + 2 \times 0.10 + 3 \times 0.05 + 4 \times 0.02 = 0.56$. The expected number of computer crashes, given that the computer is new, is $E(M|A = 1) = 0.14$, less than for the old computers.

TABLE 2.3 **Joint and Conditional Distributions of Computer Crashes (M) and Computer Age (A)**

A. Joint Distribution

	$M = 0$	$M = 1$	$M = 2$	$M = 3$	$M = 4$	**Total**
Old computer ($A = 0$)	0.35	0.065	0.05	0.025	0.01	0.50
New computer ($A = 1$)	0.45	0.035	0.01	0.005	0.00	0.50
Total	0.8	0.1	0.06	0.03	0.01	1.00

B. Conditional Distributions of M given A

	$M = 0$	$M = 1$	$M = 2$	$M = 3$	$M = 4$	**Total**
$\Pr(M|A = 0)$	0.70	0.13	0.10	0.05	0.02	1.00
$\Pr(M|A = 1)$	0.90	0.07	0.02	0.01	0.00	1.00

The conditional expectation of Y given $X = x$ is just the mean value of Y when $X = x$. In the example of Table 2.3, the mean number of crashes is 0.56 for old computers, so the conditional expectation of Y given that the computer is old is 0.56 crashes. Similarly, among new computers, the mean number of crashes is 0.14, that is, the conditional expectation of Y given that the computer is new is 0.14.

The law of iterated expectations. The mean of Y is the weighted average of the conditional expectation of Y given X, weighted by the probability distribution of X. For example, the mean height of adults is the weighted average of the mean height of men and the mean height of women, weighted by the proportions of men and women. Stated mathematically, if X takes on the l values $x_1, \ldots, x_l$, then

$$E(Y) = \sum_{i=1}^{l} E(Y|X = x_i) \Pr(X = x_i). \tag{2.17}$$

Equation (2.17) follows from Equations (2.16) and (2.15) (see Exercise 2.9).

Stated differently, the expectation of Y is the expectation of the conditional expectation of Y given X, that is,

$$E(Y) = E[E(Y|X)], \tag{2.18}$$

where the inner expectation on the right-hand side of Equation (2.18) is computed using the conditional distribution of Y given X and the outer expectation is computed using the marginal distribution of X. Equation (2.18) is known as the **law of iterated expectations**.

For example, the mean number of crashes M is the weighted average of the conditional expectation of M given that it is old and the conditional expectation of M given that it is new, so $E(M) = E(M|A = 0) \times \Pr(A = 0) + E(M|A = 1) \times \Pr(A = 1) = 0.56 \times 0.50 + 0.14 \times 0.50 = 0.35$. This is the mean of the marginal distribution of M, as calculated in Equation (2.2).

The law of iterated expectations implies that if the conditional mean of Y given X is zero, then the mean of Y is zero. This is an immediate consequence of Equation (2.18): if $E(Y|X) = 0$, then $E(Y) = E[E(Y|X)] = E[0] = 0$. Said differently, if the mean of Y given X is zero, then it must be that the probability-weighted average of these conditional means is zero, that is, the mean of Y must be zero.

Conditional variance. The **variance of Y conditional on X** is the variance of the conditional distribution of Y given X. Stated mathematically, the conditional variance of Y given X is

$$\text{var}(Y|X = x) = \sum_{i=1}^{k} [y_i - E(Y|X = x)]^2 \Pr(Y = y_i|X = x). \tag{2.19}$$

For example, the conditional variance of the number of crashes given that the computer is old is $\text{var}(M|A=0) = (0-0.56)^2 \times 0.70 + (1-0.56)^2 \times 0.13 + (2-0.56)^2 \times 0.10 + (3-0.56)^2 \times 0.05 + (4-0.56)^2 \times 0.02 \cong 0.99$. The standard deviation of the conditional distribution of M given that $A=0$ is thus $\sqrt{0.99} = 0.99$. The conditional variance of M given that $A=1$ is the variance of the distribution in the second row of Table 2.3, which is 0.22, so the standard deviation of M for new computers is $\sqrt{0.22} = 0.47$. For the conditional distributions in Table 2.3, the expected number of crashes for new computers (0.14) is less than for old computers (0.56), and the spread of the distribution of the number of crashes, as measured by the conditional standard deviation, is smaller for new computers (0.47) than for old (0.99).

Independence

Two random variables X and Y are **independently distributed**, or **independent**, if knowing the value of one of the variables provides no information about the other. Specifically, X and Y are independent if the conditional distribution of Y given X equals the marginal distribution of Y. That is, X and Y are independently distributed if, for all values of x and y,

$$\Pr(Y=y|X=x) = \Pr(Y=y) \quad \text{(independence of } X \text{ and } Y\text{).} \quad (2.20)$$

Substituting Equation (2.20) into Equation (2.15) gives an alternative expression for independent random variables in terms of their joint distribution. If X and Y are independent, then

$$\Pr(X=x, Y=y) = \Pr(X=x)\Pr(Y=y). \quad (2.21)$$

That is, the joint distribution of two independent random variables is the product of their marginal distributions.

Covariance and Correlation

Covariance.   One measure of the extent to which two random variables move together is their covariance. The **covariance** between X and Y is the expected value $E[(X-\mu_X)(Y-\mu_Y)]$, where μ_X is the mean of X and μ_Y is the mean of Y. The covariance is denoted by $\text{cov}(X,Y)$ or by σ_{XY}. If X can take on l values and Y can take on k values, then the covariance is given by the formula

$$\text{cov}(X,Y) = \sigma_{XY} = E[(X-\mu_X)(Y-\mu_Y)] =$$
$$\sum_{i=1}^{k}\sum_{j=1}^{l}(x_j-\mu_X)(y_i-\mu_Y)\Pr(X=x_j, \ Y=y_i). \quad (2.22)$$

To interpret this formula, suppose that when X is greater than its mean (so that $X - \mu_X$ is positive), then Y tends be greater than its mean (so that $Y - \mu_Y$ is positive), and when X is less than its mean (so that $X - \mu_X < 0$), then Y tends to be less than its mean (so that $Y - \mu_Y < 0$). In both cases, the product $(X - \mu_X)(Y - \mu_Y)$ tends to be positive, so the covariance is positive. In contrast, if X and Y tend to move in opposite directions (so that X is large when Y is small, and vice versa), then the covariance is negative. Finally, if X and Y are independent, then the covariance is zero (see Exercise 2.9).

Correlation.   Because the covariance is the product of X and Y, deviated from their means, its units are, awkwardly, the units of X times the units of Y. This "units" problem can make numerical values of the covariance difficult to interpret.

The correlation is an alternative measure of dependence between X and Y that solves the "units" problem of the covariance. Specifically, the **correlation** between X and Y is the covariance between X and Y, divided by their standard deviations:

$$\text{corr}(X,Y) = \frac{\text{cov}(X,Y)}{\sqrt{\text{var}(X)\,\text{var}(Y)}} = \frac{\sigma_{XY}}{\sigma_X \sigma_Y}. \tag{2.23}$$

Because the units of the numerator in Equation (2.23) are the same as those of the denominator, the units cancel and the correlation is unitless. The random variables X and Y are said to be **uncorrelated** if $\text{corr}(X,Y) = 0$.

The correlation always is between -1 and 1; that is, as proven in Appendix 2.1,

$$-1 \leq \text{corr}(X,Y) \leq 1 \text{ (correlation inequality)}. \tag{2.24}$$

Correlation and conditional mean.   If the conditional mean of Y does not depend on X, then Y and X are uncorrelated. That is,

$$\text{if } E(Y|X) = \mu_Y \text{ then cov}(Y,X) = 0 \text{ and corr}(Y,X) = 0. \tag{2.25}$$

We now show this result. First suppose that Y and X have mean zero, so that $\text{cov}(Y,X) = E[(Y - \mu_Y)(X - \mu_X)] = E(YX)$. By the law of iterated expectations (Equation (2.18)), $E(YX) = E[E(Y|X)X] = 0$ because $E(Y|X) = 0$, so $\text{cov}(Y,X) = 0$. Equation (2.25) follows by substituting $\text{cov}(Y,X) = 0$ into the definition of correlation in Equation (2.23). If Y and X do not have mean zero, first subtract off their means, then the preceding proof applies.

It is *not* necessarily true, however, that if X and Y are uncorrelated, then the conditional mean of Y given X does not depend on X. Said differently, it is possible for the conditional mean of Y to be a function of X but for Y and X nonetheless to be uncorrelated. An example is given in Exercise 2.10.

The Mean and Variance of Sums of Random Variables

The mean of the sum of two random variables, X and Y, is the sum of their means:

$$E(X + Y) = E(X) + E(Y) = \mu_X + \mu_Y. \tag{2.26}$$

The variance of the sum of X and Y is the sum of their variances, plus twice their covariance:

$$\text{var}(X + Y) = \text{var}(X) + \text{var}(Y) + 2\text{cov}(X,Y) = \sigma_X^2 + \sigma_Y^2 + 2\sigma_{XY}. \tag{2.27}$$

If X and Y are independent, then the covariance is zero and the variance of their sum is the sum of their variances:

$$\text{var}(X + Y) = \text{var}(X) + \text{var}(Y) = \sigma_X^2 + \sigma_Y^2 \text{ (if } X \text{ and } Y \text{ are independent).} \tag{2.28}$$

Useful expressions for means, variances, and covariances involving weighted sums of random variables are collected in Key Concept 2.3. The results in Key Concept 2.3 are derived in Appendix 2.1.

2.4 The Normal, Chi-Squared, $F_{m,\infty}$, and Student t Distributions

The probability distributions most often encountered in econometrics are the normal, chi-squared, $F_{m,\infty}$, and Student t distributions.

The Normal Distribution

A continuous random variable with a **normal distribution** has the familiar bell-shaped probability density shown in Figure 2.3. The specific function defining the normal probability density is given in Appendix 15.1. As Figure 2.3 shows,

Means, Variances, and Covariances of Sums of Random Variables

Let X, Y, and V be random variables, let μ_X and σ_X^2 be the mean and variance of X, let σ_{XY} be the covariance between X and Y (and so forth for the other variables), and let a, b, and c be constants. The following facts follow from the definitions of the mean, variance, and covariance:

Key Concept 2.3

$$E(a + bX + cY) = a + b\mu_X + c\mu_Y, \qquad (2.29)$$

$$\text{var}(a + bY) = b^2\sigma_Y^2, \qquad (2.30)$$

$$\text{var}(aX + bY) = a^2\sigma_X^2 + 2ab\sigma_{XY} + b^2\sigma_Y^2, \qquad (2.31)$$

$$E(Y^2) = \sigma_Y^2 + \mu_Y^2, \qquad (2.32)$$

$$\text{cov}(a + bX + cV, Y) = b\sigma_{XY} + c\sigma_{VY}, \text{ and} \qquad (2.33)$$

$$E(XY) = \sigma_{XY} + \mu_X\mu_Y. \qquad (2.34)$$

$$|\text{corr}(X,Y)| \le 1 \text{ and } |\sigma_{XY}| \le \sqrt{\sigma_X^2 \sigma_Y^2} \text{ (correlation inequality).} \qquad (2.35)$$

the normal density with mean μ and variance σ^2 is symmetric around its mean and has 95% of its probability between $\mu - 1.96\sigma$ and $\mu + 1.96\sigma$.

Some special notation and terminology have been developed for the normal distribution. The normal distribution with mean μ and variance σ^2 is expressed concisely as "$N(\mu, \sigma^2)$." The **standard normal distribution** is the normal distribution with mean $\mu = 0$ and variance $\sigma^2 = 1$ and is denoted $N(0, 1)$. Random variables that have a $N(0, 1)$ distribution are often denoted by Z, and the standard normal cumulative distribution function is denoted by the Greek letter Φ; accordingly, $\text{Pr}(Z \le c) = \Phi(c)$, where c is a constant. Values of the standard normal cumulative distribution function are tabulated in Appendix Table 1.

To compute probabilities for a normal variable with a general mean and variance, it must be **standardized** by first subtracting the mean, then dividing the result by the standard deviation. For example, suppose Y is distributed $N(1,4)$, that is, Y is normally distributed with a mean of 1 and a variance of 4. What is the probability that $Y \le 2$, that is, what is the shaded area in Figure 2.4a? The standardized version of Y is Y minus its mean, divided by its standard deviation, that is, $(Y-1)/\sqrt{4} = \frac{1}{2}(Y-1)$. Accordingly, the random variable $\frac{1}{2}(Y-1)$ is normally distributed with mean zero and variance one (see Exercise 2.4); it has the

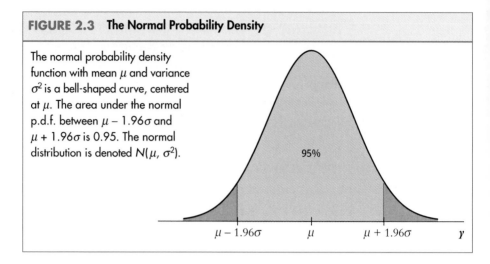

FIGURE 2.3 The Normal Probability Density

The normal probability density function with mean μ and variance σ^2 is a bell-shaped curve, centered at μ. The area under the normal p.d.f. between $\mu - 1.96\sigma$ and $\mu + 1.96\sigma$ is 0.95. The normal distribution is denoted $N(\mu, \sigma^2)$.

95%

$\mu - 1.96\sigma$ μ $\mu + 1.96\sigma$ y

standard normal distribution shown in Figure 2.4b. Now $Y \le 2$ is equivalent to $\frac{1}{2}(Y - 1) \le \frac{1}{2}(2 - 1)$, that is, $\frac{1}{2}(Y - 1) \le \frac{1}{2}$. Thus,

$$\Pr(Y \le 2) = \Pr[\tfrac{1}{2}(Y - 1) \le \tfrac{1}{2}] = \Pr(Z \le \tfrac{1}{2}) = \Phi(0.5) = 0.691, \qquad (2.36)$$

where the value 0.691 is taken from Appendix Table 1.

The same approach can be applied to compute the probability that a normally distributed random variable exceeds some value or that it falls in a certain range. These steps are summarized in Key Concept 2.4. The box, "A Bad Day on Wall Street," presents an unusual application of the cumulative normal distribution.

The multivariate normal distribution. The normal distribution can be generalized to describe the joint distribution of a set of random variables. In this case, the distribution is called the **multivariate normal distribution**, or, if only two variables are being considered, the **bivariate normal distribution**. The formula for the bivariate normal p.d.f. is given in Appendix 15.1, and the formula for the general multivariate normal p.d.f. is given in Appendix 16.1.

The multivariate normal distribution has three important properties. If X and Y have a bivariate normal distribution with covariance σ_{XY}, and if a and b are two constants, then $aX + bY$ have the normal distribution,

$$aX + bY \text{ is distributed } N(a\mu_X + b\mu_Y, \; a^2\sigma_X^2 + b^2\sigma_Y^2 + 2ab\sigma_{XY})$$
$$(X, Y \text{ bivariate normal}). \qquad (2.37)$$

FIGURE 2.4 Calculating the Probability that $Y \le 2$ When Y is Distributed $N(1, 4)$

To calculate $\Pr(Y \le 2)$, standardize Y, then use the standard normal distribution table. Y is standardized by subtracting its mean ($\mu = 1$) and dividing by its standard deviation ($\sigma_Y = 2$). The probability that $Y \le 2$ is shown in Figure 2.4a, and the corresponding probability after standardizing Y is shown in Figure 2.4b. Because the standardized random variable, $\dfrac{Y-1}{2}$, is a standard normal (Z) random variable,
$$\Pr(Y \le 2) = \Pr\left(\frac{Y-1}{2} \le \frac{2-1}{2}\right) = \Pr(Z \le 0.5).$$
From Appendix Table 1, $\Pr(Z \le 0.5) = 0.691$.

(a) $N(1, 4)$

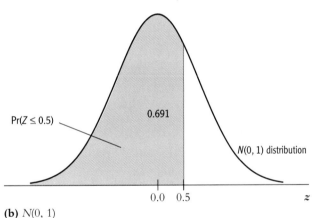

(b) $N(0, 1)$

More generally, if n random variables have a multivariate normal distribution, then any linear combination of these variables (such as their sum) is normally distributed.

Second, if a set of variables has a multivariate normal distribution, then the marginal distribution of each of the variables is normal (this follows from Equation (2.37) by setting $a = 1$ and $b = 0$).

Third, if variables with a multivariate normal distribution have covariances that equal zero, then the variables are independent. Thus, if X and Y have a bivariate normal distribution and $\sigma_{XY} = 0$, then X and Y are independent. In Section 2.3 it was stated that if X and Y are independent then, regardless of their joint distribution, $\sigma_{XY} = 0$. If X and Y are jointly normally distributed, then the converse

Key Concept 2.4

Computing Probabilities Involving Normal Random Variables

Suppose Y is normally distributed with mean μ and variance σ^2, that is, Y is distributed $N(\mu, \sigma^2)$. Then Y is standardized by subtracting its mean and dividing by its standard deviation, that is, by computing $Z = (Y - \mu)/\sigma$.

Let c_1 and c_2 denote two numbers with $c_1 < c_2$, and let $d_1 = (c_1 - \mu)/\sigma$ and $d_2 = (c_2 - \mu)/\sigma$. Then,

$$\Pr(Y \le c_2) = \Pr(Z \le d_2) = \Phi(d_2), \tag{2.38}$$

$$\Pr(Y \ge c_1) = \Pr(Z \ge d_1) = 1 - \Phi(d_1), \text{ and} \tag{2.39}$$

$$\Pr(c_1 \le Y \le c_2) = \Pr(d_1 \le Z \le d_2) = \Phi(d_2) - \Phi(d_1). \tag{2.40}$$

The normal cumulative distribution function Φ is tabulated in Appendix Table 1.

is also true. This result—that zero covariance implies independence—is a special property of the multivariate normal distribution that is not true in general.

The Chi-Squared and $F_{m,\infty}$ Distributions

The chi-squared and $F_{m,\infty}$ distributions are used when testing certain types of hypotheses in statistics and econometrics.

The **chi-squared distribution** is the distribution of the sum of m squared independent standard normal random variables. This distribution depends on m, which is called the degrees of freedom of the chi-squared distribution. For example, let Z_1, Z_2, and Z_3 be independent standard normal random variables. Then $Z_1^2 + Z_2^2 + Z_3^2$ has a chi-squared distribution with 3 degrees of freedom. The name for this distribution derives from the Greek letter used to denote it: a chi-squared distribution with m degrees of freedom is denoted χ_m^2.

Selected percentiles of the χ_m^2 distribution are given in Appendix Table 3. For example, Appendix Table 3 shows that the 95th percentile of the χ_3^2 distribution is 7.81, so $\Pr(Z_1^2 + Z_2^2 + Z_3^2 \le 7.81) = 0.95$.

A closely related distribution is the $F_{m,\infty}$ distribution. The **$F_{m,\infty}$ distribution** is the distribution of a random variable with a chi-squared distribution with m degrees of freedom, divided by m. Equivalently, the $F_{m,\infty}$ distribution is the distribution of the average of m squared standard normal random variables. For example, if Z_1, Z_2, and Z_3 are independent standard normal random variables, then $(Z_1^2 + Z_2^2 + Z_3^2)/3$ has a $F_{3,\infty}$ distribution.

A Bad Day on Wall Street

On a typical day the overall value of stocks traded on the U.S. stock market can rise or fall by 1% or even more. This is a lot—but nothing compared to what happened on Monday, October 19, 1987. On "Black Monday," the Dow Jones Industrial Average (an average of 30 large industrial stocks) fell by 25.6%! From January 1, 1980, to October 16, 1987, the standard deviation of daily returns (that is, daily percentage price changes) on the Dow was 1.16%, so the drop of 25.6% was a negative return of 22 ($= 25.6/1.16$)

standard deviations. The enormity of this drop can be seen in Figure 2.5, a plot of the daily returns on the Dow during the 1980s.

If stock returns are normally distributed, then the probability of a drop of at least 22 standard deviations is $\Pr(Z \leq -22) = \Phi(-22)$. You will not find this value in Appendix Table 1, but you can calculate it using a computer (try it!). This probability is 1.4×10^{-107}, that is, $0.000 \ldots 0.0014$, where there are a total of 106 zeros!   *continued*

FIGURE 2.5   **Daily Percentage Changes in the Dow Jones Industrial Average in the 1980s**

During the 1980s, the average percentage daily change of "the Dow" index was 0.05% and its standard deviation was 1.16%. On October 19, 1987—"Black Monday"—the index fell 25.6%, or more than 22 standard deviations.

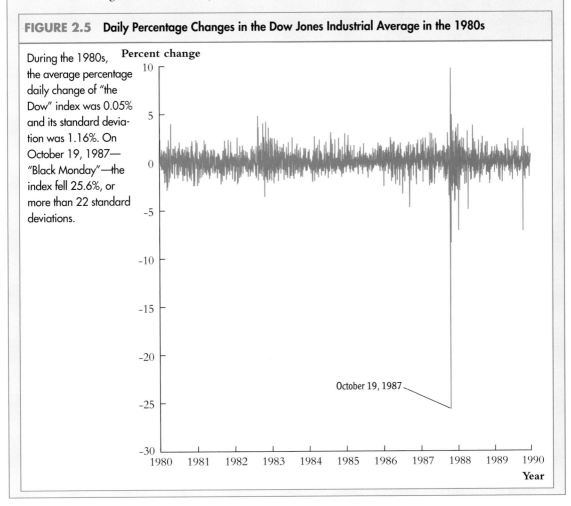

A Bad Day on Wall Street *(continued)*

How small is 1.4×10^{-107}? Consider the following:

- The world population is about 6 billion, so the probability of winning a random lottery among all living people is about one in 6 billion, or 2×10^{-10}.
- The universe is believed to have existed for 15 billion years, or about 5×10^{17} seconds, so the probability of choosing a particular second at random from all the seconds since the beginning of time is 2×10^{-18}.
- There are approximately 10^{43} molecules of gas in the first kilometer above the earth's surface. The probability of choosing one at random is 10^{-43}.

Although Wall Street *did* have a bad day, the fact that it happened at all suggests that its probability was more than 1.4×10^{-107}. In fact, stock returns have a distribution with heavier tails than the normal distribution; in other words, there are more days with large positive or large negative returns than the normal distribution would suggest. Chapter 14 presents one econometric model for stock returns used by finance professionals that is more consistent with the very bad—and very good—days we actually see on Wall Street.

Selected percentiles of the $F_{m,\infty}$ distribution are given in Appendix Table 4. For example, the 95th percentile of the $F_{3,\infty}$ distribution is 2.60, so $\Pr[(Z_1^2 + Z_2^2 + Z_3^2)/3 \leq 2.60] = 0.95$. The 95th percentile of the $F_{3,\infty}$ distribution is the 95th percentile of the χ_3^2 distribution, divided by three ($7.81/3 = 2.60$).

The Student *t* Distribution

The **Student *t* distribution** with m degrees of freedom is defined to be the distribution of the ratio of a standard normal random variable, divided by the square root of an independently distributed chi-squared random variable with m degrees of freedom divided by m. That is, let Z be a standard normal random variable, let W be a random variable with a chi-squared distribution with m degrees of freedom, and let Z and W be independently distributed. Then the random variable $Z/\sqrt{W/m}$ has a Student *t* distribution (also called the ***t* distribution**) with m degrees of freedom. This distribution is denoted t_m. Selected percentiles of the Student *t* distribution are given in Appendix Table 2.

The Student *t* distribution depends on the degrees of freedom m. Thus the 95th percentile of the t_m distribution depends on the degrees of freedom m. The Student *t* distribution has a bell shape similar to that of the normal distribution, but when m is small (20 or less) it has more mass in the tails, that is, it is a "fatter" bell shape than the normal. When m is 30 or more, the Student t distribution is well approximated by the standard normal distribution, and the t_∞ distribution equals the standard normal distribution.

2.5   Random Sampling and the Distribution of the Sample Average

Almost all the statistical and econometric procedures used in this book involve averages or weighted averages of a sample of data. Characterizing the distributions of sample averages therefore is an essential step towards understanding the performance of econometric procedures.

This section introduces some basic concepts about random sampling and the distributions of averages that are used throughout the book. We begin by discussing random sampling. The act of random sampling, that is, randomly drawing a sample from a larger population, has the effect of making the sample average itself a random variable. Because the sample average is a random variable, it has a probability distribution, which is called its sampling distribution. This section concludes with some properties of the sampling distribution of the sample average.

Random Sampling

Simple random sampling.   Suppose our student commuter from Section 2.1 aspires to be a statistician and decides to record her commuting times on various days. She selects these days at random from the school year, and her daily commuting time has the cumulative distribution function in Figure 2.2a. Because these days were selected at random, knowing the value of the commuting time on one of these randomly selected days provides no information about the commuting time on another of the days; that is, because the days were selected at random, the values of the commuting time on each of the different days are independently distributed random variables.

The situation described in the previous paragraph is an example of the simplest sampling scheme used in statistics, called **simple random sampling**, in which n objects are selected at random from a **population** (the population of commuting days) and each member of the population (each day) is equally likely to be included in the sample.

The n observations in the sample are denoted $Y_1, \ldots, Y_n$, where Y_1 is the first observation, Y_2 is the second observation, and so forth. In the commuting example, Y_1 is the commuting time on the first of her n randomly selected days and Y_i is the commuting time on the ith of her randomly selected days.

Because the members of the population included in the sample are selected at random, the values of the observations $Y_1, \ldots, Y_n$ are themselves random. If different members of the population are chosen, their values of Y will differ. Thus, the act of random sampling means that $Y_1, \ldots, Y_n$ can be treated as random variables. Before they are sampled, $Y_1, \ldots, Y_n$ can take on many possible values; after they are sampled, a specific value is recorded for each observation.

i.i.d. draws.   Because $Y_1, \ldots, Y_n$ are randomly drawn from the same population, the marginal distribution of Y_i is the same for each $i = 1, \ldots, n$; this marginal distribution is the distribution of Y in the population being sampled. When Y_i has the same marginal distribution for $i = 1, \ldots, n$, then $Y_1, \ldots, Y_n$ are said to be **identically distributed**.

Under simple random sampling, knowing the value of Y_1 provides no information about Y_2, so the conditional distribution of Y_2 given Y_1 is the same as the marginal distribution of Y_2. In other words, under simple random sampling, Y_1 is distributed independently of $Y_2, \ldots, Y_n$.

When $Y_1, \ldots, Y_n$ are drawn from the same distribution and are independently distributed, they are said to be **independently and identically distributed**, or **i.i.d**.

Simple random sampling and i.i.d. draws are summarized in Key Concept 2.5.

The Sampling Distribution of the Sample Average

The sample average, $\overline{Y}$, of the n observations $Y_1, \ldots, Y_n$ is

$$\overline{Y} = \frac{1}{n} (Y_1 + Y_2 + \cdots + Y_n) = \frac{1}{n} \sum_{i=1}^{n} Y_i. \tag{2.41}$$

An essential concept is that the act of drawing a random sample has the effect of making the sample average $\overline{Y}$ a random variable. Because the sample was drawn at random, the value of each Y_i is random. Because $Y_1, \ldots, Y_n$ are random, their average is random. Had a different sample been drawn, then the observations and their sample average would have been different: the value of $\overline{Y}$ differs from one randomly drawn sample to the next.

Simple Random Sampling and i.i.d. Random Variables

Key
Concept
2.5

In a simple random sample, n objects are drawn at random from a population and each object is equally likely to be drawn. The value of the random variable Y for the ith randomly drawn object is denoted Y_i. Because each object is equally likely to be drawn and the distribution of Y_i is the same for all i, the random variables $Y_1, \ldots, Y_n$ are independently and identically distributed (i.i.d.); that is, the distribution of Y_i is the same for all $i = 1, \ldots, n$ and Y_1 is distributed independently of $Y_2, \ldots, Y_n$ and so forth.

For example, suppose our student commuter selected five days at random to record her commute times, then computed the average of those five times. Had she chosen five different days, she would have recorded five different times—and thus would have computed a different value of the sample average.

Because $\overline{Y}$ is random, it has a probability distribution. The distribution of $\overline{Y}$ is called the **sampling distribution** of $\overline{Y}$, because it is the probability distribution associated with possible values of $\overline{Y}$ that could be computed for different possible samples $Y_1, \ldots, Y_n$.

The sampling distribution of averages and weighted averages plays a central role in statistics and econometrics. We start our discussion of the sampling distribution of $\overline{Y}$ by computing its mean and variance under general conditions on the population distribution of Y.

Mean and variance of $\overline{Y}$.   Suppose that the observations $Y_1, \ldots, Y_n$ are i.i.d., and let μ_Y and σ_Y^2 denote the mean and variance of Y_i (because the observations are i.i.d. the mean and variance is the same for all $i = 1, \ldots, n$). When $n = 2$, the mean of the sum $Y_1 + Y_2$ is given by applying Equation (2.26), that is, $E(Y_1 + Y_2) = \mu_Y + \mu_Y = 2\mu_Y$. Thus the mean of the sample average is $E[\frac{1}{2}(Y_1 + Y_2)] = \frac{1}{2} \times 2\mu_Y = \mu_Y$. In general,

$$E(\overline{Y}) = \frac{1}{n}\sum_{i=1}^{n} E(Y_i) = \mu_Y. \tag{2.42}$$

The variance of $\overline{Y}$ is found by applying Equation (2.28). For example, for $n = 2$, $\text{var}(Y_1 + Y_2) = 2\sigma_Y^2$, so (by applying Equation (2.31) with $a = b = \frac{1}{2}$ and

$\mathrm{cov}(Y_1, Y_2) = 0)$, $\mathrm{var}(\overline{Y}) = \frac{1}{2}\sigma_Y^2$. For general n, because $Y_1, \ldots, Y_n$ are i.i.d., Y_i and Y_j are independently distributed for $i \neq j$, so $\mathrm{cov}(Y_i, Y_j) = 0$. Thus,

$$\mathrm{var}(\overline{Y}) = \mathrm{var}(\frac{1}{n}\sum_{i=1}^{n} Y_i)$$

$$= \frac{1}{n^2}\sum_{i=1}^{n}\mathrm{var}(Y_i) + \frac{1}{n^2}\sum_{i=1}^{n}\sum_{j=1, j\neq i}^{n}\mathrm{cov}(Y_i, Y_j) \tag{2.43}$$

$$= \frac{\sigma_Y^2}{n}.$$

The standard deviation of $\overline{Y}$ is the square root of the variance, $\sigma_Y / \sqrt{n}$.

In summary, the mean, the variance, and the standard deviation of $\overline{Y}$ are

$$E(\overline{Y}) = \mu_Y, \tag{2.44}$$

$$\mathrm{var}(\overline{Y}) = \sigma_{\overline{Y}}^2 = \frac{\sigma_Y^2}{n}, \text{ and} \tag{2.45}$$

$$\mathrm{std.dev}(\overline{Y}) = \sigma_{\overline{Y}} = \frac{\sigma_Y}{\sqrt{n}}. \tag{2.46}$$

These results hold whatever the distribution of Y_i is; that is, the distribution of Y_i does not need to take on a specific form, such as the normal, for Equations (2.44), (2.45), and (2.46) to hold.

The notation $\sigma_{\overline{Y}}^2$ denotes the variance of the sampling distribution of the sample average $\overline{Y}$. In contrast, σ_Y^2 is the variance of each individual Y_i, that is, the variance of the population distribution from which the observation is drawn. Similarly, $\sigma_{\overline{Y}}$ denotes the standard deviation of the sampling distribution of $\overline{Y}$.

Sampling distribution of $\overline{Y}$ when Y is normally distributed.   Suppose that $Y_1, \ldots, Y_n$ are i.i.d. draws from the $N(\mu_Y, \sigma_Y^2)$ distribution. As stated following Equation (2.37), the sum of n normally distributed random variables is itself normally distributed. Because the mean of $\overline{Y}$ is μ_Y and the variance of $\overline{Y}$ is σ_Y^2/n, this means that, if $Y_1, \ldots, Y_n$ are i.i.d. draws from the $N(\mu_Y, \sigma_Y^2)$, then $\overline{Y}$ is distributed $N(\mu_Y, \sigma_Y^2/n)$.

2.6   Large-Sample Approximations to Sampling Distributions

Sampling distributions play a central role in the development of statistical and econometric procedures, so it is important to know, in a mathematical sense, what the sampling distribution of $\overline{Y}$ is. There are two approaches to characterizing sampling distributions: an "exact" approach and an "approximate" approach.

The "exact" approach entails deriving a formula for the sampling distribution that holds exactly for any value of n. The sampling distribution that exactly describes the distribution of $\overline{Y}$ for any n is called the **exact distribution** or **finite-sample distribution** of $\overline{Y}$. For example, if Y is normally distributed, and $Y_1, \ldots, Y_n$ are i.i.d., then (as discussed in Section 2.5) the exact distribution of $\overline{Y}$ is normal with mean μ_Y and variance σ_Y^2/n. Unfortunately, if the distribution of Y is not normal, then in general the exact sampling distribution of $\overline{Y}$ is very complicated and depends on the distribution of Y.

The "approximate" approach uses approximations to the sampling distribution that rely on the sample size being large. The large sample approximation to the sampling distribution is often called the **asymptotic distribution**—"asymptotic" because the approximations become exact in the limit that $n \longrightarrow \infty$. As we see in this section, these approximations can be very accurate even if the sample size is only $n = 30$ observations. Because sample sizes used in practice in econometrics typically number in the hundreds or thousands, these asymptotic distributions can be counted on to provide very good approximations to the exact sampling distribution.

This section presents the two key tools used to approximate sampling distributions when the sample size is large, the law of large numbers and the central limit theorem. The law of large numbers says that, when the sample size is large, $\overline{Y}$ will be close to μ_Y with very high probability. The central limit theorem says that, when the sample size is large, the sampling distribution of the standardized sample average, $(\overline{Y} - \mu_Y)/\sigma_{\overline{Y}}$, is approximately normal.

Although exact sampling distributions are complicated and depend on the distribution of Y, the asymptotic distributions are simple. Moreover—remarkably—the asymptotic normal distribution of $(\overline{Y} - \mu_Y)/\sigma_{\overline{Y}}$ does *not* depend on the distribution of Y. This normal approximate distribution provides enormous simplifications and underlies the theory of regression used throughout this book.

The Law of Large Numbers and Consistency

The **law of large numbers** states that, under general conditions, $\overline{Y}$ will be near μ_Y with very high probability when n is large. This is sometimes called the "law of averages." When a large number of random variables with the same mean are averaged together, the large values balance the small values and their sample average is close to their common mean.

For example, consider a simplified version of our student commuter's experiment, in which she simply records whether her commute was short (less than 20 minutes) or long. Let Y_i equal one if her commute was short on the ith randomly selected day and equal zero if it was long. Because she used simple random sampling, $Y_1, \ldots, Y_n$ are i.i.d. Thus, Y_i, $i = 1, \ldots, n$ are i.i.d. draws of a Bernoulli random variable, where (from Table 2.2) the probability that $Y_i = 1$ is 0.78. Because the expectation of a Bernoulli random variable is its success probability, $E(Y_i) = \mu_Y = 0.78$. The sample average $\overline{Y}$ is the fraction of days in her sample in which her commute was short.

Figure 2.6 shows the sampling distribution of $\overline{Y}$ for various sample sizes n. When $n = 2$ (Figure 2.6a), $\overline{Y}$ can take on only three values: 0, $\frac{1}{2}$, and 1 (neither commute was short, one was short, and both were short), none of which are particularly close to the true proportion in the population, 0.78. As n increases, however (Figures 2.6b–d), $\overline{Y}$ takes on more values and the sampling distribution becomes tightly centered on μ_Y.

The property that $\overline{Y}$ is near μ_Y with increasing probability as n increases is called **convergence in probability** or, more concisely, **consistency** (see Key Concept 2.6). The law of large numbers states that, under certain conditions, $\overline{Y}$ converges in probability to μ_Y or, equivalently, that $\overline{Y}$ is consistent for μ_Y.

The conditions for the law of large numbers that we will use in this book are that Y_i, $i = 1, \ldots, n$ are i.i.d. and that the variance of Y_i, σ_Y^2, is finite. The mathematical role of these conditions is made clear in Section 15.2, where the law of large numbers is proven. If the data are collected by simple random sampling, then the i.i.d. assumption holds. The assumption that the variance is finite says that extremely large values of Y_i are observed infrequently; otherwise the sample average would be unreliable. This assumption is plausible for the applications in this book; for example, because there is an upper limit to our student's commuting time (she could park and walk if the traffic is dreadful), the variance of the distribution of commuting times is finite.

The Central Limit Theorem

The **central limit theorem** says that, under general conditions, the distribution of $\overline{Y}$ is well approximated by a normal distribution when n is large. Recall that the mean of $\overline{Y}$ is μ_Y and its variance is $\sigma_{\overline{Y}}^2 = \sigma_Y^2/n$. According to the central limit theorem, when n is large the distribution of $\overline{Y}$ is approximately $N(\mu_Y, \sigma_{\overline{Y}}^2)$. As discussed at the end of Section 2.5, the distribution of $\overline{Y}$ is *exactly* $N(\mu_Y, \sigma_{\overline{Y}}^2)$ when the sample is drawn from a population with the normal distribution $N(\mu_Y, \sigma_Y^2)$. The central limit theorem says that this same result is *approximately* true when n is large even if $Y_1, \ldots, Y_n$ are not themselves normally distributed.

The convergence of the distribution of $\overline{Y}$ to the bell-shaped, normal approximation can be seen (a bit) in Figure 2.6. However, because the distribution gets

FIGURE 2.6   Sampling Distribution of the Sample Average of *n* Bernoulli Random Variables

(a) *n* = 2

(b) *n* = 5

(c) *n* = 25

(d) *n* = 100

The distributions are the sampling distributions of $\overline{Y}$, the sample average of *n* independent Bernoulli random variables with *p* = Pr(Y_i = 1) = 0.78 (the probability of a fast commute is 78%). The variance of the sampling distribution of $\overline{Y}$ decreases as *n* gets larger, so the sampling distribution becomes more tightly concentrated around its mean μ = 0.78 as the sample size *n* increases.

quite tight for large *n*, this requires some squinting. It would be easier to see the shape of the distribution of $\overline{Y}$ if you used a magnifying glass or had some other way to zoom in or to expand the horizontal axis of the figure.

Convergence in Probability, Consistency, and the Law of Large Numbers

Key Concept 2.6

The sample average $\overline{Y}$ converges in probability to μ_Y (or, equivalently, $\overline{Y}$ is consistent for μ_Y) if the probability that $\overline{Y}$ is in the range $\mu_Y - c$ to $\mu_Y + c$ becomes arbitrarily close to one as n increases for any constant $c > 0$. This is written as $\overline{Y} \xrightarrow{p} \mu_Y$.

The law of large numbers says that if Y_i, $i = 1, \ldots, n$ are independently and identically distributed with $E(Y_i) = \mu_Y$ and $\mathrm{var}(Y_i) = \sigma_Y^2 < \infty$, then $\overline{Y} \xrightarrow{p} \mu_Y$.

One way to do this is to standardize $\overline{Y}$, that is, to subtract its mean and divide by its standard deviation, so that it has a mean of zero and a variance of one. This leads to examining the distribution of the standardized version of $\overline{Y}$, $(\overline{Y} - \mu_Y)/\sigma_{\overline{Y}}$. According to the central limit theorem, this distribution should be well approximated by a $N(0, 1)$ distribution when n is large.

The distribution of the standardized average $(\overline{Y} - \mu_Y)/\sigma_{\overline{Y}}$ is plotted in Figure 2.7 for the distributions in Figure 2.6; the distributions in Figure 2.7 are exactly the same as in Figure 2.6, except that the scale of the horizontal axis is changed so that the standardized variable has a mean of zero and a variance of one. After this change of scale, it is easy to see that, if n is large enough, the distribution of $\overline{Y}$ is well approximated by a normal distribution.

One might ask, how large is "large enough?" That is, how large must n be for the distribution of $\overline{Y}$ to be approximately normal? The answer is "it depends." The quality of the normal approximation depends on the distribution of the underlying Y_i that make up the average. At one extreme, if the Y_i are themselves normally distributed, then $\overline{Y}$ is exactly normally distributed for all n. In contrast, when the underlying Y_i themselves have a distribution that is far from normal, then this approximation can require $n = 30$ or even more.

This point is illustrated in Figure 2.8 for a population distribution, shown in Figure 2.8a, that is quite different from the Bernoulli distribution. This distribution has a long right tail (it is "skewed" to the right). The sampling distribution of $\overline{Y}$, after centering and scaling, is shown in Figures 2.8b, c, and d for $n = 5, 25$, and 100. Although the sampling distribution is approaching the bell shape for $n = 25$, the normal approximation still has noticeable imperfections. By $n = 100$,

The Central Limit Theorem

Suppose that $Y_1, \ldots, Y_n$ are i.i.d. with $E(Y_i) = \mu_Y$ and $\mathrm{var}(Y_i) = \sigma_Y^2$, where $0 < \sigma_Y^2 < \infty$. As $n \longrightarrow \infty$, the distribution of $(\overline{Y} - \mu_Y)/\sigma_{\overline{Y}}$ (where $\sigma_{\overline{Y}}^2 = \sigma_Y^2/n$) becomes arbitrarily well approximated by the standard normal distribution.

Key

Concept

2.7

The central limit theorem is a remarkable result. While the "small n" distributions of $\overline{Y}$ in parts b and c of Figures 2.7 and 2.8 are complicated and quite different from each other, the "large n" distributions in Figures 2.7d and 2.8d are simple and, amazingly, have a similar shape. Because the distribution of $\overline{Y}$ approaches the normal as n grows large, $\overline{Y}$ is said to be **asymptotically normally distributed**.

The convenience of the normal approximation, combined with its wide applicability because of the central limit theorem, makes it a key underpinning of modern applied statistics. The central limit theorem is summarized in Key Concept 2.7.

Summary

1. The probabilities with which a random variable takes on different values are summarized by the cumulative distribution function, the probability distribution function (for discrete random variables), and the probability density function (for continuous random variables).
2. The expected value of a random variable Y (also called its mean, μ_Y), denoted $E(Y)$, is its probability-weighted average value. The variance of Y is $\sigma_Y^2 = E[(Y - \mu_Y)^2]$, and the standard deviation of Y is the square root of its variance.
3. The joint probabilities for two random variables X and Y are summarized by their joint probability distribution. The conditional probability distribution of Y given $X = x$ is the probability distribution of Y, conditional on X taking on the value x.
4. A normally distributed random variable has the bell-shaped probability density in Figure 2.3. To calculate a probability associated with a normal random variable, first standardize the variable, then use the standard normal cumulative distribution tabulated in Appendix Table 1.

5. Simple random sampling produces n random observations $Y_1, \ldots, Y_n$ that are independently and identically distributed (i.i.d.).

6. The sample average, $\overline{Y}$, varies from one randomly chosen sample to the next and thus is a random variable with a sampling distribution. If $Y_1, \ldots, Y_n$, are i.i.d., then:

a. the sampling distribution of $\overline{Y}$ has mean μ_Y and variance $\sigma_{\overline{Y}}^2 = \sigma_Y^2/n$;

b. the law of large numbers says that $\overline{Y}$ converges in probability to μ_Y; and

c. the central limit theorem says that the standardized version of $\overline{Y}$, $(\overline{Y} - \mu_Y)/\sigma_{\overline{Y}}$, has a standard normal distribution ($N(0, 1)$ distribution) when n is large.

Key Terms

Review the Concepts

2.1 Examples of random variables used in this chapter included: (a) the gender of the next person you meet, (b) the number of times a computer crashes, (c) the time it takes to commute to school, (d) whether the computer you are assigned in the library is new or old, and (e) whether it is raining or not. Explain why each can be thought of as random.

2.2 Suppose that the random variables X and Y are independent and you know their distributions. Explain why knowing the value of X tells you nothing about the value of Y.

2.3 Suppose that X denotes the amount rainfall in your hometown during a given month and Y denotes the number of children born in Los Angeles during the same month. Are X and Y independent? Explain.

2.4 An econometrics class has 80 students, and the mean student weight is 145 lbs. A random sample of 4 students is selected from the class and their average weight is calculated. Will the average weight of the students in the sample equal 145 lbs.? Why or why not? Use this example to explain why the sample average, $\overline{Y}$, is a random variable.

2.5 Suppose that $Y_1, \ldots, Y_n$ are i.i.d. random variables with a $N(1, 4)$ distribution. Sketch the probability density of $\overline{Y}$ when $n = 2$. Repeat this for $n = 10$ and $n = 100$. In words, describe how the densities differ. What is the relationship between your answer and the law of large numbers?

2.6 Suppose that $Y_1, \ldots, Y_n$ are i.i.d. random variables with the probability distribution given in Figure 2.8a. You want to calculate $\Pr(\overline{Y} \le 0.1)$. Would it be reasonable to use the normal approximation if $n = 5$? What about $n = 25$ or $n = 100$? Explain.

Exercises

Solutions to exercises denoted by * can be found on the text Web site at **www.aw.com/stock_watson**

*2.1 Use the probability distribution given in Table 2.2 to compute (a) $E(Y)$ and $E(X)$; (b) σ_X^2 and σ_Y^2; and (c) σ_{XY} and $\text{corr}(X, Y)$.

2.2 Using the random variables X and Y from Table 2.2, consider two new random variables $W = 3 + 6X$ and $V = 20 - 7Y$. Compute (a) $E(W)$ and $E(V)$; (b) σ_W^2 and σ_V^2; and (c) σ_{WV} and $\text{corr}(W, V)$.

2.3   The following table gives the joint probability distribution between employment status and college graduation among those either employed or looking for work (unemployed) in the working age U.S. population, based on the 1990 U.S. Census.

Joint Distribution of Employment Status and College Graduation in the U.S. Population Aged 25–64, 1990			
	Unemployed ($Y = 0$)	Employed ($Y = 1$)	**Total**
Non-college grads ($X = 0$)	0.045	0.709	0.754
College grads ($X = 1$)	0.005	0.241	0.246
Total	0.050	0.950	1.000

*a. Compute $E(Y)$.

b. The unemployment rate is the fraction of the labor force that is unemployed. Show that the unemployment rate is given by $1 - E(Y)$.

*c. Calculate $E(Y|X = 1)$ and $E(Y|X = 0)$.

d. Calculate the unemployment rate for (i) college graduates and (ii) non-college graduates.

*e. A randomly selected member of this population reports being unemployed. What is the probability that this worker is a college graduate? A non-college graduate?

f. Are educational achievement and employment status independent? Explain.

2.4   The random variable Y has a mean of 1 and a variance of 4. Let $Z = \frac{1}{2}(Y - 1)$. Show that $\mu_Z = 0$ and $\sigma_Z^2 = 1$.

2.5   Compute the following probabilities:

a. If Y is distributed $N(1, 4)$, find $\Pr(Y \le 3)$.

b. If Y is distributed $N(3, 9)$, find $\Pr(Y > 0)$.

*c. If Y is distributed $N(50, 25)$, find $\Pr(40 \le Y \le 52)$.

d. If Y is distributed $N(5, 2)$, find $\Pr(6 \le Y \le 8)$.

2.6   Compute the following probabilities:

a. If Y is distributed χ_1^2, find $\Pr(Y \le 6.63)$.

b. If Y is distributed χ_4^2, find $\Pr(Y \le 7.78)$.

*c. If Y is distributed $F_{10,\infty}$, find $\Pr(Y > 2.32)$.

2.7   In a population $\mu_Y = 100$ and $\sigma_Y^2 = 43$. Use the central limit theorem to answer the following questions:

a. In a random sample of size $n = 100$, find $\Pr(\overline{Y} \le 101)$.

b. In a random sample of size $n = 165$, find $\Pr(\overline{Y} > 98)$.

*c. In a random sample of size $n = 64$, find $\Pr(101 \le \overline{Y} \le 103)$.

2.8 In any year, the weather can inflict storm damage to a home. From year to year, the damage is random. Let Y denote the dollar value of damage in any given year. Suppose that in 95% of the years $Y = \$0$, but in 5% of the years $Y = \$20,000$.

   a. What is the mean and standard deviation of the damage in any year?

   b. Consider an "insurance pool" of 100 people whose homes are sufficiently dispersed so that, in any year, the damage to different homes can be viewed as independently distributed random variables. Let $\overline{Y}$ denote the average damage to these 100 homes in a year. (i) What is the expected value of the average damage $\overline{Y}$? (ii) What is the probability that $\overline{Y}$ exceeds \$2,000?

2.9 Consider two random variables X and Y. Suppose that Y takes on k values $y_1, \ldots, y_k$, and that X takes on the l values $x_1, \ldots, x_l$.

   a. Show that $\Pr(Y = y_j) = \sum_{i=1}^{l} \Pr(Y = y_j | X = x_i)\Pr(X = x_i)$. (Hint: Use the definition of $\Pr(Y = y_j | X = x_i)$.)

   b. Use your answer to (a) to verify Equation (2.17).

   c. Suppose that X and Y are independent. Show that $\sigma_{XY} = 0$ and $\text{corr}(X,Y) = 0$.

2.10 This exercise provides an example of a pair of random variables X and Y for which the conditional mean of Y given X depends on X but $\text{corr}(X,Y) = 0$. Let X and Z be two independently distributed standard normal random variables, and let $Y = X^2 + Z$.

   a. Show that $E(Y|X) = X^2$.

   b. Show that $\mu_Y = 1$.

   c. Show that $E(XY) = 0$. (*Hint:* Use the fact that the odd moments of a standard normal random variable are all zero.)

   d. Show that $\text{cov}(X,Y) = 0$ and thus $\text{corr}(X,Y) = 0$.

APPENDIX 2.1
Derivation of Results in Key Concept 2.3

This appendix derives the equations in Key Concept 2.3.

Equation (2.29) follows from the definition of the expectation.

To derive Equation (2.30), use the definition of the variance to write, $\text{var}(a + bY) = E\{[a + bY - E(a + bY)]^2\} = E\{[b(Y - \mu_Y)]^2\} = b^2 E[(Y - \mu_Y)^2] = b^2 \sigma_Y^2$.

To derive Equation (2.31), use the definition of the variance to write

$$
\begin{aligned}
\text{var}(aX + bY) &= E\{[(aX + bY) - (a\mu_X + b\mu_Y)]^2\} \\
&= E\{[a(X - \mu_X) + b(Y - \mu_Y)]^2\} \\
&= E[a^2(X - \mu_X)^2] + 2E[ab(X - \mu_X)(Y - \mu_Y)] + E[b^2(Y - \mu_Y)^2] \quad (2.47) \\
&= a^2\text{var}(X) + 2ab\text{cov}(X,Y) + b^2\text{var}(Y) \\
&= a^2\sigma_X^2 + 2ab\sigma_{XY} + b^2\sigma_Y^2,
\end{aligned}
$$

where the second equality follows by collecting terms, the third equality follows by expanding the quadratic, and the fourth equality follows by the definition of the variance and covariance.

To derive Equation (2.32), write $E(Y^2) = E\{[(Y - \mu_Y) + \mu_Y]^2\} = E[(Y - \mu_Y)^2] + 2\mu_Y E(Y - \mu_Y) + \mu_Y^2 = \sigma_Y^2 + \mu_Y^2$ because $E(Y - \mu_Y) = 0$.

To derive Equation (2.33), use the definition of the covariance to write

$$
\begin{aligned}
\text{cov}(a + bX + cV, Y) &= E\{[a + bX + cV - E(a + bX + cV)][Y - \mu_Y]\} \\
&= E\{[b(X - \mu_X) + c(V - \mu_V)][Y - \mu_Y]\} \\
&= E\{[b(X - \mu_X)][Y - \mu_Y]\} + E\{[c(V - \mu_V)][Y - \mu_Y]\} \quad (2.48) \\
&= b\sigma_{XY} + c\sigma_{VY},
\end{aligned}
$$

which is Equation (2.33).

To derive Equation (2.34), write $E(XY) = E\{[(X - \mu_X) + \mu_X][(Y - \mu_Y) + \mu_Y]\} = E[(X - \mu_X)(Y - \mu_Y)] + \mu_X E(Y - \mu_Y) + \mu_Y E(X - \mu_X) + \mu_X\mu_Y = \sigma_{XY} + \mu_X\mu_Y$.

We now prove the correlation inequality in Equation (2.35); that is, $|\text{corr}(X,Y)| \leq 1$. Let $a = -\sigma_{XY}/\sigma_X^2$ and $b = 1$. Applying Equation (2.31), we have that

$$
\begin{aligned}
\text{var}(aX + Y) &= a^2\sigma_X^2 + \sigma_Y^2 + 2a\sigma_{XY} \\
&= (-\sigma_{XY}/\sigma_X^2)^2 \sigma_X^2 + \sigma_Y^2 + 2(-\sigma_{XY}/\sigma_X^2)\sigma_{XY} \quad (2.49) \\
&= \sigma_Y^2 - \sigma_{XY}^2/\sigma_X^2.
\end{aligned}
$$

Because $\text{var}(aX + Y)$ is a variance, it cannot be negative, so from the final line of Equation (2.49) it must be that $\sigma_Y^2 - \sigma_{XY}^2/\sigma_X^2 \geq 0$. Rearranging this inequality yields

$$
\sigma_{XY}^2 \leq \sigma_X^2\sigma_Y^2 \quad \text{(covariance inequality)}. \quad (2.50)
$$

The covariance inequality implies that $\sigma_{XY}^2/(\sigma_X^2\sigma_Y^2) \leq 1$ or, equivalently, $|\sigma_{XY}/(\sigma_X\sigma_Y)| \leq 1$, which (using the definition of the correlation) proves the correlation inequality, $|\text{corr}(X,Y)| \leq 1$.

CHAPTER 3

Review of Statistics

S tatistics is the science of using data to learn about the world around us. Statistical tools help to answer questions about unknown characteristics of distributions in populations of interest. For example, what is the mean of the distribution of earnings of recent college graduates? Do mean earnings differ for men and women and, if so, by how much?

These questions relate to the distribution of earnings in the population of workers. One way to answer these questions would be to perform an exhaustive survey of the population of workers, measuring the earnings of each worker and thus finding the population distribution of earnings. In practice, however, such a comprehensive survey would be extremely expensive. The only comprehensive survey of the U.S. population is the decennial census. The 2000 U.S. Census cost $10 billion, and the process of designing the census forms, managing and conducting the surveys, and compiling and analyzing the data takes ten years. Despite this extraordinary commitment, many members of the population slip through the cracks and are not surveyed. Thus a different, more practical approach is needed.

The key insight of statistics is that one can learn about a population distribution by selecting a random sample from that population. Rather than survey the entire U.S. population, we might survey, say, 1000 members of the population, selected at random by simple random sampling. Using statistical methods, we can use this sample to reach tentative conclusions—to draw statistical inferences—about characteristics of the full population.

Three types of statistical methods are used throughout econometrics: estimation, hypothesis testing, and confidence intervals. Estimation entails computing a "best guess" numerical value for an unknown characteristic of a population distribution, such as its mean, from a sample of data. Hypothesis testing entails formulating a specific hypothesis about the population, then using sample evidence to decide whether it is true. Confidence intervals use a set of data to estimate an interval or range for an unknown population characteristic. Sections 3.1, 3.2, and 3.3 review estimation, hypothesis testing, and confidence intervals in the context of statistical inference about an unknown population mean.

Most of the interesting questions in economics involve relationships between two or more variables or comparisons between different populations. For example, is there a gap between the mean earnings for male and female recent college graduates? In Section 3.4, the methods for learning about the mean of a single population in Sections 3.1–3.3 are extended to compare means in two different populations. These methods are applied in Section 3.5, where we study evidence on the "gender gap" between earnings of male and female college graduates. The chapter concludes with a discussion of the sample correlation and scatterplots in Section 3.6.

3.1 Estimation of the Population Mean

Suppose you want to know the mean value of Y (μ_Y) in a population, such as the mean earnings of women recently graduated from college. A natural way to estimate this mean is to compute the sample average $\overline{Y}$ from a sample of n independently and identically distributed (i.i.d.) observations, $Y_1, \ldots, Y_n$ (recall that $Y_1, \ldots, Y_n$ are i.i.d. if they are collected by simple random sampling). This section discusses estimation of μ_Y and the properties of $\overline{Y}$ as an estimator of μ_Y.

Estimators and Their Properties

Estimators. The sample average $\overline{Y}$ is a natural way to estimate μ_Y; but it is not the only way. For example, another way to estimate μ_Y is simply to use the first observation, Y_1. Both $\overline{Y}$ and Y_1 are functions of the data that are designed to estimate μ_Y; using the terminology in Key Concept 3.1, both are estimators of μ_Y. When evaluated in repeated samples, $\overline{Y}$ and Y_1 take on different values (they produce different estimates) from one sample to the next. Thus, the estimators $\overline{Y}$ and

Estimators and Estimates

An **estimator** is a function of a sample of data to be drawn randomly from a population. An **estimate** is the numerical value of the estimator when it is actually computed using data from a specific sample. An estimator is a random variable because of randomness in selecting the sample, while an estimate is a nonrandom number.

Key Concept 3.1

Y_1 both have sampling distributions. There are, in fact, many estimators of μ_Y, of which $\overline{Y}$ and Y_1 are two examples.

There are many possible estimators, so what makes one estimator "better" than another? Because estimators are random variables, this question can be phrased more precisely as: What are desirable characteristics of the sampling distribution of an estimator? In general, we would like an estimator that gets as close as possible to the unknown true value, at least in some average sense; in other words, we would like the sampling distribution of an estimator to be as tightly centered around the unknown value as possible. This observation leads to three specific desirable characteristics of an estimator: unbiasedness (a lack of bias), consistency, and efficiency.

Unbiasedness.   Suppose you evaluate an estimator many times over repeated randomly drawn samples. It is reasonable to hope that, on average, you would get the right answer. Thus a desirable property of an estimator is that the mean of its sampling distribution equals μ_Y; if so, the estimator is said to be unbiased.

To state this mathematically, let $\hat{\mu}_Y$ denote some estimator of μ_Y, such as $\overline{Y}$ or Y_1. The estimator $\hat{\mu}_Y$ is unbiased if $E(\hat{\mu}_Y) = \mu_Y$, where $E(\hat{\mu}_Y)$ is the mean of the sampling distribution of $\hat{\mu}_Y$; otherwise, $\hat{\mu}_Y$ is biased.

Consistency.   Another desirable property of an estimator $\hat{\mu}_Y$ is that, when the sample size is large, the uncertainty about the value of μ_Y arising from random variations in the sample is very small. Stated more precisely, a desirable property of $\hat{\mu}_Y$ is that the probability that it is within a small interval of the true value μ_Y approaches 1 as the sample size increases, that is, $\hat{\mu}_Y$ is consistent for μ_Y (Key Concept 2.6).

Variance and efficiency. Suppose you have two candidate estimators, $\hat{\mu}_Y$ and $\tilde{\mu}_Y$, both of which are unbiased. How might you choose between them? One way to do so is to choose the estimator with the tightest sampling distribution. This suggests choosing between $\hat{\mu}_Y$ and $\tilde{\mu}_Y$ by picking the estimator with the smallest variance. If $\hat{\mu}_Y$ has a smaller variance than $\tilde{\mu}_Y$, then $\hat{\mu}_Y$ is said to be more efficient than $\tilde{\mu}_Y$. The terminology "efficiency" stems from the notion that, if $\hat{\mu}_Y$ has a smaller variance than $\tilde{\mu}_Y$, then it uses the information in the data more efficiently than does $\tilde{\mu}_Y$.

Bias, consistency, and efficiency are summarized in Key Concept 3.2.

Properties of $\overline{Y}$

How does $\overline{Y}$ fare as an estimator of μ_Y when judged by the three criteria of bias, consistency, and efficiency?

Bias and consistency. The sampling distribution of $\overline{Y}$ has already been examined in Sections 2.5 and 2.6. As shown in Section 2.5, $E(\overline{Y}) = \mu_Y$, so $\overline{Y}$ is an unbiased estimator of μ_Y. Similarly, the law of large numbers (Key Concept 2.6) states that $\overline{Y} \xrightarrow{p} \mu_Y$, that is, $\overline{Y}$ is consistent.

Efficiency. What can be said about the efficiency of $\overline{Y}$? Because efficiency entails a comparison of estimators, we need to specify the estimator or estimators to which $\overline{Y}$ is to be compared.

We start by comparing the efficiency of $\overline{Y}$ to the estimator Y_1. Because $Y_1, \ldots, Y_n$ are i.i.d., the mean of the sampling distribution of Y_1 is $E(Y_1) = \mu_Y$; thus Y_1 is an unbiased estimator of μ_Y. Its variance is $\text{var}(Y_1) = \sigma_Y^2$. From Section 2.5, the variance of $\overline{Y}$ is σ_Y^2/n. Thus, for $n \geq 2$, the variance of $\overline{Y}$ is less than the variance of Y_1; that is, $\overline{Y}$ is a more efficient estimator than Y_1 so, according to the criterion of efficiency, $\overline{Y}$ should be used instead of Y_1. The estimator Y_1 might strike you as an obviously poor estimator—why would you go to the trouble of collecting a sample of n observations only to throw away all but the first?—and the concept of efficiency provides a formal way to show that $\overline{Y}$ is a more desirable estimator than Y_1.

What about a less obviously poor estimator? Consider the weighted average in which the observations are alternately weighted by $\frac{1}{2}$ and $\frac{3}{2}$:

$$\tilde{Y} = \frac{1}{n}\left(\tfrac{1}{2}Y_1 + \tfrac{3}{2}Y_2 + \tfrac{1}{2}Y_3 + \tfrac{3}{2}Y_4 + \cdots + \tfrac{1}{2}Y_{n-1} + \tfrac{3}{2}Y_n\right), \tag{3.1}$$

Bias, Consistency, and Efficiency

Let $\hat{\mu}_Y$ be an estimator of μ_Y. Then:

- The **bias** of $\hat{\mu}_Y$ is $E(\hat{\mu}_Y) - \mu_Y$.
- $\hat{\mu}_Y$ is an **unbiased estimator** of μ_Y if $E(\hat{\mu}_Y) = \mu_Y$.
- $\hat{\mu}_Y$ is a **consistent estimator** of μ_Y if $\hat{\mu}_Y \xrightarrow{p} \mu_Y$.
- Let $\tilde{\mu}_Y$ be another estimator of μ_Y, and suppose that both $\hat{\mu}_Y$ and $\tilde{\mu}_Y$ are unbiased. Then $\hat{\mu}_Y$ is said to be more **efficient** than $\tilde{\mu}_Y$ if $\text{var}(\hat{\mu}_Y) < \text{var}(\tilde{\mu}_Y)$.

Key Concept 3.2

where the number of observations n is assumed to be even for convenience. The mean of $\tilde{Y}$ is μ_Y and its variance is $\text{var}(\tilde{Y}) = 1.25\sigma_Y^2/n$ (Exercise 3.7). Thus $\tilde{Y}$ is unbiased and, because $\text{var}(\tilde{Y}) \longrightarrow 0$ as $n \longrightarrow \infty$, $\tilde{Y}$ is consistent. However, $\tilde{Y}$ has a larger variance than $\overline{Y}$. Thus $\overline{Y}$ is more efficient than $\tilde{Y}$.

The estimators $\overline{Y}$, Y_1, and $\tilde{Y}$ have a common mathematical structure: they are weighted averages of $Y_1, \ldots, Y_n$. The comparisons in the previous two paragraphs show that the weighted averages Y_1 and $\tilde{Y}$ have larger variances than $\overline{Y}$. In fact, these conclusions reflect a more general result: $\overline{Y}$ is the most efficient estimator of *all* unbiased estimators that are weighted averages of $Y_1, \ldots, Y_n$. This result is stated in Key Concept 3.3 and is proven in Chapter 15.

$\overline{Y}$ is the least squares estimator of μ_Y.   The sample average $\overline{Y}$ provides the best fit to the data in the sense that the average squared differences between the observations and $\overline{Y}$ are the smallest of all possible estimators.

Consider the problem of finding the estimator m that minimizes

$$\sum_{i=1}^{n}(Y_i - m)^2, \tag{3.2}$$

which is a measure of the total squared gap or distance between the estimator m and the sample points. Because m is an estimator of $E(Y)$, you can think of it as a prediction of the value of Y_i, so that the gap $Y_i - m$ can be thought of as a prediction mistake. The sum of squared gaps in expression (3.2) can be thought of as the sum of squared prediction mistakes.

Efficiency of $\overline{Y}$

Key Concept 3.3

Let $\hat{\mu}_Y$ be an estimator of μ_Y that is a weighted average of $Y_1, \ldots, Y_n$, that is, $\hat{\mu}_Y = \frac{1}{n}\sum_{i=1}^{n} a_i Y_i$, where $a_1, \ldots, a_n$ are nonrandom constants. If $\hat{\mu}_Y$ is unbiased, then $\text{var}(\overline{Y}) < \text{var}(\hat{\mu}_Y)$ unless $\hat{\mu}_Y = \overline{Y}$. That is, $\overline{Y}$ is the most efficient estimator of μ_Y among all unbiased estimators that are weighted averages of $Y_1, \ldots, Y_n$.

The estimator m that minimizes the sum of squared gaps $Y_i - m$ in expression (3.2) is called the **least squares estimator**. One can imagine using trial and error to solve the least squares problem: try many values of m until you are satisfied that you have the value that makes expression (3.2) as small as possible. Alternatively, as is done in Appendix 3.2, you can use algebra or calculus to show that choosing $m = \overline{Y}$ minimizes the sum of squared gaps in expression (3.2), that is, that $\overline{Y}$ is the least squares estimator of μ_Y.

The Importance of Random Sampling

We have assumed that $Y_1, \ldots, Y_n$ are i.i.d. draws, such as those that would be obtained from simple random sampling. This assumption is important because non-random sampling can result in $\overline{Y}$ being biased. Suppose that, to estimate the monthly national unemployment rate, a statistical agency adopts a sampling scheme in which interviewers survey working-age adults sitting in city parks at 10:00 A.M. on the second Wednesday of the month. Because most employed people are at work at that hour (not sitting in the park!), the unemployed are inordinately represented among the people sitting in the park, and an estimate of the unemployment rate based on this sampling plan would be biased. This bias arises because this sampling scheme overrepresents, or oversamples, the unemployed members of the population. This example is fictitious, but the Landon Wins box gives a real-world example of biases introduced by sampling that is not entirely random.

It is important to design sample selection schemes in a way that minimizes bias. Appendix 3.1 includes a discussion of what the Bureau of Labor Statistics actually does when it conducts the U.S. Current Population Survey (CPS), the survey it uses to estimate the monthly U.S. unemployment rate.

Landon Wins!

Shortly before the 1936 Presidential election, the *Literary Gazette* published a poll indicating that Alf M. Landon would defeat the incumbent, Franklin D. Roosevelt, by a landslide—57% to 43%. The *Gazette* was right that the election was a landslide, but it was wrong about the winner: Roosevelt won by 59% to 41%!

How could the *Gazette* have made such a big mistake? The *Gazette*'s sample was chosen from telephone records and automobile registration files. But in 1936 many households did not have cars or telephones, and those that did tended to be richer—and were also more likely to be Republican. Because the telephone survey did not sample randomly from the population but instead undersampled Democrats, the estimator was biased and the *Gazette* made an embarrassing mistake.

Do you think surveys conducted over the Internet might have a similar problem with bias?

3.2   Hypothesis Tests Concerning the Population Mean

Many hypotheses about the world around us can be phrased as yes/no questions. Do the mean hourly earnings of recent U.S. college graduates equal $20/hour? Are mean earnings the same for male and female college graduates? Both these questions embody specific hypotheses about the population distribution of earnings. The statistical challenge is to answer these questions based on a sample of evidence. This section describes **testing hypotheses** concerning the population mean (Does the population mean of hourly earnings equal $20?). Hypothesis tests involving two populations (Are mean earnings the same for men and women?) are taken up in Section 3.4.

Null and Alternative Hypotheses

The starting point of statistical hypotheses testing is specifying the hypothesis to be tested, called the **null hypothesis**. Hypothesis testing entails using data to compare the null hypothesis to a second hypothesis, called the **alternative hypothesis**, that holds if the null does not.

The null hypothesis is that the population mean, $E(Y)$, takes on a specific value, denoted by $\mu_{Y,0}$. The null hypothesis is denoted H_0 and thus is

$$H_0: E(Y) = \mu_{Y,0} \tag{3.3}$$

For example, the conjecture that, on average in the population, college graduates earn \$20/hour constitutes a null hypothesis about the population distribution of hourly earnings. Stated mathematically, if Y is the hourly earning of a randomly selected recent college graduate, then the null hypothesis is that $E(Y) = 20$, that is, $\mu_{Y,0} = 20$ in Equation (3.3).

The alternative hypothesis specifies what is true if the null hypothesis is not. The most general alternative hypothesis is that $E(Y) \neq \mu_{Y,0}$; this is called a **two-sided alternative hypothesis**, because it allows $E(Y)$ to be either less than or greater than $\mu_{Y,0}$. The two-sided alternative is written as

$$H_1: E(Y) \neq \mu_{Y,0} \quad \text{(two-sided alternative)}. \tag{3.4}$$

One-sided alternatives are also possible, and these are discussed later in this section.

The problem facing the statistician is to use the evidence in a randomly selected sample of data to decide whether to accept the null hypothesis H_0 or to reject it in favor of the alternative hypothesis H_1. If the null hypothesis is "accepted," this does not mean that the statistician declares it to be true; rather, it is accepted tentatively with the recognition that it might be rejected later based on additional evidence. For this reason, statistical hypothesis testing can be posed as either rejecting the null hypothesis or failing to do so.

The p-Value

In any given sample, the sample average $\overline{Y}$ will rarely be exactly equal to the hypothesized value $\mu_{Y,0}$. Differences between $\overline{Y}$ and $\mu_{Y,0}$ can arise because the true mean in fact does not equal $\mu_{Y,0}$ (the null hypothesis is false), or because the true mean equals $\mu_{Y,0}$ (the null hypothesis is true) but $\overline{Y}$ differs from $\mu_{Y,0}$ because of random sampling. It is impossible to distinguish between these two possibilities with certainty. Although a sample of data cannot provide conclusive evidence about the null hypothesis, it is possible to do a probabilistic calculation that permits testing the null hypothesis in a way that accounts for sampling uncertainty. This calculation involves using the data to compute the p-value of the null hypothesis.

The **p-value**, also called the **significance probability**, is the probability of drawing a statistic at least as adverse to the null hypothesis as the one you actually computed in your sample, assuming the null hypothesis is correct. In the case at hand, the p-value is the probability of drawing $\overline{Y}$ at least as far in the tails of its distribution under the null hypothesis as the sample average you actually computed.

For example, suppose that, in your sample of recent college graduates, the average wage is \$22.24. The p-value is the probability of observing a value of $\overline{Y}$

at least as different from $20 (the population mean under the null) as the observed value of $22.24 by pure random sampling variation, assuming that the null hypothesis is true. If this p-value is small, say 0.5%, then it is very unlikely that this sample would have been drawn if the null hypothesis is true; thus it is reasonable to conclude that in fact the null hypothesis is not true. On the other hand, if this p-value is large, say 40%, then it is quite likely that the observed sample average of $22.24 could have arisen just by random sampling variation if the null hypothesis is true; accordingly, the evidence against the null hypothesis is weak in this probabilistic sense, and it is reasonable not to reject the null hypothesis.

To state the definition of the p-value mathematically, let $\overline{Y}^{act}$ denote the value of the sample average actually computed in the data set at hand and let $\Pr_{H_0}$ denote the probability computed under the null hypothesis (that is, computed assuming that $E(Y_i) = \mu_{Y,0}$). The p-value is

$$p\text{-value} = \Pr_{H_0}[\,|\overline{Y} - \mu_{Y,0}| > |\overline{Y}^{act} - \mu_{Y,0}|\,]. \tag{3.5}$$

That is, the p-value is the area in the tails of the distribution of $\overline{Y}$ under the null hypothesis beyond $|\overline{Y}^{act} - \mu_{Y,0}|$. If the p-value is large, then the observed value $\overline{Y}^{act}$ is consistent with the null hypothesis, but if the p-value is small, it is not.

To compute the p-value it is necessary to know the sampling distribution of $\overline{Y}$ under the null hypothesis. As discussed in Section 2.6, when the sample size is small this distribution is complicated. However, according to the central limit theorem, when the sample size is large the sampling distribution of $\overline{Y}$ is well approximated by a normal distribution. Under the null hypothesis, the mean of this normal distribution is $\mu_{Y,0}$, so under the null hypothesis $\overline{Y}$ is distributed $N(\mu_{Y,0}, \sigma_{\overline{Y}}^2)$, where $\sigma_{\overline{Y}}^2 = \sigma_Y^2/n$. This large-sample normal approximation makes it possible to compute the p-value without needing to know the population distribution of Y, as long as the sample size is large. The details of the calculation, however, depend on whether or not σ_Y^2 is known.

Calculating the p-Value When σ_Y Is Known

The calculation of the p-value when σ_Y is known is summarized in Figure 3.1. If the sample size is large, then under the null hypothesis the sampling distribution of $\overline{Y}$ is $N(\mu_{Y,0}, \sigma_{\overline{Y}}^2)$, where $\sigma_{\overline{Y}}^2 = \sigma_Y^2/n$. Thus, under the null hypothesis, the standardized version of $\overline{Y}$, $(\overline{Y} - \mu_{Y,0})/\sigma_{\overline{Y}}$, has a standard normal distribution. The p-value is the probability of obtaining a value of $\overline{Y}$ farther from $\mu_{Y,0}$ than $\overline{Y}^{act}$ under the null hypothesis or, equivalently, is the probability of obtaining $(\overline{Y} - \mu_{Y,0})/\sigma_{\overline{Y}}$ greater than $(\overline{Y}^{act} - \mu_{Y,0})/\sigma_{\overline{Y}}$ in absolute value. This probability is the shaded area shown in Figure 3.1. Written mathematically, the shaded tail probability in Figure 3.1 (that is, the p-value) is

$$p\text{-value} = \Pr_{H_0}\left(\left|\frac{\overline{Y} - \mu_{Y,0}}{\sigma_{\overline{Y}}}\right| > \left|\frac{\overline{Y}^{act} - \mu_{Y,0}}{\sigma_{\overline{Y}}}\right|\right) = 2\Phi\left(-\left|\frac{\overline{Y}^{act} - \mu_{Y,0}}{\sigma_{\overline{Y}}}\right|\right), \quad (3.6)$$

where Φ is the standard normal cumulative distribution function. That is, the p-value is the area in the tails of a standard normal distribution outside $\pm\,(\overline{Y}^{act} - \mu_{Y,0})/\sigma_{\overline{Y}}$.

The formula for the p-value in Equation (3.6) depends on the variance of the population distribution, σ_Y^2. In practice, this variance is typically unknown. (An exception is when Y_i is binary so its distribution is Bernoulli, in which case the variance is determined by the null hypothesis; see Equation (2.7)). Because in general σ_Y^2 must be estimated before the p-value can be computed, we now turn to the problem of estimating σ_Y^2.

The Sample Variance, Sample Standard Deviation, and Standard Error

The sample variance s_Y^2 is an estimator of the population variance σ_Y^2; the sample standard deviation s_Y is an estimator of the population standard deviation σ_Y; and the standard error of the sample average $\overline{Y}$ is an estimator of the standard deviation of the sampling distribution of $\overline{Y}$.

FIGURE 3.1   Calculating a p-value

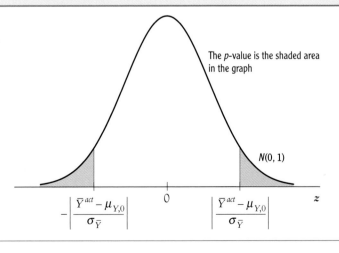

The p-value is the probability of drawing a value of $\overline{Y}$ that differs from $\mu_{Y,0}$ by at least as much as $\overline{Y}^{act}$. In large samples, $\overline{Y}$ is distributed $N(\mu_{Y,0}, \sigma_{\overline{Y}}^2)$ under the null hypothesis, so $(\overline{Y} - \mu_{Y,0})/\sigma_{\overline{Y}}$ is distributed $N(0, 1)$. Thus the p-value is the shaded standard normal tail probability outside $\pm|(\overline{Y}^{act} - \mu_{Y,0})/\sigma_{\overline{Y}}|$.

The p-value is the shaded area in the graph

$N(0, 1)$

$$-\left|\frac{\overline{Y}^{act} - \mu_{Y,0}}{\sigma_{\overline{Y}}}\right| \qquad 0 \qquad \left|\frac{\overline{Y}^{act} - \mu_{Y,0}}{\sigma_{\overline{Y}}}\right| \qquad z$$

The sample variance and standard deviation.   The **sample variance**, s_Y^2, is

$$s_Y^2 = \frac{1}{n-1} \sum_{i=1}^{n} (Y_i - \overline{Y})^2. \tag{3.7}$$

The **sample standard deviation**, s_Y, is the square root of the sample variance.

The formula for the sample variance is much like the formula for the population variance. The population variance, $E(Y - \mu_Y)^2$, is the average value of $(Y - \mu_Y)^2$ in the population distribution. Similarly, the sample variance is the sample average of $(Y_i - \mu_Y)^2$, $i = 1, \ldots, n$, with two modifications: first, μ_Y is replaced by $\overline{Y}$, and second, the average uses the divisor $n - 1$ instead of n.

The reason for the first modification—replacing μ_Y by $\overline{Y}$—is that μ_Y is unknown and thus must be estimated; the natural estimator of μ_Y is $\overline{Y}$. The reason for the second modification—dividing by $n - 1$ instead of by n—is that estimating μ_Y by $\overline{Y}$ introduces a small downward bias in $(Y_i - \overline{Y})^2$. Specifically, as is shown in Exercise 3.11, $E[(Y_i - \overline{Y})^2] = [(n-1)/n]\sigma_Y^2$. Thus, $E\sum_{i=1}^{n}(Y_i - \overline{Y})^2 = n\, E[(Y_i - \overline{Y})^2] = (n-1)\sigma_Y^2$. Dividing by $n - 1$ in Equation (3.7) instead of n corrects for this small downward bias, and as a result s_Y^2 is unbiased.

Dividing by $n - 1$ in Equation (3.7) instead of n is called a **degrees of freedom** correction: estimating the mean uses up some of the information—that is, uses up one "degree of freedom"—in the data, so that only $n - 1$ degrees of freedom remain.

Consistency of the sample variance.   The sample variance is a consistent estimator of the population variance, that is,

$$s_Y^2 \xrightarrow{p} \sigma_Y^2. \tag{3.8}$$

In other words, the sample variance is close to the population variance with high probability when n is large.

The result in Equation (3.8) is proven in Appendix 3.3 under the assumptions that $Y_1, \ldots, Y_n$ are i.i.d. and Y_i has a finite fourth moment; that is, $E(Y_i^4) < \infty$. Intuitively, the reason that s_Y^2 is consistent is that it is a sample average, so s_Y^2 obeys the Law of Large Numbers. But for s_Y^2 to obey the law of large numbers in Key Concept 2.6, $(Y_i - \mu_Y)^2$ must have finite variance, which in turn means that $E(Y_i^4)$ must be finite, that is, that Y_i must have a finite fourth moment.

The standard error of $\overline{Y}$.   Because the standard deviation of the sampling distribution of $\overline{Y}$ is $\sigma_{\overline{Y}} = \sigma_Y / \sqrt{n}$, Equation (3.8) justifies using $s_Y / \sqrt{n}$ as an estimator of $\sigma_{\overline{Y}}$. The estimator of $\sigma_{\overline{Y}}$, $s_Y/\sqrt{n}$, is called the **standard error** of $\overline{Y}$ and is denoted by $SE(\overline{Y})$ or by $\hat{\sigma}_{\overline{Y}}$ (the "^" over the symbol means that this is an estimator of $\sigma_{\overline{Y}}$). The standard error of $\overline{Y}$ is summarized as Key Concept 3.4.

Calculating the p-Value When σ_Y Is Unknown

Because s_Y^2 is a consistent estimator of σ_Y^2, the p-value can be computed by replacing $\sigma_{\overline{Y}}$ in Equation (3.6) by the standard error, $SE(\overline{Y}) = \hat{\sigma}_{\overline{Y}}$. That is, when σ_Y is unknown and $Y_1, \ldots, Y_n$ are i.i.d., the p-value is calculated using the formula

$$p\text{-value} = 2\Phi\left(-\left|\frac{\overline{Y}^{act} - \mu_{Y,0}}{SE(\overline{Y})}\right|\right). \tag{3.9}$$

The t-Statistic

The standardized sample average $(\overline{Y} - \mu_{Y,0})/SE(\overline{Y})$ plays a central role in testing statistical hypotheses and has a special name, the **t-statistic** or **t-ratio**:

$$t = \frac{\overline{Y} - \mu_{Y,0}}{SE(\overline{Y})}. \tag{3.10}$$

In general, a **test statistic** is a statistic used to perform a hypothesis test. The t-statistic is an important example of a test statistic.

Large-sample distribution of the t-statistic. When n is large, s_Y^2 is close to σ_Y^2 with high probability. Thus the distribution of the t-statistic is approximately the same as the distribution of $(\overline{Y} - \mu_{Y,0})/\sigma_{\overline{Y}}$, which in turn is well approximated by the standard normal distribution when n is large because of the central limit theorem (Key Concept 2.7). Accordingly, under the null hypothesis,

$$t \text{ is approximately distributed } N(0, 1) \text{ for large } n. \tag{3.11}$$

The formula for the p-value in Equation (3.9) can be rewritten in terms of the t-statistic. Let t^{act} denote the value of the t-statistic actually computed, that is,

$$t^{act} = \frac{\overline{Y}^{act} - \mu_{Y,0}}{SE(\overline{Y})}. \tag{3.12}$$

Accordingly, when n is large, the p-value can be calculated using

$$p\text{-value} = 2\Phi(-|t^{act}|). \tag{3.13}$$

The Standard Error of $\overline{Y}$

The **standard error** of $\overline{Y}$ is an estimator of the standard deviation of $\overline{Y}$. The standard error of $\overline{Y}$ is denoted by $SE(\overline{Y})$ or by $\hat{\sigma}_{\overline{Y}}$. When $Y_1, \ldots, Y_n$ are i.i.d.,

$$SE(\overline{Y}) = \hat{\sigma}_{\overline{Y}} = s_Y / \sqrt{n}. \qquad (3.14)$$

Key Concept 3.4

As a hypothetical example, suppose that a sample of $n = 200$ recent college graduates is used to test the null hypothesis that the mean wage, $E(Y)$, is \$20/hour. The sample average wage is $\overline{Y}^{act} = \$22.64$ and the sample standard deviation is $s_Y = \$18.14$. Then the standard error of $\overline{Y}$ is $s_Y / \sqrt{n} = 18.14 / \sqrt{200} = 1.28$. The value of the t-statistic is $t^{act} = (22.64 - 20)/1.28 = 2.06$. From Appendix Table 1, the p-value is $2\Phi(-2.06) = .039$, or 3.9%. That is, assuming the null hypothesis to be true, the probability of obtaining a sample average at least as different from the null as the one actually computed is 3.9%.

Distribution of the t-statistic when Y is normally distributed. When the population distribution is normal, the t-statistic has the Student t distribution with $n - 1$ degrees of freedom (Section 2.4), so in this special case the p-value can be computed exactly for any sample size n without relying on the central limit theorem. Because the area in the tails of the Student t distribution exceeds that of the normal distribution, p-values computed using the Student t distribution are somewhat larger than those computed using the normal distribution.

Although some statistical software computes p-values using the Student t distribution, this distribution will not be used in this book for two reasons. First, the t-statistic has a Student t distribution only if the population distribution is normal, which very often is a poor approximation to the actual distribution of economic data. Thus the advantage of this distribution holding exactly when Y is normally distributed is outweighed by the fact that it is rarely applicable. Second, the differences between the Student t distribution and the standard normal distribution are very small if the sample size is moderate and are negligible if it is large. For $n > 15$, the difference in the p-values computed using the t- and normal distributions never exceed 0.01 and for $n > 80$ they never exceed 0.002.

In modern applications, and in all the applications in this textbook, the sample sizes are in the hundreds or thousands, large enough for the difference between the Student t distribution and the standard normal distribution to be negligible.

Hypothesis Testing with a Prespecified Significance Level

Suppose it has been decided that the hypothesis will be rejected if the p-value is less than 5%. Because the area under the tails of the normal distribution outside ± 1.96 is 5%, this gives a simple rule:

$$\text{Reject } H_0 \text{ if } |t^{act}| > 1.96, \tag{3.15}$$

that is, reject if the absolute value of the t-statistic computed from the sample is greater than 1.96. If n is large enough, then under the null hypothesis the t-statistic has a $N(0, 1)$ distribution. Thus, the probability of erroneously rejecting the null hypothesis (rejecting the null hypothesis when it is in fact true) is 5%.

This framework for testing statistical hypotheses has some specialized terminology, summarized in Key Concept 3.5. The significance level of the test in Equation (3.15) is 5%, the critical value of this two-sided test is 1.96, and the rejection region is the values of the t-statistic outside ± 1.96. If the test rejects at the 5% significance level, the population mean μ_Y is said to be statistically significantly different from $\mu_{Y,0}$ at the 5% significance level.

Testing hypotheses using a prespecified significance level does not require computing p-values. In the previous example of testing the hypothesis that the mean earning of recent college graduates is \$20, the t-statistic was 2.06. This exceeds 1.96, so the hypothesis is rejected at the 5% level. Although performing the test with a 5% significance level is easy, reporting only whether the null hypothesis is rejected at a prespecified significance level conveys less information than reporting the p-value.

What significance level should you use in practice? In many cases, statisticians and econometricians use a 5% significance level. If you were to test many statistical hypotheses at the 5% level, you would incorrectly reject the null on average once in 20 cases. Sometimes a more conservative significance level might be in order. For example, legal cases sometimes involve statistical evidence, and the null hypothesis could be that the defendant is not guilty; then one would want to be quite sure that a rejection of the null (conclusion of guilt) is not just a result of random sample variation. In some legal settings the significance level used is 1%

The Terminology of Hypothesis Testing

The prespecified rejection probability of a statistical hypothesis test under the null hypothesis is the **significance level** of the test. The **critical value** of the test statistic is the value of the statistic for which the test just rejects the null hypothesis at the given significance level. The set of values of the test statistic for which the test rejects the null is the **rejection region**, and the values of the test statistic for which it does not reject the null is the **acceptance region**. The probability that the test actually incorrectly rejects the null hypothesis when the null is true is the **size** of the test, and the probability that the test correctly rejects the null when the alternative is true is the **power** of the test.

The p-value is the probability of obtaining a test statistic, by random sampling variation, at least as adverse to the null hypothesis value as is the statistic actually observed, assuming that the null hypothesis is correct. Equivalently, the p-value is the smallest significance level at which you can reject the null hypothesis.

Key Concept 3.5

or even 0.1%, to avoid this sort of mistake. Similarly, if a government agency is considering permitting the sale of a new drug, a very conservative standard might be in order so that consumers can be sure that the drugs available in the market actually work.

Being conservative, in the sense of using a very low significance level, has a cost: the smaller the significance level, the larger the critical value, and the more difficult it becomes to reject the null when the null is false. In fact, the most conservative thing to do is never to reject the null hypothesis—but if that is your view, then you never need to look at any statistical evidence, for you will never change your mind! The lower the significance level, the lower the power of the test. Many economic and policy applications can call for less conservatism than a legal case, so a 5% significance level is often considered to be a reasonable compromise.

Key Concept 3.6 summarizes hypothesis tests for the population mean against the two-sided alternative.

One-Sided Alternatives

In some circumstances, the alternative hypothesis might be that the mean exceeds $\mu_{Y,0}$. For example, one hopes that education helps in the labor market, so the

Key

Concept

3.6

Testing the Hypothesis $E(Y) = \mu_{Y,0}$ Against the Alternative $E(Y) \neq \mu_{Y,0}$

1. Compute the standard error of $\overline{Y}$, $SE(\overline{Y})$ (Equation (3.14)).

2. Compute the t-statistic (Equation (3.10)).

3. Compute the p-value (Equation (3.13)). Reject the hypothesis at the 5% significance level if the p-value is less than .05 (equivalently, if $|t^{act}| > 1.96$).

relevant alternative to the null hypothesis that earnings are the same for college graduates and nongraduates is not just that their earnings differ, but rather that graduates earn more than nongraduates. This is called a **one-sided alternative hypothesis** and can be written

$$H_1: E(Y) > \mu_{Y,0} \ \text{(one-sided alternative)}. \tag{3.16}$$

The general approach to computing p-values and to hypothesis testing is the same for one-sided alternatives as it is for two-sided alternatives, with the modification that only large positive values of the t-statistic reject, rather than values that are large in absolute value. Specifically, to test the one-sided hypothesis in Equation (3.16), construct the t-statistic in Equation (3.10). The p-value is the area under the standard normal distribution to the right of the calculated t-statistic. That is, the p-value, based on the $N(0, 1)$ approximation to the distribution of the t-statistic, is

$$p\text{-value} = \text{Pr}_{H_0}(Z > t^{act}) = 1 - \Phi(t^{act}). \tag{3.17}$$

The $N(0, 1)$ critical value for a one-sided test with a 5% significance level is 1.645. The rejection region for this test is all values of the t-statistic exceeding 1.645.

The one-sided hypothesis in Equation (3.16) concerns values of μ_Y exceeding $\mu_{Y,0}$. If instead the alternative hypothesis is that $E(Y) < \mu_{Y,0}$, then the discussion of the previous paragraph applies except that the signs are switched; for example, the 5% rejection region consists of values of the t-statistic less than -1.645.

3.3 Confidence Intervals for the Population Mean

Because of random sampling error, it is impossible to learn the exact value of the population mean of Y using only the information in a sample. However, it is possible to use data from a random sample to construct a set of values that contains the true population mean μ_Y with a certain prespecified probability. Such a set is called a **confidence set**, and the prespecified probability that μ_Y is contained in this set is called the **confidence level**. The confidence set for μ_Y turns out to be all the possible values of the mean between a lower and an upper limit, so that the confidence set is an interval, that is, a **confidence interval**.

Here is one way to construct a 95% confidence set for the population mean. Begin by picking some arbitrary value for the mean; call this $\mu_{Y,0}$. Test the null hypothesis that $\mu_Y = \mu_{Y,0}$ against the alternative that $\mu_Y \neq \mu_{Y,0}$ by computing the t-statistic; if it is less than 1.96, this hypothesized value $\mu_{Y,0}$ is not rejected at the 5% level, and write down this nonrejected value $\mu_{Y,0}$. Now pick another arbitrary value of $\mu_{Y,0}$ and test it; if you cannot reject it, write this value down on your list too. Do this again and again, and indeed, keep doing this for all possible values of the population mean. Continuing this process yields the set of all values of the population mean that cannot be rejected at the 5% level by a two-sided hypothesis test.

This list is useful because it summarizes the set of hypotheses you can and cannot reject (at the 5% level) based on your data: if someone walks up to you with a specific number in mind, you can tell him whether his hypothesis is rejected or not simply by looking up his number on your handy list. A bit of clever reasoning shows that this set of values has a remarkable property: the probability that it contains the true value of the population mean is 95%.

The clever reasoning goes like this. Suppose the true value of μ_Y is 21.5 (although we do not know this). Then $\overline{Y}$ has a normal distribution centered around 21.5, and the t-statistic testing the null hypothesis $\mu_Y = 21.5$ has a $N(0, 1)$ distribution. Thus, if n is large, the probability of rejecting the null hypothesis $\mu_Y = 21.5$ at the 5% level is 5%. But because you tested all possible values of the population mean in constructing your set, in particular you tested the true value, $\mu_Y = 21.5$. In 95% of all samples, you will correctly accept 21.5; this means that in 95% of all samples, your list will contain the true value of μ_Y. Thus, the values on your list constitute a 95% confidence set for μ_Y.

This method of constructing a confidence set is impractical, for it requires you to test all possible values of μ_Y as null hypotheses. Fortunately there is a much easier approach. According to the formula for the t-statistic in Equation (3.10), a trial value of $\mu_{Y,0}$ is rejected at the 5% level if it is more than 1.96 standard errors away from $\overline{Y}$. Thus the set of values of μ_Y that are not rejected at the 5% level consists of those values within $\pm 1.96 SE(\overline{Y})$ of $\overline{Y}$. That is, a 95% confidence interval for μ_Y is $\overline{Y} - 1.96 SE(\overline{Y}) \leq \mu_Y \leq \overline{Y} + 1.96 SE(\overline{Y})$. Key Concept 3.7 summarizes this approach.

As an example, consider the problem of constructing a 95% confidence interval for the mean hourly earnings of recent college graduates using a hypothetical random sample of 200 recent college graduates where $\overline{Y} = \$22.64$ and $SE(\overline{Y}) = 1.28$. The 95% confidence interval for mean hourly earnings is $22.64 \pm 1.96 \times 1.28 = 22.64 \pm 2.51 = (\$20.13, \$25.15)$.

This discussion so far has focused on two-sided confidence intervals. One could instead construct a one-sided confidence interval as the set of values of μ_Y that cannot be rejected by a one-sided hypothesis test. Although one-sided confidence intervals have applications in some branches of statistics, they are uncommon in applied econometric analysis.

Coverage probabilities.   The **coverage probability** of a confidence interval for the population mean is the probability, computed over repeated samples, that it contains the true population mean.

3.4 Comparing Means from Different Populations

Do recent male and female college graduates earn the same amount on average? This question involves comparing the means of two different population distributions. This section summarizes how to test hypotheses and how to construct confidence intervals for the difference in the means from two different populations.

Hypothesis Tests for the Difference Between Two Means

Let μ_w be the mean hourly earning in the population of women recently graduated from college and let μ_m be the population mean for recently graduated men. Consider the null hypothesis that earnings for these two populations differ by a

Confidence Intervals for the Population Mean

A 95% two-sided confidence interval for μ_Y is an interval constructed so that it contains the true value of μ_Y in 95% of its applications. When the sample size n is large, 95%, 90%, and 99% confidence intervals for μ_Y are:

Key Concept 3.7

95% confidence interval for $\mu_Y = \{\overline{Y} \pm 1.96 SE(\overline{Y})\}$.
90% confidence interval for $\mu_Y = \{\overline{Y} \pm 1.64 SE(\overline{Y})\}$.
99% confidence interval for $\mu_Y = \{\overline{Y} \pm 2.58 SE(\overline{Y})\}$.

certain amount, say d_0. Then the null hypothesis and the two-sided alternative hypothesis are

$$H_0: \mu_m - \mu_w = d_0 \text{ vs. } H_1: \mu_m - \mu_w \neq d_0. \tag{3.18}$$

The null hypothesis that men and women in these populations have the same earnings corresponds to H_0 in Equation (3.18) with $d_0 = 0$.

Because these population means are unknown, they must be estimated from samples of men and women. Suppose we have samples of n_m men and n_w women drawn at random from their populations. Let the sample average annual earnings be $\overline{Y}_m$ for men and $\overline{Y}_w$ for women. Then an estimator of $\mu_m - \mu_w$ is $\overline{Y}_m - \overline{Y}_w$.

To test the null hypothesis that $\mu_m - \mu_w = d_0$ using $\overline{Y}_m - \overline{Y}_w$, we need to know the distribution of $\overline{Y}_m - \overline{Y}_w$. Recall that $\overline{Y}_m$ is, according to the central limit theorem, approximately distributed $N(\mu_m, \sigma_m^2/n_m)$, where σ_m^2 is the population variance of earnings for men. Similarly, $\overline{Y}_w$ is approximately distributed $N(\mu_w, \sigma_w^2/n_w)$, where σ_w^2 is the population variance of earnings for women. Also, recall from Section 2.4 that a weighted average of two normal random variables is itself normally distributed. Because $\overline{Y}_m$ and $\overline{Y}_w$ are constructed from different randomly selected samples, they are independent random variables. Thus, $\overline{Y}_m - \overline{Y}_w$ is distributed $N[\mu_m - \mu_w, (\sigma_m^2/n_m) + (\sigma_w^2/n_w)]$.

If σ_m^2 and σ_w^2 are known, then this approximate normal distribution can be used to compute p-values for the test of the null hypothesis that $\mu_m - \mu_w = d_0$. In practice, however, these population variances are typically unknown so they must be estimated. As before, they can be estimated using the sample variances, s_m^2 and s_w^2, where s_m^2 is defined as in Equation (3.7), except that the statistic is computed only for the men in the sample, and s_w^2 is defined similarly for the women. Thus the standard error of $\overline{Y}_m - \overline{Y}_w$ is

$$SE(\overline{Y}_m - \overline{Y}_w) = \sqrt{\frac{s_m^2}{n_m} + \frac{s_w^2}{n_w}}. \tag{3.19}$$

The t-statistic for testing the null hypothesis is constructed analogously to the t-statistic for testing a hypothesis about a single population mean, that is, by subtracting the null hypothesized value of $\mu_m - \mu_w$ from the estimator $\overline{Y}_m - \overline{Y}_w$ and dividing the result by the standard error of $\overline{Y}_m - \overline{Y}_w$:

$$t = \frac{(\overline{Y}_m - \overline{Y}_w) - d_0}{SE(\overline{Y}_m - \overline{Y}_w)} \quad (t\text{-statistic for comparing two means}). \tag{3.20}$$

If both n_m and n_w are large, then this t-statistic has a standard normal distribution.[1]

Because the t-statistic in Equation (3.20) has a standard normal distribution under the null hypothesis when n_m and n_w are large, the p-value of the two-sided test is computed exactly as it was in the case of a single population; that is, the p-value is computed using Equation (3.13).

To conduct a test with a prespecified significance level, simply calculate the t-statistic in Equation (3.20) and compare it to the appropriate critical value. For example, the null hypothesis is rejected at the 5% significance level if the absolute value of the t-statistic exceeds 1.96.

If the alternative is one-sided rather than two-sided, that is, if the alternative is that $\mu_m - \mu_w > d_0$, then the test is modified as outlined in Section 3.2. The p-value is computed using Equation (3.17), and a test with a 5% significance level rejects when $t > 1.65$.

---

[1]If the two population variances are equal (i.e., $\sigma_m^2 = \sigma_w^2 = \sigma^2$), then $\overline{Y}_m - \overline{Y}_w$ is distributed $N(\mu_m - \mu_w, [(1/n_m) + (1/n_w)]\sigma^2)$. In this special case, it is possible to use the so-called pooled variance estimator of σ^2,

$$s_{pooled}^2 = \frac{1}{n_m + n_w - 2} \left[\sum_{i=1}^{n_m} (Y_i - \overline{Y}_m)^2 + \sum_{j=1}^{n_w} (Y_j - \overline{Y}_w)^2 \right],$$

where the first summation in this expression is for the observations on the men and the second summation is for the observations on the women. If the population variances differ, then the pooled variance estimator is biased and inconsistent. Therefore the pooled variance estimator should not be used in practice unless you have a good reason to believe that the population variances are the same.

Confidence Intervals for the Difference Between Two Population Means

The method for constructing confidence intervals summarized in Section 3.3 extends to constructing a confidence interval for the difference between the means, $d = \mu_m - \mu_w$. Because the hypothesized value d_0 is rejected at the 5% level if $|t| > 1.96$, d_0 will be in the confidence set if $|t| \leq 1.96$. But $|t| \leq 1.96$ means that the estimated difference, $\overline{Y}_m - \overline{Y}_w$, is less than 1.96 standard errors away from d_0. Thus, the 95% two-sided confidence interval for d consists of those values of d within ± 1.96 standard errors of $\overline{Y}_m - \overline{Y}_w$:

$$\text{95\% confidence interval for } d = \mu_m - \mu_w \text{ is } (\overline{Y}_m - \overline{Y}_w) \pm 1.96 SE(\overline{Y}_m - \overline{Y}_w). \quad (3.21)$$

With these formulas in hand, we now turn to an empirical investigation of gender differences in earnings of U.S. college graduates.

3.5 Earnings of Male and Female College Graduates in the United States

Historically men have had better access to well-paying jobs than have women. However, changes in social norms and legislation banning discrimination on the basis of gender have led to an equal role for men and women in the modern workplace—at least in theory. But what in fact are the differences, if any, in earnings of young, well-educated men and women?

Table 3.1 gives estimates of hourly earnings for college-educated full-time workers aged 25–34 in the United States. The statistics in Table 3.1 were computed from data collected as part of the Current Population Survey (CPS), which is described in Appendix 3.1. All earnings were adjusted for inflation by putting them in 1998 dollars using the Consumer Price Index.[2]

The first three columns of the table present summary information for men; the next three, for women; and the final three, for the difference between men

---

[2]Because of inflation, one dollar in 1992 was worth more than one dollar in 1998, in the sense that a dollar in 1992 could buy more goods and services than a dollar in 1998. Thus earnings in 1992 are not directly comparable to earnings in 1998 without adjusting for inflation. One way to make this adjustment is to use the Consumer Price Index (CPI), a measure of the price of a "market basket" of consumer goods and services constructed by the Bureau of Labor Statistics. Over the six years from 1992 to 1998, the price of the CPI market basket rose by 16.2%; that is, the CPI basket of goods and services costing $100 in 1992 cost $116.20 in 1998. To make earnings in 1992 and 1998 comparable in Table 3.1, 1992 earnings are inflated by the amount of overall CPI price inflation, that is, by multiplying 1992 earnings by 1.162 to put them into "1998 dollars."

TABLE 3.1 Hourly Earnings in the United States of Working College Graduates, Aged 25–34: Selected Statistics from the Current Population Survey, in 1998 Dollars

	Men			Women			Difference, Men vs. Women		
Year	$\bar{Y}_m$	s_m	n_m	$\bar{Y}_w$	s_w	n_w	$\bar{Y}_m - \bar{Y}_w$	$SE(\bar{Y}_m - \bar{Y}_w)$	95% Confidence Interval for d
1992	17.57	7.50	1591	15.22	5.97	1371	2.35**	0.25	1.87–2.84
1994	16.93	7.39	1598	15.01	6.41	1358	1.92**	0.25	1.42–2.42
1996	16.88	7.29	1374	14.42	6.07	1235	2.46**	0.26	1.94–2.97
1998	17.94	7.86	1393	15.49	6.80	1210	2.45**	0.29	1.89–3.02

These estimates are computed using data on all full-time workers aged 25–34 from the CPS for the indicated years. The difference is significantly different from zero at the *5% or **1% significance level.

and women. For example, the CPS administered in March 1999 surveyed 64,000 households, which included 1,393 men employed full time aged 25 to 34 years with a college degree. The average hourly earnings in 1998 of these 1,393 men is $17.94, and the standard deviation of these earnings is $7.86. Average hourly earnings in 1998 for the 1,210 women in that survey were $15.49, with a standard deviation of $6.80. The wage gap is $17.94 − $15.49 = $2.45 per hour. The standard error is $\sqrt{(\$7.86^2/1393) + (\$6.80^2/1210)} = \$0.29$, so the t-statistic testing that the wage gap is zero is ($2.45 − 0)/$0.29 = 8.45. This exceeds the 1% two-sided test critical value of 2.58, so this is significant at the 1% level (indeed, it is significant at the .01% level). The 95% confidence interval for this gap is $2.45 ± 1.96 × 0.29 = ($1.89, $3.02). That is, with a 95% confidence level, we estimate that the wage gap between the two populations is between $1.89 and $3.02.

The male-female wage gap is large: according to the estimates in Table 3.1, in 1998 women earned 14% less per hour than men ($2.45/$17.94). Moreover the gap did not change very much during the 1990s. It is quite unlikely that this estimated gap is simply an artifact of sampling error: $1.89 is the lowest value of the gap contained in the 95% confidence interval for 1998.

This statistical analysis documents that there is a "gender gap" in hourly earnings, but it does not say anything about its source or causes. Is this gap a consequence of gender discrimination in the labor market, or is it a reflection of differences between men and women in skills and experience, which in turn lead to differences in pay? To attack such questions we need the tools of multiple regression analysis, the topic of Part II. First, however, we must review scatterplots, the sample covariance, and the sample correlation coefficient.

3.6   Scatterplots, the Sample Covariance, and the Sample Correlation

What is the relationship between age and earnings? This question, like many others, relates one variable, X (age), to another, Y (earnings). This section reviews three ways to summarize the relationship between variables: the scatterplot, the sample covariance, and the sample correlation coefficient.

Scatterplots

A **scatterplot** is a plot of n observations on X_i and Y_i, in which each observation is represented by the point (X_i, Y_i). For example, Figure 3.2 is a scatterplot of age (X) and hourly earnings (Y) for a sample of 184 technicians without college degrees working in the communications industry from the March 1999 CPS. Each dot in Figure 3.2 corresponds to an (X, Y) pair for one of the observations. For example one of the workers in this sample is 35 years old and earns \$19.61 per hour; this worker's age and earnings are indicated by the colored dot in Figure 3.2. The scatterplot shows a positive relationship between age and earnings in this sample: older communications technicians tend to earn more than younger technicians. This relationship is not exact, however, and earnings could not be predicted perfectly using only a person's age.

Sample Covariance and Correlation

The covariance and correlation were introduced in Section 2.3 as two properties of the joint probability distribution of the random variables X and Y. Because the population distribution is unknown, in practice we do not know the population covariance or correlation. The population covariance and correlation can, however, be estimated by taking a random sample of n members of the population and collecting the data (X_i, Y_i), $i = 1, \ldots, n$.

The sample covariance and correlation are estimators of the population covariance and correlation. Like the estimators discussed previously in this chapter, they are computed by replacing a population average (the expectation) with a sample average. The **sample covariance**, denoted s_{XY}, is

$$s_{XY} = \frac{1}{n-1} \sum_{i=1}^{n} (X_i - \overline{X})(Y_i - \overline{Y}). \tag{3.22}$$

Like the sample variance, the average in Equation (3.22) is computed by dividing by $n - 1$ instead of n; here too this difference stems from using $\overline{X}$ and $\overline{Y}$ to estimate

---

FIGURE 3.2 **Scatterplot of Average Hourly Earnings vs. Age**

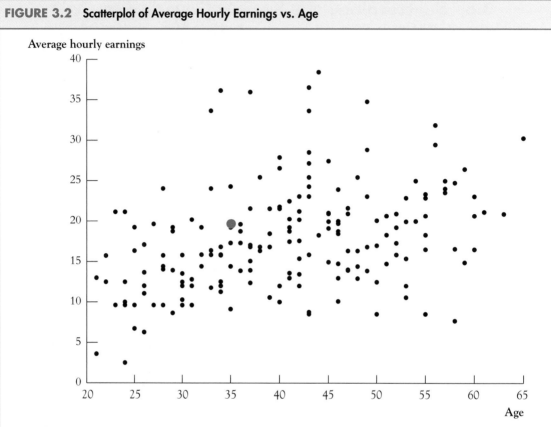

Each point in the plot represents the age and average earnings of one of the 184 workers in the sample. The colored dot corresponds to a 35-year-old worker who earns $19.61 per hour. The data are for technicians in the communications industry without college degrees from the March 1999 CPS.

---

the respective population means. When n is large, it makes little difference whether division is by n or $n - 1$.

The **sample correlation coefficient,** or **sample correlation,** is denoted r_{XY} and is the ratio of the sample covariance to the sample standard deviations:

$$r_{XY} = \frac{s_{XY}}{s_X s_Y}.$$ (3.23)

The sample correlation measures the strength of the linear association between X and Y in a sample of n observations. Like the population correlation, the sample correlation is unitless and lies between -1 and 1, that is, $|r_{XY}| \leq 1$.

The sample correlation equals 1 if $X_i = Y_i$ for all i and equals -1 if $X_i = -Y_i$ for all i. More generally, the correlation is ± 1 if the scatterplot is a straight line. If the line slopes upward, then there is a positive relationship between X and Y and the correlation is 1. If the line slopes down, then there is a negative relationship and the correlation is -1. The closer the scatterplot is to a straight line, the closer is the correlation to ± 1. A high correlation coefficient does not necessarily mean that the line has a steep slope; rather, it means that the points in the scatterplot fall very close to a straight line.

Consistency of the sample covariance and correlation.   Like the sample variance, the sample covariance is consistent. That is,

$$s_{XY} \xrightarrow{p} \sigma_{XY}. \tag{3.24}$$

In other words, in large samples the sample covariance is close to the population covariance with high probability.

The proof of the result in Equation (3.24) under the assumption that (X_i, Y_i) are i.i.d. and that X_i and Y_i have finite fourth moments is similar to the proof in Appendix 3.3 that the sample covariance is consistent, and is left as an exercise (Exercise 15.2).

Because the sample variance and sample covariance are consistent, the sample correlation coefficient is consistent, that is, $r_{XY} \xrightarrow{p} \mathrm{corr}(X_i, Y_i)$.

Example.   As an example, consider the data on age and earnings in Figure 3.2. For these 184 workers, the sample standard deviation of age is $s_A = 10.49$ years and the sample standard deviation of earnings is $s_E = \$6.44/\mathrm{hour}$. The covariance between age and earnings is $s_{AE} = 24.29$ (the units are years $\times$ dollars per hour, not readily interpretable). Thus, the correlation coefficient is $r_{AE} = 24.29/(10.49 \times 6.44) = 0.36$ or 36%. The correlation of 0.36 means that there is a positive relationship between age and earnings, but as is evident in the scatterplot, this relationship is far from perfect.

To verify that the correlation does not depend on the units of measurement, suppose that earnings had been reported in cents, in which case the sample standard deviations of earnings is 644¢/hour and the covariance between age and earnings is 2429 (units are years $\times$ cents/hour); then the correlation is $2429/(10.49 \times 644) = 0.36$ or 36%.

Figure 3.3 gives additional examples of scatterplots and correlation. Figure 3.3a shows a strong positive linear relationship between these variables, and the sample correlation is 0.9. Figure 3.3b shows a strong negative relationship with a sample correlation of −0.8. Figure 3.3c shows a scatterplot with no evident relationship, and the sample correlation is zero. Figure 3.3d shows a clear relationship: as X increases, Y initially increases but then decreases. Despite this discernable relation-

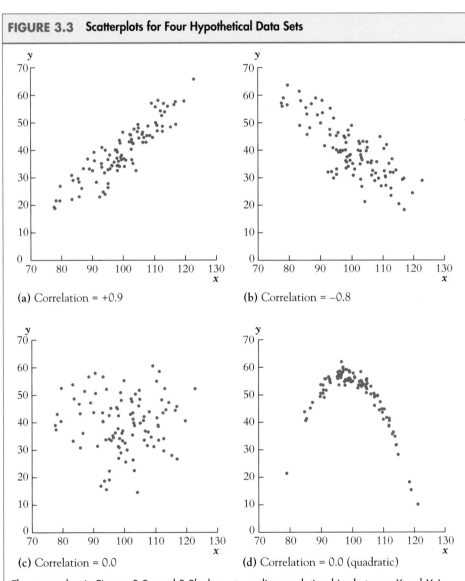

FIGURE 3.3   Scatterplots for Four Hypothetical Data Sets

(a) Correlation = +0.9

(b) Correlation = −0.8

(c) Correlation = 0.0

(d) Correlation = 0.0 (quadratic)

The scatterplots in Figures 3.3a and 3.3b show strong linear relationships between X and Y. In Figure 3.3c, X is independent of Y and the two variables are uncorrelated. In Figure 3.3d, the two variables also are uncorrelated even though they are related nonlinearly.

ship between X and Y, the sample correlation is zero; the reason is that, for these data, small values of Y are associated with *both* large and small values of X.

This final example emphasizes an important point: the correlation coefficient is a measure of *linear* association. There is a relationship in Figure 3.3d, but it is not linear.

Summary

1. The sample average, $\overline{Y}$, is an estimator of the population mean, μ_Y. When $Y_1, \ldots, Y_n$ are i.i.d.,
   a. the sampling distribution of $\overline{Y}$ has mean μ_Y and variance $\sigma_{\overline{Y}}^2 = \sigma_Y^2/n$;
   b. $\overline{Y}$ is unbiased;
   c. by the law of large numbers, $\overline{Y}$ is consistent; and
   d. by the central limit theorem, $\overline{Y}$ has an approximately normal sampling distribution when the sample size is large.
2. The t-statistic is used to test the null hypothesis that the population mean takes on a particular value. If n is large, the t-statistic has a standard normal sampling distribution when the null hypothesis is true.
3. The t-statistic can be used to calculate the p-value associated with the null hypothesis. A small p-value is evidence that the null hypothesis is false.
4. A 95% confidence interval for μ_Y is an interval constructed so that it contains the true value of μ_Y in 95% of repeated samples.
5. Hypothesis tests and confidence intervals for the difference in the means of two populations are conceptually similar to tests and intervals for the mean of a single population.
6. The sample correlation coefficient is an estimator of the population correlation coefficient and measures the linear relationship between two variables, that is, how well their scatterplot is approximated by a straight line.

Key Terms

estimator (57)

estimate (57)

bias, consistency, and efficiency (59)

least squares estimator (60)

hypothesis test (61)

null and alternative hypotheses (61)

two-sided alternative hypothesis (62)

p-value (62)

sample variance (65)

sample standard deviation (65)

Review the Concepts

3.1 Explain the difference between the sample average $\overline{Y}$ and the population mean.

3.2 Explain the difference between an estimator and an estimate. Provide an example of each.

3.3 A population distribution has a mean of 10 and a variance of 16. Determine the mean and variance of $\overline{Y}$ from an i.i.d. sample from this population for (a) $n = 10$; (b) $n = 100$; and (c) $n = 1000$. Relate your answers to the law of large numbers.

3.4 What role does the central limit theorem play in statistical hypothesis testing? In the construction of confidence intervals?

3.5 What is the difference between a null and alternative hypothesis? Among size, significance level, and power? Between a one-sided and two-sided alternative hypothesis?

3.6 Why does a confidence interval contain more information than the result of a single hypothesis test?

3.7 Sketch a hypothetical scatterplot for a sample of size 10 for two random variables with a population correlation of (a) 1.0; (b) −1.0; (c) 0.9; (d) −0.5; (e) 0.0.

Exercises

3.1 In a population $\mu_Y = 100$ and $\sigma_Y^2 = 43$. Use the central limit theorem to answer the following questions:

*a. In a random sample of size $n = 100$, find $\Pr(\overline{Y} < 101)$.

b. In a random sample of size $n = 64$, find $\Pr(101 < \overline{Y} < 103)$.

c. In a random sample of size $n = 165$, find $\Pr(\overline{Y} > 98)$.

3.2 Let Y be a Bernoulli random variable with success probability $\Pr(Y = 1) = p$, and let $Y_1, \ldots, Y_n$ be i.i.d. draws from this distribution. Let $\hat{p}$ be the fraction of successes (1s) in this sample.

a. Show that $\hat{p} = \overline{Y}$.

b. Show that $\hat{p}$ is an unbiased estimator of p.

c. Show that $\text{var}(\hat{p}) = p(1 - p)/n$.

3.3 In a survey of 400 likely voters, 215 responded that they would vote for the incumbent and 185 responded that they would vote for the challenger. Let p denote the fraction of all likely voters that preferred the incumbent at the time of the survey, and let $\hat{p}$ be the fraction of survey respondents that preferred the incumbent.

*a. Use the survey results to estimate p.

*b. Use the estimator of the variance of $\hat{p}$, $\hat{p}(1 - \hat{p})/n$, to calculate the standard error of your estimator.

*c. What is the p-value for the test H_0: $p = 0.5$ vs. H_1: $p \neq 0.5$?

d. What is the p-value for the test H_0: $p = 0.5$ vs. H_1: $p > 0.5$?

e. Why do the results from (c) and (d) differ?

f. Did the survey contain statistically significant evidence that the incumbent was ahead of the challenger at the time of the survey? Explain.

3.4 Using the data in Exercise 3.3:

a. Construct a 95% confidence interval for p.

b. Construct a 99% confidence interval for p.

c. Why is the interval in (b) wider than the interval in (a)?

d. Without doing any additional calculations, test the hypothesis H_0: $p = 0.50$ vs. H_1: $p \neq 0.50$ at the 5% significance level.

3.5 Suppose that a light bulb manufacturing plant produces bulbs with a mean life of 2000 hours and a standard deviation of 200 hours. An inventor claims to have developed an improved process that produces bulbs with a longer mean life and the same standard deviation. The plant manager randomly selects 100 bulbs produced by the process. She says that she will believe the inventor's claim if the sample mean life of the bulbs is greater that 2100 hours, otherwise she will conclude that the new process is no better than the old process. Let μ denote the mean of the new process. Consider the null and alternative hypothesis H_0: $\mu = 2000$ vs. H_1: $\mu > 2000$.

*a.   What is the size of the plant manager's testing procedure?

b.   Suppose that the new process is in fact better and has a mean bulb life of 2150 hours. What is the power of the plant manager's testing procedure?

c.   What testing procedure should the plant manager use if she wants the size of her test to be 5%?

3.6   Suppose a new standardized test is given to 100 randomly selected third-grade students in New Jersey. The sample average score $\overline{Y}$ on the test is 58 points and the sample standard deviation, s_Y, is 8 points.

a.   The authors plan to administer the test to all third–grade students in New Jersey. Construct a 95% confidence interval for the mean score of all New Jersey third graders.

b.   Suppose the same test is given to 200 randomly selected third graders from Iowa, producing a sample average of 62 points and sample standard deviation of 11 points. Construct a 90% confidence interval for the difference in mean scores between Iowa and New Jersey.

c.   Can you conclude with a high degree of confidence that the population means for Iowa and New Jersey students are different? (What is the standard error of the difference in the two sample means? What is the p-value of the test of no difference in means versus some difference?)

3.7   Consider the estimator $\widetilde{Y}$, defined in Equation (3.1). Show that (a) $E(\widetilde{Y}) = \mu_Y$ and (b) $\text{var}(\widetilde{Y}) = 1.25\sigma_Y^2/n$.

3.8   To investigate possible gender discrimination in a firm, a sample of 100 men and 64 women with similar job descriptions are selected at random. A summary of the resulting monthly salaries are:

	Average Salary ($\overline{Y}$)	Standard Deviation (s_Y)	n
Men	$3100	$200	100
Women	$2900	$320	64

a. What do these data suggest about wage differences in the firm? Do they represent statistically significant evidence that wages of men and women are different? (To answer this question, first state the null and alternative hypothesis; second, compute the relevant t-statistic; third, compute the p-value associated with the t-statistic; and finally use the p-value to answer the question.)

b. Do these data suggest that the firm is guilty of gender discrimination in its compensation policies? Explain.

3.9 Data on fifth-grade test scores (reading and mathematics) for 420 school districts in California yield $\overline{Y} = 654.2$ and standard deviation $s_Y = 19.5$.

*a.** Construct a 95% confidence interval for the mean test score in the population.

Class Size	Average Score ($\overline{Y}$)	Standard Deviation (s_Y)	n
Small	657.4	19.4	238
Large	650.0	17.9	182

*b.** When the districts were divided into districts with small classes (< 20 students per teacher) and large classes (≥ 20 students per teacher), the following results were found:

Is there statistically significant evidence that the districts with smaller classes have higher average test scores? Explain.

3.10 Values of height in inches (X) and weight in pounds (Y) are recorded from a sample of 300 male college students. The resulting summary statistics are $\overline{X} = 70.5$ inches; $\overline{Y} = 158$ lbs; $s_X = 1.8$ inches; $s_Y = 14.2$ lbs; $s_{XY} = 21.73$ inches $\times$ lbs, and $r_{XY} = 0.85$. Convert these statistics to the metric system (meters and kilograms).

3.11 This exercise shows that the sample variance is an unbiased estimator of the population variance when $Y_1, \ldots, Y_n$ are i.i.d. with mean μ_Y and variance σ_Y^2.

a. Use Equation (2.27) to show that $E[(Y_i - \overline{Y})^2] = \text{var}(Y_i) - 2\text{cov}(Y_i, \overline{Y}) + \text{var}(\overline{Y})$.

*b.** Use Equation (2.33) to show that $\text{cov}(\overline{Y}, Y_i) = \sigma_Y^2/n$.

c. Use the results in parts (a) and (b) to show that $E(s_Y^2) = \sigma_Y^2$.

3.1 The U.S. Current Population Survey

Each month the Bureau of Labor Statistics in the U.S. Department of Labor conducts the "Current Population Survey" (CPS), which provides data on labor force characteristics of the population, including the level of employment, unemployment, and earnings. Approximately 65,000 U.S. households are surveyed each month. The sample is chosen by randomly selecting addresses from a database comprised of addresses from the most recent decennial census augmented with data on new housing units constructed after the last census. The exact random sampling scheme is rather complicated (first small geographical areas are randomly selected, then housing units within these areas are randomly selected); details can be found in the *Handbook of Labor Statistics* and on the Bureau of Labor Statistics website (www.bls.gov).

The survey conducted each March is more detailed than in other months and asks questions about earnings during the previous year. The statistics in Table 3.1 were computed using the March surveys. The CPS earnings data are for full-time workers, defined to be somebody employed more than 35 hours per week for at least 48 weeks in the previous year.

3.2 Two Proofs That $\overline{Y}$ Is the Least Squares Estimator of μ_Y

This appendix provides two proofs, one using calculus and one not, that $\overline{Y}$ minimizes the sum of squared prediction mistakes in Equation (3.2), that is, that $\overline{Y}$ is the least squares estimator of $E(Y)$.

Calculus proof. To minimize the sum of squared prediction mistakes, take its derivative and set it to zero:

$$\frac{d}{dm} \sum_{i=1}^{n}(Y_i - m)^2 = -2\sum_{i=1}^{n}(Y_i - m) = -2\sum_{i=1}^{n}Y_i + 2nm = 0. \qquad (3.25)$$

Solving for the final equation for m shows that $\sum_{i=1}^{n}(Y_i - m)^2$ is minimized when $m = \overline{Y}$.

Non-calculus proof.   The strategy is to show that the difference between the least squares estimator and $\overline{Y}$ must be zero, from which it follows that $\overline{Y}$ is the least squares estimator. Let $d = \overline{Y} - m$, so that $m = \overline{Y} - d$. Then $(Y_i - m)^2 = (Y_i - [\overline{Y} - d])^2 = ([Y_i - \overline{Y}] + d)^2 = (Y_i - \overline{Y})^2 + 2d(Y_i - \overline{Y}) + d^2$. Thus, the sum of squared prediction mistakes (Equation (3.2)) is,

$$\sum_{i=1}^{n}(Y_i - m)^2 = \sum_{i=1}^{n}(Y_i - \overline{Y})^2 + 2d\sum_{i=1}^{n}(Y_i - \overline{Y}) + nd^2 = \sum_{i=1}^{n}(Y_i - \overline{Y})^2 + nd^2, \quad (3.26)$$

where the second equality uses the fact that $\sum_{i=1}^{n}(Y_i - \overline{Y}) = 0$. Because both terms in the final line of Equation (3.26) are nonnegative and because the first term does not depend on d, $\sum_{i=1}^{n}(Y_i - m)^2$ is minimized by choosing d to make the second term, nd^2, as small as possible. This is done by setting $d = 0$, that is, by setting $m = \overline{Y}$, so that $\overline{Y}$ is the least squares estimator of $E(Y)$.

APPENDIX

3.3

A Proof That the Sample Variance Is Consistent

This appendix uses the law of large numbers to prove that the sample variance s_Y^2 is a consistent estimator of the population variance σ_Y^2, as stated in Equation (3.8), when $Y_1, \ldots, Y_n$ are i.i.d. and $E(Y_i^4) < \infty$.

First, add and subtract μ_Y to write $(Y_i - \overline{Y})^2 = [(Y_i - \mu_Y) - (\overline{Y} - \mu_Y)]^2 = (Y_i - \mu_Y)^2 - 2(Y_i - \mu_Y)(\overline{Y} - \mu_Y) + (\overline{Y} - \mu_Y)^2$. Substituting this expression for $(Y_i - \overline{Y})^2$ into the definition of s_Y^2 (Equation (3.7)), we have that

$$s_Y^2 = \frac{1}{n-1}\sum_{i=1}^{n}(Y_i - \overline{Y})^2$$

$$= \frac{1}{n-1}\sum_{i=1}^{n}(Y_i - \mu_Y)^2 - \frac{2}{n-1}\sum_{i=1}^{n}(Y_i - \mu_Y)(\overline{Y} - \mu_Y) + \frac{1}{n-1}\sum_{i=1}^{n}(\overline{Y} - \mu_Y)^2$$

$$= \left(\frac{n}{n-1}\right)\left[\frac{1}{n}\sum_{i=1}^{n}(Y_i - \mu_Y)^2\right] - \left(\frac{n}{n-1}\right)(\overline{Y} - \mu_Y)^2, \quad (3.27)$$

where the final equality follows from the definition of $\overline{Y}$ (which implies that $\sum_{i=1}^{n}(Y_i - \mu_Y) = n(\overline{Y} - \mu_Y)$) and by collecting terms.

The law of large numbers can now be applied to the two terms in the final line of Equation (3.27). Define $W_i = (Y_i - \mu_Y)^2$. Now $E(W_i) = \sigma_Y^2$ (by the definition of the variance). Because the random variables $Y_1, \ldots, Y_n$ are i.i.d., the random variables $W_1, \ldots, W_n$ are i.i.d. In addition, $E(W_i^2) = E[(Y_i - \mu_Y)^4] < \infty$ because, by assumption, $E(Y_i^4) < \infty$. Thus $W_1, \ldots, W_n$ are i.i.d. and $\text{var}(W_i) < \infty$, so $\overline{W}$ satisfies the conditions for the law of large numbers in Key Concept 2.6 and $\overline{W} \xrightarrow{p} E(W_i)$. But $\overline{W} = \frac{1}{n}\sum_{i=1}^{n}(Y_i - \mu_Y)^2$ and $E(W_i) = \sigma_Y^2$, so $\frac{1}{n}\sum_{i=1}^{n}(Y_i - \mu_Y)^2 \xrightarrow{p} \sigma_Y^2$. Also, $n/(n-1) \longrightarrow 1$, so the first term in Equation (3.27) converges in probability to σ_Y^2. Because $\overline{Y} \xrightarrow{p} \mu_Y$, $(\overline{Y} - \mu_Y)^2 \xrightarrow{p} 0$ so the second term converges in probability to zero. Combining these results yields $s_Y^2 \xrightarrow{p} \sigma_Y^2$.

PART TWO | Fundamentals of Regression Analysis

CHAPTER 4

Linear Regression with One Regressor

Astate implements tough new penalties on drunk drivers; what is the effect on highway fatalities? A school district cuts the size of its elementary school classes; what is the effect on its students' standardized test scores? You successfully complete one more year of college classes; what is the effect on your future earnings?

All three of these questions are about the unknown effect of changing one variable, X (X being penalties for drunk driving, class size, or years of schooling), on another variable, Y (Y being highway deaths, student test scores, or earnings).

This chapter introduces the linear regression model relating one variable, X, to another, Y. This model postulates a linear relationship between X and Y; the slope of the line relating X and Y is the effect of a one-unit change in X on Y. Just as the mean of Y is an unknown characteristic of the population distribution of Y, the slope of the line relating X and Y is an unknown characteristic of the population joint distribution of X and Y. The econometric problem is to estimate this slope—that is, to estimate the effect on Y of a unit change in X—using a sample of data on these two variables.

This chapter describes methods for making statistical inferences about this regression model using a random sample of data on X and Y. For instance, using data on class sizes and test scores from different school districts, we show how to estimate the expected effect on test scores of reducing class sizes by, say, one student per class. The slope and the intercept of the line relating X and Y can be estimated by a method called ordinary least squares (OLS). Moreover, the OLS estimator can be used to test hypotheses about the population value of the slope—for example, testing the hypothesis that cutting class size has no effect whatsoever on test scores—and to create confidence intervals for the slope.

4.1 The Linear Regression Model

The superintendent of an elementary school district must decide whether to hire additional teachers and she wants your advice. If she hires the teachers, she will reduce the number of students per teacher (the student-teacher ratio) by two. She faces a tradeoff. Parents want smaller classes so that their children can receive more individualized attention. But hiring more teachers means spending more money, which is not to the liking of those paying the bill! So she asks you: If she cuts class sizes, what will the effect be on student performance?

In many school districts, student performance is measured by standardized tests, and the job status or pay of some administrators can depend in part on how well their students do on these tests. We therefore sharpen the superintendent's question: If she reduces the average class size by two students, what will the effect be on standardized test scores in her district?

A precise answer to this question requires a quantitative statement about changes. If the superintendent *changes* the class size by a certain amount, what would she expect the *change* in standardized test scores to be? We can write this as a mathematical relationship using the Greek letter beta, $\beta_{ClassSize}$, where the subscript "ClassSize" distinguishes the effect of changing the class size from other effects. Thus,

$$\beta_{ClassSize} = \frac{\text{change in TestScore}}{\text{change in ClassSize}} = \frac{\Delta TestScore}{\Delta ClassSize}, \tag{4.1}$$

where the Greek letter Δ (delta) stands for "change in." That is, $\beta_{ClassSize}$ is the change in the test score that results from changing the class size, divided by the change in the class size.

If you were lucky enough to know $\beta_{ClassSize}$, you would be able to tell the superintendent that decreasing class size by one student would change districtwide test scores by $\beta_{ClassSize}$. You could also answer the superintendent's actual question, which concerned changing class size by two students per class. To do so, rearrange Equation (4.1) so that

$$\Delta TestScore = \beta_{ClassSize} \times \Delta ClassSize. \tag{4.2}$$

Suppose that $\beta_{ClassSize} = -0.6$. Then a reduction in class size of two students per class would yield a predicted change in test scores of $(-0.6) \times (-2) = 1.2$; that is, you would predict that test scores would *rise* by 1.2 points as a result of the *reduction* in class sizes by two students per class.

Equation (4.1) is the definition of the slope of a straight line relating test scores and class size. This straight line can be written

$$TestScore = \beta_0 + \beta_{ClassSize} \times ClassSize, \qquad (4.3)$$

where β_0 is the intercept of this straight line, and, as before, $\beta_{ClassSize}$ is the slope. According to Equation (4.3), if you knew β_0 and $\beta_{ClassSize}$, not only would you be able to determine the *change* in test scores at a district associated with a *change* in class size, you also would be able to predict the average test score itself for a given class size.

When you propose Equation (4.3) to the superintendent, she tells you that something is wrong with this formulation. She points out that class size is just one of many facets of elementary education, and that two districts with the same class sizes will have different test scores for many reasons. One district might have better teachers or it might use better textbooks. Two districts with comparable class sizes, teachers, and textbooks still might have very different student populations; perhaps one district has more immigrants (and thus fewer native English speakers) or wealthier families. Finally, she points out that, even if two districts are the same in all these ways, they might have different test scores for essentially random reasons having to do with the performance of the individual students on the day of the test. She is right, of course; for all these reasons, Equation (4.3) will not hold exactly for all districts. Instead, it should be viewed as a statement about a relationship that holds *on average* across the population of districts.

A version of this linear relationship that holds for *each* district must incorporate these other factors influencing test scores, including each district's unique characteristics (quality of their teachers, background of their students, how lucky the students were on test day, etc.). One approach would be to list the most important factors and to introduce them explicitly into Equation (4.3) (an idea we return to in Chapter 5). For now, however, we simply lump all these "other factors" together and write the relationship for a given district as

$$TestScore = \beta_0 + \beta_{ClassSize} \times ClassSize + \text{other factors}. \qquad (4.4)$$

Thus, the test score for the district is written in terms of one component, $\beta_0 + \beta_{ClassSize} \times ClassSize,$ that represents the average effect of class size on scores in the population of school districts and a second component that represents all other factors.

Although this discussion has focused on test scores and class size, the idea expressed in Equation (4.4) is much more general, so it is useful to introduce more general notation. Suppose you have a sample of n districts. Let Y_i be the average test score in the ith district, let X_i be the average class size in the ith district, and let u_i denote the other factors influencing the test score in the ith district. Then Equation (4.4) can be written more generally as

$$Y_i = \beta_0 + \beta_1 X_i + u_i, \tag{4.5}$$

for each district, that is, $i = 1, \ldots, n$, where β_0 is the intercept of this line and β_1 is the slope. (The general notation "β_1" is used for the slope in Equation (4.5) instead of "$\beta_{ClassSize}$" because this equation is written in terms of a general variable X_i.)

Equation (4.5) is the **linear regression model with a single regressor**, in which Y is the **dependent variable** and X is the **independent variable** or the **regressor**.

The first part of Equation (4.5), $\beta_0 + \beta_1 X_i$, is the **population regression line** or the **population regression function**. This is the relationship that holds between Y and X on average over the population. Thus, if you knew the value of X, according to this population regression line you would predict that the value of the dependent variable, Y, is $\beta_0 + \beta_1 X$.

The **intercept** β_0 and the **slope** β_1 are the **coefficients** of the population regression line, also known as the **parameters** of the population regression line. The slope β_1 is the change in Y associated with a unit change in X. The intercept is the value of the population regression line when $X = 0$; it is the point at which the population regression line intersects the Y axis. In some econometric applications, such as the application in Section 4.7, the intercept has a meaningful economic interpretation. In other applications, however, the intercept has no real-world meaning; for example when X is the class size, strictly speaking the intercept is the predicted value of test scores when there are no students in the class! When the real-world meaning of the intercept is nonsensical it is best to think of it mathematically as the coefficient that determines the level of the regression line.

The term u_i in Equation (4.5) is the **error term**. The error term incorporates all of the factors responsible for the difference between the ith district's average test score and the value predicted by the population regression line. This error term contains all the other factors besides X that determine the value of the dependent variable, Y, for a specific observation, i. In the class size example, these other factors include all the unique features of the ith district that affect the performance of its students on the test, including teacher quality, student economic background, luck, and even any mistakes in grading the test.

The linear regression model and its terminology are summarized in Key Concept 4.1.

Figure 4.1 summarizes the linear regression model with a single regressor for seven hypothetical observations on test scores (Y) and class size (X). The population regression line is the straight line $\beta_0 + \beta_1 X$. The population regression line slopes down, that is, $\beta_1 < 0$, which means that districts with lower student-teacher ratios (smaller classes) tend to have higher test scores. The intercept β_0 has a mathematical meaning as the value of the Y axis intersected by the population regression line, but, as mentioned earlier, it has no real-world meaning in this example.

Because of the other factors that determine test performance, the hypothetical observations in Figure 4.1 do not fall exactly on the population regression line. For example, the value of Y for district #1, Y_1, is above the population regression line. This means that test scores in district #1 were better than predicted by the population regression line, so the error term for that district, u_1, is positive. In contrast, Y_2 is below the population regression line, so test scores for that district were worse than predicted, and $u_2 < 0$.

FIGURE 4.1   Scatter Plot of Test Score vs. Student-Teacher Ratio (Hypothetical Data)

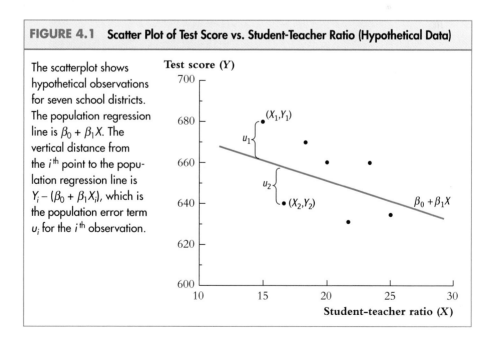

The scatterplot shows hypothetical observations for seven school districts. The population regression line is $\beta_0 + \beta_1 X$. The vertical distance from the ith point to the population regression line is $Y_i - (\beta_0 + \beta_1 X_i)$, which is the population error term u_i for the ith observation.

Terminology for the Linear Regression Model with a Single Regressor

The linear regression model is:

$$Y_i = \beta_0 + \beta_1 X_i + u_i,$$

where:

the subscript i runs over observations, $i = 1, \ldots, n$;

Y_i is the *dependent variable*, the *regressand*, or simply the *left-hand variable*;

X_i is the *independent variable*, the *regressor*, or simply the *right-hand variable*;

$\beta_0 + \beta_1 X$ is the *population regression line* or *population regression function*;

β_0 is the *intercept* of the population regression line;

β_1 is the *slope* of the population regression line; and

u_i is the *error term*.

Now return to your problem as advisor to the superintendent: What is the expected effect on test scores of reducing the student-teacher ratio by two students per teacher? The answer is easy: the expected change is $(-2) \times \beta_{ClassSize}$. But what is the value of $\beta_{ClassSize}$?

4.2 Estimating the Coefficients of the Linear Regression Model

In a practical situation, such as the application to class size and test scores, the intercept β_0 and slope β_1 of the population regression line are unknown. Therefore, we must use data to estimate the unknown slope and intercept of the population regression line.

This estimation problem is similar to others you have faced in statistics. For example, suppose you want to compare the mean earnings of men and women who recently graduated from college. Although the population mean earnings are unknown, we can estimate the population means using a random sample of male and female college graduates. Then the natural estimator of the unknown population mean earnings for women, for example, is the average earnings of the female college graduates in the sample.

The same idea extends to the linear regression model. We do not know the population value of $\beta_{ClassSize}$, the slope of the unknown population regression line relating X (class size) and Y (test scores). But just as it was possible to learn about the population mean using a sample of data drawn from that population, so is it possible to learn about the population slope $\beta_{ClassSize}$ using a sample of data.

The data we analyze here consist of test scores and class sizes in 1998 in 420 California school districts that serve kindergarten through eighth grade. The test score is the districtwide average of reading and math scores for fifth graders. Class size can be measured in various ways. The measure used here is one of the broadest, which is the number of students in the district divided by the number of teachers, that is, the districtwide student-teacher ratio. These data are described in more detail in Appendix 4.1.

Table 4.1 summarizes the distributions of test scores and class sizes for this sample. The average student-teacher ratio is 19.6 students per teacher and the standard deviation is 1.9 students per teacher. The 10th percentile of the distribution of the student-teacher ratio is 17.3 (that is, only 10% of districts have student-teacher ratios below 17.3), while the district at the 90th percentile has a student-teacher ratio of 21.9.

A scatterplot of these 420 observations on test scores and the student-teacher ratio is shown in Figure 4.2. The sample correlation is -0.23, indicating a weak negative relationship between the two variables. Although larger classes in this sample tend to have lower test scores, there are other determinants of test scores that keep the observations from falling perfectly along a straight line.

Despite this low correlation, if one could somehow draw a straight line through these data, then the slope of this line would be an estimate of $\beta_{ClassSize}$ based on these data. One way to draw the line would be to take out a pencil and a ruler and to "eyeball" the best line you could. While this method is easy, it is very unscientific and different people will create different estimated lines.

TABLE 4.1   **Summary of the Distribution of Student-Teacher Ratios and Fifth-Grade Test Scores for 420 K–8 Districts in California in 1998**

| | Average | Standard Deviation | Percentile | | | | | | |
			10%	25%	40%	50% (median)	60%	75%	90%
Student-teacher ratio	19.6	1.9	17.3	18.6	19.3	19.7	20.1	20.9	21.9
Test score	654.2	19.1	630.4	640.0	649.1	654.5	659.4	666.7	679.1

FIGURE 4.2   **Scatterplot of Test Score vs. Student-Teacher Ratio (California School District Data)**

Data from 420 California school districts. There is a weak negative relationship between the student-teacher ratio and test scores: the sample correlation is –0.23.

How, then, should you choose among the many possible lines? By far the most common way is to choose the line that produces the "least squares" fit to these data, that is, to use the ordinary least squares (OLS) estimator.

The Ordinary Least Squares Estimator

The OLS estimator chooses the regression coefficients so that the estimated regression line is as close as possible to the observed data, where closeness is measured by the sum of the squared mistakes made in predicting Y given X.

As discussed in Section 3.1, the sample average, $\overline{Y}$, is the least squares estimator of the population mean, $E(Y)$; that is, $\overline{Y}$ minimizes the total squared estimation mistakes $\sum_{i=1}^{n}(Y_i - m)^2$ among all possible estimators m (see expression (3.2)).

The OLS estimator extends this idea to the linear regression model. Let b_0 and b_1 be some estimators of β_0 and β_1. The regression line based on these estimators is $b_0 + b_1 X$, so the value of Y_i predicted using this line is $b_0 + b_1 X_i$. Thus, the mistake made in predicting the ith observation is $Y_i - (b_0 + b_1 X_i) = Y_i - b_0 - b_1 X_i$. The sum of these squared prediction mistakes over all n observations is

$$\sum_{i=1}^{n}(Y_i - b_0 - b_1 X_i)^2. \tag{4.6}$$

The sum of the squared mistakes for the linear regression model in expression (4.6) is the extension of the sum of the squared mistakes for the problem of estimating the mean in expression (3.2). In fact, if there is no regressor, then b_1 does not enter expression (4.6) and the two problems are identical except for the different notation (m in expression (3.2), b_0 in expression (4.6)). Just as there is a unique estimator, $\overline{Y}$, that minimizes the expression (3.2), so is there a unique pair of estimators of β_0 and β_1 that minimize expression (4.6).

The estimators of the intercept and slope that minimize the sum of squared mistakes in expression (4.6) are called the **ordinary least squares (OLS) estimators** of β_0 and β_1.

OLS has its own special notation and terminology. The OLS estimator of β_0 is denoted $\hat{\beta}_0$, and the OLS estimator of β_1 is denoted $\hat{\beta}_1$. The **OLS regression line** is the straight line constructed using the OLS estimators, that is, $\hat{\beta}_0 + \hat{\beta}_1 X$. The **predicted value** of Y_i given X_i, based on the OLS regression line, is $\hat{Y}_i = \hat{\beta}_0 + \hat{\beta}_1 X_i$. The **residual** for the ith observation is the difference between Y_i and its predicted value, that is, the residual is $\hat{u}_i = Y_i - \hat{Y}_i$.

You could compute the OLS estimators $\hat{\beta}_0$ and $\hat{\beta}_1$ by trying different values of b_0 and b_1 repeatedly until you find those that minimize the total squared mistakes in expression (4.6); they are the least squares estimates. This method would be quite tedious, however. Fortunately there are formulas, derived by minimizing expression (4.6) using calculus, that streamline the calculation of the OLS estimators.

The OLS formulas and terminology are collected in Key Concept 4.2. These formulas are implemented in virtually all statistical and spreadsheet programs. These formulas are derived in Appendix 4.2.

OLS Estimates of the Relationship Between Test Scores and the Student-Teacher Ratio

When OLS is used to estimate a line relating the student-teacher ratio to test scores using the 420 observations in Figure 4.2, the estimated slope is −2.28 and the estimated intercept is 698.9. Accordingly, the OLS regression line for these 420 observations is

$$\widehat{TestScore} = 698.9 - 2.28 \times STR, \tag{4.7}$$

where *TestScore* is the average test score in the district and *STR* is the student-teacher ratio. The symbol "^" over *TestScore* in Equation (4.7) indicates that this is the predicted value based on the OLS regression line. Figure 4.3 plots this OLS regression line superimposed over the scatterplot of the data previously shown in Figure 4.2.

Key Concept 4.2

The OLS Estimator, Predicted Values, and Residuals

The OLS estimators of the slope β_1 and the intercept β_0 are:

$$\hat{\beta}_1 = \frac{\sum_{i=1}^{n}(X_i - \overline{X})(Y_i - \overline{Y})}{\sum_{i=1}^{n}(X_i - \overline{X})^2} = \frac{s_{XY}}{s_X^2} \tag{4.8}$$

$$\hat{\beta}_0 = \overline{Y} - \hat{\beta}_1\overline{X}. \tag{4.9}$$

The OLS predicted values $\hat{Y}_i$ and residuals $\hat{u}_i$ are:

$$\hat{Y}_i = \hat{\beta}_0 + \hat{\beta}_1 X_i,\ i = 1, \ldots, n \tag{4.10}$$

$$\hat{u}_i = Y_i - \hat{Y}_i,\ i = 1, \ldots, n. \tag{4.11}$$

The estimated intercept ($\hat{\beta}_0$), slope ($\hat{\beta}_1$), and residual ($\hat{u}_i$) are computed from a sample of n observations of X_i and Y_i, $i = 1, \ldots, n$. These are estimates of the unknown true population intercept (β_0), slope (β_1), and error term (u_i).

The slope of −2.28 means that an increase in the student-teacher ratio by one student per class is, on average, associated with a decline in districtwide test scores by 2.28 points on the test. A decrease in the student-teacher ratio by 2 students per class is, on average, associated with an increase in test scores of 4.56 points (= −2 × (−2.28)). The negative slope indicates that more students per teacher (larger classes) is associated with poorer performance on the test.

It is now possible to predict the districtwide test score given a value of the student-teacher ratio. For example, for a district with 20 students per teacher, the predicted test score is 698.9 − 2.28 × 20 = 653.3. Of course, this prediction will not be exactly right because of the other factors that determine a district's performance. But the regression line does give a prediction (the OLS prediction) of what test scores would be for that district, based on their student-teacher ratio, absent those other factors.

Is this estimate of the slope large or small? To answer this, we return to the superintendent's problem. Recall that she is contemplating hiring enough teachers to reduce the student-teacher ratio by 2. Suppose her district is at the median of the California districts. From Table 4.1, the median student-teacher ratio is

---

FIGURE 4.3   **The Estimated Regression Line for the California Data**

The estimated regression line shows a negative relationship between test scores and the student-teacher ratio. If class sizes fall by 1 student, the estimated regression predicts that test scores will increase by 2.28 points.

19.7 and the median test score is 654.5. A reduction of 2 students per class, from 19.7 to 17.7, would move her student-teacher ratio from the 50th percentile to very near the 10th percentile. This is a big change, and she would need to hire many new teachers. How would it affect test scores?

According to Equation (4.7), cutting the student-teacher ratio by 2 is predicted to increase test scores by approximately 4.6 points; if her district's test scores are at the median, 654.5, they are predicted to increase to 659.1. Is this improvement large or small? According to Table 4.1, this improvement would move her district from the median to just short of the 60th percentile. Thus, a decrease in class size that would place her district close to the 10% with the smallest classes would move her test scores from the 50th to the 60th percentile. According to these estimates, at least, cutting the student-teacher ratio by a large amount (2 students per teacher) would help and might be worth doing depending on her budgetary situation, but it would not be a panacea.

What if the superintendent were contemplating a far more radical change, such as reducing the student-teacher ratio from 20 students per teacher to 5? Unfortunately, the estimates in Equation (4.7) would not be very useful to her. This regression was estimated using the data in Figure 4.2, and as the figure shows, the smallest student-teacher ratio in these data is 14. These data contain no information on how districts with extremely small classes perform, so these data alone are not a reliable basis for predicting the effect of a radical move to such an extremely low student-teacher ratio.

The "Beta" of a Stock

A fundamental idea of modern finance is that an investor needs a financial incentive to take a risk. Said differently, the expected return[1] on a risky investment, R, must exceed the return on a safe, or risk-free, investment, R_f. Thus the expected excess return, $R - R_f$, on a risky investment, like owning stock in a company, should be positive.

At first it might seem like the risk of a stock should be measured by its variance. Much of that risk, however, can be reduced by holding other stocks in a "portfolio," that is, by diversifying your financial holdings. This means that the right way to measure the risk of a stock is not by its *variance* but rather by its *covariance* with the market.

The capital asset pricing model (CAPM) formalizes this idea. According to the CAPM, the expected excess return on an asset is proportional to the expected excess return on a portfolio of all available assets (the "market portfolio"). That is, the CAPM says that

$$R - R_f = \beta(R_m - R_f), \qquad (4.12)$$

where R_m is the expected return on the market portfolio and β is the coefficient in the population regression of $R - R_f$ on $R_m - R_f$. In practice, the risk-free return is often taken to be the rate of interest on short-term U.S. government debt. According to the CAPM, a stock with a $\beta < 1$ has less risk than the market portfolio and therefore has a lower expected excess return than the market portfolio. In contrast, a stock with a $\beta > 1$ is riskier than the market portfolio and thus comands a higher expected excess return.

The "beta" of a stock has become a workhorse of the investment industry, and you can obtain estimated β's for hundreds of stocks on investment firm web sites. Those β's typically are estimated by OLS regression of the actual excess return on the stock against the actual excess return on a broad market index.

The table below gives estimated β's for six U.S. stocks. Low-risk consumer products firms like Kellogg have stocks with low β's; risky high-tech stocks like Microsoft have high β's.

Company	Estimated β
Kellogg (breakfast cereal)	0.24
Waste Management (waste disposal)	0.38
Sprint (long distance telephone)	0.59
Walmart (discount retailer)	0.89
Barnes and Noble (book retailer)	1.03
Best Buy (electronic equipment retailer)	1.80
Microsoft (software)	1.83

Source: Yahoo.com

[1]The return on an investment is the change in its price plus any payout (dividend) from the investment as a percentage of its initial price. For example, a stock bought on January 1 for $100, that paid a $2.50 dividend during the year and sold on December 31 for $105, would have a return of $R = [(\$105 - \$100) + \$2.50] / \$100 = 7.5\%$.

Why Use the OLS Estimator?

There are both practical and theoretical reasons to use the OLS estimators $\hat{\beta}_0$ and $\hat{\beta}_1$. Because OLS is the dominant method used in practice, it has become the common language for regression analysis throughout economics, finance (see the box), and the social sciences more generally. Presenting results using OLS (or its variants discussed later in this book) means that you are "speaking the same language" as other economists and statisticians. The OLS formulas are built into virtually all spreadsheet and statistical software packages, making OLS easy to use.

The OLS estimators also have desirable theoretical properties. For example, the sample average $\overline{Y}$ is an unbiased estimator of the mean $E(Y)$, that is, $E(\overline{Y}) = \mu_Y$; $\overline{Y}$ is a consistent estimator of μ_Y; and in large samples the sampling distribution of $\overline{Y}$ is approximately normal (Section 3.1). The OLS estimators $\hat{\beta}_0$ and $\hat{\beta}_1$ also have these properties. Under a general set of assumptions (stated in Section 4.3), $\hat{\beta}_0$ and $\hat{\beta}_1$ are unbiased and consistent estimators of β_0 and β_1 and their sampling distribution is approximately normal. These results are discussed in Section 4.4.

An additional desirable theoretical property of $\overline{Y}$ is that it is efficient among estimators that are linear functions of $Y_1, \ldots, Y_n$: it has the smallest variance of all estimators that are weighted averages of $Y_1, \ldots, Y_n$ (Section 3.1). A similar result is also true of the OLS estimator, but this result requires an additional assumption beyond those in Section 4.3 so we defer its discussion to Section 4.9.

4.3 The Least Squares Assumptions

This section presents a set of three assumptions on the linear regression model and the sampling scheme under which OLS provides an appropriate estimator of the unknown regression coefficients, β_0 and β_1. Initially these assumptions might appear abstract. They do, however, have natural interpretations, and understanding these assumptions is essential for understanding when OLS will—and will not—give useful estimates of the regression coefficients.

Assumption #1: The Conditional Distribution of u_i Given X_i Has a Mean of Zero

The first **least squares assumption** is that the conditional distribution of u_i given X_i has a mean of zero. This assumption is a formal mathematical statement about the "other factors" contained in u_i and asserts that these other factors are unrelated to X_i in the sense that, given a value of X_i, the mean of the distribution of these other factors is zero.

This is illustrated in Figure 4.4. The population regression is the relationship that holds on average between class size and test scores in the population, and the error term u_i represents the other factors that lead test scores at a given district to differ from the prediction based on the population regression line. As shown in Figure 4.4, at a given value of class size, say 20 students per class, sometimes these

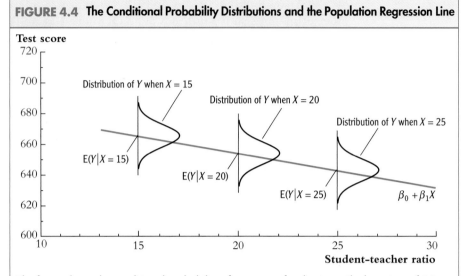

FIGURE 4.4 The Conditional Probability Distributions and the Population Regression Line

The figure shows the conditional probability of test scores for districts with class sizes of 15, 20, and 25 students. The mean of the conditional distribution of test scores, given the student-teacher ratio, $E(Y|X)$, is the population regression line $\beta_0 + \beta_1 X$. At a given value of X, Y is distributed around the regression line and the error, $u = Y - (\beta_0 + \beta_1 X)$, has a conditional mean of zero for all values of X.

other factors lead to better performance than predicted ($u_i > 0$) and sometimes to worse ($u_i < 0$), but on average over the population the prediction is right. In other words, given $X_i = 20$, the mean of the distribution of u_i is zero. In Figure 4.4, this is shown as the distribution of u_i being centered around the population regression line at $X_i = 20$ and, more generally, at other values x of X_i as well. Said differently, the distribution of u_i, conditional on $X_i = x$, has a mean of zero; stated mathematically, $E(u_i | X_i = x) = 0$ or, in somewhat simpler notation, $E(u_i | X_i) = 0$.

As shown in Figure 4.4, the assumption that $E(u_i | X_i) = 0$ is equivalent to assuming that the population regression line is the conditional mean of Y_i given X_i (a mathematical proof of this is left as Exercise 4.3).

Correlation and conditional mean.   Recall from Section 2.3 that if the conditional mean of one random variable given another is zero, then the two random variables have zero covariance and thus are uncorrelated (Equation (2.25)). Thus, the conditional mean assumption $E(u_i | X_i) = 0$ implies that X_i and u_i are uncorrelated, or $\text{corr}(X_i, u_i) = 0$. Because correlation is a measure of linear association, this implication does not go the other way; even if X_i and u_i are uncorrelated, the conditional mean of u_i given X_i might be nonzero. However, if X_i and u_i are correlated, then it must be the case that $E(u_i | X_i)$ is nonzero. It is therefore often convenient to discuss the conditional mean assumption in terms of possible correlation between X_i and u_i. If X_i and u_i are correlated, then the conditional mean assumption is violated.

Assumption #2: (X_i, Y_i), $i = 1, \ldots, n$ Are Independently and Identically Distributed

The second least squares assumption is that (X_i, Y_i), $i = 1, \ldots, n$ are independently and identically distributed (i.i.d.) across observations. As discussed in Section 2.5 (Key Concept 2.5), this is a statement about how the sample is drawn. If the observations are drawn by simple random sampling from a single large population, then (X_i, Y_i), $i = 1, \ldots, n$ are i.i.d. For example, let X be the age of a worker and Y be his or her earnings, and imagine drawing a person at random from the population of workers. That randomly drawn person will have a certain age and earnings (that is, X and Y will take on some values). If a sample of n workers is drawn from this population, then (X_i, Y_i), $i = 1, \ldots, n$, necessarily have the same distribution, and if they are drawn at random they are also distributed independently from one observation to the next, that is, they are i.i.d.

The i.i.d. assumption is a reasonable one for many data collection schemes. For example, survey data from a randomly chosen subset of the population typically can be treated as i.i.d.

Not all sampling schemes produce i.i.d. observations on (X_i, Y_i), however. One example is when the values of X are not drawn from a random sample of the population but rather are set by a researcher as part of an experiment. For example, suppose a horticulturalist wants to study the effects of different organic weeding methods (X) on tomato production (Y) and accordingly grows different plots of tomatoes using different organic weeding techniques. If she picks the techniques (the level of X) to be used on the ith plot and applies the same technique to the ith plot in all repetitions of the experiment, then the value of X_i does not change from one sample to the next. Thus X_i is nonrandom (although the outcome Y_i is random), so the sampling scheme is not i.i.d. The results presented in this chapter developed for i.i.d. regressors are also true if the regressors are nonrandom (this is discussed further in Chapter 15). The case of a nonrandom regressor is, however, quite special. For example, modern experimental protocols would have the horticulturalist assign the level of X to the different plots using a computerized random number generator, thereby circumventing any possible bias by the horticulturalist (she might use her favorite weeding method for the tomatoes in the sunniest plot). When this modern experimental protocol is used, the level of X is random and (X_i, Y_i) are i.i.d.

Another example of non–i.i.d. sampling is when observations refer to the same unit of observation over time. For example, we might have data on inventory levels (Y) at a firm and the interest rate at which the firm can borrow (X), where these data are collected over time from a specific firm; for example, they might be recorded four times a year (quarterly) for 30 years. This is an example of time series data, and a key feature of time series data is that observations falling close to each other in time are not independent but rather tend to be correlated with each other; if interest rates are low now, they are likely to be low next quarter. This pattern of correlation violates the "independence" part of the i.i.d. assumption. Time series data introduce a set of complications that are best handled after developing the basic tools of regression analysis, so we defer further discussion of time series analysis to Part IV.

Assumption #3: X_i and u_i Have Four Moments

The third least squares assumption is that the fourth moments of X_i and u_i are nonzero and finite $(0 < E(X_i^4) < \infty$ and $0 < E(u_i^4) < \infty)$ or, equivalently, that the fourth moments of X_i and Y_i are nonzero and finite. This assumption limits the probability of drawing an observation with extremely large values of X_i or u_i. Were we to draw an observation with extremely large X_i or Y_i—that is, with X_i or Y_i far outside the normal range of the data—then that observation would be given great importance in an OLS regression and would make the regression results misleading.

The assumption of finite fourth moments is used in the mathematics that justify the large-sample approximations to the distributions of the OLS test statistics. We encountered this assumption in Chapter 3 when discussing the consistency of the sample variance. Specifically, Equation (3.8) states that the sample variance s_Y^2 is a consistent estimator of the population variance σ_Y^2 (that is, that $s_Y^2 \xrightarrow{p} \sigma_Y^2$). If $Y_1, \ldots, Y_n$ are i.i.d. and the fourth moment of Y_i is finite, then the law of large numbers in Key Concept 2.6 applies to the average, $\frac{1}{n}\sum_{i=1}^{n}(Y_i - \mu_Y)^2$, a key step in the proof in Appendix 3.3 showing that s_Y^2 is consistent. The role of the fourth moments assumption in the mathematical theory of OLS regression is discussed further in Section 15.3.

One could argue that this assumption is a technical fine point that regularly holds in practice. Class size is capped by the physical capacity of a classroom; the best you can do on a standardized test is to get all the questions right and the worst you can do is to get all the questions wrong. Because class size and test scores have a finite range, they necessarily have finite fourth moments. More generally, commonly used distributions such as the normal have four moments. Still, as a mathematical matter, some distributions have infinite

The Least Squares Assumptions

$$Y_i = \beta_0 + \beta_1 X_i + u_i,\ i = 1, \ldots, n,\ \text{where:}$$

Key Concept 4.3

1. The error term u_i has conditional mean zero given X_i, that is, $E(u_i | X_i) = 0$;

2. (X_i, Y_i), $i = 1, \ldots, n$ are independent and identically distributed (i.i.d.) draws from their joint distribution; and

3. (X_i, u_i) have nonzero finite fourth moments.

fourth moments, and this assumption rules out those distributions. If this assumption holds then it is unlikely that statistical inferences using OLS will be dominated by a few observations.

Use of the Least Squares Assumptions

The three least squares assumptions for the linear regression model are summarized in Key Concept 4.3. The least squares assumptions play twin roles, and we return to them repeatedly throughout this textbook.

Their first role is mathematical: if these assumptions hold, then, as is shown in the next section, in large samples the OLS estimators have sampling distributions that are normal. In turn, this large-sample normal distribution lets us develop methods for hypothesis testing and constructing confidence intervals using the OLS estimators.

Their second role is to organize the circumstances that pose difficulties for OLS regression. As we will see, the first least squares assumption is the most important to consider in practice. One reason why the first least squares assumption might not hold in practice is discussed in Section 4.10 and Chapter 5, and additional reasons are discussed in Section 7.2.

It is also important to consider whether the second assumption holds in an application. Although it plausibly holds in many cross-sectional data sets, it is inappropriate for time series data. Therefore, the i.i.d. assumption will be replaced by a more appropriate assumption when we discuss regression with time series data in Part IV.

We treat the third assumption as a technical condition that commonly holds in practice so we do not dwell on it further.

4.4   Sampling Distribution of the OLS Estimators

Because the OLS estimators $\hat{\beta}_0$ and $\hat{\beta}_1$ are computed from a randomly drawn sample, the estimators themselves are random variables with a probability distribution—the sampling distribution—that describes the values they could take over different possible random samples. This section presents these sampling distributions. In small samples, these distributions are complicated, but in large samples, they are approximately normal because of the central limit theorem.

The Sampling Distribution of the OLS Estimators

Review of the sampling distribution of $\overline{Y}$.   Recall the discussion in Sections 2.5 and 2.6 about the sampling distribution of the sample average, $\overline{Y}$, an estimator of the unknown population mean of Y, μ_Y. Because $\overline{Y}$ is calculated using a randomly drawn sample, $\overline{Y}$ is a random variable that takes on different values from one sample to the next; the probability of these different values is summarized in its sampling distribution. Although the sampling distribution of $\overline{Y}$ can be complicated when the sample size is small, it is possible to make certain statements about it that hold for all n. In particular, the mean of the sampling distribution is μ_Y, that is, $E(\overline{Y}) = \mu_Y$, so $\overline{Y}$ is an unbiased estimator of μ_Y. If n is large, then more can be said about the sampling distribution. In particular, the central limit theorem (Section 2.6) states that this distribution is approximately normal.

The sampling distribution of $\hat{\beta}_0$ and $\hat{\beta}_1$.   These ideas carry over to the OLS estimators $\hat{\beta}_0$ and $\hat{\beta}_1$ of the unknown intercept β_0 and slope β_1 of the population regression line. Because the OLS estimators are calculated using a random sample, $\hat{\beta}_0$ and $\hat{\beta}_1$ are random variables that take on different values from one sample to the next; the probability of these different values is summarized in their sampling distributions.

Although the sampling distribution of $\hat{\beta}_0$ and $\hat{\beta}_1$ can be complicated when the sample size is small, it is possible to make certain statements about it that hold for all n. In particular, the mean of the sampling distributions of $\hat{\beta}_0$ and $\hat{\beta}_1$ are β_0 and β_1. In other words, under the least squares assumptions in Key Concept 4.3,

$$E(\hat{\beta}_0) = \beta_0 \text{ and } E(\hat{\beta}_1) = \beta_1, \tag{4.13}$$

that is, $\hat{\beta}_0$ and $\hat{\beta}_1$ are unbiased estimators of β_0 and β_1. The proof that $\hat{\beta}_1$ is unbiased is given in Appendix 4.3 and the proof that $\hat{\beta}_0$ is unbiased is left as Exercise 4.4.

If the sample is sufficiently large, by the central limit theorem the sampling distribution of $\hat{\beta}_0$ and $\hat{\beta}_1$ is well approximated by the bivariate normal distribution (Section 2.4.). This implies that the marginal distributions of $\hat{\beta}_0$ and $\hat{\beta}_1$ are normal in large samples.

This argument invokes the central limit theorem. Technically, the central limit theorem concerns the distribution of averages (like $\overline{Y}$). If you examine the numerator in Equation (4.8) for $\hat{\beta}_1$, you will see that it, too, is a type of average—not a simple average, like $\overline{Y}$, but an average of the product, $(Y_i - \overline{Y})(X_i - \overline{X})$. As discussed further in Appendix 4.3, the central limit theorem applies to this average so that, like the simpler average $\overline{Y}$, it is normally distributed in large samples.

The normal approximation to the distribution of the OLS estimators in large samples is summarized in Key Concept 4.4. (Appendix 4.3 summarizes the derivation of these formulas.) A relevant question in practice is how large n must be for these approximations to be reliable. In Section 2.6 we suggested that $n = 100$ is sufficiently large for the sampling distribution of $\overline{Y}$ to be well approximated by a normal distribution, and sometimes smaller n suffices. This criterion carries over to the more complicated averages appearing in regression analysis. In virtually all modern econometric applications $n > 100$, so we will treat the normal approximations to the distributions of the OLS estimators as reliable unless there are good reasons to think otherwise.

The results in Key Concept 4.4 imply that the OLS estimators are consistent, that is, when the sample size is large, $\hat{\beta}_0$ and $\hat{\beta}_1$ will be close to the true population coefficients β_0 and β_1 with high probability. This is because the variances $\sigma^2_{\hat{\beta}_0}$ and $\sigma^2_{\hat{\beta}_1}$ of the estimators decrease to zero as n increases (n appears in the denominator of the formulas for the variances), so the distribution of the OLS estimators will be tightly concentrated around their means, β_0 and β_1, when n is large.

Another implication of the distributions in Key Concept 4.4 is that, in general, the larger is the variance of X_i, the smaller is the variance $\sigma^2_{\hat{\beta}_1}$ of $\hat{\beta}_1$. Mathematically, this arises because the variance of $\hat{\beta}_1$ in Equation (4.14) is inversely proportional to the square of the variance of X_i: the larger is var(X_i), the larger is the denominator in Equation (4.14) so the smaller is $\sigma^2_{\hat{\beta}_1}$. To get a better sense of why this is so, look at Figure 4.5, which presents a scatterplot of 150 artificial data points on X and Y. The data points indicated by the colored dots are the 75 observations closest to $\overline{X}$. Suppose you were asked to draw a line as accurately as

Key Concept 4.4

Large-Sample Distributions of $\hat{\beta}_0$ and $\hat{\beta}_1$

If the least squares assumptions in Key Concept 4.3 hold, then in large samples $\hat{\beta}_0$ and $\hat{\beta}_1$ have a jointly normal sampling distribution. The large-sample normal distribution of $\hat{\beta}_1$ is $N(\beta_1, \sigma^2_{\hat{\beta}_1})$, where the variance of this distribution, $\sigma^2_{\hat{\beta}_1}$, is

$$\sigma^2_{\hat{\beta}_1} = \frac{1}{n} \frac{\text{var}[(X_i - \mu_X)u_i]}{[\text{var}(X_i)]^2}. \tag{4.14}$$

The large-sample normal distribution of $\hat{\beta}_0$ is $N(\beta_0, \sigma^2_{\hat{\beta}_0})$, where

$$\sigma^2_{\hat{\beta}_0} = \frac{1}{n} \frac{\text{var}(H_i u_i)}{[E(H_i^2)]^2}, \quad \text{where } H_i = 1 - \left(\frac{\mu_X}{E(X_i^2)}\right)X_i. \tag{4.15}$$

possible through *either* the colored or the black dots—which would you choose? It would be easier to draw a precise line through the black dots, which have a larger variance than the colored dots. Similarly, the larger the variance of X, the more precise is $\hat{\beta}_1$.

The normal approximation to the sampling distribution of $\hat{\beta}_0$ and $\hat{\beta}_1$ is a powerful tool. With this approximation in hand, we are able to develop methods for making inferences about the true population values of the regression coefficients using only a sample of data.

4.5 Testing Hypotheses About One of the Regression Coefficients

Your client, the superintendent, calls you with a problem. She has an angry taxpayer in her office who asserts that cutting class size will not help test scores, so that reducing them further is a waste of money. Class size, the taxpayer claims, has no effect on test scores.

The taxpayer's claim can be rephrased in the language of regression analysis. Because the effect on test scores of a unit change in class size is $\beta_{ClassSize}$, the taxpayer is asserting that the population regression line is flat, that is, that the slope $\beta_{ClassSize}$ of the population regression line is zero. Is there, the superintendent asks, evidence in your sample of 420 observations on California school districts that

FIGURE 4.5   **The Variance of $\hat{\beta}_1$ and the Variance of X**

The colored dots represent a set of X_i's with a small variance. The black dots represent a set of X_i's with a large variance. The regression line can be estimated more accurately with the black dots than with the colored dots.

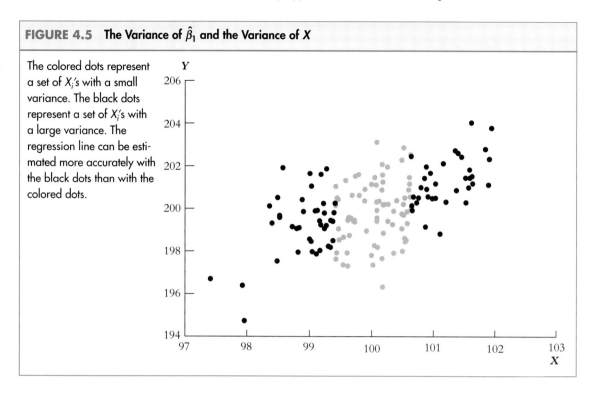

this slope is nonzero? Can you reject the taxpayer's hypothesis that $\beta_{ClassSize} = 0$, or must you accept it, at least tentatively pending further new evidence?

This section discusses tests of hypotheses about the slope β_1 or intercept β_0 of the population regression line. We start by discussing two-sided tests of the slope β_1 in detail, then turn to one-sided tests and to tests of hypotheses regarding the intercept β_0.

Two-Sided Hypotheses Concerning β_1

The general approach to testing hypotheses about these coefficients is the same as to testing hypotheses about the population mean, so we begin with a brief review.

Testing hypotheses about the population mean.   Recall from Section 3.2 that the null hypothesis that the mean of Y is a specific value $\mu_{Y,0}$ can be written as $H_0: E(Y) = \mu_{Y,0}$, and the two-sided alternative is $H_1: E(Y) \neq \mu_{Y,0}$.

The test of the null hypothesis H_0 against the two-sided alternative proceeds as in the three steps summarized in Key Concept 3.6. The first is to compute the standard error of $\overline{Y}$, $SE(\overline{Y})$, which is an estimator of the standard deviation of the sampling distribution of $\overline{Y}$. The second step is to compute the t-statistic, which has the general form given in Key Concept 4.5; applied here, the t-statistic is $t = (\overline{Y} - \mu_{Y,0})/SE(\overline{Y})$.

The third step is to compute the p-value, which is the smallest significance level at which the null hypothesis could be rejected, based on the test statistic actually observed; equivalently, the p-value is the probability of obtaining a statistic, by random sampling variation, at least as different from the null hypothesis value as is the statistic actually observed, assuming that the null hypothesis is correct (Key Concept 3.5). Because the t-statistic has a standard normal distribution in large samples under the null hypothesis, the p-value for a two–sided hypothesis test is $2\Phi(-|t^{act}|)$, where t^{act} is the value of the t-statistic actually computed and Φ is the cumulative standard normal distribution tabulated in Appendix Table 1. Alternatively, the third step can be replaced by simply comparing the t-statistic to the critical value appropriate for the test with the desired significance level; for example, a two–sided test with a 5% significance level would reject the null hypothesis if $|t^{act}| > 1.96$. In this case, the population mean is said to be statistically significantly different than the hypothesized value at the 5% significance level.

Testing hypotheses about the slope β_1.   At a theoretical level, the critical feature justifying the foregoing testing procedure for the population mean is that, in large samples, the sampling distribution of $\overline{Y}$ is approximately normal. Because $\hat{\beta}_1$ also has a normal sampling distribution in large samples, hypotheses about the true value of the slope β_1 can be tested using the same general approach.

The null and alternative hypotheses need to be stated precisely before they can be tested. The angry taxpayer's hypothesis is that $\beta_{ClassSize} = 0$. More generally, under the null hypothesis the true population slope β_1 takes on some specific value, $\beta_{1,0}$. Under the two–sided alternative, β_1 does not equal $\beta_{1,0}$. That is, the **null hypothesis** and the **two–sided alternative hypothesis** are

$$H_0\colon \beta_1 = \beta_{1,0} \text{ vs. } H_1\colon \beta_1 \neq \beta_{1,0} \text{ (two–sided alternative).} \quad (4.16)$$

To test the null hypothesis H_0, we follow the same three steps as for the population mean.

The first step is to compute the **standard error of $\hat{\beta}_1$**, $SE(\hat{\beta}_1)$. The standard error of $\hat{\beta}_1$ is an estimator of $\sigma_{\hat{\beta}_1}$, the standard deviation of the sampling distribution of $\hat{\beta}_1$. Specifically,

$$SE(\hat{\beta}_1) = \sqrt{\hat{\sigma}^2_{\hat{\beta}_1}}, \quad (4.17)$$

General Form of the *t*-Statistic

Key Concept 4.5

In general, the *t*-statistic has the form

$$t = \frac{\text{estimator} - \text{hypothesized value}}{\text{standard error of the estimator}}. \tag{4.18}$$

where

$$\hat{\sigma}_{\hat{\beta}_1}^2 = \frac{1}{n} \times \frac{\frac{1}{n-2}\sum_{i=1}^{n}(X_i - \overline{X})^2 \hat{u}_i^2}{\left[\frac{1}{n}\sum_{i=1}^{n}(X_i - \overline{X})^2\right]^2}. \tag{4.19}$$

The estimator of the variance in Equation (4.19) is discussed in Appendix 4.4. Although the formula for $\hat{\sigma}_{\hat{\beta}_1}^2$ is complicated, in applications the standard error is computed by regression software so that it is easy to use in practice.

The second step is to compute the **t-statistic**,

$$t = \frac{\hat{\beta}_1 - \beta_{1,0}}{SE(\hat{\beta}_1)}. \tag{4.20}$$

The third step is to compute the **p-value**, that is, the probability of observing a value of $\hat{\beta}_1$ at least as different from $\beta_{1,0}$ as the estimate actually computed ($\hat{\beta}_1^{act}$), assuming that the null hypothesis is correct. Stated mathematically,

$$p\text{-value} = \Pr_{H_0}\left[|\hat{\beta}_1 - \beta_{1,0}| > |\hat{\beta}_1^{act} - \beta_{1,0}|\right]$$

$$= \Pr_{H_0}\left[\left|\frac{\hat{\beta}_1 - \beta_{1,0}}{SE(\hat{\beta}_1)}\right| > \left|\frac{\hat{\beta}_1^{act} - \beta_{1,0}}{SE(\hat{\beta}_1)}\right|\right] = \Pr_{H_0}(|t| > |t^{act}|), \tag{4.21}$$

where, $\Pr_{H_0}$ denotes the probability computed under the null hypothesis, the second equality follows by dividing by $SE(\hat{\beta}_1)$, and t^{act} is the value of the *t*-statistic actually computed. Because $\hat{\beta}_1$ is approximately normally distributed in large samples, under the null hypothesis the *t*-statistic is approximately distributed as a standard normal random variable, so in large samples,

$$p\text{-value} = \Pr(|Z| > |t^{act}|) = 2\Phi(-|t^{act}|). \tag{4.22}$$

A small value of the *p*-value, say less than 5%, provides evidence against the null hypothesis in the sense that the chance of obtaining a value of $\hat{\beta}_1$ by pure random variation from one sample to the next is less than 5% if in fact the null hypothesis is correct. If so, the null hypothesis is rejected at the 5% significance level.

Alternatively, the hypothesis can be tested at the 5% significance level simply by comparing the value of the *t*-statistic to ± 1.96, the critical value for a two-sided test, and rejecting the null hypothesis at the 5% level if $|t^{act}| > 1.96$.

These steps are summarized in Key Concept 4.6.

Application to test scores.   The OLS estimator of the slope coefficient, estimated using the 420 observations in Figure 4.2 and reported in Equation (4.7), is -2.28. Its standard error is 0.52, that is, $SE(\hat{\beta}_1) = 0.52$. Thus, to test the null hypothesis that $\beta_{ClassSize} = 0$, we construct the *t*-statistic using Equation (4.20); accordingly, $t^{act} = (-2.28 - 0)/0.52 = -4.38$.

This *t*-statistic exceeds the 1% two-sided critical value of 2.58, so the null hypothesis is rejected in favor of the two-sided alternative at the 1% significance level. Alternatively, we can compute the *p*-value associated with $t = -4.38$. This probability is the area in the tails of standard normal distribution, as shown in Figure 4.6. This probability is extremely small, approximately .00001, or .001%. That is, if the null hypothesis $\beta_{ClassSize} = 0$ is true, the probability of obtaining a value of $\hat{\beta}_1$ as far from the null as the value we actually obtained is extremely small, less than .001%. Because this event is so unlikely, it is reasonable to conclude that the null hypothesis is false.

One-Sided Hypotheses Concerning β_1

The discussion so far has focused on testing the hypothesis that $\beta_1 = \beta_{1,0}$ against the hypothesis that $\beta_1 \neq \beta_{1,0}$. This is a two-sided hypothesis test, because under the alternative β_1 could be either larger or smaller than $\beta_{1,0}$. Sometimes, however, it is appropriate to use a one-sided hypothesis test. For example, in the student-teacher ratio/test score problem, many people think that smaller classes provide a better learning environment. Under that hypothesis, β_1 is negative: smaller classes lead to higher scores. It might make sense, therefore, to test the null hypothesis that $\beta_1 = 0$ (no effect) against the one-sided alternative that $\beta_1 < 0$.

For a one-sided test, the null hypothesis and the one-sided alternative hypothesis are

$$H_0: \beta_1 = \beta_{1,0} \text{ vs. } H_1: \beta_1 < \beta_{1,0}, \text{ (one-sided alternative).} \tag{4.23}$$

Testing the Hypothesis $\beta_1 = \beta_{1,0}$ Against the Alternative $\beta_1 \neq \beta_{1,0}$

1. Compute the standard error of $\hat{\beta}_1$, $SE(\hat{\beta}_1)$ (Equation (4.17)).
2. Compute the t-statistic (Equation (4.20)).
3. Compute the p-value (Equation (4.22)). Reject the hypothesis at the 5% significance level if the p-value is less than .05 or, equivalently, if $|t^{act}| > 1.96$.

The standard error and (typically) the t-statistic and p-value testing $\beta_1 = 0$ are computed automatically by regression software.

Key Concept 4.6

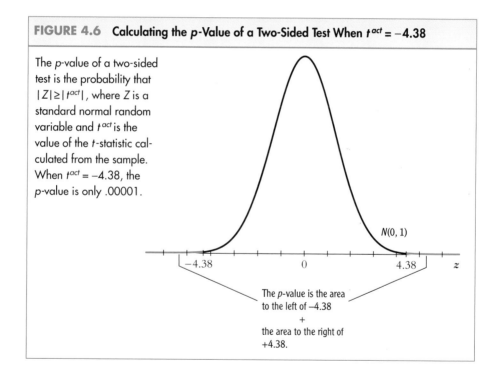

FIGURE 4.6   Calculating the p-Value of a Two-Sided Test When $t^{act} = -4.38$

The p-value of a two-sided test is the probability that $|Z| \geq |t^{act}|$, where Z is a standard normal random variable and t^{act} is the value of the t-statistic calculated from the sample. When $t^{act} = -4.38$, the p-value is only .00001.

$N(0, 1)$

-4.38 0 4.38 z

The p-value is the area to the left of -4.38
+
the area to the right of $+4.38$.

where $\beta_{1,0}$ is the value of β_1 under the null (0 in the student–teacher ratio example) and the alternative is that β_1 is less than $\beta_{1,0}$. If the alternative is that β_1 is greater than $\beta_{1,0}$, the inequality in Equation (4.23) is reversed.

Because the null hypothesis is the same for a one- and a two-sided hypothesis test, the construction of the t-statistic is the same. The only difference between a one- and two-sided hypothesis test is how you interpret the t-statistic. For the one-sided alternative in (4.23), the null hypothesis is rejected against the one-sided alternative for large negative, but not large positive, values of the t-statistic: instead of rejecting if $|t^{act}| > 1.96$, the hypothesis is rejected at the 5% significance level if $t^{act} < -1.645$.

The p-value for a one-sided test is obtained from the cumulative standard normal distribution as

$$p\text{-value} = \Pr(Z < t^{act}) = \Phi(t^{act}) \quad (p\text{-value, one-sided left-tail test}). \quad (4.24)$$

If the alternative hypothesis is that β_1 is greater than $\beta_{1,0}$, the inequalities in Equations (4.23) and (4.24) are reversed, so the p-value is the right-tail probability, $\Pr(Z > t^{act})$.

When should a one-sided test be used?   In practice, one-sided alternative hypotheses should be used when there is a clear reason for β_1 being on a certain side of the null value $\beta_{1,0}$ under the alternative. This reason could stem from economic theory, prior empirical evidence, or both. However, even if it initially seems that the relevant alternative is one-sided, upon reflection this might not necessarily be so. A newly formulated drug undergoing clinical trials actually could prove harmful because of previously unrecognized side effects. In the class size example, we are reminded of the graduation joke that a university's secret of success is to admit talented students and then make sure that the faculty stays out of their way and does as little damage as possible. In practice, such ambiguity often leads econometricians to use two-sided tests.

Application to test scores.   The t-statistic testing the hypothesis that there is no effect of class size on test scores (so $\beta_{1,0} = 0$ in Equation (4.23)) is $t^{act} = -4.38$. This is less than -2.33 (the critical value for a one-sided test with a 1% significance level), so the null hypothesis is rejected against the one-sided alternative at the 1% level. In fact, the p-value is less than .0006%. Based on these data, you can reject the angry taxpayer's assertion that the negative estimate of the slope arose purely because of random sampling variation at the 1% significance level.

Testing Hypotheses About the Intercept β_0

This discussion has focused on testing hypotheses about the slope, β_1. Occasionally, however, the hypothesis concerns the intercept, β_0. The null hypothesis concerning the intercept and the two-sided alternative are

$$H_0: \beta_0 = \beta_{0,0} \text{ vs. } H_1: \beta_0 \neq \beta_{0,0} \quad (\text{two-sided alternative}). \quad (4.25)$$

The general approach to testing this null hypothesis consists of the three steps in Key Concept 4.6, applied to β_0 (the formula for the standard error of $\hat{\beta}_0$ is given in Appendix 4.4). If the alternative is one-sided, this approach is modified as was discussed in the previous subsection for hypotheses about the slope.

Hypothesis tests are useful if you have a specific null hypothesis in mind (as did our angry taxpayer). Being able to accept or to reject this null hypothesis based on the statistical evidence provides a powerful tool for coping with the uncertainty inherent in using a sample to learn about the population. Yet, there are many times that no single hypothesis about a regression coefficient is dominant, and instead one would like to know a range of values of the coefficient that are consistent with the data. This calls for constructing a confidence interval.

4.6   Confidence Intervals for a Regression Coefficient

Because any statistical estimate of the slope β_1 necessarily has sampling uncertainty, we cannot determine the true value of β_1 exactly from a sample of data. It is, however, possible to use the OLS estimator and its standard error to construct a confidence interval for the slope β_1 or for the intercept β_0.

Confidence interval for β_1.   Recall that a **95% confidence interval** for β_1 has two equivalent definitions. First, it is the set of values that cannot be rejected using a two-sided hypothesis test with a 5% significance level. Second, it is an interval that has a 95% probability of containing the true value of β_1; that is, in 95% of possible samples that might be drawn, the confidence interval will contain the true value of β_1. Because this interval contains the true value in 95% of all samples, it is said to have a **confidence level** of 95%.

The reason these two definitions are equivalent is as follows. A hypothesis test with a 5% significance level will, by definition, reject the true value of β_1 in only 5% of all possible samples, that is, in 95% of all possible samples the true value of β_1 will *not* be rejected. Because the 95% confidence interval (as defined in the first definition) is the set of all values of β_1 that are *not* rejected at the 5% significance level, it follows that the true value of β_1 will be contained in the confidence interval in 95% of all possible samples.

As in the case of a confidence interval for the population mean (Section 3.3), in principle a 95% confidence interval can be computed by testing all possible values of β_1 (that is, testing the null hypothesis $\beta_1 = \beta_{1,0}$ for all values of $\beta_{1,0}$) at the

5% significance level using the t-statistic. The 95% confidence interval is then the collection of all the values of β_1 that are not rejected. But constructing the t-statistic for all values of β_1 would take forever.

An easier way to construct the confidence interval is to note that the t-statistic will reject the hypothesized value $\beta_{1,0}$ whenever $\beta_{1,0}$ is outside the range $\hat{\beta}_1 \pm 1.96SE(\hat{\beta}_1)$. That is, the 95% confidence interval for β_1 is the interval $(\hat{\beta}_1 - 1.96SE(\hat{\beta}_1), \hat{\beta}_1 + 1.96SE(\hat{\beta}_1))$. This argument parallels the argument used to develop a confidence interval for the population mean.

The construction of a confidence interval for β_1 is summarized as Key Concept 4.7.

Confidence interval for β_0.   A 95% confidence interval for β_0 is constructed as in Key Concept 4.7, with $\hat{\beta}_0$ and $SE(\hat{\beta}_0)$ replacing $\hat{\beta}_1$ and $SE(\hat{\beta}_1)$.

Application to test scores.   The OLS regression of the test score against the student-teacher ratio, reported in Equation (4.7), yielded $\hat{\beta}_0 = 698.7$ and $\hat{\beta}_1 = -2.28$. The standard errors of these estimates are $SE(\hat{\beta}_0) = 10.4$ and $SE(\hat{\beta}_1) = 0.52$.

Because of the importance of the standard errors, we will henceforth include them when reporting OLS regression lines in parentheses below the estimated coefficients:

$$\widehat{TestScore} = 698.9 - 2.28 \times STR. \qquad (4.26)$$
$$(10.4) \quad (0.52)$$

The 95% two-sided confidence interval for β_1 is $\{-2.28 \pm 1.96 \times 0.52\}$, that is, $-3.30 \leq \beta_1 \leq -1.26$. The value $\beta_1 = 0$ is not contained in this confidence interval, so (as we knew already from Section 4.5) the hypothesis $\beta_1 = 0$ can be rejected at the 5% significance level.

Confidence intervals for predicted effects of changing X.   The **95% confidence interval** for β_1 can be used to construct a 95% confidence interval for the predicted effect of a general change in X.

Consider changing X by a given amount, Δx. The predicted change in Y associated with this change in X is $\beta_1 \Delta x$. The population slope β_1 is unknown, but because we can construct a confidence interval for β_1, we can construct a confidence interval for the predicted effect $\beta_1 \Delta x$. Because one end of a 95% confidence interval for β_1 is $\hat{\beta}_1 - 1.96SE(\hat{\beta}_1)$, the predicted effect of the change Δx using this estimate of β_1 is $(\hat{\beta}_1 - 1.96SE(\hat{\beta}_1)) \times \Delta x$. The other end of the confidence interval

Confidence Intervals for β_1

Key Concept 4.7

A 95% two-sided confidence interval for β_1 is an interval that contains the true value of β_1 with a 95% probability, that is, it contains the true value of β_1 in 95% of all possible randomly drawn samples. Equivalently, it is also the set of values of β_1 that cannot be rejected by a 5% two-sided hypothesis test. When the sample size is large, it is constructed as

$$95\% \text{ confidence interval for } \beta_1 = (\hat{\beta}_1 - 1.96SE(\hat{\beta}_1), \hat{\beta}_1 + 1.96SE(\hat{\beta}_1)). \quad (4.27)$$

is $\hat{\beta}_1 + 1.96SE(\hat{\beta}_1)$, and the predicted effect of the change using that estimate is $(\hat{\beta}_1 + 1.96SE(\hat{\beta}_1)) \times \Delta x$. Thus a 95% confidence interval for the effect of changing x by the amount Δx can be expressed as

$$95\% \text{ confidence interval for } \beta_1 \Delta x =$$
$$(\hat{\beta}_1 \Delta x - 1.96SE(\hat{\beta}_1) \times \Delta x, \hat{\beta}_1 \Delta x + 1.96SE(\hat{\beta}_1) \times \Delta x). \quad (4.28)$$

For example, our hypothetical superintendent is contemplating reducing the student–teacher ratio by 2. Because the 95% confidence interval for β_1 is $(-3.30, -1.26)$, the effect of reducing the student–teacher ratio by 2 could be as great as $-3.30 \times (-2) = 6.60$, or as little as $-1.26 \times (-2) = 2.52$. Thus decreasing the student–teacher ratio by 2 is predicted to increase test scores by between 2.52 and 6.60 points, with a 95% confidence level.

4.7 Regression When *X* Is a Binary Variable

The discussion so far has focused on the case that the regressor is a continuous variable. Regression analysis can also be used when the regressor is binary, that is, when it takes on only two values, 0 or 1. For example, X might be a worker's gender (= 1 if female, = 0 if male), whether a school district is urban or rural (= 1 if urban, = 0 if rural), or whether the district's class size is small or large (= 1 if small, = 0 if large). A binary variable is also called an **indicator variable** or sometimes a **dummy variable**.

Interpretation of the Regression Coefficients

The mechanics of regression with a binary regressor are the same as if it is continuous. The interpretation of β_1, however, is different, and it turns out that regression with a binary variable is equivalent to performing a difference of means analysis, as described in Section 3.4.

To see this, suppose you have a variable D_i that equals either 0 or 1, depending on whether the student-teacher ratio is less than 20:

$$D_i = \begin{cases} 1 \text{ if the student-teacher ratio in } i^{\text{th}} \text{ district} < 20 \\ 0 \text{ if the student-teacher ratio in } i^{\text{th}} \text{ district} \geq 20. \end{cases} \quad (4.29)$$

The population regression model with D_i as the regressor is

$$Y_i = \beta_0 + \beta_1 D_i + u_i, \, i = 1, \ldots, n. \quad (4.30)$$

This is the same as the regression model with the continuous regressor X_i, except that now the regressor is the binary variable D_i. Because D_i is not continuous, it is not useful to think of β_1 as a slope; indeed, because D_i can take on only two values, there is no "line" so it makes no sense to talk about a slope. Thus we will not refer to β_1 as the slope in Equation (4.30); instead we will simply refer to β_1 as the **coefficient multiplying D_i** in this regression or, more compactly, the **coefficient on D_i**.

If β_1 in Equation (4.30) is not a slope, then what is it? The best way to interpret β_0 and β_1 in a regression with a binary regressor is to consider, one at a time, the two possible cases, $D_i = 0$ and $D_i = 1$. If the student-teacher ratio is high, then $D_i = 0$ and Equation (4.30) becomes

$$Y_i = \beta_0 + u_i \quad (D_i = 0). \quad (4.31)$$

Because $E(u_i | D_i) = 0$, the conditional expectation of Y_i when $D_i = 0$ is $E(Y_i | D_i = 0) = \beta_0$, that is, β_0 is the population mean value of test scores when the student-teacher ratio is high. Similarly, when $D_i = 1$,

$$Y_i = \beta_0 + \beta_1 + u_i \quad (D_i = 1). \quad (4.32)$$

Thus, when $D_i = 1$, $E(Y_i | D_i = 1) = \beta_0 + \beta_1$; that is, $\beta_0 + \beta_1$ is the population mean value of test scores when the student-teacher ratio is low.

Because $\beta_0 + \beta_1$ is the population mean of Y_i when $D_i = 1$ and β_0 is the population mean of Y_i when $D_i = 0$, the difference $(\beta_0 + \beta_1) - \beta_0 = \beta_1$ is the difference between these two means. In other words, β_1 is the difference between the conditional expectation of Y_i when $D_i = 1$ and when $D_i = 0$, or $\beta_1 = E(Y_i | D_i = 1) - E(Y_i | D_i = 0)$. In the test score example, β_1 is the difference between mean test score in districts with low student-teacher ratios and the mean test score in districts with high student-teacher ratios.

Because β_1 is the difference in the population means, it makes sense that the OLS estimator β_1 is the difference between the sample averages of Y_i in the two groups, and in fact this is the case.

Hypothesis tests and confidence intervals.   If the two population means are the same, then β_1 in Equation (4.30) is zero. Thus, the null hypothesis that the two population means are the same can be tested against the alternative hypothesis that they differ by testing the null hypothesis $\beta_1 = 0$ against the alternative $\beta_1 \neq 0$. This hypothesis can be tested using the procedure outlined in Section 4.5. Specifically, the null hypothesis can be rejected at the 5% level against the two-sided alternative when the OLS t-statistic $t = \hat{\beta}_1 / SE(\hat{\beta}_1)$ exceeds 1.96 in absolute value. Similarly, a 95% confidence interval for β_1, constructed as $\hat{\beta}_1 \pm 1.96 SE(\hat{\beta}_1)$ as described in Section 4.6, provides a 95% confidence interval for the difference between the two population means.

Application to Test Scores.   As an example, a regression of the test score against the student-teacher ratio binary variable D defined in Equation (4.29) estimated by OLS using the 420 observations in Figure 4.2, yields

$$\widehat{TestScore} = 650.0 + 7.4D$$
$$(1.3) \quad (1.8) \tag{4.33}$$

where the standard errors of the OLS estimates of the coefficients β_0 and β_1 are given in parentheses below the OLS estimates. Thus the average test score for the subsample with student-teacher ratios greater than or equal to 20 (that is, for which $D = 0$) is 650.0, and the average test score for the subsample with student-teacher ratios less than 20 (so $D = 1$) is $650.0 + 7.4 = 657.4$. Thus the difference between the sample average test scores for the two groups is 7.4. This is the OLS estimate of β_1, the coefficient on the student-teacher ratio binary variable D.

Is the difference in the population mean test scores in the two groups statistically significantly different from zero at the 5% level? To find out, construct the t-statistic on β_1: $t = 7.4/1.8 = 4.04$. This exceeds 1.96 in absolute value, so the hypothesis that the population mean test scores in districts with high and low student-teacher ratios is the same can be rejected at the 5% significance level.

The OLS estimator and its standard error can be used to construct a 95% confidence interval for the true difference in means. This is $7.4 \pm 1.96 \times 1.8 = (3.9, 10.9)$. This confidence interval excludes $\beta_1 = 0$, so that (as we know from the previous paragraph) the hypothesis $\beta_1 = 0$ can be rejected at the 5% significance level.

4.8   The R^2 and the Standard Error of the Regression

The R^2 and the standard error of the regression are two measures of how well the OLS regression line fits the data. The R^2 ranges between zero and one and measures the fraction of the variance of Y_i that is explained by variation in X_i. The standard error of the regression measures how far Y_i typically is from its predicted value.

The R^2

The **regression R^2** is the fraction of the sample variance of Y_i explained by (or predicted by) X_i. The definitions of the predicted value and the residual (see Key Concept 4.2) allow us to write the dependent variable Y_i as the sum of the predicted value, $\hat{Y}_i$, plus the residual $\hat{u}_i$:

$$Y_i = \hat{Y}_i + \hat{u}_i. \tag{4.34}$$

In this notation, the R^2 is the ratio of the sample variance of $\hat{Y}_i$ to the sample variance of Y_i.

Mathematically, the R^2 can be written as the ratio of the explained sum of squares to the total sum of squares. The **explained sum of squares**, or **ESS**, is the sum of squared deviations of the predicted values of Y_i, $\hat{Y}_i$, from their average, and the **total sum of squares**, or **TSS**, is the sum of squared deviations of Y_i from its average:

$$ESS = \sum_{i=1}^{n}(\hat{Y}_i - \overline{Y})^2 \text{ and} \tag{4.35}$$

$$TSS = \sum_{i=1}^{n}(Y_i - \overline{Y})^2 , \tag{4.36}$$

where Equation (4.35) uses the fact that $\overline{Y}$ equals the sample average OLS predicted value (proven in Appendix 4.3).

The R^2 is the ratio of the explained sum of squares to the total sum of squares:

$$R^2 = \frac{ESS}{TSS}. \tag{4.37}$$

Alternatively, the R^2 can be written in terms of the fraction of the variance of Y_i *not* explained by X_i. The **sum of squared residuals**, or **SSR**, is the sum of the squared OLS residuals:

$$SSR = \sum_{i=1}^{n} \hat{u}_i^2. \tag{4.38}$$

It is shown in Appendix 4.3 that $TSS = ESS + SSR$. Thus the R^2 also can be expressed as one minus the ratio of the sum of squared residuals to the total sum of squares:

$$R^2 = 1 - \frac{SSR}{TSS}. \tag{4.39}$$

Finally, the R^2 of the regression of Y on the single regressor X is the square of the correlation coefficient between Y and X.

The R^2 ranges between zero and one. If $\hat{\beta}_1 = 0$, then X_i explains none of the variation of Y_i and the predicted value of Y_i based on the regression is just the sample average of Y_i. In this case, the explained sum of squares is zero and the sum of squared residuals equals the total sum of squares; thus the R^2 is zero. In contrast, if X_i explains all of the variation of Y_i, then $Y_i = \hat{Y}_i$ for all i and every residual is zero (that is, $\hat{u}_i = 0$), so that $ESS = TSS$ and $R^2 = 1$. In general the R^2 does not take on the extreme values of zero or one but falls somewhere in between. An R^2 near one indicates that the regressor is good at predicting Y_i, while an R^2 near zero indicates that the regressor is not very good at predicting Y_i.

The Standard Error of the Regression

The **standard error of the regression**, or **SER**, is an estimator of the standard deviation of the regression error u_i. Because the regression errors $u_1, \ldots, u_n$ are unobserved, the SER is computed using their sample counterparts, the OLS residuals $\hat{u}_1, \ldots, \hat{u}_n$. The formula for the SER is

$$SER = s_{\hat{u}}, \text{ where } s_{\hat{u}}^2 = \frac{1}{n-2} \sum_{i=1}^{n} \hat{u}_i^2 = \frac{SSR}{n-2}, \tag{4.40}$$

where the formula for $s_{\hat{u}}^2$ uses the fact (proven in Appendix 4.3) that the sample average of the OLS residuals is zero.

The formula for the *SER* in Equation (4.40) is the same as the formula for the sample standard deviation of Y given in Equation (3.7) in Section 3.2, except that $Y_i - \overline{Y}$ in Equation (3.7) is replaced by $\hat{u}_i$, and the divisor in Equation (3.7) is $n - 1$, whereas here it is $n - 2$. The reason for using the divisor $n - 2$ here (instead of n) is the same as the reason for using the divisor $n - 1$ in Equation (3.7): it corrects for a slight downward bias introduced because two regression coefficients were estimated. This is called a "degrees of freedom" correction; because two coefficients were estimated (β_0 and β_1), two "degrees of freedom" of the data were lost, so the divisor in this factor is $n - 2$. (The mathematics behind this is discussed in Section 15.4.) When n is large, the difference between dividing by n, by $n - 1$, or by $n - 2$ is negligible.

4.9 Heteroskedasticity and Homoskedasticity

Our only assumption about the distribution of u_i conditional on X_i is that it has a mean of zero (the first least squares assumption). If, furthermore, the *variance* of this conditional distribution does not depend on X_i, then the errors are said to be homoskedastic. This section discusses homoskedasticity, its theoretical implications, the simplified formulas for the standard errors of the OLS estimators that arise if the errors are homoskedastic, and the risks you run if you use these simplified formulas in practice.

What Are Heteroskedasticity and Homoskedasticity?

Definitions of heteroskedasticity and homoskedasticity.   The error term u_i is **homoskedastic** if the variance of the conditional distribution of u_i given X_i is constant for $i = 1, \ldots , n$ and in particular does not depend on X_i. Otherwise, the error term is **heteroskedastic**.

As an illustration, return to Figure 4.4. The distribution of the errors u_i is shown for various values of x. Because this distribution applies specifically for the indicated value of x, this is the conditional distribution of u_i given $X_i = x$. As drawn in that figure, all these conditional distributions have the same spread; more precisely, the variance of these distributions is the same for the various values of x. That is, in Figure 4.4, the conditional variance of u_i given $X_i = x$ does not depend on x, so the errors illustrated in Figure 4.4 are homoskedastic.

In contrast, Figure 4.7 illustrates a case in which the conditional distribution of u_i spreads out as x increases. For small values of x, this distribution is tight, but for larger values of x, it has a greater spread. Thus, in Figure 4.7 the variance of u_i given $X_i = x$ increases with x, so that the errors in Figure 4.7 are heteroskedastic.

The definitions of heteroskedasticity and homoskedasticity are summarized in Key Concept 4.8.

Example.   These terms are a mouthful and the definitions might seem abstract. To help clarify them with an example, we digress from the student-teacher ratio/test score problem and instead return to the example of earnings of male versus female college graduates considered in Section 3.5. Let $MALE_i$ be a binary variable that equals 1 for male college graduates and equals 0 for female graduates. The binary variable regression model relating someone's earnings to his or her gender is

$$Earnings_i = \beta_0 + \beta_1 MALE_i + u_i \tag{4.41}$$

for $i = 1, \ldots, n$. Because the regressor is binary, β_1 is the difference in the population means of the two groups, in this case, the difference in mean earnings between men and women who graduated from college.

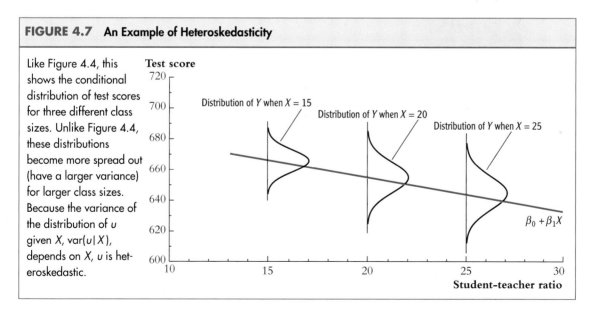

FIGURE 4.7   An Example of Heteroskedasticity

Like Figure 4.4, this shows the conditional distribution of test scores for three different class sizes. Unlike Figure 4.4, these distributions become more spread out (have a larger variance) for larger class sizes. Because the variance of the distribution of u given X, $var(u|X)$, depends on X, u is heteroskedastic.

Heteroskedasticity and Homoskedasticity

Key Concept 4.8

The error term u_i is homoskedastic if the variance of the conditional distribution of u_i given X_i, $\text{var}(u_i | X_i = x)$, is constant for $i = 1, \ldots, n$, and in particular does not depend on x; otherwise, the error term is heteroskedastic.

The definition of homoskedasticity states that the variance of u_i does not depend on the regressor. Here the regressor is $MALE_i$, so at issue is whether the variance of the error term depends on $MALE_i$. In other words, is the variance of the error term the same for men and for women? If so, the error is homoskedastic; if not, it is heteroskedastic.

Deciding whether the variance of u_i depends on $MALE_i$ requires thinking hard about what the error term actually is. In this regard, it is useful to write Equation (4.41) as two separate equations, one for men and one for women:

$$Earnings_i = \beta_0 + u_i \text{ (women) and} \tag{4.42}$$

$$Earnings_i = \beta_0 + \beta_1 + u_i \text{ (men).} \tag{4.43}$$

Thus, for women, u_i is the deviation of the ith woman's earnings from the population mean earnings for women (β_0), and for men, u_i is the deviation of the ith man's earnings from the population mean earnings for men ($\beta_0 + \beta_1$). It follows that the statement, "the variance of u_i does not depend on $MALE$," is equivalent to the statement, "the variance of earnings is the same for men as it is for women." In other words, in this example, the error term is homoskedastic if the variance of the population distribution of earnings is the same for men and women; if these variances differ, the error term is heteroskedastic.

Mathematical Implications of Homoskedasticity

The OLS estimators remain unbiased and asymptotically normal. Because the least squares assumptions in Key Concept 4.3 place no restrictions on the conditional variance, they apply to both the general case of heteroskedasticity and the special case of homoskedasticity. Therefore, the OLS estimators remain unbiased and consistent even if the errors are homoskedastic. In addition, the OLS estimators have sampling distributions that are normal in large samples even if the errors are homoskedastic. Whether the errors are homoskedastic or heteroskedastic, the OLS estimator is unbiased, consistent, and asymptotically normal.

Efficiency of the OLS estimator.   If the least squares assumptions in Key Concept 4.3 hold and in addition the errors are homoskedastic, then the OLS estimators $\hat{\beta}_0$ and $\hat{\beta}_1$ are efficient among all estimators that are linear in $Y_1, \ldots, Y_n$ and are unbiased, conditional on $X_1, \ldots, X_n$. That is, the OLS estimators have the smallest variance of all unbiased estimators that are weighted averages of $Y_1, \ldots, Y_n$. In other words, if, in addition to the least squares assumptions, the errors are homoskedastic, then the OLS estimators $\hat{\beta}_0$ and $\hat{\beta}_1$ are the **best linear unbiased estimators**, or **BLUE**. This result was stated for the sample average $\overline{Y}$ in Key Concept 3.3 and it extends to OLS under homoskedasticity. This result, which is known as the Gauss-Markov theorem, is proven in Chapter 15.

If the errors are heteroskedastic, then OLS is no longer BLUE. In theory, if the errors are heteroskedastic then it is possible to construct an estimator that has a smaller variance than the OLS estimator. This method is called **weighted least squares**, in which the observations are weighted by the inverse of the square root of the conditional variance of u_i given X_i. Because of this weighting, the errors in this weighted regression are homoskedastic so OLS, applied to this weighted regression, is BLUE. Although theoretically elegant, the problem with weighted least squares in practice is that you must know how the conditional variance of u_i actually depends on X_i, which is rarely known in applications. Because weighted least squares is mainly of theoretical interest, we defer further discussion to Chapter 15.

Homoskedasticity-only variance formula.   If the error term is homoskedastic, then the formulas for the variances of $\hat{\beta}_0$ and $\hat{\beta}_1$ in Key Concept 4.4 simplify. Consequently, if the errors are homoskedastic, then there is a specialized formula that can be used for the standard errors of $\hat{\beta}_0$ and $\hat{\beta}_1$. These formulas are given in Appendix 4.4. In the special case that X is a binary variable, the estimator of the variance of $\hat{\beta}_1$ under homoskedasticity (that is, the square of the standard error of $\hat{\beta}_1$ under homoskedasticity) is the so-called pooled variance formula for the difference in means, discussed in footnote 1 in Section 3.4.

Because these alternative formulas are derived for the special case that the errors are homoskedastic and do not apply if the errors are heteroskedastic, they will be referred to as the "homoskedasticity-only" formulas for the variance and standard error of the OLS estimators. As the name suggests, if the errors are heteroskedastic then the **homoskedasticity-only standard errors** are inappropriate. Specifically, if the errors are heteroskedastic, then the t-statistic computed using the homoskedasticity-only standard error does not have a standard normal distribution, even in large samples. In fact, the correct critical values to use for this homoskedasticity-only t-statistic depend on the precise nature of the heteroskedasticity, so those critical values cannot be tabulated. Similarly, if the errors are heteroskedastic but a confidence interval is constructed as ±1.96 homoskedasticity-only standard errors, in general the probability that this interval contains the true value of the coefficient is not 95%, even in large samples.

In contrast, because homoskedasticity is a special case of heteroskedasticity, the estimators $\hat{\sigma}_{\hat{\beta}_1}^2$ and $\hat{\sigma}_{\hat{\beta}_0}^2$ of the variances of $\hat{\beta}_1$ and $\hat{\beta}_0$ given in Equations (4.19) and (4.59) produce valid statistical inferences whether the errors are heteroskedastic or homoskedastic. Thus hypothesis tests and confidence intervals based on those standard errors are valid whether or not the errors are heteroskedastic. Because the standard errors we have used so far (i.e., those based on Equations (4.19) and (4.59)) lead to statistical inferences that are valid whether or not the errors are heteroskedastic, they are called **heteroskedasticity-robust standard errors.** Because such formulas were proposed by Eicker (1967), Huber (1967) and White (1980), they are also referred to as Eicker-Huber-White standard errors.

What Does This Mean in Practice?

Which is more realistic, heteroskedasticity or homoskedasticity? The answer to this question depends on the application. However, the issues can be clarified by returning to the example of the gender gap in earnings among college graduates. Familiarity with how people are paid in the world around us gives some clues as to which assumption is more sensible. For many years—and, to a lesser extent, today—women were not found in the top-paying jobs: there have always been poorly paid men, but there have rarely been highly paid women. This suggests that the distribution of earnings among women is tighter than among men. In other words, the variance of the error term in Equation (4.42) for women is plausibly less than the variance of the error term in Equation (4.43) for men. Thus, the presence of a "glass ceiling" for women's jobs and pay suggests that the error term in the binary variable regression model in Equation (4.41) is heteroskedastic. Unless there are compelling reasons to the contrary—and we can think of none—it makes sense to treat the error term in this example as heteroskedastic.

As this example of modeling earnings illustrates, heteroskedasticity arises in many econometric applications. At a general level, economic theory rarely gives any reason to believe that the errors are homoskedastic. It therefore is prudent to assume that the errors might be heteroskedastic unless you have compelling reasons to believe otherwise.

Practical implications. The main issue of practical relevance in this discussion is whether one should use heteroskedasticity-robust or homoskedasticity-only standard errors. In this regard, it is useful to imagine computing both, then choosing between them. If the homoskedasticity-only and heteroskedasticity-robust standard errors are the same, nothing is lost by using the heteroskedasticity-robust standard errors; if they differ, however, then you should use the more reliable ones that allow for heteroskedasticity. The simplest thing, then, is always to use the heteroskedasticity-robust standard errors.

For historical reasons, many software programs use the homoskedasticity-only standard errors as their default setting, so it is up to the user to specify the option of heteroskedasticity-robust standard errors. The details of how to implement heteroskedasticity-robust standard errors depend on the software package you use.

All the empirical examples in this book employ heteroskedasticity-robust standard errors unless explicitly stated otherwise.[2]

4.10 Conclusion

Return for a moment to the problem that started this chapter, the superintendent who is considering hiring additional teachers to cut the student-teacher ratio. What have we learned that she might find useful?

Our regression analysis, based on the 420 observations for 1998 in the California test score data set, showed that there was a negative relationship between the student-teacher ratio and test scores: districts with smaller classes have higher test scores. The coefficient is moderately large, in a practical sense: districts with 2 fewer students per teacher have, on average, test scores that are 4.6 points higher. This corresponds to moving a district at the 50th percentile of the distribution of test scores to approximately the 60th percentile.

---

[2]In case this book is used in conjunction with other texts, it might be helpful to note that some textbooks add homoskedasticity to the list of least squares assumptions. As just discussed, however, this additional assumption is not needed for the validity of OLS regression analysis as long as heteroskedasticity-robust standard errors are used.

The coefficient on the student-teacher ratio is statistically significantly different from 0 at the 5% significance level. The population coefficient might be 0, and we might simply have estimated our negative coefficient by random sampling variation. However, the probability of doing so (and of obtaining a t-statistic on β_1 as large as we did) purely by random variation over potential samples is exceedingly small, approximately 0.001%. A 95% confidence interval for β_1 is $-3.30 \leq \beta_1 \leq -1.26$.

We have made considerable progress towards answering the superintendent's question. Yet, a nagging concern remains. We estimated a negative relationship between the student-teacher ratio and test scores, but is this relationship necessarily the *causal* one that the superintendent needs to make her decision? We have found that districts with lower student-teacher ratios have, on average, higher test scores. But does this mean that reducing the student-teacher ratio will in fact increase scores?

There is, in fact, reason to worry that it might not. Hiring more teachers, after all, costs money, so wealthier school districts can better afford smaller classes. But students at wealthier schools also have other advantages over their poorer neighbors, including better facilities, newer books, and better-paid teachers. Moreover, students at wealthier schools tend themselves to come from more affluent families, and thus have other advantages not directly associated with their school. For example, California has a large immigrant community; these immigrants tend to be poorer than the overall population and, in many cases, their children are not native English speakers. It thus might be that our negative estimated relationship between test scores and the student-teacher ratio is a consequence of small classes being found in conjunction with many other factors that are, in fact, the real cause of the lower test scores.

These other factors, or "omitted variables," could mean that the OLS analysis done so far in fact has little value to the superintendent. Indeed, it could be misleading: changing the student-teacher ratio alone would not change these other factors that determine a child's performance at school. To address this problem, we need a method that will allow us to isolate the effect on test scores of changing the student-teacher ratio, *holding these other factors constant*. That method is multiple regression analysis, the topic of Chapter 5.

Summary

1. The population regression line, $\beta_0 + \beta_1 X$, is the mean of Y as a function of the value of X. The slope, β_1, is the expected change in Y associated with a 1-unit change in X. The intercept, β_0, determines the level (or height) of the regression

line. Key Concept 4.1 summarizes the terminology of the population linear regression model.

2. The population regression line can be estimated using sample observations (Y_i, X_i), $i = 1, \ldots, n$ by ordinary least squares (OLS). The OLS estimators of the regression intercept and slope are denoted by $\hat{\beta}_0$ and $\hat{\beta}_1$.

3. There are three key assumptions for the linear regression model: (1) The regression errors, u_i, have a mean of zero conditional on the regressors X_i; (2) the sample observations are i.i.d. random draws from the population; and (3) the random variables have four moments. If these assumptions hold, the OLS estimators $\hat{\beta}_0$ and $\hat{\beta}_1$ are (1) unbiased; (2) consistent; and (3) normally distributed when the sample is large.

4. Hypothesis testing for regression coefficients is analogous to hypothesis testing for the population mean: use the t-statistic to calculate the p-values and either accept or reject the null hypothesis. Like a confidence interval for the population mean, a 95% confidence interval for a regression coefficient is computed as the estimator ± 1.96 standard errors.

5. When X is binary, the regression model can be used to estimate and test hypotheses about the difference between the population means of the "$X = 0$" group and the "$X = 1$" group.

6. The R^2 and standard error of the regression (SER) are measures of how close the values of Y_i are to the estimated regression line. The R^2 is between zero and one, with a larger value indicating that the Y_i's are closer to the line. The standard error of the regression is an estimator of the standard deviation of the regression error.

7. In general the error u_i is heteroskedastic, that is, the variance of u_i at a given value of X_i, $\text{var}(u_i \,|\, X_i = x)$ depends on x. A special case is when the error is homoskedastic, that is, $\text{var}(u_i \,|\, X_i = x)$ is constant. Homoskedasticity-only standard errors do not produce valid statistical inferences when the errors are heteroskedastic, but heteroskedasticity-robust standard errors do.

Key Terms

linear regression model with
   a single regressor (94)
dependent variable (94)
independent variable (94)
regressor (94)
population regression line (94)
population regression function (94)

population intercept and
   slope (94)
population coefficients (94)
parameters (94)
error term (94)
ordinary least squares (OLS) estimator (99)
OLS regression line (99)

Review the Concepts

4.1 Explain the difference between $\hat{\beta}_1$ and β_1; between the residual $\hat{u}_i$ and the regression error u_i; and between the OLS predicted value $\hat{Y}_i$ and $E(Y_i | X_i)$.

4.2 Outline the procedures for computing the p-value of a two-sided test of $H_0: \mu_Y = 0$ using an i.i.d. set of observations Y_i, $i = 1, \ldots, n$. Outline the procedures for computing the p-value of a two-sided test of $H_0: \beta_1 = 0$ in a regression model using an i.i.d. set of observations (Y_i, X_i), $i = 1, \ldots, n$.

4.3 Explain how you could use a regression model to estimate the wage gender gap using the data from Section 3.5. What are the dependent and independent variables?

4.4 Sketch a hypothetical scatterplot of data for an estimated regression with $R^2 = 0.9$. Sketch a hypothetical scatterplot of data for a regression with $R^2 = 0.5$.

Exercises

Solutions to exercises denoted by * can be found on the text Web site at **www.aw.com/stock_watson.**

*4.1 Suppose that a researcher, using data on class size (CS) and average test scores from 100 third-grade classes, estimates the OLS regression,

$$\widehat{TestScore} = 520.4 - 5.82 \times CS, \ R^2 = 0.08, \ SER = 11.5.$$
$$(20.4) \ (2.21)$$

  a. A classroom has 22 students. What is the regression's prediction for that classroom's average test score?

  b. Last year a classroom had 19 students, and this year it has 23 students. What is the regression's prediction for the change in the classroom average test score?

  c. Construct a 95% confidence interval for β_1, the regression slope coefficient.

  d. Calculate the p-value for the two-sided test of the null hypothesis $H_0: \beta_1 = 0$. Do you reject the null hypothesis at the 5% level? At the 1% level?

  e. The sample average class size across the 100 classrooms is 21.4. What is the sample average of the test scores across the 100 classrooms? (*Hint:* Review the formulas for the OLS estimators.)

  f. What is the sample standard deviation of test scores across the 100 classrooms? (*Hint:* Review the formulas for the R^2 and *SER*.)

4.2 Suppose that a researcher, using wage data on 250 randomly selected male workers and 280 female workers, estimates the OLS regression,

$$\widehat{Wage} = 12.68 + 2.79 \, Male, \; R^2 = 0.06, \; SER = 3.10$$
$$\phantom{\widehat{Wage} = } (0.18) \;\; (0.84)$$

where *Wage* is measured in \$/hour and *Male* is a binary variable that is equal to one if the person is a male and 0 if the person is a female. Define the wage gender gap as the difference in mean earnings between men and women.

  a. What is the estimated gender gap?

  b. Is the estimated gender gap significantly different from zero? (Compute the p-value for testing the null hypothesis that there is no gender gap.)

  c. Construct a 95% confidence interval for the gender gap.

  d. In the sample, what is the mean wage of women? Of men?

  e. Another researcher uses these same data, but regresses *Wages* on *Female*, a variable that is equal to one if the person is female and zero if the person a male. What are the regression estimates calculated from this regression?

$$\widehat{Wage} = \underline{} + \underline{} \, Female, \; R^2 = \underline{}, \; SER = \underline{}.$$

*4.3 Show that the first least squares assumption, $E(u_i \,|\, X_i) = 0$, implies that $E(Y_i \,|\, X_i) = \beta_0 + \beta_1 X_i$.

4.4   Show t hat $\hat{\beta}_0$ is an unbiased estimator of β_0. (Hint: use the fact that $\hat{\beta}_1$ is unbiased, which is shown in Appendix 4.3).

4.5   Suppose that a random sample of 200 20-year-old men is selected from a population and their height and weight is recorded. A regression of weight on height yields:

$$\widehat{Weight} = -99.41 + 3.94 \; Height, \; R^2 = 0.81, \; SER = 10.2,$$
$$\qquad\qquad (2.15) \quad (0.31)$$

where *Weight* is measured in pounds and *Height* is measured in inches.

   a.   What is the regression's weight prediction for someone who is 70 inches tall? 65 inches tall? 74 inches tall?

   b.   A person has a late growth spurt and grows 1.5 inches over the course of a year. What is the regression's prediction for the increase in the person's weight?

   c.   Construct a 99% confidence interval for the weight gain in (b).

   d.   Suppose that instead of measuring weight and height in pounds and inches, they are measured in kilograms and centimeters. What are the regression estimates from this new kilogram-centimeter regression? (Give all results, estimated coefficients, standard errors, R^2, and *SER*.)

4.6   Starting from Equation (4.15), derive the variance of $\hat{\beta}_0$ under homoskedasticity given in Equation (4.61) in Appendix 4.4.

APPENDIX

4.1 | The California Test Score Data Set

The California Standardized Testing and Reporting data set contains data on test performance, school characteristics, and student demographic backgrounds. The data used here are from all 420 K–6 and K–8 districts in California with data available for 1998 and 1999.

Test scores are the average of the reading and math scores on the Stanford 9 Achievement Test, a standardized test administered to fifth-grade students. School characteristics (averaged across the district) include enrollment, number of teachers (measured as "full-time-equivalents"), number of computers per classroom, and expenditures per student. The student-teacher ratio used here is the number of full-time equivalent teachers in the district, divided by the number of students. Demographic variables for the students also are averaged across the district. The demographic variables include the percentage of students in the public assistance program CalWorks (formerly AFDC), the percentage of students that qualify for a reduced price lunch, and the percentage of students that are English learners (that is, students for whom English is a second language). All of these data were obtained from the California Department of Education (www.cde.ca.gov).

4.2 | Derivation of the OLS Estimators

This appendix uses calculus to derive the formulas for the OLS estimators given in Key Concept 4.2. To minimize the sum of squared prediction mistakes $\sum_{i=1}^{n}(Y_i - b_0 - b_1 X_i)^2$ (Equation (4.6)), first take the partial derivatives with respect to b_0 and b_1:

$$\frac{\partial}{\partial b_0} \sum_{i=1}^{n}(Y_i - b_0 - b_1 X_i)^2 = -2\sum_{i=1}^{n}(Y_i - b_0 - b_1 X_i) \text{ and} \tag{4.44}$$

$$\frac{\partial}{\partial b_1} \sum_{i=1}^{n}(Y_i - b_0 - b_1 X_i)^2 = -2\sum_{i=1}^{n}(Y_i - b_0 - b_1 X_i)X_i. \tag{4.45}$$

The OLS estimators, $\hat{\beta}_0$ and $\hat{\beta}_1$, are the values of b_0 and b_1 that minimize $\sum_{i=1}^{n}(Y_i - b_0 - b_1 X_i)^2$ or, equivalently, the values of b_0 and b_1 for which the derivatives in Equations (4.44) and (4.45) equal zero. Accordingly, setting these derivatives equal to zero, collecting terms, and dividing by n shows that the OLS estimators, $\hat{\beta}_0$ and $\hat{\beta}_1$, must satisfy the two equations,

$$\overline{Y} - \hat{\beta}_0 - \hat{\beta}_1 \overline{X} = 0 \text{ and} \tag{4.46}$$

$$\frac{1}{n}\sum_{i=1}^{n}X_i Y_i - \hat{\beta}_0 \overline{X} - \hat{\beta}_1 \frac{1}{n}\sum_{i=1}^{n}X_i^2 = 0. \tag{4.47}$$

Solving this pair of equations for $\hat{\beta}_0$ and $\hat{\beta}_1$ yields

$$\hat{\beta}_1 = \frac{\frac{1}{n}\sum_{i=1}^{n} X_i Y_i - \overline{X}\,\overline{Y}}{\frac{1}{n}\sum_{i=1}^{n} X_i^2 - (\overline{X})^2} = \frac{\sum_{i=1}^{n}(X_i - \overline{X})(Y_i - \overline{Y})}{\sum_{i=1}^{n}(X_i - \overline{X})^2} \tag{4.48}$$

$$\hat{\beta}_0 = \overline{Y} - \hat{\beta}_1\,\overline{X}. \tag{4.49}$$

Equations (4.48) and (4.49) are the formulas for $\hat{\beta}_0$ and $\hat{\beta}_1$ given in Key Concept 4.2; the formula $\hat{\beta}_1 = s_{XY}/s_X^2$ is obtained by dividing the numerator and denominator in Equation (4.48) by $n-1$.

Sampling Distribution of the OLS Estimator

In this appendix, we show that the OLS estimator $\hat{\beta}_1$ is unbiased and, in large samples, has the normal sampling distribution given in Key Concept 4.4.

Representation of $\hat{\beta}_1$ in Terms of the Regressors and Errors

We start by providing an expression for $\hat{\beta}_1$ in terms of the regressors and errors. Because $Y_i = \beta_0 + \beta_1 X_i + u_i$, $Y_i - \overline{Y} = \beta_1(X_i - \overline{X}) + u_i - \overline{u}$, so the numerator of the formula for $\hat{\beta}_1$ in Equation (4.48) is

$$\sum_{i=1}^{n}(X_i - \overline{X})(Y_i - \overline{Y}) = \sum_{i=1}^{n}(X_i - \overline{X})[\beta_1(X_i - \overline{X}) + (u_i - \overline{u})]$$

$$= \beta_1\sum_{i=1}^{n}(X_i - \overline{X})^2 + \sum_{i=1}^{n}(X_i - \overline{X})(u_i - \overline{u}). \tag{4.50}$$

Now $\sum_{i=1}^{n}(X_i - \overline{X})(u_i - \overline{u}) = \sum_{i=1}^{n}(X_i - \overline{X})u_i - \sum_{i=1}^{n}(X_i - \overline{X})\overline{u} = \sum_{i=1}^{n}(X_i - \overline{X})u_i$, where the final equality follows from the definition of $\overline{X}$, which implies that $\sum_{i=1}^{n}(X_i - \overline{X})\overline{u} = \left[\sum_{i=1}^{n} X_i - n\overline{X}\right]\overline{u} = 0$. Substituting $\sum_{i=1}^{n}(X_i - \overline{X})(u_i - \overline{u}) = \sum_{i=1}^{n}(X_i - \overline{X})u_i$ into the final expression in Equation (4.50) yields $\sum_{i=1}^{n}(X_i - \overline{X})(Y_i - \overline{Y}) = \beta_1\sum_{i=1}^{n}(X_i - \overline{X})^2 + \sum_{i=1}^{n}(X_i - \overline{X})u_i$. Substituting this expression in turn into the formula for $\hat{\beta}_1$ in Equation (4.48) yields

$$\hat{\beta}_1 = \beta_1 + \frac{\dfrac{1}{n}\sum_{i=1}^{n}(X_i - \overline{X})u_i}{\dfrac{1}{n}\sum_{i=1}^{n}(X_i - \overline{X})^2}. \tag{4.51}$$

Proof That $\hat{\beta}_1$ Is Unbiased

The expectation of $\hat{\beta}_1$ is obtained by taking the expectation of both sides of Equation (4.51). Thus,

$$E(\hat{\beta}_1) = \beta_1 + E\left[\frac{\dfrac{1}{n}\sum_{i=1}^{n}(X_i - \overline{X})u_i}{\dfrac{1}{n}\sum_{i=1}^{n}(X_i - \overline{X})^2}\right]$$

$$\tag{4.52}$$

$$= \beta_1 + E\left[\frac{\dfrac{1}{n}\sum_{i=1}^{n}(X_i - \overline{X})E(u_i \mid X_1, \ldots, X_n)}{\dfrac{1}{n}\sum_{i=1}^{n}(X_i - \overline{X})^2}\right] = \beta_1,$$

where the second equality in Equation (4.52) follows by using the law of iterated expectations (Section 2.3). By the second least squares assumption, u_i is distributed independently of X for all observations other than i, so $E(u_i \mid X_1, \ldots, X_n) = E(u_i \mid X_i)$. By the first least squares assumption, however, $E(u_i \mid X_i) = 0$. Thus, the numerator in the final term in Equation (4.52) is zero, so $E(\hat{\beta}_1) = \beta_1$, that is, the OLS estimator is unbiased.

Large-Sample Normal Distribution of the OLS Estimator

The large-sample normal approximation to the limiting distribution of $\hat{\beta}_1$ (Key Concept 4.4) is obtained by considering the behavior of the final term in Equation (4.51).

First consider the numerator of this term. Because $\overline{X}$ is consistent, if the sample size is large, $\overline{X}$ is nearly equal to μ_X. Thus, to a close approximation, the term in the numerator of Equation (4.51) is the sample average $\bar{v}$, where $v_i = (X_i - \mu_X)u_i$. By the first least squares assumption, v_i has a mean of zero. By the second least squares assumption, v_i is i.i.d. The variance of v_i is $\sigma_v^2 = \text{var}[(X_i - \mu_X)u_i]$ which, by the third least squares assumption, is nonzero and finite. Therefore, $\bar{v}$ satisfies all the requirements of the central limit theorem (Key Concept 2.7). Thus, $\bar{v}/\sigma_{\bar{v}}$ is, in large samples, distributed $N(0, 1)$, where $\sigma_{\bar{v}}^2 = \sigma_v^2/n$. Thus the distribution of $\bar{v}$ is well approximated by the $N(0, \sigma_v^2/n)$ distribution.

Next consider the expression in the denominator in Equation (4.51); this is the sample variance of X (except dividing by n rather than $n - 1$, which is inconsequential if n is large). As discussed in Section 3.2 (Equation (3.8)), the sample variance is a consistent estimator of the population variance, so in large samples it is arbitrarily close to the population variance of X.

Combining these two results, we have that, in large samples, $\hat{\beta}_1 - \beta_1 \cong \bar{v}/\text{var}(X_i)$, so that the sampling distribution of $\hat{\beta}_1$ is, in large samples, $N(\beta_1, \sigma_{\hat{\beta}_1}^2)$, where $\sigma_{\hat{\beta}_1}^2 = \text{var}(\bar{v})/[\text{var}(X_i)]^2 = \text{var}[(X_i - \mu_X)u_i]/\{n[\text{var}(X_i)]^2\}$, which is the expression in Equation (4.14).

Some Additional Algebraic Facts About OLS

The OLS residuals and predicted values satisfy:

$$\frac{1}{n}\sum_{i=1}^{n} \hat{u}_i = 0, \tag{4.53}$$

$$\frac{1}{n}\sum_{i=1}^{n} \hat{Y}_i = \overline{Y}, \tag{4.54}$$

$$\sum_{i=1}^{n} \hat{u}_i X_i = 0 \text{ and } s_{\hat{u}X} = 0, \text{ and} \tag{4.55}$$

$$TSS = SSR + ESS. \tag{4.56}$$

Equations (4.53) through (4.56) say that the sample average of the OLS residuals is zero; the sample average of the OLS predicted values equals $\overline{Y}$; the sample covariance $s_{\hat{u}X}$ between the OLS residuals and the regressors is zero; and the total sum of squares is the sum of the sum of squared residuals and the explained sum of squares (the ESS, TSS, and SSR are defined in Equations (4.35), (4.36), and (4.38)).

To verify Equation (4.53), note that the definition of $\hat{\beta}_0$ lets us write the OLS residuals as $\hat{u}_i = Y_i - \hat{\beta}_0 - \hat{\beta}_1 X_i = (Y_i - \overline{Y}) - \hat{\beta}_1(X_i - \overline{X})$; thus

$$\sum_{i=1}^{n} \hat{u}_i = \sum_{i=1}^{n} (Y_i - \overline{Y}) - \hat{\beta}_1 \sum_{i=1}^{n} (X_i - \overline{X}).$$

But the definition of $\overline{Y}$ and $\overline{X}$ imply that $\sum_{i=1}^{n}(Y_i - \overline{Y}) = 0$ and $\sum_{i=1}^{n}(X_i - \overline{X}) = 0$, so $\sum_{i=1}^{n}\hat{u}_i = 0$.

To verify Equation (4.54), note that $Y_i = \hat{Y}_i + \hat{u}_i$, so $\sum_{i=1}^{n}Y_i = \sum_{i=1}^{n}\hat{Y}_i + \sum_{i=1}^{n}\hat{u}_i = \sum_{i=1}^{n}\hat{Y}_i$, where the second equality is a consequence of Equation (4.53).

To verify Equation (4.55), note that $\sum_{i=1}^{n}\hat{u}_i = 0$ implies $\sum_{i=1}^{n}\hat{u}_i X_i = \sum_{i=1}^{n}\hat{u}_i(X_i - \overline{X})$, so

$$\sum_{i=1}^{n}\hat{u}_i X_i = \sum_{i=1}^{n}[(Y_i - \overline{Y}) - \hat{\beta}_1(X_i - \overline{X})](X_i - \overline{X})$$

$$= \sum_{i=1}^{n}(Y_i - \overline{Y})(X_i - \overline{X}) - \hat{\beta}_1\sum_{i=1}^{n}(X_i - \overline{X})^2 = 0, \tag{4.57}$$

where the final equality in Equation (4.57) is obtained using the formula for $\hat{\beta}_1$ in Equation (4.48). This result, combined with the preceding results, implies that $s_{\hat{u}X} = 0$.

Equation (4.56) follows from the previous results and some algebra:

$$TSS = \sum_{i=1}^{n}(Y_i - \overline{Y})^2 = \sum_{i=1}^{n}(Y_i - \hat{Y}_i + \hat{Y}_i - \overline{Y})^2$$

$$= \sum_{i=1}^{n}(Y_i - \hat{Y}_i)^2 + \sum_{i=1}^{n}(\hat{Y}_i - \overline{Y})^2 + 2\sum_{i=1}^{n}(Y_i - \hat{Y}_i)(\hat{Y}_i - \overline{Y})$$

$$= SSR + ESS + 2\sum_{i=1}^{n}\hat{u}_i\hat{Y}_i = SSR + ESS, \tag{4.58}$$

where the final equality follows from $\sum_{i=1}^{n}\hat{u}_i\hat{Y}_i = \sum_{i=1}^{n}\hat{u}_i(\hat{\beta}_0 + \hat{\beta}_1 X_i) = \hat{\beta}_0\sum_{i=1}^{n}\hat{u}_i + \hat{\beta}_1\sum_{i=1}^{n}\hat{u}_i X_i = 0$ by the previous results.

APPENDIX
4.4 | Formulas for OLS Standard Errors

This appendix discusses the formulas for OLS standard errors. These are first presented under the least squares assumptions in Key Concept 4.3, which allow for heteroskedasticity; these are the "heteroskedasticity-robust" standard errors. Formulas for the variance of the OLS estimators and the associated standard errors are then given for the special case of homoskedasticity.

Heteroskedasticity-Robust Standard Errors

The estimator $\hat{\sigma}^2_{\hat{\beta}_1}$ defined in Equation (4.19) is obtained by replacing the population variances in Equation (4.14) by the corresponding sample variances, with a modification. The variance in the numerator of Equation (4.14) is estimated by $\frac{1}{n-2}\sum_{i=1}^{n}(X_i - \overline{X})^2\hat{u}_i^2$, where the divisor $n - 2$ (instead of n) incorporates a degrees-of-freedom adjustment to correct for downward bias, analogously to the degrees-of-freedom adjustment used in the definition of the *SER* in Section 4.8. The variance in the denominator is estimated by $\frac{1}{n}\sum_{i=1}^{n}(X_i - \overline{X})^2$. Replacing $\text{var}[(X_i - \mu_X)u_i]$ and $\text{var}(X_i)$ in Equation (4.14) by these two estimators yields $\hat{\sigma}_{\hat{\beta}_1}^2$ in Equation(4.19). The consistency of heteroskedasticity-robust standard errors is discussed in Section 15.3.

The estimator of the variance of $\hat{\beta}_0$ is

$$\hat{\sigma}_{\hat{\beta}_0}^2 = \frac{1}{n} \times \frac{\frac{1}{n-2}\sum_{i=1}^{n}\hat{H}_i^2\hat{u}_i^2}{\left(\frac{1}{n}\sum_{i=1}^{n}\hat{H}_i^2\right)^2}, \tag{4.59}$$

where $\hat{H}_i = 1 - [\overline{X}/\frac{1}{n}\sum_{i=1}^{n}X_i^2]X_i$. The standard error of $\hat{\beta}_0$ is $SE(\hat{\beta}_0) = \sqrt{\hat{\sigma}_{\hat{\beta}_0}^2}$. The reasoning behind the estimator $\hat{\sigma}_{\hat{\beta}_0}^2$ is the same as behind $\hat{\sigma}_{\hat{\beta}_1}^2$ and stems from replacing population expectations with sample averages.

Homoskedasticity-Only Variances

Under homoskedasticity, the conditional variance of u_i given X_i is a constant, that is, $\text{var}(u_i | X_i) = \sigma_u^2$. If the errors are homoskedastic, the formulas in Key Concept 4.4 simplify to

$$\sigma_{\hat{\beta}_1}^2 = \frac{\sigma_u^2}{n\sigma_X^2} \quad \text{and} \tag{4.60}$$

$$\sigma_{\hat{\beta}_0}^2 = \frac{E(X_i^2)}{n\sigma_X^2}\sigma_u^2. \tag{4.61}$$

To derive Equation (4.60), write the numerator in Equation (4.14) as $\text{var}[(X_i - \mu_X)u_i] = E(\{(X_i - \mu_X)u_i - E[(X_i - \mu_X)u_i]\}^2) = E\{[(X_i - \mu_X)u_i]^2\} = E[(X_i - \mu_X)^2 u_i^2] = E[(X_i - \mu_X)^2\text{var}(u_i | X_i)]$, where the second equality follows because $E[(X_i - \mu_X)u_i] = 0$ (by the first least squares assumption) and where the final equality follows from the law of iterated expectations (Section 2.3). If u_i is homoskedastic, then $\text{var}(u_i | X_i) = \sigma_u^2$ so $E[(X_i - \mu_X)^2\text{var}(u_i | X_i)] = \sigma_u^2 E[(X_i - \mu_X)^2] = \sigma_u^2\sigma_X^2$. The result in Equation (4.60) follows by substituting this expression into the numerator of Equation (4.14) and simplifying. A similar calculation yields Equation (4.61).

Homoskedasticity-Only Standard Errors

The homoskedasticity-only standard errors are obtained by substituting sample means and variances for the population means and variances in Equations (4.60) and (4.61), and by estimating the variance of u_i by the square of the *SER*. The homoskedasticity-only estimators of these variances are

$$\tilde{\sigma}^2_{\hat{\beta}_1} = \frac{s^2_{\hat{u}}}{\sum\limits_{i=1}^{n} (X_i - \overline{X})^2} \quad \text{(homoskedasticity-only) and} \tag{4.62}$$

$$\tilde{\sigma}^2_{\hat{\beta}_0} = \frac{\left(\dfrac{1}{n} \sum\limits_{i=1}^{n} X_i^2\right) s^2_{\hat{u}}}{\sum\limits_{i=1}^{n} (X_i - \overline{X})^2} \quad \text{(homoskedasticity-only)}, \tag{4.63}$$

where $s^2_{\hat{u}}$ is given in Equation (4.40). The homoskedasticity-only standard errors are the square roots of $\tilde{\sigma}^2_{\hat{\beta}_0}$ and $\tilde{\sigma}^2_{\hat{\beta}_1}$.

CHAPTER 5

Linear Regression with Multiple Regressors

C hapter 4 ended on a worried note. Although school districts with lower student-teacher ratios tend to have higher test scores in the California data set, perhaps students from districts with small classes have other advantages that help them perform well on standardized tests. Could this have produced misleading results and, if so, what can be done?

Omitted factors, such as student characteristics, can in fact make the ordinary least squares (OLS) estimator of the effect of class size on test scores misleading or, more precisely, biased. This chapter explains this "omitted variable bias" and introduces multiple regression, a method that can eliminate omitted variable bias. The key idea of multiple regression is that, if we have data on these omitted variables, then we can include them as additional regressors and thereby estimate the effect of one regressor (the student-teacher ratio) while holding constant the other variables (such as student characteristics).

This chapter explains how to estimate the coefficients of the multiple linear regression model. It examines how to perform statistical inference, that is, how to test hypotheses about the multiple regression coefficients and how to construct confidence intervals for those coefficients. Many aspects of multiple regression parallel those of regression with a single regressor, studied in Chapter 4. The coefficients of the multiple regression model can be estimated from data using OLS; the OLS estimators in multiple regression are random variables because they depend on data from a random sample; in large samples the sampling distributions of the OLS estimators are approximately normal; and the OLS estimators can be used to test hypotheses and to construct confidence intervals for the population regression coefficients. One such testable hypothesis is that reducing the student-teacher ratio has no effect on test scores, holding constant measurable characteristics of students in the district.

5.1 Omitted Variable Bias

By focusing only on the student-teacher ratio, the empirical analysis in Chapter 4 ignored some potentially important determinants of test scores by collecting their influences in the regression error term. These omitted factors include school characteristics, such as teacher quality and computer usage, and student characteristics, such as family background. We begin by considering an omitted student characteristic that is particularly relevant in California because of its large immigrant population: the prevalence in the school district of students who are still learning English.

By ignoring the percentage of English learners in the district, the OLS estimator of the slope in the regression of test scores on the student-teacher ratio could be biased; that is, the mean of the sampling distribution of the OLS estimator might not equal the true effect on test scores of a unit change in the student-teacher ratio. Here is the reasoning. Students who are still learning English might perform worse on standardized tests than native English speakers. If districts with large classes also have many students still learning English, then the OLS regression of test scores on the student-teacher ratio could erroneously find a correlation and produce a large estimated coefficient, when in fact the true causal effect of cutting class sizes on test scores is small, even zero. Accordingly, based on the analysis of Chapter 4, the superintendent might hire enough new teachers to reduce the student-teacher ratio by two, but her hoped-for improvement in test scores will fail to materialize if the true coefficient is small or zero.

A look at the California data lends credence to this concern. The correlation between the student-teacher ratio and the percentage of English learners (students who are not native English speakers and who have not yet mastered English) in the district is 0.19. This small but positive correlation suggests that districts with more English learners tend to have a higher student-teacher ratio (larger classes). If the student-teacher ratio were unrelated to the percentage of English learners, then it would be safe to ignore English proficiency in the regression of test scores against the student-teacher ratio. But because the student-teacher ratio and the percentage of English learners are correlated, it is possible that the OLS coefficient in the regression of test scores on the student teacher ratio reflects that influence.

Definition of Omitted Variable Bias

If the regressor (the student-teacher ratio) is correlated with a variable that has been omitted from the analysis (the percentage of English learners) but that determines, in part, the dependent variable (test scores), then the OLS estimator will have **omitted variable bias**.

Omitted variable bias occurs when two conditions are true: first, the omitted variable is correlated with the included regressor; second, the omitted variable is a determinant of the dependent variable. To illustrate these conditions, consider three examples of variables that are omitted from the regression of test scores on the student-teacher ratio.

Example #1: Percentage of English learners. Because the percentage of English learners is correlated with the student-teacher ratio, the first condition for omitted variable bias holds. It is plausible that students who are still learning English will do worse on standardized tests than native English speakers, in which case the percentage of English learners is a determinant of test scores and the second condition for omitted variable bias holds. Thus, the OLS estimator in the regression of test scores on the student-teacher ratio could incorrectly reflect the influence of the omitted variable, the percentage of English learners. That is, omitting the percentage of English learners may introduce omitted variable bias.

Example #2: Time of day of the test. Another variable omitted from the analysis is the time of day that the test was administered. For this omitted variable, it is plausible that the first condition for omitted variable bias does not hold but the second condition does. For example, if the time of day of the test varies from one district to the next in a way that is unrelated to class size, then the time of day and class size would be uncorrelated so the first condition does not hold. On the other hand, the time of day of the test could affect scores (alertness varies through the school day), so the second condition holds. However, because in this example the time that the test is administered is uncorrelated with the student-teacher ratio, the student-teacher ratio could not be incorrectly picking up the "time of day" effect. Thus omitting the time of day of the test does not result in omitted variable bias.

Example #3: Parking lot space per pupil. Another omitted variable is parking lot space per pupil (the area of the teacher parking lot divided by the number of students). This variable satisfies the first but not the second condition for omitted variable bias. Specifically, schools with more teachers per pupil probably have more teacher parking space, so the first condition would be satisfied.

However, under the assumption that learning takes place in the classroom, not the parking lot, parking lot space has no direct effect on learning; thus the second condition does not hold. Because parking lot space per pupil is not a determinant of test scores, omitting it from the analysis does not lead to omitted variable bias.

Omitted variable bias is summarized in Key Concept 5.1.

Omitted variable bias and the first least squares assumption. Omitted variable bias means that the first least squares assumption—that $E(u_i | X_i) = 0$, as listed in Key Concept 4.3—is incorrect. To see why, recall that the error term u_i in the linear regression model with a single regressor represents all factors, other than X_i, that are determinants of Y_i. If one of these other factors is correlated with X_i, this means that the error term (which contains this factor) is correlated with X_i. In other words, if an omitted variable is a determinant of Y_i, then it is in the error term, and if it is correlated with X_i, then the error term is correlated with X_i. Because u_i and X_i are correlated, the conditional mean of u_i given X_i is nonzero. This correlation therefore violates the first least squares assumption, and the consequence is serious: the OLS estimator is biased. This bias does not vanish even in very large samples, and the OLS estimator is inconsistent.

A Formula for Omitted Variable Bias

The discussion of the previous section about omitted variable bias can be summarized mathematically by a formula for this bias. Let the correlation between X_i and u_i be $\text{corr}(X_i, u_i) = \rho_{Xu}$. Suppose that the second and third least squares assumptions hold, but the first does not because ρ_{Xu} is nonzero. Then the OLS estimator has the limit (derived in Appendix 5.1),

$$\hat{\beta}_1 \xrightarrow{p} \beta_1 + \rho_{Xu} \frac{\sigma_u}{\sigma_X}. \tag{5.1}$$

That is, as the sample size increases, $\hat{\beta}_1$ is close to $\beta_1 + \rho_{Xu}(\sigma_u/\sigma_X)$ with increasingly high probability.

The formula in Equation (5.1) summarizes several of the ideas discussed above about omitted variable bias:

1. Omitted variable bias is a problem whether the sample size is large or small. Because $\hat{\beta}_1$ does not converge in probability to the true value β_1, $\hat{\beta}_1$ is inconsistent; that is, $\hat{\beta}_1$ is not a consistent estimator of β_1 when there is omitted variable bias. The term $\rho_{Xu}(\sigma_u/\sigma_X)$ in Equation (5.1) is the bias in $\hat{\beta}_1$ that persists even in large samples.

Key

Concept

5.1

Omitted Variable Bias in Regression with a Single Regressor

Omitted variable bias is the bias in the OLS estimator that arises when the regressor, X, is correlated with an omitted variable. For omitted variable bias to occur, two conditions must be true:

1. X is correlated with the omitted variable; and

2. the omitted variable is a determinant of the dependent variable, Y.

2. Whether this bias is large or small in practice depends on the correlation ρ_{Xu} between the regressor and the error term. The larger is $|\rho_{Xu}|$, the larger is the bias.

3. The direction of the bias in $\hat{\beta}_1$ depends on whether X and u are positively or negatively correlated. For example, we speculated that the percentage of students learning English has a *negative* effect on district test scores (students still learning English have lower scores), so that the percentage of English learners enters the error term with a negative sign. In our data, the fraction of English learners is *positively* correlated with the student-teacher ratio (districts with more English learners have larger classes). Thus the student-teacher ratio (X) would be *negatively* correlated with the error term (u), so $\rho_{Xu} < 0$ and the coefficient on the student-teacher ratio $\hat{\beta}_1$ would be biased toward a negative number. In other words, having a small percentage of English learners is associated both with *high* test scores and *low* student-teacher ratios, so one reason that the OLS estimator suggests that small classes improve test scores may be that the districts with small classes have fewer English learners.

Addressing Omitted Variable Bias by Dividing the Data into Groups

What can you do about omitted variable bias? Our superintendent is considering increasing the number of teachers in her district, but she has no control over the fraction of immigrants in her community. As a result, she is interested in the effect of the student-teacher ratio on test scores, *holding constant* other factors, including the percentage of English learners. This new way of posing her question suggests that, instead of using data for all districts, perhaps we should focus on districts

The Mozart Effect: Omitted Variable Bias?

A study published in *Nature* in 1993 (Rauscher, Shaw and Ky, 1993) suggested that listening to Mozart for 10–15 minutes could temporarily raise your IQ by 8 or 9 points. That study made big news—and politicians and parents saw an easy way to make their children smarter. For a while, the state of Georgia even distributed classical music CDs to all infants in the state.

What is the evidence for the "Mozart effect"? A review of dozens of studies found that students who take optional music or arts courses in high school do in fact have higher English and math test scores than those who don't.[1] A closer look at these studies, however, suggests that the real reason for the better test performance has little to do with those courses. Instead, the authors of the review suggested that the correlation between testing well and taking art or music could arise from any number of things. For example, the academically better students might have more time to take optional music courses or more interest in doing so, or those schools with a deeper music curriculum might just be better schools across the board.

In the terminology of regression, the estimated relationship between test scores and taking optional music courses appears to have omitted variable bias. By omitting factors such as the student's innate ability or the overall quality of the school, studying music appears to have an effect on test scores when in fact it has none.

So is there a Mozart effect? One way to find out is to do a randomized controlled experiment. (As discussed further in Chapter 11, randomized controlled experiments eliminate omitted variable bias by randomly assigning participants to "treatment" and "control" groups.) Taken together, the many controlled experiments on the Mozart effect fail to show that listening to Mozart improves IQ or general test performance. For reasons not fully understood, however, it seems that listening to classical music *does* help temporarily in one narrow area: folding paper and visualizing shapes. So the next time you cram for an origami exam, try to fit in a little Mozart too.

---

[1]See the *Journal of Aesthetic Education* 34: 3–4 (Fall/Winter 2000), especially the article by Ellen Winner and Monica Cooper, (pp. 11–76) and the one by Lois Hetland (pp. 105–148).

with percentages of English learners comparable to hers. Among this subset of districts, do those with smaller classes do better on standardized tests?

Table 5.1 reports evidence on the relationship between class size and test scores within districts with comparable percentages of English learners. Districts are divided into eight groups. First, the districts are broken into four categories that correspond to the quartiles of the distribution of the percentage of English learners across districts. Second, within each of these four categories, districts are further broken down into two groups, depending on whether the student-teacher ratio is small ($STR < 20$) or large ($STR \geq 20$).

TABLE 5.1 Differences in Test Scores for California School Districts with Low and High Student Teacher Ratios, by the Percentage of English Learners in the District

	Student-Teacher Ratio < 20		Student-Teacher Ratio ≥ 20		Difference in Test Scores, Low vs. High STR	
	Average Test Score	n	Average Test Score	n	Difference	t-statistic
All Districts	657.4	238	650.0	182	7.4	4.04
Percent of English Learners						
< 2.2%	664.1	78	665.4	27	−1.3	−0.44
2.2–8.8%	666.1	61	661.8	44	4.3	1.44
8.8–23.0%	654.6	55	649.7	50	4.9	1.64
> 23.0%	636.7	44	634.8	61	1.9	0.68

The first row in Table 5.1 reports the overall difference in average test scores between districts with low and high student-teacher ratios, that is, the difference in test scores between these two groups without breaking them down further into the quartiles of English learners. (Recall that this difference was previously reported in regression form in Equation (4.33) as the OLS estimate of the coefficient on D_i in the regression of *TestScore* on D_i, where D_i is a binary regressor that equals one if $STR_i < 20$ and equals 0 otherwise.) Over the full sample of 420 districts, the average test score is 7.4 points higher in districts with a low student-teacher ratio than a high one; the *t*-statistic is 4.04, so the null hypothesis that the mean test score is the same in the two groups is rejected at the 1% significance level.

The final four rows in Table 5.1 report the difference in test scores between districts with low and high student-teacher ratios, broken down by the quartile of the percentage of English learners. This evidence presents a different picture. Of the districts with the fewest English learners (< 2.2%), the average test score for those 78 with low student-teacher ratios is 664.1 and the average for the 27 with high student-teacher ratios is 665.4. Thus, for the districts with the fewest English learners, test scores were on average 1.3 points *lower* in the districts with low student-teacher ratios! In the second quartile, districts with low student-teacher ratios had test scores that averaged 4.3 points higher than those with high student-teacher ratios; this gap was 4.9 points for the third quartile and only 1.9 points for the quartile of districts with the most English learners. Once we hold the percentage of English learners constant, the difference in performance between districts with high and low student-teacher ratios is perhaps half (or less) of the overall estimate of 7.4 points.

At first this finding might seem puzzling. How can the overall effect of test scores be twice the effect of test scores within any quartile? The answer is that the districts with the most English learners tend to have *both* the highest student-teacher ratios *and* the lowest test scores. The difference in the average test score between districts in the lowest and highest quartile of the percentage of English learners is large, approximately 30 points. The districts with few English learners tend to have lower student teacher ratios: 74% (78 of 105) of the districts in the first quartile of English learners have small classes (*STR* < 20), while only 42% (44 of 105) of the districts in the quartile with the most English learners have small classes. So, the districts with the most English learners have lower test scores and also have higher student-teacher ratios than the other districts.

This analysis reinforces the superintendent's worry that omitted variable bias is present in the regression of test scores against the student-teacher ratio. By looking within quartiles of the percentage of English learners, the test score differences in the second part of Table 5.1 improve upon the simple difference-of-means analysis in the first line of Table 5.1. Still, this analysis does not yet provide the superintendent with a useful estimate of the effect on test scores of changing class size, holding constant the fraction of English learners. Such an estimate can be provided, however, using the method of multiple regression.

5.2 The Multiple Regression Model

The **multiple regression model** extends the single variable regression model of Chapter 4 to include additional variables as regressors. This model permits estimating the effect on Y_i of changing one variable (X_{1i}) while holding the other regressors (X_{2i}, X_{3i}, and so forth) constant. In the class size problem, the multiple regression model provides a way to isolate the effect on test scores (Y_i) of the student-teacher ratio (X_{1i}) while holding constant the percentage of students in the district who are English learners (X_{2i}).

The Population Regression Line

Suppose for the moment that there are only two independent variables, X_{1i} and X_{2i}. In the linear multiple regression model, the average relationship between these two independent variables and the dependent variable, Y, is given by the linear function

$$E(Y_i \mid X_{1i} = x_1, X_{2i} = x_2) = \beta_0 + \beta_1 x_1 + \beta_2 x_2, \tag{5.2}$$

where $E(Y_i | X_{1i} = x_1, X_{2i} = x_2)$ is the conditional expectation of Y_i given that $X_{1i} = x_1$ and $X_{2i} = x_2$. That is, if the student–teacher ratio in the ith district (X_{1i}) equals some value x_1 and the percentage of English learners in the ith district (X_{2i}) equals x_2, then the expected value of Y_i given the student–teacher ratio and the percentage of English learners is given by Equation (5.2).

Equation (5.2) is the **population regression line** or **population regression function** in the multiple regression model. The coefficient β_0 is the **intercept**, the coefficient β_1 is the **slope coefficient of X_{1i}** or, more simply, the **coefficient on X_{1i}**, and the coefficient β_2 is the **slope coefficient of X_{2i}** or, more simply, the **coefficient on X_{2i}**. One or more of the independent variables in the multiple regression model are sometimes referred to as **control variables**.

The interpretation of the coefficient β_1 in Equation (5.2) is different than it was when X_{1i} was the only regressor: in Equation (5.2), β_1 is the effect on Y of a unit change in X_1, **holding X_2 constant** or **controlling for X_2**.

This interpretation of β_1 follows from the definition that the expected effect on Y of a change in X_1, ΔX_1, holding X_2 constant, is the difference between the expected value of Y when the independent variables take on the values $X_1 + \Delta X_1$ and X_2 and the expected value of Y when the independent variables take on the values X_1 and X_2. Accordingly, write the population regression function in Equation (5.2) as $Y = \beta_0 + \beta_1 X_1 + \beta_2 X_2$, and imagine changing X_1 by the amount ΔX_1 while not changing X_2, that is, while holding X_2 constant. Because X_1 has changed, Y will change by some amount, say ΔY. After this change, the new value of Y, $Y + \Delta Y$, is

$$Y + \Delta Y = \beta_0 + \beta_1(X_1 + \Delta X_1) + \beta_2 X_2. \tag{5.3}$$

An equation for ΔY in terms of ΔX_1 is obtained by subtracting the equation, $Y = \beta_0 + \beta_1 X_1 + \beta_2 X_2$ from Equation (5.3), yielding $\Delta Y = \beta_1 \Delta X_1$. That is,

$$\beta_1 = \frac{\Delta Y}{\Delta X_1}, \text{ holding } X_2 \text{ constant.} \tag{5.4}$$

The coefficient β_1 is the effect on Y (the expected change in Y) of a unit change in X_1, holding X_2 fixed. Another phrase used to describe β_1 is the **partial effect** on Y of X_1, holding X_2 fixed.

The interpretation of the intercept in the multiple regression model, β_0, is similar to the interpretation of the intercept in the single–regressor model: it is the expected value of Y_i when X_{1i} and X_{2i} are zero. Simply put, the intercept β_0 determines how far up the Y axis the population regression line starts.

The Population Multiple Regression Model

The population regression line in Equation (5.2) is the relationship between Y and X_1 and X_2 that holds on average in the population. Just as in the case of regression with a single regressor, however, this relationship does not hold exactly because many other factors influence the dependent variable. In addition to the student-teacher ratio and the fraction of students still learning English, for example, test scores are also influenced by school characteristics, other student characteristics, and luck. Thus the population regression function in Equation (5.2) needs to be augmented to incorporate these additional factors.

Just as in the case of regression with a single regressor, the factors that determine Y_i in addition to X_{1i} and X_{2i} are incorporated into Equation (5.2) as an "error" term u_i. This error term is the deviation of a particular observation (test scores in the ith district in our example) from the average population relationship. Accordingly, we have

$$Y_i = \beta_0 + \beta_1 X_{1i} + \beta_2 X_{2i} + u_i, \; i = 1, \ldots, n, \tag{5.5}$$

where the subscript i indicates the ith of the n observations (districts) in the sample.

Equation (5.5) is the **population multiple regression model** when there are two regressors, X_{1i} and X_{2i}.

In regression with binary regressors it can be useful to treat β_0 as the coefficient on a regressor that always equals one; think of β_0 as the coefficient on X_{0i}, where $X_{0i} = 1$ for $i = 1, \ldots, n$. Accordingly, the population multiple regression model in Equation (5.5) can alternatively be written as

$$Y_i = \beta_0 X_{0i} + \beta_1 X_{1i} + \beta_2 X_{2i} + u_i, \text{ where } X_{0i} = 1, \; i = 1, \ldots, n. \tag{5.6}$$

The two ways of writing the population regression model, Equations (5.5) and (5.6), are equivalent.

The discussion so far has focused on the case of a single additional variable, X_2. In practice, however, there might be multiple factors omitted from the single-regressor model. For example, ignoring the students' economic background might result in omitted variable bias, just as ignoring the fraction of English learners did. This reasoning leads us to consider a model with three regressors or, more generally, a model that includes k regressors. The multiple regression model with k regressors, $X_{1i}, X_{2i}, \ldots, X_{ki}$, is summarized as Key Concept 5.2.

Key Concept 5.2

The Multiple Regression Model

The multiple regression model is

$$Y_i = \beta_0 + \beta_1 X_{1i} + \beta_2 X_{2i} + \cdots + \beta_k X_{ki} + u_i, \, i = 1, \ldots, n. \qquad (5.7)$$

where:

- Y_i is i^{th} observation on the dependent variable; $X_{1i}, X_{2i}, \ldots, X_{ki}$ are the ith observations on each of the k regressors; and u_i is the error term.

- The population regression line is the relationship that holds between Y and the X's on average in the population:

$$E(Y \mid X_{1i} = x_1, X_{2i} = x_2, \ldots, X_{ki} = x_k) = \beta_0 + \beta_1 x_1 + \beta_2 x_2 + \cdots + \beta_k x_k.$$

- β_1 is the slope coefficient on X_1, β_2 is the coefficient on X_2, etc. The coefficient β_1 is the expected change in Y_i resulting from changing X_{1i} by one unit, holding constant $X_{2i}, \ldots, X_{ki}$. The coefficients on the other X's are interpreted similarly.

- The intercept β_0 is the expected value of Y when all the X's equal zero. The intercept can be thought of as the coefficient on a regressor, X_{0i}, that equals one for all i.

The definitions of homoskedasticity and heteroskedasticity in the multiple regression model are similar to their definitions in the single-regressor model. The error term u_i in the multiple regression model is **homoskedastic** if the variance of the conditional distribution of u_i given $X_{1i}, \ldots, X_{ki}$, $\text{var}(u_i \mid X_{1i}, \ldots, X_{ki})$, is constant for $i = 1, \ldots, n$ and thus does not depend on the values of $X_{1i}, \ldots, X_{ki}$. Otherwise, the error term is **heteroskedastic**.

The multiple regression model holds out the promise of providing just what the superintendent wants to know: the effect of changing the student-teacher ratio, holding constant other factors that are beyond her control. These factors include not just the percentage of English learners, but other measurable factors that might affect test performance, including the economic background of the students. To be of practical help to the superintendent, however, we need to provide her with estimates of the unknown population coefficients $\beta_0, \ldots, \beta_k$ of the population regression model calculated using a sample of data. Fortunately, these coefficients can be estimated using ordinary least squares.

5.3   The OLS Estimator in Multiple Regression

This section describes how the coefficients of the multiple regression model can be estimated using OLS.

The OLS Estimator

Section 4.2 shows how to estimate the intercept and slope coefficients in the single-regressor model by applying OLS to a sample of observations of Y and X. The key idea is that these coefficients can be estimated by minimizing the sum of squared prediction mistakes, that is, by choosing the estimators b_0 and b_1 so as to minimize $\sum_{i=1}^{n}(Y_i - b_0 - b_1 X_i)^2$; the estimators that do so are the OLS estimators, $\hat{\beta}_0$ and $\hat{\beta}_1$.

The method of OLS also can be used to estimate the coefficients $\beta_0, \beta_1, \ldots, \beta_k$ in the multiple regression model. Let $b_0, b_1, \ldots, b_k$ be estimators of $\beta_0, \beta_1, \ldots, \beta_k$. The predicted value of Y_i, calculated using these estimators, is $b_0 + b_1 X_{1i} + \cdots + b_k X_{ki}$, and the mistake in predicting Y_i is $Y_i - (b_0 + b_1 X_{1i} + \cdots + b_k X_{ki}) = Y_i - b_0 - b_1 X_{1i} - \cdots - b_k X_{ki}$. The sum of these squared prediction mistakes over all n observations thus is

$$\sum_{i=1}^{n} (Y_i - b_0 - b_1 X_{1i} - \cdots - b_k X_{ki})^2. \tag{5.8}$$

The sum of the squared mistakes for the linear regression model in expression (5.8) is the extension of the sum of the squared mistakes given in Equation (4.6) for the linear regression model with a single regressor.

The estimators of the coefficients $\beta_0, \beta_1, \ldots, \beta_k$ that minimize the sum of squared mistakes in expression (5.8) are called the **ordinary least squares (OLS) estimators** of $\beta_0, \beta_1, \ldots, \beta_k$. The OLS estimators are denoted $\hat{\beta}_0, \hat{\beta}_1, \ldots, \hat{\beta}_k$.

The terminology of OLS in the linear multiple regression model is the same as in the linear regression model with a single regressor. The **OLS regression line** is the straight line constructed using the OLS estimators, that is, $\hat{\beta}_0 + \hat{\beta}_1 X_1 + \cdots + \hat{\beta}_k X_k$. The **predicted value** of Y_i given $X_{1i}, \ldots, X_{ki}$, based on the OLS regression line, is $\hat{Y}_i = \hat{\beta}_0 + \hat{\beta}_1 X_{1i} + \cdots + \hat{\beta}_k X_{ki}$. The **OLS residual** for the ith observation is the difference between Y_i and its OLS predicted value, that is, the OLS residual is $\hat{u}_i = Y_i - \hat{Y}_i$.

The OLS estimators could be computed by trial and error, repeatedly trying different values of $b_0, \ldots, b_k$ until you are satisfied that you have minimized the total sum of squares in expression (5.8). It is far easier, however, to use explicit formulas for the OLS estimators that are derived using calculus. The formulas for the OLS estimators in the multiple regression model are similar to those in Key Concept 4.2 for the single-regressor model. These formulas are incorporated into modern statistical software. In the multiple regression model, the formulas are best expressed and discussed using matrix notation, so their presentation is deferred to Section 16.1.

The definitions and terminology of OLS in multiple regression are summarized in Key Concept 5.3.

Application to Test Scores and the Student-Teacher Ratio

In Section 4.2, we used OLS to estimate the intercept and slope coefficient of the regression relating test scores (*TestScore*) to the student-teacher ratio (*STR*), using our 420 observations for California school districts; the estimated OLS regression line, reported in Equation (4.7), is

$$\widehat{TestScore} = 698.9 - 2.28 \times STR. \tag{5.9}$$

Our concern has been that this relationship is misleading because the student-teacher ratio might be picking up the effect of having many English learners in districts with large classes. That is, it is possible that the OLS estimator is subject to omitted variable bias.

We are now in a position to address this concern by using OLS to estimate a multiple regression in which the dependent variable is the test score (Y_i) and there are two regressors: the student-teacher ratio (X_{1i}) and the percentage of English learners in the school district (X_{2i}) for our 420 districts ($i = 1, \ldots, 420$). The estimated OLS regression line for this multiple regression is

$$\widehat{TestScore} = 686.0 - 1.10 \times STR - 0.65 \times PctEL, \tag{5.10}$$

where *PctEL* is the percentage of students in the district who are English learners. The OLS estimate of the intercept ($\hat{\beta}_0$) is 686.0, the OLS estimate of the coefficient on the student-teacher ratio ($\hat{\beta}_1$) is −1.10, and the OLS estimate of the coefficient on the percentage English learners ($\hat{\beta}_2$) is −0.65.

The estimated effect on test scores of a change in the student-teacher ratio in the multiple regression is approximately half as large as when the student-teacher ratio is the only regressor: in the single-regressor equation (Equation (5.9)), a unit decrease in the *STR* is estimated to increase test scores by 2.28 points, but in the multiple regression equation (Equation (5.10)), it is estimated

The OLS Estimators, Predicted Values, and Residuals in the Multiple Regression Model

The OLS estimators $\hat{\beta}_0, \hat{\beta}_1, \ldots, \hat{\beta}_k$ are the values of $b_0, b_1, \ldots, b_k$ that minimize the sum of squared prediction mistakes $\sum_{i=1}^{n} (Y_i - b_0 - b_1 X_{1i} - \cdots - b_k X_{ki})^2$. The OLS predicted values $\hat{Y}_i$ and residuals $\hat{u}_i$ are:

$$\hat{Y}_i = \hat{\beta}_0 + \hat{\beta}_1 X_{1i} + \cdots + \hat{\beta}_k X_{ki}, i = 1, \ldots, n, \text{ and} \qquad (5.11)$$

$$\hat{u}_i = Y_i - \hat{Y}_i, i = 1, \ldots, n. \qquad (5.12)$$

The OLS estimators $\hat{\beta}_0, \hat{\beta}_1, \ldots, \hat{\beta}_k$ and residual $\hat{u}_i$ are computed from a sample of n observations of $(X_{1i}, \ldots, X_{ki}, Y_i)$, $i = 1, \ldots, n$. These are estimators of the unknown true population coefficients $\beta_0, \beta_1, \ldots, \beta_k$ and error term, u_i.

Key Concept 5.3

to increase test scores by only 1.10 points. This difference occurs because the coefficient on *STR* in the multiple regression is the effect of a change in *STR*, holding constant (or controlling for) *PctEL*, whereas in the single-regressor regression, *PctEL* is not held constant.

These two estimates can be reconciled by concluding that there is omitted variable bias in the estimate in the single-regressor model in Equation (5.9). In Section 5.1, we saw that districts with a high percentage of English learners tend to have not only low test scores but also a high student-teacher ratio. If the fraction of English learners is omitted from the regression, reducing the student-teacher ratio is estimated to have a larger effect on test scores, but this estimate reflects *both* the effect of a change in the student-teacher ratio *and* the omitted effect of having fewer English learners in the district.

We have reached the same conclusion that there is omitted variable bias in the relationship between test scores and the student-teacher ratio by two different paths: the tabular approach of dividing the data into groups (Section 5.1) and the multiple regression approach (Equation (5.10)). Of these two methods, multiple regression has two important advantages. First, it provides a quantitative estimate of the effect of a unit decrease in the student-teacher ratio, which is what the superintendent needs to make her decision. Second, it readily extends to more than two regressors, so that multiple regression can be used to control for measurable factors other than just the percentage of English learners.

The rest of this chapter is devoted to understanding and to using OLS in the multiple regression model. Much of what you learned about the OLS estimator with a single regressor carries over to multiple regression with few or no modifications, so we will focus on that which is new with multiple regression. We begin by extending the least squares assumptions to the multiple regression model.

5.4 The Least Squares Assumptions in Multiple Regression

There are four least squares assumptions in the multiple regression model. The first three are those of Section 4.3 for the single regressor model (Key Concept 4.3), extended to allow for multiple regressors, and these are discussed only briefly. The fourth assumption is new and is discussed in more detail.

Assumpion #1: The Conditional Distribution of u_i Given $X_{1i}, X_{2i}, \ldots, X_{ki}$ Has a Mean of Zero

The first assumption is that the conditional distribution of u_i given $X_{1i}, \ldots, X_{ki}$ has a mean of zero. This assumption extends the first least squares assumption with a single regressor to multiple regressors. This assumption means that sometimes Y_i is above the population regression line and sometimes Y_i is below the population regression line, but on average over the population Y_i falls on the population regression line. Therefore, for any value of the regressors, the expected value of u_i is zero. As is the case for regression with a single regressor, this is the key assumption that makes the OLS estimators unbiased. We return to omitted variable bias in multiple regression in Section 5.11.

Assumption #2: $(X_{1i}, X_{2i}, \ldots, X_{ki}, Y_i)$, $i = 1, \ldots, n$ Are i.i.d.

The second assumption is that $(X_{1i}, \ldots, X_{ki}, Y_i)$, $i = 1, \ldots, n$ are independently and identically distributed (i.i.d.) random variables. This assumption holds automatically if the data are collected by simple random sampling. The comments on this assumption appearing in Section 4.3 for a single regressor also apply to multiple regressors.

Assumption #3: X_{1i}, X_{2i}, . . . , X_{ki} and u_i Have Four Moments

The third assumption is that X_{1i}, . . . , X_{ki}, and u_i have four moments. Like the third assumption for the single-regressor model, this assumption limits the probability of observing extremely large values of X_{1i}, . . . , X_{ki}, or u_i. This assumption is a technical condition used in the proofs of the properties of OLS statistics in large samples.

Assumption #4: No Perfect Multicollinearity

The fourth assumption is new to the multiple regression model. It rules out an inconvenient situation, called perfect multicollinearity, in which it is impossible to compute the OLS estimator. The regressors are said to be **perfectly multicollinear** (or to exhibit **perfect multicollinearity**) if one of the regressors is a perfect linear function of the other regressors. The fourth least squares assumption is that the regressors are not perfectly multicollinear.

To illustrate what perfect multicollinearity is and to show why it poses a problem, consider three examples of hypothetical regressions in which a third regressor is added to the regression of test scores on the student-teacher ratio and the percentage of English learners in Equation (5.10).

Example #1: Fraction of English learners. Let $FracEL_i$ be the *fraction* of English learners in the ith district, which varies between zero and one. If the variable $FracEL_i$ were included as a third regressor in addition to STR_i and $PctEL_i$, the regressors would be perfectly multicollinear. The reason is that $PctEL$ is the *percentage* of English learners, so that $PctEL_i = 100 \times FracEL_i$ for every district. Thus one of the regressors ($PctEL_i$) can be written as a perfect linear function of another regressor ($FracEL_i$).

Because of this perfect multicollinearity, it is impossible to compute the OLS estimates of the regression of $TestScore_i$ on STR_i, $PctEL_i$, and $FracEL_i$. Depending on how your software package handles perfect multicollinearity, if you try to estimate this regression the software will do one of three things: it will drop one of the variables (arbitrarily making the choice of which to drop); it will refuse to calculate the OLS estimates and give an error message; or it will crash. The mathematical reason for this is that perfect multicollinearity produces division by zero in the OLS formulas.

At an intuitive level, the reason that perfect multicollinearity is a problem is that you are asking the regression to answer an illogical question. Recall that the coefficient on $PctEL_i$ is the effect on test scores of a unit change in $PctEL$, holding the other variables constant. If one of the other variables is $FracEL$, you are asking, what is the effect of a unit change in the *percentage* of English learners, holding constant the *fraction* of English learners? Because the percentage of English learners and the fraction of English learners move together in a perfect linear relationship, this question makes no sense and OLS cannot answer it.

Example #2: "Not very small" classes.   Let NVS_i be a binary variable that equals one if the student-teacher ratio in the ith district is "not very small," specifically, NVS_i equals one if $STR_i \geq 12$ and equals zero otherwise. This regression also exhibits perfect multicollinearity, but for a more subtle reason than the regression in the previous example. There are in fact no districts in our data set with $STR_i < 12$; as you can see in the scatterplot in Figure 4.2, the smallest value of STR is 14. Thus, $NVS_i = 1$ for all observations. Now recall that the linear regression model with an intercept can equivalently be thought of as including a regressor, X_{0i}, that equals one for all i, as is shown in Equation (5.6). Thus we can write $NVS_i = 1 \times X_{0i}$ for all the observations in our data set; that is, NVS_i can be written as a perfect linear combination of the regressors; specifically, it equals X_{0i}.

This illustrates two important points about perfect multicollinearity. First, when the regression includes an intercept, then one of the regressors that can be implicated in perfect multicollinearity is the "constant" regressor X_{0i}. Second, perfect multicollinearity is a statement about the data set you have on hand. While it is possible to imagine a school district with fewer than 12 students per teacher, there are no such districts in our data set so we cannot analyze them in our regression.

Example #3: Percentage of English speakers.   Let $PctES_i$ be the percentage of "English speakers" in the ith district, defined to be the percentage of students who are *not* English learners. Again the regressors will be perfectly multicollinear. Like the previous example, the perfect linear relationship among the regressors involves the "constant" regressor X_{0i}: for every district, $PctES_i = 100 \times X_{0i} - PctEL_i$.

This example illustrates another point: perfect multicollinearity is a feature of the entire set of regressors. If either the intercept (i.e., the regressor X_{0i}) or $PctEL_i$ were excluded from this regression, the regressors would not be perfectly multicollinear.

Solutions to perfect multicollinearity.   Perfect multicollinearity typically arises when a mistake has been made in specifying the regression. Sometimes the mistake is easy to spot (as in the first example) but sometimes it is not (as in the

**The Least Squares Assumptions in
the Multiple Regression Model**

$Y_i = \beta_0 + \beta_1 X_{1i} + \beta_2 X_{2i} + \cdots + \beta_k X_{ki} + u_i$, $i = 1, \ldots, n$, where:

**Key
Concept
5.4**

1. u_i has conditional mean zero given $X_{1i}, X_{2i}, \ldots, X_{ki}$, that is,
   $E(u_i \mid X_{1i}, X_{2i}, \ldots, X_{ki}) = 0$;
2. $(X_{1i}, X_{2i}, \ldots, X_{ki}, Y_i)$, $i = 1, \ldots, n$ are independently and identically distributed (i.i.d.) draws from their joint distribution;
3. $(X_{1i}, X_{2i}, \ldots, X_{ki}, u_i)$ have nonzero finite fourth moments; and
4. there is no perfect multicollinearity.

second example). In one way or another your software will let you know if you make such a mistake because it cannot compute the OLS estimator if you have.

When your software lets you know that you have perfect multicollinearity, it is important that you modify your regression to eliminate it. Some software is unreliable when there is perfect multicollinearity, and at a minimum you will be ceding control over your choice of regressors to your computer if your regressors are perfectly multicollinear.

Imperfect multicollinearity.   Despite its similar name, imperfect multicollinearity is conceptually quite different than perfect multicollinearity. **Imperfect multicollinearity** means that two or more of the regressors are highly correlated, in the sense that there is a linear function of the regressors that is highly correlated with another regressor. Imperfect multicollinearity does not pose any problems for the theory of the OLS estimators; indeed, a purpose of OLS is to sort out the independent influences of the various regressors when these regressors are potentially correlated.

The least squares assumptions for the multiple regression model are summarized in Key Concept 5.4.

5.5   The Distribution of the OLS Estimators in Multiple Regression

Because the data differ from one sample to the next, different samples produce different values of the OLS estimators. This variation across possible samples gives rise to the uncertainty associated with the OLS estimators of the population regression coefficients, $\beta_0, \beta_1, \ldots, \beta_k$. Just as in the case of regression with a single regressor, this variation is summarized in the sampling distribution of the OLS estimators.

Recall from Section 4.4 that, under the least squares assumptions, the OLS estimators ($\hat{\beta}_0$ and $\hat{\beta}_1$) are unbiased and consistent estimators of the unknown coefficients (β_0 and β_1) in the linear regression model with a single regressor. In addition, in large samples, the sampling distribution of $\hat{\beta}_0$ and $\hat{\beta}_1$ is well approximated by a bivariate normal distribution.

These results carry over to multiple regression analysis. That is, under the least squares assumptions of Key Concept 5.4, the OLS estimators $\hat{\beta}_0, \hat{\beta}_1, \ldots, \hat{\beta}_k$ are unbiased and consistent estimators of $\beta_0, \beta_1, \ldots, \beta_k$ in the linear multiple regression model. In large samples, the joint sampling distribution of $\hat{\beta}_0, \hat{\beta}_1, \ldots, \hat{\beta}_k$ is well approximated by a multivariate normal distribution, which is the extension of the bivariate normal distribution to the general case of two or more jointly normal random variables (Section 2.4).

Although the algebra is more complicated when there are multiple regressors, the central limit theorem applies to the OLS estimators in the multiple regression model for the same reason that it applies to $\overline{Y}$ and to the OLS estimators when there is a single regressor: the OLS estimators $\hat{\beta}_0, \hat{\beta}_1, \ldots, \hat{\beta}_k$ are averages of the randomly sampled data, and if the sample size is sufficiently large the sampling distribution of those averages becomes normal. Because the multivariate normal distribution is best handled mathematically using matrix algebra, the expressions for the joint distribution of the OLS estimators are deferred to Chapter 16.

Key Concept 5.5 summarizes the result that, in large samples, the distribution of the OLS estimators in multiple regression is approximately jointly normal. In general, the OLS estimators are correlated; this correlation arises from the correlation between the regressors. The joint sampling distribution of the OLS estimators is discussed in more detail for the case that there are two regressors and homoskedastic errors in Appendix 5.2, and the general case is discussed in Section 16.2.

Standard Errors for the OLS Estimators

Recall that, in the case of a single regressor, it was possible to estimate the variance of the OLS estimator by substituting sample averages for expectations, which led to the estimator $\hat{\sigma}^2_{\hat{\beta}_1}$ given in Equation (4.19). Under the least squares assumptions, the law of large numbers implies that these sample averages converge to their population counterparts, so for example $\hat{\sigma}^2_{\hat{\beta}_1}/\sigma^2_{\hat{\beta}_1} \xrightarrow{p} 1$. The square root of $\hat{\sigma}^2_{\hat{\beta}_1}$ is the standard error of $\hat{\beta}_1$, $SE(\hat{\beta}_1)$, an estimator of the standard deviation of the sampling distribution of $\hat{\beta}_1$.

Large Sample Distribution of $\hat{\beta}_0, \hat{\beta}_1, \ldots, \hat{\beta}_k$

If the least squares assumptions (Key Concept 5.4) hold, then in large samples the OLS estimators $\hat{\beta}_0, \hat{\beta}_1, \ldots, \hat{\beta}_k$ are jointly normally distributed and each $\hat{\beta}_j$ is distributed $N(\beta_j, \sigma_{\hat{\beta}_j}^2), j = 0, \ldots, k$.

Key Concept 5.5

All this extends directly to multiple regression. The OLS estimator $\hat{\beta}_j$ of the jth regression coefficient has a standard deviation, and this standard deviation is estimated by its standard error, $SE(\hat{\beta}_j)$. The formula for the standard error is most easily stated using matrices, so it is given in Section 16.2. The important point is that, as far as standard errors are concerned, there is nothing conceptually different between the single- or multiple-regressor cases. The key ideas—the large-sample normality of the estimators and the ability to estimate consistently the standard deviation of their sampling distribution—are the same whether one has one, two, or 12 regressors.

5.6   Hypothesis Tests and Confidence Intervals for a Single Coefficient

This section describes how to test hypotheses and construct confidence intervals for a single coefficient in a multiple regression equation.

Hypothesis Tests for a Single Coefficient

Suppose that you want to test the hypothesis that a change in the student-teacher ratio has no effect on test scores, holding constant the percentage of English learners in the district. This corresponds to hypothesizing that the true coefficient β_1 on the student-teacher ratio is zero in the population regression of test scores on STR and $PctEL$. More generally, we might want to test the hypothesis that the true coefficient β_j on the jth regressor takes on some specific value, $\beta_{j,0}$. The null value $\beta_{j,0}$ comes either from economic theory or, as in the student-teacher ratio example, from the decision-making context of the application. If the alternative hypothesis is two-sided, then the two hypotheses can be written mathematically as

$$H_0: \beta_j = \beta_{j,0} \text{ vs. } H_1: \beta_j \neq \beta_{j,0} \quad \text{(two-sided alternative).} \quad (5.13)$$

For example, if the first regressor is STR, then the null hypothesis that changing the student-teacher ratio has no effect on class size corresponds to the null hypothesis that $\beta_1 = 0$ (so $\beta_{1,0} = 0$). Our task is to test the null hypothesis H_0 against the alternative H_1 using a sample of data.

Key Concept 4.6 gives a procedure for testing this null hypothesis when there is a single regressor. The first step in this procedure is to calculate the standard error of the coefficient. The second step is to calculate the t-statistic using the general formula in Key Concept 4.5. The third step is to compute the p-value of the test using the cumulative normal distribution in Appendix Table 1 or, alternatively, to compare the t-statistic to the critical value corresponding to the desired significance level of the test. The theoretical underpinning of this procedure is that the OLS estimator has a large-sample normal distribution which, under the null hypothesis, has as its mean the hypothesized true value, and that the variance of this distribution can be estimated consistently.

This underpinning is present in multiple regression as well. As stated in Key Concept 5.5, the sampling distribution of $\hat{\beta}_j$ is approximately normal. Under the null hypothesis the mean of this distribution is $\beta_{j,0}$. The variance of this distribution can be estimated consistently. Therefore we can simply follow the same procedure as in the single-regressor case to test the null hypothesis in Equation (5.13).

The procedure for testing a hypothesis on a single coefficient in multiple regression is summarized as Key Concept 5.6. The t-statistic actually computed is denoted t^{act} in the Key Concept. However it is customary to denote this simply as t, and we adopt this simplified notation for the rest of the book.

Confidence Intervals for a Single Coefficient

The method for constructing a confidence interval in the multiple regression model is also the same as in the single-regressor model. This method is summarized as Key Concept 5.7.

The method for conducting a hypothesis test in Key Concept 5.6 and the method for constructing a confidence interval in Key Concept 5.7 rely on the large-sample normal approximation to the distribution of the OLS estimator $\hat{\beta}_j$. Accordingly, it should be kept in mind that these methods for quantifying the sampling uncertainty are only guaranteed to work in large samples.

Testing the Hypothesis $\beta_j = \beta_{j,0}$ Against the Alternative $\beta_j \neq \beta_{j,0}$

1. Compute the standard error of $\hat{\beta}_j$, $SE(\hat{\beta}_j)$.

2. Compute the t-statistic,

$$t = \frac{\hat{\beta}_j - \beta_{j,0}}{SE(\hat{\beta}_j)}. \tag{5.14}$$

3. Compute the p-value,

$$p\text{-value} = 2\Phi(-|t^{act}|), \tag{5.15}$$

where t^{act} is the value of the t-statistic actually computed. Reject the hypothesis at the 5% significance level if the p-value is less than 0.05 or, equivalently, if $|t^{act}| > 1.96$.

The standard error and (typically) the t-statistic and p-value testing $\beta_j = 0$ are computed automatically by regression software.

Key Concept 5.6

Application to Test Scores and the Student-Teacher Ratio

Can we reject the null hypothesis that a change in the student-teacher ratio has no effect on test scores, once we control for the percentage of English learners in the district? What is a 95% confidence interval for the effect on test scores of a change in the student-teacher ratio, controlling for the percentage of English learners? We are now able to find out. The regression of test scores against *STR* and *PctEL*, estimated by OLS, was given in Equation (5.10) and is restated here with standard errors in parentheses below the coefficients:

$$\widehat{TestScore} = 686.0 - 1.10 \times STR - 0.650 \times PctEL. \tag{5.16}$$
$$\quad\quad\quad (8.7) \quad (0.43) \quad\quad\quad (0.031)$$

To test the hypothesis that the true coefficient on *STR* is 0, we first need to compute the t-statistic in Equation (5.14). Because the null hypothesis says that the true value of this coefficient is zero, the t-statistic is $t = (-1.10 - 0)/0.43 = -2.54$. The associated p-value is $2\Phi(-2.54) = 1.1\%$; that is, the smallest signifi-

Key Concept 5.7

Confidence Intervals for a Single Coefficient in Multiple Regression

A 95% two-sided confidence interval for the coefficient β_j is an interval that contains the true value of β_j with a 95% probability; that is, it contains the true value of β_j in 95% of all possible randomly drawn samples. Equivalently, it is also the set of values of β_j that cannot be rejected by a 5% two-sided hypothesis test. When the sample size is large, the 95% confidence interval is:

$$95\% \text{ confidence interval for } \beta_j = (\hat{\beta}_j - 1.96SE(\hat{\beta}_j), \hat{\beta}_j + 1.96SE(\hat{\beta}_j)). \quad (5.17)$$

A 90% confidence interval is obtained by replacing 1.96 in Equation (5.17) with 1.645.

cance level at which we can reject the null hypothesis is 1.1%. Because the p-value is less than 5%, the null hypothesis can be rejected at the 5% significance level (but not quite at the 1% significance level).

A 95% confidence interval for the population coefficient on STR is $-1.10 \pm 1.96 \times 0.43 = (-1.95, -0.26)$; that is, we can be 95% confident that the true value of the coefficient is between -1.95 and -0.26. Interpreted in the context of the superintendent's interest in decreasing the student-teacher ratio by 2, the 95% confidence interval for the effect on test scores of this reduction is $(-1.95 \times 2, -0.26 \times 2) = (-3.90, -0.52)$.

Adding expenditures per pupil to the equation   Your analysis of the multiple regression in Equation (5.16) has persuaded the superintendent that, based on the evidence so far, reducing class size will help test scores in her district. Now, however, she moves on to a more nuanced question. If she is to hire more teachers, she can pay for those teachers either through cuts elsewhere in the budget (no new computers, reduced maintenance, etc.), or by asking for an increase in her budget, which taxpayers do not favor. What, she asks, is the effect on test scores of reducing the student-teacher ratio, holding expenditures per pupil (and the percentage of English learners) constant?

This question can be addressed by estimating a regression of test scores on the student-teacher ratio, total spending per pupil, and the percentage of English learners. The OLS regression line is

$$\widehat{TestScore} = 649.6 - 0.29 \times STR + 3.87 \times Expn - 0.656 \times PctEL, \qquad (5.18)$$
$$(15.5) \quad (0.48) \qquad\quad (1.59) \qquad\qquad (0.032)$$

where *Expn* is total annual expenditures per pupil in the district in thousands of dollars.

The result is striking. Holding expenditures per pupil and the percentage of English learners constant, changing the student-teacher ratio is estimated to have a very small effect on test scores: the estimated coefficient on *STR* is −1.10 in Equation (5.16) but, after adding *Expn* as a regressor in Equation (5.18), it is only −0.29. Moreover, the *t*-statistic for testing that the true value of the coefficient is zero is now $t = (-0.29 - 0)/0.48 = -0.60$, so the hypothesis that the population value of this coefficient is indeed zero cannot be rejected even at the 10% significance level ($|-0.60| < 1.645$). Thus Equation (5.18) provides no evidence that hiring more teachers improves test scores if overall expenditures per pupil are held constant.

Note that the standard error on *STR* increased when *Expn* was added, from 0.43 in Equation (5.16) to 0.48 in Equation (5.18). This illustrates the general point that a correlation between regressors (the correlation between *STR* and *Expn* is −0.62) can make the OLS estimators less precise (see Appendix 5.2 for further discussion).

What about our angry taxpayer? He asserts that the population values of *both* the coefficient on the student-teacher ratio (β_1) *and* the coefficient on spending per pupil (β_2) are zero, that is, he hypothesizes that both $\beta_1 = 0$ and $\beta_2 = 0$. Although it might seem that we can reject this hypothesis because the *t*-statistic testing $\beta_2 = 0$ in Equation (5.18) is $t = 3.87/1.59 = 2.43$, this reasoning is flawed. The taxpayer's hypothesis is a joint hypothesis, and to test it we need a new tool, the *F*-statistic.

5.7 Tests of Joint Hypotheses

This section describes how to formulate joint hypotheses on multiple regression coefficients and how to test them using an *F*-statistic.

Testing Hypotheses on Two or More Coefficients

Joint null hypotheses.   Consider the regression in Equation (5.18) of the test score against the student-teacher ratio, expenditures per pupil, and the percentage of English learners. Our angry taxpayer hypothesizes that neither the student-teacher ratio nor expenditures per pupil have an effect on test scores, once we control for the percentage of English learners. Because *STR* is the first regressor in Equation (5.18) and *Expn* is the second, we can write this hypothesis mathematically as

$$H_0: \beta_1 = 0 \text{ and } \beta_2 = 0 \text{ vs. } H_1: \beta_1 \neq 0 \text{ and/or } \beta_2 \neq 0. \tag{5.19}$$

The hypothesis that *both* the coefficient on the student-teacher ratio (β_1) *and* the coefficient on expenditures per pupil (β_2) are zero is an example of a joint hypothesis on the coefficients in the multiple regression model. In this case, the null hypothesis restricts the value of two of the coefficients, so as a matter of terminology we can say that the null hypothesis in Equation (5.19) imposes two **restrictions** on the multiple regression model: that $\beta_1 = 0$ *and* that $\beta_2 = 0$.

In general, a **joint hypothesis** is a hypothesis that imposes two or more restrictions on the regression coefficients. We consider joint null and alternative hypotheses of the form

$$H_0: \beta_j = \beta_{j,0}, \beta_m = \beta_{m,0}, \text{ etc., for a total of } q \text{ restrictions, vs.}$$

$$H_1: \text{one or more of the } q \text{ restrictions under } H_0 \text{ does not hold,} \tag{5.20}$$

where β_j, β_m, etc., refer to different regression coefficients, and $\beta_{j,0}$, $\beta_{m,0}$, etc., refer to the values of these coefficients under the null hypothesis. The null hypothesis in Equation (5.19) is an example of Equation (5.20). Another example is that, in a regression with $k = 6$ regressors, the null hypothesis is that the coefficients on the 2nd, 4th, and 5th regressors are zero; that is, $\beta_2 = 0$, $\beta_4 = 0$, and $\beta_5 = 0$, so that there are $q = 3$ restrictions. In general, under the null hypothesis H_0 there are q such restrictions.

If any one (or more than one) of the equalities under the null hypothesis H_0 in Equation (5.20) is false, then the joint null hypothesis itself is false. Thus, the alternative hypothesis is that at least one of the equalities in the null hypothesis H_0 does not hold.

Why can't I just test the individual coefficients one at a time? Although it seems it should be possible to test a joint hypothesis by using the usual *t*-statistics to test the restrictions one at a time, the following calculation shows that this approach is unreliable. Specifically, suppose that you are interested in testing the joint null hypothesis in Equation (5.18) that $\beta_1 = 0$ and $\beta_2 = 0$. Let t_1 be the *t*-statistic for testing the null hypothesis that $\beta_1 = 0$, and let

t_2 be the t-statistic for testing the null hypothesis that $\beta_2 = 0$. What happens when you use the "one at a time" testing procedure: reject the joint null hypothesis if either t_1 or t_2 exceeds 1.96 in absolute value?

Because this question involves the two random variables t_1 and t_2, answering it requires characterizing the joint sampling distribution of t_1 and t_2. As mentioned in Section 5.5, in large samples $\hat{\beta}_1$ and $\hat{\beta}_2$ have a joint normal distribution, so under the joint null hypothesis the t-statistics t_1 and t_2 have a bivariate normal distribution, where each t-statistic has mean equal to zero and variance equal to one.

First consider the special case in which the t-statistics are uncorrelated and thus are independent. What is the size of the "one at a time" testing procedure; that is, what is the probability that you will reject the null hypothesis when it is true? More than 5%! In this special case we can calculate the rejection probability of this method exactly. The null is *not* rejected only if both $|t_1| \leq 1.96$ and $|t_2| \leq 1.96$. Because the t-statistics are independent, $\Pr(|t_1| \leq 1.96 \text{ and } |t_2| \leq 1.96) = \Pr(|t_1| \leq 1.96) \times \Pr(|t_2| \leq 1.96) = 0.95^2 = 0.9025 = 90.25\%$. So the probability of rejecting the null hypothesis when it is true is $1 - 0.95^2 = 9.75\%$. This "one at a time" method rejects the null too often because it gives you too many chances: if you fail to reject using the first t-statistic, you get to try again using the second.

If the regressors are correlated the situation is even more complicated. The size of the "one at a time" procedure depends on the value of the correlation between the regressors. Because the "one at a time" testing approach has the wrong size—that is, its rejection rate under the null hypothesis does not equal the desired significance level—a new approach is needed.

One approach is to modify the "one at a time" method so that it uses different critical values that ensure that its size equals its significance level. This method, called the Bonferroni method, is described in Appendix 5.3. The advantage of the Bonferroni method is that it applies very generally. Its disadvantage is that it can have low power; it frequently fails to reject the null hypothesis when in fact the alternative hypothesis is true.

Fortunately, there is another approach to testing joint hypotheses that is more powerful, especially when the regressors are highly correlated. That approach is based on the F-statistic.

The *F*-Statistic

The **F-statistic** is used to test joint hypothesis about regression coefficients. The formulas for the F-statistic are integrated into modern regression software. We first discuss the case of two restrictions, then turn to the general case of q restrictions.

The F-statistic with q = 2 restrictions.   When the joint null hypothesis has the two restrictions that $\beta_1 = 0$ and $\beta_2 = 0$, the F-statistic combines the two t-statistics t_1 and t_2 using the formula

$$F = \frac{1}{2}\left(\frac{t_1^2 + t_2^2 - 2\hat{\rho}_{t_1,t_2}t_1 t_2}{1 - \hat{\rho}_{t_1,t_2}^2}\right), \tag{5.21}$$

where $\hat{\rho}_{t_1,t_2}$ is an estimator of the correlation between the two t-statistics.

To understand the F-statistic in Equation (5.21), first suppose that we know that the t-statistics are uncorrelated so we can drop the terms involving $\hat{\rho}_{t_1,t_2}$. If so, Equation (5.21) simplifies and $F = \frac{1}{2}(t_1^2 + t_2^2)$; that is, the F statistic is the average of the squared t-statistics. Under the null hypothesis, t_1 and t_2 are independent standard normal random variables (because the t-statistics are uncorrelated by assumption), so under the null hypothesis F has a $F_{2,\infty}$ distribution (Section 2.4). Under the alternative hypothesis that either β_1 is nonzero or β_2 is nonzero (or both), then either t_1^2 or t_2^2 (or both) will be large, leading the test to reject the null hypothesis.

In general the t-statistics are correlated, and the formula for the F-statistic in Equation (5.21) adjusts for this correlation. This adjustment is made so that, under the null hypothesis, the F-statistic has a $F_{2,\infty}$ distribution in large samples whether or not the t-statistics are correlated.

The F-statistic with q restrictions.   The formula for the F-statistic testing the q restrictions of the joint null hypothesis in Equation (5.20) is given in Section 16.3. This formula is incorporated into regression software, making the F-statistic easy to compute in practice.

Under the null hypothesis, the F-statistic has a sampling distribution that, in large samples, is given by the $F_{q,\infty}$ distribution. That is, in large samples, under the null hypothesis

$$\text{the } F\text{-statistic is distributed } F_{q,\infty}. \tag{5.22}$$

Thus the critical values for the F-statistic can be obtained from the tables of the $F_{q,\infty}$ distribution in Appendix Table 4 for the appropriate value of q and the desired significance level.

Computing the p-value using the F-statistic.   The p-value of the F-statistic can be computed using the large-sample chi-squared approximation to its distribution. Let F^{act} denote the value of the F-statistic actually computed. Because the F-statistic has a large-sample $F_{q,\infty}$ distribution under the null hypothesis, the p-value is

$$p\text{-value} = \Pr[F_{q,\infty} > F^{act}]. \tag{5.23}$$

The p-value in Equation (5.23) can be evaluated using a table of the $F_{q,\infty}$ distribution (or, alternatively, a table of the χ_q^2 distribution, because a χ_q^2-distributed random variable is q times a $F_{q,\infty}$-distributed random variable). Alternatively, the p-value can be evaluated using a computer, because formulas for the cumulative chi-squared and F distributions have been incorporated into most modern statistical software.

The "overall" regression F-statistic.   The "overall" regression F-statistic tests the joint hypothesis that *all* the slope coefficients are zero. That is, the null and alternative hypotheses are

$$H_0\text{: } \beta_1 = 0, \beta_2 = 0, \ldots, \beta_k = 0 \text{ vs. } H_1\text{: } \beta_j \neq 0, \text{ at least one } j, j = 1, \ldots, k. \tag{5.24}$$

Under this null hypothesis, none of the regressors explain any of the variation in Y_i, although the intercept (which under the null hypothesis is the mean of Y_i) can be nonzero. The null hypothesis in Equation (5.24) is a special case of the general null hypothesis in Equation (5.20), and the overall regression F-statistic is the F-statistic computed for the null hypothesis in Equation (5.24). In large samples, the overall regression F-statistic has a $F_{k,\infty}$ distribution.

The F-statistic when q = 1.   When $q = 1$, the F-statistic tests a single restriction. Then the joint null hypothesis reduces to the null hypothesis on a single regression coefficient, and the F-statistic is the square of the t-statistic.

Heteroskedasticity and homoskedasticity again.   Recall from Section 4.9 that, for historical reasons, statistical software sometimes computes the homoskedasticity-only standard errors as the default, so the user must specify that the heteroskedasticity-robust standard errors be used instead. This warning applies to F-statistics as well: to ensure that you use the heteroskedasticity-robust F-statistic, in some regression packages you must select a "robust" option so that robust estimates of the "covariance matrix" are used. If the homoskedasticity-only version of the F-statistic (discussed in Appendix 5.3) is used but the errors are heteroskedastic, then the F-statistic will not have the $F_{q,\infty}$ distribution in Equation (5.22) under the null hypothesis, leading to misleading statistical inferences.

Application to Test Scores and the Student-Teacher Ratio

We are now able to test the null hypothesis that the coefficients on *both* the student-teacher ratio *and* expenditures per pupil are zero, against the alternative that at least one coefficient is nonzero, controlling for the percentage of English learners in the district.

To test this hypothesis, we need to compute the *F*-statistic of the test that $\beta_1 = 0$ and $\beta_2 = 0$ using the regression of *TestScore* on *STR*, *Expn*, and *PctEL* reported in Equation (5.18). This *F*-statistic is 5.43. Under the null hypothesis, in large samples this statistic has a $F_{2,\infty}$ distribution. The 5% critical value of the $F_{2,\infty}$ distribution is 3.00 (Appendix Table 4), and the 1% critical value is 4.61. The value of the *F*-statistic computed from the data, 5.43, exceeds 4.61, so the null hypothesis is rejected at the 1% level. It is very unlikely that we would have drawn a sample that produced an *F*-statistic as large as 5.43 if the null hypothesis really were true (the *p*-value is 0.005). Based on the evidence in Equation (5.18) as summarized in this *F*-statistic, we can reject the taxpayer's hypothesis that *neither* the student-teacher ratio *nor* expenditures per pupil have an effect on test scores (holding constant the percentage of English learners).

5.8 Testing Single Restrictions Involving Multiple Coefficients

Sometimes economic theory suggests a single restriction that involves two or more regression coefficients. For example, theory might suggest a null hypothesis of the form $\beta_1 = \beta_2$; that is, the effects of the first and second regressor are the same. In this case, the task is to test this null hypothesis against the alternative that the two coefficients differ, that is,

$$H_0: \beta_1 = \beta_2 \text{ vs. } H_1: \beta_1 \neq \beta_2. \tag{5.25}$$

This null hypothesis has a single restriction, so $q = 1$, but that restriction involves multiple coefficients (β_1 and β_2). We need to modify the methods presented so far to test this hypothesis. There are two approaches; which one will be easiest depends on your software.

Approach #1: Test the restriction directly.   Some statistical packages have a specialized command designed to test restrictions like Equation (5.25) and the result is an F-statistic that, because $q = 1$, has a $F_{1,\infty}$ distribution under the null hypothesis. (Recall from Section 2.4 that the square of a standard normal random variable has a $F_{1,\infty}$ distribution, so the 95% percentile of the $F_{1,\infty}$ distribution is $1.96^2 = 3.84$.)

Approach #2: Transform the regression.   If your statistical package cannot test the restriction directly, the hypothesis in Equation (5.25) can be tested using a trick in which the original regression equation is rewritten to turn the restriction in Equation (5.25) into a restriction on a single regression coefficient. To be concrete, suppose there are only two regressors, X_{1i} and X_{2i} in the regression, so the population regression has the form

$$Y_i = \beta_0 + \beta_1 X_{1i} + \beta_2 X_{2i} + u_i. \tag{5.26}$$

Here is the trick: by subtracting and adding $\beta_2 X_{1i}$, we have that $\beta_1 X_{1i} + \beta_2 X_{2i} = \beta_1 X_{1i} - \beta_2 X_{1i} + \beta_2 X_{1i} + \beta_2 X_{2i} = (\beta_1 - \beta_2)X_{1i} + \beta_2(X_{1i} + X_{2i}) = \gamma_1 X_{1i} + \beta_2 W_i$, where $\gamma_1 = \beta_1 - \beta_2$ and $W_i = X_{1i} + X_{2i}$. Thus, the population regression in Equation (5.26) can be rewritten as

$$Y_i = \beta_0 + \gamma_1 X_{1i} + \beta_2 W_i + u_i. \tag{5.27}$$

Because the coefficient γ_1 in this equation is $\gamma_1 = \beta_1 - \beta_2$, under the null hypothesis in Equation (5.25), $\gamma_1 = 0$, while under the alternative, $\gamma_1 \neq 0$. Thus, by turning Equation (5.26) into Equation (5.27), we have turned a restriction on two regression coefficients into a restriction on a single regression coefficient.

Because the restriction now involves the single coefficient γ_1, the null hypothesis in Equation (5.25) can be tested using the t-statistic method of Section 5.6. In practice, this is done by first constructing the new regressor W_i as the sum of the two original regressors, then estimating the regression of Y_i on X_{1i} and W_i. A 95% confidence interval for the difference in the coefficients $\beta_1 - \beta_2$ can be calculated as $\hat{\gamma}_1 \pm 1.96 SE(\hat{\gamma}_1)$.

This method can be extended to other restrictions on regression equations using the same trick (see Exercise 5.8).

The two methods (Approaches #1 and #2) are equivalent, in the sense that the F-statistic from the first method equals the square of the t-statistic from the second method.

Extension to q > 1. In general it is possible to have q restrictions under the null hypothesis in which some or all of these restrictions involve multiple coefficients. The F-statistic of Section 5.7 extends to this type of joint hypothesis. The F-statistic can be computed by either of the two methods just discussed for $q = 1$. Precisely how best to do this in practice depends on the specific regression package being used.

5.9 Confidence Sets for Multiple Coefficients

This section explains how to construct a confidence set for two or more multiple regression coefficients. The method is conceptually similar to the method in Section 5.6 for constructing a confidence set for a single coefficient using the t-statistic, except that the confidence set for multiple coefficients is based on the F-statistic.

A **95% confidence set** for two or more coefficients is a set that contains the true population values of these coefficients in 95% of randomly drawn samples. Thus, a confidence set is the generalization to two or more coefficients of a confidence interval for a single coefficient.

Recall that a 95% confidence interval is computed by finding the set of values of the coefficients that are not rejected using a t-statistic at the 5% significance level. This approach can be extended to the case of multiple coefficients. To make this concrete, suppose you are interested in constructing a confidence set for two coefficients, β_1 and β_2. Section 5.7 showed how to use the F-statistic to test a joint null hypothesis that $\beta_1 = \beta_{1,0}$ and $\beta_2 = \beta_{2,0}$. Suppose you were to test every possible value of $\beta_{1,0}$ and $\beta_{2,0}$ at the 5% level. For each pair of candidates $(\beta_{1,0}, \beta_{2,0})$, you construct the F-statistic and reject if it exceeds the 5% critical value of 3.00. Because the test has a 5% significance level, the true population values of β_1 and β_2 will be not be rejected in 95% of all samples. Thus, the set of values not rejected at the 5% level by this F-statistic constitutes a 95% confidence set for β_1 and β_2.

Although this method of trying all possible values of $\beta_{1,0}$ and $\beta_{2,0}$ works in theory, in practice it is much simpler to use an explicit formula for the confidence set. This formula for the confidence set for an arbitrary number of coefficients is based on the formula for the F-statistic in Section 16.3. When there are two coefficients, the resulting confidence sets are ellipses.

As an illustration, Figure 5.1 shows a 95% confidence set (confidence ellipse) for the coefficients on the student-teacher ratio and expenditure per pupil, holding constant the percentage of English learners, based on the estimated regression in Equation (5.18). This ellipse does not include the point (0,0). This means that the null hypothesis that these two coefficients are both zero is rejected using the F-statistic at the 5% significance level, which we already knew from Section 5.7. The confidence ellipse is a fat sausage with the long part of the sausage oriented in the lower-left/upper-right direction. The reason for this orientation is that the estimated correlation between $\hat{\beta}_1$ and $\hat{\beta}_2$ is positive, which in turn arises because the correlation between the regressors *STR* and *Expn* is negative (schools that spend more per pupil tend to have fewer students per teacher).

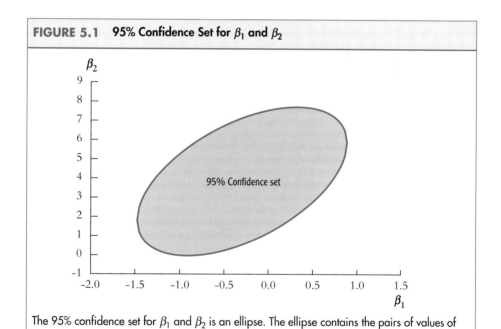

FIGURE 5.1   95% Confidence Set for β_1 and β_2

The 95% confidence set for β_1 and β_2 is an ellipse. The ellipse contains the pairs of values of β_1 and β_2 that cannot be rejected using the F-statistic at the 5% significance level.

5.10 Additional Regression Statistics

Three commonly used summary statistics in multiple regression are the standard error of the regression, the regression R^2, and the adjusted R^2 (also known as $\overline{R}^2$). All three statistics measure how well the OLS estimate of the multiple regression line describes, or "fits," the data.

The Standard Error of the Regression (SER)

The standard error of the regression estimates the standard deviation of the error term u_i. Thus, the SER is a measure of the spread of the distribution of Y around the regression line. In multiple regression, the SER is

$$SER = s_{\hat{u}}, \text{ where } s_{\hat{u}}^2 = \frac{1}{n-k-1} \sum_{i=1}^{n} \hat{u}_i^2 = \frac{SSR}{n-k-1}, \tag{5.28}$$

where the SSR is the sum of squared residuals, $SSR = \sum_{i=1}^{n} \hat{u}_i^2$.

The only difference between the definition in Equation (5.28) and the definition of the SER in Section 4.8 for the single-regressor model is that here the divisor is $n - k - 1$ rather than $n - 2$. In Section 4.8, the divisor $n - 2$ (rather than n) adjusts for the downward bias introduced by estimating two coefficients (the slope and intercept of the regression line). Here, the divisor $n - k - 1$ adjusts for the downward bias introduced by estimating $k + 1$ coefficients (the k slope coefficients plus the intercept). As in Section 4.8, using $n - k - 1$ rather than n is called a degrees-of-freedom adjustment. If there is a single regressor, then $k = 1$, so the formula in Section 4.8 is the same as in Equation (5.28). When n is large, the effect of the degrees-of-freedom adjustment is negligible.

The R^2

The regression **R^2** is the fraction of the sample variance of Y_i explained by (or predicted by) the regressors. Equivalently, the R^2 is one minus the fraction of the variance of Y_i *not* explained by the regressors.

The mathematical definition of the R^2 is the same as for regression with a single regressor:

$$R^2 = \frac{ESS}{TSS} = 1 - \frac{SSR}{TSS}, \tag{5.29}$$

where the explained sum of squares is $ESS = \sum_{i=1}^{n} (\hat{Y}_i - \overline{Y})^2$ and the total sum of squares is $TSS = \sum_{i=1}^{n} (Y_i - \overline{Y})^2$.

In multiple regression, the R^2 increases whenever a regressor is added, unless the new regressor is perfectly multicollinear with the original regressors. To see this, think about starting with one regressor and then adding a second. When you use OLS to estimate the model with both regressors, OLS finds the values of the coefficients that minimize the sum of squared residuals. If OLS happens to choose the coefficient on the new regressor to be exactly zero, then the SSR will be the same whether or not the second variable is included in the regression. But if OLS chooses any value other than zero, then it must be that this value reduced the SSR relative to the regression that excludes this regressor. In practice it is extremely unusual for an estimated coefficient to be exactly zero, so in general the SSR will decrease when a new regressor is added. But this means that the R^2 generally increases (and never decreases) when a new regressor is added.

The "Adjusted R^2"

Because the R^2 increases when a new variable is added, an increase in the R^2 does not mean that adding a variable actually improves the fit of the model. In this sense, the R^2 gives an inflated estimate of how well the regression fits the data. One way to correct for this is to deflate or reduce the R^2 by some factor, and this is what the adjusted R^2, or $\overline{R}^2$, does.

The **adjusted R^2**, or $\overline{R}^2$, is a modified version of the R^2 that does not necessarily increase when a new regressor is added. The $\overline{R}^2$ is

$$\overline{R}^2 = 1 - \frac{n-1}{n-k-1} \frac{SSR}{TSS} = 1 - \frac{s_{\hat{u}}^2}{s_Y^2}. \tag{5.30}$$

The difference between this formula and the second definition of the R^2 in Equation (5.29) is that the ratio of the sum of squared residuals to the total sum of squares is multiplied by the factor $(n-1)/(n-k-1)$. As the second expression in Equation (5.30) shows, this makes the adjusted R^2 one minus the ratio of the sample variance of the OLS residuals (with the degrees-of-freedom correction in Equation (5.28)) to the sample variance of Y.

There are three useful things to know about the $\overline{R}^2$. First, $(n-1)/(n-k-1)$ is always greater than one, so $\overline{R}^2$ is always less than R^2.

Second, adding a regressor has two opposite effects on the $\overline{R}^2$. On the one hand, the SSR falls, which increases the $\overline{R}^2$. On the other hand, the factor $(n-1)/(n-k-1)$ increases. Whether the $\overline{R}^2$ increases or decreases depends on which of these two effects is stronger.

Third, the $\overline{R}^2$ can be negative. This happens when the regressors, taken together, reduce the sum of squared residuals by such a small amount that this reduction fails to offset the factor $(n-1)/(n-k-1)$.

Interpreting the R^2 and the Adjusted R^2 in Practice

An R^2 or an $\overline{R}^2$ near one means that the regressors are good at predicting the values of the dependent variable in the sample, and an R^2 or an $\overline{R}^2$ near zero means they are not. This makes these statistics useful summaries of the predictive ability of the regression. However, it is easy to read more into them than they deserve.

There are four potential pitfalls to guard against when using the R^2 or $\overline{R}^2$:

1. **An increase in the R^2 or $\overline{R}^2$ does not necessarily mean that an added variable is statistically significant.** The R^2 increases whenever you add a regressor, whether or not it is statistically significant. The $\overline{R}^2$ does not always increase, but if it does this does not necessarily mean that the coefficient on that added regressor is statistically significant. To ascertain whether an added variable is statistically significant, you need to perform a hypothesis test using the t-statistic.

2. **A high R^2 or $\overline{R}^2$ does not mean that the regressors are a true cause of the dependent variable.** Imagine regressing test scores against parking lot area per pupil. Parking lot area is correlated with the student-teacher ratio, with whether the school is in a suburb or a city, and possibly with district income—all things that are correlated with test scores. Thus the regression of test scores on parking lot area per pupil could have a high R^2 and $\overline{R}^2$, but the relationship is not causal (try telling the superintendent that the way to increase test scores is to increase parking space!).

3. **A high R^2 or $\overline{R}^2$ does not mean there is no omitted variable bias.** Recall the discussion of Section 5.1, which concerned omitted variable bias in the regression of test scores on the student-teacher ratio. The R^2 of the regression never came up because it played no logical role in this discussion. Omitted variable bias can occur in regressions with a low R^2, a moderate R^2, or a high R^2. Conversely, a low R^2 does not imply that there necessarily is omitted variable bias.

4. **A high R^2 or $\overline{R}^2$ does not necessarily mean you have the most appropriate set of regressors, nor does a low R^2 or $\overline{R}^2$ necessarily mean you have an inappropriate set of regressors.** The question of what constitutes the right set of regressors in multiple regression is difficult and we return to it throughout this textbook. Decisions about the regressors must weigh issues of omitted variable bias, data availability, data quality, and, most importantly, economic theory and the nature of the substantive questions being addressed. None of these questions can be answered simply by having a high (or low) regression R^2 or $\overline{R}^2$.

These points are summarized in Key Concept 5.8.

R^2 and $\overline{R}^2$: What They Tell You—and What They Don't

The R^2 and $\overline{R}^2$ tell you whether the regressors are good at predicting, or "explaining," the values of the dependent variable in the sample of data on hand. If the R^2 (or $\overline{R}^2$) is nearly one, then the regressors produce good predictions of the dependent variable in that sample, in the sense that the variance of the OLS residual is small compared to the variance of the dependent variable. If the R^2 (or $\overline{R}^2$) is nearly zero, the opposite is true.

The R^2 and $\overline{R}^2$ do NOT tell you whether:

Key Concept 5.8

1. an included variable is statistically significant;

2. the regressors are a true cause of the movements in the dependent variable;

3. there is omitted variable bias; or

4. you have chosen the most appropriate set of regressors.

5.11 Omitted Variable Bias and Multiple Regression

The OLS estimators of the coefficients in multiple regression will have omitted variable bias if an omitted determinant of Y_i is correlated with at least one of the regressors. For example, students from affluent families often have more learning opportunities than do their less affluent peers, which could lead to better test scores. Moreover, if the district is a wealthy one then the schools will tend to have larger budgets and lower student-teacher ratios. If so, the affluence of the students and the student-teacher ratio would be negatively correlated, and the OLS estimate of the coefficient on the student-teacher ratio would pick up the effect of average district income, even after controlling for the percentage of English learners. In short, omitting the students' economic background could lead to omitted variable bias in the regression of test scores on the student-teacher ratio and the percentage of English learners.

The general conditions for omitted variable bias in multiple regression are similar to those for a single regressor: if an omitted variable is a determinant of Y_i and if it is correlated with at least one of the regressors, then the OLS estimators will have omitted variable bias. As was discussed in Section 5.6, the OLS estimators are correlated, so in general the OLS estimators of all the coefficients will be

Omitted Variable Bias in Multiple Regression

Omitted variable bias is the bias in the OLS estimator that arises when one or more included regressors are correlated with an omitted variable. For omitted variable bias to arise, two things must be true:

1. at least one of the included regressors must be correlated with the omitted variable; and

2. the omitted variable must be a determinant of the dependent variable, Y.

biased. The two conditions for omitted variable bias in multiple regression are summarized in Key Concept 5.9.

At a mathematical level, if the two conditions for omitted variable bias are satisfied, then at least one of the regressors is correlated with the error term. This means that the conditional expectation of u_i given $X_{1i}, \ldots, X_{ki}$ is nonzero, so that the first least squares assumption is violated. As a result, the omitted variable bias persists even if the sample size is large, that is, omitted variable bias implies that the OLS estimators are inconsistent.

Model Specification in Theory and in Practice

In theory, when data are available on the omitted variable, the solution to omitted variable bias is to include the omitted variable in the regression. In practice, however, deciding whether to include a particular variable can be difficult and requires judgment.

Our approach to the challenge of potential omitted variable bias is twofold. First, a core or base set of regressors should be chosen using a combination of expert judgment, economic theory, and knowledge of how the data were collected; the regression using this base set of regressors is sometimes referred to as a **base specification**. This base specification should contain the variables of primary interest and the control variables suggested by expert judgment and economic theory. Expert judgment and economic theory are rarely decisive, however, and often the variables suggested by economic theory are not the ones on which you have data. Therefore the next step is to develop a list of candidate **alternative specifications**, that is, alternative sets of regressors. If the estimates of the coefficients of interest are numerically similar across the alternative specifications, then this provides evidence that the estimates from your base specification are reliable. If, on the other hand, the estimates of the coefficients of interest change substantially across specifications, this often provides evidence that the original specification had omitted variable bias. We elaborate on this approach to model specification in Section 7.2 after studying some tools for specifying regressions.

5.12 Analysis of the Test Score Data Set

This section presents an analysis of the effect on test scores of the student-teacher ratio using the California data set. Our primary purpose is to provide an example in which multiple regression analysis is used to mitigate omitted variable bias. Our secondary purpose is to demonstrate how to use a table to summarize regression results.

This analysis focuses on estimating the effect on test scores of a change in the student-teacher ratio, holding constant student characteristics that the superintendent cannot control. Earlier in this chapter, we estimated regressions that included both the student-teacher ratio and expenditures per pupil. The coefficient on the student-teacher ratio in that regression was the effect of a change in the student-teacher ratio, holding expenditures per pupil constant, and our estimates suggested that this effect is small and not statistically significantly different from zero. The regressions reported here do not include expenditures per pupil, so the effect of the student-teacher ratio estimated here does *not* hold spending per pupil constant.

Many factors potentially affect the average test score in a district. Some of the factors that could affect test scores are correlated with the student-teacher ratio, so omitting them from the regression will result in omitted variable bias. If data are available on these omitted variables, the solution to this problem is to include them as additional regressors in the multiple regression. When we do this, the coefficient on the student-teacher ratio is the effect of a change in the student-teacher ratio, holding constant these other factors.

Here we consider three variables that control for background characteristics of the students that could affect test scores. One of these control variables is the one we have used previously, the fraction of students who are still learning English. The two other variables are new and control for the economic background of the students. There is no perfect measure of economic background in the data set, so instead we use two imperfect indicators of low income in the district. The first new variable is the percentage of students who are eligible for obtaining a subsidized or free lunch at school. Students are eligible for this program if their family income is less than a certain threshold (approximately 150% of the poverty line). The second new variable is the percentage of students in the district whose families qualify for a California income assistance program. Families are eligible for this income assistance program depending in part on their family income, but the threshold is lower (stricter) than the threshold for the subsidized lunch program. These two variables thus measure the fraction of economically disadvantaged children in the district; although they are related, they are not perfectly correlated (their correlation coefficient is 0.74). Although theory suggests that economic background could be an important omitted factor, theory and expert judgment do not really help us decide which of these two variables (percentage eligible for a subsidized lunch or percentage eligible for income assistance) is a better measure of background. For our base specification, we choose the percentage eligible for a subsidized lunch as the economic background variable, but we consider an alternative specification that includes the other variable as well.

Scatterplots of tests scores and these variables are presented in Figure 5.2. Each of these variables exhibits a negative correlation with test scores. The correlation between test scores and the percentage of English learners is −0.64; between test scores and the percentage eligible for a subsidized lunch is −0.87; and between test scores and the percentage qualifying for income assistance is −0.63.

We are now faced with a communication problem. What is the best way to show the results from several multiple regressions that contain different subsets of the possible regressors? So far, we have presented regression results by writing out the estimated regression equations, as in Equation (5.18). This is fine when there are only a few regressors and only a few equations, but with more regressors and equations this method of presentation can be confusing. A better way to communicate the results of several regressions is in a table.

Table 5.2 summarizes the results of regressions of the test score on various sets of regressors. Each column summarizes a separate regression. Each regression has the same dependent variable, test score. The entries in the first 5 rows are the estimated regression coefficients, with their standard errors below them in parentheses. The asterisks indicate whether the t-statistics, testing the hypothesis that the relevant coefficient is zero, is significant at the 5% level (1 asterisk) or the 1% level (2 asterisks). The final three rows contain summary statistics for the regression (the standard error of the regression, *SER*, and the adjusted R^2, $\overline{R}^2$) and the sample size (which is the same for all of the regressions, 420 observations).

All the information that we have presented so far in equation format appears as a column of this table. For example, consider the regression of the test score

FIGURE 5.2 **Scatterplots of Test Scores vs. Three Student Characteristics**

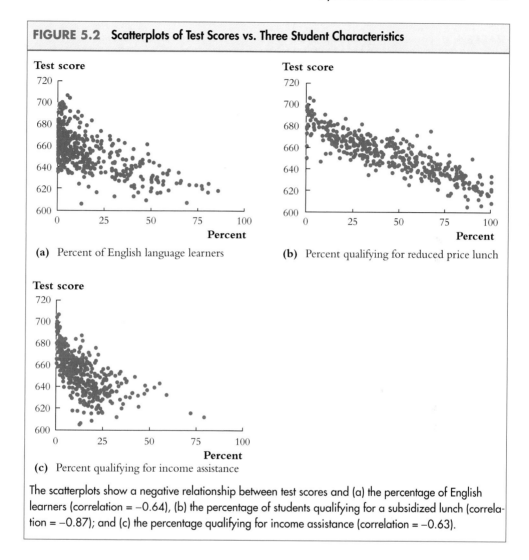

(a) Percent of English language learners

(b) Percent qualifying for reduced price lunch

(c) Percent qualifying for income assistance

The scatterplots show a negative relationship between test scores and (a) the percentage of English learners (correlation = −0.64), (b) the percentage of students qualifying for a subsidized lunch (correlation = −0.87); and (c) the percentage qualifying for income assistance (correlation = −0.63).

against the student-teacher ratio, with no control variables. In equation form, this regression is

$$\widehat{TestScore} = 698.9 - 2.28 \times STR, \ \overline{R}^2 = 0.049, \ SER = 19.26, \ n = 420. \quad (5.31)$$
$$\phantom{\widehat{TestScore} = }(10.4) \ (0.52)$$

All this information appears in column (1) of Table 5.2. The estimated coefficient on the student-teacher ratio (−2.28) appears in the first row of numerical entries, and its standard error (0.52) appears in parentheses just below the estimated coefficient. The intercept (698.9) and its standard error (10.4) are given in the row labeled

TABLE 5.2 Results of Regressions of Test Scores on the Student-Teacher Ratio and Student Characteristic Control Variables Using California Elementary School Districts

Dependent variable: Average test score in the district.

Regressor	(1)	(2)	(3)	(4)	(5)
Student-teacher ratio (X_1)	−2.28**	−1.10*	−1.00**	−1.31**	−1.01**
	(0.52)	(0.43)	(0.27)	(0.34)	(0.27)
Percent English learners (X_2)		−0.650**	−0.122**	−0.488**	−0.130**
		(0.031)	(0.033)	(0.030)	(0.036)
Percent eligible for subsidized lunch (X_3)			−0.547**		−0.529**
			(0.024)		(0.038)
Percent on public income assistance (X_4)				−0.790**	0.048
				(0.068)	(0.059)
Intercept	698.9**	686.0**	700.2**	698.0**	700.4**
	(10.4)	(8.7)	(5.6)	(6.9)	(5.5)
Summary Statistics					
SER	18.58	14.46	9.08	11.65	9.08
$\overline{R}^2$	0.049	0.424	0.773	0.626	0.773
n	420.0	420.0	420.0	420.0	420.0

These regressions were estimated using the data on K-8 school districts in California, described in Appendix 4.1. Standard errors are given in parentheses under coefficients. The individual coefficient is statistically significant at the *5% level or **1% significance level using a two-sided test.

"Intercept." (Sometimes you will see this row labeled "constant" because, as discussed in Section 5.2, the intercept can be viewed as the coefficient on a regressor that is always equal to one.) Similarly, the $\overline{R}^2$ (.049), the SER (18.58), and the sample size n (420) appear in the final rows. The blank entries in the rows of the other regressors indicate that those regressors are not included in this regression.

Although the table does not report t-statistics, these can be computed from the information provided; for example, the t-statistic testing the hypothesis that the coefficient on the student-teacher ratio in column (1) is zero is −2.28/0.52 = −4.38. This hypothesis is rejected at the 1% level, which is indicated by the double asterisk next to the estimated coefficient in the table.

Regressions that include the control variables measuring student characteristics are reported in columns (2)–(5). Column (2), which reports the regression of test scores on the student-teacher ratio and on the percentage of English learners, was previously stated as Equation (5.16).

Column (3) presents the base specification, in which the regressors are the student-teacher ratio and two control variables, the percentage of English learners and the percentage of students eligible for a free lunch.

Columns (4) and (5) present alternative specifications that examine the effect of changes in the way the economic background of the students is measured. In column (4), the percentage of students on public assistance is included as a regressor, and in column (5) both of the economic background variables are included.

These results suggest three conclusions:

1. Controlling for these student characteristics cuts the effect of the student-teacher ratio on test scores approximately in half. This estimated effect is not very sensitive to which specific control variables are included in the regression. In all cases the coefficient on the student-teacher ratio remains statistically significant at the 5% level. In the four specifications with control variables, regressions (2)–(5), reducing the student-teacher ratio by one student per teacher is estimated to increase average test scores by approximately one point, holding constant student characteristics.

2. The student characteristic variables are very useful predictors of test scores. The student-teacher ratio alone explains only a small fraction of the variation in test scores: the $\overline{R}^2$ in column (1) is 0.049. The $\overline{R}^2$ jumps, however, when the student characteristic variables are added. For example, the $\overline{R}^2$ in the base specification, regression (3), is 0.773. The sign of the coefficients on the student demographic variables is consistent with the patterns seen in Figure 5.2: districts with many English learners and districts with many poor children have lower test scores.

3. The control variables are not always individually statistically significant: in specification (5), the hypothesis that the coefficient on the percentage qualifying for income assistance is zero is not rejected at the 5% level (the t-statistic is −0.82). Because adding this control variable to the base specification (3) has a negligible effect on the estimated coefficient and its standard error, and because the coefficient on this control variable is not significant in specification (5), this additional control variable is redundant, at least for the purposes of this analysis.

5.13 Conclusion

This chapter began with a concern: in the regression of test scores against the student-teacher ratio, omitted student characteristics that influence test scores might be correlated with the student-teacher ratio in the district, and if so the student-teacher ratio in the district would pick up the effect on test scores of these omitted student characteristics. Thus, the OLS estimator would have omitted variable bias. To mitigate this potential omitted varible bias, we augmented the regression by including variables that control for various student characteristics (the percentage of English learners and two measures of student economic background). Doing so cuts the estimated effect of a unit change in the student-teacher ratio in half, although it remains possible to reject the null hypothesis that the population effect of test scores, holding these control variables constant, is zero at the 5% significance level. Because they eliminate omitted variable bias arising from these student characteristics, these multiple regression estimates (and the associated confidence intervals) are much more useful for advising the superintendent than the single-regressor estimates of Chapter 4.

The analysis in this chapter has presumed that the population regression function is linear in the regressors, that is, that the conditional expectation of Y_i given the regressors is a straight line. There is, however, no particular reason to think this is so. In fact, the effect of reducing the student-teacher ratio might be quite different in districts with large classes than in districts that already have small classes. If so, the population regression line is not linear in the X's but rather is a nonlinear function of the X's. To extend our analysis to regression functions that are nonlinear in the X's, however, we need the tools developed in the next chapter.

Summary

1. Omitted variable bias occurs when an omitted variable (1) is correlated with an included regressor and (2) is a determinant of Y.
2. The multiple regression model is a linear regression model that includes multiple regressors, $X_1, X_2, \ldots, X_k$. Associated with each regressor is a regression coefficient, $\beta_1, \beta_2, \ldots, \beta_k$. The coefficient β_1 is the expected change in Y associated with a one-unit change in X_1, holding the other regressors constant. The other regression coefficients have an analogous interpretation.
3. The coefficients in multiple regression can be estimated by OLS. When the four least squares assumptions in Key Concept 5.4 are satisfied, the OLS estimators are unbiased, consistent, and normally distributed in large samples.
4. Hypothesis tests and confidence intervals for a single regression coefficient are carried out using essentially the same procedures that were used in the one-variable linear regression model of Chapter 4. For example, a 95% confidence interval for β_1 is given by $\hat{\beta}_1 \pm 1.96 SE(\hat{\beta}_1)$.
5. Hypotheses involving more than one restriction on the coefficients are called joint hypotheses. Joint hypotheses can be tested using an F-statistic.
6. The standard error of the regression, the R^2, and the $\overline{R}^2$ are summary statistics for the multiple regression model.

Key Terms

omitted variable bias (144)

multiple regression model (149)

population regression line (150)

population regression function (150)

intercept (150)

coefficient on X_{1i} (150)

control variable (150)

partial effect (150)

population multiple regression

    model (151)

homoskedastic (152)

heteroskedastic (152)

OLS estimators of $\beta_0, \beta_1, \ldots, \beta_k$ (153)

OLS regression line (153)

predicted value (153)

OLS residual (153)

perfect multicollinearity (157)

imperfect multicollinearity (159)

restrictions (166)

joint hypothesis (166)

F-statistic (167)

95% confidence set (172)

R^2 and adjusted R^2 ($\overline{R}^2$) (174, 175)

base specification (178)

alternative specifications (178)

rule-of-thumb F-statistic (193)

Review the Concepts

5.1 A researcher is interested in the effect on test scores of computer usage. Using school district data like that used in this chapter, she regresses district average test scores on the number of computers per student. Will $\hat{\beta}_1$ be an unbiased estimator of the effect on test scores of increasing the number of computers per student? Why or why not? If you think $\hat{\beta}_1$ is biased, is it biased up or down? Why?

5.2 A multiple regression includes two regressors: $Y_i = \beta_0 + \beta_1 X_{1i} + \beta_2 X_{2i} + u_i$. What is the expected change in Y if X_1 increases by 3 units and X_2 is unchanged? What is the expected change in Y if X_2 decreases by 5 units and X_1 is unchanged? What is the expected change in Y if X_1 increases by 3 units and X_2 decreases by 5 units?

5.3 Explain why two perfectly multicollinear regressors cannot be included in a linear multiple regression. Give two examples of a pair of perfectly multi-collinear regressors.

5.4 Explain how you would test the null hypothesis that $\beta_1 = 0$ in the multiple regression model, $Y_i = \beta_0 + \beta_1 X_{1i} + \beta_2 X_{2i} + u_i$. Explain how you would test the null hypothesis that $\beta_2 = 0$. Explain how you would test the joint hypothesis that $\beta_1 = 0$ *and* $\beta_2 = 0$. Why isn't the result of the joint test implied by the results of the first two tests?

5.5 Provide an example of a regression that arguably would have a high value of R^2 but would produce biased and inconsistent estimators of the regression coefficient(s). Explain why the R^2 is likely to be high. Explain why the OLS estimators would be biased and inconsistent.

Exercises

The first seven exercises refer to the table of estimated regressions below, computed using data for 1998 from the CPS. The data set consists of information on 4,000 full-time full-year workers. The highest educational achievement for

Results of Regressions of Average Hourly Earnings on Gender and Education Binary Variables and other characteristics using 1998 data from the Current Population Survey

Dependent variable: Average Hourly Earnings (AHE).

Regressor	(1)	(2)	(3)
College (X_1)	5.46	5.48	5.44
	(0.21)	(0.21)	(0.21)
Female (X_2)	−2.64	−2.62	−2.62
	(0.20)	(0.20)	(0.20)
Age (X_3)		0.29	0.29
		(0.04)	(0.04)
Northeast (X_4)			0.69
			(0.30)
Midwest (X_5)			0.60
			(0.28)
South (X_6)			−0.27
			(0.26)
Intercept	12.69	4.40	3.75
	(0.14)	(1.05)	(1.06)
Summary Statistics and Joint Tests			
F-Statistic for regional effects = 0			6.10
SER	6.27	6.22	6.21
R^2	0.176	0.190	0.194
$\overline{R}^2$			
n	4000.0	4000.0	4000.0

each worker was either a high school diploma or a bachelor's degree. The worker's ages ranged from 25–34 years. The data set also contained information on the region of the country where the person lived, marital status, and number of children. For the purposes of this exercises let

AHE = average hourly earnings (in 1998 dollars)

$College$ = binary variable (1 if college, 0 if high school)

$Female$ = binary variable (1 if female, 0 if male)

Age = age (in years)

$Ntheast$ = binary variable (1 if Region = Northeast, 0 otherwise)

$Midwest$ = binary variable (1 if Region = Midwest, 0 otherwise)

$South$ = binary variable (1 if Region = South, 0 otherwise)

$West$ = binary variable (1 if Region = West, 0 otherwise)

5.1 Add "*" (5%) and "**" (1%) to the table to indicate statistical significance of the coefficients.

5.2 Compute $\overline{R}^2$ for each of the regressions.

5.3 Using the regression results in column (1):

*a. Do workers with college degrees earn more, on average, than workers with only high school degrees? How much more? Is the earnings difference estimated from this regression statistically significant at the 5% level?

b. Do men earn more than women on average? How much more? Is the earnings difference estimated from this regression statistically significant at the 5% level?

5.4 Using the regression results in column (2):

a. Is age an important determinant of earnings? Explain.

b. Sally is 29-year-old female college graduate. Betsy is a 34-year-old female college graduate. Predict Sally's and Betsy's earnings and construct a 95% confidence interval for the expected difference between their earnings.

5.5 Using the regression results in column (3):

*a. Do there appear to be important regional differences?

b. Why is the regressor *West* omitted from the regression? What would happen if it was included?

*c. Juanita is a 28-year-old female college graduate from the South. Molly is a 28-year-old female college graduate from the West. Jennifer is a 28-year-old female college graduate from the Midwest.

    ci. Construct a 95% confidence interval for the difference in expected earnings between Juanita and Molly.

    cii. Calculate the expected difference in earnings between Juanita and Jennifer.

    ciii. Explain how you would construct a 95% confidence interval for the difference in expected earnings between Juanita and Jennifer. (*Hint:* What would happen if you included *West* and excluded *Midwest* from the regression?)

5.6 The regression shown in column (2) was estimated again, this time using data from 1992. (4,000 observations selected at random from the March 1993 CPS, converted into 1998 dollars using the consumer price index.) The results are

$$\widehat{AHE} = 0.77 + 5.29College - 2.59Female + 0.40Age, \ SER = 5.85, \ \overline{R}^2 = 0.21$$
$$\quad\ \ (0.98) \ \ (0.20) \qquad\quad (0.18) \qquad\quad (0.03)$$

Comparing this regression to the regression for 1998 shown in column (2), was there a statistically significant change in the coefficient on *College*?

*5.7 Evaluate the following statement: "In all of the regressions, the coefficient on *Female* is negative, large, and statistically significant. This provides strong statistical evidence of gender discrimination in the U.S. labor market."

5.8 Consider the regression model $Y_i = \beta_0 + \beta_1 X_{1i} + \beta_2 X_{2i} + u_i$. Use "Approach #2" from Section 5.8 to transform the regression so that you can use a *t*-statistic to test

    a. $\beta_1 = \beta_2$;

    b. $\beta_1 + a\beta_2 = 0$, where *a* is a constant;

    c. $\beta_1 + \beta_2 = 1$. (*Hint:* You must redefine the dependent variable in the regression.)

5.9 Appendix 5.3 shows two formulas for the rule-of-thumb *F*-statistic, Equations (5.38) and (5.39). Show that the two formulas are equivalent.

Derivation of Equation (5.1)

This appendix presents a derivation of the formula for omitted variable bias in Equation (5.1). Equation (4.51) in Appendix 4.3 states that

$$\hat{\beta}_1 = \beta_1 + \frac{\frac{1}{n}\sum_{i=1}^{n}(X_i - \overline{X})u_i}{\frac{1}{n}\sum_{i=1}^{n}(X_i - \overline{X})^2}. \tag{5.32}$$

Under the least squares assumptions in Key Concept 5.4, $\frac{1}{n}\sum_{i=1}^{n}(X_i - \overline{X})^2 \xrightarrow{p} \sigma_X^2$ and $\frac{1}{n}\sum_{i=1}^{n}(X_i - \overline{X})u_i \xrightarrow{p} \text{cov}(u_i, X_i) = \rho_{Xu}\sigma_u\sigma_X$. Substitution of these limits into Equation (5.32) yields Equation(5.1).

Distribution of the OLS Estimators When There Are Two Regressors and Homoskedastic Errors

Although the general formula for the variance of the OLS estimators in multiple regression is complicated, if there are two regressors ($k = 2$) and the errors are homoskedastic then the formula simplifies enough to provide some insights into the distribution of the OLS estimators.

Because the errors are homoskedastic, the conditional variance of u_i can be written as $\text{var}(u_i | X_{1i}, X_{2i}) = \sigma_u^2$. When there are two regressors, X_{1i} and X_{2i}, and the error term is homoskedastic, in large samples the sampling distribution of $\hat{\beta}_1$ is $N(\beta_1, \sigma_{\hat{\beta}_1}^2)$, where the variance of this distribution, $\sigma_{\hat{\beta}_1}^2$, is

$$\sigma_{\hat{\beta}_1}^2 = \frac{1}{n}\left[\frac{1}{1 - \rho_{X_1, X_2}^2}\right]\frac{\sigma_u^2}{\sigma_{X_1}^2}, \tag{5.33}$$

where ρ_{X_1,X_2} is the population correlation between the two regressors X_1 and X_2 and $\sigma^2_{X_1}$ is the population variance of X_1.

The variance $\sigma^2_{\hat{\beta}_1}$ of the sampling distribution of $\hat{\beta}_1$ depends on the squared correlation between the regressors. If X_1 and X_2 are highly correlated, either positively or negatively, then $\rho^2_{X_1,X_2}$ is close to one, and thus the term $1 - \rho^2_{X_1,X_2}$ in the denominator of Equation (5.33) is small and the variances of $\hat{\beta}_1$ and $\hat{\beta}_2$ are larger than they would be if ρ_{X_1,X_2} were close to zero. This has an intuitive interpretation. Recall that the coefficient on X_1 is the effect of a unit change in the first regressor, holding the second constant. If the two regressors are highly correlated, then it is difficult to estimate the partial effect of the first regressor, holding the second constant, because the two regressors move together in the population.

For example, suppose we want to estimate the separate effects on test scores of having more teachers (lower STR), holding spending per pupil constant, and having more spending per pupil, holding STR constant. Because teacher salaries make up a very large share of the budget of an elementary school, STR and spending per pupil are strongly negatively correlated (more teachers means lower STR and more spending per pupil). Because these two variables are strongly negatively correlated, it could be difficult using a sample of data to estimate their separate effects precisely. This is reflected mathematically in a large variance of $\hat{\beta}_1$.

Another feature of the joint normal large-sample distribution of the OLS estimators is that $\hat{\beta}_1$ and $\hat{\beta}_2$ are in general correlated. When the errors are homoskedastic, the correlation between the OLS estimators $\hat{\beta}_1$ and $\hat{\beta}_2$ is the negative of the correlation between the two regressors:

$$\text{corr}(\hat{\beta}_1, \hat{\beta}_2) = -\rho_{X_1,X_2}. \tag{5.34}$$

APPENDIX

5.3 | Two Other Ways to Test Joint Hypotheses

The method of Section 5.7 is the preferred way to test joint hypotheses in multiple regression. However, if the author of a study presents regression results but did not test a joint restriction in which you are interested, and you do not have the original data, then you will not be able to compute the F-statistic of Section 5.7.

This appendix describes two other ways to test joint hypotheses that can be used when you only have a table of regression results. The first of these, the Bonferroni test, is an application of a very general testing approach based on Bonferroni's inequality. The second, a rule-of-thumb F-statistic, is a specialized approach for multiple regression that is theoretically justified only if the errors are homoskedastic; the rule-of-thumb F-statistic is the F-statistic counterpart of the t-statistic calculated using homoskedasticity-only standard errors.

The Bonferroni Test

The Bonferroni test is a test of a joint hypotheses based on the t-statistics for the individual hypotheses; that is, the Bonferroni test is the one-at-a-time t-statistic test of Section 5.7 done properly. The **Bonferroni test** of the joint null hypothesis $\beta_1 = \beta_{1,0}$ and $\beta_2 = \beta_{2,0}$ based on the critical value $c > 0$ uses the rule:

$$\text{Accept if } |t_1| \leq c \text{ and if } |t_2| \leq c; \text{ otherwise, reject} \tag{5.35}$$
$$\text{(Bonferroni one-at-a-time } t\text{-statistic test)},$$

where t_1 and t_2 are the t-statistics that respectively test the restrictions on β_1 and β_2.

The trick is to choose the critical value c in such a way that the probability that the one-at-a-time test rejects when the null hypothesis is true is no more than the desired significance level, say 5%. This is done by using Bonferroni's inequality to choose the critical value c to allow both for the fact that two restrictions are being tested and for any possible correlation between t_1 and t_2.

Bonferroni's Inequality

Bonferroni's inequality is a basic result of probability theory. Let A and B be events. Let $A \cap B$ be the event "both A and B" (the intersection of A and B), and let $A \cup B$ be the event "A or B or both" (the union of A and B). Then $\Pr(A \cup B) = \Pr(A) + \Pr(B) - \Pr(A \cap B)$. Because $\Pr(A \cap B) \geq 0$, it follows that $\Pr(A \cup B) \leq \Pr(A) + \Pr(B)$. This inequality in turn implies that $1 - \Pr(A \cup B) \geq 1 - [\Pr(A) + \Pr(B)]$. Let A^c and B^c be the complements of A and B, that is, the events "not A" and "not B." Because the complement of $A \cup B$ is $A^c \cap B^c$, $1 - \Pr(A \cup B) = \Pr(A^c \cap B^c)$, which yields Bonferroni's inequality, $\Pr(A^c \cap B^c) \geq 1 - [\Pr(A) + \Pr(B)]$.

Now let A be the event that $|t_1| > c$ and B be the event that $|t_2| > c$. Then the inequality $\Pr(A \cup B) \leq \Pr(A) + \Pr(B)$ yields

$$\Pr(|t_1| > c \text{ or } |t_2| > c \text{ or both}) \leq \Pr(|t_1| > c) + \Pr(|t_2| > c). \tag{5.36}$$

Bonferroni Tests

Because the event "$|t_1| > c$ or $|t_2| > c$ or both" is the rejection region of the one-at-a-time test, Equation (5.36) provides a way to choose the critical value c so that the "one at a time" t-statistic has the desired significance level in large samples. Under the null hypothesis in large samples, $\Pr(|t_1| > c) = \Pr(|t_2| > c) = \Pr(|Z| > c)$. Thus Equation (5.36) implies that, in large samples, the probability that the one-at-a-time test rejects under the null is

$$\Pr_{H_0}(\text{one-at-a-time test rejects}) \leq 2\Pr(|Z| > c). \tag{5.37}$$

The inequality in Equation (5.37) provides a way to choose critical value c so that the probability of rejection under the null hypothesis equals the desired significance level. The Bonferroni approach can be extended to more than two coefficients; if there are q restrictions under the null, the factor of 2 on the right hand side of in Equation (5.37) is replaced by q.

Table 5.3 presents critical values c for the one-at-a-time Bonferroni test for various significance levels and $q = 2, 3,$ and 4. For example, suppose the desired significance level is 5% and $q = 2$. According to Table 5.3, the critical value c is 2.241. This critical value is the 1.25% percentile of the standard normal distribution, so $\Pr(|Z| > 2.241) = 2.5\%$. Thus Equation (5.37) tells us that, in large samples, the one-at-a-time test in Equation (5.35) will reject at most 5% of the time under the null hypothesis.

The critical values in Table 5.3 are larger than the critical values for testing a single restriction. For example, with $q = 2$, the one-at-a-time test rejects if at least one t-statistic exceeds 2.241 in absolute value. This critical value is greater than 1.96 because it properly corrects for the fact that, by looking at two t-statistics, you get a second chance to reject the joint null hypothesis, as discussed in Section 5.7.

If the individual t-statistics are based on heteroskedasticity-robust standard errors, then the Bonferroni test is valid whether or not there is heteroskedasticity, but if the

TABLE 5.3	Bonferroni Critical Values c for the One-at-a-time t-Statistic Test of a Joint Hypothesis		
	Significance Level		
Number of restrictions (q)	**10%**	**5%**	**1%**
2	1.960	2.241	2.807
3	2.128	2.394	2.935
4	2.241	2.498	3.023

t-statistics are based on homoskedasticity-only standard errors, the Bonferroni test is valid only under homoskedasticity.

Application to Test Scores

The *t*-statistics testing the joint null hypothesis that the true coefficients on test scores and expenditures per pupil in Equation (5.18) are, respectively, $t_1 = -0.60$ and $t_2 = 2.43$. Although $|t_1| < 2.241$, because $|t_2| > 2.241$, we can reject the joint null hypothesis at the 5% significance level using the Bonferroni test. However, both t_1 and t_2 are less than 2.807 in absolute value, so we cannot reject the joint null hypothesis at the 1% significance level using the Bonferroni test. In contrast, using the *F*-statistic in Section 5.7, we were able to reject this hypothesis at the 1% significance level.

The Rule-of-Thumb *F*-Statistic

The rule-of-thumb *F*-statistic is computed using a simple formula based on the sum of squared residuals from two regressions. In the first regression, called the **restricted regression**, the null hypothesis is forced to be true. When the null hypothesis is of the type in Equation (5.20) where all the hypothesized values are zero, the restricted regression is the regression in which those coefficients are set to zero, that is, the relevant regressors are excluded from the regression. In the second regression, called the **unrestricted regression**, the alternative hypothesis is allowed to be true. If the sum of squared residuals is sufficiently smaller in the unrestricted than the restricted regression, then the test rejects the null hypothesis.

The **rule-of-thumb *F*-statistic** is given by the formula

$$F = \frac{(SSR_{restricted} - SSR_{unrestricted})/q}{SSR_{unrestricted}/(n - k_{unrestricted} - 1)}, \tag{5.38}$$

where $SSR_{restricted}$ is the sum of squared residuals from the restricted regression, $SSR_{unrestricted}$ is the sum of squared residuals from the unrestricted regression, q is the number of restrictions under the null hypothesis, and $k_{unrestricted}$ is the number of regressors in the unrestricted regression. An alternative equivalent formula for the rule-of-thumb *F*-statistic is based on the R^2 of the two regressions:

$$F = \frac{(R^2_{unrestricted} - R^2_{restricted})/q}{(1 - R^2_{unrestricted})/(n - k_{unrestricted} - 1)}. \tag{5.39}$$

If the errors are homoskedastic, then the difference between the rule-of-thumb *F*-statistic computed using Equation (5.38) and the *F*-statistic used in Section 5.7 vanishes as the sample size n increases. Thus, if the errors are homoskedastic, the sampling distribution of the rule-of-thumb F-statistic under the null hypothesis is, in large samples, $F_{q,\infty}$.

These rule-of-thumb formulas are easy to compute and have an intuitive interpretation in terms of how well the unrestricted and restricted regressions fit the data. Unfortunately, they are valid only if the errors are homoskedastic. Because homoskedasticity is a special case that cannot be counted on in applications with economic data, or more generally with data sets typically found in the social sciences, the rule-of-thumb F-statistic is not a satisfactory substitute for the heteroskedasticity-robust F-statistic of Section 5.7.

Application to Test Scores and the Student-Teacher Ratio

To test the null hypothesis that the population coefficients on STR and $Expn$ are 0, controlling for $PctEL$, we need to compute the SSR (or R^2) for the restricted and unrestricted regression. The unrestricted regression has the regressors STR, $Expn$, and $PctEL$, and is given in Equation (5.18); its R^2 is .4366; that is, $R^2_{unrestricted} = .4366$. The restricted regression imposes the joint null hypothesis that the true coefficients on STR and $Expn$ are zero; that is, under the null hypothesis STR and $Expn$ do not enter the population regression, although $PctEL$ does (the null hypothesis does not restrict the coefficient on $PctEL$). The restricted regression, estimated by OLS, is

$$\widehat{TestScore} = 664.7 - 0.671 \times PctEL, \ R^2 = 0.4149. \tag{5.40}$$
$$\phantom{\widehat{TestScore} = 66}(1.0) \ \ (0.032)$$

so $R^2_{restricted} = .4149$. The number of restrictions is $q = 2$, the number of observations is $n = 420$, and the number of regressors in the unrestricted regression is $k = 3$. The rule-of-thumb F-statistic, computed using Equation (5.39), is

$$F = [(0.4366 - 0.4149)/2]/[(1 - 0.4366)/(420 - 3 - 1)] = 8.01.$$

Because 8.01 exceeds the 1% critical value of 4.61, the hypothesis is rejected at the 1% level using this rule-of-thumb approach.

This example illustrates the advantages and disadvantages of the rule-of-thumb F-statistic. Its advantage is that it can be computed using a calculator. Its disadvantage is that the value of the rule-of-thumb F-statistic can be very different than the heteroskedasticity-robust F-statistic used in Section 5.7: the heteroskedasticity-robust F-statistic testing this joint hypothesis is 5.43, quite different than the less reliable homoskedasticity-only rule-of-thumb value of 8.01.

CHAPTER 6

Nonlinear Regression Functions

In Chapters 4 and 5, the population regression function was assumed to be linear. In other words, the slope of the population regression function was constant, so that the effect on Y of a unit change in X does not itself depend on the value of X. But what if the effect on Y of a change in X does depend on the value of one or more of the independent variables? If so, the population regression function is nonlinear.

This chapter develops two groups of methods for detecting and modeling nonlinear population regression functions. The methods in the first group are useful when the effect on Y of a change in one independent variable, X_1, depends on the value of X_1 itself. For example, reducing class sizes by one student per teacher might have a greater effect if class sizes are already manageably small than if they are so large that the teacher can do little more than keep the class under control. If so, the test score (Y) is a nonlinear function of the student-teacher ratio (X_1), where this function is steeper when X_1 is small. An example of a nonlinear regression function with this feature is shown in Figure 6.1. Whereas the linear population regression function in Figure 6.1a has a constant slope, the nonlinear population regression function in Figure 6.1b has a steeper slope when X_1 is small than when it is large. This first group of methods is presented in Section 6.2.

The methods in the second group are useful when the effect on Y of a change in X_1 depends on the value of another independent variable, say X_2. For example, students still learning English might especially benefit from having more one-on-one attention; if so, the effect on test scores of reducing the student-teacher ratio will be greater in districts with many students still learning English than in districts with few English learners. In this example, the effect

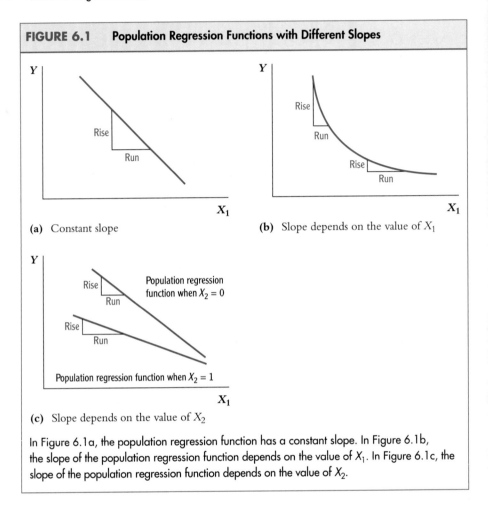

FIGURE 6.1   Population Regression Functions with Different Slopes

(a) Constant slope

(b) Slope depends on the value of X_1

(c) Slope depends on the value of X_2

Population regression function when $X_2 = 0$

Population regression function when $X_2 = 1$

In Figure 6.1a, the population regression function has a constant slope. In Figure 6.1b, the slope of the population regression function depends on the value of X_1. In Figure 6.1c, the slope of the population regression function depends on the value of X_2.

on test scores (Y) of a reduction in the student–teacher ratio (X_1) depends on the percentage of English learners in the district (X_2). As shown in Figure 6.1c, the slope of this type of population regression function depends on the value of X_2. This second group of methods is presented in Section 6.3.

In the models of this chapter, the population regression function is a nonlinear function of the independent variables, that is, the conditional expectation $E(Y_i \mid X_{1i}, \ldots, X_{ki})$ is a nonlinear function of one or more of the X's. Although they are nonlinear in the X's, these models are linear functions of the unknown coefficients (or parameters) of the population regression model and thus are versions of the multiple regression model of Chapter 5. Therefore, the unknown coefficients of these nonlinear regression functions can be estimated and tested using OLS and the methods of Chapter 5.

Sections 6.1 and 6.2 introduce nonlinear regression functions in the context of regression with a single independent variable, and Section 6.3 extends this to two independent variables. To keep things simple, additional control variables are omitted in the empirical examples of Sections 6.1–6.3. In practice, however, it is important to analyze nonlinear regression functions in models that control for omitted variable bias by including control variables as well. In Section 6.4, we combine nonlinear regression functions and additional control variables when we take a close look at possible nonlinearities in the relationship between test scores and the student-teacher ratio, holding student characteristics constant.

6.1   A General Strategy for Modeling Nonlinear Regression Functions

This section lays out a general strategy for modeling nonlinear population regression functions. In this strategy, the nonlinear models are extensions of the multiple regression model and therefore can be estimated and tested using the tools of Chapter 5. First, however, we return to the California test score data and consider the relationship between test scores and district income.

Test Scores and District Income

In Chapter 5, we found that the economic background of the students is an important factor in explaining performance on standardized tests. That analysis used two economic background variables (the percentage of students qualifying for a subsidized lunch and the percentage of district families qualifying for income assistance) to measure the fraction of students in the district coming from poor families. A different, broader measure of economic background is the average annual per capita income in the school district ("district income"). The California data set includes district income measured in thousands of 1998 dollars. The sample contains a wide range of income levels: for the 420 districts in our sample, the median district income is 13.7 (that is, $13,700 per person), and it ranges from 5.3 ($5,300 per person) to 55.3 ($55,300 per person).

Figure 6.2 shows a scatterplot of fifth-grade test scores against district income for the California data set, along with the OLS regression line relating these two variables. Test scores and average income are strongly positively correlated, with a correlation coefficient of 0.71; students from affluent districts do better on the tests than students from poor districts. But this scatterplot has a peculiarity: most of the points are below the OLS line when income is very low (under $10,000) or very high (over $40,000), but are above the line when income is between $15,000 and $30,000. There seems to be some curvature in the relationship between test scores and income that is not captured by the linear regression.

In short, it seems that the relationship between district income and test scores is not a straight line. Rather, it is nonlinear. A nonlinear function is a function with a slope that is not constant: the function $f(X)$ is linear if the slope of $f(X)$ is the same for all values of X, but if the slope depends on the value of X, then $f(X)$ is nonlinear.

If a straight line is not an adequate description of the relationship between district income and test scores, what is? Imagine drawing a curve that fits the points in Figure 6.2. This curve would be steep for low values of district income, then would flatten out as district income gets higher. One way to approximate such a curve mathematically is to model the relationship as a quadratic function. That is, we could model test scores as a function of income *and* the square of income.

A quadratic population regression model relating test scores and income is written mathematically as

$$TestScore_i = \beta_0 + \beta_1 Income_i + \beta_2\, Income_i^2 + u_i, \tag{6.1}$$

where β_0, β_1, and β_2 are coefficients, $Income_i$ is the income in the ith district, $Income_i^2$, is the square of income in the ith district, and u_i is an error term that, as usual, represents all the other factors that determine test scores. Equation (6.1) is called the **quadratic regression model** because the population regression function, $E(TestScore_i \mid Income_i) = \beta_0 + \beta_1 Income_i + \beta_2 Income_i^2$, is a quadratic function of the independent variable, *Income*.

If you knew the population coefficients β_0, β_1, and β_2 in Equation (6.1), you could predict the test score of a district based on its average income. But these population coefficients are unknown and therefore must be estimated using a sample of data.

At first, it might seem difficult to find the coefficients of the quadratic function that best fits the data in Figure 6.2. If you compare Equation (6.1) with the

---

FIGURE 6.2   Scatterplot of Test Score vs. District Income with a Linear OLS Regression Function

There is a positive correlation between test scores and district income (correlation = 0.71), but the linear OLS regression line does not adequately describe the relationship between these variables.

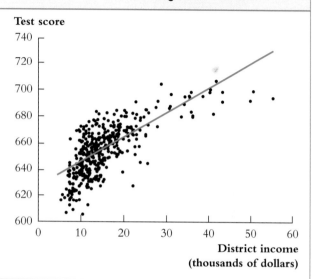

multiple regression model in Key Concept 5.2, however, you will see that Equation (6.1) is in fact a version of the multiple regression model with two regressors: the first regressor is *Income*, and the second regressor is $Income^2$. Thus, after defining the regressors as *Income* and $Income^2$, the nonlinear model in Equation (6.1) is simply a multiple regression model with two regressors!

Because the quadratic regression model is a variant of multiple regression, its unknown population coefficients can be estimated and tested using the OLS methods described in Chapter 5. Estimating the coefficients of Equation (6.1) using OLS for the 420 observations in Figure 6.2 yields

$$\widehat{TestScore} = 607.3 + 3.85 Income - 0.0423 Income^2, \ \overline{R}^2 = 0.554, \quad (6.2)$$
$$\qquad\qquad (2.9) \ \ (0.27) \qquad\quad (0.0048)$$

where (as usual) standard errors of the estimated coefficients are given in parentheses. The estimated regression function (6.2) is plotted in Figure 6.3, superimposed over the scatterplot of the data. The quadratic function captures the curvature in the scatterplot: it is steep for low values of district income but flattens out when district income is high. In short, the quadratic regression function seems to fit the data better than the linear one.

We can go one step beyond this visual comparison and formally test the hypothesis that the relationship between income and test scores is linear, against

FIGURE 6.3   **Scatterplot of Test Score vs. District Income with Linear and Quadratic Regression Functions**

The quadratic OLS regression function fits the data better than the linear OLS regression function.

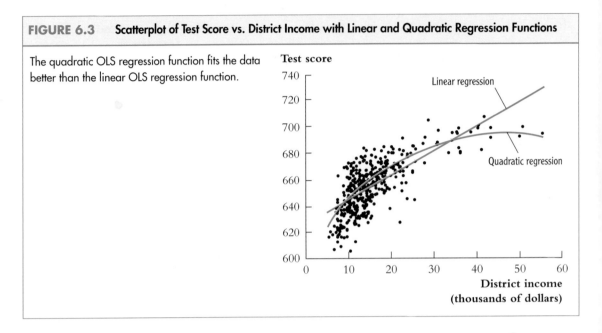

the alternative that it is nonlinear. If the relationship is linear, then the regression function is correctly specified as Equation (6.1), except that the regressor $Income^2$ is absent; that is, if the relationship is linear, then Equation (6.1) holds with $\beta_2 = 0$. Thus, we can test the null hypothesis that the population regression function is linear against the alternative that it is quadratic by testing the null hypothesis that $\beta_2 = 0$ against the alternative that $\beta_2 \neq 0$.

Because Equation (6.1) is just a variant of the multiple regression model, the null hypothesis that $\beta_2 = 0$ can be tested by constructing the t-statistic for this hypothesis. This t-statistic is $t = (\hat{\beta}_2 - 0)/SE(\hat{\beta}_2)$, which from Equation (6.2) is $t = -0.0423/0.0048 = -8.81$. In absolute value, this exceeds the 5% critical value of this test (which is 1.96). Indeed the p-value for the t-statistic is less than .01%, so we can reject the hypothesis that $\beta_2 = 0$ at all conventional significance levels. Thus this formal hypothesis test supports our informal inspection of Figures 6.2 and 6.3: the quadratic model fits the data better than the linear model.

The Effect on Y of a Change in X in Nonlinear Specifications

Put aside the test score example for a moment and consider a general problem. You want to know how the dependent variable Y is expected to change when the independent variable X_1 changes by the amount ΔX_1, holding constant other independent variables $X_2, \ldots, X_k$. When the population regression function is linear, this effect is easy to calculate: as shown in Equation (5.4), the expected change in Y is $\Delta Y = \beta_1 \Delta X_1$, where β_1 is the population regression coefficient multiplying X_1. When the regression function is nonlinear, however, the expected change in Y is more complicated to calculate because it can depend on the values of the independent variables.

A general formula for a nonlinear population regression function.[1]   The nonlinear population regression models considered in this chapter are of the form

$$Y_i = f(X_{1i}, X_{2i}, \ldots, X_{ki}) + u_i, \, i = 1, \ldots, n, \tag{6.3}$$

where $f(X_{1i}, X_{2i}, \ldots, X_{ki})$ is the population **nonlinear regression function**, a possibly nonlinear function of the independent variables $X_{1i}, X_{2i}, \ldots, X_{ki}$, and u_i is the error term. For example, in the quadratic regression model in Equation (6.1), only one independent variable is present, so X_1 is *Income* and the population regression function is $f(Income_i) = \beta_0 + \beta_1 Income_i + \beta_2 Income_i^2$.

Because the population regression function is the conditional expectation of Y_i given $X_{1i}, X_{2i}, \ldots, X_{ki}$, in Equation (6.3) we allow for the possibility that this conditional expectation is a nonlinear function of $X_{1i}, X_{2i}, \ldots, X_{ki}$, that is, $E(Y_i \mid X_{1i}, X_{2i}, \ldots, X_{ki}) = f(X_{1i}, X_{2i}, \ldots, X_{ki})$, where f can be a nonlinear function. If the population regression function is linear, then $f(X_{1i}, X_{2i}, \ldots, X_{ki}) = \beta_0 + \beta_1 X_{1i} + \beta_2 X_{2i} + \cdots + \beta_k X_{ki}$, and Equation (6.3) becomes the linear regression model in Key Concept 5.2. However, Equation (6.3) allows for nonlinear regression functions as well.

The effect on Y of a change in X_1.   As discussed in Section 5.2, the effect on Y of a change in X_1, ΔX_1, holding $X_2, \ldots, X_k$ constant, is the difference in the expected value of Y when the independent variables take on the values $X_1 + \Delta X_1, X_2, \ldots, X_k$ and the expected value of Y when the independent variables take on the values $X_1, X_2, \ldots, X_k$. The difference between these two expected values, say ΔY, is what happens to Y on average in the population when X_1 changes by an amount ΔX_1, holding constant the other variables

---

[1]The term "nonlinear regression" applies to two conceptually different families of models. In the first family, the population regression function is a nonlinear function of the X's but is a linear function of the unknown parameters (the β's). In the second family, the population regression function is a nonlinear function of the unknown parameters and may or may not be a nonlinear function of the X's. The models in this chapter are all in the first family. We encounter models from the second family when we take up regression with a binary dependent variable in Chapter 9.

$X_2, \ldots, X_k$. In the nonlinear regression model of Equation (6.3), this effect on Y is $\Delta Y = f(X_1 + \Delta X_1, X_2, \ldots, X_k) - f(X_1, X_2, \ldots, X_k)$.

Because the regression function f is unknown, the population effect on Y of a change in X_1 is also unknown. To estimate the population effect, first estimate the population regression function. At a general level, denote this estimated function by $\hat{f}$; an example of such an estimated function is the estimated quadratic regression function in Equation (6.2). The estimated effect on Y (denoted $\Delta \hat{Y}$) of the change in X_1 is the difference between the predicted value of Y when the independent variables take on the values $X_1 + \Delta X_1, X_2, \ldots, X_k$ and the predicted value of Y when they take on the values $X_1, X_2, \ldots, X_k$.

The method for calculating the expected effect on Y of a change in X_1 is summarized in Key Concept 6.1.

Application to test scores and income.   What is the predicted change in test scores associated with a change in district income of $1,000, based on the estimated quadratic regression function in Equation (6.2)? Because that regression function is quadratic, this effect depends on the initial district income. We therefore consider two cases: an increase in district income from 10 to 11 (i.e., from $10,000 per capita to $11,000) and an increase in district income from 40 to 41.

To compute $\Delta \hat{Y}$ associated with the change in income from 10 to 11, we can apply the general formula in Equation (6.6) to the quadratic regression model. Doing so yields

$$\Delta \hat{Y} = (\hat{\beta}_0 + \hat{\beta}_1 \times 11 + \hat{\beta}_2 \times 11^2) - (\hat{\beta}_0 + \hat{\beta}_1 \times 10 + \hat{\beta}_2 \times 10^2), \qquad (6.4)$$

where $\hat{\beta}_0$, $\hat{\beta}_1$, and $\hat{\beta}_2$ are the OLS estimators.

The term in the first set of parentheses in Equation (6.4) is the predicted value of Y when $Income = 11$, and the term in the second set of parentheses is the predicted value of Y when $Income = 10$. These predicted values are calculated using the OLS estimates of the coefficients in Equation (6.2). Accordingly, when $Income = 10$, the predicted value of test scores is $607.3 + 3.85 \times 10 - 0.0423 \times 10^2 = 641.57$. When $Income = 11$, the predicted value is $607.3 + 3.85 \times 11 - 0.0423 \times 11^2 = 644.53$. The difference in these two predicted values is $\Delta \hat{Y} = 644.53 - 641.57 = 2.96$ points, that is, the predicted difference in test scores between a district with average income of $11,000 and one with average income of $10,000 is 2.96 points. In the second case, when income changes from $40,000 to $41,000, the difference in the predicted values in Equation (6.4) is $\Delta \hat{Y} = (607.3 + 3.85 \times 41 -$

> ## The Expected Effect on Y of a Change in X_1 in the Nonlinear Regression Model (6.3)
>
> The expected change in Y, ΔY, associated with the change in X_1, ΔX_1, holding $X_2, \ldots, X_k$ constant, is the difference between the value of the population regression function before and after changing X_1, holding $X_2, \ldots, X_k$ constant. That is, the expected change in Y is the difference:
>
> $$\Delta Y = f(X_1 + \Delta X_1, X_2, \ldots, X_k) - f(X_1, X_2, \ldots, X_k). \qquad (6.5)$$
>
> The estimator of this unknown population difference is the difference between the predicted values for these two cases. Let $\hat{f}(X_1, X_2, \ldots, X_k)$ be the predicted value of Y based on the estimator $\hat{f}$ of the population regression function. Then the predicted change in Y is
>
> $$\Delta \hat{Y} = \hat{f}(X_1 + \Delta X_1, X_2, \ldots, X_k) - \hat{f}(X_1, X_2, \ldots, X_k). \qquad (6.6)$$

Key Concept 6.1

$0.0423 \times 41^2) - (607.3 + 3.85 \times 40 - 0.0423 \times 40^2) = 694.04 - 693.62 = 0.42$ points. Thus, a change of income of \$1,000 is associated with a larger change in predicted test scores if the initial income is \$10,000 than if it is \$40,000 (the predicted changes are 2.96 points versus 0.42 points). Said differently, the slope of the estimated quadratic regression function in Figure 6.3 is steeper at low values of income (like \$10,000) than at the higher values of income (like \$40,000).

Standard errors of estimated effects. The estimator of the effect on Y of changing X_1 depends on the estimator of the population regression function, $\hat{f}$, which varies from one sample to the next. Therefore the estimated effect contains sampling error. One way to quantify the sampling uncertainty associated with the estimated effect is to compute a confidence interval for the true population effect. To do so, we need to compute the standard error of $\Delta \hat{Y}$ in Equation (6.6).

It is easy to compute a standard error for $\Delta \hat{Y}$ when the regression function is linear. The estimated effect of a change in X_1 is $\hat{\beta}_1 \Delta X_1$, so a 95% confidence interval for the estimated change is $\hat{\beta}_1 \Delta X_1 \pm 1.96 SE(\hat{\beta}_1) \Delta X_1$.

In the nonlinear regression models of this chapter, the standard error of $\Delta \hat{Y}$ can be computed using the tools introduced in Section 5.8 for testing a single restriction involving multiple coefficients. To illustrate this method, consider the estimated change in test scores associated with a change in income from 10 to 11 in Equation (6.4), which is $\Delta\hat{Y} = \hat{\beta}_1 \times (11 - 10) + \hat{\beta}_2 \times (11^2 - 10^2) = \hat{\beta}_1 + 21\hat{\beta}_2$. The standard error of the predicted change therefore is

$$SE(\Delta\hat{Y}) = SE(\hat{\beta}_1 + 21\hat{\beta}_2). \tag{6.7}$$

Thus, if we can compute the standard error of $\hat{\beta}_1 + 21\hat{\beta}_2$, then we have computed the standard error of $\Delta\hat{Y}$. There are two methods for doing this using standard regression software, which correspond to the two approaches in Section 5.8 for testing a single restriction on multiple coefficients.[2]

The first method is to use "approach #1" of Section 5.8, which is to compute the F-statistic testing the hypothesis that $\beta_1 + 21\beta_2 = 0$. The standard error of $\Delta\hat{Y}$ is then given by[3]

$$SE(\Delta\hat{Y}) = \frac{|\Delta\hat{Y}|}{\sqrt{F}}. \tag{6.8}$$

When applied to the quadratic regression in Equation (6.2), the F-statistic testing the hypothesis that $\beta_1 + 21\beta_2 = 0$ is $F = 299.94$. Because $\Delta\hat{Y} = 2.96$, applying Equation (6.8) gives $SE(\Delta\hat{Y}) = 2.96/\sqrt{299.94} = 0.17$. Thus a 95% confidence interval for the change in the expected value of Y is $2.96 \pm 1.96 \times 0.17$ or $(2.63, 3.29)$.

The second method is to use "approach #2" of Section 5.8, which entails transforming the regressors so that, in the transformed regression, one of the coefficients is $\beta_1 + 21\beta_2$. Doing this transformation is left as an exercise (Exercise 6.4).

A comment on interpreting coefficients in nonlinear specifications. In the multiple regression model of Chapter 5, the regression coefficients had a natural interpretation. For example, β_1 is the expected change in Y associated with a change in X_1, holding the other regressors constant. But, as we have seen, this is not generally the case in a nonlinear model. That is, it is not very helpful to think of β_1 in Equation (6.1) as being the effect of changing the district's income, holding the square of the district's income constant. This means that in nonlinear models, the regression function is best interpreted by graphing it and by calculating the predicted effect on Y of changing one or more of the independent variables.

---

[2]These two approaches are different ways to use regression software to implement the general formulas for the standard errors of predicted effects presented in Section 16.2.

[3]Equation (6.8) is derived by noting that the F-statistic is the square of the t-statistic testing this hypothesis, that is, $F = t^2 = [(\hat{\beta}_1 + 21\hat{\beta}_2)/SE(\hat{\beta}_1 + 21\hat{\beta}_2)]^2 = [\Delta\hat{Y}/SE(\Delta\hat{Y})]^2$, and solving for $SE(\Delta\hat{Y})$.

A General Approach to Modeling Nonlinearities Using Multiple Regression

The general approach to modeling nonlinear regression functions taken in this chapter has five elements:

1. *Identify a possible nonlinear relationship.* The best thing to do is to use economic theory and what you know about the application to suggest a possible nonlinear relationship. Before you even look at the data, ask yourself whether the slope of the regression function relating Y and X might reasonably depend on the value of X or on another independent variable. Why might such nonlinear dependence exist? What nonlinear shapes does this suggest? For example, thinking about classroom dynamics with 11-year-olds suggests that cutting class size from 18 students to 17 could have a greater effect than cutting it from 30 to 29.

2. *Specify a nonlinear function and estimate its parameters by OLS.* Sections 6.2 and 6.3 contain various nonlinear regression functions that can be estimated by OLS. After working through these sections you will understand the characteristics of each of these functions.

3. *Determine whether the nonlinear model improves upon a linear model.* Just because you think a regression function is nonlinear does not mean it really is! You must determine empirically whether your nonlinear model is appropriate. Most of the time you can use t-statistics and F-statistics to test the null hypothesis that the population regression function is linear against the alternative that it is nonlinear.

4. *Plot the estimated nonlinear regression function.* Does the estimated regression function describe the data well? Looking at Figures 6.2 and 6.3 suggested that the quadratic model fit the data better than the linear model.

5. *Estimate the effect on Y of a change in X.* The final step is to use the estimated regression to calculate the effect on Y of a change in one or more regressors X using the method in Key Concept 6.1.

6.2 Nonlinear Functions of a Single Independent Variable

This section provides two methods for modeling a nonlinear regression function. To keep things simple, we develop these methods for a nonlinear regression function that involves only one independent variable, X. As we see in Section 6.4, however, these models can be modified to include multiple independent variables.

The first method discussed in this section is polynomial regression, an extension of the quadratic regression used in the last section to model the relationship between test scores and income. The second method uses logarithms of X and/or Y. Although these methods are presented separately, they can be used in combination.

Polynomials

One way to specify a nonlinear regression function is to use a polynomial in X. In general, let r denote the highest power of X that is included in the regression. The **polynomial regression model** of degree r is

$$Y_i = \beta_0 + \beta_1 X_i + \beta_2 X_i^2 + \cdots + \beta_r X_i^r + u_i. \tag{6.9}$$

When $r = 2$, Equation (6.9) is the quadratic regression model discussed in Section 6.1. When $r = 3$, so that the highest power of X included is X^3, Equation (6.9) is called the **cubic regression model**.

The polynomial regression model is similar to the multiple regression model of Chapter 5, except that in Chapter 5 the regressors were distinct independent variables whereas here the regressors are powers of the same dependent variable, X, that is, the regressors are X, X^2, X^3, etc. Thus the techniques for estimation and inference developed for multiple regression can be applied here. In particular, the unknown coefficients $\beta_0, \beta_1, \ldots, \beta_r$ in Equation (6.9) can be estimated by OLS regression of Y_i against $X_i, X_i^2, \ldots, X_i^r$.

Testing the null hypothesis that the population regression function is linear. If the population regression function is linear, then the quadratic and higher order terms do not enter the population regression function. Accordingly, the null hypothesis (H_0) that the regression is linear and the alternative (H_1) that it is a polynomial of degree r correspond to

$$H_0: \beta_2 = 0, \beta_3 = 0, \ldots, \beta_r = 0 \text{ vs. } H_1: \text{at least one } \beta_j \neq 0, j = 2, \ldots, r. \tag{6.10}$$

The null hypothesis that the population regression function is linear can be tested against the alternative that it is a polynomial of degree r by testing H_0 against H_1 in Equation (6.10). Because H_0 is a joint null hypothesis with $q = r - 1$ restrictions on the coefficients of the population polynomial regression model, it can be tested using the *F*-statistic as described in Section 5.7.

What degree polynomial should I use? That is, how many powers of *X* should be included in a polynomial regression? The answer balances a trade-off between flexibility and statistical precision. Increasing the degree *r* introduces more flexibility into the regression function and allows it to match more shapes; a polynomial of degree *r* can have up to *r* − 1 bends (that is, inflection points) in its graph. But increasing *r* means adding more regressors, which can reduce the precision of the estimated coefficients.

Thus the answer to the question of how many terms to include is that you should include enough to model the nonlinear regression function adequately, but no more. Unfortunately, this answer is not very useful in practice!

A practical way to determine the degree of the polynomial is to ask whether the coefficients in Equation (6.9) associated with largest values of *r* are zero. If so, then these terms can be dropped from the regression. This procedure, which is called sequential hypothesis testing because individual hypotheses are tested sequentially, is summarized in the following steps:

1. Pick a maximum value of *r* and estimate the polynomial regression for that *r*.

2. Use the *t*-statistic to test the hypothesis that the coefficient on X^r (β_r in Equation (6.9)) is zero. If you reject this hypothesis, then X^r belongs in the regression, so use the polynomial of degree *r*.

3. If you do not reject $\beta_r = 0$ in step 2, eliminate X^r from the regression and estimate a polynomial regression of degree *r* − 1. Test whether the coefficient on X^{r-1} is zero. If you reject, use the polynomial of degree *r* − 1.

4. If you do not reject $\beta_{r-1} = 0$ in step 3, continue this procedure until the coefficient on the highest power in your polynomial is statistically significant.

This recipe has one missing ingredient: the initial degree *r* of the polynomial. In many applications involving economic data, the nonlinear functions are smooth, that is, they do not have sharp jumps or "spikes." If so, then it is appropriate to choose a small maximum order for the polynomial, such as 2, 3, or 4, that is, begin with *r* = 2 or 3 or 4 in step 1.[4]

---

[4] A different way to choose *r* is to use an "information criterion," which is described in Chapter 12 in the context of time series analysis. In practice, the information criterion approach and the sequential hypothesis testing approach described here often yield similar results.

Application to district income and test scores. The estimated cubic regression function relating district income to test scores is

$$\widehat{TestScore} = 600.1 + 5.02 Income - 0.096 Income^2 + 0.00069 Income^3,$$
$$\quad\quad\quad (5.1) \quad (0.71) \quad\quad (0.029) \quad\quad\quad (0.00035) \quad\quad\quad (6.11)$$

$$\bar{R}^2 = 0.555.$$

The t-statistic on $Income^3$ is 1.97, so the null hypothesis that the regression function is a quadratic is rejected against the alternative that it is a cubic at the 5% level. Moreover, the F-statistic testing the joint null hypothesis that the coefficients on $Income^2$ and $Income^3$ are both zero is 37.7, with a p-value less than 0.01%, so the null hypothesis that the regression function is linear is rejected against the alternative that it is a cubic.

Interpretation of coefficients in polynomial regression models. The coefficients in polynomial regressions do not have a simple interpretation. The best way to interpret polynomial regressions is to plot the estimated regression function and to calculate the estimated effect on Y associated with a change in X for one or more values of X.

Logarithms

Another way to specify a nonlinear regression function is to use the natural logarithm of Y and/or X. Logarithms convert changes in variables into percentage changes, and many relationships are naturally expressed in terms of percentages. Here are some examples:

- Section 3.5 examined the wage gap between male and female college graduates. In that discussion, the wage gap was measured in terms of dollars. However, it is easier to compare wage gaps across professions and over time when they are expressed in percentage terms.

- In Section 6.1, we found that district income and test scores were nonlinearly related. Would this relationship be linear using percentage changes? That is, might it be that a change in district income of 1%—rather than $1,000—is associated with a change in test scores that is approximately constant for different values of income?

- In the economic analysis of consumer demand, it is often assumed that a 1% increase in price leads to a certain *percentage* decrease in the quantity demanded. The percentage change in demand resulting from a 1% increase in price is called the price **elasticity**.

Regression specifications that use natural logarithms allow regression models to estimate percentage relationships such as these. Before introducing those specifications, we review the exponential and natural logarithm functions.

The exponential function and the natural logarithm. The exponential function and its inverse, the natural logarithm, play an important role in modeling nonlinear regression functions. The **exponential function** of x is e^x, that is, e raised to the power x, where e is the constant $2.71828\ldots$; the exponential function is also written as $\exp(x)$. The **natural logarithm** is the inverse of the exponential function, that is, the natural logarithm is the function for which $x = \ln(e^x)$ or, equivalently, $x = \ln[\exp(x)]$. The base of the natural logarithm is e. Although there are logarithms in other bases, such as base 10, in this book we only consider logarithms in base e, that is, the natural logarithm, so when we use the term "logarithm" we always mean "natural logarithm."

The logarithm function, $y = \ln(x)$, is graphed in Figure 6.4. Note that the logarithm function is only defined for positive values of x. The logarithm function has a slope that is steep at first, then flattens out (although the function continues to increase). The slope of the logarithm function $\ln(x)$ is $1/x$.

The logarithm function has the following useful properties:

$$\ln(1/x) = -\ln(x); \tag{6.12}$$

$$\ln(ax) = \ln(a) + \ln(x); \tag{6.13}$$

$$\ln(x/a) = \ln(x) - \ln(a); \text{ and} \tag{6.14}$$

$$\ln(x^a) = a\ln(x). \tag{6.15}$$

Logarithms and percentages. The link between the logarithm and percentages relies on a key fact: when Δx is small, the difference between the logarithm of $x + \Delta x$ and the logarithm of x is approximately $\frac{\Delta x}{x}$, the percentage change in x divided by 100. That is,

$$\ln(x + \Delta x) - \ln(x) \cong \frac{\Delta x}{x} \left(\text{when } \frac{\Delta x}{x} \text{ is small}\right), \tag{6.16}$$

where "$\cong$" means "approximately equal to." The derivation of this approximation relies on calculus, but it is readily demonstrated by trying out some values of x and Δx. For example, when $x = 100$ and $\Delta x = 1$, then $\Delta x / x = 1/100 = 0.01$ (or 1%), while $\ln(x + \Delta x) - \ln(x) = \ln(101) - \ln(100) = 0.00995$ (or 0.995%). Thus $\Delta x / x$ (which is 0.01) is very close to $\ln(x + \Delta x) - \ln(x)$ (which is 0.00995). When $\Delta x = 5$, $\Delta x / x = 5/100 = 0.05$, while $\ln(x + \Delta x) - \ln(x) = \ln(105) - \ln(100) = 0.04879$.

FIGURE 6.4   The Logarithm Function, Y = ln(X)

The logarithmic function
$Y = \ln(X)$ is steeper for small
than for large values of X,
is only defined for $X > 0$, and
has slope $1/X$.

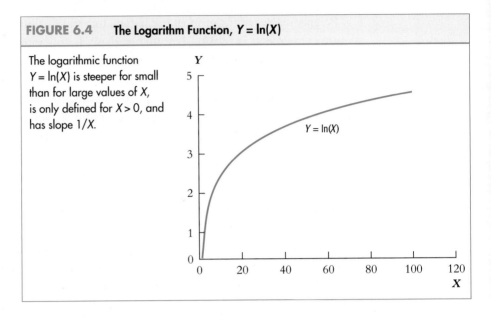

The three logarithmic regression models.   There are three different cases in which logarithms might be used: when X is transformed by taking its logarithm but Y is not; when Y is transformed to its logarithm but X is not; and when both Y and X are transformed to their logarithms. The interpretation of the regression coefficients is different in each case. We discuss these three cases in turn.

Case I: X is in logarithms, Y is not.   In this case, the regression model is

$$Y_i = \beta_0 + \beta_1 \ln(X_i) + u_i, \; i = 1, \ldots, n. \tag{6.17}$$

Because Y is not in logarithms but X is, this is sometimes referred to as a **linear-log model**.

In the linear-log model, a 1% change in X is associated with a change in Y of $0.01\beta_1$. To see this, consider the difference between the population regression function at values of X that differ by ΔX: this is $[\beta_0 + \beta_1\ln(X + \Delta X)] - [\beta_0 + \beta_1\ln(X)] = \beta_1[\ln(X + \Delta X) - \ln(X)] \cong \beta_1(\Delta X/X)$ where the final step uses the approximation in Equation (6.16). If X changes by 1%, then $\Delta X/X = 0.01$; thus, in this model a 1% change in X is associated with a change of Y of $0.01\beta_1$.

The only difference between the regression model in Equation (6.17) and the regression model of Chapter 4 with a single regressor is that the right-hand variable is now the logarithm of X rather than X itself. To estimate the coefficients β_0 and β_1 in Equation (6.17), first compute a new variable, $\ln(X)$; this is readily done using a spreadsheet or statistical software. Then β_0 and β_1 can be estimated by the OLS regression of Y_i on $\ln(X_i)$, hypotheses about β_1 can be tested using the t-statistic, and a 95% confidence interval for β_1 can be constructed as $\hat{\beta}_1 \pm 1.96SE(\hat{\beta}_1)$.

As an example, return to the relationship between district income and test scores. Instead of the quadratic specification, we could use the linear-log specification in Equation (6.17). Estimating this regression by OLS yields

$$\widehat{TestScore} = 557.8 + 36.42\ln(Income), \overline{R}^2 = 0.561. \qquad (6.18)$$
$$\qquad\quad (3.8) \quad (1.40)$$

According to Equation (6.18), a 1% increase in income is associated with an increase in test scores of $0.01 \times 36.42 = 0.36$ points.

To estimate the effect on Y of a change in X in its original units of thousands of dollars (not in logarithms), we can use the method in Key Concept 6.1. For example, what is the predicted difference in test scores for districts with average incomes of $10,000 versus $11,000? The estimated value of ΔY is the difference between the predicted values: $\Delta\hat{Y} = [557.8 + 36.42\ln(11)] - [557.8 + 36.42\ln(10)] = 36.42 \times [\ln(11) - \ln(10)] = 3.47$. Similarly, the predicted difference between a district with average income of $40,000 and a district with average income of $41,000 is $36.42 \times [\ln(41) - \ln(40)] = 0.90$. Thus, like the quadratic specification, this regression predicts that a $1,000 increase in income has a larger effect on test scores in poor districts than it does in affluent districts.

The estimated linear-log regression function in Equation (6.18) is plotted in Figure 6.5. Because the regressor in Equation (6.18) is the natural logarithm of income rather than income, the estimated regression function is not a straight line. Like the quadratic regression function in Figure 6.3, it is initially steep but then flattens out for higher levels of income.

Case II: Y is in logarithms, X is not.   In this case, the regression model is

$$\ln(Y_i) = \beta_0 + \beta_1 X_i + u_i. \qquad (6.19)$$

Because Y is in logarithms but X is not, this is referred to as a **log-linear model.**

In the log-linear model, a one-unit change in X ($\Delta X = 1$) is associated with a $100 \times \beta_1\%$ change in Y. To see this, compare the expected values of $\ln(Y)$ for values of X that differ by ΔX. The expected value of $\ln(Y)$ given X is $\ln(Y) = \beta_0 + \beta_1 X$. When X is $X + \Delta X$, the expected value is given by $\ln(Y + \Delta Y) = \beta_0 + \beta_1(X + \Delta X)$. Thus the difference between these expected values is $\ln(Y + \Delta Y) - \ln(Y) = [\beta_0 + \beta_1(X + \Delta X)] - [\beta_0 + \beta_1 X] = \beta_1\Delta X$. From the approximation in Equation (6.16),

---

FIGURE 6.5   The Linear-Log Regression Function

The estimated linear-log regression function $\hat{Y} = \hat{\beta}_0 + \hat{\beta}_1\ln(X)$ captures much of the nonlinear relation between test scores and district income.

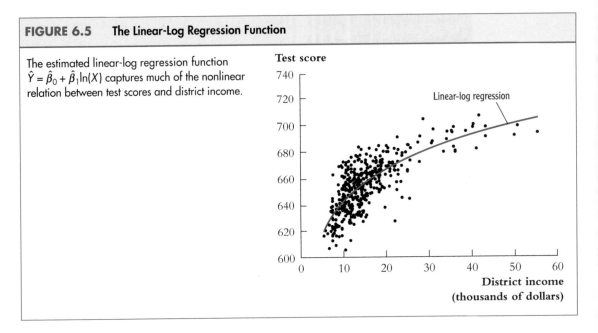

however, if $\beta_1\Delta X$ is small, then $\ln(Y + \Delta Y) - \ln(Y) \cong \Delta Y/Y$. Thus, $\Delta Y/Y \cong \beta_1\Delta X$. If $\Delta X = 1$, so that X changes by one unit, then $\Delta Y/Y$ changes by β_1. Translated into percentages, a unit change in X is associated with a $100 \times \beta_1\%$ change in Y.

As an illustration, we return to the empirical example of Section 3.6, the relationship between age and earnings of college graduates. Many employment contracts specify that, for each additional year of service, a worker gets a certain percentage increase in his or her wage. This percentage relationship suggests estimating the log-linear specification in Equation (6.19) so that each additional year of age (X) is, on average in the population, associated with some constant percentage increase in earnings (Y). By first computing the new dependent variable, $\ln(Earnings_i)$, the unknown coefficients β_0 and β_1 can be estimated by the OLS regression of $\ln(Earnings_i)$ against Age_i. When estimated using the 12,077 observations on college graduates in the 1999 Current Population Survey (the data are described in Appendix 3.1), this relationship is

$$\widehat{\ln(Earnings)} = 2.453 + 0.0128Age, \ \overline{R}^2 = 0.0387. \tag{6.20}$$
$$(0.024) \ \ (0.0006)$$

According to this regression, earnings are predicted to increase by 1.28% ($(100 \times 0.0128)\%$) for each additional year of age.

Case III: both X and Y are in logarithms. In this case, the regression model is

$$\ln(Y_i) = \beta_0 + \beta_1\ln(X_i) + u_i. \tag{6.21}$$

Because both Y and X are specified in logarithms, this is referred to as a **log-log model**.

In the log-log model, a 1% change in X is associated with a β_1% change in Y. Thus, in this specification β_1 is the elasticity of Y with respect to X. To see this, again apply Key Concept 6.1; thus $\ln(Y + \Delta Y) - \ln(Y) = [\beta_0 + \beta_1\ln(X + \Delta X)] - [\beta_0 + \beta_1\ln(X)] = \beta_1[\ln(X + \Delta X) - \ln(X)]$. Application of the approximation in Equation (6.16) to both sides of this equation yields

$$\frac{\Delta Y}{Y} \cong \beta_1\frac{\Delta X}{X} \text{ or}$$

$$\beta_1 = \frac{\Delta Y/Y}{\Delta X/X} = \frac{100 \times (\Delta Y/Y)}{100 \times (\Delta X/X)} = \frac{\text{percentage change in } Y}{\text{percentage change in } X}. \tag{6.22}$$

Thus, in the log-log specification β_1 is the ratio of the percentage change in Y associated with the percentage change in X. If the percentage change in X is 1% (that is, if $\Delta X = 0.01X$), then β_1 is the percentage change in Y associated with a 1% change in X. That is, β_1 is the elasticity of Y with respect to X.

As an illustration, return to the relationship between income and test scores. When this relationship is specified in this form, the unknown coefficients are estimated by a regression of the logarithm of test scores against the logarithm of income. The resulting estimated equation is

$$\widehat{\ln(TestScore)} = 6.336 + 0.0554\ln(Income), \overline{R}^2 = 0.557. \tag{6.23}$$
$$(0.006) \quad (0.0021)$$

According to this estimated regression function, a 1% increase in income is estimated to correspond to a 0.0554% increase in test scores.

The estimated log-log regression function in Equation (6.23) is plotted in Figure 6.6. Because Y is in logarithms, the vertical axis in Figure 6.6 is the logarithm of the test score, and the scatterplot is the logarithm of test scores versus district income. For comparison purposes, Figure 6.6 also shows the estimated regression function for a log-linear specification, which is

$$\widehat{\ln(TestScore)} = 6.439 + 0.00284Income, \overline{R}^2 = 0.497. \tag{6.24}$$
$$(0.003) \quad (0.00018)$$

Because the vertical axis is in logarithms, the regression function in Equation (6.24) is the straight line in Figure 6.6.

As you can see in Figure 6.6, the log-log specification fits slightly better than the log-linear specification. This is consistent with the higher $\overline{R}^2$ for the log-log regression (0.557) than for the log-linear regression (0.497). Even so, the log-log specification does not fit the data especially well: at the lower values of income, most of the observations fall below the log-log curve, while in the middle income range most of the observations fall above the estimated regression function.

The three logarithmic regression models are summarized in Key Concept 6.2.

A difficulty with comparing logarithmic specifications. Which of the log regression models best fits the data? As we saw in the discussion of Equations (6.23) and (6.24), the $\overline{R}^2$ can be used to compare the log-linear and log-log models; as it happened, the log-log model had the higher $\overline{R}^2$. Similarly, the $\overline{R}^2$ can be used to compare the linear-log regression in Equation (6.18) and the linear regression of Y against X. In the test score and income regression, the linear-log regression has an $\overline{R}^2$ of 0.561 while the linear regression has an $\overline{R}^2$ of 0.508, so the linear-log model fits the data better.

How can we compare the linear-log model and the log-log model? Unfortunately, the $\overline{R}^2$ *cannot* be used to compare these two regressions because their

FIGURE 6.6 **The Log-Linear and Log-Log Regression Functions**

In the log-linear regression function, ln(Y) is a linear function of X. In the log-log regression function, ln(Y) is a linear function of ln(X).

Logarithms in Regression: Three Cases

Logarithms can be used to transform the dependent variable Y, an independent variable X, or both (but they must be positive). The following table summarizes these three cases and the interpretation of the regression coefficient β_1. In each case, β_1 can be estimated by applying OLS after taking the logarithm of the dependent and/or independent variable.

Key Concept 6.2

Case	Regression Specification	Interpretation of β_1
I	$Y_i = \beta_0 + \beta_1 \ln(X_i) + u_i$	A 1% change in X is associated with a change in Y of $0.01\beta_1$.
II	$\ln(Y_i) = \beta_0 + \beta_1 X_i + u_i$	A change in X by 1 unit ($\Delta X = 1$) is associated with a $100\beta_1$% change in Y.
III	$\ln(Y_i) = \beta_0 + \beta_1 \ln(X_i) + u_i$	A 1% change in X is associated with a β_1% change in Y, so β_1 is the elasticity of Y with respect to X.

dependent variables are different (one is Y_i, the other is $\ln(Y_i)$). Recall that the $\overline{R}^2$ measures the fraction of the variance of the dependent variable explained by the regressors. Because the dependent variables in the log-log and linear-log models are different, it does not make sense to compare their $\overline{R}^2$'s.

Because of this problem, the best thing to do in a particular application is to decide, using economic theory and either your or other experts' knowledge of the problem, whether it makes sense to specify Y in logarithms. For example, labor economists typically model earnings using logarithms because wage comparisons, contract wage increases, and so forth are often most naturally discussed in percentage terms. In modeling test scores, it seems (to us, anyway) natural to discuss test results in terms of points on the test rather than percentage increases in the test scores, so we focus on models in which the dependent variable is the test score rather than its logarithm.

Computing predicted values of Y when Y is in logarithms.[5]   If the dependent variable Y has been transformed by taking logarithms, the estimated regression can be used to compute directly the predicted value of $\ln(Y)$. However, it is a bit trickier to compute the predicted value of Y itself.

---

[5]This material is more advanced and can be skipped without loss of continuity.

To see this, consider the log-linear regression model in Equation (6.19), and rewrite it so that it is specified in terms of Y rather than $\ln(Y)$. To do so, take the exponential function of both sides of the Equation (6.19); the result is

$$Y_i = \exp(\beta_0 + \beta_1 X_i + u_i) = e^{\beta_0 + \beta_1 X_i} e^{u_i}. \tag{6.25}$$

If u_i is distributed independently of X_i, then the expected value of Y_i given X_i is $E(Y_i | X_i) = E(e^{\beta_0 + \beta_1 X_i} e^{u_i} | X_i) = e^{\beta_0 + \beta_1 X_i} E(e^{u_i})$. The problem is that even if $E(u_i) = 0$, $E(e^{u_i}) \neq 1$. Thus, the appropriate predicted value of Y_i is not simply obtained by taking the exponential function of $\hat{\beta}_0 + \hat{\beta}_1 X_i$, that is, by setting $\hat{Y}_i = e^{\hat{\beta}_0 + \hat{\beta}_1 X_i}$: this predicted value is biased because of the missing factor $E(e^{u_i})$.

One solution to this problem is to estimate the factor $E(e^{u_i})$ and to use this estimate when computing the predicted value of Y, but this gets complicated and we do not pursue it further.

Another "solution," which is the approach used in this book, is to compute predicted values of the logarithm of Y but not to transform them to their original units. In practice, this is often acceptable because when the dependent variable is specified as a logarithm, it is often most natural just to use the logarithmic specification (and the associated percentage interpretations) throughout the analysis.

Polynomial and Logarithmic Models of Test Scores and District Income

In practice, economic theory or expert judgment might suggest a functional form to use, but in the end the true form of the population regression function is unknown. In practice, fitting a nonlinear function therefore entails deciding which method or combination of methods works best. As an illustration, we compare logarithmic and polynomial models of the relationship between district income and test scores.

Polynomial specifications.   We considered two polynomial specifications specified using powers of *Income*, quadratic (Equation (6.2)) and cubic (Equation (6.11)). Because the coefficient on *Income*^{3} in Equation (6.11) was significant at the 5% level, the cubic specification provided an improvement over the quadratic, so we select the cubic model as the preferred polynomial specification.

Logarithmic specifications.   The logarithmic specification in Equation (6.18) seemed to provide a good fit to these data, but we did not test this formally. One way to do so is to augment it with higher powers of the logarithm of income. If these additional terms are not statistically different from zero, then we can conclude that the specification in Equation (6.18) is adequate in the sense that it cannot be rejected against a polynomial function of the logarithm. Accordingly, the estimated cubic regression (specified in powers of the logarithm of income) is

$$\widehat{TestScore} = 486.1 + 113.4\ln(Income) - 26.9[\ln(Income)]^2$$
$$\quad\quad (79.4) \quad (87.9) \quad\quad\quad (31.7)$$
$$+ \; 3.06[\ln(Income)]^3, \; \overline{R}^2 = 0.560.$$
$$(3.74)$$

$$(6.26)$$

The t-statistic on the coefficient on the cubic term is 0.818, so the null hypothesis that the true coefficient is zero is not rejected at the 10% level. The F-statistic testing the joint hypothesis that the true coefficients on the quadratic and cubic term are both zero is 0.44, with a p-value of 0.64, so this joint null hypothesis is not rejected at the 10% level. Thus the cubic logarithmic model in Equation (6.26) does not provide a statistically significant improvement over the model in Equation (6.18), which is linear in the logarithm of income.

Comparing the cubic and linear-log specifications. Figure 6.7 plots the estimated regression functions from the cubic specification in Equation (6.11) and the linear-log specification in Equation (6.18). The two estimated regression functions are quite similar. One statistical tool for comparing these specifications is the $\overline{R}^2$. The $\overline{R}^2$ of the logarithmic regression is 0.561 and for the cubic regression it is 0.555. Because the logarithmic specification has a slight edge in terms of the $\overline{R}^2$, and because this specification does not need higher order polynomials in the logarithm of income to fit these data, we adopt the logarithmic specification in Equation (6.18).

6.3   Interactions Between Independent Variables

In the introduction to this chapter we wondered whether reducing the student-teacher ratio might have a bigger effect on test scores in districts where many students are still learning English than in those with few still learning English. This could arise, for example, if students who are still learning English benefit differentially from one-on-one or small-group instruction. If so, the presence of many English learners in a district would interact with the student-teacher ratio in such a way that the effect on test scores of a change in the student-teacher ratio would depend on the fraction of English learners.

FIGURE 6.7 **The Linear-Log and Cubic Regression Functions**

The estimated cubic regression function (Equation (6.11)) and the estimated linear-log regression function (Equation (6.18)) are nearly identical in this sample.

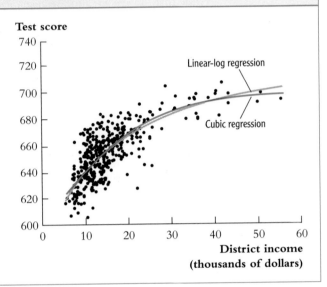

This section explains how to incorporate such interactions between two independent variables into the multiple regression model. The possible interaction between the student–teacher ratio and the fraction of English learners is an example of the more general situation in which the effect on Y of a change in one independent variable depends on the value of another independent variable. We consider three cases: when both independent variables are binary, when one is binary and the other is continuous, and when both are continuous.

Interactions Between Two Binary Variables

Consider the population regression of log earnings (Y_i, where $Y_i = \ln(Earnings_i)$) against two binary variables, the individual's gender (D_{1i}, which $= 1$ if the ith person is female) and whether he or she has a college degree (D_{2i}, where $D_{2i} = 1$ if the ith person graduated from college). The population linear regression of Y_i on these two binary variables is

$$Y_i = \beta_0 + \beta_1 D_{1i} + \beta_2 D_{2i} + u_i. \tag{6.27}$$

In this regression model, β_1 is the effect on log earnings of being female, holding schooling constant, and β_2 is the effect of having a college degree, holding gender constant.

The specification in Equation (6.27) has an important limitation: the effect of having a college degree in this specification, holding constant gender, is the same for men and women. There is, however, no reason that this must be so. Phrased mathematically, the effect of D_{2i} on Y_i, holding D_{1i} constant, could depend on the value of D_{1i}. In other words, there could be an interaction between gender and having a college degree so that the value in the job market of a degree is different for men and women.

Although the specification in Equation (6.27) does not allow for this interaction between gender and acquiring a college degree, it is easy to modify the specification so that it does by introducing another regressor, the product of the two binary variables, $D_{1i} \times D_{2i}$. The resulting regression is

$$Y_i = \beta_0 + \beta_1 D_{1i} + \beta_2 D_{2i} + \beta_3 (D_{1i} \times D_{2i}) + u_i. \tag{6.28}$$

The new regressor, the product $D_{1i} \times D_{2i}$, is called an **interaction term** or an **interacted regressor**, and the population regression model in Equation (6.28) is called a binary variable **interaction regression model**.

The interaction term in Equation (6.28) allows the population effect on log earnings (Y_i) of having a college degree (changing D_{2i} from $D_{2i} = 0$ to $D_{2i} = 1$) to depend on gender (D_{1i}). To show this mathematically, calculate the population effect of a change in D_{2i} using the general method laid out in Key Concept 6.1. The first step is to compute the conditional expectation of Y_i for $D_{2i} = 0$, given a value of D_{1i}; this is $E(Y_i | D_{1i} = d_1, D_{2i} = 0) = \beta_0 + \beta_1 \times d_1 + \beta_2 \times 0 + \beta_3 \times (d_1 \times 0) = \beta_0 + \beta_1 d_1$. The next step is to compute the conditional expectation of Y_i after the change, that is, for $D_{2i} = 1$, given the same value of D_{1i}; this is $E(Y_i | D_{1i} = d_1, D_{2i} = 1) = \beta_0 + \beta_1 \times d_1 + \beta_2 \times 1 + \beta_3 \times (d_1 \times 1) = \beta_0 + \beta_1 d_1 + \beta_2 + \beta_3 d_1$. The effect of this change is the difference of expected values (that is, the difference in Equation (6.6)), which is

$$E(Y_i | D_{1i} = d_1, D_{2i} = 1) - E(Y_i | D_{1i} = d_1, D_{2i} = 0) = \beta_2 + \beta_3 d_1. \tag{6.29}$$

Thus, in the binary variable interaction specification in Equation (6.28), the effect of acquiring a college degree (a unit change in D_{2i}) depends on the person's gender (the value of D_{1i}, which is d_1 in Equation (6.29)). If the person is male ($d_1 = 0$), the effect of acquiring a college degree is β_2, but if the person is female ($d_1 = 1$), the effect is $\beta_2 + \beta_3$. The coefficient β_3 on the interaction term is the difference in the effect of acquiring a college degree for women versus men.

Although this example was phrased using log earnings, gender, and acquiring a college degree, the point is a general one. The binary variable interaction regression allows the effect of changing one of the binary independent variables to depend on the value of the other binary variable.

The method we used here to interpret the coefficients was, in effect, to work through each possible combination of the binary variables. This method, which applies to all regressions with binary variables, is summarized in Key Concept 6.3.

Application to the student-teacher ratio and the percentage of English learners.   Let $HiSTR_i$ be a binary variable that equals one if the student-teacher ratio is 20 or more and equals zero otherwise, and let $HiEL_i$ be a binary variable that equals one if the percentage of English learners is 10% or more and equals zero otherwise. The interacted regression of test scores against $HiSTR_i$ and $HiEL_i$ is

$$\widehat{TestScore} = 664.1 - 18.2HiEL - 1.9HiSTR - 3.5(HiSTR \times HiEL),$$
$$(1.4)\quad(2.3)(1.9)(3.1) \tag{6.30}$$

$$\overline{R}^2 = 0.290.$$

The predicted effect of moving from a district with a low student-teacher ratio to one with a high student-teacher ratio, holding constant whether the percentage of English learners is high or low, is given by Equation (6.29), with estimated coefficients replacing the population coefficients. According to the estimates in Equation (6.30), this effect thus is $-1.9 - 3.5HiEL$. That is, if the fraction of English learners is low ($HiEL = 0$), then the effect on test scores of moving from $HiSTR = 0$ to $HiSTR = 1$ is for test scores to decline by 1.9 points. If the fraction of English learners is high, test scores are estimated to decline by $1.9 + 3.5 = 5.4$ points.

The estimated regression in Equation (6.30) also can be used to estimate the mean test scores for each of the four possible combinations of the binary variables. This is done using the procedure in Key Concept 6.3. Accordingly, the sample average test score for districts with low student-teacher ratios ($HiSTR_i = 0$) and low fractions of English learners ($HiEL_i = 0$) is 664.1. For districts with $HiSTR_i = 1$ (high student-teacher ratios) and $HiEL_i = 0$ (low fractions of English learners), the sample average is 662.2 ($= 664.1 - 1.9$). When $HiSTR_i = 0$ and $HiEL_i = 1$, the sample average is 645.9 ($= 664.1 - 18.2$), and when $HiSTR_i = 1$ and $HiEL_i = 1$, the sample average is 640.5 ($= 664.1 - 18.2 - 1.9 - 3.5$).

Interactions Between a Continuous and a Binary Variable

Next consider the population regression of log earnings ($Y_i = \ln(Earnings_i)$) against one continuous variable, the individual's years of work experience (X_i) and one binary variable, whether the worker has a college degree (D_i, where $D_i = 1$ if the ith person is a college graduate). As shown in Figure 6.8, there are three different ways that the population regression line relating Y and the continuous variable X can depend on the binary variable D.

In Figure 6.8a, the two regression lines differ only in their intercept. The corresponding population regression model is

$$Y_i = \beta_0 + \beta_1 X_i + \beta_2 D_i + u_i. \qquad (6.31)$$

This is the familiar multiple regression model with a population regression function that is linear in X_i and D_i. When $D_i = 0$, the population regression function is $\beta_0 + \beta_1 X_i$, so the intercept is β_0 and the slope is β_1. When $D_i = 1$, the population regression function is $\beta_0 + \beta_1 X_i + \beta_2$, so the slope remains β_1 but the intercept is $\beta_0 + \beta_2$. Thus β_2 is the difference between the intercepts of the two regression lines, as shown in Figure 6.8a. Stated in terms of the earnings example, β_1 is the effect on log earnings of an additional year of work experience, holding college degree status constant, and β_2 is the effect of a college degree on log earnings, holding years of experience constant. In this specification, the effect of an additional year of work experience is the same for college graduates and nongraduates, that is, the two lines in Figure 6.8a have the same slope.

In Figure 6.8b, the two lines have different slopes and intercepts. The different slopes permit the effect of an additional year of work to differ for college graduates and nongraduates. To allow for different slopes, add an interaction term to Equation (6.31):

$$Y_i = \beta_0 + \beta_1 X_i + \beta_2 D_i + \beta_3 (X_i \times D_i) + u_i, \qquad (6.32)$$

FIGURE 6.8   **Regression Functions Using Binary and Continuous Variables**

(a) Different intercepts, same slope

(b) Different intercepts, different slopes

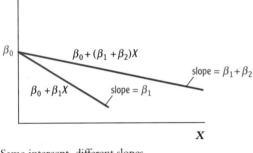

(c) Same intercept, different slopes

Interactions of binary variables and continuous variables can produce three different population regression functions: (a) $\beta_0 + \beta_1 X + \beta_2 D$ allows for different intercepts but has the same slope; (b) $\beta_0 + \beta_1 X + \beta_2 D + \beta_3 (X \times D)$ allows for different intercepts and different slopes; and (c) $\beta_0 + \beta_1 X + \beta_2 (X \times D)$ has the same intercept but allows for different slopes.

---

where $X_i \times D_i$ is a new variable, the product of X_i and D_i. To interpret the coefficients of this regression, apply the procedure in Key Concept 6.3. Doing so shows that, if $D_i = 0$, the population regression function is $\beta_0 + \beta_1 X_i$, whereas if $D_i = 1$, the population regression function is $(\beta_0 + \beta_2) + (\beta_1 + \beta_3)X_i$. Thus, this specification allows for two different population regression functions relating Y_i and X_i, depending on the value of D_i, as is shown in Figure 6.8b. The difference between the two intercepts is β_2, and the difference between the two slopes is β_3. In the earnings example, β_1 is the effect of an additional year of work experience for nongraduates $(D_i = 0)$ and $\beta_1 + \beta_3$ is this effect for graduates, so β_3 is the *difference* in the effect of an additional year of work experience for college graduates versus nongraduates.

A third possibility, shown in Figure 6.8c, is that the two lines have different slopes but the same intercept. The interacted regression model for this case is

$$Y_i = \beta_0 + \beta_1 X_i + \beta_2(X_i \times D_i) + u_i. \tag{6.33}$$

The coefficients of this specification also can be interpreted using Key Concept 6.3. In terms of the earnings example, this specification allows for different effects of experience on log earnings between college graduates and nongraduates, but requires that expected log earnings be the same for both groups when they have no prior experience. Said differently, this specification corresponds to the population mean entry-level wage being the same for college graduates and nongraduates. This does not make much sense in this application, and in practice this specification is used less frequently than Equation (6.32), which allows for different intercepts and slopes.

All three specifications, Equations (6.31), (6.32), and (6.33), are versions of the multiple regression model of Chapter 5 and, once the new variable $X_i \times D_i$ is created, the coefficients of all three can be estimated by OLS.

The three regression models with a binary and a continuous independent variable are summarized in Key Concept 6.4.

Application to the student-teacher ratio and the percentage of English learners. Does the effect on test scores of cutting the student-teacher ratio depend on whether the percentage of students still learning English is high or low? One way to answer this question is to use a specification that allows for two different regression lines, depending on whether there are a high or low percentage of English learners. This is achieved using the different intercept/different slope specification:

$$\widehat{TestScore} = 682.2 - 0.97 STR + 5.6 HiEL - 1.28(STR \times HiEL)$$
$$\phantom{\widehat{TestScore} = } (11.9)\ (0.59) \quad\ \ (19.5) \qquad (0.97) \tag{6.34}$$

$$\overline{R}^2 = 0.305,$$

where the binary variable $HiEL_i$ equals one if the percentage of students still learning English in the district is greater than 10% and equals zero otherwise.

For districts with a low fraction of English learners ($HiEL_i = 0$), the estimated regression line is $682.2 - 0.97 STR_i$. For districts with a high fraction of English learners ($HiEL_i = 1$), the estimated regression line is $682.2 + 5.6 - 0.97 STR_i - 1.28 STR_i = 687.8 - 2.25 STR_i$. According to these estimates, reducing the student-teacher ratio by one is predicted to increase test scores by 0.97 points in

Interactions Between Binary and Continuous Variables

Key Concept 6.4

Through the use of the interaction term $X_i \times D_i$, the population regression line relating Y_i and the continuous variable X_i can have a slope that depends on the binary variable D_i. There are three possibilities:

1. Different intercept, same slope (Figure 6.8a):
$$Y_i = \beta_0 + \beta_1 X_i + \beta_2 D_i + u_i;$$

2. Different intercept and slope (Figure 6.8b):
$$Y_i = \beta_0 + \beta_1 X_i + \beta_2 D_i + \beta_3(X_i \times D_i) + u_i;$$

3. Same intercept, different slope (Figure 6.8c):
$$Y_i = \beta_0 + \beta_1 X_i + \beta_2(X_i \times D_i) + u_i.$$

districts with low fractions of English learners but by 2.25 points in districts with high fractions of English learners. The difference between these two effects, 1.28 points, is the coefficient on the interaction term in Equation (6.34).

The OLS regression in Equation (6.34) can be used to test several hypotheses about the population regression line. First, the hypothesis that the two lines are in fact the same can be tested by computing the F-statistic testing the joint hypothesis that the coefficient on $HiEL_i$ and the coefficient on the interaction term $STR_i \times HiEL_i$ are both zero. This F-statistic is 89.9, which is significant at the 1% level.

Second, the hypothesis that two lines have the same slope can be tested by testing whether the coefficient on the interaction term is zero. The t-statistic, $-1.28/0.97 = -1.32$, is less than 1.645 in absolute value, so the null hypothesis that the two lines have the same slope cannot be rejected using a two-sided test at the 10% significance level.

Third, the hypothesis that the lines have the same intercept can be tested by testing whether the population coefficient on $HiEL$ is zero. The t-statistic is $t = 5.6/19.5 = 0.29$, so the hypothesis that the lines have the same intercept cannot be rejected at the 5% level.

These three tests produce seemingly contradictory results: the joint test using the F-statistic rejects the joint hypothesis that the slope and the intercept are the same, but the tests of the individual hypotheses using the t-statistic fail to reject. The reason for this is that the regressors, $HiEL$ and $STR \times HiEL$, are highly correlated. This results in large standard errors on the individual coefficients. Even though it is impossible to tell which of the coefficients is nonzero, there is strong evidence against the hypothesis that *both* are zero.

Finally, the hypothesis that the student-teacher ratio does not enter this specification can be tested by computing the F-statistic for the joint hypothesis that the coefficients on STR and on the interaction term are both zero. This F-statistic is 5.64, which has a p-value of 0.004. Thus, the coefficients on the student-teacher ratio are statistically significant at the 1% significance level.

Interactions Between Two Continuous Variables

Now suppose that both independent variables (X_{1i} and X_{2i}) are continuous. An example is when Y_i is log earnings of the ith worker, X_{1i} is his or her years of work experience, and X_{2i} is the number of years he or she went to school. If the population regression function is linear, the effect on wages of an additional year of experience does not depend on the number of years of education or, equivalently, the effect of an additional year of education does not depend on the number of years of work experience. In reality, however, there might be an interaction between these two variables so that the effect on wages of an additional year of experience depends on the number of years of education. This interaction can be modeled by augmenting the linear regression model with an interaction term that is the product of X_{1i} and X_{2i}:

$$Y_i = \beta_0 + \beta_1 X_{1i} + \beta_2 X_{2i} + \beta_3 (X_{1i} \times X_{2i}) + u_i. \tag{6.35}$$

The interaction term allows the effect of a unit change in X_1 to depend on X_2. To see this, apply the general method for computing effects in nonlinear regression models in Key Concept 6.1. The difference in Equation (6.6), computed for the interacted regression function in Equation (6.35), is $\Delta Y = (\beta_1 + \beta_3 X_2) \Delta X_1$ (Exercise 6.5(a)). Thus, the effect on Y of a change in X_1, holding X_2 constant, is

$$\frac{\Delta Y}{\Delta X_1} = \beta_1 + \beta_3 X_2, \tag{6.36}$$

which depends on X_2. For example, in the earnings example, if β_3 is positive then the effect on log earnings of an additional year of experience is greater, by the amount β_3, for each additional year of education the worker has.

The Demand for Economics Journals

Professional economists follow the most recent research in their areas of specialization. Most research in economics first appears in economics journals, so economists—or their libraries—subscribe to economics journals.

How elastic is the demand by libraries for economics journals? To find out, we analyzed the relationship between the number of subscriptions to a journal at U.S. libraries (Y_i) and its library subscription price using data for the year 2000 for 180 economics journals. Because the product of a journal is not the paper on which it is printed but rather the ideas it contains, its price is logically measured not in dollars per year or dollars per page but instead in dollars per idea. Although we cannot measure "ideas" directly, a good indirect measure is the number of times that articles in a journal are subsequently cited by other researchers.
(Continued)

FIGURE 6.9   Library Subscriptions and Prices of Economics Journals

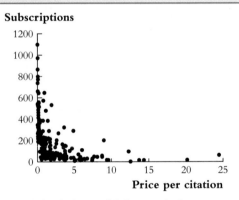

(a) Subscriptions and Price per citation

(b) ln(Subscriptions) and ln(Price per citation)

(c) ln(Subscriptions) and ln(Price per citation)

There is a nonlinear inverse relation between the number of U.S. library subscriptions (quantity) and the library price per citation (price), as shown in Figure 6.9a for 180 economics journals in 2000. But as seen in Figure 6.9b, the relation between log quantity and log price appears to be approximately linear. Figure 6.9c shows that demand is more elastic for young journals (*Age* = 5) than for old journals (*Age* = 80).

Accordingly, we measure price as the "price per citation" in the journal. The price range is enormous, from $\frac{1}{2}¢$ per citation (the *American Economic Review*) to 20¢ per citation or more. Some journals are expensive per citation because they have few citations, others because their library subscription price per year is very high: in 2000, a library subscription to the *Journal of Econometrics* cost almost $1,900, 40 times the price of a subscription to the *American Economic Review*!

Because we are interested in estimating elasticities, we use a log-log specification (Key Concept 6.2). The scatterplots in Figure 6.9a and 6.9b provide empirical support for this transformation. Because some of the oldest and most prestigious journals are the cheapest per citation, a regression of log quantity

(Continued)

TABLE 6.1 Estimates of the Demand for Economic Journals

Dependent Variable: Logarithm of Subscriptions at U.S. Libraries in the Year 2000; 180 Observations.

Regressor	(1)	(2)	(3)	(4)
ln(*Price per citation*)	−0.533** (0.034)	−0.408** (0.044)	−0.961** (0.160)	−0.899** (0.145)
[ln(*Price per citation*)]^2			0.017 (0.025)	
[ln(*Price per citation*)]^3			0.0037 (0.0055)	
ln(*Age*)		0.424** (0.119)	0.373** (0.118)	0.374** (0.118)
ln(*Age*) × ln(*Price per citation*)			0.156** (0.052)	0.141** (0.040)
ln(*Characters* ÷ 1,000,000)		0.206* (0.098)	0.235* (0.098)	0.229* (0.096)
Intercept	4.77** (0.055)	3.21** (0.38)	3.41** (0.38)	3.43** (0.38)
F-statistics and Summary Statistics				
F-statistic testing coefficients on quadratic and cubic terms (*p*-value)			0.25 (0.779)	
SER	0.750	0.705	0.691	0.688
$\overline{R}^2$	0.555	0.607	0.622	0.626

The *F*-statistic tests the hypothesis that the coefficients on [ln(*Price per citation*)]^2 and [ln(*Price per citation*)]^3 are both zero. Standard errors are given in parentheses under coefficients, and *p*-values are given in parentheses under *F*-statistics. Individual coefficients are statistically significant at the *5% level or **1% level.

against log price could have omitted variable bias. Our regressions therefore include two control variables, the logarithm of age and the logarithm of the number of characters per year in the journal.

The regression results are summarized in Table 6.1. Those results yield the following conclusions (see if you can find the basis for these conclusions in the table!):

1. Demand is less elastic for older than for newer journals;
2. The evidence supports a linear, rather than a cubic, function of log price; and
3. Demand is greater for journals with more characters, holding price and age constant.

So what is the elasticity of demand for economics journals? It depends on the age of the journal.

Demand curves for an 80-year-old journal and a 5-year-old upstart are superimposed on the scatterplot in Figure 6.9c; the older journal's demand elasticity is −0.28 ($SE = 0.06$), while the younger journal's is −0.67 ($SE = 0.08$).

This demand is very inelastic: demand is very insensitive to price, especially for older journals. For libraries, having the most recent research on hand is a necessity, not a luxury. By way of comparison, experts estimate the demand elasticity for cigarettes to be in the range of −0.3 to −0.5. Economics journals are, it seems, as addictive as cigarettes—but a lot better for your health![6]

[6]These data were graciously provided by Professor Theodore Bergstrom of the Department of Economics at the University of California, Santa Barbara. If you are interested in learning more about the economics of economics journals, see Bergstrom (2001).

A similar calculation shows that the effect on Y of a change ΔX_2 in X_2, holding X_1 constant, is $\frac{\Delta Y}{\Delta X_2} = (\beta_2 + \beta_3 X_1)$.

Putting these two effects together shows that the coefficient β_3 on the interaction term is the effect of a unit increase in X_1 *and* X_2, above and beyond the sum of the effects of a unit increase in X_1 alone and a unit increase in X_2 alone. That is, if X_1 changes by ΔX_1 *and* X_2 changes by ΔX_2, then the expected change in Y is $\Delta Y = (\beta_1 + \beta_3 X_2)\Delta X_1 + (\beta_2 + \beta_3 X_1)\Delta X_2 + \beta_3 \Delta X_1 \Delta X_2$ (Exercise 6.5(c)). The first term is the effect from changing X_1 holding X_2 constant; the second term is the effect from changing X_2 holding X_1 constant; and the final term, $\beta_3 \Delta X_1 \Delta X_2$, is the extra effect from changing both X_1 and X_2.

Interactions between two variables are summarized as Key Concept 6.5.

When interactions are combined with logarithmic transformations, they can be used to estimate price elasticities when the price elasticity depends on the characteristics of the good (see the box for an example).

Application to the student-teacher ratio and the percentage of English learners. The previous examples considered interactions between the student-teacher ratio and a binary variable indicating whether the percentage of English learners is large or small. A different way to study this interaction is to examine

Interactions in Multiple Regression

The interaction term between the two independent variables X_1 and X_2 is their product $X_1 \times X_2$. Including this interaction term allows the effect on Y of a change in X_1 to depend on the value of X_2 and, conversely, allows the effect of a change in X_2 to depend on the value of X_1.

Key Concept 6.5

The coefficient on $X_1 \times X_2$ is the effect of a unit increase in X_1 *and* X_2, above and beyond the sum of the individual effects of a unit increase in X_1 alone and a unit increase in X_2 alone. This is true whether X_1 and/or X_2 are continuous or binary.

the interaction between the student-teacher ratio and the continuous variable, the percentage of English learners (*PctEL*). The estimated interaction regression is

$$\widehat{TestScore} = 686.3 - 1.12STR - 0.67PctEL + 0.0012(STR \times PctEL),$$
$$\qquad\qquad (11.8) \quad (0.59) \qquad (0.37) \qquad\quad (0.019) \qquad\qquad\qquad (6.37)$$

$$\overline{R}^2 = 0.422.$$

When the percentage of English learners is at the median (*PctEL* = 8.85), the slope of the line relating test scores and the student-teacher ratio is estimated to be −1.11 (= −1.12 + 0.0012 × 8.85). When the percentage of English learners is at the 75th percentile (*PctEL* = 23.0), this line is estimated to be flatter, with a slope of −1.09 (= −1.12 + 0.0012 × 23.0). That is, for a district with 8.85% English learners, the estimated effect of a unit reduction in the student-teacher ratio is to increase test scores by 1.11 points, but for a district with 23.0% English learners, reducing the student-teacher ratio by one unit is predicted to increase test scores by only 1.09 points. The difference between these estimated effects is not statistically significant, however: the *t*-statistic testing whether the coefficient on the interaction term is zero is $t = 0.0012/0.019 = 0.06$, which is not significant at the 10% level.

To keep the discussion focused on nonlinear models, the specifications in Sections 6.1–6.3 exclude additional control variables such as the students' economic background. Consequently, these results arguably are subject to omitted variable bias. To draw substantive conclusions about the effect on test scores of reducing the student-teacher ratio, these nonlinear specifications must be augmented with control variables, and it is to such an exercise that we now turn.

6.4 Nonlinear Effects on Test Scores of the Student-Teacher Ratio

This section addresses three specific questions about test scores and the student-teacher ratio. First, after controlling for differences in economic characteristics of different districts, does the effect on test scores of reducing the student-teacher ratio depend on the fraction of English learners? Second, does this effect depend on the value of the student-teacher ratio? Third, and most important, after taking economic factors and nonlinearities into account, what is the estimated effect on test scores of reducing the student-teacher ratio by two students per teacher, as our superintendent from Chapter 4 proposes to do?

We answer these questions by considering nonlinear regression specifications of the type discussed in Sections 6.2 and 6.3, extended to include two measures of the economic background of the students: the percentage of students eligible for a subsidized lunch and the logarithm of average district income. The logarithm of income is used because the empirical analysis of Section 6.2 suggests that this specification captures the nonlinear relationship between test scores and income. As in Section 5.12, we do not include expenditures per pupil as a regressor and in so doing we are considering the effect of decreasing the student-teacher ratio, allowing expenditures per pupil to increase (that is, we are not holding expenditures per pupil constant).

Discussion of Regression Results

The OLS regression results are summarized in Table 6.2. The columns labeled (1) through (7) each report separate regressions. The entries in the table are the coefficients, standard errors, certain F-statistics and their p-values, and summary statistics, as indicated by the description in each row.

The first column of regression results, labeled regression (1) in the table, is regression (4) in Table 5.2 repeated here for convenience. This regression does not control for income, so the first thing we do is check whether the results change substantially when log income is included as an additional economic control variable. The results are given in regression (2) in Table 6.2. The log of income is statistically significant at the 1% level and the coefficient on the student-teacher ratio becomes somewhat closer to zero, falling from -1.00 to -0.73, although it remains statistically significant at the 1% level. The change in the coefficient on STR is large enough between regressions (1) and (2) to warrant including the logarithm of income in the remaining regressions as a deterrent to omitted variable bias.

TABLE 6.2   Nonlinear Regression Models of Test Scores

Dependent Variable: Average Test Score in District; 420 Observations.

Regressor	(1)	(2)	(3)	(4)	(5)	(6)	(7)
Student-teacher ratio (STR)	−1.00** (0.27)	−0.73** (0.26)	−0.97 (0.59)	−0.53 (0.34)	64.33** (24.86)	83.70** (28.50)	65.29** (25.26)
STR^2					−3.42** (1.25)	−4.38** (1.44)	−3.47** (1.27)
STR^3					0.059** (0.021)	0.075** (0.024)	0.060** (0.021)
% English Learners	−0.122** (0.033)	−0.176** (0.034)					−0.166** (0.034)
% English Learners ≥10%? (Binary, $HiEL$)			5.64 (19.51)	5.50 (9.80)	−5.47** (1.03)	816.1* (327.7)	
$HiEL \times STR$			−1.28 (0.97)	−0.58 (0.50)		−123.3* (50.2)	
$HiEL \times STR^2$						6.12* (2.54)	
$HiEL \times STR^3$						−0.101* (0.043)	
% Eligible for subsidized lunch	−0.547** (0.024)	−0.398** (0.033)		−0.411** (0.029)	−0.420** (0.029)	−0.418** (0.029)	−0.402** (0.033)
Average district income (logarithm)		11.57** (1.81)		12.12** (1.80)	11.75** (1.78)	11.80** (1.78)	11.51** (1.81)
Intercept	700.1** (5.6)	658.6** (8.6)	682.2** (11.9)	653.6** (9.9)	252.0 (163.6)	122.3 (185.5)	244.8 (165.7)

F-statistics and p-values on Joint Hypotheses

(a) all STR variables and interactions = 0			5.64 (0.004)	5.92 (0.003)	6.31 (<0.001)	4.96 (<0.001)	5.91 (0.001)
(b) STR^2, STR^3 = 0					6.17 (<0.001)	5.81 (0.003)	5.96 (0.003)
(c) $HiEL \times STR$, $HiEL \times STR^2$, $HiEL \times STR^3$ = 0						2.69 (0.046)	
SER	9.08	8.64	15.88	8.63	8.56	8.55	8.57
$\overline{R}^2$	0.773	0.794	0.305	0.795	0.798	0.799	0.798

These regressions were estimated using the data on K–8 school districts in California, described in Appendix 4.1. Standard errors are given in parentheses under coefficients, and p-values are given in parentheses under F-statistics. Individual coefficients are statistically significant at the *5% or **1% significance level.

Regression (3) in Table 6.2 is the interacted regression in Equation (6.34) with the binary variable for a high or low percentage of English learners, but with no economic control variables. When the economic control variables (percentage eligible for subsidized lunch and log income) are added (regression (4) in the table), the coefficients change, but in neither case is the coefficient on the interaction term significant at the 5% level. Based on the evidence in regression (4), the hypothesis that the effect of STR is the same for districts with low and high percentages of English learners cannot be rejected at the 5% level (the t-statistic is $t = -0.58/0.50 = -1.16$).

Regression (5) examines whether the effect of changing the student-teacher ratio depends on the value of the student-teacher ratio by including a cubic specification in STR in addition to the other control variables in regression (4) (the interaction term, $HiEL \times STR$, was dropped because it was not significant in regression (4) at the 10% level). The estimates in regression (5) are consistent with the student-teacher ratio having a nonlinear effect. The null hypothesis that the relationship is linear is rejected at the 1% significance level against the alternative that it is cubic (the F-statistic testing the hypothesis that the true coefficients on STR^2 and STR^3 are zero is 6.17, with a p-value of <0.001).

Regression (6) further examines whether the effect of the student-teacher ratio depends not just on the value of the student-teacher ratio but also on the fraction of English learners. By including interactions between $HiEL$ and STR, STR^2, and STR^3, we can check whether the (possibly cubic) population regressions functions relating test scores and STR are different for low and high percentages of English learners. To do so, we test the restriction that the coefficients on the three interaction terms are zero. The resulting F-statistic is 2.69, which has a p-value of 0.046 and thus is significant at the 5% but not the 1% significance level. This provides some evidence that the regression functions are different for districts with high and low percentages of English learners; however, comparing regressions (6) and (4) makes it clear that these differences are ones associated with the quadratic and cubic terms.

Regression (7) is a modification of regression (5), in which the continuous variable $PctEL$ is used instead of the binary variable $HiEL$ to control for the percentage of English learners in the district. The coefficients on the other regressors do not change substantially when this modification is made, indicating that the results in regression (5) are not sensitive to what measure of the percentage of English learners is actually used in the regression.

In all the specifications, the hypothesis that the student-teacher ratio does not enter the regressions is rejected at the 1% level.

FIGURE 6.10   Three Regression Functions Relating Test Scores and Student-Teacher Ratio

The cubic regressions from columns (5) and (7) of Table 6.2 are nearly identical. They indicate a small amount of nonlinearity in the relation between test scores and student-teacher ratio.

The nonlinear specifications in Table 6.2 are most easily interpreted graphically. Figure 6.10 graphs the estimated regression functions relating test scores and the student-teacher ratio for the linear specification (2) and the cubic specifications (5) and (7), along with a scatterplot of the data.[7] These estimated regression functions show the predicted value of test scores as a function of the student-teacher ratio, holding fixed other values of the independent variables in the regression. The estimated regression functions are all close to each other, although the cubic regressions flatten out for large values of the student-teacher ratio.

Regression (6) indicates a statistically significant difference in the cubic regression functions relating test scores and STR, depending on whether the percentage of English learners in the district is large or small. Figure 6.11 graphs these two estimated regression functions so that we can see whether this difference, in addition to being statistically significant, is of practical importance. As Figure 6.11 shows, for student-teacher ratios between 17 and 23—a range that

---

[7]For each curve, the predicted value was computed by setting each independent variable, other than STR, to its sample average value and computing the predicted value by multiplying these fixed values of the independent variables by the respective estimated coefficients from Table 6.2. This was done for various values of STR and the graph of the resulting adjusted predicted values is the estimated regression line relating test scores and the STR, holding the other variables constant at their sample averages.

FIGURE 6.11   **Regression Functions for Districts with High and Low Percentages of English Learners**

Districts with low percentages of English learners (HiEL = 0) are shown by gray dots and districts with HiEL = 1 are shown by colored dots. The cubic regression function for HiEL = 1 from regression (6) in Table 6.2 is approximately 10 points below the cubic regression function for HiEL = 0 for $17 \leq STR \leq 23$, but otherwise the two functions have similar shapes and slopes in this range. The slopes of the regression functions differ most for very large and small values of STR, where there are few observations.

---

includes 88% of the observations—the two functions are separated by approximately ten points but otherwise are very similar; that is, for STR between 17 and 23, districts with a lower percentage of English learners do better, holding constant the student-teacher ratio, but the effect of a change in the student-teacher ratio is essentially the same for the two groups. The two regression functions are different for student-teacher ratios below 16.5, but we must be careful not to read more into this than is justified. The districts with STR < 16.5 constitute only 6% of the observations, so the differences between the nonlinear regression functions are reflecting differences in these very few districts with very low student-teacher ratios. Thus, based on Figure 6.11, we conclude that the effect on test scores of a change in the student-teacher ratio does not depend on the percentage of English learners for the range of student-teacher ratios for which we have the most data.

Summary of Findings

These results let us answer the three questions raised at the start of this section.

First, after controlling for economic background, whether there are many or few English learners in the district does not have a substantial influence on the effect on test scores of a change in the student-teacher ratio. In the linear specifications, there is no statistically significant evidence of such a difference. The cubic specification in regression (6) provides statistically significant evidence (at the 5% level) that the regression functions are different for districts with high and low percentages of English learners; as shown in Figure 6.11, however, the estimated regression functions have similar slopes in the range of student-teacher ratios containing most of our data.

Second, after controlling for economic background, there is evidence of a nonlinear effect on test scores of the student-teacher ratio. This effect is statistically significant at the 1% level (the coefficients on STR^2 and STR^3 are always significant at the 1% level).

Third, we now can return to the superintendent's problem that opened Chapter 4. She wants to know the effect on test scores of reducing the student-teacher ratio by two students per teacher. In the linear specification (2), this effect does not depend on the student-teacher ratio itself, and the estimated effect of this reduction is to improve test scores by 1.46 ($= -0.73 \times -2$) points. In the nonlinear specifications, this effect depends on the value of the student-teacher ratio. If her district currently has a student-teacher ratio of 20, and she is considering cutting it to 18, then based on regression (5) the estimated effect of this reduction is to improve test scores by 3.00 points, while based on regression (7) this estimate is 2.93. If her district currently has a student-teacher ratio of 22, and she is considering cutting it to 20, then based on regression (5) the estimated effect of this reduction is to improve test scores by 1.93 points, while based on regression (7) this estimate is 1.90. The estimates from the nonlinear specifications suggest that cutting the student-teacher ratio has a somewhat greater effect if this ratio is already small.

6.5   Conclusion

This chapter presented several ways to model nonlinear regression functions. Because these models are variants of the multiple regression model, the unknown coefficients can be estimated by OLS, and hypotheses about their values can be tested using t- and F-statistics as described in Chapter 5. In these models, the expected effect on Y of a change in one of the independent variables, X_1, holding the other independent variables $X_2, \ldots, X_k$ constant, in general depends on the values of $X_1, X_2, \ldots, X_k$.

There are many different models in this chapter, and you could not be blamed for being a bit bewildered about which to use in a given application. How should you analyze possible nonlinearities in practice? Section 6.1 laid out a general approach for such an analysis, but this approach requires you to make decisions and exercise judgment along the way. It would be convenient if there were a single recipe you could follow that would always work in every application, but in practice data analysis is rarely that simple.

The single most important step in specifying nonlinear regression functions is to "use your head." Before you look at the data, can you think of a reason, based on economic theory or expert judgment, why the slope of the population regression function might depend on the value of that, or another, independent variable? If so, what sort of dependence might you expect? And, most importantly, what nonlinearities (if any) could have major implications for the substantive issues addressed by your study? Careful answers to these questions will focus your analysis. In the test score application, for example, such reasoning led us to investigate whether hiring more teachers might have a greater effect in districts with a large percentage of students still learning English, perhaps because those students would differentially benefit from more personal attention. By making the question precise, we were able to find a precise answer: after controlling for the economic background of the students, we found no statistically significant evidence of such an interaction.

Summary

1. In a nonlinear regression the slope of the population regression function depends on the value of one or more of the independent variables.
2. The effect on Y of a change in the independent variable(s) can be computed by evaluating the regression function at two values of the independent variable(s). The procedure is summarized in Key Concept 6.1.
3. A polynomial regression includes powers of X as regressors. A quadratic regression includes X and X^2, and a cubic regression includes X, X^2, and X^3.
4. Small changes in logarithms can be interpreted as proportional or percentage changes in a variable. Regressions involving logarithms are used to estimate proportional changes and elasticities.
5. The product of two variables is called an interaction term. When interaction terms are included as regressors, they allow the regression slope of one variable to depend on the value of another variable.

Key Terms

quadratic regression model (198)

nonlinear regression function (201)

polynomial regression model (206)

cubic regression model (206)

elasticity (208)

exponential function (209)

natural logarithm (209)

linear-log model (210)

log-linear model (211)

log-log model (213)

interaction term (219)

interacted regressor (219)

interaction regression model (219)

Review the Concepts

6.1 Sketch a regression function that is increasing (has a positive slope) and is steep for small values of X but less steep for large values of X. Explain how you would specify a nonlinear regression to model this shape. Can you think of an economic relationship with a shape like this?

6.2 A "Cobb-Douglas" production function relates production (Q) to factors of production, capital (K), labor (L), and raw materials (M), and an error term u using the equation $Q = \lambda K^{\beta_1} L^{\beta_2} M^{\beta_3} e^u$, where λ, β_1, β_2, and β_3 are production parameters. Suppose you have data on production and the factors of production from a random sample of firms with the same Cobb-Douglas production function. How would you use regression analysis to estimate the production parameters?

6.3 A standard "money demand" function used by macroeconomists has the form $\ln(m) = \beta_0 + \beta_1 \ln(GDP) + \beta_2 R$, where m is the quantity of (real) money, GDP is the value of (real) gross domestic product, and R is the value of the nominal interest rate measured in percent per year. Suppose that $\beta_1 = 1.0$ and $\beta_2 = -0.02$. What will happen to the value of m if GDP increases by 2%? What will happen to m if the interest rate increases from 4% to 5%?

6.4 You have estimated a linear regression model relating Y to X. Your professor says, "I think that the relationship between Y and X is nonlinear." Explain how you would test the adequacy of your linear regression.

6.5 Suppose that in problem 6.2 you thought that the value of β_2 was not constant, but rather increased when K increased. How could you use an interaction term to capture this effect?

Exercises

6.1 Sales in a company are $196 million in 2001 and increase to $198 million in 2002.

a. Compute the percentage increase in sales using the usual formula $100 \times \frac{Sales_{2002} - Sales_{2001}}{Sales_{2001}}$. Compare this value to the approximation $100 \left(\ln(Sales_{2002}) - \ln(Sales_{2001}) \right)$.

b. Repeat part (a) assuming $Sales_{2002} = 205$; $Sales_{2002} = 250$; $Sales_{2002} = 500$.

c. How good is the approximation when the change is small? Does the quality of the approximation deteriorate as the percentage change increases?

6.2 Suppose that a researcher collects data on houses that have sold in a particular neighborhood over the past year and obtains the regression results in the table shown below.

*a. Using the results in column (1), what is the expected change in price of building a 500-square-foot addition to a house? Construct a 95% confidence interval for the percentage change in price.

b. Comparing columns (1) and (2), is it better to use *Size* or ln(*Size*) to explain house prices?

*c. Using column (2) what is the estimated effect of pool on price? (Make sure you get the units right.) Construct a 95% confidence interval for this effect.

d. The regression in column (3) adds the number of bedrooms to the regression. How large is the estimated effect of an additional bedroom? Is the effect statistically significant? Why do you think the estimated effect is so small? (*Hint:* What other variables are being held constant?)

*e. Is the quadratic term $\ln(Size)^2$ important?

f. Use the regression in column (5) to compute the expected change in price when a pool is added to a house without a view. Repeat the exercise for a house with a view. Is there a large difference? Is the difference statistically significant?

Dependent Variable: ln(Price)

Regressor	(1)	(2)	(3)	(4)	(5)
Size	0.00042 (0.000038)				
ln*(size)*		0.69 (0.054)	0.68 (0.087)	0.57 (2.03)	0.69 (0.055)
ln*(size)*²				0.0078 (0.14)	
Bedrooms			0.0036 (0.037)		
Pool	0.082 (0.032)	0.071 (0.034)	0.071 (0.034)	0.071 (0.036)	0.071 (0.035)
View	0.037 (0.029)	0.027 (0.028)	0.026 (0.026)	0.027 (0.029)	0.027 (0.030)
Pool × view					0.0022 (0.10)
Condition	0.13 (0.045)	0.12 (0.035)	0.12 (0.035)	0.12 (0.036)	0.12 (0.035)
Intercept	10.97 (0.069)	6.60 (0.39)	6.63 (0.53)	7.02 (7.50)	6.60 (0.40)
Summary Statistics					
SER	0.102	0.098	0.099	0.099	0.099
$\overline{R}^2$	0.72	0.74	0.73	0.73	0.73

Variable definitions: *Price* = sale price ($'s); *Size* = house size (in square feet); *Bedrooms* = number of bedrooms; *Pool* = binary variable (1 if house has a swimming pool, 0 if not); *View* = binary variable (1 if house has a nice view, 0 if not); *Condition* = binary variable (1 if realtor reports house is in excellent condition, 0 if not).

6.3 After reading this chapter's analysis of test scores and class size, an educator comments, "In my experience, student performance depends on class size, but not in the way your regressions say. Rather, students do well when class size is less than 20 students and do very poorly when class size is greater than 25. There are no gains from reducing class size below 20 students, the relationship is constant in the intermediate region between 20 and 25 students, and there is no loss to increasing class size when it is already greater than 25." The educator is describing a "threshold effect" in which performance is constant for class sizes less than 20, then jumps and is constant for class sizes between 20 and 25, and then jumps again for class sizes greater than 25. To model these threshold effects, define the binary variables

$$STRsmall = 1 \text{ if } STR < 20, \text{ and } STRsmall = 0 \text{ otherwise}$$

$$STRmoderate = 1 \text{ if } 20 \leq STR \leq 25, \text{ and } STRmoderate = 0 \text{ otherwise}$$

$$STRlarge = 1 \text{ if } STR > 25, \text{ and } STRmoderate = 0 \text{ otherwise.}$$

a. Consider the regression $TestScore_i = \beta_0 + \beta_1 STRsmall_i + \beta_2 STRlarge_i + u_i$. Sketch the regression function relating $TestScore$ to STR for hypothetical values of the regression coefficients that are consistent with the educator's statement.

b. A researcher tries to estimate the regression $TestScore_i = \beta_0 + \beta_1 STRsmall_i + \beta_2 STRmoderate_i + \beta_3 STRlarge_i + u_i$ and finds that her computer crashes. Why?

*6.4 Explain how you would use "Approach #2" of section 5.8 to calculate the confidence interval discussed below Equation (6.8). (*Hint:* This requires estimating a new regression using a different definition of the regressors and the dependent variable. See Exercise (5.8).)

6.5 Consider the regression model $Y_i = \beta_0 + \beta_1 X_{1i} + \beta_2 X_{2i} + \beta_3(X_{1i} \times X_{2i}) + u_i$. Use Key Concept 6.1 to show:

a. $\dfrac{\Delta Y}{\Delta X_1} = \beta_1 + \beta_3 X_2$ (effect of change in X_1 holding X_2 constant).

b. $\dfrac{\Delta Y}{\Delta X_2} = \beta_2 + \beta_3 X_1$ (effect of change in X_2 holding X_1 constant).

c. If X_1 changes by ΔX_1 *and* X_2 changes by ΔX_2, then $\Delta Y = (\beta_1 + \beta_3 X_2)\Delta X_1 + (\beta_2 + \beta_3 X_1)\Delta X_2 + \beta_3 \Delta X_1 \Delta X_2$.

CHAPTER 7

Assessing Studies Based on Multiple Regression

The preceding three chapters explain how to use multiple regression to analyze the relationship among variables in a data set. In this chapter, we step back and ask, What makes a study that uses multiple regression reliable or unreliable? We focus on statistical studies that have the objective of estimating the causal effect of a change in some independent variable, such as class size, on a dependent variable, such as test scores. For such studies, when will multiple regression provide a useful estimate of the causal effect and, just as importantly, when will it fail to do so?

To answer this question, this chapter presents a framework for assessing statistical studies in general, whether or not they use regression analysis. This framework relies on the concepts of internal and external validity. A study is internally valid if its statistical inferences about causal effects are valid for the population and setting studied; it is externally valid if its inferences can be generalized to other populations and settings. In Sections 7.1 and 7.2, we discuss internal and external validity, list a variety of possible threats to internal and external validity, and discuss how to identify those threats in practice. Some of those threats cannot be handled using the econometric tools introduced so far, and this chapter provides a preview of methods, studied in the remaining chapters of this book, for handling these threats.

As an illustration of the framework of internal and external validity, in Section 7.3 we assess the internal and external validity of the study of the effect on test scores of cutting the student–teacher ratio presented in Chapters 4–6.

7.1   Internal and External Validity

The concepts of internal and external validity, defined in Key Concept 7.1, provide a framework for evaluating whether a statistical or econometric study is useful for answering a specific question of interest.

Internal and external validity distinguish between the population and setting studied and the population and setting to which the results are generalized. The **population studied** is the population of entities—people, companies, school districts, and so forth—from which the sample was drawn. The population to which the results are generalized, or the **population of interest**, is the population of entities to which the causal inferences from the study are to be applied. For example, a high school (grades 9–12) principal might want to generalize our findings on class sizes and test scores in California elementary school districts (the population studied) to the population of high schools (the population of interest).

By "setting" we mean the institutional, legal, social, and economic environment. For example, it would be important to know whether the findings of a laboratory experiment assessing methods for growing organic tomatoes could be generalized to the field, that is, whether the organic methods that work in the setting of a laboratory also work in the setting of the real world. We provide other examples of differences in populations and settings later in this section.

Threats to Internal Validity

Internal validity has two components. First, the estimator of the causal effect should be unbiased and consistent. For example, if $\hat{\beta}_{STR}$ is the OLS estimator of the effect on test scores of a unit change in the student-teacher ratio in a certain regression, then $\hat{\beta}_{STR}$ should be an unbiased and consistent estimator of the true population causal effect of a change in the student-teacher ratio, β_{STR}.

Second, hypothesis tests should have the desired significance level (the actual rejection rate of the test under the null hypothesis should equal its desired significance level), and confidence intervals should have the desired confidence level. For example, if a confidence interval is constructed as $\hat{\beta}_{STR} \pm 1.96 SE(\hat{\beta}_{STR})$, this confidence interval should contain the true population causal effect, β_{STR}, with probability 95% over repeated samples.

In regression analysis, causal effects are estimated using the estimated regression function and hypothesis tests are performed using the estimated regression coefficients and their standard errors. Accordingly, in a study based on OLS regression, the requirements for internal validity are that the OLS estimator is unbiased and consistent, and that standard errors are computed in a way that makes confidence

Internal and External Validity

A statistical analysis is **internally valid** if the statistical inferences about causal effects are valid for the population being studied. The analysis is **externally valid** if its inferences and conclusions can be generalized from the population and setting studied to other populations and settings.

Key Concept 7.1

intervals have the desired confidence level. There are various reasons this might not happen, and these reasons constitute threats to internal validity. These threats lead to failures of one or more of the least squares assumptions in Key Concept 5.4. For example, one threat that we have discussed at length is omitted variable bias; this leads to correlation between one or more regressors and the error term, which violates the first least squares assumption. If data on the omitted variable are available, then this threat can be avoided by including that variable as an additional regressor.

Section 7.2 provides a detailed discussion of the various threats to internal validity in multiple regression analysis and how to mitigate them.

Threats to External Validity

Potential threats to external validity arise from differences between the population and setting studied and the population and setting of interest.

Differences in populations. Differences between the population studied and the population of interest can pose a threat to external validity. For example, laboratory studies of the toxic effects of chemicals typically use animal populations like mice (the population studied), but the results are used to write health and safety regulations for human populations (the population of interest). Whether mice and men differ sufficiently to threaten the external validity of such studies is a matter of debate.

More generally, the true causal effect might not be the same in the population studied and the population of interest. This could be because the population was chosen in way that makes it different from the population of interest, because of differences in characteristics of the populations, because of geographical differences, or because the study is out of date.

Differences in settings. Even if the population being studied and the population of interest are identical, it might not be possible to generalize the study results if the **settings** differ. For example, a study of the effect on college binge drinking of an antidrinking advertising campaign might not generalize to another identical group of college students if the legal drinking ages at the two colleges differ. In this case, the legal setting in which the study was conducted differs from the legal setting to which its results are applied.

More generally, examples of differences in settings include differences in the institutional environment (public universities versus religious universities), differences in laws (differences in legal drinking ages), or differences in the physical environment (tailgate-party binge drinking in southern California versus Fairbanks, Alaska).

Application to test scores and the student-teacher ratio. Chapters 5 and 6 reported statistically significant, but substantively small, estimated improvements in test scores resulting from reducing the student-teacher ratio. This analysis was based on test results for California school districts. Suppose for the moment that these results are internally valid. To what other populations and settings of interest could this finding be generalized?

The closer are the population and setting of the study to those of interest, the stronger is the case for external validity. For example, college students and college instruction are very different than elementary school students and instruction, so it is implausible that the effect of reducing class sizes estimated using the California elementary school district data would generalize to colleges. On the other hand, elementary school students, curriculum, and organization are broadly similar throughout the United States, so it is plausible that the California results might generalize to performance on standardized tests in other U.S. elementary school districts.

How to assess the external validity of a study. External validity must be judged using specific knowledge of the populations and settings studied and those of interest. Important differences between the two will cast doubt on the external validity of the study.

Sometimes there are two or more studies on different but related populations. If so, the external validity of both studies can be checked by comparing their results. For example, in Section 7.3 we analyze test score and class size data for elementary school districts in Massachusetts and compare the Massachusetts and California results. In general, similar findings in two or more studies bolster claims to external validity, while differences in their findings that are not readily explained cast doubt on their external validity.[1]

How to design an externally valid study.   Because threats to external validity stem from a lack of comparability of populations and settings, these threats are best minimized at the early stages of a study, before the data are collected. Study design is beyond the scope of this textbook, and the interested reader is referred to Shadish, Cook, and Campbell (2002).

7.2.   Threats to Internal Validity of Multiple Regression Analysis

Studies based on regression analysis are internally valid if the estimated regression coefficients are unbiased and consistent, and if their standard errors yield confidence intervals with the desired confidence level. This section surveys five reasons why the OLS estimator of the multiple regression coefficients might be biased, even in large samples: omitted variables, misspecification of the functional form of the regression function, imprecise measurement of the independent variables ("errors in variables"), sample selection, and simultaneous causality. All five sources of bias arise because the regressor is correlated with the error term in the population regression, violating the first least squares assumption in Key Concept 5.4. For each, we discuss what can be done to reduce this bias. The section concludes with a discussion of circumstances that lead to inconsistent standard errors and what can be done about it.

Omitted Variable Bias

Recall that omitted variable bias arises when a variable that both determines Y and is correlated with one or more of the included regressors is omitted from the

---

[1]A comparison of many related studies on the same topic is called a meta-analysis. The discussion in the box on the "Mozart effect" in Chapter 5 is based on a meta-analysis, for example. Performing a meta-analysis of many studies has its own challenges. How do you sort the good studies from the bad? How do you compare studies when the dependent variables differ? Should you put more weight on a large study than a small study? A discussion of meta-analysis and its challenges goes beyond the scope of this textbook. The interested reader is referred to Hedges and Olkin (1985) and Cooper and Hedges (1994).

regression. This bias persists even in large samples, so that the OLS estimator is inconsistent. How best to minimize omitted variable bias depends on whether or not data are available for the potential omitted variable.

Solutions to omitted variable bias when the omitted variable is observed.

If you have data on the omitted variable, then you can include this variable in a multiple regression, thereby addressing the problem. However, adding a new variable has both costs and benefits. On the one hand, omitting the variable could result in omitted variable bias. On the other hand, including the variable when it does not belong (that is, when its population regression coefficient is zero) reduces the precision of the estimators of the other regression coefficients. In other words, the decision to include a variable or not involves a trade-off between bias and variance of the coefficients of interest. In practice, there are four steps that can help you decide whether or not to include a variable or set of variables in a regression.

The first step is to identify the key coefficients of interest in your regression. In the test score regressions, this is the coefficient on the student-teacher ratio, because the question originally posed concerns the effect on test scores of reducing the student-teacher ratio.

The second step is to ask yourself: What are the most likely sources of important omitted variable bias in this regression? Answering this requires applying economic theory and expert knowledge, and should occur before you actually run any regressions; because this is done before analyzing the data, this is referred to as *a priori* ("before the fact") reasoning. In the test score example, this step entails identifying those determinants of test scores that, if ignored, could bias our estimator of the class size effect. The result of this step is a base regression specification, the starting point for your empirical regression analysis, and a list of additional "questionable" variables that might help to mitigate possible omitted variable bias.

The third step is to augment your base specification with the additional questionable variables identified in the second step and to test the hypotheses that their coefficients are zero. If the coefficients on the additional variables are statistically significant, or if the estimated coefficients of interest change appreciably when the additional variables are included, then they should remain in the specification and you should modify your base specification. If not, then these variables can be excluded from the regression.

The fourth step is to present an accurate summary of your results in tabular form. This provides "full disclosure" to a potential skeptic, who can then draw his or her own conclusions. Tables 5.2 and 6.2 are examples of this strategy. For example, in Table 6.2, we could have presented only the regression in column (7), because that regression summarizes the relevant effects and nonlinearities in the other regressions in that table. Presenting the other regressions, however, permits the skeptical reader to draw his or her own conclusions.

These steps are summarized in Key Concept 7.2.

Solutions to omitted variable bias when the omitted variable is not observed. Adding an omitted variable to a regression is not an option if you do not have data on that variable. Still, there are three other ways to solve omitted variable bias. Each of these three solutions circumvents omitted variable bias through the use of different types of data.

The first solution is to use data in which the same observational unit is observed at different points in time. For example, test score and related data might be collected for the same districts in 1995, then again in 2000. Data in this form is called panel data. As explained in Chapter 8, panel data make it possible to control for unobserved omitted variables as long as those omitted variables do not change over time.

The second solution is to use instrumental variables regression. This method relies on a new variable, called an instrumental variable. Instrumental variables regression is discussed in Chapter 10.

The third solution is to use a study design in which the effect of interest (for example, the effect of reducing class size on student achievement) is studied using a randomized controlled experiment. Randomized controlled experiments are discussed in Chapter 11.

Misspecification of the Functional Form of the Regression Function

If the true population regression function is nonlinear but the estimated regression is linear, then this **functional form misspecification** makes the OLS estimator biased. This bias is a type of omitted variable bias, in which the omitted variables are the terms that reflect the missing nonlinear aspects of the regression function. For example, if the population regression function is a quadratic polynomial, then a regression that omits the square of the independent variable would suffer from omitted variable bias.

Solutions to functional form misspecification. When the dependent variable is continuous (like test scores), this problem of potential nonlinearity can be solved using the methods of Chapter 6. If, however, the dependent variable is discrete or binary (for example, Y_i equals one if the ith person attended college and equals zero otherwise), things are more complicated. Regression with a discrete dependent variable is discussed in Chapter 9.

Should I Include More Variables in My Regression?

Key Concept 7.2

If you include another variable in your multiple regression, you will eliminate the possibility of omitted variable bias from excluding that variable but the variance of the estimator of the coefficients of interest can increase. Here are some guidelines to help you decide whether to include an additional variable:

1. Be specific about the coefficient or coefficients of interest.

2. Use *a priori* reasoning to identify the most important potential sources of omitted variable bias, leading to a base specification and some "questionable" variables.

3. Test whether additional questionable variables have nonzero coefficients.

4. Provide "full disclosure" representative tabulations of your results so that others can see the effect of including the questionable variables on the coefficient(s) of interest. Do your results change if you include a questionable variable?

Errors-in-Variables

Suppose that in our regression of test scores against the student-teacher ratio we had inadvertently mixed up our data, so that we ended up regressing test scores for fifth graders on the student-teacher ratio for tenth graders in that district. Although the student-teacher ratio for elementary school students and tenth graders might be correlated, they are not the same, so this mix-up would lead to bias in the estimated coefficient. This is an example of **errors-in-variables bias** because its source is an error in the measurement of the independent variable. This bias persists even in very large samples, so that the OLS estimator is inconsistent if there is measurement error.

There are many possible sources of measurement error. If the data are collected through a survey, a respondent might give the wrong answer. For example, one question in the Current Population Survey involves last year's earnings. A respondent might not know his exact earnings, or he might misstate it for some other reason. If instead the data are obtained from computerized administrative records, there might have been typographical errors when the data were first entered.

To see that errors-in-variables bias results in correlation between the regressor and the error term, suppose there is a single regressor X_i (say, actual income) but that X_i is measured imprecisely by $\widetilde{X}_i$ (the respondent's estimate of income). Because $\widetilde{X}_i$, not X_i, is observed, the regression equation actually estimated is the one based on $\widetilde{X}_i$. Written in terms of the imprecisely measured variable $\widetilde{X}_i$, the population regression equation $Y_i = \beta_0 + \beta_1 X_i + u_i$ is

$$Y_i = \beta_0 + \beta_1 \widetilde{X}_i + [\beta_1(X_i - \widetilde{X}_i) + u_i]$$
$$= \beta_0 + \beta_1 \widetilde{X}_i + v_i, \tag{7.1}$$

where $v_i = \beta_1(X_i - \widetilde{X}_i) + u_i$. Thus, the population regression equation written in terms of $\widetilde{X}_i$ has an error term that contains the difference between X_i and $\widetilde{X}_i$. If this difference is correlated with the measured value $\widetilde{X}_i$, then the regressor $\widetilde{X}_i$ will be correlated with the error term and $\hat{\beta}_1$ will be biased and inconsistent.

The precise size and direction of the bias in $\hat{\beta}_1$ depends on the correlation between $\widetilde{X}_i$ and $(X_i - \widetilde{X}_i)$. This correlation depends, in turn, on the specific nature of the measurement error.

As an example, suppose that the survey respondent provides their best guess or recollection of the actual value of the independent variable X_i. A convenient way to represent this mathematically is to suppose that the measured value of X_i equals the actual, unmeasured value, plus a purely random component, w_i. Accordingly, the measured value of the variable, denoted by $\widetilde{X}_i$, is $\widetilde{X}_i = X_i + w_i$. Because the error is purely random, we might suppose that w_i has mean zero and variance σ_w^2 and is uncorrelated with X_i and the regression error u_i. Under this assumption, a bit of algebra[2] shows that $\hat{\beta}_1$ has the probability limit

$$\hat{\beta}_1 \xrightarrow{p} \frac{\sigma_X^2}{\sigma_X^2 + \sigma_w^2} \beta_1. \tag{7.2}$$

That is, if the measurement imprecision has the effect of simply adding a random element to the actual value of the independent variable, then $\hat{\beta}_1$ is inconsistent. Because the ratio $\frac{\sigma_X^2}{\sigma_X^2 + \sigma_w^2}$ is less than one, $\hat{\beta}_1$ will be biased towards zero, even in large samples. In the extreme case that the measurement error is so large that essentially no information about X_i remains, the ratio of the variances in the final expression in Equation (7.2) is zero and $\hat{\beta}_1$ converges in probability to zero. In the other extreme, when there is no measurement error, $\sigma_w^2 = 0$ so $\hat{\beta}_1 \xrightarrow{p} \beta_1$.

---

[2]Under this measurement error assumption, $v_i = \beta_1(X_i - \widetilde{X}_i) + u_i = -\beta_1 w_i + u_i$, $\text{cov}(\widetilde{X}_i, u_i) = 0$, and $\text{cov}(\widetilde{X}_i, w_i) = \text{cov}(X_i + w_i, w_i) = \sigma_w^2$, so $\text{cov}(\widetilde{X}_i, v_i) = -\beta_1 \text{cov}(\widetilde{X}_i, w_i) + \text{cov}(\widetilde{X}_i, u_i) = -\beta_1 \sigma_w^2$. Thus, from Equation (5.1), $\hat{\beta}_1 \xrightarrow{p} \beta_1 - \beta_1 \sigma_w^2 / \sigma_{\widetilde{X}}^2$. Now $\sigma_{\widetilde{X}}^2 = \sigma_X^2 + \sigma_w^2$, so $\hat{\beta}_1 \xrightarrow{p} \beta_1 - \beta_1 \sigma_w^2 / (\sigma_X^2 + \sigma_w^2) = [\sigma_X^2 / (\sigma_X^2 + \sigma_w^2)]\beta_1$.

Although the result in Equation (7.2) is specific to this particular type of measurement error, it illustrates the more general proposition that if the independent variable is measured imprecisely then the OLS estimator is biased, even in large samples. Errors-in-variables bias is summarized in Key Concept 7.3.

Solutions to errors-in-variables bias. The best way to solve the errors-in-variables problem is to get an accurate measure of X. If this is impossible, however, there are econometric methods that can be used to mitigate errors-in-variables bias.

One such method is instrumental variables regression. This relies on having another variable (the "instrumental" variable) that is correlated with the actual value X_i but is uncorrelated with the measurement error. This method is studied in Chapter 10.

A second method is to develop a mathematical model of the measurement error and, if possible, to use the resulting formulas to adjust the estimates. For example, if a researcher believes that the measured variable is in fact the sum of the actual value and a random measurement error term, and if she knows or can estimate the ratio σ_w^2 / σ_X^2, then she can use Equation (7.2) to compute an estimator of β_1 that corrects for the downward bias. Because this approach requires specialized knowledge about the nature of the measurement error, the details typically are specific to a given data set and its measurement problems and we shall not pursue this approach further in this textbook.

Sample Selection

Sample selection bias occurs when the availability of the data is influenced by a selection process that is related to the value of the dependent variable. This selection process can introduce correlation between the error term and the regressor, which leads to bias in the OLS estimator.

Sample selection that is unrelated to the value of the dependent variable does not introduce bias. For example, if data are collected from a population by simple random sampling, the sampling method (being drawn at random from the population) has nothing to do with the value of the dependent variable. Such sampling does not introduce bias.

Bias can be introduced when the method of sampling is related to the value of the dependent variable. An example of sample selection bias in polling was given in the box in Chapter 2. In that example, the sample selection method (randomly selected phone numbers of automobile owners) was related to the dependent variable (who the individual supported for president in 1936), because in 1936 car owners with phones were more likely to be Republicans.

Errors-in-Variables Bias

Errors-in-variables bias in the OLS estimator arises when an independent variable is measured imprecisely. This bias depends on the nature of the measurement error and persists even if the sample size is large. If the measured variable equals the actual value plus a mean-zero, independently distributed measurement error term, then the OLS estimator in a regression with a single right-hand variable is biased towards zero, and its probability limit is given in Equation (7.2).

Key Concept 7.3

An example of sample selection in economics arises in using a regression of wages on education to estimate the effect on wages of an additional year of education. Only individuals who have a job have wages, by definition. The factors (observable and unobservable) that determine whether someone has a job—education, experience, where one lives, ability, luck, and so forth—are similar to the factors that determine how much that person earns when employed. Thus, the fact that someone has a job suggests that, all else equal, the error term in the wage equation for that person is positive. Said differently, whether someone has a job is in part determined by the omitted variables in the error term in the wage regression. Thus, the simple fact that someone has a job, and thus appears in the data set, provides information that the error term in the regression is positive, at least on average, and could be correlated with the regressors. This too can lead to bias in the OLS estimator.

Sample selection bias is summarized in Key Concept 7.4.

Solutions to selection bias.   The methods we have discussed so far cannot eliminate sample selection bias. The methods for estimating models with sample selection are beyond the scope of this book. Those methods build on the techniques introduced in Chapter 9, where further references are provided.

Simultaneous Causality

So far, we have assumed that causality runs from the regressors to the dependent variable (X causes Y). But what if causality also runs from the dependent variable to one or more regressors (Y causes X)? If so, causality runs "backwards" as well as forwards, that is, there is **simultaneous causality**. If there is simultaneous causality, an OLS regression picks up both effects so the OLS estimator is biased and inconsistent.

Sample Selection Bias

Sample selection bias arises when a selection process influences the availability of data and that process is related to the dependent variable. Sample selection induces correlation between one or more regressors and the error term, leading to bias and inconsistency of the OLS estimator.

Key Concept 7.4

For example, our study of test scores focused on the effect on test scores of reducing the student-teacher ratio, so that causality is presumed to run from the student-teacher ratio to test scores. Suppose, however, that a government initiative subsidized hiring teachers in school districts with poor test scores. If so, causality would run in both directions: for the usual educational reasons low student-teacher ratios arguably lead to high test scores, but because of the government program low test scores would lead to low student-teacher ratios.

Simultaneous causality leads to correlation between the regressor and the error term. In the test score example, suppose there is an omitted factor that leads to poor test scores; because of the government program, this factor that produces low scores in turn results in a low student-teacher ratio. Thus, a negative error term in the population regression of test scores on the student-teacher ratio reduces test scores, but because of the government program it also leads to a decrease in the student-teacher ratio. In other words, the student-teacher ratio is positively correlated with the error term in the population regression. This in turn leads to simultaneous causality bias and inconsistency of the OLS estimator.

This correlation between the error term and the regressor can be made precise mathematically by introducing an additional equation that describes the reverse causal link. For convenience, consider just the two variables X and Y and ignore other possible regressors. Accordingly, there are two equations, one in which X causes Y, and one in which Y causes X:

$$Y_i = \beta_0 + \beta_1 X_i + u_i \text{ and} \tag{7.3}$$

$$X_i = \gamma_0 + \gamma_1 Y_i + v_i. \tag{7.4}$$

Equation (7.3) is the familiar one in which β_1 is the effect on Y of a change in X, where u represents other factors. Equation (7.4) represents the reverse causal effect of Y on X. In the test score problem, Equation (7.3) represents the educational effect of class size on test scores, while Equation (7.4) represents the reverse causal effect of test scores on class size induced by the government program.

Simultaneous causality leads to correlation between X_i and the error term u_i in Equation (7.3). To see this, imagine that u_i is negative, which decreases Y_i. However, this lower value of Y_i effects the value of X_i through the second of these equations, and if γ_1 is positive, a low value of Y_i will lead to a low value of X_i. Thus, if γ_1 is positive, X_i and u_i will be positively correlated.[3]

Because this can be expressed mathematically using a system of two simultaneous equations, the simultaneous causality bias is sometimes called **simultaneous equations bias**. Simultaneous causality bias is summarized in Key Concept 7.5.

Solutions to simultaneous causality bias. There are two ways to mitigate simultaneous causality bias. One is to use instrumental variables regression, the topic of Chapter 10. The second is to design and to implement a randomized controlled experiment in which the reverse causality channel is nullified, and such experiments are discussed in Chapter 11.

Sources of Inconsistency of OLS Standard Errors

Inconsistent standard errors pose a different threat to internal validity. Even if the OLS estimator is consistent and the sample is large, inconsistent standard errors will produce hypothesis tests with size that differs from the desired significance level and "95%" confidence intervals that fail to include the true value in 95% of repeated samples.

There are two main reasons for inconsistent standard errors: improperly handled heteroskedasticity and correlation of the error term across observations.

Heteroskedasticity. As discussed in Section 4.9, for historical reasons some regression software report homoskedasticity-only standard errors. If, however, the regression error is heteroskedastic, those standard errors are not a reliable basis for hypothesis tests and confidence intervals. The solution to this problem is to use heteroskedasticity-robust standard errors and to construct F-statistics using a het-

---

[3]To show this mathematically, note that Equation (7.4) implies that $\mathrm{cov}(X_i, u_i) = \mathrm{cov}(\gamma_0 + \gamma_1 Y_i + v_i, u_i) = \gamma_1 \mathrm{cov}(Y_i, u_i) + \mathrm{cov}(v_i, u_i)$. Assuming that $\mathrm{cov}(v_i, u_i) = 0$, by Equation (7.3) this in turn implies that $\mathrm{cov}(X_i, u_i) = \gamma_1 \mathrm{cov}(Y_i, u_i) = \gamma_1 \mathrm{cov}(\beta_0 + \beta_1 X_i + u_i, u_i) = \gamma_1 \beta_1 \mathrm{cov}(X_i, u_i) + \gamma_1 \sigma_u^2$. Solving for $\mathrm{cov}(X_i, u_i)$ then yields the result $\mathrm{cov}(X_i, u_i) = \gamma_1 \sigma_u^2 / (1 - \gamma_1 \beta_1)$.

Simultaneous Causality Bias

Key Concept 7.5

Simultaneous causality bias, also called simultaneous equations bias, arises in a regression of Y on X when, in addition to the causal link of interest from X to Y, there is a causal link from Y to X. This reverse causality makes X correlated with the error term in the population regression of interest.

eroskedasticity-robust variance estimator. Heteroskedasticity-robust standard errors are provided as an option in modern software packages.

Correlation of the error term across observations. In some settings, the population regression error can be correlated across observations. This will not happen if the data are obtained by sampling at random from the population because the randomness of the sampling process ensures that the errors are independently distributed from one observation to the next. Sometimes, however, sampling is only partially random. The most common circumstance is when the data are repeated observations on the same entity over time, for example, the same school district for different years. If the omitted variables that comprise the regression error are persistent (like district demographics) then this induces "serial" correlation in the regression error over time. Another example is when sampling is based on a geographical unit. If there are omitted variables that reflect geographic influences, these omitted variables could result in correlation of the regression errors for adjacent observations.

Correlation of the regression error across observations does not make the OLS estimator biased or inconsistent, but it does violate the second least squares assumption in Key Concept 5.4. The consequence is that the OLS standard errors—both homoskedasticy-only *and* heteroskedasticity-robust—are incorrect in the sense that they do not produce confidence intervals with the desired confidence level.

In many cases, this problem can be fixed by using an alternative formula for standard errors. We provide such a formula for computing standard errors that are robust to both heteroskedasticity and serial correlation in the discussion in Chapter 12 of regression with time series data.

7.3   Example: Test Scores and Class Size

The framework of internal and external validity helps us to take a critical look at what we have learned—and what we have not—from our analysis of the California test score data.

External Validity

Whether the California analysis can be generalized—that is, whether it is externally valid—depends on the population and setting to which the generalization is made. Here, we consider whether the results can be generalized to performance on other standardized tests in other elementary public school districts in the United States.

Section 7.1 noted that having more than one study on the same topic provides an opportunity to assess the external validity of both studies by comparing their results. In the case of test scores and class size, other comparable data sets are, in fact, available. In this section, we examine a different data set, based on standardized test results for fourth graders in 220 public school districts in Massachusetts in 1998. Both the Massachusetts and California tests are broad measures of student knowledge and academic skills, although the details differ. Similarly, the organization of classroom instruction is broadly similar at the elementary school level in the two states (as it is in most U.S. elementary school districts), although aspects of elementary school funding and curriculum differ. Thus, finding similar results about the effect of the student-teacher ratio on test performance in the California and Massachusetts data would be evidence of external validity of the findings in California. Conversely, finding different results in the two states would raise questions about the internal or external validity of at least one of the studies.

Comparison of the California and Massachusetts data.   Like the California data, the Massachusetts data are at the school district level. The definitions of the variables in the Massachusetts data set are the same as those in the California data set, or nearly so. More information on the Massachusetts data set, including definitions of the variables, is given in Appendix 7.1.

Table 7.1 presents summary statistics for the California and Massachusetts samples. The average test score is higher in Massachusetts, but the test is different, so a direct comparison of scores is not appropriate. The average student-teacher ratio is higher in California (19.6 versus 17.3). Average district income is 20% higher in Massachusetts, but the standard deviation of income is greater in California, that is, there is a greater spread in average district incomes in California than in

TABLE 7.1   Summary Statistics for California and Massachusetts Test Score Data Sets

	California		Massachusetts	
	Average	**Standard Deviation**	**Average**	**Standard Deviation**
Test scores	654.1	19.1	709.8	15.1
Student–teacher ratio	19.6	1.9	17.3	2.3
% English learners	15.8%	18.3%	1.1%	2.9%
% Receiving lunch subsidy	44.7%	27.1%	15.3%	15.1%
Average district income ($)	$15,317	$7,226	$18,747	$5,808
Number of observations	420		220	
Year	1999		1998	

Massachusetts. The average percentage of students still learning English and the average percentage of students receiving subsidized lunches are both much higher in the California than in the Massachusetts districts.

Test scores and average district income. To save space, we do not present scatterplots of all the Massachusetts data. Because it was a focus in Chapter 6, however, it is interesting to examine the relationship between test scores and average district income in Massachusetts. This scatterplot is presented in Figure 7.1. The general pattern of this scatterplot is similar to that in Figure 6.2 for the California data: the relationship between income and test scores appears to be steep for low values of income and flatter for high values. Evidently, the linear regression plotted in the figure misses this apparent nonlinearity. Cubic and logarithmic regression functions are also plotted in Figure 7.1. The cubic regression function has a slightly higher $\overline{R}^2$ than the logarithmic specification (0.486 versus 0.455). Comparing Figures 6.7 and 7.1 shows that the general pattern of nonlinearity found in the California income and test score data is also present in the Massachusetts data. The precise functional forms that best describe this nonlinearity differ, however, with the cubic specification fitting best in Massachusetts but the linear-log specification fitting best in California.

Multiple regression results. Regression results for the Massachusetts data are presented in Table 7.2. The first regression, reported in column (1) in the table, has only the student–teacher ratio as a regressor. The slope is negative (−1.72), and the hypothesis that the coefficient is zero can be rejected at the 1% significance level ($t = -1.72/0.50 = -3.44$).

FIGURE 7.1   **Test Scores vs. Income for Massachusetts Data**

The estimated linear regression function does not capture the nonlinear relation between income and test scores in the Massachusetts data. The estimated linear-log and cubic regression functions are similar for district incomes between $13,000 and $30,000, the region containing most of the observations.

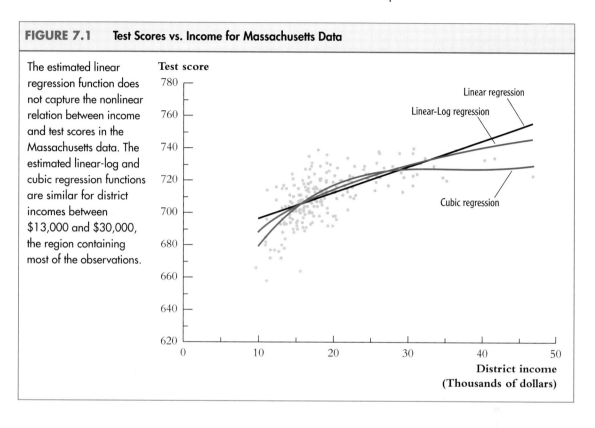

The remaining columns report the results of including additional variables that control for student characteristics and of introducing nonlinearities into the estimated regression function. Controlling for the percentage of English learners, the percentage of students eligible for a free lunch, and average district income reduces the estimated coefficient on the student-teacher ratio by 60%, from −1.72 in regression (1) to −0.69 in regression (2) and −0.64 in regression (3).

Comparing the $\overline{R}^2$'s of regressions (2) and (3) indicates that the cubic specification (3) provides a better model of the relationship between test scores and income than does the logarithmic specification (2), even holding constant the student-teacher ratio. There is no statistically significant evidence of a nonlinear relationship between test scores and the student-teacher ratio: the F-statistic in regression (4) testing whether the population coefficients on STR^2 and STR^3 are zero has a p-value of 0.641. Similarly, there is no evidence that a reduction in the student-teacher ratio has a different effect in districts with many English learners than with few (the t-statistic on $HiEL \times STR$ in regression (5) is $0.80/0.56 = 1.43$). Finally, regression (6) shows that the estimated coefficient on the student-teacher ratio does not change substantially when the percentage of English learners

TABLE 7.2 Multiple Regression Estimates of the Student-Teacher Ratio and Test Scores: Data from Massachusetts

Dependent Variable: Average Combined English, Math, and Science Test Score in the School District, Fourth Grade; 220 Observations.

Regressor	(1)	(2)	(3)	(4)	(5)	(6)
Student-teacher ratio (*STR*)	−1.72** (0.50)	−0.69* (0.27)	−0.64* (0.27)	12.4 (14.0)	−1.02** (0.37)	−0.67* (0.27)
STR^2				−0.680 (0.737)		
STR^3				0.011 (0.013)		
% English learners		−0.411 (0.306)	−0.437 (0.303)	−0.434 (0.300)		
% English learners > median? (Binary, *HiEL*)					−12.6 (9.8)	
$HiEL \times STR$					0.80 (0.56)	
% Eligible for free lunch		−0.521** (0.077)	−0.582** (0.097)	−0.587** (0.104)	−0.709** (0.091)	−0.653** (0.72)
District income (logarithm)		16.53** (3.15)				
District income			−3.07 (2.35)	−3.38 (2.49)	−3.87* (2.49)	−3.22 (2.31)
District income^2			0.164 (0.085)	0.174 (0.089)	0.184* (0.090)	0.165 (0.085)
District income^3				−0.0022* (0.0010)	−0.0023* (0.0010)	−0.0023* (0.0010)	−0.0022* (0.0010)
Intercept	739.6** (8.6)	682.4** (11.5)	744.0** (21.3)	665.5** (81.3)	759.9** (23.2)	747.4** (20.3)

(Table 7.2 continued)

(which is insignificant in regression (3)) is excluded. In short, the results in regression (3) are not sensitive to the changes in functional form and specification considered in regressions (4)–(6) in Table 7. 2. Therefore we adopt regression (3) as our base estimate of the effect in test scores of a change in the student-teacher ratio based on the Massachusetts data.

(Table 7.2 continued)

F-statistics and p-values Testing Exclusion of Groups of Variables

	(1)	(2)	(3)	(4)	(5)	(6)
all STR variables and interactions = 0				2.86 (0.038)	4.01 (0.020)	
STR^2, STR^3 = 0				0.45 (0.641)		
$Income^2$, $Income^3$			7.74 (< 0.001)	7.75 (< 0.001)	5.85 (0.003)	6.55 (0.002)
HiEL, HiEL × STR					1.58 (0.208)	
SER	14.64	8.69	8.61	8.63	8.62	8.64
$\bar{R}^2$	0.063	0.670	0.676	0.675	0.675	0.674

These regressions were estimated using the data on Massachusetts elementary school districts described in Appendix 7.1. Standard errors are given in parentheses under the coefficients, and p-values are given in parentheses under the F-statistics. Individual coefficients are statistically significant at the *5% level or **1% level.

Comparison of Massachusetts and California results.   For the California data, we found:

a. Adding variables that control for student background characteristics reduced the coefficient on the student-teacher ratio from −2.28 (Table 5.2, regression (1)) to −0.73 (Table 6.2, regression (2)), a reduction of 68%.

b. The hypothesis that the true coefficient on the student-teacher ratio is zero was rejected at the 1% significance level, even after adding variables that control for student background and district economic characteristics.

c. The effect of cutting the student-teacher ratio did not depend in an important way on the percentage of English learners in the district.

d. There is some evidence that the relationship between test scores and the student-teacher ratio is nonlinear.

Do we find the same things in Massachusetts? For findings (a), (b), and (c), the answer is yes. Including the additional control variables reduces the coefficient on the student-teacher ratio from −1.72 (Table 7.2, regression (1)) to −0.69 (Table 7.2, regression (2)), a reduction of 60%. The coefficients on the student-teacher ratio remain significant after adding the control variables. Those coefficients are only significant at the 5% level in the Massachusetts data, whereas they are significant at the 1% level in the California data. However, there are nearly twice as many observations in the California data, so it is not surprising that the California estimates are more precise. As in the California data, there is no statistically significant evidence in the Massachusetts data of an interaction between the student-teacher ratio and the binary variable indicating a large percentage of English learners in the district.

Finding (d), however, does not hold up in the Massachusetts data: the hypothesis that the relationship between the student-teacher ratio and test scores is linear cannot be rejected at the 5% significance level when tested against a cubic specification.

Because the two standardized tests are different, the coefficients themselves cannot be compared directly: one point on the Massachusetts test is not the same as one point on the California test. If, however, the test scores are put into the same units, then the estimated class size effects can be compared. One way to do this is to transform the test scores by standardizing them: subtract the sample average and divide by the standard deviation so that they have a mean of zero and a variance of one. The slope coefficients in the regression with the transformed test score equal the slope coefficients in the original regression, divided by the standard deviation of the test. Thus the coefficient on the student-teacher ratio, divided by the standard deviation of test scores, can be compared across the two data sets.

This comparison is undertaken in Table 7.3. The first column reports the OLS estimates of the coefficient on the student-teacher ratio in a regression with the percentage of English learners, the percentage of students eligible for a free lunch, and the average district income included as control variables. The second column reports the standard deviation of the test scores across districts. The final two columns report the estimated effect on test scores of reducing the student-teacher ratio by two students per teacher (our superintendent's proposal), first in the units of the test, and second in standard deviation units. For the linear specification, the OLS coefficient estimate using California data is -0.73, so cutting the student-teacher ratio by two is estimated to increase district test scores by $-0.73 \times (-2) = 1.46$ points. Because the standard deviation of test scores is 19.1 points, this corresponds to $1.46/19.1 = 0.076$ standard deviations of the distribution of test scores across districts. The standard error of this estimate is $0.26 \times 2/19.1 = 0.027$. The estimated effects for the nonlinear models and their standard errors were computed using the method described in Section 6.1.

Based on the linear model using California data, a reduction of two students per teacher is estimated to increase test scores by 0.076 standard deviation units, with a standard error of 0.027. The nonlinear models for California data suggest a somewhat larger effect, with the specific effect depending on the initial student-

---

TABLE 7.3   **Student-Teacher Ratios and Test Scores: Comparing the Estimates from California and Massachusetts**

| | OLS Estimate $\hat{\beta}_{STR}$ | Standard Deviation of Test Scores Across Districts | Estimated Effect of 2 Fewer Students Per Teacher, In Units of: | |
			Points on the Test	Standard Deviations
California				
Linear: Table 6.2(2)	−0.73 (0.26)	19.1	1.46 (0.52)	0.076 (0.027)
Cubic: Table 6.2(7) *Reduce STR from 20 to 18*	—	19.1	2.93 (0.70)	0.153 (0.037)
Cubic: Table 6.2(7) *Reduce STR from 22 to 20*	—	19.1	1.90 (0.69)	0.099 (0.036)
Massachusetts				
Linear: Table 7.2(3)	−0.64 (0.27)	15.1	1.28 (0.54)	0.085 (0.036)

Standard errors are given in parentheses.

teacher ratio. Based on the Massachusetts data, this estimated effect is 0.085 standard deviation units, with a standard error of 0.036.

These estimates are essentially the same. Cutting the student-teacher ratio is predicted to raise test scores, but the predicted improvement is small. In the California data, for example, the difference in test scores between the median district and a district at the 75th percentile is 12.2 test score points (Table 4.1), or 0.64 (= 12.2/19.1) standard deviations. The estimated effect from the linear model is just over one-tenth this size; in other words, according to this estimate, cutting the student teacher-ratio by two would move a district only one-tenth of the way from the median to the 75th percentile of the distribution of test scores across districts. Reducing the student-teacher ratio by two is a large change for a district, but the estimated benefits shown in Table 7.3, while nonzero, are small.

This analysis of Massachusetts data suggests that the California results are externally valid, at least when generalized to elementary school districts elsewhere in the United States.

Internal Validity

The similarity of the results for California and Massachusetts does not ensure their *internal* validity. Section 7.2 listed five possible threats to internal validity that could induce bias in the estimated effect on test scores on class size. We consider these threats in turn.

Omitted variables. The multiple regressions reported in this and previous chapters control for a student characteristic (the percentage of English learners), a family economic characteristic (the percentage of students receiving a subsidized lunch), and a broader measure of the affluence of the district (average district income).

Possible omitted variables remain, such as other school and student characteristics, and their omission might cause omitted variables bias. For example, if the student-teacher ratio is correlated with teacher quality (perhaps because better teachers are attracted to schools with smaller student-teacher ratios), and if teacher quality affects test scores, then omission of teacher quality could bias the coefficient on the student-teacher ratio. Similarly, districts with a low student-teacher ratio might also offer many extracurricular learning opportunities. Also, districts with a low student-teacher ratio might attract families that are more committed to enhancing their children's learning at home. Such omitted factors could lead to omitted variable bias.

One way to eliminate omitted variable bias, at least in theory, is to conduct an experiment. For example, students could be randomly assigned to different size classes, and their subsequent performance on standardized tests could be compared. Such a study was in fact conducted in Tennessee, and we examine it in Chapter 11.

Functional form. The analysis here and in Chapter 6 explored a variety of functional forms. We found that some of the possible nonlinearities investigated were not statistically significant, while those that were did not substantially alter the estimated effect of reducing the student-teacher ratio. Although further functional form analysis could be carried out, this suggests that the main findings of these studies are unlikely to be sensitive to using different nonlinear regression specifications.

Errors-in-variables. The average student-teacher ratio in the district is a broad and potentially inaccurate measure of class size. For example, because students move in and out of districts, the student-teacher ratio might not accurately represent the actual class sizes experienced by the students taking the test, which in turn could lead to the estimated class size effect being biased toward zero. Another variable with potential measurement error is average district income. Those data were taken from the 1990 census, while the other data pertain to 1998 (Massachusetts) or 1999 (California). If the economic composition of the district changed substantially over the 1990s, this would be an imprecise measure of the actual average district income.

Selection.   The California and the Massachusetts data cover all the public elementary school districts in the state that satisfy minimum size restrictions, so there is no reason to believe that sample selection is a problem here.

Simultaneous causality.   Simultaneous causality would arise if the performance on standardized tests affected the student-teacher ratio. This could happen, for example, if there is a bureaucratic or political mechanism for increasing the funding of poorly performing schools or districts, which in turn resulted in hiring more teachers. In Massachusetts, no such mechanism for equalization of school financing was in place during the time of these tests. In California, a series of court cases led to some equalization of funding, but this redistribution of funds was not based on student achievement. Thus, in neither Massachusetts nor California does simultaneous causality appear to be a problem.

Heteroskedasticity and correlation of the error term across observations. All of the results reported here and in earlier chapters use heteroskedastic-robust standard errors, so heteroskedasticity does not threaten internal validity. Correlation of the error term across observations, however, could threaten the consistency of the standard errors because simple random sampling was not used (the sample consists of all elementary school districts in the state). Although there are alternative standard error formulas that could be applied to this situation, the details are complicated and specialized and we leave them to more advanced texts.

Discussion and Implications

The similarity between the Massachusetts and California results suggest that these studies are externally valid, in the sense that the main findings can be generalized to performance on standardized tests at other elementary school districts in the United States.

   Some of the most important potential threats to internal validity have been addressed by controlling for student background, family economic background, and district affluence, and by checking for nonlinearities in the regression function. Still, some potential threats to internal validity remain. A leading candidate is omitted variable bias, perhaps arising because the control variables do not capture other characteristics of the school districts or extracurricular learning opportunities.

Based on both the California and the Massachusetts data, we are able to answer the superintendent's question from Chapter 4.1: after controlling for family economic background, student characteristics, and district affluence, and after modeling nonlinearities in the regression function, cutting the student-teacher ratio by two students per teacher is predicted to increase test scores by approximately 0.08 standard deviations of the distribution of test scores across districts. This effect is statistically significant, but it is quite small. This small estimated effect is in line with the results of the many studies that have investigated the effects on test scores of class size reductions.[4]

The superintendent can now use this estimate to help her decide whether to reduce class sizes. In making this decision, she will need to weigh the costs of the proposed reduction against the benefits. The costs include teacher salaries and expenses for additional classrooms. The benefits include improved academic performance, which we have measured by performance on standardized tests, but there are other potential benefits that we have not studied, including lower dropout rates and enhanced future earnings. The estimated effect of the proposal on standardized test performance is one important input into her calculation of costs and benefits.

7.4 Conclusion

The concepts of internal and external validity provide a framework for assessing what has been learned from an econometric study.

A study based on multiple regression is internally valid if the estimated coefficients are unbiased and consistent, and if standard errors are consistent. Threats to the internal validity of such a study include omitted variables, misspecification of functional form (nonlinearities), imprecise measurement of the independent variables (errors-in-variables), sample selection, and simultaneous causality. Each of these introduces correlation between the regressor and the error term, which in turn makes OLS estimators biased and inconsistent. If the errors are correlated

---

[4]If you are interested in learning more about the relationship between class size and test scores, see the reviews by Ehrenberg, Brewer, Gamoran, and Willms (2001a, 2001b).

across observations, as they can be with time series data, or if they are heteroskedastic but the standard errors are computed using the homoskedasticity-only formula, then internal validity is compromised because the standard errors will be inconsistent. These latter problems can be addressed by computing the standard errors properly.

A study using regression analysis, like any statistical study, is externally valid if its findings can be generalized beyond the population and setting studied. Sometimes it can help to compare two or more studies on the same topic. Whether or not there are two or more such studies, however, assessing external validity requires making judgments about the similarities of the population and setting studied and the population and setting to which the results are being generalized.

The next two parts of this textbook develop ways to address threats to internal validity that cannot be mitigated by multiple regression analysis alone. Part III extends the multiple regression model in ways designed to mitigate all five sources of potential bias in the OLS estimator; Part III also discusses a different approach to obtaining internal validity, randomized controlled experiments. Part IV develops methods for analyzing time series data and for using time series data to estimate so-called dynamic causal effects, which are causal effects that vary over time.

Summary

1. Statistical studies are evaluated by asking whether the analysis is internally and externally valid. A study is internally valid if the statistical inferences about causal effects are valid for the population being studied. A study is externally valid if its inferences and conclusions can be generalized from the population and setting studied to other populations and settings.

2. In regression analysis, there are two main threats to internal validity. First, OLS estimators will be inconsistent if the regressors and error terms are correlated. Second, confidence intervals and hypothesis tests are not valid when the standard errors are incorrect.

3. Regressors and error terms may be correlated when there are omitted variables, an incorrect functional form, one or more of the regressors is measured with error, the sample is chosen nonrandomly from the population, or there is simultaneous causality between the regressors and dependent variables.

4. Standard errors are incorrect when the errors are heteroskedastic and the computer software uses the homoskedasticity-only standard errors, or when the error term is correlated across different observations.

Key Terms

population studied (242)

population of interest (242)

internal validity (243)

external validity (243)

functional form misspecification (247)

errors-in-variables bias (248)

sample selection bias (250)

simultaneous causality bias (251)

simultaneous equations bias (253)

Review the Concepts

7.1 What is the difference between internal and external validity? Between the population studied and the population of interest?

7.2 Key Concept 7.2 describes the problem of variable selection in terms of a tradeoff between bias and variance. What is this tradeoff? Why could including an additional regressor decrease bias? Increase variance?

7.3 Economic variables are often measured with error. Does this mean that regression analysis is unreliable? Explain.

7.4 Suppose that a state offered voluntary standardized tests to all of its third graders, and these data were used in a study of class size on student performance. Explain how sample selection bias might invalidate the results.

7.5 A researcher estimates the effect on crime rates of spending on police using city-level data. Explain how simultaneous causality might invalidate the results.

7.6 A researcher estimates a regression using two different software packages. The first uses the homoskedasticity-only formula for standard errors. The second uses the heteroskedasticity-robust formula. The standard errors are very different. Which should you use? Why?

Exercises

*7.1 Suppose that you have just read a careful statistical study of the effect of advertising on the demand for cigarettes. Using data from New York during the 1970s, it concluded that advertising on buses and subways was more effective than print advertising. Use the concept of external validity to determine if these results are likely to apply to Boston in the 1970s; Los Angeles in the 1970s; New York in 2002.

7.2 Consider the one-variable regression model: $Y_i = \beta_0 + \beta_1 X_i + u_i$, and suppose that it satisfies the assumption in Key Concept 4.3. Suppose that Y_i is measured with error, so that the data are $\widetilde{Y}_i = Y_i + w_i$, where w_i is the measurement error which is i.i.d. and independent of Y_i and X_i. Consider the population regression $\widetilde{Y}_i = \beta_0 + \beta_1 X_i + v_i$, where v_i is the regression error using the mismeasured dependent variable, $\widetilde{Y}_i$.

    a. Show that $v_i = u_i + w_i$.

    b. Show that the regression $\widetilde{Y}_i = \beta_0 + \beta_1 X_i + v_i$ satisfies the assumptions in Key Concept 4.3. (Assume that w_i is independent of Y_j and X_j for all values of i and j and has a finite fourth moment.)

    c. Are the OLS estimators consistent?

    d. Can confidence intervals be constructed in the usual way?

    e. Evaluate the statement: "Measurement error in the X's is a serious problem. Measurement error in Y is not."

7.3 Labor economists studying the determinants of women's earnings discovered a puzzling empirical result. Using randomly selected employed women, they regressed earnings on the women's number of children and a set of control variables (age, education, occupation, etc.) They found that women with more children had higher wages, controlling for these other factors. Explain how sample selection might be the cause of this result. (*Hint:* Notice that the sample includes only women who are working.) (This empirical puzzle motivated James Heckman's research on sample selection that led to his 2000 Nobel Prize in economics.)

APPENDIX

7.1 | The Massachusetts Elementary School Testing Data

The Massachusetts data are districtwide averages for public elementary school districts in 1998. The test score is taken from the Massachusetts Comprehensive Assessment System (MCAS) test administered to all fourth-graders in Massachusetts public schools in the spring of 1998. The test is sponsored by the Massachusetts Department of Education and is mandatory for all public schools. The data analyzed here are the overall total score, which is the sum of the scores on the English, Math, and Science portions of the test.

Data on the student-teacher ratio, the percentage of students receiving a subsidized lunch, and the percentage of students still learning English are averages for each elementary school district for the 1997–1998 school year, and were obtained from the Massachusetts Department of Education. Data on average district income were obtained from the 1990 U.S. Census.

CHAPTER 8

Regression with Panel Data

M ultiple regression is a powerful tool for controlling for the effect of variables on which we have data. If data are not available for some of the variables, however, they cannot be included in the regression and the OLS estimators of the regression coefficients could have omitted variable bias.

This chapter describes a method for controlling for some types of omitted variables without actually observing them. This method requires a specific type of data, called panel data, in which each observational unit, or entity, is observed at two or more time periods. By studying *changes* in the dependent variable over time, it is possible to eliminate the effect of omitted variables that differ across entities but are constant over time.

The empirical application in this chapter concerns drunk driving: what are the effects of alcohol taxes and drunk driving laws on traffic fatalities? We address this question using data on traffic fatalities, alcohol taxes, drunk driving laws, and related variables for the 48 contiguous U.S. states for each of the seven years from 1982 to 1988. This panel data set lets us control for unobserved variables that differ from one state to the next, such as prevailing cultural attitudes towards drinking and driving, but do not change over time. It also allows us to control for variables that vary through time, like improvements in the safety of new cars, but do not vary across states.

Section 8.1 describes the structure of panel data and introduces the drunk driving data set. Fixed effects regression, the main tool for regression analysis of panel data, is an extension of multiple regression that exploits panel data to control for variables that differ across entities but are constant over time. Fixed effects regression is introduced in Sections 8.2 and 8.3, first for the case of only two time periods, then for multiple time periods. In Section 8.4, these methods are extended to incorporate so-called time fixed effects, which control for unobserved variables that are constant across entities but change over time. In Section 8.5, we use these methods to study the effect of alcohol taxes and drunk driving laws on traffic deaths.

8.1   Panel Data

Recall from Section 1.3 that **panel data** (also called longitudinal data) refers to data for n different entities observed at T different time periods. The state traffic fatality data studied in this chapter are panel data. Those data are for $n = 48$ entities (states), where each entity is observed in $T = 7$ time periods (each of the years 1982, ... , 1988), for a total of $7 \times 48 = 336$ observations.

When describing cross-sectional data it was useful to use a subscript to denote the entity, for example Y_i referred to the variable Y for the ith entity. When describing panel data, we need some additional notation to keep track of both the entity and the time period. This is done by using two subscripts rather than one: the first, i, refers to the entity, and the second, t, refers to the time period of the observation. Thus Y_{it} denotes the variable Y observed for the ith of n entities in the tth of T periods. This notation is summarized in Key Concept 8.1.

Some additional terminology associated with panel data describes whether some observations are missing. A **balanced panel** has all its observations, that is, the variables are observed for each entity and each time period. A panel that has some missing data for at least one time period for at least one entity is called an **unbalanced panel**. The traffic fatality data set has data for all 48 U.S. states for all seven years, so it is balanced. If, however, some data were missing (for example, if we did not have data on fatalities for some states in 1983), then the data set would be unbalanced. The methods presented in this chapter are described for a balanced panel; however, all these methods can be used with an unbalanced panel, although precisely how to do so in practice depends on the regression software being used.

Example: Traffic Deaths and Alcohol Taxes

There are approximately 40,000 highway traffic fatalities each year in the United States. Approximately one-third of fatal crashes involve a driver who was drinking, and this fraction rises during peak drinking periods. One study (Levitt and Porter, 2001) estimates that as many as 25% of drivers on the road between 1 A.M.

Notation for Panel Data

Panel data consists of observations on the same n entities at two or more time periods T. If the data set contains observations on the variables X and Y, then the data are denoted

$$(X_{it}, Y_{it}), \ i = 1, \dots, n \text{ and } t = 1, \dots, T, \qquad (8.1)$$

where the first subscript, i, refers to the entity being observed, and the second subscript, t, refers to the date at which it is observed.

and 3 A.M. have been drinking, and that a driver who is legally drunk is at least 13 times as likely to cause a fatal crash as a driver who has not been drinking.

In this chapter, we study how effective various government policies designed to discourage drunk driving actually are in reducing traffic deaths. The panel data set contains variables related to traffic fatalities and alcohol, including the number of traffic fatalities in each state in each year, the type of drunk driving laws in each state in each year, and the tax on beer in each state. The measure of traffic deaths we use is the fatality rate, which is the number of annual traffic deaths per 10,000 people in the population in the state. The measure of alcohol taxes we use is the "real" tax on a case of beer, which is the beer tax, put into 1988 dollars by adjusting for inflation.[1] The data are described in more detail in Appendix 8.1.

Figure 8.1a is a scatterplot of the data for 1982 on two of these variables, the fatality rate and the real tax on a case of beer. A point in this scatterplot represents the fatality rate in 1982 and the real beer tax in 1982 for a given state. The OLS regression line obtained by regressing the fatality rate on the real beer tax is also plotted in the figure; the estimated regression line is

$$\widehat{FatalityRate} = 2.01 + 0.15 BeerTax \quad (1982 \text{ data}). \qquad (8.2)$$
$$\qquad\qquad\quad (0.15) \quad (0.13)$$

The coefficient on the real beer tax is positive, but not statistically significant at the 10% level.

---

[1]To make the taxes comparable over time, they are put into "1988 dollars" using the Consumer Price Index (CPI). For example, because of inflation a tax of $1 in 1982 corresponds to a tax of $1.23 in 1988 dollars.

FIGURE 8.1 **The Traffic Fatality Rate and the Tax on Beer**

Panel a is a scatterplot of traffic fatality rates and the real tax on a case of beer (in 1988 dollars) for 48 states in 1982. Panel b shows the data for 1988. Both plots show a positive relationship between the fatality rate and the real beer tax.

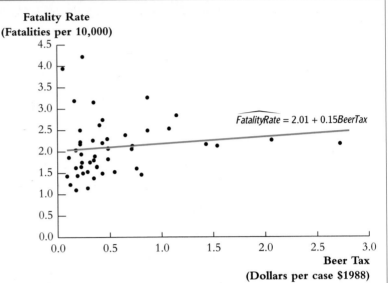

FatalityRate = 2.01 + 0.15BeerTax

(a) 1982 data

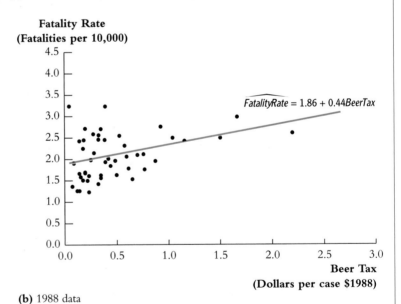

FatalityRate = 1.86 + 0.44BeerTax

(b) 1988 data

Because we have data for more than one year, we can reexamine this relationship for another year. This is done in Figure 8.1b, which is the same scatterplot as before, except that it uses the data for 1988. The OLS regression line through these data is

$$\widehat{FatalityRate} = 1.86 + 0.44 BeerTax \quad \text{(1988 data).} \quad (8.3)$$
$$\qquad\qquad\quad (0.11) \quad (0.13)$$

In contrast to the regression using the 1982 data, the coefficient on the real beer tax is statistically significant at the 1% level (the t-statistic is 3.43). Curiously, the estimated coefficient for the 1982 and the 1988 data is *positive*: taken literally, higher real beer taxes are associated with *more*, not fewer, traffic fatalities.

Should we conclude that an increase in the tax on beer leads to more traffic deaths? Not necessarily, because these regressions could have substantial omitted variable bias. Many factors affect the fatality rate, including the quality of the automobiles driven in the state, whether the state highways are in good repair, whether most driving is rural or urban, the density of cars on the road, and whether it is socially acceptable to drink and drive. Any of these factors may be correlated with alcohol taxes; and if they are, they will lead to omitted variable bias. One approach to these potential sources of omitted variable bias would be to collect data on all of these variables and add them to the annual cross-sectional regressions in Equations (8.2) and (8.3). Unfortunately, some of these variables, such as the cultural acceptance of drinking and driving, might be very hard or even impossible to measure.

If these factors remain constant over time in a given state, however, then another route is available. Because we have panel data, we can in effect hold these factors constant, even though we cannot measure them. To do so, we use OLS regression with fixed effects.

8.2   Panel Data with Two Time Periods: "Before and After" Comparisons

When data for each state are obtained for $T = 2$ time periods, it is possible to compare values of the dependent variable in the second period to values in the first period. By focusing on *changes* in the dependent variable, this "before and after" comparison in effect holds constant the unobserved factors that differ from one state to the next but do not change over time within the state.

Let Z_i be a variable that determines the fatality rate in the ith state, but does not change over time (so the t subscript is omitted). For example, Z_i might be the local cultural attitude towards drinking and driving, which changes slowly and thus could be considered to be constant between 1982 and 1988. Accordingly, the population linear regression relating Z_i and the real beer tax to the fatality rate is

$$FatalityRate_{it} = \beta_0 + \beta_1 BeerTax_{it} + \beta_2 Z_i + u_{it}, \tag{8.4}$$

where u_{it} is the error term and $i = 1, \ldots, n$ and $t = 1, \ldots, T$.

Because Z_i does not change over time, in the regression model in Equation (8.4) it will not produce any *change* in the fatality rate between 1982 and 1988. Thus, in this regression model, the influence of Z_i can be eliminated by analyzing the change in the fatality rate between the two periods. To see this mathematically, consider Equation (8.4) for each of the two years, 1982 and 1988:

$$FatalityRate_{i1982} = \beta_0 + \beta_1 BeerTax_{i1982} + \beta_2 Z_i + u_{i1982}, \tag{8.5}$$

$$FatalityRate_{i1988} = \beta_0 + \beta_1 BeerTax_{i1988} + \beta_2 Z_i + u_{i1988}. \tag{8.6}$$

Subtracting Equation (8.5) from Equation (8.6) eliminates the effect of Z_i:

$$\begin{aligned} FatalityRate_{i1988} &- Fatality\ Rate_{i1982} \\ &= \beta_1(BeerTax_{i1988} - BeerTax_{i1982}) + u_{i1988} - u_{i1982}. \end{aligned} \tag{8.7}$$

This specification has an intuitive interpretation. Cultural attitudes towards drinking and driving affect the level of drunk driving and thus the traffic fatality rate in a state. If, however, they did not change between 1982 and 1988, then they did not produce any *change* in fatalities in the state. Rather, any changes in traffic fatalities over time must have arisen from other sources. In Equation (8.7), these other sources are changes in the tax on beer or changes in the error term (which captures changes in other factors that determine traffic deaths).

Specifying the regression in changes in Equation (8.7) eliminates the effect of the unobserved variables Z_i that are constant over time. In other words, analyzing changes in Y and X has the effect of controlling for variables that are constant over time, thereby eliminating this source of omitted variable bias.

Figure 8.2 presents a scatterplot of the *change* in the fatality rate between 1982 and 1988 against the *change* in the real beer tax between 1982 and 1988 for the 48 states in our data set. A point in Figure 8.2 represents the change in the fatality rate and the change in the real beer tax between 1982 and 1988 for a given state. The OLS regression line, estimated using these data and plotted in the figure, is

$$
\begin{aligned}
\overline{FatalityRate_{1988}} &- FatalityRate_{1982} \\
&= -0.072 - 1.04(BeerTax_{1988} - BeerTax_{1982}), \\
&\ (0.065)\ \ (0.36)
\end{aligned}
\tag{8.8}
$$

where including an intercept allows for the possibility that the mean change in the fatality rate, in the absence of a change in the real beer tax, is nonzero.

In contrast to the cross-sectional regression results, the estimated effect of a change in the real beer tax is negative, as predicted by economic theory. The

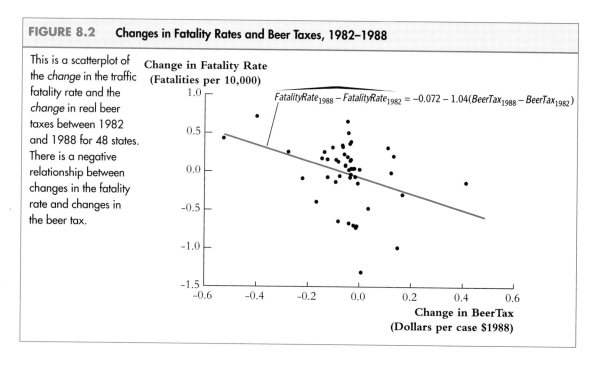

FIGURE 8.2   **Changes in Fatality Rates and Beer Taxes, 1982–1988**

This is a scatterplot of the *change* in the traffic fatality rate and the *change* in real beer taxes between 1982 and 1988 for 48 states. There is a negative relationship between changes in the fatality rate and changes in the beer tax.

hypothesis that the population slope coefficient is zero is rejected at the 5% significance level. According to this estimated coefficient, an increase in the real beer tax by $1 per case reduces the traffic fatality rate by 1.04 deaths per 10,000 people. This estimated effect is very large: the average fatality rate is approximately two in these data (that is, two fatalities per year per 10,000 members of the population), so the estimate suggests that traffic fatalities can be cut in half merely by increasing the real tax on beer by $1 per case.

By examining changes in the fatality rate over time, the regression in Equation (8.8) controls for fixed factors such as cultural attitudes towards drinking and driving. But there are many factors that influence traffic safety, and if they change over time and are correlated with the real beer tax, then their omission will produce omitted variable bias. In Section 8.5, we undertake a more careful analysis that controls for several such factors, so for now it is best to refrain from drawing any substantive conclusions about the effect of real beer taxes on traffic fatalities.

This "before and after" analysis works when the data are observed in two different years. Our data set, however, contains observations for seven different years, and it seems foolish to discard that potentially useful additional data. But the "before and after" method does not apply directly when $T > 2$. To analyze all the observations in our panel data set, we use the method of fixed effects regression.

8.3 Fixed Effects Regression

Fixed effects regression is a method for controlling for omitted variables in panel data when the omitted variables vary across entities (states) but do not change over time. Unlike the "before and after" comparisons of Section 8.2, fixed effects regression can be used when there are two or more time observations for each entity.

The fixed effects regression model has n different intercepts, one for each entity. These intercepts can be represented by a set of binary (or indicator) variables. These binary variables absorb the influences of all omitted variables that differ from one entity to the next but are constant over time.

The Fixed Effects Regression Model

Consider the regression model in Equation (8.4) with the dependent variable (*FatalityRate*) and observed regressor (*BeerTax*) denoted as Y_{it} and X_{it}:

$$Y_{it} = \beta_0 + \beta_1 X_{it} + \beta_2 Z_i + u_{it}, \tag{8.9}$$

where Z_i is an unobserved variable that varies from one state to the next but does not change over time (for example, Z_i represents cultural attitudes towards drinking and driving). We want to estimate β_1, the effect on Y of X holding constant the unobserved state characteristics Z.

Because Z_i varies from one state to the next but is constant over time, the population regression model in Equation (8.9) can be interpreted as having n intercepts, one for each state. Specifically, let $\alpha_i = \beta_0 + \beta_2 Z_i$. Then Equation (8.9) becomes

$$Y_{it} = \beta_1 X_{it} + \alpha_i + u_{it}. \tag{8.10}$$

Equation (8.10) is the **fixed effects regression model**, in which $\alpha_1, \ldots, \alpha_n$ are treated as unknown intercepts to be estimated, one for each state. The interpretation of α_i as a state-specific intercept in Equation (8.10) comes from considering the population regression line for the ith state; this population regression line is $\alpha_i + \beta_1 X_{it}$. The slope coefficient of the population regression line, β_1, is the same for all states, but the intercept of the population regression line varies from one state to the next. The source of the variation in the intercept is the variable Z_i, which varies from one state to the next but is constant over time.

The state-specific intercepts in the fixed effects regression model also can be expressed using binary variables to denote the individual states. Section 6.3 considered the case in which the observations belong to one of two groups and the population regression line has the same slope for both groups but different intercepts (see Figure 6.8a). That population regression line was expressed mathematically using a single binary variable indicating one of the groups (specification #1 in Key Concept 6.4). If we only had two states in our data set, that binary variable regression model would apply here. Because we have more than two states, however, we need to add additional binary variables to capture all the state-specific intercepts in Equation (8.10).

To develop the fixed effects regression model using binary variables, let $D1_i$ be a binary variable that equals one when $i = 1$ and equals zero otherwise, let $D2_i$ equal one when $i = 2$ and equal zero otherwise, etc. We cannot include all n binary variables plus a common intercept, for if we do the regressors will be perfectly multicollinear (Exercise 8.2), so we arbitrarily omit the binary variable $D1_i$ for the first group. Accordingly, the fixed effects regression model in Equation (8.10) can be written equivalently as

$$Y_{it} = \beta_0 + \beta_1 X_{it} + \gamma_2 D2_i + \gamma_3 D3_i + \cdots + \gamma_n Dn_i + u_{it}, \tag{8.11}$$

where $\beta_0, \beta_1, \gamma_2, \ldots, \gamma_n$ are unknown coefficients to be estimated. To derive the relationship between the coefficients in Equation (8.11) and the intercepts in Equation (8.10), compare the population regression lines for each state in the two equations. In Equation (8.11), the population regression equation for the first state is $\beta_0 + \beta_1 X_{it}$, so $\alpha_1 = \beta_0$. For the second and remaining states, it is $\beta_0 + \beta_1 X_{it} + \gamma_i$, so $\alpha_i = \beta_0 + \gamma_i$ for $i \geq 2$.

Thus, there are two equivalent ways to write the fixed effects regression model, Equations (8.10) and (8.11). In Equation (8.10), it is written in terms of n state-specific intercepts. In Equation (8.11), the fixed effects regression model has a common intercept and $n - 1$ binary regressors. In both formulations, the slope coefficient on X is the same from one state to the next. The state-specific intercepts in Equation (8.10) and the binary regressors in Equation (8.11) have the same source: the unobserved variable Z_i that varies across states but not over time.

Extension to multiple X's. If there are other observed determinants of Y that are correlated with X and that change over time, then these should also be included in the regression to avoid omitted variable bias. Doing so results in the fixed effects regression model with multiple regressors, summarized in Key Concept 8.2.

Least squares assumptions for the fixed effects regression model. There are five least squares assumptions for the fixed effects regression model: the four assumptions for the multiple regression model in Key Concept 5.4 (modified for panel data), plus a fifth, new assumption. In cross-sectional data, the errors are uncorrelated across entities, conditional on the regressors, and the fifth assumption extends this to panel data by assuming that the errors are uncorrelated across time as well as entities, conditional on the regressors. These assumptions are conceptually similar to the least squares assumptions for the multiple regression model, but their mathematical statements are rather complicated because of the necessarily complicated notation associated with panel data sets. The assumptions are stated and discussed in Appendix 8.2.

Estimation and Inference

In principle the binary-variable specification of the fixed effects regression model (Equation (8.13)) can be estimated by OLS. This regression, however, has $k + n$ regressors (the k X's, the $n - 1$ binary variables, and the intercept), so in practice this OLS regression is tedious or, in some software packages, impossible to implement if the number of entities is large. Econometric software therefore has special routines for OLS estimation of fixed effects regression models. These special

The Fixed Effects Regression Model

The fixed effects regression model is

$$Y_{it} = \beta_1 X_{1,it} + \cdots + \beta_k X_{k,it} + \alpha_i + u_{it}, \qquad (8.12)$$

where $i = 1, \ldots, n$ and $t = 1, \ldots, T$, where $X_{1,it}$ is the value of the first regressor for entity i in time period t, $X_{2,it}$ is the value of the second regressor, and so forth, and $\alpha_1, \ldots, \alpha_n$ are entity-specific intercepts.

Equivalently, the fixed effects regression model can be written in terms of a common intercept, the X's, and $n - 1$ binary variables representing all but one entity:

$$\begin{aligned} Y_{it} = \beta_0 + \beta_1 X_{1,it} + \cdots &+ \beta_k X_{k,it} + \gamma_2 D2_i \\ &+ \gamma_3 D3_i + \cdots + \gamma_n Dn_i + u_{it}, \end{aligned} \qquad (8.13)$$

where $D2_i = 1$ if $i = 2$ and zero otherwise, and so forth.

Key Concept 8.2

routines are equivalent to using OLS on the full binary variable regression, but are faster because they employ some mathematical simplifications that arise in the algebra of fixed effects regression.

The "entity-demeaned" OLS algorithm. Regression software typically computes the OLS fixed effects estimator in two steps. In the first step, the entity-specific average is subtracted from each variable. In the second step, the regression is estimated using "entity-demeaned" variables. Specifically, consider the case of a single regressor in the version of the fixed effects model in Equation (8.10) and take the average of both sides of Equation (8.10); then $\overline{Y}_i = \beta_1 \overline{X}_i + \alpha_i + \overline{u}_i$, where $\overline{Y}_i = \frac{1}{T}\sum_{t=1}^{T} Y_{it}$, and $\overline{X}_i$ and $\overline{u}_i$ are defined similarly. Thus Equation (8.10) implies that $Y_{it} - \overline{Y}_i = \beta_1(X_{it} - \overline{X}_i) + (u_{it} - \overline{u}_i)$. Let $\widetilde{Y}_{it} = Y_{it} - \overline{Y}_i$, $\widetilde{X}_{it} = X_{it} - \overline{X}_i$, and $\widetilde{u}_{it} = u_{it} - \overline{u}_i$; accordingly,

$$\widetilde{Y}_{it} = \beta_1 \widetilde{X}_{it} + \widetilde{u}_{it}. \qquad (8.14)$$

Thus β_1 can be estimated by the OLS regression of the "entity-demeaned" variables $\widetilde{Y}_{it}$ on $\widetilde{X}_{it}$. In fact, this estimator is identical to the OLS estimator of β_1 obtained by estimation of the fixed effects model in Equation (8.10) using $n - 1$ binary variables (Exercise 16.6).

The "before and after" regression vs. fixed effects estimation. Although Equation (8.11) with its binary variables looks quite different than the "before and after" regression model in Equation (8.7), in the special case that $T = 2$ the OLS estimator β_1 from the binary variable specification and from the "before and after" specification are identical. Thus, when $T = 2$, there are three ways to estimate β_1 by OLS: the "before and after" specification in Equation (8.7), the binary variable specification in Equation (8.11), and the "entity-demeaned" specification in Equation (8.14). These three methods are equivalent, that is, they produce identical OLS estimates.

Standard errors and statistical inference. Under the least squares assumptions in Appendix 8.2, the usual heteroskedasticity-robust OLS standard errors produce inference that is reliable in large samples. That is, hypothesis tests constructed using the usual standard errors will have a size equal to the desired significance level, and confidence intervals with a desired 95% confidence level will contain the true value of β_1 in 95% of repeated samples.

Application to Traffic Deaths

The OLS estimate of the fixed effects regression line relating the real beer tax to the fatality rate, based on all seven years of data (336 observations), is

$$\widehat{FatalityRate} = -0.66\, BeerTax + StateFixedEffects, \qquad (8.15)$$
$$(0.20)$$

where, as is conventional, the estimated state fixed intercepts are not listed to save space and because they are not of primary interest in this application.

Like the "differences" specification in Equation (8.8), the estimated coefficient in the fixed effects regression in Equation (8.15) is negative, so that, as predicted by economic theory, higher real beer taxes are associated with fewer traffic deaths—the opposite of what we found in the initial cross-sectional regressions of Equations (8.2) and (8.3). The two regressions are not identical because the "differences" regression in Equation (8.8) uses only the data for 1982 and 1988 (specifically, the difference between those two years), whereas the fixed effects regression in Equation (8.15) uses the data for all seven years. Because of the additional observations, the standard error is smaller in Equation (8.15) than in Equation (8.8).

Including state fixed effects in the fatality rate regression lets us avoid omitted variables bias arising from omitted factors, such as cultural attitudes towards drinking and driving, that vary across states but are constant over time within a state. Still, a skeptic might suspect that there are other factors that could lead to omitted variables bias. For example, over this period cars were getting safer and occupants were increasingly wearing seat belts; if the real tax on beer rose on average during the mid–1980s, then it could be picking up the effect of overall automobile safety improvements. If, however, safety improvements evolved over time but were the same for all states, then we can eliminate their influence by including time fixed effects.

8.4 Regression with Time Fixed Effects

Just as fixed effects for each entity can control for variables that are constant over time but differ across entities, so can time fixed effects control for variables that are constant across entities but evolve over time.

Because safety improvements in new cars are introduced nationally, they serve to reduce traffic fatalities in all states. So, it is plausible to think of automobile safety as an omitted variable that changes over time but has the same value for all states. The population regression in Equation (8.9) can be modified to include the effect of automobile safety, which we will denote by S_t:

$$Y_{it} = \beta_0 + \beta_1 X_{it} + \beta_2 Z_i + \beta_3 S_t + u_{it}, \tag{8.16}$$

where S_t is unobserved, where the single "t" subscript emphasizes that safety changes over time but is constant across states. Because $\beta_3 S_t$ represents variables that determine Y_{it}, if S_t is correlated with X_{it}, then omitting S_t from the regression leads to omitted variable bias.

Time Effects Only

For the moment, suppose that the variables Z_i are not present, so that the term $\beta_2 Z_i$ can be dropped from Equation (8.16), although the term $\beta_3 S_t$ remains. Our objective is to estimate β_1, controlling for S_t.

Although S_t is unobserved, its influence can be eliminated because it varies over time but not over states, just as it is possible to eliminate the effect of Z_i, which varies across states but not over time. That is, $\beta_3 S_t$ can be replaced by a set of T binary variables, each indicating a different year. Specifically, let $B1_t = 1$ if t is the first time period in the sample and equal zero otherwise; let $B2_t = 1$ if t is the second time period; and so forth. The binary variables $B1_t, \ldots, BT_t$ are referred to as **time effects**.

The **time effects regression model** with a single X regressor and $T - 1$ time effects is

$$Y_{it} = \beta_0 + \beta_1 X_{it} + \delta_2 B2_t + \cdots + \delta_T BT_t + u_{it}, \tag{8.17}$$

where $\delta_2, \ldots, \delta_T$ are unknown coefficients. As in the fixed effects regression model in Equation (8.11), in this version of the time effects model the intercept is included, and the first binary variable ($B1_t$) is omitted to prevent perfect multicollinearity.

In the traffic fatalities regression, the time fixed effects specification in Equation (8.17) allows us to eliminate bias arising from omitted variables like nationally introduced safety standards that change over time but are the same across states in a given year.

Both Time and State Fixed Effects

If some omitted variables are constant over time but vary across states (such as cultural norms), while others are constant across states but vary over time (such as national safety standards), then it is appropriate to include *both* state *and* time effects. This is done by including both $n - 1$ state binary variables and $T - 1$ time binary variables in the regression, along with the intercept. The combined **time and entity fixed effects regression model** is

$$Y_{it} = \beta_0 + \beta_1 X_{it} + \gamma_2 D2_i + \cdots + \gamma_n Dn_i + \delta_2 B2_t + \cdots + \delta_T BT_t + u_{it}, \tag{8.18}$$

where $\beta_0, \beta_1, \gamma_2, \ldots, \gamma_n, \delta_2, \ldots, \delta_T$ are unknown coefficients.

The combined time and state fixed effects regression model eliminates omitted variables bias arising both from unobserved variables that are constant over time and from unobserved variables that are constant across states.

When there are additional observed "X" regressors, then these appear in Equation (8.18) as well.

Estimation.   The time fixed effects model and the time and entity (state) fixed effects model are both variants of the multiple regression model. Thus their coefficients can be estimated by OLS by including the additional time binary variables. Some software incorporates algorithms for computing combined time and entity fixed effects regressions that are computationally more efficient than OLS estimation of the full binary variable model in Equation (8.18).

Application to traffic deaths.   Adding time effects to the state fixed effects regression results in the OLS estimate of the regression line:

$$\widehat{FatalityRate} = -0.64BeerTax + StateFixedEffects + TimeFixedEffects. \quad (8.19)$$
$$(0.25)$$

This specification includes the beer tax, 47 state binary variables (state fixed effects), 6 year binary variables (time fixed effects), and an intercept, so that this regression actually has $1 + 47 + 6 + 1 = 55$ right-hand variables! The coefficients on the time and state binary variables and the intercept are not reported because they are not of primary interest.

Including the time effects has little impact on the estimated relationship between the real beer tax and the fatality rate (compare Equations (8.15) and (8.19)), and the coefficient on the real beer tax remains significant at the 5% level $(t = -0.64/0.25 = -2.56)$.

This estimated relationship between the real beer tax and traffic fatalities is immune to omitted variable bias from variables that are constant either over time or across states. However, many important determinants of traffic deaths do not fall into this category, so this specification could still be subject to omitted variable bias. With the tool of fixed effects regression in hand, we therefore undertake a more complete empirical analysis of these data.

8.5   Drunk Driving Laws and Traffic Deaths

Alcohol taxes are only one way to discourage drinking and driving. States differ in their punishments for drunk driving, and a state that cracks down on drunk driving could do so across the board by toughening laws as well as raising taxes. If so, omitting these laws could produce omitted variable bias in the OLS estimator of the effect of real beer taxes on traffic fatalities, even in regressions with state and time fixed effects. In addition, because vehicle use depends in part on whether drivers have jobs and because tax changes can reflect economic conditions (a state budget deficit can lead to tax hikes), omitting state economic conditions also could result in omitted variable bias.

In this section, we extend the preceding analysis to study the effect on traffic fatalities of drinking laws (including beer taxes), holding economic conditions constant. This is done by estimating panel data regressions that include regressors representing other drunk driving laws and state economic conditions.

The results are summarized in Table 8.1. The format of the table is the same as that of the tables of regression results in Chapters 5, 6, and 7: each column reports a different regression and each row reports a coefficient estimate and standard error, F-statistic, and p-value, or other information about the regression.

Column (1) in Table 8.1 presents results for the OLS regression of the fatality rate on the real beer tax without state and time fixed effects. As in the cross-sectional regressions for 1982 and 1988 (Equations (8.2) and (8.3)), the coefficient on the real beer tax is *positive* (0.36) and the column (1) estimate is statistically significantly different from zero at the 5% level: according to this estimate, increasing beer taxes *increases* traffic fatalities! However, the regression in column (2) (reported previously as Equation (8.15)), which includes state fixed effects, suggests that the positive coefficient in regression (1) is the result of omitted variable bias (the coefficient on the real beer tax is −0.66). The regression $\overline{R}^2$ jumps from 0.090 to 0.889 when fixed effects are included; evidently, the state fixed effects account for a large amount of the variation in the data.

Little changes when time effects are added, as reported in column (3) (reported previously as Equation (8.19)). The results in columns (1)–(3) are consistent with the omitted fixed variables—historical and cultural factors, general road conditions, population density, attitudes towards drinking and driving, and so forth—being important factors that determine the variation in traffic fatalities across states.

The final three regressions in Table 8.1 include additional potential determinants of fatalities rates, along with time and state effects. The base specification, reported in column (4), includes two sets of legal variables related to drunk driving plus variables that control for the amount of driving and overall state economic conditions. The first set of variables is the minimum legal drinking age, represented by three binary variables for a minimum legal drinking age of 18, 19, and 20 (so the "omitted group" is a minimum legal drinking age of 21 or higher). The second set of legal variables is punishments associated with the first conviction for driving under the influence of alcohol, either mandatory jail time or mandatory community service (the omitted group is less severe punishment). The three measures of driving and economic conditions are average vehicle miles per driver, the unemployment rate, and the logarithm of real (1988 dollars) personal income per capita (using the logarithm of income permits the coefficient to be interpreted in terms of percentage changes of income; see Section 6.2).

The regression in column (4) has four interesting results.

1. Including the additional variables reduces the estimated coefficient on the real beer tax, relative to the regression in column (3). The estimated

TABLE 8.1   Regression Analysis of the Effect of Drunk Driving Laws on Traffic Deaths

Dependent Variable: Traffic Fatality Rate (Deaths Per 10,000).

Regressor	(1)	(2)	(3)	(4)	(5)	(6)
Beer tax	0.36** (0.05)	−0.66** (0.20)	−0.64* (0.25)	−0.45* (0.22)	−0.70** (0.25)	−0.46* (0.22)
Drinking age 18				0.028 (0.066)	−0.011 (0.064)	
Drinking age 19				−0.019 (0.040)	−0.078 (0.049)	
Drinking age 20				0.031 (0.046)	−0.102* (0.046)	
Drinking age						−0.002 (0.017)
Mandatory jail?				0.013 (0.032)	−0.026 (0.065)	
Mandatory community service?				0.033 (0.115)	0.147 (0.137)	
Mandatory jail or community service?						0.031 (0.076)
Average vehicle miles per driver				0.008 (0.008)	0.017 (0.010)	0.009 (0.008)
Unemployment rate				−0.063** (0.012)		−0.063** (0.012)
Real income per capita (logarithm)				1.81** (0.47)		1.79** (0.45)
State effects?	no	yes	yes	yes	yes	yes
Time effects?	no	no	yes	yes	yes	yes
F-statistics and p-values Testing Exclusion of Groups of Variables:						
Time effects = 0			2.47 (0.024)	11.44 (<0.001)	2.28 (0.037)	11.59 (<0.001)
Drinking age coefficients = 0				0.48 (0.696)	2.09 (0.102)	
Jail, community service coefficients = 0				0.17 (0.845)	0.59 (0.557)	
Unemployment rate, income per capita = 0				38.29 (<0.001)		40.12 (<0.001)
$\overline{R}^2$	0.090	0.889	0.891	0.926	0.893	0.926

These regressions were estimated using panel data for 48 U.S. states from 1982 to 1988 (336 observations total), described in Appendix 8.1. Standard errors are given in parentheses under the coefficients, and p-values are given in parentheses under the F-statistics. The individual coefficient is statistically significant at the *5% level or **1% significance level.

coefficient (−0.45) continues to be negative and statistically significant at the 5% significance level. One way to evaluate the magnitude of the coefficient is to imagine a state with an average real beer tax doubling its tax; because the average real beer tax in these data is approximately $0.50/case, this entails increasing the tax by $0.50/case. According to the estimate in column (4), the effect of a $0.50 increase (in 1988 dollars) in the beer tax is a decrease in the expected fatality rate by 0.45 × 0.50 = 0.23 deaths per 10,000. This estimated effect is large: because the average fatality rate is 2 per 10,000, a reduction of 0.23 corresponds to decreasing the fatality rate to 1.77 per 10,000. This said, the estimate is quite imprecise: because the standard error on this coefficient is 0.22, the 95% confidence interval for this effect is −0.45 × 0.50 ± 1.96 × 0.22 × 0.050 = (−0.44, −0.01). This wide 95% confidence interval includes values of the true effect that are very nearly zero.

2. The minimum legal drinking age is estimated to have very little effect on traffic fatalities. The joint hypothesis that the coefficients on the minimum legal drinking age variables are zero cannot be rejected at the 10% significance level: the F-statistic testing the joint hypothesis that the three coefficients are zero is 0.48, with a p-value of 0.696. Moreover, the estimates are small in magnitude. For example, a state with a minimum legal drinking age of 18 is estimated to have a fatality rate higher by 0.028 deaths per 10,000 than a state with a minimum legal drinking age of 21, holding the other factors in the regression constant.

3. The coefficients on the first offense punishment variables are also estimated to be small and jointly insignificantly different from zero at the 10% significance level (the F-statistic is 0.17).

4. The economic variables have considerable explanatory power for traffic fatalities. High unemployment rates are associated with fewer fatalities: an increase in the unemployment rate by one percentage point is estimated to reduce traffic fatalities by 0.063 deaths per 10,000. Similarly, high values of real per capita income are associated with high fatalities: the coefficient is 1.81, so a 1% increase in real per capita income is associated with an increase in traffic fatalities of 0.0181 deaths per 10,000 (see Case I in Key Concept 6.2 for interpreting this coefficient). According to these estimates, good economic conditions are associated with higher fatalities, perhaps because of increased traffic density when the unemployment rate is low or greater alcohol consumption when income is high. The two economic variables are jointly significant at the 0.1% significance level (the F-statistic is 38.29).

The final two columns of Table 8.1 report regressions that check the sensitivity of these conclusions to changes in the base specification. The regression in column (5) drops the variables that control for economic conditions. The result is an increase in the estimated effect of the real beer tax, but no appreciable change in the other coefficients; the sensitivity of the estimated beer tax coefficient to including the economic variables, combined with the statistical significance of the coefficients on those variables, indicates that the economic variables should remain in the base specification. The regression in column (6) examines the sensitivity of the results to using a different functional form for the drinking age (replacing the three indicator variables with the drinking age itself) and combining the two binary punishment variables. The results of regression (4) are not sensitive to these changes.

The strength of this analysis is that including state and time fixed effects mitigates the threat of omitted variable bias arising from unobserved variables that either do not change over time (like cultural attitudes towards drinking and driving) or do not vary across states (like safety innovations). As always, however, it is important to think about possible limitations of this analysis. One potential source of omitted variable bias is that the measure of alcohol taxes used here, the real tax on beer, could move with other alcohol taxes; this suggests interpreting the results as pertaining more broadly than just to beer. A subtler possibility is that hikes in the real beer tax could be associated with public education campaigns, perhaps in response to political pressure. If so, changes in the real beer tax could pick up the effect of a broader campaign to reduce drunk driving.

These results present a provocative picture of measures to control drunk driving and traffic fatalities. According to these estimates, neither stiff punishments nor increasing the minimum legal drinking age have important effects on fatalities. In contrast, there is evidence that increasing alcohol taxes, as measured by the real tax on beer, does reduce traffic deaths. The magnitude of this effect, however, is imprecisely estimated.[2]

8.6   Conclusion

This chapter showed how multiple observations over time on the same entity can be used to control for unobserved omitted variables that differ across entities but are constant over time. The key insight is that if the unobserved variable does not change over time, then any changes in the dependent variable must be

---

[2]If you are interested in seeing further analysis of these data, see Ruhm (1996). If you are interested in learning more about drunk driving and alcohol, and about the economics of alcohol more generally, see Cook and Moore (2000).

due to influences other than these fixed characteristics. If cultural attitudes towards drinking and driving do not change appreciably over seven years within a state, then explanations for changes in the traffic fatality rate over those seven years must lie elsewhere.

To exploit this insight, you need data in which the same entity is observed at two or more time periods, that is, you need panel data. With panel data, the multiple regression model of Part II can be extended to include a full set of binary variables, one for each entity; this is the fixed effects regression model, which can be estimated by OLS. A twist on the fixed effects regression model is to include time fixed effects, which control for unobserved variables that change over time but are constant across entities. Both entity and time fixed effects can be included in the regression to control for variables that vary across entities but are constant over time and for variables that vary over time but are constant across entities.

Despite these virtues, entity and time fixed effects regression cannot control for omitted variables that vary *both* across entities *and* over time. And, obviously, panel data methods require panel data, which often are not available. Thus there remains a need for a method that can eliminate the influence of unobserved omitted variables when panel data methods cannot do the job. A powerful and general method for doing so is instrumental variables regression, the topic of Chapter 10.

Summary

1. Panel data consists of observations on multiple (n) entities—states, firms, people, etc.—where each entity is observed at two or more time periods (T).

2. Regression with entity fixed effects controls for unobserved variables that differ from one entity to the next but are constant over time.

3. When there are two time periods, fixed effect regression can be estimated by a "before and after" regression of the change in Y from the first period to the second on the change in X.

4. Entity fixed effects regression can be estimated by including binary variables for $n - 1$ entities, plus the observable independent variables (the X's) and an intercept.

5. Time fixed effects control for unobserved variables that are the same across entities but vary over time.

6. A regression with time and entity fixed effects can be estimated by including binary variables for $n - 1$ entities, binary variables for $T - 1$ time periods, plus the X's and an intercept.

Key Terms

panel data (272)

balanced panel (272)

unbalanced panel (272)

fixed effects regression model (279)

time fixed effects (283)

time effects regression model (284)

time and entity fixed effects regression
model (284)

Review the Concepts

8.1 Why is it necessary to use two subscripts, i and t, to describe panel data? What does i refer to? What does t refer to?

8.2 A researcher is using a panel data set on $n = 1,000$ workers over $T = 10$ years (from 1991–2000) that contains the workers' earnings, gender, education, and age. The researcher is interested in the effect of education on earnings. Give some examples of unobserved person-specific variables that are correlated with both education and earnings. Can you think of examples of time-specific variables that might be correlated with education and earnings? How would you control for these person-specific and time-specific effects in a panel data regression?

8.3 Can the regression that you suggested in response to question 8.2 be used to estimate the effect of gender on an individual's earnings? Can that regression be used to estimate the effect of the national unemployment rate on an individual's earnings? Explain.

Exercises

8.1 This question refers to the drunk driving panel data regression summarized in Table 8.1.

*a. New Jersey has a population of 8.1 million people. Suppose that New Jersey increased the tax on a case of beer by $1 (in $1988). Use the results in column (4) to predict the number of lives that would be saved over the next year. Construct a 95% confidence interval for your answer.

b. The drinking age in New Jersey is 21. Suppose that New Jersey lowered its drinking age to 18. Use the results in column (4) to predict the change in the number of traffic fatalities in the next year. Construct a 95% confidence interval for your answer.

*__c.__ Suppose that real income per capita in New Jersey increases by 1% in the next year. Use the results in column (4) to predict the change in the number of traffic fatalities in the next year. Construct a 90% confidence interval for your answer.

d. Should time effects be included in the regression? Why or why not?

*__e.__ The estimate of the coefficient on beer tax in column (5) is significant at the 1% level. The estimate in column (4) is significant at the 5% level. Does this mean that the estimate in (5) is more reliable?

f. A researcher conjectures that the unemployment rate has a different effect on traffic fatalities in the western states than the other states. How would you test this hypothesis? (Be specific about the specification of the regression and the statistical test you would use.)

8.2 Consider the binary variable version of the fixed effects model in Equation (8.11), except with an additional regressor, $D1_i$; that is, let

$$Y_{it} = \beta_0 + \beta_1 X_{it} + \gamma_1 D1_i + \gamma_2 D2_i + \cdots + \gamma_n Dn_i + u_{it}. \qquad (8.20)$$

a. Suppose that $n = 3$. Show that the binary regressors and the "constant" regressor are perfectly multicollinear, that is, express one of the variables $D1_i$, $D2_i$, $D3_i$, and $X_{0,it}$ as a perfect linear function of the others, where $X_{0,it} = 1$ for all i, t.

b. Show the result in (a) for general n.

c. What will happen if you try to estimate the coefficients of the regression in Equation (8.20) by OLS?

8.3 Section 7.2 gave a list of five potential threats to the internal validity of a regression study. Apply this list to the empirical analysis in Section 8.5 and thereby draw conclusions about its internal validity.

The State Traffic Fatality Data Set

The data are for the "lower 48" U.S. states (excluding Alaska and Hawaii), annually for 1982 through 1988. The traffic fatality rate is the number of traffic deaths in a given state in a given year, per 10,000 people living in that state in that year. Traffic fatality data were obtained from the U.S. Department of Transportation Fatal Accident Reporting System. The beer tax is the tax on a case of beer, which is a measure of state alcohol taxes more generally. The drinking age variables in Table 8.1 are binary variables indicating whether the legal drinking age is 18, 19, or 20. The two binary punishment variables in Table 8.1 describe the state's minimum sentencing requirements for an initial drunk driving conviction: "Mandatory jail?" equals one if the state requires jail time and equals zero otherwise, and "Mandatory community service?" equals one if the state requires community service and equals zero otherwise. Data on the total vehicle miles traveled annually by state were obtained from the Department of Transportation. Personal income was obtained from the U.S. Bureau of Economic Analysis, and the unemployment rate was obtained from the U.S. Bureau of Labor Statistics.

These data were graciously provided to us by Professor Christopher J. Ruhm of the Department of Economics at the University of North Carolina.

The Fixed Effects Regression Assumptions

There are five least squares assumptions for the fixed effects regression model of Key Concept 8.2. Stated for a single regressor, the five assumptions are:

1. $E(u_{it} | X_{i1}, X_{i2}, \ldots, X_{iT}, \alpha_i) = 0$;
2. $(X_{i1}, X_{i2}, \ldots, X_{iT}, Y_{i1}, Y_{i2}, \ldots, Y_{iT})$, $i = 1, \ldots, n$ are i.i.d. draws from their joint distribution;

3. (X_{it}, u_{it}) have nonzero finite fourth moments;

4. there is no perfect multicollinearity; and

5. $\mathrm{cov}(u_{it}, u_{is} \mid X_{it}, X_{is}, \alpha_i) = 0$ for $t \neq s$.

For multiple regressors, X_{it} should be replaced by the full list $X_{1,it}, X_{2,it}, \ldots, X_{k,it}$.

The first assumption is that the error term has a conditional mean of zero, given the regressors. This is the same as the first least squares assumption in Key Concept 5.4, extended to include the binary regressors and all T observations on X over time for the ith entity, and the discussion of this assumption in Part II extends directly.

The second assumption extends the multiple regression i.i.d. assumption to panel data. This assumption holds if entities are selected by simple random sampling from the population. Thus, the variables at one entity are distributed identically to, but independently of, the variables at another entity; that is, the variables are i.i.d. for $i = 1, \ldots, n$. So far, this reasoning is the same as for cross-sectional data. In panel data, however, the entities are followed over time, and it does not necessarily make sense to think of the variables *within* an entity as independently distributed over time. For example, because real beer taxes typically change only slightly from year to year, knowledge of the real beer tax in a state in 1982 provides quite a bit of information about the real beer tax in that state in 1983. Thus the appropriate sampling concept is that, in a panel data set, the entire stream of variables (that is, the variables over all time periods) are i.i.d. draws from the joint distribution of the stream of variables across entities.

The third and fourth assumptions are exactly the same as in Key Concept 5.4 for the multiple regression model.

The fifth assumption is that the errors u_{it} in the fixed effects regression model are uncorrelated over time, conditional on the regressors. For example, in some states (say, Minnesota), one winter might be especially snowy, making driving especially treacherous and resulting in an unusually high number of fatal accidents. Moreover, the amount of snow has nothing to do with the tax on beer, and snowfall in one winter plausibly is distributed independently of the snowfall in another. Thus the amount of snow in one Minnesota winter is uncorrelated with the amount of snow the next winter, given the tax on beer in Minnesota. Stated more generally, if u_{it} consists of random factors (like snowfall) that vary independently from one year to the next, conditional on the regressors (the beer tax), then u_{it} is uncorrelated from year to year, conditional on the regressors. In this case, the fifth assumption holds.

The only role of the fifth assumption is to provide conditions under which the usual (heteroskedasticity-robust) OLS standard errors of Chapter 5 lead to valid statistical inferences. If the fifth assumption holds, as is assumed in this chapter, then conventional (heteroskedasticity-robust) standard errors produce hypothesis tests in which the size equals the desired significance level.

In some applications, this fifth assumption does not plausibly hold. For example, if some of the omitted factors in u_{it} change slowly over time, then u_{it} will be correlated with its value in other time periods in the same state (same i), that is, u_{it} and u_{is} will be correlated for $t \neq s$, conditional on the regressors. In this case, the fifth assumption does not hold and a new formula must be used to compute standard errors (so-called heteroskedasticity- and autocorrelation-consistent standard errors). Because this formula is rather complicated, further discussion of it is postponed to Chapter 13.

CHAPTER 9

Regression with a Binary Dependent Variable

Two people, identical but for their race, walk into a bank and apply for a mortgage, a large loan so that each can buy an identical house. Does the bank treat them the same way? Are they both equally likely to have their mortgage application accepted? By law they must receive identical treatment. But whether or not they do is a matter of great concern among bank regulators.

Loans are made and denied for many legitimate reasons. For example, if the proposed loan payments take up most or all of the applicant's monthly income, then a loan officer might justifiably deny the loan. Also, even loan officers are human and they can make honest mistakes, so the denial of a single minority applicant does not prove anything about discrimination. Many studies of discrimination thus look for statistical evidence of discrimination, that is, evidence contained in large data sets showing that whites and minorities are treated differently.

But how, precisely, should one check for statistical evidence of discrimination in the mortgage market? A start is to compare the fraction of minority and white applicants who were denied a mortgage. In the data examined in this chapter, gathered from mortgage applications in 1990 in the Boston, Massachusetts, area, 28% of black applicants were denied mortgages but only 9% of white applicants were denied. But this comparison does not really answer the question that opened this chapter, because the black and white applicants were not necessarily "identical but for their race." Instead, we need a method for comparing rates of denial, *holding other applicant characteristics constant*.

This sounds like a job for multiple regression analysis—and it is, but with a twist. The twist is that the dependent variable—whether or not the applicant is denied—is binary. In Part II, we regularly used binary variables as regressors, and they caused no particular problems. But when the dependent variable is binary, things are more difficult: what does it mean to fit a line to a dependent variable that can take on only two values, zero and one?

The answer to this question is to interpret the regression function as a predicted probability. This interpretation is discussed in Section 9.1, and it allows us to apply the multiple regression models from Part II to binary dependent variables. Section 9.1 goes over this "linear probability model." But the predicted probability interpretation also suggests that alternative, nonlinear regression models can do a better job modeling these probabilities. These methods, called "probit" and "logit" regression, are discussed in Section 9.2. Section 9.3, which is optional, discusses the method used to estimate the coefficients of the probit and logit regressions, the method of maximum likelihood estimation. In Section 9.4, we apply these methods to the Boston mortgage application data set to see whether there is evidence of racial bias in mortgage lending.

The binary dependent variable considered in this chapter is an example of a dependent variable with a limited range, in other words, it is a **limited dependent variable**. Models for other types of limited dependent variables, for example, dependent variables that take on multiple discrete values, are surveyed in Appendix 9.3.

9.1   Binary Dependent Variables and the Linear Probability Model

Whether a mortgage application is accepted or denied is one example of a binary variable. Many other important questions also concern binary outcomes. What is the effect of a tuition subsidy on an individual's decision to go to college? What determines whether a teenager takes up smoking? What determines whether or not a country receives foreign aid? What determines whether a job applicant is successful? In all these examples, the outcome of interest is binary: the student does or does not go to college, the teenager does or does not take up smoking, a country does or does not receive foreign aid, the applicant does or does not get a job.

This section discusses what distinguishes regression with a binary dependent variable from regression with a continuous dependent variable, then turns to the simplest model to use with binary dependent variables, the linear probability model.

Binary Dependent Variables

The application examined in this chapter is whether race is a factor in denying a mortgage application; the binary dependent variable is whether or not a mortgage application is denied. The data are a subset of a larger data set compiled by researchers at the Federal Reserve Bank of Boston under the Home Mortgage Disclosure Act (HMDA), and relate to mortgage applications filed in the Boston, Massachusetts, area in 1990. The Boston HMDA data are described in Appendix 9.1.

Mortgage applications are complicated, and so is the process by which the bank loan officer decides. The loan officer must forecast whether or not the applicant will make his or her loan payments. One important piece of information is the size of the required loan payments relative to the applicant's income. As anyone who has borrowed money knows, it is much easier to make payments that are 10% of your income than 50%! We therefore begin by looking at the relationship between two variables: the binary dependent variable *deny*, which equals one if the mortgage application was denied and equals zero if it was accepted, and the continuous variable *P/I ratio*, which is the ratio of the applicant's anticipated total monthly loan payments to his or her monthly income.

Figure 9.1 presents a scatterplot of *deny* versus *P/I ratio* for 127 of the 2,380 observations in the data set. (The scatterplot is easier to read using this subset of the data.) This scatterplot looks different than the scatterplots of Part II because the variable *deny* is binary. Still, it seems to show a relationship between *deny* and *P/I ratio*: few applicants with a payment-to-income ratio less than 0.3 have their application denied, but most applicants with a payment-to-income ratio exceeding 0.4 are denied.

This positive relationship between *P/I ratio* and *deny* (the higher the *P/I ratio*, the greater the fraction of denials) is summarized in Figure 9.1 by the OLS regression line estimated using these 127 observations. As usual, this line plots the predicted value of *deny* as a function of the regressor, the payment-to-income ratio. For example, when *P/I ratio* = 0.3, the predicted value of deny is 0.20. But what, precisely, does it mean for the predicted value of the binary variable *deny* to be 0.20?

The key to answering this question—and more generally to understanding regression with a binary dependent variable—is to interpret the regression as modeling the *probability* that the dependent variable equals one. Thus, the predicted

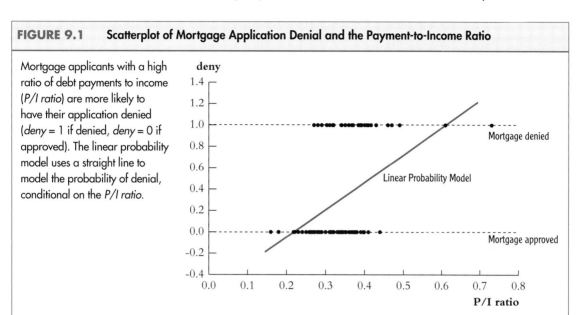

FIGURE 9.1   Scatterplot of Mortgage Application Denial and the Payment-to-Income Ratio

Mortgage applicants with a high ratio of debt payments to income (*P/I ratio*) are more likely to have their application denied (*deny* = 1 if denied, *deny* = 0 if approved). The linear probability model uses a straight line to model the probability of denial, conditional on the *P/I ratio*.

value of 0.20 is interpreted as meaning that, when *P/I ratio* is 0.3, the probability of denial is estimated to be 20%. Said differently, if there were many applications with *P/I ratio* = 0.3, then 20% of them would be denied.

This interpretation follows from two facts. First, from Part II, the population regression function is the expected value of Y given the regressors, $E(Y|X_1, \ldots, X_k)$. Second, from Section 2.2, if Y is a 0–1 binary variable, then its expected value (or mean) is the probability that $Y = 1$, that is, $E(Y) = \Pr(Y = 1)$. In the regression context the expected value is conditional on the value of the regressors, so the probability is conditional on X. Thus for a binary variable, $E(Y|X_1, \ldots, X_k) = \Pr(Y = 1|X_1, \ldots, X_k)$. In short, for a binary variable the predicted value from the population regression is the probability that $Y = 1$, given X.

The linear multiple regression model applied to a binary dependent variable is called the linear probability model: "linear" because it is a straight line, and "probability model" because it models the probability that the dependent variable equals one, in our example, the probability of loan denial.

The Linear Probability Model

The **linear probability model** is the name for the multiple regression model of Part II when the dependent variable is binary rather than continuous. Because the dependent variable Y is binary, the population regression function corresponds to the probability that the dependent variable equals one, given X. The population coefficient β_1 on a regressor X is the *change in the probability* that $Y = 1$ associated with a *unit change* in X. Similarly, the OLS predicted value, $\hat{Y}_i$, computed using the estimated regression function, is the predicted probability that the dependent variable equals one, and the OLS estimator $\hat{\beta}_1$ estimates the change in the probability that $Y = 1$ associated with a unit change in X.

Almost all of the tools of Part II carry over to the linear probability model. The coefficients can be estimated by OLS. Ninety-five percent confidence intervals can be formed as ±1.96 standard errors; hypotheses concerning several coefficients can be tested using the F-statistic discussed in Chapter 5; and interactions between variables can be modeled using the methods of Section 6.3. Because the errors of the linear probability model are always heteroskedastic (Exercise 9.3), it is essential that heteroskedasticity-robust standard errors be used for inference.

One tool that does not carry over is the R^2. When the dependent variable is continuous, it is possible to imagine a situation in which the R^2 equals one: all the data lie exactly on the regression line. This is impossible when the dependent variable is binary, unless the regressors are also binary. Accordingly, the R^2 is not a particularly useful statistic here. We return to measures of fit in the next section.

The linear probability model is summarized in Key Concept 9.1.

Application to the Boston HMDA data.   The OLS regression of the binary dependent variable, *deny*, against the payment-to-income ratio, *P/I ratio*, estimated using all 2,380 observations in our data set is

$$\widehat{deny} = -0.080 + 0.604 P/I\ ratio. \tag{9.1}$$
$$(0.032)\quad(0.098)$$

The estimated coefficient on *P/I ratio* is positive, and the population coefficient is statistically significantly different from zero at the 1% level (the t-statistic is 6.13). Thus, applicants with higher debt payments as a fraction of income are more likely to have their application denied. This coefficient can be used to compute the predicted change in the probability of denial, given a change in the regressor. For example, according to Equation (9.1), if the *P/I ratio* increases by 0.1, then the probability of denial increases by $0.604 \times 0.1 \cong 0.060$, that is, by 6.0 percentage points.

The estimated linear probability model in Equation (9.1) can be used to compute predicted denial probabilities as a function of the *P/I ratio*. For example, if projected debt payments are 30% of an applicant's income, then the *P/I ratio* is 0.3 and the predicted value from Equation (9.1) is $-0.080 + 0.604 \times 0.3 = 0.101$. That is, according to this linear probability model, an applicant whose projected debt payments are 30% of income has a probability of 10.1% that their applica-

The Linear Probability Model

The linear probability model is the linear multiple regression model

$$Y_i = \beta_0 + \beta_1 X_{1i} + \beta_2 X_{2i} + \cdots + \beta_k X_{ki} + u_i, \tag{9.2}$$

where Y_i is binary, so that

$$\Pr(Y = 1 \mid X_1, X_2, \ldots, X_k) = \beta_0 + \beta_1 X_1 + \beta_2 X_2 + \cdots + \beta_k X_k.$$

The regression coefficient β_1 is the change in the probability that $Y = 1$ associated with a unit change in X_1, holding constant the other regressors, and so forth for β_2, etc. The regression coefficients can be estimated by OLS, and the usual (heteroskedasticity-robust) OLS standard errors can be used for confidence intervals and hypothesis tests.

Key Concept 9.1

tion will be denied. (This is different than the probability of 20% based on the regression line in Figure 9.1, because that line was estimated using only 127 of the 2,380 observations used to estimate Equation (9.1).)

What is the effect of race on the probability of denial, holding constant the *P/I ratio*? To keep things simple, we focus on differences between black and white applicants. To estimate the effect of race, holding constant the *P/I ratio*, we augment Equation (9.1) with a binary regressor that equals one if the applicant is black and equals zero if the applicant is white. The estimated linear probability model is

$$\widehat{deny} = -0.091 + 0.559 P/I\ ratio + 0.177 black. \tag{9.3}$$
$$\quad\ (0.029)\ \ (0.089) \qquad\qquad (0.025)$$

The coefficient on *black*, 0.177, indicates that an African-American applicant has a 17.7% higher probability of having a mortgage application denied than a white, holding constant their payment-to-income ratio. This coefficient is significant at the 1% level (the *t*-statistic is 7.11).

Taken literally, this estimate suggests that there might be racial bias in mortgage decisions, but such a conclusion would be premature. Although the payment-to-income ratio plays a role in the loan officer's decision, so do many other factors, such as the applicant's earning potential and the individual's credit history. If any of these variables are correlated with the regressors *black* or *P/I ratio*, then their omission from Equation (9.3) will cause omitted variable bias. Thus we must defer any conclusions about discrimination in mortgage lending until we complete the more thorough analysis in Section 9.3.

Shortcomings of the linear probability model.   The linearity that makes the linear probability model easy to use is also its major flaw. Look again at Figure 9.1: the estimated line representing the predicted probabilities drops below zero for very low values of the *P/I ratio* and exceeds one for high values! But this is nonsense: a probability cannot be less than zero or greater than one. This nonsensical feature is an inevitable consequence of the linear regression. To address this problem, we introduce new nonlinear models specifically designed for binary dependent variables, the probit and logit regression models.

9.2   Probit and Logit Regression

Probit and **logit**[1] regression are nonlinear regression models specifically designed for binary dependent variables. Because a regression with a binary dependent variable Y models the probability that $Y = 1$, it makes sense to adopt a nonlinear formulation that forces the predicted values to be between zero and one. Because cumulative probability distribution functions (c.d.f.'s) produce probabilities between zero and one (Section 2.1), they are used in logit and probit regressions. Probit regression uses the standard normal c.d.f. Logit regression, also called **logistic regression,** uses the "logistic" c.d.f.

Probit Regression

Probit regression with a single regressor.   The probit regression model with a single regressor X is

$$\Pr(Y = 1 \mid X) = \Phi(\beta_0 + \beta_1 X), \qquad (9.4)$$

where Φ is the cumulative standard normal distribution function (tabulated in Appendix Table 1).

For example, suppose Y is the binary mortgage denial variable, *deny*, X is the payment-to-income ratio (*P/I ratio*), $\beta_0 = -2$, and $\beta_1 = 3$. What then is the probability of denial if *P/I ratio* = 0.4? According to Equation (9.4), this probability is

---

[1]Pronounced prō–bit and lō–jit.

$\Phi(\beta_0 + \beta_1 P/I \; ratio) = \Phi(-2 + 3P/I \; ratio) = \Phi(-2 + 3 \times 0.4) = \Phi(-0.8)$. According to the cumulative normal distribution table (Appendix Table 1), $\Phi(-0.8) =$ $\Pr(Z \le -0.8) = 21.2\%$. That is, when the $P/I \; ratio$ is 0.4, the predicted probability that the application will be denied is 21.2%, computed using the probit model with the coefficients $\beta_0 = -2$ and $\beta_1 = 3$.

In the probit model, the term, $\beta_0 + \beta_1 X$, plays the role of "z" in the cumulative standard normal distribution table in Appendix Table 1. Thus, the calculation in the previous paragraph can, equivalently, be done by first computing the "z-value," $z = \beta_0 + \beta_1 X = -2 + 3 \times 0.4 = -0.8$, then looking up the probability in the tail of the normal distribution to the left of $z = -0.8$, which is 21.2%.

If β_1 in Equation (9.4) is positive, then an increase in X increases the probability that $Y = 1$; if β_1 is negative, an increase in X decreases the probability that $Y = 1$. Beyond this, however, it is not easy to interpret the probit coefficients β_0 and β_1 directly. Instead, the coefficients are best interpreted indirectly by computing probabilities and/or changes in probabilities. When there is just one regressor, the easiest way to interpret a probit regression is to plot the probabilities.

Figure 9.2 plots the estimated regression function produced by the probit regression of *deny* on *P/I ratio* for the 127 observations in the scatterplot. The estimated probit regression function has a stretched "S" shape: it is nearly zero and flat for small values of *P/I ratio*; it turns and increases for intermediate values; and it flattens out again and is nearly one for large values. For small values of the payment-to-income ratio, the probability of denial is small. For example, for *P/I ratio* = 0.2, the estimated probability of denial based on the estimated probit function in Figure 9.2 is $\Pr(deny = 1 \,|\, P/I \; ratio = 0.2) = 2.1\%$. When the *P/I ratio* is 0.3, the estimated probability of denial is 16.1%. When the *P/I ratio* is 0.4, the probability of denial increases sharply to 51.9%, and when the *P/I ratio* is 0.6, the denial probability is 98.3%. According to this estimated probit model, for applicants with high payment-to-income ratios, the probability of denial is nearly one.

Probit regression with multiple regressors.   In all the regression problems we have studied so far, leaving out a determinant of Y that is correlated with the included regressors results in omitted variable bias. Probit regression is no exception. In linear regression, the solution is to include the additional variable as a regressor. This is also the solution to omitted variable bias in probit regression.

The probit model with multiple regressors extends the single-regressor probit model by adding regressors to compute the z value. Accordingly, the probit population regression model with two regressors, X_1 and X_2, is

$$\Pr(Y = 1 \,|\, X_1, X_2) = \Phi(\beta_0 + \beta_1 X_1 + \beta_2 X_2). \tag{9.5}$$

FIGURE 9.2   **Probit Model of the Probability of Denial, Given the P/I Ratio**

The probit model uses the cumulative normal distribution function to model the probability of denial given the payment-to-income ratio or, more generally, to model $\Pr(Y = 1|X)$. Unlike the linear probability model, the probit conditional probabilities are always between zero and one.

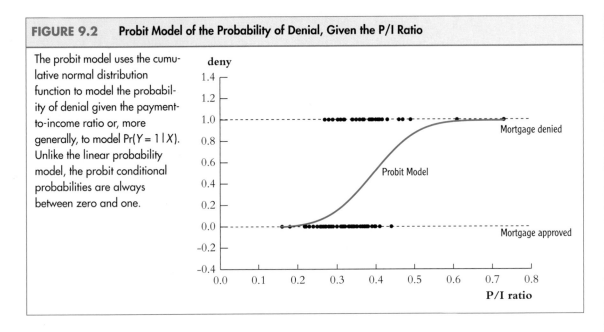

For example, suppose $\beta_0 = -1.6$, $\beta_1 = 2$, and $\beta_2 = 0.5$. If $X_1 = 0.4$ and $X_2 = 1$, then the z-value is $z = -1.6 + 2 \times 0.4 + 0.5 \times 1 = -0.3$. So, the probability that $Y = 1$ given $X_1 = 0.4$ and $X_2 = 1$ is $\Pr(Y = 1 | X_1 = 0.4, X_2 = 1) = \Phi(-0.3) = 38\%$.

Effect of a change in X.   In general, the effect on Y of a change in X is the expected change in Y arising from a change in X. When Y is binary, its conditional expectation is the conditional probability that it equals one, so the expected change in Y arising from a change in X is the change in the probability that $Y = 1$.

Recall from Section 6.1 that, when the population regression function is a nonlinear function of X, this expected change is estimated in three steps: first, compute the predicted value at the original value of X using the estimated regression function; next, compute the predicted value at the changed value of X, $X + \Delta X$; then compute the difference between the two predicted values. This procedure is summarized in Key Concept 6.1. As emphasized in Section 6.1, this method *always* works for computing predicted effects of a change in X, no matter how complicated the nonlinear model. When applied to the probit model, the method of Key Concept 6.1 yields the estimated effect on the probability that $Y = 1$ of a change in X.

The probit regression model, predicted probabilities, and estimated effects are summarized in Key Concept 9.2.

The Probit Model, Predicted Probabilities, and Estimated Effects

Key Concept 9.2

The population probit model with multiple regressors is

$$\Pr(Y = 1 \mid X_1, X_2, \ldots, X_k) = \Phi(\beta_0 + \beta_1 X_1 + \beta_2 X_2 + \cdots + \beta_k X_k), \quad (9.6)$$

where the dependent variable Y is binary, Φ is the cumulative standard normal distribution function and X_1, X_2, etc., are regressors. The probit coefficients β_0, β_1, etc., do not have simple interpretations. The model is best interpreted by computing predicted probabilities and the effect of a change in a regressor.

The predicted probability that $Y = 1$, given values of $X_1, X_2, \ldots, X_k$ is calculated by computing the z-value, $z = \beta_0 + \beta_1 X_1 + \beta_2 X_2 + \cdots + \beta_k X_k$, and then looking up this z-value in the normal distribution table (Appendix Table 1).

The effect of a change in a regressor is computed by: (1) computing the predicted probability for the initial value of the regressors; (2) computing the predicted probability for the new or changed value of the regressors; and (3) taking their difference.

Application to the mortgage data.   As an illustration, we fit a probit model to the 2,380 observations in our data set on mortgage denial (*deny*) and the payment-to-income ratio (*P/I ratio*):

$$\Pr(deny = 1 \mid P/I\ ratio) = \Phi(-2.19 + 2.97 P/I\ ratio). \quad (9.7)$$
$$(0.16) \quad (0.47)$$

The estimated coefficients of -2.19 and 2.97 are difficult to interpret because they affect the probability of denial via the z-value. Indeed, the only thing that can be readily concluded from the estimated probit regression in Equation (9.7) is that the *P/I ratio* is positively related to probability of denial (the coefficient on the *P/I ratio* is positive) and this relationship is statistically significant ($t = 2.97/0.47 = 6.32$).

What is the change in the predicted probability that an application will be denied when the payment-to-income ratio increases from 0.3 to 0.4? To answer this, we follow the procedure in Key Concept 6.1: compute the probability of denial for *P/I ratio* = 0.3, then for *P/I ratio* = 0.4, and then compute the difference. The probability of denial when *P/I ratio* = 0.3 is $\Phi(-2.19 + 2.97 \times 0.3) = \Phi(-1.30) = 0.097$. The probability of denial when *P/I ratio* = 0.4 is $\Phi(-2.19 + 2.97 \times 0.4) = \Phi(-1.00) = 0.159$.

The estimated change in the probability of denial is $0.159 - 0.097 = 0.062$. That is, an increase in the payment-to-income ratio from 0.3 to 0.4 is associated with an increase in the probability of denial of 6.2 percentage points, from 9.7% to 15.9%.

Because the probit regression function is nonlinear, the effect of a change in X depends on the starting value of X. For example, if P/I ratio $= 0.5$, then the estimated denial probability based on Equation (9.7) is $\Phi(-2.19 + 2.97 \times 0.5) = \Phi(-0.71) = 0.239$. Thus the change in the predicted probability when P/I ratio increases from 0.4 to 0.5 is $0.239 - 0.159$, or 8.0 percentage points, larger than the increase of 6.2 percentage points when the P/I ratio increases from 0.3 to 0.4.

What is the effect of race on the probability of mortgage denial, holding constant the payment-to-income ratio? To estimate this effect, we estimate a probit regression with both P/I ratio and black as regressors:

$$\Pr(deny = 1 \mid P/I \ ratio, \ black) = \Phi(-2.26 + 2.74 P/I \ ratio + 0.71 black). \quad (9.8)$$
$$\qquad\qquad\quad (0.16) \quad (0.44) \qquad\qquad (0.083)$$

Again, the values of the coefficients are difficult to interpret but the sign and statistical significance are not. The coefficient on black is positive, indicating that an African-American applicant has a higher probability of denial than a white applicant, holding constant their payment-to-income ratio. This coefficient is statistically significant at the 1% level (the t-statistic on black is 8.55). For a white applicant with P/I ratio $= 0.3$, the predicted denial probability is 7.5%, while for a black applicant with P/I ratio $= 0.3$ it is 23.3%; the difference in denial probabilities between these two hypothetical applicants is 15.8 percentage points.

Estimation of the probit coefficients. The probit coefficients reported here were estimated using the method of maximum likelihood, which produces efficient (minimum variance) estimators in a wide variety of applications, including regression with a binary dependent variable. The maximum likelihood estimator is consistent and normally distributed in large samples, so that t-statistics and confidence intervals for the coefficients can be constructed in the usual way.

Regression software for estimating probit models typically uses maximum likelihood estimation, so this is a simple method to apply in practice. Standard errors produced by such software can be used in the same way as the standard errors of regression coefficients; for example, a 95% confidence interval for the true probit coefficient can be constructed as the estimated coefficient ± 1.96 standard errors. Similarly, F-statistics computed using maximum likelihood estimators

Logit Regression

Key Concept 9.3

The population logit model of the binary dependent variable Y with multiple regressors is

$$\Pr(Y = 1 \mid X_1, X_2, \ldots, X_k) = F(\beta_0 + \beta_1 X_1 + \beta_2 X_2 + \cdots + \beta_k X_k)$$

$$= \frac{1}{1 + e^{-(\beta_0 + \beta_1 X_1 + \beta_2 X_2 + \cdots + \beta_k X_k)}}. \tag{9.9}$$

Logit regression is similar to probit regression, except that the cumulative distribution function is different.

can be used to test joint hypotheses. Maximum likelihood estimation is discussed further in Section 9.3, with additional details given in Appendix 9.2.

Logit Regression

The logit regression model.   The logit regression model is similar to the probit regression model, except that the cumulative standard normal distribution function Φ in Equation (9.6) is replaced by the cumulative standard logistic distribution function, which we denote by F. Logit regression is summarized in Key Concept 9.3. The logistic cumulative distribution function has a specific functional form, defined in terms of the exponential function, which is given as the final expression in Equation (9.9).

As with probit, the logit coefficients are best interpreted by computing predicted probabilities and differences in predicted probabilities.

The coefficients of the logit model can be estimated by maximum likelihood. The maximum likelihood estimator is consistent and normally distributed in large samples, so that t-statistics and confidence intervals for the coefficients can be constructed in the usual way.

The logit and probit regression functions are similar. This is illustrated in Figure 9.3, which graphs the probit and logit regression functions for the dependent variable *deny* and the single regressor *P/I ratio*, estimated by maximum likelihood using the same 127 observations as in Figures 9.1 and 9.2. The differences between the two functions are small.

FIGURE 9.3 **Probit and Logit Models of the Probability of Denial, Given the P/I Ratio**

These logit and probit models produce nearly identical estimates of the probability that a mortgage application will be denied, given the payment-to-income ratio.

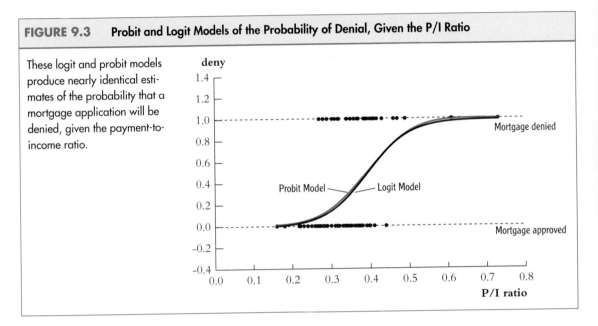

Historically, the main motivation for logit regression was that the logistic cumulative distribution function could be computed faster than the normal cumulative distribution function. With the advent of more efficient computers, this distinction is no longer important.

Application to the Boston HMDA data. A logit regression of *deny* against *P/I ratio* and *black*, using the 2,380 observations in the data set, yields the estimated regression function

$$\Pr(deny = 1 \mid P/I\ ratio,\ black) = F(-4.13 + 5.37 P/I\ ratio + 1.27 black). \quad (9.10)$$
$$(0.35)\ \ (0.96) (0.15)$$

The coefficient on *black* is positive and statistically significant at the 1% level (the *t*-statistic is 8.47). The predicted denial probability of a white applicant with *P/I ratio* = 0.3 is $1/[1 + e^{-(-4.13+5.37\times0.3+1.27\times0)}] = 1/[1 + e^{2.52}] = 0.074$, or 7.4%. The predicted denial probability of an African-American applicant with *P/I ratio* = 0.3 is $1/[1 + e^{1.25}] = 0.222$, or 22.2%, so the difference between the two probabilities is 14.8 percentage points.

Comparing the Linear Probability, Probit, and Logit Models

All three models—linear probability, probit, and logit—are just approximations to the unknown population regression function $E(Y|X) = \Pr(Y = 1|X)$. The linear probability model is easiest to use and to interpret, but it cannot capture the nonlinear nature of the true population regression function. Probit and logit regressions model this nonlinearity in the probabilities, but their regression coefficients are more difficult to interpret. So which should you use in practice?

There is no one right answer, and different researchers use different models. Probit and logit regressions frequently produce similar results. For example, according to the estimated probit model in Equation (9.8) the difference in denial probabilities between a black and white applicant with *P/I ratio* = 0.3 was estimated to be 15.8 percentage points, whereas the logit estimate of this gap, based on Equation (9.10), was 14.9 percentage points. For practical purposes the two estimates are very similar. One way to choose between logit and probit is to pick the method that is easiest to use in your statistical software.

The linear probability model provides the least sensible approximation to the nonlinear population regression function. Even so, in some data sets there may be few extreme values of the regressors, in which case the linear probability model still can provide an adequate approximation. In the denial probability regression in Equation (9.3), the estimated black/white gap from the linear probability model is 17.7 percentage points, larger than the probit and logit estimates but still qualitatively similar. The only way to know this, however, is to estimate both a linear and nonlinear model and to compare their predicted probabilities.

9.3   Estimation and Inference in the Logit and Probit Models[2]

The nonlinear models studied in Chapter 6 are nonlinear functions of the independent variables but are linear functions of the unknown coefficients ("parameters"). Consequently, the unknown coefficients of those nonlinear regression functions can be estimated by OLS. In contrast, the probit and logit regression

---

[2]This section contains more advanced material that can be skipped without loss of continuity.

functions are a nonlinear function of the coefficients. That is, the probit coefficients β_0, β_1, etc., in Equation (9.6) appear *inside* the cumulative standard normal distribution function Φ, and the logit coefficients in Equation (9.9) appear inside the cumulative standard logistic distribution function F. Because the population regression function is a nonlinear function of the coefficients β_0, β_1, etc., those coefficients cannot be estimated by OLS.

This section provides an introduction to the standard method for estimation of probit and logit coefficients, maximum likelihood; additional mathematical details are given in Appendix 9.2. Because it is built into modern statistical software, maximum likelihood estimation of the probit coefficients is easy in practice. The theory of maximum likelihood estimation, however, is more complicated than the theory of least squares. We therefore first discuss another estimation method, nonlinear least squares, before turning to maximum likelihood.

Nonlinear Least Squares Estimation

Nonlinear least squares is a general method for estimating the unknown coefficients of a regression function when, like the probit coefficients, those coefficients enter the population regression function nonlinearly.

Recall the discussion in Section 5.3 of the OLS estimator of the coefficients of the linear multiple regression model. The OLS estimator minimizes the sum of squared residuals prediction mistakes in Equation (5.8), $\sum_{i=1}^{n}[Y_i - (b_0 + b_1 X_{1i} + \cdots + b_k X_{ki})]^2$. In principal, the OLS estimator can be computed by checking many trial values of $b_0, \ldots, b_k$ and settling on the values that minimize the sum of squared mistakes.

This same approach can be used to estimate the probit coefficients. Because the regression model is nonlinear in the coefficients, this method is called nonlinear least squares. For a set of trial coefficient values b_0, b_1, etc., construct the sum of squared prediction mistakes,

$$\sum_{i=1}^{n}[Y_i - \Phi(b_0 + b_1 X_{1i} + \cdots + b_k X_{ki})]^2, \tag{9.11}$$

which is the same as for the linear regression model except that the regression function is given by the probit model. The **nonlinear least squares estimator** of the probit coefficients are the values of $b_0, b_1, \ldots, b_k$ that minimize the sum of squared prediction mistakes in Equation (9.11). Similarly, the nonlinear least squares estimator of the logit coefficients minimizes the sum of squared prediction mistakes, with the logistic distribution function F replacing Φ in Equation (9.11).

In the linear regression model, there is a fortuitous formula that expresses the OLS estimator as a function of the data. Unfortunately, there is no such formula for the probit model, so the nonlinear least squares estimator must be found numerically by the computer. Regression software typically incorporates sophisticated algorithms for solving this minimization problem, which simplifies the task of computing the nonlinear least squares estimator in practice.

The nonlinear least squares estimator of the probit coefficients shares two key properties with the OLS estimator in linear regression: it is consistent (the probability that it is close to the true value approaches one as the sample size gets large) and it is normally distributed in large samples. There are, however, estimators that have a smaller variance than the nonlinear least squares estimator, that is, the nonlinear least squares estimator is inefficient. For this reason, the nonlinear least squares estimator of the probit coefficients is rarely used in practice, and instead the parameters are estimated by maximum likelihood.

Maximum Likelihood Estimation

The **likelihood function** is the joint probability distribution of the data, treated as a function of the unknown coefficients. The **maximum likelihood estimator (MLE)** of the unknown coefficients consists of the values of the coefficients that maximize the likelihood function. Because the MLE chooses the unknown coefficients to maximize the likelihood function, which is in turn the joint probability distribution, in effect the MLE chooses the values of the parameters to maximize the probability of drawing the data that are actually observed. In this sense, the MLEs are the parameter values "most likely" to have produced the data.

To illustrate maximum likelihood estimation, consider two i.i.d. observations, Y_1 and Y_2, on a binary dependent variable with no regressors. Thus, Y is a Bernoulli random variable and the only unknown parameter to estimate is the probability p that $Y = 1$, which is also the mean of Y.

To obtain the maximum likelihood estimator we need an expression for the likelihood function, which in turn requires an expression for the joint probability distribution of the data. The joint probability distribution of the two observations Y_1 and Y_2 is $\Pr(Y_1 = y_1, Y_2 = y_2)$. Because Y_1 and Y_2 are independently distributed, the joint distribution is the product of the individual distributions (Equation (2.21)), so $\Pr(Y_1 = y_1, Y_2 = y_2) = \Pr(Y_1 = y_1)\Pr(Y_2 = y_2)$. The Bernoulli distribution can be summarized in the formula $\Pr(Y = y) = p^y(1 - p)^{1-y}$: when $y = 1$, $\Pr(Y = 1) = p^1(1 - p)^0 = p$ and when $y = 0$, $\Pr(Y = 0) = p^0(1 - p)^1 = 1 - p$. Thus, the joint probability distribution of Y_1 and Y_2 is $\Pr(Y_1 = y_1, Y_2 = y_2) = [p^{y_1}(1 - p)^{1-y_1}] \times [p^{y_2}(1 - p)^{1-y_2}] = p^{(y_1+y_2)}(1 - p)^{2-(y_1+y_2)}$.

The likelihood function is the joint probability distribution, treated as a function of the unknown coefficients. For $n = 2$ i.i.d. observations on Bernoulli random variables, the likelihood function is

$$f(p; Y_1, Y_2) = p^{(Y_1 + Y_2)}(1 - p)^{2 - (Y_1 + Y_2)}. \tag{9.12}$$

The maximum likelihood estimator of p is the value of p that maximizes the likelihood function in Equation (9.12). As with all maximization or minimization problems, this can be done by trial and error; that is, you can try different values of p and compute the likelihood $f(p; Y_1, Y_2)$ until you are satisfied that you have maximized this function. In this example, however, maximizing the likelihood function using calculus produces a simple formula for the MLE: the MLE is $\hat{p} = \frac{1}{2}(Y_1 + Y_2)$. In other words, the MLE of p is just the sample average! In fact, for general n, the MLE $\hat{p}$ of the Bernoulli probability p is the sample average, that is, $\hat{p} = \overline{Y}$ (this is shown in Appendix 9.2). In this example, the MLE is the usual estimator of p, the fraction of times $Y_i = 1$ in the sample.

This example is similar to the problem of estimating the unknown coefficients of the probit and logit regression models. In those models, the success probability p is not constant, but rather depends on X; that is, it is the success probability conditional on X, which is given in Equation (9.6) for the probit model and Equation (9.9) for the logit model. Thus, the probit and logit likelihood functions are similar to the likelihood function in Equation (9.12), except that the success probability varies from one observation to the next (because it depends on X_i). Expressions for the probit and logit likelihood functions are given in Appendix 9.2.

Like the nonlinear least squares estimator, the MLE is consistent and normally distributed in large samples. Because regression software commonly computes the MLE of the probit coefficients, this estimator is easy to use in practice. All the estimated probit and logit coefficients reported in this chapter are MLEs.

Statistical inference based on the MLE.   Because the MLE is normally distributed in large samples, statistical inference about the probit and logit coefficients based on the MLE proceeds in the same way as inference about the linear regression function coefficients based on the OLS estimator. That is, hypothesis tests are performed using the *t*-statistic and 95% confidence intervals are formed as ±1.96 standard errors. Tests of joint hypotheses on multiple coefficients use the *F*-statistic, in a way similar to that discussed in Chapter 5 for the linear regression model. All of this is completely analogous to statistical inference in the linear regression model.

An important practical point is that some statistical software reports tests of joint hypotheses using the F-statistic, while other software uses the chi-squared statistic. The chi-squared statistic is $q \times F$, where q is the number of restrictions being tested. Because the F-statistic is, under the null hypothesis, distributed as χ_q^2/q in large samples, $q \times F$ is distributed as χ_q^2 in large samples. Because the two approaches differ only in whether they divide by q, they produce identical inferences, but you need to know which approach is implemented in your software so that you use the correct critical values.

Measures of Fit

In Section 9.1, it was mentioned that the R^2 is a poor measure of fit for the linear probability model. This is also true for probit and logit regression. Two measures of fit for models with binary dependent variables are the "fraction correctly predicted" and the "pseudo-R^2." The **fraction correctly predicted** uses the following rule: if $Y_i = 1$ and the predicted probability exceeds 50%, or if $Y_i = 0$ and the predicted probability is less than 50%, then Y_i is said to be correctly predicted. Otherwise, Y_i is said to be incorrectly predicted. The "fraction correctly predicted" is the fraction of the n observations $Y_1, \ldots, Y_n$ that are correctly predicted.

An advantage of this measure of fit is that it is easy to understand. A disadvantage is that it does not reflect the quality of the prediction: if $Y_i = 1$, the observation is treated as correctly predicted whether the predicted probability is 51% or 90%.

The **pseudo-R^2** measures the fit of the model using the likelihood function. Because the MLE maximizes the likelihood function, adding another regressor to a probit or logit model increases the value of the maximized likelihood, just like adding a regressor necessarily reduces the sum of squared residuals in linear regression by OLS. This suggests measuring the quality of fit of a probit model by comparing values of the maximized likelihood function with all the regressors to the value of the likelihood with none. This is, in fact, what the pseudo-R^2 does. A formula for the pseudo-R^2 is given in Appendix 9.2.

9.4   Application to the Boston HMDA Data

The regressions of the previous two sections indicated that denial rates were higher for black than white applicants, holding constant their payment-to-income ratio. Loan officers, however, legitimately weigh many factors when deciding on a mortgage application, and if any of those other factors differ systematically by race then the estimators considered so far have omitted variable bias.

In this section, we take a closer look at whether there is statistical evidence of discrimination in the Boston HMDA data. Specifically, our objective is to estimate the effect of race on the probability of denial, holding constant those applicant characteristics that a loan officer might legally consider when deciding on a mortgage application.

The most important variables available to loan officers through the mortgage applications in the Boston HMDA data set are listed in Table 9.1; these are the variables we will focus on in our empirical models of loan decisions. The first two variables are direct measures of the financial burden the proposed loan would place on the applicant, measured in terms of his or her income. The first of these is the *P/I ratio*; the second is the ratio of housing-related expenses to income. The next variable is the size of the loan, relative to the assessed value of the home; if the loan-to-value ratio is nearly one, then the bank might have trouble recouping the full amount of the loan if the applicant defaults on the loan and the bank forecloses. The final three financial variables summarize the applicant's credit history. If an applicant has been unreliable paying off debts in the past, then the loan officer legitimately might worry about his or her ability or desire to make mortgage payments in the future. The three variables measure different types of credit histories, which the loan officer might weigh differently. The first concerns consumer credit, such as credit card debt; the second, previous mortgage payment history; and the third measures credit problems so severe that they appeared in a public legal record, such as filing for bankruptcy.

Table 9.1 also lists some other variables relevant to the loan officer's decision. Sometimes the applicant must apply for private mortgage insurance.[3] The loan officer knows whether that application was denied, and that denial would weigh negatively with the loan officer. The next three variables, which concern the employment status, marital status, and educational attainment of the applicant, relate to the prospective ability of the applicant to repay. In the event of foreclosure, characteristics of the property are relevant as well and the next variable indicates whether the property is a condominium. The final two variables in Table 9.1 are whether the applicant is black or white, and whether the application was denied or accepted. In these data, 14.2% of applicants are black and 12.0% of applications are denied.

---

[3]Mortgage insurance is an insurance policy under which the insurance company makes the monthly payment to the bank if the borrower defaults. During the period of this study, if the loan-to-value ratio exceeds 80% the applicant typically was required to buy mortgage insurance.

TABLE 9.1 Variables Included in Regression Models of Mortgage Decisions

Variable	Definition	Sample Average
Financial Variables		
P/I ratio	Ratio of total monthly debt payments to total monthly income	0.331
housing expense-to-income ratio	Ratio of monthly housing expenses to total monthly income	0.255
loan-to-value ratio	Ratio of size of loan to assessed value of property	0.738
consumer credit score	1 if no "slow" payments or delinquencies 2 if one or two slow payments or delinquencies 3 if more than two slow payments 4 if insufficient credit history for determination 5 if delinquent credit history with payments 60 days overdue 6 if delinquent credit history with payments 90 days overdue	2.1
mortgage credit score	1 if no late mortgage payments 2 if no mortgage payment history 3 if one or two late mortgage payments 4 if more than two late mortgage payments	1.7
public bad credit record	1 if any public record of credit problems (bankruptcy, charge-offs, collection actions) 0 otherwise	0.074
Additional Applicant Characteristics		
denied mortgage insurance	1 if applicant applied for mortgage insurance and was denied, 0 otherwise	0.020
self-employed	1 if self-employed, 0 otherwise	0.116
single	1 if applicant reported being single, 0 otherwise	0.393
high school diploma	1 if applicant graduated from high school, 0 otherwise	0.984
unemployment rate	1989 Massachusetts unemployment rate in the applicant's industry	3.8
condominium	1 if unit is a condominium, 0 otherwise	0.288
black	1 if applicant is black, 0 if white	0.142
deny	1 if mortgage application denied, 0 otherwise	0.120

Table 9.2 presents regression results based on these variables. The base specifications, reported in columns (1)–(3), include the financial variables in Table 9.1 plus the variables indicating whether private mortgage insurance was denied and

whether the applicant is self-employed. Loan officers commonly use thresholds, or cutoff values, for the loan-to-value ratio, so the base specification for that variable uses binary variables for whether the loan-to-value ratio is high (≥ 0.95), medium (between 0.8 and 0.95), or low (< 0.8; this case is omitted to avoid perfect multicollinearity). The regressors in the first three columns are similar to those in the base specification considered by the Federal Reserve Bank of Boston in their original analysis of these data.[4] The regressions in columns (1)–(3) differ only in how the denial probability is modeled, respectively using a linear probability model, a logit model, and a probit model.

Because the regression in column (1) is a linear probability model, its coefficients are estimated changes in predicted probabilities arising from a unit change in the independent variable. Accordingly, an increase in the *P/I ratio* of 0.1 is estimated to increase the probability of denial by 4.5 percentage points (the coefficient on *P/I ratio* in column (1) is 0.449, and $0.449 \times 0.1 \cong 0.045$). Similarly, having a high loan-to-value ratio increases the probability of denial: a loan-to-value ratio exceeding 95% is associated with a 18.9 percentage point increase (the coefficient is 0.189) in the denial probability, relative to the omitted case of a loan-to-value ratio less than 80%, holding the other variables in column (1) constant. Applicants with a poor credit rating also have a more difficult time getting a loan, all else being constant, although interestingly the coefficient on consumer credit is statistically significant but the coefficient on mortgage credit is not. Applicants with a public record of credit problems, such as filing for bankruptcy, have much greater difficulty obtaining a loan: all else equal, a public bad credit record is estimated to increase the probability of denial by 0.197, or 19.7 percentage points. Being denied private mortgage insurance is estimated to be virtually decisive: the estimated coefficient of 0.702 means that being denied mortgage insurance increases your chance of being denied a mortgage by 70.2 percentage points, all else equal. Of the nine variables (other than race) in the regression, the coefficients on all but two are statistically significant at the 5% level, which is consistent with loan officers' considering many factors when they make their decisions.

The coefficient on *black* in regression (1) is 0.084, indicating that the difference in denial probabilities for black and white applicants is 8.4 percentage points,

---

[4]The difference between the regressors in columns (1)–(3) and those in Munnell et al. (1996), table 2(1), is that Munnell et al. include additional indicators for the location of the home and the identity of the lender, data which are not publicly available; an indicator for a multifamily home, which is irrelevant here because our subset focuses on single-family homes; and net wealth, which we omit because this variable has a few very large positive and negative values and thus risks making the results sensitive to a few specific "outlier" observations.

TABLE 9.2 Mortgage Denial Regressions Using the Boston HMDA Data

Dependent Variable: *deny* = 1 If Mortgage Application Is Denied, = 0 If Accepted; 2,380 observations.

Regression Model Regressor	LPM (1)	Logit (2)	Probit (3)	Probit (4)	Probit (5)	Probit (6)
black	0.084** (0.023)	0.688** (0.182)	0.389** (0.098)	0.371** (0.099)	0.363** (0.100)	0.246 (0.448)
P/I ratio	0.449** (0.114)	4.76** (1.33)	2.44** (0.61)	2.46** (0.60)	2.62** (0.61)	2.57** (0.66)
housing expense-to- income ratio	−0.048 (.110)	−0.11 (1.29)	−0.18 (0.68)	−0.30 (0.68)	−0.50 (0.70)	−0.54 (0.74)
medium loan-to-value ratio (0.80 ≤ loan-value ratio ≤ 0.95)	0.031* (0.013)	0.46** (0.16)	0.21** (0.08)	0.22** (0.08)	0.22** (0.08)	0.22** (0.08)
high loan-to-value ratio (loan-value ratio ≥ 0.95)	0.189** (0.050)	1.49** (0.32)	0.79** (0.18)	0.79** (0.18)	0.84** (0.18)	0.79** (0.18)
consumer credit score	0.031** (0.005)	0.29** (0.04)	0.15** (0.02)	0.16** (0.02)	0.34** (0.11)	0.16** (0.02)
mortgage credit score	0.021 (0.011)	0.28* (0.14)	0.15* (0.07)	0.11 (0.08)	0.16 (0.10)	0.11 (0.08)
public bad credit record	0.197** (0.035)	1.23** (0.20)	0.70** (0.12)	0.70** (0.12)	0.72** (0.12)	0.70** (0.12)
denied mortgage insurance	0.702** (0.045)	4.55** (0.57)	2.56** (0.30)	2.59** (0.29)	2.59** (0.30)	2.59** (0.29)
self-employed	0.060** (0.021)	0.67** (0.21)	0.36** (0.11)	0.35** (0.11)	0.34** (0.11)	0.35** (0.11)
single				0.23** (0.08)	0.23** (0.08)	0.23** (0.08)
high school diploma				−0.61** (0.23)	−0.60* (0.24)	−0.62** (0.23)
unemployment rate				0.03 (0.02)	0.03 (0.02)	0.03 (0.02)
condominium					−0.05 (0.09)	
black × P/I ratio						−0.58 (1.47)
black × housing expense-to- income ratio						1.23 (1.69)
Additional credit rating indicator variables	no	no	no	no	yes	no
constant	−0.183** (0.028)	−5.71** (0.48)	−3.04** (0.23)	−2.57** (0.34)	−2.90** (0.39)	−2.54** (0.35)

(Table 9.2 continued)

(Table 9.2 continued)

F-statistics and p-values Testing Exclusion of Groups of Variables

	(1)	(2)	(3)	(4)	(5)	(6)
Applicant single; HS diploma; industry unemployment rate				5.85 (<0.001)	5.22 (0.001)	5.79 (<0.001)
Additional credit rating indicator variables					1.22 (0.291)	
Race interactions and black						4.96 (0.002)
Race interactions only						0.27 (0.766)
Difference in predicted probability of denial, white vs. black (percentage points)	8.4%	6.0%	7.1%	6.6%	6.3%	6.5%

These regressions were estimated using the $n = 2,380$ observations in the Boston HMDA data set described in Appendix 9.1. The linear probability model was estimated by OLS, and probit and logit regressions were estimated by maximum likelihood. Standard errors are given in parentheses under the coefficients and p-values are given in parentheses under the F-statistics. The change in predicted probability in the final row was computed for a hypothetical applicant whose values of the regressors, other than race, equal the sample mean. Individual coefficients are statistically significant at the [*]5% or [**]1% level.

holding constant the other variables in the regression. This is statistically significant at the 1% significance level ($t = 3.65$).

The logit and probit estimates reported in columns (2) and (3) yield similar conclusions. In the logit and probit regressions, eight of the nine coefficients on variables other than race are individually statistically significantly different from zero at the 5% level, and the coefficient on *black* is statistically significant at the 1% level. As discussed in Section 9.2, because these models are nonlinear, specific values of all the regressors must be chosen to compute the difference in predicted probabilities for white and black applicants. A conventional way to make this choice is to consider an "average" applicant who has the sample average values of all the regressors other than race. The final row in Table 9.2 reports this estimated difference in probabilities, evaluated for this average applicant. The estimated racial differentials are similar to each other: 8.4 percentage points for the linear probability model (column (1)), 6.0 percentage points for the logit model (column (2)), and 7.1 percentage points for the probit model (column (3)). These estimated race effects and the coefficients on *black* are less than in the regressions of the previous sections, in which the only regressors were *P/I ratio* and *black*, indicating that those earlier estimates had omitted variable bias.

The regressions in columns (4)–(6) investigate the sensitivity of the results in column (3) to changes in the regression specification. Column (4) modifies column (3) by including additional applicant characteristics. These characteristics help to predict whether the loan is denied; for example, having at least a high school diploma reduces the probability of denial (the estimate is negative and the coefficient is statistically significant at the 1% level). However, controlling for these personal characteristics does not change the estimated coefficient on *black* or the estimated difference in denial probabilities (6.6%) in an important way.

Column (5) breaks out the six consumer credit categories and four mortgage credit categories to test the null hypothesis that these two variables enter linearly; this regression also adds a variable indicating whether the property is a condominium. The null hypothesis that the credit rating variables enter the expression for the z-value linearly is not rejected, nor is the condominium indicator significant, at the 5% level. Most importantly, the estimated racial difference in denial probabilities (6.3%) is essentially the same as in columns (3) and (4).

Column (6) examines whether there are interactions. Are different standards applied to evaluating the payment-to-income and housing expense-to-income ratios for black versus white applicants? The answer appears to be no: the interaction terms are not jointly statistically significant at the 5% level. However, race continues to have a significant effect, because the race indicator and the interaction terms are jointly statistically significant at the 1% level. Again, the estimated racial difference in denial probabilities (6.5%) is essentially the same as in the other probit regressions.

In all six specifications, the effect of race on the denial probability, holding other applicant characteristics constant, is statistically significant at the 1% level. The estimated difference in denial probabilities between black and white applicants ranges from 6.0 percentage points to 8.4 percentage points.

One way to assess whether this differential is large or small is to return to a variation on the question posed at the beginning of this chapter. Suppose two individuals apply for a mortgage, one white and one black but otherwise having the same values of the other independent variables in regression (3); specifically, aside from race, the values of the other variables in regression (3) are the sample average values in the HMDA data set. The white applicant faces a 7.4% chance of denial, but the black applicant faces a 14.5% chance of denial. The estimated racial difference in denial probabilities, 7.1 percentage points, means that the black applicant is nearly twice as likely to be denied as the white applicant.

The results in Table 9.2 (and in the original Boston Fed study) provide statistical evidence of racial patterns in mortgage denial that, by law, ought not be there. This evidence played an important role in spurring policy changes by bank regulators.[5] But economists love a good argument, and not surprisingly these results have also stimulated a vigorous debate.

Because the suggestion that there is (or was) racial discrimination in lending is charged, we briefly review some points of this debate. In so doing, it is useful to adopt the framework of Chapter 7, that is, to consider the internal and external validity of the results in Table 9.2, which are representative of previous analyses of the Boston HMDA data. A number of the criticisms made of the original Federal Reserve Bank of Boston study concern internal validity: possible errors in the data, alternative nonlinear functional forms, additional interactions, and so forth. The original data were subjected to a careful audit, some errors were found, and the results reported here (and in the final published Boston Fed study) are based on the "cleaned" data set. Estimation of other specifications—different functional forms and/or additional regressors—also produces estimates of racial differentials comparable to those in Table 9.2. A potentially more difficult issue of internal validity is whether there is relevant nonracial financial information obtained during in-person loan interviews, not recorded on the loan application itself, that is correlated with race; if so, there still might be omitted variable bias in the Table 9.2 regressions. Finally, some have questioned external validity: even if there was racial discrimination in Boston in 1990, it is wrong to implicate lenders elsewhere today. The only way to resolve the question of external validity is to consider data from other locations and years.[6]

9.5 Summary

When the dependent variable Y is binary, the population regression function is the probability that $Y = 1$, conditional on the regressors. Estimation of this population regression function entails finding a functional form that does justice to its probability interpretation, estimating the unknown parameters of that func-

---

[5]These policy shifts include changes in the way that fair lending examinations were done by Federal bank regulators, changes in inquiries made by the U.S. Department of Justice, and enhanced education programs for banks and other home loan origination companies.

[6]If you are interested in further reading on this topic, a good place to start is the symposium on racial discrimination and economics in the Spring 1998 issue of the *Journal of Economic Perspectives*. The article in that symposium by Helen Ladd (1998) surveys the evidence and debate on racial discrimination in mortgage lending. A more detailed treatment is given in Goering and Wienk (1996).

James J. Heckman and Daniel L. McFadden, Nobel Laureates

The 2000 Nobel Prize in economics was awarded jointly to two econometricians, James J. Heckman of the University of Chicago and Daniel L. McFadden of the University of California at Berkeley, for fundamental contributions to the analysis of data on individuals and firms. Much of their work addressed difficulties that arise with limited dependent variables.

Heckman was awarded the prize for developing tools for handling sample selection. As discussed in Section 7.2, sample selection bias occurs when the availability of data are influenced by a selection process related to the value of dependent variable. For example, suppose you want to estimate the relationship between earnings and some regressor, X, using a random sample from the population. If you estimate the regression using the subsample of employed workers—that is, those reporting positive earnings—the OLS estimate could be subject to selection bias. Heckman's solution was to specify a preliminary equation with a binary dependent variable indicating whether the worker is in or out of the labor force (in or out of the subsample) and to treat this equation and the earnings equation as a system of simultaneous equations. This general strategy has been extended to selection problems that arise in many fields, ranging from labor economics to industrial organization to finance.

McFadden was awarded the prize for developing models for analyzing discrete choice data (does a high school graduate join the military, go to college, or get a job?). He started by considering the problem of an individual maximizing the expected utility of each possible choice, which could depend on observable variables (such as wages, job characteristics, and family background). He then derived models for the individual choice probabilities with unknown coefficients, which in turn could be estimated by maximum likelihood. These models and their extensions have proven widely useful in analyzing discrete choice data in many fields, including labor economics, health economics, and transportation economics.

For more information on these and other Nobel laureates in economics, visit the Nobel Foundation Web site, www.nobel.se/economics.

tion, and interpreting the results. The resulting predicted values are predicted probabilities, and the estimated effect of a change in a regressor X is the estimated change in the probability that $Y = 1$ arising from the change in X.

A natural way to model the probability that $Y = 1$ given the regressors is to use a cumulative distribution function, where the argument of the c.d.f. depends on the regressors. Probit regression uses a normal c.d.f. as the regression function, and logit regression uses a logistic c.d.f. Because these models are nonlinear functions of the unknown parameters, those parameters are more complicated to estimate than linear regression coefficients. The standard estimation method is maximum likelihood. In practice, statistical inference using the maximum likelihood estimates proceeds the same way as it does in linear multiple regression; for example, 95% confidence intervals for a coefficient are constructed as the estimated coefficient ± 1.96 standard errors.

Despite its intrinsic nonlinearity, sometimes the population regression function can be adequately approximated by a linear probability model, that is, by the straight line produced by linear multiple regression. The linear probability model, probit regression, and logit regression all give similar "bottom line" answers when they are applied to the Boston HMDA data: all three methods estimate substantial differences in mortgage denial rates for otherwise similar black and white applicants.

Binary dependent variables are the most common example of limited dependent variables, which are dependent variables with a limited range. The final quarter of the twentieth century saw important advances in econometric methods for analyzing other limited dependent variables (see the Nobel Laureates box). Some of these methods are reviewed in Appendix 9.3.

Summary

1. When Y is a binary variable, the linear multiple regression model is called the linear probability model. The population regression line shows the probability that $Y = 1$ given the value of the regressors, $X_1, X_2, \ldots, X_k$.

2. Probit and logit regression models are nonlinear regression models used when Y is a binary variable. Unlike the linear probability model, probit and logit regression ensure that the predicted probability that $Y = 1$ is between zero and one for all values of X.

3. Probit regression uses the standard normal cumulative distribution function. Logit regression uses the logistic cumulative distribution function. Logit and probit coefficients are estimated by maximum likelihood.

4. The values of coefficients in probit and logit regressions are not easy to interpret. Changes in the probability that $Y = 1$ associated with changes in one or more of the X's can be calculated using the general procedure for nonlinear models outlined in Key Concept 6.1.

5. Hypothesis tests on coefficients in the linear probability, logit, and probit models are performed using the usual t- and F-statistics.

Key Terms

limited dependent variable (297)

linear probability model (299)

probit (302)

logit (302)

nonlinear least squares estimator (310)

likelihood function (311)

maximum likelihood estimator (MLE)
   (311)

fraction correctly predicted (313)

pseudo-R^2 (313)

Review the Concepts

9.1 Suppose that a linear probability model yields a predicted value of Y that is equal to 1.3. Explain why this is nonsensical.

9.2 In Table 9.2 the estimated coefficient on *black* is 0.084 in column (1), 0.688 in column (2), and 0.389 in column (3). In spite of these large differences, all 3 models yield similar estimates of the marginal effect of race on the probability of mortgage denial. How can this be?

9.3 One of your friends is using data on individuals to study the determinants of smoking at your university. She asks you whether she should use a probit, logit, or linear probability model. What advice do you give her? Why?

9.4 Why are the coefficients of probit and logit models estimated by maximum likelihood instead of OLS?

Exercises

*9.1 Use the estimated probit model in Equation (9.8) to answer the following questions:

   a. A black mortgage applicant has a *P/I ratio* of 0.35. What is the probability that his application will be denied?

   b. Suppose that the applicant reduced this ratio to 0.30. What effect would this have on his probability of being denied a mortgage?

   c. Repeat parts (a) and (b) for a white applicant.

   d. Does the marginal effect of the *P/I ratio* on the probability of mortgage denial depend on race? Explain.

9.2 Repeat question 9.1 using the logit model in Equation (9.10). Are the logit and probit results similar? Explain.

9.3 Consider the linear probability model $Y_i = \beta_0 + \beta_1 X_i + u_i$, where $\Pr(Y_i = 1 \mid X_i) = \beta_0 + \beta_1 X_i$.

    a. Show that $E(u_i \mid X_i) = 0$.

    b. Show that $\text{var}(u_i \mid X_i) = (\beta_0 + \beta_1 X_i)[1 - (\beta_0 + \beta_1 X_i)]$.
    (*Hint:* Review Equation (2.7).)

    c. Is u_i heteroskedastic? Explain.

    d. (Requires Section 9.3) Derive the likelihood function.

9.4 Use the estimated linear probability model shown in column (1) of Table 9.2 to answer the following:

    a. Two applicants, one white and one black, apply for a mortgage. They have the same values for all the regressors other than race. How much more likely is the black applicant to be denied a mortgage?

    b. Construct a 95% confidence interval for your answer to (a).

    c. Think of an important omitted variable that might bias the answer in (a). What is it and how would it bias the results?

9.5 (Requires Section 9.3 and calculus) Suppose that a random variable Y has the following probability distribution: $\Pr(Y = 1) = p$, $\Pr(Y = 2) = q$, and $\Pr(Y = 3) = 1 - p - q$. A random sample of size n is drawn from this distribution and the random variables are denoted $Y_1, Y_2, \ldots, Y_n$.

    a. Derive the likelihood function for the parameters p and q.

    b. Derive formulas for the MLE of p and q.

APPENDIX 9.1 | The Boston HMDA Data Set

The Boston HMDA data set was collected by researchers at the Federal Reserve Bank of Boston. The data set combines information from mortgage applications and a follow-up survey of the banks and other lending institutions that received these mortgage applications. The data pertain to mortgage applications made in 1990 in the greater Boston metropolitan area. The full data set has 2,925 observations, consisting of all mortgage applications by blacks and Hispanics plus a random sample of mortgage applications by whites.

To narrow the scope of the analysis in this chapter, we use a subset of the data for single-family residences only (thereby excluding data on multifamily homes) and for black and white applicants only (thereby excluding data on applicants from other minority groups). This leaves 2,380 observations. Definitions of the variables used in this chapter are given in Table 9.1.

These data were graciously provided to us by Geoffrey Tootell of the Research Department of the Federal Reserve Bank of Boston. More information about this data set, along with the conclusions reached by the Federal Reserve Bank of Boston researchers, is available in the article by Alicia H. Munnell, Geoffrey M.B. Tootell, Lynne E. Browne, and James McEneaney, "Mortgage Lending in Boston: Interpreting HMDA Data," *American Economic Review*, 1996, pp. 25–53.

APPENDIX

9.2 | Maximum Likelihood Estimation

This appendix provides a brief introduction to maximum likelihood estimation in the context of the binary response models discussed in this chapter. We start by deriving the MLE of the success probability p for n i.i.d. observations of a Bernoulli random variable. We then turn to the probit and logit models and discuss the pseudo-R^2. We conclude with a discussion of standard errors for predicted probabilities. This appendix uses calculus at two points.

MLE for n I.I.D. Bernoulli Random Variables

The first step in computing the MLE is to derive the joint probability distribution. For n i.i.d. observations on a Bernoulli random variable, this joint probability distribution is the extension of the $n = 2$ case in Section 9.3 to general n:

$$\Pr(Y_1 = y_1, Y_2 = y_2, \ldots, Y_n = y_n) =$$
$$[p^{y_1}(1 - p)^{(1-y_1)}] \times [p^{y_2}(1 - p)^{(1-y_2)}] \times \cdots \times [p^{y_n}(1 - p)^{(1-y_n)}] = \qquad (9.13)$$
$$p^{(y_1 + \cdots + y_n)}(1 - p)^{n - (y_1 + \cdots + y_n)}.$$

The likelihood function is the joint probability distribution, treated as a function of the unknown coefficients. Let $S = \sum_{i=1}^{n} Y_i$; then the likelihood function is

$$f_{Bernoulli}(p; Y_1, \ldots, Y_n) = p^S(1-p)^{n-S}. \tag{9.14}$$

The MLE of p is the value of p that maximizes the likelihood in Equation (9.14). The likelihood function can be maximized using calculus. It is convenient to maximize not the likelihood but its logarithm (because the logarithm is a strictly increasing function, maximizing the likelihood or its logarithm gives the same estimator). The log likelihood is $S\ln(p) + (n - S)\ln(1 - p)$, and the derivative of the log likelihood with respect to p is

$$\frac{d}{dp}\ln[f_{Bernoulli}(p; Y_1, \ldots, Y_n)] = \frac{S}{p} - \frac{n-S}{1-p}. \tag{9.15}$$

Setting the derivative in Equation (9.15) to zero and solving for p yields the MLE $\hat{p} = S/n = \overline{Y}$.

MLE for the Probit Model

For the probit model, the probability that $Y_i = 1$, conditional on $X_{1i}, \ldots, X_{ki}$, is $p_i = \Phi(\beta_0 + \beta_1 X_{1i} + \cdots + \beta_k X_{ki})$. The conditional probability distribution for the ith observation is $\Pr[Y_i = y_i | X_{1i}, \ldots, X_{ki}] = p_i^{y_i}(1 - p_i)^{1-y_i}$. Assuming that $(X_{1i}, \ldots, X_{ki}, Y_i)$ are i.i.d., $i = 1, \ldots, n$, the joint probability distribution of $Y_1, \ldots, Y_n$, conditional on the X's, is

$$\Pr(Y_1 = y_1, \ldots, Y_n = y_n | X_{1i}, \ldots, X_{ki}, i = 1, \ldots, n)$$
$$= \Pr(Y_1 = y_1 | X_{11}, \ldots, X_{k1}) \times \cdots \times \Pr(Y_n = y_n | X_{1n}, \ldots, X_{kn}) \tag{9.16}$$
$$= p_1^{y_1}(1 - p_1)^{1-y_1} \times \cdots \times p_n^{y_n}(1 - p_n)^{1-y_n}.$$

The likelihood function is the joint probability distribution, treated as a function of the unknown coefficients. It is conventional to consider the logarithm of the likelihood. Accordingly, the log likelihood function is

$$\ln[f_{probit}(\beta_0, \ldots, \beta_k; Y_1, \ldots, Y_n | X_{1i}, \ldots, X_{ki}, i = 1, \ldots, n)] =$$
$$\sum_{i=1}^{n} Y_i \ln[\Phi(\beta_0 + \beta_1 X_{1i} + \cdots + \beta_k X_{ki})] \tag{9.17}$$
$$+ \sum_{i=1}^{n} (1 - Y_i) \ln[1 - \Phi(\beta_0 + \beta_1 X_{1i} + \cdots + \beta_k X_{ki})],$$

where this expression incorporates the probit formula for the conditional probability, $p_i = \Phi(\beta_0 + \beta_1 X_{1i} + \cdots + \beta_k X_{ki})$.

The MLE for the probit model maximizes the likelihood function or, equivalently, the logarithm of the likelihood function given in Equation (9.17). Because there is no simple formula for the MLE, the probit likelihood function must be maximized using a numerical algorithm on the computer.

Under general conditions, maximum likelihood estimators are consistent and have a normal sampling distribution in large samples.

MLE for the Logit Model

The likelihood for the logit model is derived in the same way as the likelihood for the probit model. The only difference is that the conditional success probability p_i for the logit model is given by Equation (9.9). Accordingly, the log likelihood of the logit model is given by Equation (9.17), with $\Phi(\beta_0 + \beta_1 X_{1i} + \cdots + \beta_k X_{ki})$ replaced by $[1 + e^{-(\beta_0 + \beta_1 X_{1i} + \beta_2 X_{2i} + \cdots + \beta_k X_{ki})}]^{-1}$. Like the probit model, there is no simple formula for the MLE of the logit coefficients, so the log likelihood must be maximized numerically.

Pseudo-R^2

The pseudo-R^2 compares the value of the likelihood of the estimated model to the value of the likelihood when none of the X's are included as regressors. Specifically, the pseudo-R^2 is

$$\text{pseudo-}R^2 = 1 - \frac{\ln(f_{probit}^{\max})}{\ln(f_{Bernoulli}^{\max})}, \tag{9.18}$$

where $f_{probit}^{\max}$ is the value of the maximized probit likelihood (which includes the X's) and $f_{Bernoulli}^{\max}$ is the value of the maximized Bernoulli likelihood (the probit model excluding all the X's).

Standard Errors for Predicted Probabilities

For simplicity, consider the case of a single regressor in the probit model. Then the predicted probability at a fixed value of that regressor, x, is $\hat{p}(x) = \Phi(\hat{\beta}_0^{MLE} + \hat{\beta}_1^{MLE} x)$, where $\hat{\beta}_0^{MLE}$ and $\hat{\beta}_1^{MLE}$ are the MLEs of the two probit coefficients. Because this predicted probability depends on the estimators $\hat{\beta}_0^{MLE}$ and $\hat{\beta}_1^{MLE}$, and because those estimators have a sampling distribution, the predicted probability will also have a sampling distribution.

The variance of the sampling distribution of $\hat{p}(x)$ is calculated by approximating the function $\Phi(\hat{\beta}_0^{MLE} + \hat{\beta}_1^{MLE} x)$, a nonlinear function of $\hat{\beta}_0^{MLE}$ and $\hat{\beta}_1^{MLE}$, by a linear function of $\hat{\beta}_0^{MLE}$ and $\hat{\beta}_1^{MLE}$. Specifically, let

$$\hat{p}(x) = \Phi(\hat{\beta}_0^{MLE} + \hat{\beta}_1^{MLE} x) \cong c + a_0 \hat{\beta}_0^{MLE} + a_1 \hat{\beta}_1^{MLE}, \tag{9.19}$$

where the constant c and factors a_0 and a_1 depend on x and are obtained from calculus. (Equation (9.19) is a first order Taylor series expansion; $c = \Phi(\beta_0 + \beta_1 x)$, and a_0 and a_1 are the partial derivatives, $a_0 = \partial\Phi(\beta_0 + \beta_1 x)/\partial\beta_0|_{\hat{\beta}_0^{MLE}, \hat{\beta}_1^{MLE}}$ and $a_1 = \partial\Phi(\beta_0 + \beta_1 x)/\partial\beta_1|_{\hat{\beta}_0^{MLE}, \hat{\beta}_1^{MLE}}$.) The variance of $\hat{p}(x)$ now can be calculated using the approximation in Equation (9.19) and the expression for the variance of the sum of two random variables in Equation (2.31):

$$
\begin{aligned}
\mathrm{var}[\hat{p}(x)] &\cong \mathrm{var}(c + a_0\hat{\beta}_0^{MLE} + a_1\hat{\beta}_1^{MLE}) \\
&= a_0^2\mathrm{var}(\hat{\beta}_0^{MLE}) + a_1^2\mathrm{var}(\hat{\beta}_1^{MLE}) + 2a_0a_1\mathrm{cov}(\hat{\beta}_0^{MLE}, \hat{\beta}_1^{MLE}).
\end{aligned}
\tag{9.20}
$$

Using Equation (9.20), the standard error of $\hat{p}(x)$ can be calculated using estimates of the variances and covariance of the MLE's.

APPENDIX

9.3 | Other Limited Dependent Variable Models

This appendix surveys some models for limited dependent variables, other than binary variables, found in econometric applications. In most cases the OLS estimators of the parameters of limited dependent variable models are inconsistent, and estimation is routinely done using maximum likelihood. There are several advanced references available to the reader interested in further details; see for example Ruud (2000) and Maddala (1983).

Censored and Truncated Regression Models

Suppose you have cross-sectional data on car purchases by individuals in a given year. Car buyers have positive expenditures, which can reasonably be treated as continuous random variables, but nonbuyers spent $0. Thus the distribution of car expenditures is a combination of a discrete distribution (at zero) and a continuous distribution.

Nobel laureate James Tobin developed a useful model for a dependent variable with a partly continuous and partly discrete distribution (Tobin, 1958). Tobin suggested modeling the ith individual in the sample as having a desired level of spending, Y_i^*, that is related to the regressors (for example, family size) according to a linear regression model. That is, when there is a single regressor, the desired level of spending is

$$
Y_i^* = \beta_0 + \beta_1 X_i + u_i, \quad i = 1, \ldots, n.
\tag{9.21}
$$

If Y_i^* (what the consumer wants to spend) exceeds some cutoff, such as the minimum price of a car, then the consumer buys the car and spends $Y_i = Y_i^*$, which is observed. However, if Y_i^* is less than the cutoff, then spending of $Y_i = 0$ is observed instead of Y_i^*.

When Equation (9.21) is estimated using observed expenditures Y_i in place of Y_i^*, the OLS estimator is inconsistent. Tobin solved this problem by deriving the likelihood function using the additional assumption that u_i has a normal distribution, and the resulting MLE has been used by applied econometricians to analyze many problems in economics. In Tobin's honor, Equation (9.21), combined with the assumption of normal errors, is called the **tobit** regression model. The tobit model is an example of a **censored regression model**, so-called because the dependent variable has been "censored" above or below a certain cutoff.

Sample Selection Models

In the censored regression model, there are data on buyers and nonbuyers, as there would be were the data obtained by simple random sampling of the adult population. If, however, the data are collected from sales tax records then the data would include only buyers: there would be no data at all for nonbuyers. Data in which observations are unavailable above or below a threshold (data for buyers only) are called truncated data. The **truncated regression model** is a regression model applied to data in which observations are simply unavailable when the dependent variable is above or below a certain cutoff.

The truncated regression model is an example of a sample selection model, in which the selection mechanism (an individual is in the sample by virtue of buying a car) is related to the value of the dependent variable (the price of the car). As discussed in the box in Section 9.4, one approach to estimation of sample selection models is to develop two equations, one for Y_i^* and one for whether or not Y_i^* is observed. The parameters of the model can then be estimated by maximum likelihood, or in a stepwise procedure, estimating the selection equation first, then estimating the equation for Y_i^*. For additional discussion, see Ruud (2000, Chapter 28) or Greene (2000, Section 20.4).

Count Data

Count data arises when the dependent variable is a counting number, for example the number of restaurant meals eaten by a consumer in a week. When these numbers are large, the variable can be treated as approximately continuous, but when they are small, the continuous approximation is a poor one. The linear regression model, estimated by OLS, can be used for count data, even if the number of counts is small. Predicted values from the regression are interpreted as the expected value of the dependent variable, conditional on the regressors. So, when the dependent variable is the number of restaurant meals eaten, a predicted value of 1.7 means, on average, 1.7 restaurant meals per week. As in the binary regression model, however, OLS does not take advantage of the special structure of count data and can yield nonsense predictions, for example −0.2 restaurant meals per week. Just as probit and logit eliminate nonsense predictions when the dependent variable is binary, special models do so for count data. The two most widely used models are the Poisson and negative binomial regression models.

Ordered Responses

Ordered response data arise when mutually exclusive qualitative categories have a natural ordering, such as obtaining a high school degree, some college education (but not graduating), or graduating from college. Like count data, ordered response data have a natural ordering, but unlike count data they do not have natural numerical values.

Because there are no natural numerical values for ordered response data, OLS is inappropriate. Instead, ordered data are often analyzed using a generalization of probit called the **ordered probit model**, in which the probabilities of each outcome (e.g., a college education), conditional on the independent variables (such as parents' income) are modeled using the cumulative normal distribution.

Discrete Choice Data

A **discrete choice** or **multiple choice** variable can take on multiple unordered qualitative values. One example in economics is the mode of transport chosen by a commuter: she might take the subway, ride the bus, drive, or make her way under her own power (walk, bicycle). If we were to analyze these choices, the dependent variable would have four possible outcomes (subway, bus, car, human-powered). These outcomes are not ordered in any natural way. Instead, the outcomes are a choice among distinct qualitative alternatives.

The econometric task is to model the probability of choosing the various options, given various regressors such as individual characteristics (how far the commuter's house is from the subway station) and the characteristics of each option (the price of the subway). As discussed in the box in Section 9.3, models for analysis of discrete choice data can be developed from principles of utility maximization. Individual choice probabilities can be expressed in probit or logit form, and those models are called **multinomial probit** and **multinomial logit** regression models.

CHAPTER 10

Instrumental Variables Regression

C hapter 7 discussed several problems, including omitted variables, errors-in-variables, and simultaneous causality, that make the error term correlated with the regressor. Omitted variable bias can be addressed directly by including the omitted variable in a multiple regression, but this is only feasible if you have data on the omitted variable. And sometimes, such as when causality runs *both* from X to Y *and* from Y to X, so that there is simultaneous causality bias, multiple regression simply cannot eliminate the bias. If a direct solution to these problems is either infeasible or unavailable, then a new method is required.

Instrumental variables (IV) regression is a general way to obtain a consistent estimator of the unknown coefficients of the population regression function when the regressor, X, is correlated with the error term, u. To understand how IV regression works, think of the variation in X as having two parts: one part that, for whatever reason, is correlated with u (this is the part that causes the problems), and a second part that is uncorrelated with u. If you had information that allowed you to isolate the second part, then you could focus on those variations in X that are uncorrelated with u and disregard the variations in X that bias the OLS estimates. This is, in fact, what IV regression does. The information about the movements in X that are uncorrelated with u is gleaned from one or more additional variables, called **instrumental variables** or simply **instruments**. Instrumental variables regression uses these additional variables as tools or "instruments" to isolate the movements in X that are uncorrelated with u, which in turn permit consistent estimation of the regression coefficients.

The first two sections of this chapter describe the mechanics and assumptions of IV regression: why IV regression works, what is a valid instrument, and how to implement and to interpret the most common IV regression method, two stage least squares. The key to successful empirical analysis using instrumental variables is finding valid instruments, and Section 10.3 takes up the question of how to assess whether a set of instruments is valid. As an illustration, Section 10.4 uses IV regression to estimate the elasticity of demand for cigarettes. Finally, Section 10.5 turns to the difficult question of where valid instruments come from in the first place.

10.1 The IV Estimator with a Single Regressor and a Single Instrument

We start with the case of a single regressor, X, which might be correlated with the regression error, u. If X and u are correlated, then the OLS estimator is inconsistent, that is, it may not be close to the true value of the regression coefficient even when the sample is very large (see Equation (5.1)). As discussed in Section 7.2, this correlation between X and u can stem from various sources, including omitted variables, errors in variables (measurement errors in the regressors), or simultaneous causality (when causality runs "backwards" from Y to X as well as "forwards" from X to Y). Whatever the source of the correlation between X and u, if there is a valid instrumental variable, Z, then the effect on Y of a unit change in X can be estimated using the instrumental variables estimator.

The IV Model and Assumptions

The population regression model relating the dependent variable Y_i and regressor X_i is

$$Y_i = \beta_0 + \beta_1 X_i + u_i, \ i = 1, \ldots, n, \tag{10.1}$$

where as usual u_i is the error term representing omitted factors that determine Y_i. If X_i and u_i are correlated, the OLS estimator is inconsistent. Instrumental variables estimation uses an additional, "instrumental" variable Z to isolate that part of X that is uncorrelated with u_i.

Endogeneity and exogeneity.   Instrumental variables regression has some specialized terminology to distinguish variables that are correlated with the population error term u from ones that are not. Variables correlated with the error term are called **endogenous** variables, while variables uncorrelated with the error term are called **exogenous** variables. The historical source of these terms traces to models with multiple equations, in which an "endogenous" variable is determined within the model while an "exogenous" variable is determined outside the model. For example, Section 7.2 considered the possibility that, if low test scores produced decreases in the student-teacher ratio because of political intervention and increased funding, then causality would run *both* from the student-teacher ratio to test scores *and* from test scores to the student-teacher ratio. This was represented mathematically as a system of two simultaneous equations (Equations (7.3) and (7.4)), one for each causal connection. As discussed in Section 7.2, because both test scores and the student-teacher ratio are determined within the model, both are correlated with the population error term u; that is, in this example, both variables are endogenous. In contrast, an exogenous variable, which is determined outside the model, is uncorrelated with u.

The two conditions for a valid instrument.   A valid instrumental variable ("instrument") must satisfy two conditions, known as **instrument relevance** and **instrument exogeneity**:

1. **Instrument Relevance:** $\text{corr}(Z_i, X_i) \neq 0$.
2. **Instrument Exogeneity:** $\text{corr}(Z_i, u_i) = 0$.

If an instrument is relevant, then variation in the instrument is related to variation in X_i. If in addition the instrument is exogenous, then that part of the variation of X_i captured by the instrumental variable is exogenous. Thus, an instrument that is relevant and exogenous can capture movements in X_i that are exogenous. This exogenous variation can in turn be used to estimate the population coefficient β_1.

The two conditions for a valid instrument are vital for instrumental variables regression, and we return to them (and a version of them relevant for multiple regressors and multiple instruments) repeatedly throughout this chapter.

The Two Stage Least Squares Estimator

If the instrument Z satisfies the conditions of instrument relevance and exogeneity, then the coefficient β_1 can be estimated using an IV estimator called **two stage least squares** (**TSLS**). As the name suggests, the two stage least squares estimator is calculated in two stages. The first stage decomposes X into two components: a problematic component that may be correlated with the regression error, and another problem-free component that is uncorrelated with the error. The second stage uses the problem-free component to estimate β_1.

The first stage begins with a population regression linking X and Z:

$$X_i = \pi_0 + \pi_1 Z_i + v_i, \tag{10.2}$$

where π_0 is the intercept, π_1 is the slope, and v_i is the error term. This regression provides the needed decomposition of X_i. One component is $\pi_0 + \pi_1 Z_i$, the part of X_i that can be predicted by Z_i. Because Z_i is exogenous, this component of X_i is uncorrelated with u_i, the error term in Equation (10.1). The other component of X_i is v_i, which is the problematic component of X_i that is correlated with u_i.

The idea behind TSLS is to use the problem-free component of X_i, $\pi_0 + \pi_1 Z_i$, and to disregard v_i. The only complication is that the values of π_0 and π_1 are unknown, so $\pi_0 + \pi_1 Z_i$ cannot be calculated. Accordingly, the first stage of TSLS applies OLS to Equation (10.2) and uses the predicted value from the OLS regression, $\hat{X}_i = \hat{\pi}_0 + \hat{\pi}_1 Z_i$, where $\hat{\pi}_0$ and $\hat{\pi}_1$ are the OLS estimates.

The second stage of TSLS is easy: regress Y_i on $\hat{X}_i$ using OLS. The resulting estimators from the second stage regression are the TSLS estimators, $\hat{\beta}_0^{TSLS}$ and $\hat{\beta}_1^{TSLS}$.

Why Does IV Regression Work?

Two examples provide some intuition for why IV regression solves the problem of correlation between X_i and u_i.

Example #1: Philip Wright's problem. The method of instrumental variables estimation was first published in 1928 in an appendix to a book written by Philip G. Wright (Wright, 1928); this appendix is thought to have been written with or by his son, Sewall Wright, an important statistician. Philip Wright was concerned with an important economic problem of his day: how to set an import tariff (a tax on imported goods) on animal and vegetable oils and fats, such as butter and soy oil. In the 1920s, import tariffs were a major source of tax revenue for the United States. The key to understanding the economic effect of a tariff was having quantitative estimates of the demand and supply curves of the goods. Recall that the supply elasticity is the percentage change in the quantity supplied arising from a 1% increase in the price, and the demand elasticity is the percentage change in the quantity demanded arising from a 1% increase in the price. Philip Wright needed estimates of these elasticities of supply and demand.

To be concrete, consider the problem of estimating the elasticity of demand for butter. Recall from Key Concept 6.2 that the coefficient in a linear equation relating $\ln(Y_i)$ to $\ln(X_i)$ has the interpretation of the elasticity of Y with respect to X. In the Wrights' problem, this suggests the demand equation

$$\ln(Q_i^{butter}) = \beta_0 + \beta_1 \ln(P_i^{butter}) + u_i, \tag{10.3}$$

where Q_i^{butter} is the ith observation on the quantity of butter consumed, P_i^{butter} is its price, and u_i represents other factors that affect demand, such as income and consumer tastes. In Equation (10.3), a 1% increase in the price of butter yields a β_1 percent change in demand, so β_1 is the demand elasticity.

The Wrights had data on total annual butter consumption and its average annual price in the United States for 1912 to 1922. It would have been easy to use these data to estimate the demand elasticity by applying OLS to Equation (10.3), but they had a key insight: because of the interactions between supply and demand, the regressor, $\ln(P_i^{butter})$, was likely to be correlated with the error term.

To see this, look at Figure 10.1a, which shows the market demand and supply curves for butter for three different years. The demand and supply curves for the first period are denoted D_1 and S_1, and the first period's equilibrium price and quantity are determined by their intersection. In year two, demand increases from D_1 to D_2 (say, because of an increase in income) and supply decreases from S_1 to S_2 (because of an increase in the cost of producing butter); the equilibrium price and quantity are determined by the intersection of the new supply and demand curves. In year three, the factors affecting demand and supply change again; demand increases again to D_3, supply increases to S_3, and a new equilibrium quantity and price are determined. Figure 10.1b shows the equilibrium quantity and price pairs for these three periods and for eight subsequent years, where in each year the supply and demand curves are subject to shifts associated with factors other than price that affect market supply and demand. This scatterplot is like the one that the Wrights would have seen when they plotted their data. As they reasoned, fitting a line to these points by OLS will estimate neither a demand curve nor a supply curve, because the points have been determined by changes in both demand and supply.

The Wrights realized that a way to get around this problem was to find some third variable that shifted supply but did not shift demand. Figure 10.1c shows what happens when such a variable shifts the supply curve, but demand remains stable. Now all of the equilibrium price and quantity pairs lie on a stable demand curve, and the slope of the demand curve is easily estimated. In the instrumental variable formulation of Wright's problem, this third variable—the instrumental

---

FIGURE 10.1

(a) Price and quantity are determined by the intersection of the supply and demand curves. The equilibrium in the first period is determined by the intersection of the demand curve D_1 and the supply curve S_1. Equilibrium in the second period is the intersection of D_2 and S_2, and equilibrium in the third period is the intersection of D_3 and S_3.

(a) Demand and Supply in Three Time Periods

(b) This scatterplot shows equilibrium price and quantity in eleven different time periods. The demand and supply curves are hidden. Can you determine the demand and supply curves from the points on the scatterplot?

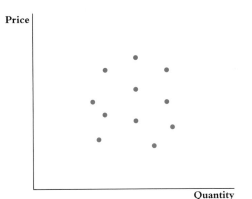

(b) Equilibrium Price and Quantity for Eleven Time Periods

(c) When the supply curve shifts from S_1 to S_2 to S_3 but the demand curve remains at D_1, the equilibrium prices and quantities trace out the demand curve.

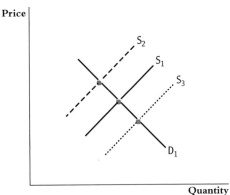

(c) Equilibrium Price and Quantity When Only the Supply Curve Shifts variable—is correlated with price (it shifts the supply curve, which leads to a change in price) but is uncorrelated with u (the demand curve remains stable). The Wrights discussed several potential instrumental variables; one was the weather. For example, below-average rainfall in a dairy region could impair grazing and thus reduce butter production at a given price (it would shift the supply curve to the left and increase the equilibrium price), so dairy-region rainfall satisfies the condition for instrument relevance. But dairy-region rainfall should not have a direct influence on the demand for butter, so the correlation between dairy-region rainfall and u_i would be zero; that is, dairy-region rainfall satisfies the condition for instrument exogeneity.

Example #2: Estimating the effect on test scores of class size.   Despite controlling for student and district characteristics, the estimates of the effect on test scores of class size reported in Part II still might have omitted variables bias resulting from unmeasured variables such as learning opportunities outside school or the quality of the teachers. If data on these variables are unavailable, this omitted variables bias cannot be addressed by including the variables in the multiple regressions.

Instrumental variables regression provides an alternative approach to this problem. Consider the following hypothetical example: some California schools are forced to close for repairs because of a summer earthquake. Districts close to the epicenter are most severely affected. A district with some closed schools needs to "double up" their students, temporarily increasing class size. This means that distance from the epicenter satisfies the condition for instrument relevance because it is correlated with class size. But if distance to the epicenter is unrelated to any of the other factors affecting student performance (such as whether the students are still learning English), then it will be exogenous because it is uncorrelated with the error term. Thus the instrumental variable, distance to the epicenter, could be used to circumvent omitted variables bias and to estimate the effect of class size on test scores.

The Sampling Distribution of the TSLS Estimator

The exact distribution of the TSLS estimator in small samples is complicated. However, like the OLS estimator, its distribution in large samples is simple: the TSLS estimator is consistent and is normally distributed.

Formula for the TSLS estimator.   Although the two stages of TSLS make the estimator seem complicated, when there is a single X and a single instrument Z, as we assume in this section, there is a simple formula for the TSLS estimator.

Let s_{ZY} be the sample covariance between Z and Y and let s_{ZX} be the sample covariance between Z and X. As shown in Appendix 10.2, the TSLS estimator with a single instrument is

$$\hat{\beta}_1^{TSLS} = \frac{s_{ZY}}{s_{ZX}}. \tag{10.4}$$

That is, the TSLS estimator of β_1 is the ratio of the sample covariance between Z and Y to the sample covariance between Z and X.

Sampling distribution of $\hat{\beta}_1^{TSLS}$ when the sample size is large.

The formula in Equation (10.4) can be used to show that $\hat{\beta}_1^{TSLS}$ is consistent and, in large samples, normally distributed. The argument is summarized here, with mathematical details given in Appendix 10.3.

The argument that $\hat{\beta}_1^{TSLS}$ is consistent combines the assumptions that Z_i is relevant and exogenous with the consistency of sample covariances for population covariances. To begin, note that because $Y_i = \beta_0 + \beta_1 X_i + u_i$ in Equation (10.1),

$$\text{cov}(Z_i, Y_i) = \text{cov}(Z_i, \beta_0 + \beta_1 X_i + u_i) = \beta_1 \text{cov}(Z_i, X_i) + \text{cov}(Z_i, u_i), \tag{10.5}$$

where the second equality follows from the properties of covariances (Equation (2.33)). By the instrument exogeneity assumption, $\text{cov}(Z_i, u_i) = 0$, and by the instrument relevance assumption, $\text{cov}(Z_i, X_i) \neq 0$. Thus, if the instrument is valid,

$$\beta_1 = \frac{\text{cov}(Z_i, Y_i)}{\text{cov}(Z_i, X_i)}. \tag{10.6}$$

That is, the population coefficient β_1 is the ratio of the population covariance between Z and Y to the population covariance between Z and X.

As discussed in Section 3.6, the sample covariance is a consistent estimator of the population covariance, that is, $s_{ZY} \xrightarrow{p} \text{cov}(Z_i, Y_i)$ and $s_{ZX} \xrightarrow{p} \text{cov}(Z_i, X_i)$. It follows from Equations (10.4) and (10.6) that the TSLS estimator is consistent:

$$\hat{\beta}_1^{TSLS} = \frac{s_{ZY}}{s_{ZX}} \xrightarrow{p} \frac{\text{cov}(Z_i, Y_i)}{\text{cov}(Z_i, X_i)} = \beta_1. \tag{10.7}$$

The formula in Equation (10.4) also can be used to show that the sampling distribution of $\hat{\beta}_1^{TSLS}$ is normal in large samples. The reason is the same as for every other least squares estimator we have considered: the TSLS estimator is an average of random variables, and when the sample size is large the central limit theorem tells us that averages of random variables are normally distributed. Specifically, the numerator of the expression for $\hat{\beta}_1^{TSLS}$ in Equation (10.4) is $s_{ZY} = \frac{1}{n-1}\sum_{i=1}^{n}(Z_i - \overline{Z})(Y_i - \overline{Y})$, an average of $(Z_i - \overline{Z})(Y_i - \overline{Y})$. A bit of algebra, sketched out in Appendix 10.3, shows that because of this averaging the central limit theorem implies that, in large samples, $\hat{\beta}_1^{TSLS}$ has a sampling distribution that is approximately $N(\beta_1, \sigma^2_{\hat{\beta}_1^{TSLS}})$, where

$$\sigma^2_{\hat{\beta}_1^{TSLS}} = \frac{1}{n}\frac{\text{var}[(Z_i - \mu_Z)u_i]}{[\text{cov}(Z_i, X_i)]^2}. \tag{10.8}$$

Statistical inference using the large-sample distribution.   The variance $\sigma^2_{\hat{\beta}_1^{TSLS}}$ can be estimated by estimating the variance and covariance terms appearing in Equation (10.8), and the square root of the estimate of $\sigma^2_{\hat{\beta}_1^{TSLS}}$ is the standard error of the IV estimator. This is done automatically in TSLS regression commands in econometric software packages. Because $\hat{\beta}_1^{TSLS}$ is normally distributed in large samples, hypothesis tests about β_1 can be performed by computing the t-statistic, and a 95% large-sample confidence interval is given by $\hat{\beta}_1^{TSLS} \pm 1.96SE(\hat{\beta}_1^{TSLS})$.

Application to the Demand for Cigarettes

The Wrights were interested in the demand elasticity of butter, but today other commodities, such as cigarettes, figure more prominently in public policy debates. One tool in the quest for reducing illnesses and deaths from smoking—and the costs, or externalities, imposed by those illnesses on the rest of society—is to tax cigarettes so heavily that current smokers cut back and potential new smokers are discouraged from taking up the habit. But precisely how big a tax hike is needed to make a dent in cigarette consumption? For example, what would the after-tax sales price of cigarettes need to be to achieve a 20% reduction in cigarette consumption?

The answer to this question depends on the elasticity of demand for cigarettes. If the elasticity is −1, then the 20% target in consumption can be achieved by a 20% increase in price. If the elasticity is −0.5, then the price must rise 40% to decrease consumption by 20%. Of course, we do not know what the demand elasticity of cigarettes is in the abstract: we must estimate it from data on prices and sales. But, as with butter, because of the interactions between supply and demand, the elasticity of demand for cigarettes cannot be estimated consistently by an OLS regression of log quantity on log price.

We therefore use TSLS to estimate the elasticity of demand for cigarettes using annual data for the 48 continental U.S. states for 1985–1995 (the data are described in Appendix 10.1). For now, all the results are for the cross section of states in 1995; results using data for earlier years (panel data) are presented in Section 10.4.

The instrumental variable, $SalesTax_i$, is the portion of the tax on cigarettes arising from the general sales tax, measured in dollars per pack (in real dollars, deflated by the Consumer Price Index). Cigarette consumption ($Q_i^{cigarettes}$) is the number of packs of cigarettes sold per capita in the state, and the price, $P_i^{cigarettes}$, is the average real price per pack of cigarettes including all taxes.

Before using TSLS it is essential to ask whether the two conditions for instrument validity hold. We return to this topic in detail in Section 10.3, where we provide some statistical tools that help in this assessment. Even with those statistical tools, judgment plays an important role, so it is useful to think about whether the sales tax on cigarettes plausibly satisfies the two conditions.

First consider instrument relevance. Because a high sales tax increases the total sales price $P_i^{cigarettes}$, the sales tax per pack plausibly satisfies the condition for instrument relevance.

Next consider instrument exogeneity. For the sales tax to be exogenous, it must be uncorrelated with the error in the demand equation; that is, the sales tax must affect the demand for cigarettes only indirectly through the price. This seems plausible: general sales tax rates vary from state to state, but they do so mainly because different states choose different mixes of sales, income, property, and other taxes to finance public undertakings. Those choices about public finance are driven by political considerations, not by factors related to the demand for cigarettes. We discuss the credibility of this assumption more in Section 10.4, but for now we keep it as a working hypothesis.

In modern statistical software, the first stage of TSLS is estimated automatically so you do not need to run this regression yourself to compute the TSLS estimator. Just this once, however, we present the first-stage regression explicitly; using data for the 48 states in 1995, this is

$$\widehat{\ln(P_i^{cigarettes})} = 4.63 + 0.031 \ SalesTax_i. \tag{10.9}$$
$$(0.03) \quad (0.005)$$

The R^2 of this regression is 47%, so the variation in sales tax on cigarettes explains 47% of the variance of cigarette prices across states.

In the second stage of TSLS, $\ln(Q_i^{cigarettes})$ is regressed on $\widehat{\ln(P_i^{cigarettes})}$ using OLS. The resulting estimated regression function is

$$\widehat{\ln(Q_i^{cigarettes})} = 9.72 - 1.08 \ \widehat{\ln(P_i^{cigarettes})}. \tag{10.10}$$

This estimated regression function is written using the regressor in the second stage, the predicted value $\widehat{\ln(P_i^{cigarettes})}$. It is, however, conventional and less cumbersome simply to report the estimated regression function with $\ln(P_i^{cigarettes})$ rather than $\widehat{\ln(P_i^{cigarettes})}$. Reported in this notation, the TSLS estimates and heteroskedasticity-robust standard errors are

$$\widehat{\ln(Q_i^{cigarettes})} = 9.72 - 1.08\ln(P_i^{cigarettes}). \tag{10.11}$$
$$(1.53) \quad (0.32)$$

The TSLS estimate suggests that the demand for cigarettes is surprisingly elastic, in light of their addictive nature: an increase in the price of 1% reduces consumption by 1.08%. But, recalling our discussion of instrument exogeneity, perhaps this estimate should not yet be taken too seriously. Even though the elasticity was estimated using an instrumental variable, there might still be omitted variables that are correlated with the sales tax per pack. A leading candidate is income: states with higher incomes might depend relatively less on a sales tax and more on an income tax to finance state government. Moreover, the demand for cigarettes presumably depends on income. Thus we would like to reestimate our demand equation including income as an additional regressor. To do so, however, we must first extend the IV regression model to include additional regressors.

10.2 The General IV Regression Model

The general IV regression model has four types of variables: the dependent variable, Y; problematic endogenous regressors, like the price of cigarettes, which are potentially correlated with the error term and which we will label X; additional regressors that are not correlated with the error term, called **included exogenous variables**, which we will label W; and instrumental variables, Z. In general, there can be multiple endogenous regressors (X's), multiple included exogenous regressors (W's), and multiple instrumental variables (Z's).

For IV regression to be possible, there must be at least as many instrumental variables (Z's) as endogenous regressors (X's). In Section 10.1, there was a single endogenous regressor and a single instrument. Having (at least) one instrument for this single endogenous regressor was essential. Without the instrument we could not have computed the instrumental variables estimator: there would be no first-stage regression in TSLS.

The General Instrumental Variables Regression Model and Terminology

Key Concept 10.1

The general IV regression model is

$$Y_i = \beta_0 + \beta_1 X_{1i} + \cdots + \beta_k X_{ki} + \beta_{k+1} W_{1i} + \cdots + \beta_{k+r} W_{ri} + u_i, \qquad (10.12)$$

$i = 1, \ldots, n$, where:

- Y_i is the dependent variable;
- u_i is the error term, which represents measurement error and/or omitted factors;
- $X_{1i}, \ldots, X_{ki}$ are k endogenous regressors, which are potentially correlated with u_i;
- $W_{1i}, \ldots, W_{ri}$ are r included exogenous regressors, which are uncorrelated with u_i;
- $\beta_0, \beta_1, \ldots, \beta_{k+r}$ are unknown regression coefficients;
- $Z_{1i}, \ldots, Z_{mi}$ are m instrumental variables.

The coefficients are overidentified if there are more instruments than endogenous regressors ($m > k$); they are underidentified if $m < k$; and they are exactly identified if $m = k$. Estimation of the IV regression model requires exact identification or overidentification.

The relationship between the number of instruments and the number of endogenous regressors is sufficiently important to have its own terminology. The regression coefficients are said to be **exactly identified** if the number of instruments (m) equals the number of endogenous regressors (k), that is, $m = k$. The coefficients are **overidentified** if the number of instruments exceeds the number of endogenous regressors, that is, $m > k$; and they are **underidentified** if the number of instruments is less than the number of endogenous regressors, that is,

$m < k$. The coefficients must be either exactly identified or overidentified if they are to be estimated by IV regression.

The general IV regression model and its terminology is summarized in Key Concept 10.1.

TSLS in the General IV Model

TSLS with a single endogenous regressor. When there is a single endogenous regressor X and some additional included exogenous variables, the equation of interest is

$$Y_i = \beta_0 + \beta_1 X_i + \beta_2 W_{1i} + \cdots + \beta_{1+r} W_{ri} + u_i, \qquad (10.13)$$

where, as before, X_i might be correlated with the error term, but $W_{1i}, \ldots, W_{ri}$ are not.

The population first-stage regression of TSLS relates X to the exogenous variables, that is, the W's and the instruments Z:

$$X_i = \pi_0 + \pi_1 Z_{1i} + \cdots + \pi_m Z_{mi} + \pi_{m+1} W_{1i} + \cdots + \pi_{m+r} W_{ri} + v_i, \quad (10.14)$$

where $\pi_0, \pi_1, \ldots, \pi_{m+r}$ are unknown regression coefficients and v_i is an error term.

Equation (10.14) is sometimes called the **reduced form** equation for X. It relates the endogenous variable X to all the available exogenous variables, both those included in the regression of interest (W) and the instruments (Z).

In the first stage of TSLS, the unknown coefficients in Equation (10.14) are estimated by OLS, and the predicted values from this regression are $\hat{X}_1, \ldots, \hat{X}_n$.

In the second stage of TSLS, Equation (10.13) is estimated by OLS, except that X_i is replaced by its predicted values from the first stage. That is, Y_i is regressed on $\hat{X}_i$, $W_{1i}, \ldots, W_{ri}$ using OLS. The resulting estimator of $\beta_0, \beta_1, \ldots, \beta_{1+r}$ is the TSLS estimator.

Extension to multiple endogenous regressors. When there are multiple endogenous regressors $X_{1i}, \ldots, X_{ki}$, the TSLS algorithm is similar, except that each endogenous regressor requires its own first-stage regression. Each of these first-stage regressions has the same form as Equation (10.14), that is, the dependent variable is one of the X's and the regressors are all the instruments (Z's) and all the included exogenous variables (W's). Together, these first-stage regressions produce predicted values of each of the endogenous regressors.

Two Stage Least Squares

Key Concept 10.2

The TSLS estimator in the general IV regression model in Equation (10.12) with multiple instrumental variables is computed in two stages:

1. **First-stage regression(s):** Regress X_{1i} on the instrumental variables $(Z_{1i}, \ldots, Z_{mi})$ and the included exogenous variables $(W_{1i}, \ldots, W_{ri})$ using OLS. Compute the predicted values from this regression; call these $\hat{X}_{1i}$. Repeat this for all the endogenous regressors $X_{2i}, \ldots, X_{ki}$, thereby computing the predicted values $\hat{X}_{1i}, \ldots, \hat{X}_{ki}$.

2. **Second-stage regression:** Regress Y_i on the predicted values of the endogenous variables $(\hat{X}_{1i}, \ldots, \hat{X}_{ki})$ and the included exogenous variables $(W_{1i}, \ldots, W_{ri})$ using OLS. The TSLS estimators $\hat{\beta}_0^{TSLS}, \ldots, \hat{\beta}_{k+r}^{TSLS}$ are the estimators from the second-stage regression.

In practice, the two stages are done automatically within TSLS estimation commands in modern econometric software.

In the second stage of TSLS, Equation (10.12) is estimated by OLS, except that the endogenous regressors (X's) are replaced by their respective predicted values ($\hat{X}$'s). The resulting estimator of $\beta_0, \beta_1, \ldots, \beta_{k+r}$ is the TSLS estimator.

In practice, the two stages of TSLS are done automatically within TSLS estimation commands in modern econometric software. The general TSLS estimator is summarized in Key Concept 10.2.

Instrument Relevance and Exogeneity in the General IV Model

The conditions of instrument relevance and exogeneity need to be modified for the general IV regression model.

When there is one included endogenous variable but multiple instruments, the condition for instrument relevance is that at least one Z is useful for predicting X, given W. When there are multiple included endogenous variables, this condition is more complicated because we must rule out perfect multicollinearity in the population regression. Intuitively, when there are multiple included endogenous variables, the instruments must provide enough information about the exogenous movements in these variables to sort out their separate effects on Y.

The Two Conditions for Valid Instruments

A set of m instruments $Z_{1i}, \ldots, Z_{mi}$ must satisfy the following two conditions to be valid:

1. Instrument Relevance

- *In general*, let $\hat{X}_{1i}^*$ be the predicted value of X_{1i} from the population regression of X_{1i} on the instruments (Z's) and the included exogenous regressors (W's), and let "1" denote a regressor that takes on the value "1" for all observations (its coefficient is the intercept). Then $(\hat{X}_{1i}^*, \ldots, \hat{X}_{ki}^*, W_{1i}, \ldots, W_{ri}, 1)$ are not perfectly multicollinear.

- *If there is only one* X, then at least one Z must enter the population regression of X on the Z's and the W's.

2. Instrument Exogeneity

The instruments are uncorrelated with the error term, that is,
$$\text{corr}(Z_{1i}, u_i) = 0, \ldots, \text{corr}(Z_{mi}, u_i) = 0.$$

The general statement of the instrument exogeneity condition is that each instrument must be uncorrelated with the error term u_i. The general conditions for valid instruments are given in Key Concept 10.3.

The IV Regression Assumptions and Sampling Distribution of the TSLS Estimator

Under the IV regression assumptions, the TSLS estimator is consistent and has a sampling distribution that, in large samples, is approximately normal.

The IV regression assumptions.   The IV regression assumptions are modifications of the least squares assumptions for the multiple regression model in Key Concept 5.4.

The first IV regression assumption modifies the conditional mean assumption in Key Concept 5.4 to apply to the included exogenous variables only. Just like the second least squares assumption for the multiple regression model, the second IV regression assumption is that the draws are i.i.d., as they are if the data are collected by simple random sampling. Similarly, the third IV assumption is that all

The IV Regression Assumptions

Key Concept 10.4

The variables and errors in the IV regression model in Key Concept 10.1 satisfy

1. $E(u_i | W_{1i}, \ldots, W_{ri}) = 0$;

2. $(X_{1i}, \ldots, X_{ki}, W_{1i}, \ldots, W_{ri}, Z_{1i}, \ldots, Z_{mi}, Y_i)$ are i.i.d. draws from their joint distribution;

3. The X's, W's, Z's, and u all have nonzero, finite fourth moments;

4. The W's are not perfectly multicollinear; and

5. The two conditions for a valid instrument in Key Concept 10.3 hold.

the variables have four moments, and the fourth IV regression assumption is that the included exogenous regressors are not perfectly multicollinear.

The fifth IV regression assumption is that the two conditions for instrument validity in Key Concept 10.3 hold. The IV regression assumptions are summarized in Key Concept 10.4.

Sampling distribution of the TSLS estimator. Under the IV regression assumptions, the TSLS estimator is consistent and normally distributed in large samples. This is shown in Section 10.1 (and Appendix 10.3) for the special case of a single endogenous regressor, a single instrument, and no included exogenous variables. Conceptually, the reasoning in Section 10.1 carries over to the general case of multiple instruments and multiple included endogenous variables. The expressions in the general case are complicated, however, and the reader is referred to Greene (2000, Chapter 9) for the details.

Inference Using the TSLS Estimator

Because the sampling distribution of the TSLS estimator is normal in large samples, the general procedures for statistical inference (hypothesis tests and confidence intervals) in regression models extend to TSLS regression. For example, 95% confidence intervals are constructed as the TSLS estimator ± 1.96 standard errors. Similarly, joint hypotheses about the population values of the coefficients can be tested using the F-statistic, as described in Section 5.7.

Calculation of TSLS standard errors. There are two points to bear in mind about TSLS standard errors. First, the standard errors reported by OLS estimation of the second-stage regression are incorrect because they do not recognize that it is the second stage of a two-stage process. Specifically, the second-stage OLS standard errors fail to adjust for the fact that the second-stage regression uses the predicted values of the included endogenous variables. Formulas for standard errors that make the necessary adjustment are incorporated into (and automatically used by) TSLS regression commands in econometric software. Therefore this issue is not a concern in practice if you use a specialized TSLS regression command.

Second, as always the error u might be heteroskedastic. It is therefore important to use heteroskedasticity-robust versions of the standard errors, for precisely the same reason as it is important to use heteroskedasticity-robust standard errors for the OLS estimators of the multiple regression model.

Application to the Demand for Cigarettes

In Section 10.1, we estimated the elasticity of demand for cigarettes using data on annual consumption in 48 U.S. states in 1995 using TSLS with a single regressor (the logarithm of the real price per pack) and a single instrument (the real sales tax per pack). Income also affects demand, however, so it is part of the error term of the population regression. As discussed in Section 10.1, if the state sales tax is related to state income, then it is correlated with a variable in the error term of the cigarette demand equation, which violates the instrument exogeneity condition. If so, the IV estimator in Section 10.1 is inconsistent. That is, the IV regression suffers from a version of omitted variable bias. To solve this problem, we need to include income in the regression.

We therefore consider an alternative specification in which the logarithm of income is included in the demand equation. In the terminology of Key Concept 10.1, the dependent variable Y is the logarithm of consumption, $\ln(Q_i^{cigarettes})$; the endogenous regressor X is the logarithm of the real price, $\ln(P_i^{cigarettes})$; the included exogenous variable W is the logarithm of real per capita state income, $\ln(Inc_i)$; and the instrument Z is the real sales tax per pack, $SalesTax_i$. The TSLS estimates and (heteroskedasticity-robust) standard errors are

$$\widehat{\ln(Q_i^{cigarettes})} = 9.43 - 1.14\ln(P_i^{cigarettes}) + 0.21\ln(Inc_i). \qquad (10.15)$$
$$(1.26) \quad (0.37) \qquad\qquad (0.31)$$

This regression uses a single instrument, $SalesTax_i$, but in fact another candidate instrument is available. In addition to general sales taxes, states levy special taxes that apply only to cigarettes and other tobacco products. These cigarette-specific taxes ($CigTax_i$) constitute a possible second instrumental variable. The cigarette-specific tax increases the price of cigarettes paid by the consumer, so it arguably meets the condition for instrument relevance. If it is uncorrelated with the error term in the state cigarette demand equation, it is an exogenous instrument.

With this additional instrument in hand, we now have two instrumental variables, the real sales tax per pack and the real state cigarette-specific tax per pack. With two instruments and a single endogenous regressor, the demand elasticity is overidentified, that is, the number of instruments ($SalesTax_i$ and $CigTax_i$, so $m = 2$) exceeds the number of included endogenous variables ($P_i^{cigarettes}$, so $k = 1$). We can estimate the demand elasticity using TSLS, where the regressors in the first-stage regression are the included exogenous variable, $\ln(Inc_i)$, and both instruments.

The resulting TSLS estimate of the regression function using the two instruments $SalesTax_i$ and $CigTax_i$ is

$$\widehat{\ln(Q_i^{cigarettes})} = 9.89 - 1.28\ln(P_i^{cigarettes}) + 0.28\ln(Inc_i). \qquad (10.16)$$
$$\quad (0.96)\ (0.25) \qquad\qquad\qquad (0.25)$$

Compare Equations (10.15) and (10.16): the standard error of the estimated price elasticity is smaller by one-third in Equation (10.16) (0.25 in Equation (10.16) versus 0.37 in Equation (10.15)). The reason the standard error is smaller in Equation (10.16) is that this estimate uses more information than Equation (10.15): in Equation (10.15), only one instrument is used (the sales tax), but in Equation (10.16), two instruments are used (the sales tax and the cigarette-specific tax). Using two instruments explains more of the variation in cigarette prices than using just one, and this is reflected in smaller standard errors on the estimated demand elasticity.

Are these estimates credible? Ultimately, credibility depends on whether the set of instrumental variables—here, the two taxes—plausibly satisfies the two conditions for valid instruments. It is therefore vital that we assess whether these instruments are valid, and it is to this topic that we now turn.

10.3 Checking Instrument Validity

Whether instrumental variables regression is useful in a given application hinges on whether the instruments are valid: invalid instruments produce meaningless results. It therefore is essential to assess whether a given set of instruments is valid in a particular application.

Assumption #1: Instrument Relevance

The role of the instrument relevance condition in IV regression is subtle. One way to think of instrument relevance is that it plays a role akin to the sample size: the more relevant the instruments—that is, the more the variation in X is explained by the instruments—the more information is available for use in IV regression. A more relevant instrument produces a more accurate estimator, just as a larger sample size produces a more accurate estimator. Moreover, statistical inference using TSLS is predicated on the TSLS estimator having a normal sampling distribution, but according to the central limit theorem the normal distribution is a good approximation in large—but not necessarily small—samples. If having a more relevant instrument is like having a larger sample size, this suggests that for the normal distribution to provide a good approximation to the sampling distribution of the TSLS estimator, the instruments should not just be relevant, but be highly relevant.

Instruments that explain little of the variation in X are called **weak instruments**. In the cigarette example, the distance of the state from cigarette manufacturing plants arguably would be a weak instrument: although a greater distance increases shipping costs (thus shifting the supply curve in and raising the equilibrium price), cigarettes are lightweight, so shipping costs are a small component of the price of cigarettes. Thus the amount of price variation explained by shipping costs, and thus distance to manufacturing plants, probably is quite small.

This section discusses why weak instruments are a problem, how to check for weak instruments, and what to do if you have weak instruments. It is assumed throughout that the instruments are exogenous.

Why weak instruments are a problem. If the instruments are weak, then the normal distribution provides a poor approximation to the sampling distribution of the TSLS estimator, even if the sample size is large. Thus there is no theoretical justification for the usual methods for performing statistical inference, even in large samples. In fact, if instruments are weak, then the TSLS estimator can be badly biased, and 95% confidence intervals constructed as the TSLS estimator ± 1.96 standard errors can contain the true value of the coefficient far less than 95% of the time. In short, if instruments are weak, TSLS is no longer reliable.

To see that there is a problem with the large-sample normal approximation to the sampling distribution of the TSLS estimator, consider the special case, considered in Section 10.1, of a single included endogenous variable, a single instrument, and no included exogenous regressor. If the instrument is valid, then $\hat{\beta}_1^{TSLS}$

A Rule of Thumb for Checking for Weak Instruments

Key Concept 10.5

The first-stage F-statistic is the F-statistic testing the hypothesis that the coefficients on the instruments $Z_{1i}, \ldots, Z_{mi}$ equal zero in the first stage of two stage least squares. When there is a single endogenous regressor, a first-stage F less than 10 indicates that the instruments are weak, in which case the TSLS estimator is biased (even in large samples), and TSLS t-statistics and confidence intervals are unreliable.

is consistent because the sample covariances s_{ZY} and s_{ZX} are consistent; that is, $\hat{\beta}_1^{TSLS} = s_{ZY}/s_{ZX} \xrightarrow{p} \text{cov}(Z_i, Y_i)/\text{cov}(Z_i, X_i) = \beta_1$ (Equation (10.7)). But now suppose that the instrument is not just weak but irrelevant, so that $\text{cov}(Z_i, X_i) = 0$. Then $s_{ZX} \xrightarrow{p} \text{cov}(Z_i, X_i) = 0$, so, taken literally, the denominator on the right-hand side of the limit $\text{cov}(Z_i, Y_i)/\text{cov}(Z_i, X_i)$ is zero! Clearly, the argument that $\hat{\beta}_1^{TSLS}$ is consistent breaks down when the instrument relevance condition fails. As shown in Appendix 10.4, this breakdown results in the TSLS estimator having a nonnormal sampling distribution, even if the sample size is very large. In fact, when the instrument is irrelevant, the large-sample distribution of $\hat{\beta}_1^{TSLS}$ is not that of a normal random variable, rather, it is the distribution of a *ratio* of two normal random variables!

While this circumstance of totally irrelevant instruments might not be encountered in practice, it raises a question: How relevant must the instruments be for the normal distribution to provide a good approximation in practice? The answer to this question in the general IV model is complicated. Fortunately, however, there is a simple rule of thumb available for the most common situation in practice, the case of a single endogenous regressor.

Checking for weak instruments when there is a single endogenous regressor. One way to check for weak instruments when there is a single endogenous regressor is to compute the F-statistic testing the hypothesis that the coefficients on the instruments are all zero in the first-stage regression of TSLS. This **first-stage F-statistic** provides a measure of the information content contained in the instruments: the more information content, the larger is the expected value of the F-statistic. One simple rule of thumb is that you do not need to worry about weak instruments if the first-stage F-statistic exceeds 10. (Why 10? See Appendix 10.4.) This is summarized in Key Concept 10.5.

A Scary Regression

One way to estimate the percentage increase in earnings from going to school for another year (the "return to education") is to regress the logarithm of earnings against years of school using data on individuals. But if more able individuals are both more successful in the labor market and attend school longer (perhaps because they find it easier), then years of schooling will be correlated with the omitted variable, innate ability, and the OLS estimator of the return to education will be biased. Because innate ability is extremely difficult to measure and thus cannot be used as a regressor, some labor economists have turned to IV regression to estimate the return to education. But what variable is correlated with years of education but not the error term in the earnings regression—that is, what is a valid instrumental variable?

Your birthday, suggested labor economists Joshua Angrist and Alan Krueger. Because of mandatory schooling laws, they reasoned, your birthday is correlated with your years of education: if the law requires you to attend school until your 16th birthday and you turn 16 in January while you are in tenth grade, you might drop out—but if you turn 16 in July you already will have completed tenth grade. If so, your birthday satisfies the instrument relevance condition. But being born in January or July should have no *direct* effect on your earnings (other than through years of education), so your birthday satisfies the instrument exogeneity condition. They implemented this idea by using the individual's quarter (three-month period) of birth as an instrumental variable. They used a very large sample of data from the U.S. Census (their regressions had at least 329,000 observations!), and they controlled for other variables such as the worker's age.

But John Bound, another labor economist, was skeptical. He knew that weak instruments cause TSLS to be unreliable and worried that, despite the extremely large sample size, the quarter of birth might be a weak instrument in some of their specifications. So when Bound and Krueger next met over lunch, the conversation inevitably turned to whether the Angrist-Krueger instruments were weak. Krueger thought not, and suggested a creative way to find out: why not rerun the regressions using a truly irrelevant instrument—replace each individual's real quarter of birth by a fake quarter of birth, randomly generated by the computer—and compare the results using the real and fake instruments? What they found was amazing: it didn't matter whether you used the real quarter of birth or the fake one as the instrument—TSLS gave basically the same answer!

This was a scary regression for labor econometricians. The TSLS standard error computed using the real data suggests that the return to education is precisely estimated—but so does the standard error computed using the fake data. Of course, the fake data *cannot* estimate the return to education precisely, because the fake instrument is totally irrelevant. The worry, then, is that the TSLS estimates based on the real data are just as unreliable as those based on the fake data.

The problem is that the instruments are in fact very weak in some of Angrist and Krueger's regressions. In some of their specifications, the first-stage F-statistic is less than two, far less than the rule-of-thumb cutoff of 10. In other specifications, Angrist and Krueger have larger first-stage F-statistics, and in those cases the TSLS inferences are not subject to the problem of weak instruments. By the way, in those specifications the return to education is estimated to be approximately 8%, somewhat *greater* than estimated by OLS.[1]

---

[1]The original IV regressions are reported in Angrist and Krueger (1991), and the re-analysis using the fake instruments is published in Bound, Jaeger, and Baker (1995).

What do I do if I have weak instruments? It depends. If you have many instruments, then some of those instruments are probably weaker than others. If you have a small number of strong instruments and many weak ones, you will be better off to discard the weakest instruments and use the most relevant subset for your TSLS analysis. Your TSLS standard errors might increase when you drop weak instruments, but keep in mind that your original standard errors were not meaningful anyway!

If, however, you have only a few instruments or if the coefficients are exactly identified, then discarding weak instruments will not help. In this case, there are two recourses: find additional, stronger instruments, or use some advanced tools designed specifically for use with weak instruments. The first requires an intimate knowledge of the problem at hand and can entail redesigning the data set and the nature of the empirical study. The second requires procedures that are less sensitive to weak instruments than TSLS. One estimator that is less sensitive to weak instruments than TSLS is limited information maximum likelihood (LIML); see Hayashi (2000, Section 8.6) or Greene (2000, Chapter 16). The development of procedures that are reliable when instruments are weak is currently an area of active research.

Assumption #2: Instrument Exogeneity

If the instruments are not exogenous, then TSLS is inconsistent: the TSLS estimator converges in probability to something other than the population coefficient in the regression. After all, the idea of instrumental variables regression is that the instrument contains information about variation in X_i that is unrelated to the error term u_i. If, in fact, the instrument is not exogenous, then it cannot pinpoint this exogenous variation in X_i, and it stands to reason that IV regression fails to provide a consistent estimator. The math behind this argument is summarized in Appendix 10.4.

Can you test statistically the assumption that the instruments are exogenous? No. More precisely, suppose that you have as many instruments as endogenous regressors (the coefficients are exactly identified). Then it is impossible to develop a statistical test of the hypothesis that the instruments are in fact exogenous. That is, empirical evidence cannot be brought to bear on the question of whether these instruments satisfy the exogeneity restriction. In this case, the only way to assess whether the instruments are exogenous is to draw on expert opinion and your personal knowledge of the empirical problem at hand. For example, the Wrights' knowledge of agricultural supply and demand led them to suggest that below average rainfall would plausibly shift the supply curve for butter but would not directly shift the demand curve.

Assessing whether the instruments are exogenous *necessarily* requires making an expert judgment based on personal knowledge of the application. If, however, there are more instruments than endogenous regressors, then there is a statistical tool that can be helpful in this process, the so-called test of overidentifying restrictions.

The overidentifying restrictions test.   Suppose you have a single endogenous regressor, two instruments, and no included exogenous variables. Then you could compute two different TSLS estimators, one using the first instrument, the other using the second. These two estimators will not be the same because of sampling variation, but if both instruments are exogenous then they will tend to be close to each other. But what if these two instruments produce very different estimates? Then you might sensibly conclude that there is something wrong with one or the other of the instruments—or both. That is, it would be reasonable to conclude that one or the other, or both, of the instruments is not exogenous.

The **test of overidentifying restrictions** implicitly makes this comparison. We say implicitly, because the test is carried out without actually computing all of the different possible IV estimates. Here is the idea. Exogeneity of the instruments means that they are uncorrelated with u_i. This suggests that the instruments should be approximately uncorrelated with $\hat{u}_i^{TSLS}$, where $\hat{u}_i^{TSLS} = Y_i - (\hat{\beta}_0^{TSLS} + \hat{\beta}_1^{TSLS}X_{1i} + \cdots + \hat{\beta}_{k+r}^{TSLS}W_{ri})$ is the residual from the estimated TSLS regression using all the instruments (approximately rather than exactly because of sampling variation). (Note that these residuals are constructed using the true X's rather than their first-stage predicted values.) Accordingly, if the instruments are in fact exogenous, then the coefficients on the instruments in a regression of $\hat{u}_i^{TSLS}$ on the instruments and the included exogenous variables should all be zero, and this hypothesis can be tested.

This method for computing the overidentifying restriction test is summarized in Key Concept 10.6. This statistic is computed using the homoskedasticity-only F-statistic. The test statistic is commonly called the J-statistic.

In large samples, if the instruments are not weak and the errors are homoskedastic, then, under the null hypothesis that the instruments are exogenous, the J-statistic has a chi-squared distribution with $m - k$ degrees of freedom (χ_{m-k}^2). It is important to remember that even though the number of restrictions being tested is m, the degrees of freedom of the asymptotic distribution of the J-statistic is $m - k$. The reason is that it is only possible to test the *over*identifying restrictions, of which there are $m - k$.

The Overidentifying Restrictions Test (the *J*-Statistic)

Key Concept 10.6

Let $\hat{u}_i^{TSLS}$ be the residuals from TSLS estimation of Equation (10.12). Use OLS to estimate the regression coefficients in

$$\hat{u}_i^{TSLS} = \delta_0 + \delta_1 Z_{1i} + \cdots + \delta_m Z_{mi} + \delta_{m+1} W_{1i} + \cdots + \delta_{m+r} W_{ri} + e_i, \tag{10.17}$$

where e_i is the regression error term. Let F denote the homoskedasticity-only F-statistic testing the hypothesis that $\delta_1 = \cdots = \delta_m = 0$. The overidentifying restrictions test statistic is $J = mF$. Under the null hypothesis that all the instruments are exogenous, then in large samples J is distributed χ^2_{m-k}, where $m - k$ is the "degree of overidentification," that is, the number of instruments minus the number of endogenous regressors.

The easiest way to see that you cannot test the exogeneity of the regressors when the coefficients are exactly identified ($m = k$) is to consider the case of a single included endogenous variable ($k = 1$). If there are two instruments, then you can compute two TSLS estimators, one for each instrument, and you can compare them to see if they are close. But if you have only one instrument, then you can compute only one TSLS estimator and you have nothing to compare it to. In fact, if the coefficients are exactly identified, so that $m = k$, then the overidentifying test statistic J is exactly zero.

10.4 Application to the Demand for Cigarettes[2]

Our attempt to estimate the elasticity of demand for cigarettes left off with the TSLS estimates summarized in Equation (10.16), in which income was an included exogenous variable and there were two instruments, the general sales tax and the cigarette-specific tax. We can now undertake a more careful evaluation of these instruments.

---

[2]This section assumes knowledge of the material in Sections 8.1 and 8.2 on panel data with $T = 2$ time periods.

The Externalities of Smoking

Smoking imposes costs that are not fully borne by the smoker, that is, it generates externalities. One economic justification for taxing cigarettes therefore is to "internalize" these externalities. In theory, the tax on a pack of cigarettes should equal the dollar value of the externalities created by smoking that pack. But what, precisely, are the externalities of smoking, measured in dollars per pack?

Several studies have used econometric methods to estimate the externalities of smoking. The negative externalities—costs—borne by others include medical costs paid by the government to care for ill smokers, health care costs of nonsmokers associated with secondhand smoke, and fires caused by cigarettes.

But, from a purely economic point of view, smoking also has *positive* externalities, or benefits. The biggest benefit of smoking is that smokers tend to pay much more in Social Security (public pension) taxes than they ever get back. There are also large savings in nursing home expenditures on the very old—smokers tend not to live that long. Because the negative externalities of smoking occur while the smoker is alive but the positive ones accrue

after death, the net present value of the per-pack externalities (the value of the net costs per pack, discounted to the present) depend on the discount rate.

The studies do not agree on a specific dollar value of the net externalities. Some suggest the net externalities, properly discounted, are quite small, less than current taxes. In fact, the most extreme estimates suggest that the net externalities are *positive*, so smoking should be subsidized! Other studies, which incorporate costs that are probably important but difficult to quantify (such as caring for babies who are unhealthy because their mothers smoke) suggest that externalities might be $1 per pack, possibly even more. But all the studies agree that, by tending to die in late middle age, smokers pay far more in taxes than they ever get back in their brief retirement.[3]

_____

[3]An early calculation of the externalities of smoking was reported by Willard G. Manning et al. (1989). A calculation suggesting that health care costs would go *up* if everyone stopped smoking is presented in Barendregt et al. (1997). Other studies of the externalities of smoking are reviewed by Chaloupka and Warner (2000).

As in Section 10.1, it makes sense that the two instruments are relevant because taxes are a big part of the price of cigarettes, and shortly we will look at this empirically. First, however, we focus on the difficult question of whether the two tax variables are plausibly exogenous.

The first step in assessing whether an instrument is exogenous is to think through the arguments for why it may or may not be. This requires thinking about what factors account for the error term in the cigarette demand equation and whether these factors are plausibly related to the instruments.

Why do some states have higher per capita cigarette consumption than others? One reason might be variation in incomes across states, but state income is included in Equation (10.16), so this is not part of the error term. Another reason is that there are historical factors influencing demand. For example, states that grow tobacco have higher rates of smoking than most other states. Could this factor be related to taxes? Quite possibly: if tobacco farming and cigarette production are important industries in a state, then these industries could exert influence to keep cigarette-specific taxes low. This suggests that an omitted factor in cigarette demand—whether the state grows tobacco and produces cigarettes—could be correlated with cigarette-specific taxes.

One solution to this possible correlation between the error term and the instrument would be to include information on the size of the tobacco and cigarette industry in the state; this is the approach we took when we included income as a regressor in the demand equation. But because we have panel data on cigarette consumption, a different approach is available that does not require this information. As discussed in Chapter 8, panel data makes it possible to eliminate the influence of variables that vary across entities (states) but do not change over time, such as the climate and historical circumstances that lead to a large tobacco and cigarette industry in a state. Two methods for doing this were given in Chapter 8: constructing data on *changes* in the variables between two different time periods, and using fixed effects regression. To keep the analysis here as simple as possible, we adopt the former approach and perform regressions of the type described in Section 8.2, based on the changes in the variables between two different years.

The time span between the two different years influences how the estimated elasticities are to be interpreted. Because cigarettes are addictive, changes in price will take some time to alter behavior. At first, an increase in the price of cigarettes might have little effect on demand. Over time, however, the price increase might contribute to some smokers' desire to quit and, importantly, it could discourage nonsmokers from taking up the habit. Thus the response of demand to a price increase could be small in the short run but large in the long run. Said differently, for an addictive product like cigarettes, demand might be inelastic in the short run, that is, it might have a short-run elasticity near zero, but it might be more elastic in the long run.

In this analysis, we focus on estimating the long-run price elasticity. We do this by considering quantity and price changes that occur over ten-year periods. Specifically, in the regressions considered here, the ten-year change in log quantity, $\ln(Q^{cigarettes}_{i,1995}) - \ln(Q^{cigarettes}_{i,1985})$, is regressed against the ten-year change in log price, $\ln(P^{cigarettes}_{i,1995}) - \ln(P^{cigarettes}_{i,1985})$, and the ten-year change in log income, $\ln(Inc_{i,1995}) - \ln(Inc_{i,1985})$. Two instruments are used: the change in the sales tax over ten years, $SalesTax_{i,1995} - SalesTax_{i,1985}$, and the change in the cigarette-specific tax over ten years, $CigTax_{i,1995} - CigTax_{i,1985}$.

TABLE 10.1 Two Stage Least Squares Estimates of the Demand for Cigarettes Using Panel Data for 48 U.S. States

Dependent variable: $\ln(Q_{i,1995}^{cigarettes}) - \ln(Q_{i,1985}^{cigarettes})$

Regressor	(1)	(2)	(3)
$\ln(P_{i,1995}^{cigarettes}) - \ln(P_{i,1985}^{cigarettes})$	−0.94**	−1.34**	−1.20**
	(0.21)	(0.23)	(0.20)
$\ln(Inc_{i,1995}) - \ln(Inc_{i,1985})$	0.53	0.43	0.46
	(0.34)	(0.30)	(0.31)
Intercept	0.21	0.45**	0.37**
	(0.13)	(0.14)	(0.12)
Instrumental variable(s)	Sales tax	Cigarette-specific tax	Both sales tax and cigarette-specific tax
First-stage F-statistic	33.70	107.20	88.60
Overidentifying restrictions J-test and p-value	–	–	4.93 (0.026)

These regressions were estimated using data for 48 U.S. states (48 observations on the ten-year differences). The data are described in Appendix 10.1. The J-test of overidentifying restrictions is described in Key Concept 10.6 (its p-value is given in parentheses), and the first-stage F-statistic is described in Key Concept 10.5. Individual coefficients are statistically significant at the *5% level or **1% significance level.

The results are presented in Table 10.1. As usual, each column in the table presents the results of a different regression. All regressions have the same regressors, and all coefficients are estimated using TSLS; the only difference between the three regressions is the set of instruments used. In column (1), the only instrument is the sales tax; in column (2), the only instrument is the cigarette-specific tax; and in column (3), both taxes are used as instruments.

In IV regression, the reliability of the coefficient estimates hinge on the validity of the instruments, so the first things to look at in Table 10.1 are the diagnostic statistics assessing the validity of the instruments.

First, are the instruments relevant? The first-stage F-statistics in the three regressions are 33.7, 107.2, and 88.6, so in all three cases the first-stage F-statistics exceed 10. We conclude that the instruments are not weak, so that we can rely on the standard methods for statistical inference (hypothesis tests, confidence intervals) using the estimated coefficients and standard errors.

Second, are the instruments exogenous? Because the regressions in columns (1) and (2) each have a single instrument and a single included endogenous regressor, the coefficients in those regressions are exactly identified. Thus we cannot deploy the J-test in either of those regressions. The regression in column (3), however, is overidentified because there are two instruments and a single included endogenous regressor, so there is one ($m - k = 2 - 1 = 1$) overidentifying restriction. The J-statistic is 4.93; this has a χ_1^2 distribution, so the 5% critical value is 3.84 (Appendix Table 3) and the null hypothesis that both the instruments are exogenous is rejected at the 5% significance level (this deduction can be made directly from the p-value of 0.026, reported in the table).

The reason the J-statistic rejects is that the two instruments produce rather different estimated coefficients. When the only instrument is the sales tax (column (1)), the estimated price elasticity is -0.94, but when the only instrument is the cigarette-specific tax, the estimated price elasticity is -1.34. Recall the basic idea of the J-statistic: if both instruments are exogenous, then the two TSLS estimators using the individual instruments are consistent and differ from each other only because of random sampling variation. If, however, one of the instruments is exogenous and one is not, then the estimator based on the endogenous instrument is inconsistent, which is detected by the J-statistic. In this application, the difference between the two estimated price elasticities is sufficiently large that it is unlikely to be the result of pure sampling variation, so the J-statistic rejects the null hypothesis that both the instruments are exogenous.

The J-statistic rejection means that the regression in column (3) is based on invalid instruments (the instrument exogeneity condition fails). What does this imply about the estimates in columns (1) and (2)? The J-statistic rejection says that at least one of the instruments is endogenous, so there are three logical possibilities: the sales tax is exogenous but the cigarette-specific tax is not, in which case the column (1) regression is reliable; the cigarette-specific tax is exogenous but the sales tax is not, so the column (2) regression is reliable; or neither tax is exogenous, so neither regression is reliable. The statistical evidence cannot tell us which possibility is correct, so we must use our judgment.

We think that the case for the exogeneity of the general sales tax is stronger than for the cigarette-specific tax, because the political process can link changes in the cigarette-specific tax to changes in the cigarette market and smoking policy. For example, if smoking decreases in a state because it becomes out of fashion, there will be fewer smokers and a weakened lobby against cigarette-specific tax increases, which in turn could lead to higher cigarette-specific taxes. Thus, changes in tastes (which are part of u) could be correlated with changes in cigarette-specific taxes (the instrument). This suggests discounting the IV estimates that use the cigarette-only tax as an instrument. This suggests adopting only the price elasticity estimated using the general sales tax as an instrument, -0.94.

The estimate of −0.94 indicates that cigarette consumption is not very inelastic: an increase in price of 1% leads to a decrease in consumption of 0.94%. This may seem surprising for an addictive product like cigarettes. But remember that this elasticity is computed using changes over a ten-year period, so it is a long-run elasticity. This estimate suggests that increased taxes can make a substantial dent in cigarette consumption, at least in the long run.

When the elasticity is estimated using five-year changes from 1985 to 1990, rather than the ten-year changes reported in Table 10.1, the elasticity (estimated with the general sales tax as the instrument) is −0.79; for changes from 1990 to 1995, the elasticity is −0.68. These estimates suggest that demand is less elastic over horizons of five years than ten. This finding of greater price elasticity at longer horizons is consistent with the large body of research on cigarette demand. Demand elasticity estimates in that literature typically fall in the range −0.3 to −0.5, but these are mainly short-run elasticities; some recent studies suggest that the long-run elasticity could be perhaps twice the short-run elasticity.[4]

10.5 Where Do Valid Instruments Come From?

In practice the most difficult aspect of IV estimation is finding instruments that are both relevant and exogenous. There are two main approaches, which reflect two different perspectives on econometric and statistical modeling.

The first approach is to use economic theory to suggest instruments. For example, the Wrights' understanding of the economics of agricultural markets led them to look for an instrument that shifted the supply curve but not the demand curve; this in turn led them to consider weather conditions in agricultural regions. One area where this approach has been particularly successful is the field of financial economics. Some economic models of investor behavior involve statements about how investors forecast, which then imply sets of variables that are uncorrelated with the error term. Those models sometimes are nonlinear in the data and in the parameters, in which case the IV estimators discussed in this chapter cannot be used. An extension of IV methods to nonlinear models, called generalized method of moments estimation, is used instead. Economic theories are, however, abstractions that often do not take into account the nuances and details necessary for analyzing a particular data set. Thus this approach does not always work.

---

[4]If you are interested in learning more about the economics of smoking, see Chaloupka and Warner (2000) and Gruber (2001).

The second approach to constructing instruments is to look for some exogenous source of variation in X arising from what is, in effect, a random phenomenon that induces shifts in the endogenous regressor. For example, in our hypothetical example in Section 10.1, earthquake damage increased average class size in some school districts, and this variation in class size was unrelated to potential omitted variables that affect student achievement. This approach typically requires knowledge of the problem being studied and careful attention to the details of the data, and is best explained through examples.

Three Examples

We now turn to three empirical applications of IV regression that provide examples of how different researchers used their expert knowledge of their empirical problem to find instrumental variables.

Does putting criminals in jail reduce crime?   This is a question only an economist would ask. After all, a criminal cannot commit a crime outside jail while in prison, and the fact that some criminals are caught and jailed serves to deter others. But the magnitude of the combined effect—the change in the crime rate associated with a 1% increase in the prison population—is an empirical question.

One strategy for estimating this effect is to regress crime rates (crimes per 100,000 members of the general population) against incarceration rates (prisoners per 100,000), using annual data at a suitable level of jurisdiction (for example, U.S. states). This regression could include some control variables measuring economic conditions (crime increases when general economic conditions worsen), demographics (youths commit more crimes than the elderly), and so forth. There is, however, a serious potential for simultaneous causality bias that undermines such an analysis: if the crime rate goes up and the police do their job, there will be more prisoners. On the one hand, increased incarceration reduces the crime rate; on the other hand, an increased crime rate increases incarceration. As in the butter example in Figure 10.1, because of this simultaneous causality an OLS regression of the crime rate on the incarceration rate will estimate some complicated combination of these two effects. This problem cannot be solved by finding better control variables.

This simultaneous causality bias, however, can be eliminated by finding a suitable instrumental variable and using TSLS. The instrument must be correlated with the incarceration rate (it must be relevant), but it must also be uncorrelated with the error term in the crime rate equation of interest (it must be exogenous). That is, it must affect the incarceration rate but be unrelated to any of the unobserved factors that determine the crime rate.

Where does one find something that affects incarceration but has no direct effect on the crime rate? One place is exogenous variation in the capacity of existing prisons. Because it takes time to build a prison, short-term capacity restrictions can force states to release prisoners prematurely or otherwise reduce incarceration rates. Using this reasoning, Levitt (1996) suggested that lawsuits aimed at reducing prison overcrowding could serve as an instrumental variable, and he implemented this idea using panel data for the U.S. states from 1972 to 1993.

Are variables measuring overcrowding litigation valid instruments? Although Levitt did not report first-stage F-statistics, the prison overcrowding litigation slowed the growth of prisoner incarcerations in his data, suggesting that this instrument is relevant. To the extent that overcrowding litigation is induced by prison conditions but not by the crime rate or its determinants, this instrument is exogenous. Because Levitt breaks down overcrowding legislation into several types, and thus has several instruments, he is able to test the overidentifying restrictions and fails to reject them using the J-test, which bolsters the case that his instruments are valid.

Using these instruments and TSLS, Levitt estimated the effect on the crime rate of incarceration to be substantial. This estimated effect was three times larger than the effect estimated using OLS, suggesting that OLS suffered from large simultaneous causality bias.

Does cutting class sizes increase test scores?   As we saw in the empirical analysis of Part II, schools with small classes tend to be wealthier, and their students have access to enhanced learning opportunities both in and out of the classroom. In Part II, we used multiple regression to tackle the threat of omitted variables bias by controlling for various measures of student affluence, ability to speak English, and so forth. Still, a skeptic could wonder whether we did enough: if we left out something important, our estimates of the class size effect would still be biased.

This potential omitted variables bias could be addressed by including the right control variables, but if these data are unavailable (some, like outside learning opportunities, are hard to measure) then an alternative approach is to use IV regression. This regression requires an instrumental variable correlated with class size (relevance) but uncorrelated with the omitted determinants of test performance that make up the error term, such as parental interest in learning, learning opportunities outside the classroom, quality of the teachers and school facilities, etc. (exogeneity).

Where does one look for an instrument that induces random, exogenous variation in class size, but is unrelated to the other determinants of test performance?

Hoxby (2000) suggested biology. Because of random fluctuations in timings of births, the size of the incoming kindergarten class varies from one year to the next. Although the actual number of children entering kindergarten might be endogenous (recent news about the school might influence whether parents send a child to a private school), she argued that the *potential* number of children entering kindergarten—the number of four-year-olds in the district—is mainly a matter of random fluctuations in the birth dates of children.

Is potential enrollment a valid instrument? Whether it is exogenous depends on whether it is correlated with unobserved determinants of class size. Surely biological fluctuations in potential enrollment are exogenous, but potential enrollment also fluctuates because parents with young children choose to move into an improving school district and out of one in trouble. If so, an increase in potential enrollment could be correlated with unobserved factors such as the quality of school management, rendering this instrument invalid. Hoxby addressed this problem by reasoning that growth or decline in the potential student pool for this reason would occur smoothly over several years, whereas random fluctuations in birth dates would produce short-term "spikes" in potential enrollment. Thus, she used as her instrument not potential enrollment, but the deviation of potential enrollment from its long-term trend. These deviations satisfy the criterion for instrument relevance (the first-stage F-statistics all exceed 100). She makes a good case that this instrument is exogenous, but, as in all IV analysis, the credibility of this assumption is ultimately a matter of judgment.

Hoxby implemented this strategy using detailed panel data on elementary schools in Connecticut in the 1980s and 1990s. The panel data set permitted her to include school fixed effects, which, in addition to the instrumental variables strategy, attacks the problem of omitted variables bias at the school level. Her TSLS estimates suggested that the effect on test scores of class size is small; most of her estimates were statistically insignificantly different from zero.

Does aggressive treatment of heart attacks prolong lives?   New aggressive treatments for victims of heart attacks (technically, acute myocardial infarctions, or AMI) hold the potential for saving lives. Before a new medical procedure—in this example, cardiac catheterization[5]—is approved for general use, it goes through clinical trials, a series of randomized controlled experiments designed to measure its effects and side effects. But strong performance in a clinical trial is one thing; actual performance in the real world is another.

---

[5]Cardiac catheterization is a procedure in which a catheter, or tube, is inserted into a blood vessel and guided all the way to the heart to obtain information about the heart and coronary arteries.

A natural starting point for estimating the real-world effect of cardiac catheterization is to compare patients who received the treatment to those who did not. This leads to regressing the length of survival of the patient against the binary treatment variable (whether the patient received cardiac catheterization) and other control variables that affect mortality (age, weight, other measured health conditions, etc.). The population coefficient on the indicator variable is the increment to the patient's life expectancy provided by the treatment. Unfortunately, the OLS estimator is subject to bias: cardiac catheterization does not "just happen" to a patient randomly; rather, it is performed because the doctor and patient decide that it might be effective. If their decision is based in part on unobserved factors relevant to health outcomes not in the data set, then the treatment decision will be correlated with the regression error term. If the healthiest patients are the ones who receive the treatment, the OLS estimator will be biased (treatment is correlated with an omitted variable), and the treatment will appear more effective than it really is.

This potential bias can be eliminated by IV regression using a valid instrumental variable. The instrument must be correlated with treatment (must be relevant) but must be uncorrelated with the omitted health factors that affect survival (must be exogenous).

Where does one look for something that affects treatment but not the health outcome, other than through its effect on treatment? McClellan, McNeil, and Newhouse (1994) suggested geography. Most hospitals in their data set did not specialize in cardiac catheterization, so many patients were closer to "regular" hospitals that did not offer this treatment than to cardiac catheterization hospitals. McClellan, McNeil, and Newhouse therefore used as an instrumental variable the difference between the distance from the AMI patient's home to the nearest cardiac catheterization hospital and the distance to the nearest hospital of any sort; this distance is zero if the nearest hospital is a cardiac catheterization hospital, otherwise it is positive. If this relative distance affects the probability of receiving this treatment, then it is relevant. If it is distributed randomly across AMI victims, then it is exogenous.

Is relative distance to the nearest cardiac catheterization hospital a valid instrument? McClellan, McNeil, and Newhouse do not report first-stage *F*-statistics, but they do provide other empirical evidence that it is not weak. Is this distance measure exogenous? They make two arguments. First, they draw on their medical expertise and knowledge of the health care system to argue that distance to a hospital is plausibly uncorrelated with any of the unobservable variables that determine AMI outcomes. Second, they have data on some of the additional variables that affect AMI outcomes, such as the weight of the patient, and in their sample distance is uncorrelated with these *observable* determinants of survival; this, they argue, makes it more credible that distance is uncorrelated with the *unobservable* determinants in the error term as well.

Using 205,021 observations on Americans aged at least 64 who had an AMI in 1987, McClellan, McNeil, and Newhouse reached a striking conclusion: their TSLS estimates suggest that cardiac catheterization has a small, possibly zero effect on health outcomes, that is, cardiac catheterization does not substantially prolong life. In contrast, the OLS estimates suggest a large positive effect. They interpret this difference as evidence of bias in the OLS estimates.

McClellan, McNeil, and Newhouse's IV method has an interesting interpretation. The OLS analysis used actual treatment as the regressor, but because actual treatment is itself the outcome of a decision by patient and doctor, they argue that the actual treatment is correlated with the error term. Instead, TSLS uses *predicted* treatment, where the variation in predicted treatment arises because of variation in the instrumental variable: patients closer to a cardiac catheterization hospital are more likely to receive this treatment.

This interpretation has two implications. First, the IV regression actually estimates the effect of the treatment not on a "typical" randomly selected patient, but rather on patients for whom distance is an important consideration in the treatment decision. The effect on those patients might differ from the effect on a typical patient, which provides one explanation of the greater estimated effectiveness of the treatment in clinical trials than in McClellan, McNeil, and Newhouse's IV study. Second, it suggests a general strategy for finding instruments in this type of setting: find an instrument that affects the probability of treatment, but does so for reasons that are unrelated to the outcome except through their effect on the likelihood of treatment. Both these implications have applicability to experimental and "quasi-experimental" studies, the topic of Chapter 11.

10.6 Conclusion

From the humble start of estimating how much less butter people will buy if its price rises, IV methods have evolved into a general approach for estimating regressions when one or more variables are correlated with the error term. Instrumental variables regression uses the instruments to isolate variation in the endogenous regressors that is uncorrelated with the error in the regression of interest; this is the first stage of two stage least squares. This in turn permits estimation of the effect of interest in the second stage of two stage least squares.

Successful IV regression requires valid instruments, that is, instruments that are both relevant (not weak) and exogenous. If the instruments are weak, then the TSLS estimator can be biased, even in large samples, and statistical inferences based on TSLS t-statistics and confidence intervals can be misleading. Fortunately, when there is a single endogenous regressor it is possible to check for weak instruments simply by checking the first-stage F-statistic.

If the instruments are not exogenous, that is, if one or more instruments is correlated with the error term, then the TSLS estimator is inconsistent. If there are more instruments than endogenous regressors, then instrument exogeneity can be examined by testing the overidentifying restrictions. However, the core assumption—that there are at least as many exogenous instruments as there are endogenous regressors—cannot be tested. It is therefore incumbent on both the empirical analyst and the critical reader to use their own understanding of the empirical application to evaluate whether this assumption is reasonable.

The interpretation of IV regression as a way to exploit known exogenous variation in the endogenous regressor can be used to guide the search for potential instrumental variables in a particular application. This interpretation underlies much of the empirical analysis in the area that goes under the broad heading of program evaluation, in which experiments or quasi-experiments are used to estimate the effect of programs, policies, or other interventions on some outcome measure. A variety of additional issues arises in those applications, for example the interpretation of IV results when, as in the cardiac catheterization example, different "patients" might have different responses to the same "treatment." These and other aspects of empirical program evaluation are taken up in Chapter 11.

Summary

1. Instrumental variables regression is a way to estimate regression coefficients when one or more regressor is correlated with the error term.
2. Endogenous variables are correlated with the error term in the equation of interest; exogenous variables are uncorrelated with this error term.
3. For an instrument to be valid, it must (1) be correlated with the included endogenous variable and (2) be exogenous.
4. IV regression requires at least as many instruments as included endogenous variables.
5. The TSLS estimator has two stages: first, the included endogenous variables are regressed against the included exogenous variables and the instruments; second, the

dependent variable is regressed against the included exogenous variables and the predicted values of the included endogenous variables from the first-stage regression(s).

6. Weak instruments (instruments that are nearly uncorrelated with the included endogenous variables) make the TSLS estimator biased and TSLS confidence intervals and hypothesis tests unreliable.

7. If an instrument is not exogenous, then the TSLS estimator is inconsistent.

Key Terms

instrumental variables (IV) regression (331)
instrumental variable (instrument) (331)
endogenous variable (333)
exogenous variable (333)
instrument relevance condition (333)
instrument exogeneity condition (333)
two stage least squares (333)
included exogenous variables (341)
exact identification (342)

overidentification (342)
underidentification (342)
reduced form (343)
first-stage regression (344)
second-stage regression (344)
weak instruments (349)
first-stage F-statistic (350)
test of overidentifying restrictions (353)

Review the Concepts

10.1 In the demand curve regression model of Equation (10.3), is $\ln(P_i^{butter})$ positively or negatively correlated with the error, u_i? If β_1 is estimated by OLS, would you expect the estimated value to be larger or smaller than the true value of β_1? Explain.

10.2 In the study of cigarette demand in this chapter, suppose that we used as an instrument the number of trees per capita in the state. Is this instrument relevant? Is it exogenous? Is it a valid instrument?

10.3 In his study of the effect of incarceration on crime rates, suppose that Levitt had used the number of lawyers per capita as an instrument. Is this instrument relevant? Is it exogenous? Is it a valid instrument?

10.4 In their study of the effectiveness of cardiac catheterization, McClellan, McNeil, and Newhouse (1994) used as an instrument the difference in distance to cardiac catheterization and regular hospitals. How could you determine whether this instrument is relevant? How could you determine whether this instrument is exogenous?

Exercises

*10.1 This question refers to the panel data regressions summarized in Table 10.1.

a. Suppose that Federal government is considering a new tax on cigarettes that is estimated to increase the retail price by $0.10 per pack. If the current price per pack is $2.00, use the regression in column (1) to predict the change in demand. Construct a 95% confidence interval for the change in demand.

b. Suppose that the United States enters a recession and income falls by 2%. Use the regression in column (1) to predict the change in demand.

c. Recessions typically last less than one year. Do you think that that the regression in column (1) will provide a reliable answer to the question in (b)? Why or why not?

d. Suppose that the F-statistic in column (1) was 3.6 instead of 33.6. Would the regression provide a reliable answer to the question posed in (a)? Why or why not?

10.2 Consider the regression model with a single regressor: $Y_i = \beta_0 + \beta_1 X_i + u_i$. Suppose that the assumptions in Key Concept 4.3 are satisfied.

a. Show that X_i is a valid instrument. That is, show that Key Concept 10.3 is satisfied with $Z_i = X_i$.

b. Show that the IV regression assumptions in Key Concept 10.4 are satisfied with this choice of Z_i.

c. Show that the IV estimator constructed using $Z_i = X_i$ is identical to the OLS estimator.

10.3 A classmate is interested in estimating the variance of the error term in Equation (10.1).

a. Suppose that she uses the estimator from the second-stage regression of TSLS: $\hat{\sigma}_a^2 = \frac{1}{n-2}\sum_{i=1}^{n}(Y_i - \hat{\beta}_0^{TSLS} - \hat{\beta}_1^{TSLS}\hat{X}_i)^2$, where $\hat{X}_i$ is the fitted value from the first-stage regression. Is this estimator consistent? (For the purposes of this question suppose that the sample is very large and the TSLS estimators are essentially identical to β_0 and β_1.)

b. Is $\hat{\sigma}_b^2 = \frac{1}{n-2}\sum_{i=1}^{n}(Y_i - \hat{\beta}_0^{TSLS} - \hat{\beta}_1^{TSLS}X_i)^2$ consistent?

10.4 Consider TSLS estimation with a single included endogenous variable and a single instrument. Then the predicted value from the first-stage regression is $\hat{X}_i = \hat{\pi}_0 + \hat{\pi}_1 Z_i$. Use the definition of the sample variance and covariance to show that $s_{\hat{X}Y} = \hat{\pi}_1 s_{ZY}$ and $s_{\hat{X}}^2 = \hat{\pi}_1^2 s_Z^2$. Use this result to fill in the steps of the derivation in Appendix 10.2 of Equation (10.4).

The Cigarette Consumption Panel Data Set

The data set consists of annual data for the 48 continental U.S. states from 1985–1995. Quantity consumed is measured by annual per capita cigarette sales in packs per fiscal year, as derived from state tax collection data. The price is the average retail cigarette price per pack during the fiscal year, including taxes. Income is per capita income. The general sales tax is the average tax, in cents per pack, due to the broad-based state sales tax applied to all consumption goods. The cigarette-specific tax is the tax applied to cigarettes only. All prices, income, and taxes used in the regressions in this chapter are deflated by the Consumer Price Index and thus are in constant (real) dollars. We are grateful to Professor Jonathan Gruber of MIT for providing us with these data.

Derivation of the Formula for the TSLS Estimator in Equation (10.4)

The first stage of TSLS is to regress X_i on the instrument Z_i by OLS, and to compute the OLS predicted value $\hat{X}_i$, and the second stage is to regress Y_i on $\hat{X}_i$ by OLS. Accordingly, the formula for the TSLS estimator, expressed in terms of the predicted value $\hat{X}_i$, is the formula for the OLS estimator in Key Concept 4.2, with $\hat{X}_i$ replacing X_i. That is, $\hat{\beta}_1^{TSLS} = s_{\hat{X}Y}/s_{\hat{X}}^2$, where $s_{\hat{X}}^2$ is the sample variance of $\hat{X}_i$ and $s_{\hat{X}Y}$ is the sample covariance between Y_i and $\hat{X}_i$.

Because $\hat{X}_i$ is the predicted value of X_i from the first-stage regression, $\hat{X}_i = \hat{\pi}_0 + \hat{\pi}_1 Z_i$, the definitions of sample variances and covariances imply that $s_{\hat{X}Y} = \hat{\pi}_1 s_{ZY}$ and $s_{\hat{X}}^2 = \hat{\pi}_1^2 s_Z^2$

(Exercise 10.4). Thus, the TSLS estimator can be written as $\hat{\beta}_1^{TSLS} = s_{\hat{X}Y}/s_{\hat{X}}^2 = s_{ZY}/(\hat{\pi}_1 s_Z^2)$. Finally, $\hat{\pi}_1$ is the OLS slope coefficient from the first stage of TSLS, so $\hat{\pi}_1 = s_{ZX}/s_Z^2$. Substitution of this formula for $\hat{\pi}_1$ into the formula $\hat{\beta}_1^{TSLS} = s_{ZY}/(\hat{\pi}_1 s_Z^2)$, yields the formula for the TSLS estimator in Equation (10.4).

APPENDIX 10.3 | Large-Sample Distribution of the TSLS Estimator

This appendix studies the large-sample distribution of the TSLS estimator in the case considered in Section 10.1, that is, with a single instrument, a single included endogenous variable, and no included exogenous variables.

To start, we derive a formula for the TSLS estimator in terms of the errors that forms the basis for the remaining discussion, similar to the expression for the OLS estimator in Equation (4.51) in Appendix 4.3. From Equation (10.1), $Y_i - \overline{Y} = \beta_1(X_i - \overline{X}) + (u_i - \overline{u})$. Accordingly, the sample covariance between Z and Y can be expressed as

$$
\begin{aligned}
s_{ZY} &= \frac{1}{n-1} \sum_{i=1}^{n} (Z_i - \overline{Z})(Y_i - \overline{Y}) \\
&= \frac{1}{n-1} \sum_{i=1}^{n} (Z_i - \overline{Z})[\beta_1(X_i - \overline{X}) + (u_i - \overline{u})] \\
&= \beta_1 s_{ZX} + \frac{1}{n-1} \sum_{i=1}^{n} (Z_i - \overline{Z})(u_i - \overline{u}) \\
&= \beta_1 s_{ZX} + \frac{1}{n-1} \sum_{i=1}^{n} (Z_i - \overline{Z})u_i,
\end{aligned}
\tag{10.18}
$$

where $s_{ZX} = \frac{1}{n-1}\sum_{i=1}^{n}(Z_i - \overline{Z})(X_i - \overline{X})$ and where the final equality follows because $\sum_{i=1}^{n}(Z_i - \overline{Z}) = 0$. Substituting the definition of s_{ZX} and the final expression in Equation (10.18) into the definition of $\hat{\beta}_1^{TSLS}$ and multiplying the numerator and denominator by $(n-1)/n$ yields

$$
\hat{\beta}_1^{TSLS} = \beta_1 + \frac{\dfrac{1}{n}\sum_{i=1}^{n}(Z_i - \overline{Z})u_i}{\dfrac{1}{n}\sum_{i=1}^{n}(Z_i - \overline{Z})(X_i - \overline{X})}.
\tag{10.19}
$$

Large-Sample Distribution of $\hat{\beta}_1^{TSLS}$ When the IV Regression Assumptions in Key Concept 10.4 Hold

Equation (10.19) for the TSLS estimator is similar to Equation (4.51) in Appendix 4.3 for the OLS estimator, with the exceptions that Z rather than X appears in the numerator, and the denominator is the covariance between Z and X rather than the variance of X. Because of these similarities, and because Z is exogenous, the argument in Appendix 4.2 that the OLS estimator is normally distributed in large samples extends to $\hat{\beta}_1^{TSLS}$.

Specifically, when the sample is large, $\overline{Z} \cong \mu_Z$, so the numerator is approximately $\overline{q} = \frac{1}{n}\sum_{i=1}^{n}q_i$, where $q_i = (Z_i - \mu_Z)u_i$. Because the instrument is exogenous, $E(q_i) = 0$. By the IV regression assumptions in Key Concept 10.4, q_i is i.i.d. with variance $\sigma_q^2 = \text{var}[(Z_i - \mu_Z)u_i]$. It follows that $\text{var}(\overline{q}) = \sigma_{\overline{q}}^2 = \sigma_q^2/n$ and, by the central limit theorem, $\overline{q}/\sigma_{\overline{q}}$ is, in large samples, distributed $N(0,1)$.

Because the sample covariance is consistent for the population covariance, $s_{ZX} \xrightarrow{p}$ $\text{cov}(Z_i, X_i)$, which, because the instrument is relevant, is nonzero. Thus, by Equation (10.19) $\hat{\beta}_1^{TSLS} \cong \beta_1 + \overline{q}/\text{cov}(Z_i, X_i)$, so that in large samples $\hat{\beta}_1^{TSLS}$ is approximately distributed $N(\beta_1, \sigma_{\hat{\beta}_1^{TSLS}}^2)$, where $\sigma_{\hat{\beta}_1^{TSLS}}^2 = \sigma_{\overline{q}}^2/[\text{cov}(Z_i, X_i)]^2 = (1/n)\text{var}[(Z_i - \mu_Z)u_i]/[\text{cov}(Z_i, X_i)]^2$, which is the expression given in Equation (10.8).

APPENDIX

10.4

Large-Sample Distribution of the TSLS Estimator When the Instrument Is Not Valid

This appendix considers the large-sample distribution of the TSLS estimator in the set-up of Section 10.1 (one X, one Z) when one or the other of the conditions for instrument validity fail. If the instrument relevance condition fails (that is, the instrument is weak), the large-sample distribution of TSLS estimator is not normal; in fact, its distribution is that of a ratio of two normal random variables. If the instrument exogeneity condition fails, the TSLS estimator is inconsistent.

Large-Sample Distribution of $\hat{\beta}_1^{TSLS}$ When the Instrument Is Weak

First consider the case that the instrument is irrelevant, so that $\text{cov}(Z_i, X_i) = 0$. Then the argument in Appendix 10.3 entails division by zero. To avoid this problem, we need to take a closer look at the behavior of the term in the denominator of Equation (10.19) when the population covariance is zero.

We start by rewriting Equation (10.19). Because of the consistency of the sample average, in large samples, $\overline{Z}$ is close to μ_Z and $\overline{X}$ is close to μ_X. Thus, the term in the denominator of Equation (10.19) is approximately $\frac{1}{n}\sum_{i=1}^{n}(Z_i - \mu_Z)(X_i - \mu_X) = \frac{1}{n}\sum_{i=1}^{n}r_i = \overline{r}$, where $r_i = (Z_i - \mu_Z)(X_i - \mu_X)$. Let $\sigma_r^2 = \text{var}[(Z_i - \mu_Z)(X_i - \mu_X)]$, let $\sigma_{\overline{r}}^2 = \sigma_r^2/n$ and let $\overline{q}$, $\sigma_{\overline{q}}^2$, and σ_q^2 be as defined in Appendix 10.3. Then Equation (10.19) implies that, in large samples,

$$\hat{\beta}_1^{TSLS} \cong \beta_1 + \frac{\overline{q}}{\overline{r}} = \beta_1 + \left(\frac{\sigma_{\overline{q}}}{\sigma_{\overline{r}}}\right)\left(\frac{\overline{q}/\sigma_{\overline{q}}}{\overline{r}/\sigma_{\overline{r}}}\right) = \beta_1 + \left(\frac{\sigma_q}{\sigma_r}\right)\left(\frac{\overline{q}/\sigma_{\overline{q}}}{\overline{r}/\sigma_{\overline{r}}}\right). \tag{10.20}$$

If the instrument is irrelevant, $E(r_i) = \text{cov}(Z_i, X_i) = 0$. Thus, $\overline{r}$ is the sample average of the random variables r_i, $i = 1, \ldots, n$, which are i.i.d. (by the second least squares assumption), have variance $\sigma_r^2 = \text{var}[(Z_i - \mu_Z)(X_i - \mu_X)]$ (which is finite by the third IV regression assumption), and have a mean of zero (because the instruments are irrelevant). It follows that the central limit theorem applies to $\overline{r}$, specifically, $\overline{r}/\sigma_{\overline{r}}$ is approximately distributed $N(0, 1)$. Therefore, the final expression of Equation (10.20) implies that, in large samples, the distribution of $\hat{\beta}_1^{TSLS} - \beta_1$ is the distribution of aS, where $a = \sigma_q/\sigma_r$ and S is the ratio of two random variables, each of which has a standard normal distribution (these two standard normal random variables are correlated).

In other words, when the instrument is irrelevant, the central limit theorem applies to the denominator as well as the numerator of the TSLS estimator, so that in large samples the distribution of the TSLS estimator is the distribution of the ratio of two normal random variables. Because X_i and u_i are correlated, these normal random variables are correlated, and the large-sample distribution of the TSLS estimator when the instrument is irrelevant is complicated. In fact, the large-sample distribution of the TSLS estimator with irrelevant instruments is centered around the probability limit of the OLS estimator. Thus, when the instrument is irrelevant, TSLS does not eliminate the bias in OLS and, moreover, has a nonnormal distribution, even in large samples.

When the instrument is weak but not irrelevant, the distribution of the TSLS estimator continues to be nonnormal, so the general lesson here about the extreme case of an irrelevant instrument carries over to weak instruments. For example, it is possible to show that the mean of the sampling distribution of the TSLS estimator is, in large samples, approximately equal to $\beta_1 + (\beta_1^{OLS} - \beta_1)/[E(F) - 1]$, where β_1^{OLS} is the (probability) limit of the OLS estimator, that is $\hat{\beta}_1 \xrightarrow{p} \beta_1^{OLS}$ and $E(F)$ is the expectation of the first-stage F-statistic. This expression for the mean of the TSLS estimator is the source of the cutoff value suggested in Key Concept 10.5 for the rule-of-thumb diagnostic for weak instruments. Specifically, if $E(F) = 10$, then the large-sample bias of TSLS, relative to the large-sample bias of OLS, is $1/9$, or just over 10%, small enough to be acceptable in many applications.

Large-Sample Distribution of $\hat{\beta}_1^{TSLS}$ When the Instrument Is Endogenous

The numerator in the final expression in Equation (10.19) converges in probability to $\text{cov}(Z_i, u_i)$. If the instrument is exogenous, this is zero, and the TSLS estimator is consistent (assuming the instrument is not weak). If, however, the instrument is not exogenous, then if the instrument is not weak, $\hat{\beta}_1^{TSLS} \xrightarrow{p} \beta_1 + \text{cov}(Z_i, u_i)/\text{cov}(Z_i, X_i) \neq \beta_1$. That is, if the instrument is not exogenous, then the TSLS estimator is inconsistent.

CHAPTER 11 | Experiments and Quasi-Experiments

In many fields, such as psychology and medicine, causal effects are commonly estimated using experiments. Before being approved for widespread medical use, for example, a new drug must be subjected to experimental trials in which some patients are randomly selected to receive the drug while others are given a harmless ineffective substitute (a "placebo"); the drug is approved only if this randomized controlled experiment provides convincing statistical evidence that the drug is safe and effective.

Although randomized controlled experiments in economics are rare, there are three reasons to study them in an econometrics course. First, at a conceptual level, the notion of an ideal randomized controlled experiment provides a benchmark against which to judge estimates of causal effects in practice. Second, when experiments are actually conducted their results can be very influential, so it is important to understand the limitations and threats to validity of actual experiments, as well as their strengths. Third, external circumstances sometimes produce what appears to be randomization; that is, because of external events, the treatment of some individual occurs "as if" it is random. For example, suppose that a law is passed in one state but not its neighboring state. If the state of residence of the individual is thought of "as if" it is randomly assigned, then when the law passes it is "as if" some people are randomly subjected to the law (the treatment group) while others are not (the control group). Thus passage of the law produces a "quasi-experiment," also referred to as a "natural experiment," and many of the lessons learned by studying actual experiments can be applied (with some modifications) to quasi-experiments.

This chapter examines experiments and quasi-experiments in economics. The statistical tools used in this chapter are multiple regression analysis, regression analysis of panel data, and instrumental variables (IV) regression. What distinguishes the discussion in this chapter is not the tools used, but rather the type of data analyzed and the special opportunities and challenges posed when analyzing experiments and quasi-experiments.

The methods developed in this chapter are often used for program evaluation. **Program evaluation** is the field of study that concerns estimating the effect of a program, policy, or some other intervention or "treatment." What is the effect on earnings of going through a job training program? What is the effect on employment of low-skilled workers of an increase in the minimum wage? What is the effect on college attendance of making low-cost student aid loans available to middle-class students? This chapter discusses how such programs or policies can be evaluated using experiments or quasi-experiments.

We begin in Section 11.1 by elaborating on the discussion in Chapter 1 of an ideal randomized controlled experiment and causal effects. In reality, actual experiments with human subjects encounter practical problems that constitute threats to their internal and external validity, and these threats are discussed in Section 11.2. As discussed in Section 11.3, some of these threats can be addressed or evaluated using regression methods, including the "differences-in-differences" estimator and instrumental variables regression. Section 11.4 uses these methods to analyze a randomized controlled experiment in which elementary students were randomly assigned to different sized classes in the state of Tennessee in the late 1980s.

Section 11.5 turns to quasi-experiments and the estimation of causal effects using quasi-experiments. Threats to the validity of quasi-experiments are discussed in Section 11.6. One issue that arises in both experiments and quasi-experiments is that treatment effects can differ from one member of the population to the next, and the matter of interpreting the resulting estimates of causal effects when the population is heterogeneous is taken up in Section 11.7.

11.1 Idealized Experiments and Causal Effects

Recall from Section 1.2 that a randomized controlled experiment randomly selects subjects (individuals or, more generally, entities) from a population of interest, then randomly assigns them either to a treatment group, which receives the experimental treatment, or to a control group, which does not receive the treatment. The causal effect of the treatment is the expected effect on the outcome of interest of the treatment as measured in an ideal randomized controlled experiment.

Ideal Randomized Controlled Experiments

Initially, one might think that an ideal experiment would take two otherwise identical individuals, treat one of them, and compare the difference in their outcomes while holding constant all other influences. This is not, however, a practical experimental design, for it is impossible to find two identical individuals: even identical twins have different life experiences, so they are not identical in every way.

The central idea of an ideal randomized experiment is that the causal effect can be measured by randomly selecting individuals from a population and then randomly giving some of the individuals the treatment. If the treatment is assigned at random—for example, by flipping a coin, or by using a computerized random number generator—then the treatment level is distributed independently of any of the other determinants of the outcome, thereby eliminating the possibility of omitted variable bias (Key Concept 5.1). Suppose, for example, that individuals are randomly assigned to attend a job training program. An individual's prior work experience will influence his or her chances of getting a job after the training program ends, but as long as participation in the job training program (the "treatment") is randomly assigned, the distribution of work experience is the same in the treatment and control groups; that is, participation is distributed independently of previous work experience. Thus participation and previous work experience are uncorrelated, so omitting previous work experience from the analysis will not cause omitted variables bias in the estimator of the effect on future employment of the training program.

The role of random assignment can be restated in terms of the regression model with a single regressor,

$$Y_i = \beta_0 + \beta_1 X_i + u_i, \tag{11.1}$$

where X_i is the treatment level and, as usual, u_i contains all the additional determinants of the outcome Y_i. If the treatment is the same for all members of the treatment group, then X_i is binary, where $X_i = 1$ indicates that the ith individual received the treatment and $X_i = 0$ indicates that he or she did not receive the treatment. If the treatment level varies among those in the treatment group, then X_i is the level of treatment received. For example, X_i might be the dose of a drug or the number of weeks in a job training program, where $X_i = 0$ if the treatment is not received (a dose of zero). If X_i is binary, then the linear regression function in Equation (11.1) does not impose functional form restrictions. If X_i can take on multiple values, then Equation (11.1) treats the population regression function as linear (nonlinearities can be addressed using the methods of Section 6.2).

If X_i is randomly assigned, then X_i is distributed independently of the omitted factors in u_i. Because these omitted factors and X_i are independently distributed, $E(Y_i|X_i) = \beta_0 + \beta_1 X_i$ in Equation (11.1); said differently, the conditional mean of u_i given X_i does not depend on X_i; that is, $E(u_i|X_i) = 0$. Thus random assignment of X_i implies that the first least squares assumption in the regression model with a single regressor (Key Concept 4.3) holds automatically.

The causal effect.   The **causal effect** on Y of treatment level x is the difference in the conditional expectations, $E(Y|X = x) - E(Y|X = 0)$, where $E(Y|X = x)$ is the expected value of Y for the treatment group receiving treatment level x in an ideal randomized controlled experiment and $E(Y|X = 0)$ is the expected value of Y for the control group. In the context of experiments, the causal effect is also called the **treatment effect**. Because of random assignment, $E(u_i|X_i) = 0$ in Equation (11.1), so β_1 in Equation (11.1) is the causal effect of a unit change in X as measured by the expected difference in outcomes between the treatment and control groups.

The Differences Estimator

The causal effect is a difference in expected values and thus is an unknown characteristic of a population. The causal effect can be estimated using data from a randomized controlled experiment. Suppose that the treatment X_i is binary. Because the treatment is randomly assigned, the causal effect can be estimated by the difference in the sample average outcomes between the treatment and control groups. Equivalently, as discussed in Section 4.7, β_1 can be estimated by the OLS estimator $\hat{\beta}_1$ from the regression of Y_i on X_i. Because $E(u_i|X_i) = 0$ in Equation (11.1), $\hat{\beta}_1$ is unbiased. We refer to the OLS estimator $\hat{\beta}_1$ from the regression of Y_i on X_i as the **differences estimator** because, when the treatment is binary, it is the difference between the sample average outcome of the treatment group and the sample average outcome of the control group.

By randomly assigning treatment, an ideal randomized controlled experiment eliminates correlation between the treatment X_i and the error term u_i, so the differences estimator is unbiased and consistent. In practice, however, real-world experiments deviate from an ideal experiment, and problems arise that can introduce correlation between X_i and u_i.

11.2 Potential Problems with Experiments in Practice

Recall from Key Concept 7.1 that a statistical study is *internally valid* if the statistical inferences about causal effects are valid for the population being studied; it is *externally valid* if its inferences and conclusions can be generalized from the population and setting studied to other populations and settings. Various real-world problems pose threats to the internal and external validity of the statistical analysis of actual experiments with human subjects.

Threats to Internal Validity

Threats to the internal validity of randomized controlled experiments include failure to randomize, failure to follow the treatment protocol, attrition, experimental effects, and small sample sizes.

Failure to randomize.   Random assignment to the treatment and control group is the fundamental feature of a randomized controlled experiment that makes it possible to estimate the causal effect. If the treatment is not assigned randomly, but instead is based in part on the characteristics or preferences of the subject, then experimental outcomes will reflect both the effect of the treatment and the effect of the nonrandom assignment. For example, suppose that participants in a job training program experiment are assigned to the treatment group depending on whether their last name falls in the first or second half of the alphabet. Because of ethnic differences in last names, ethnicity could differ systematically between the treatment and control groups. To the extent that work experience, education, and other labor market characteristics differ by ethnicity, there could be systematic differences between the treatment and control groups in these omitted factors that affect outcomes.

More generally, nonrandom assignment can lead to correlation between the treatment X_i and the error term because receiving the treatment is determined in part by individual characteristics that enter the error term. In general, nonrandom assignment leads to bias in the differences estimator.

Failure to follow treatment protocol.   In an actual experiment, people do not always do what they are told. In a job training program experiment, for example, some of the subjects assigned to the treatment group might not show up for the training sessions and thus not receive the treatment. Similarly, subjects assigned to the control group might somehow receive the training anyway, perhaps by making a special request to an instructor or administrator.

Thus even if the treatment *assigned* is random, the treatment *actually received* might not be random. Instead, the treatment the subject actually receives is partly determined by random assignment (being made eligible for the job training program), and partly determined by individual characteristics (the subject's desire to receive the job training). As teachers and students know, you can require a student to take a course, but it is tougher to make him show up for class.

The failure of individuals to follow completely the randomized treatment protocol is called **partial compliance** with the treatment protocol. In some cases, the experimenter knows whether the treatment was actually received (for example, the trainee attended class), and the treatment actually received is recorded as X_i. Because there is an element of choice in whether the subject receives the treatment, X_i (the treatment actually received) will be correlated with u_i (which includes motivation and innate ability) even if there is random assignment. In other words, with partial compliance the treatment and control groups no longer are random samples from the larger population from which the subjects were originally drawn; instead, the treatment and control groups have an element of self-selection. Thus, failure to follow the treatment protocol leads to bias in the OLS estimator.

In other cases the experimenter might not know whether the treatment is actually received. For example, if a subject in a medical experiment is provided with the drug but, unbeknownst to the researchers, simply does not take it, then the recorded treatment ("received drug") is incorrect. Incorrect measurement of the treatment actually received also leads to bias in the differences estimator.

Attrition.   **Attrition** refers to subjects dropping out of the study after being randomly assigned to the treatment or control group. Sometimes attrition occurs for reasons unrelated to the treatment program; for example, a participant in a job training study might need to leave town to care for a sick relative. But if the reason for attrition is related to the treatment itself, then the attrition results in bias in the OLS estimator of the causal effect. For example, suppose the most able trainees drop out of the job training program experiment because they get out-of-town jobs acquired using the job training skills, so that at the end of the experiment only the least able members of the treatment group remain. Then the distribution of other characteristics (ability) will differ between the control and treatment groups (the treatment enabled the ablest trainees to leave town). In other words, the treatment X_i will be correlated with u_i (which includes ability) for those who remain in the sample at the end of the experiment and the differences estimator will be biased. Because attrition results in a nonrandomly selected sample, attrition that is related to the treatment leads to selection bias (Key Concept 7.4).

Experimental effects.   In experiments with human subjects, the mere fact that the subjects are in an experiment can change their behavior, a phenomenon sometimes called the **Hawthorne effect** (see the box on the following page). For example, the excitement created by or the attention resulting from being in an experimental program might bring forth extra effort that could affect outcomes.

In some experiments, a "double-blind" protocol can mitigate the effect of being in an experiment: although subjects and experimenters both know that they are in an experiment, neither knows whether a subject is in the treatment or control group. In a medical drug experiment, for example, sometimes the drug and the placebo can be made to look the same so that neither the medical professional dispensing the drug nor the patient knows whether the administered drug is the real thing or the placebo. If the experiment is double blind, then both the treatment and control groups should experience the same experimental effects, so different outcomes between the two groups can be attributed to the drug.

Double-blind experiments are clearly infeasible in real-world experiments in economics: both the experimental subject and instructor know whether the subject is attending the job training program. In a poorly designed experiment, this experimental effect could be substantial. For example, teachers in an experimental program might try especially hard to make their program a success if they run the risk of losing their jobs if the program performs poorly in the experiment. Deciding whether experimental results are biased because of the experimental effects requires making judgments based on what the experiment is evaluating and on the details of how the experiment was conducted.

Small samples.   Because experiments with human subjects can be very expensive, sometimes the sample sizes are small. A small sample size does not bias estimators of the causal effect, but it does mean that the causal effect is estimated imprecisely.

The Hawthorne Effect

During the 1920s and 1930s, the General Electric Company conducted a series of studies of worker productivity at their Hawthorne plant. In one set of experiments, they varied light bulb wattage to see how lighting affected the productivity of women assembling electrical parts. In other experiments they increased or decreased rest periods, changed the workroom layout, and shortened workdays. Influential early reports on these studies concluded that productivity continued to rise whether the lights were dimmer or brighter, whether workdays were longer or shorter, whether conditions improved or worsened. Researchers concluded that the productivity improvements were not the consequence of changes in the workplace, but instead came about because their special role in the experiment made the workers feel noticed and valued, so they worked harder and harder. Over the years, the idea that being in an experiment influences subject behavior has come to be known as the Hawthorne effect.

But there is a glitch to this story: careful examination of the actual Hawthorne data reveals no Hawthorne effect (Gillespie, 1991; Jones, 1992)! Still, in some experiments, especially ones in which the subjects have a stake in the outcome, merely being in an experiment could affect behavior. The Hawthorne effect and experimental effects more generally can pose threats to internal validity—even though the Hawthorne effect is not evident in the original Hawthorne data.

Threats to External Validity

Threats to external validity compromise the ability to generalize the results of the study to other populations and settings. Two such threats are when the experimental sample is not representative of the population of interest and when the treatment being studied is not representative of the treatment that would be implemented more broadly.

Nonrepresentative sample.   The population studied and the population of interest must be sufficiently similar to justify generalizing the experimental results. If a job training program is evaluated in an experiment with former prison inmates, then it might be possible to generalize the study results to other former prison inmates. Because a criminal record weighs heavily on the minds of potential employers, however, the results might not generalize to workers who have never committed a crime.

Another example of a nonrepresentative sample can arise when the experimental participants are volunteers. Even if the volunteers are randomly assigned to treatment and control groups, these volunteers might be more motivated than the overall population and, for them, the treatment could have a greater effect. More generally, selecting the sample nonrandomly from the greater population of interest can compromise the ability to generalize the results from the population studied (such as volunteers) to the population of interest.

Nonrepresentative program or policy. The policy or program of interest also must be sufficiently similar to the program studied to permit generalizing the results. One important feature is that the program in a small-scale, tightly monitored experiment could be quite different than the program actually implemented. If the program actually implemented is widely available, the scaled-up program might not provide the same quality control as the experimental version or it might be funded at a lower level; either possibility could result in the full-scale program being less effective than the smaller experimental program. Another difference between an experimental program and an actual program is its duration: the experimental program only lasts for the length of the experiment, while the actual program under consideration might be available for longer periods of time.

General equilibrium effects. An issue related to scale and duration concerns what economists call "general equilibrium" effects. Turning a small, temporary experimental program into a widespread, permanent program might change the economic environment sufficiently that the results from the experiment cannot be generalized. A small, experimental job training program, for example, might supplement training by employers, but if the program were made widely available it could displace employer-provided training, thereby reducing the net benefits of the program. Similarly, a widespread educational reform, such as school vouchers or sharply reducing class sizes, could increase the demand for teachers and change the type of person who is attracted to teaching, so the eventual net effect of the widespread reform would reflect these induced changes in school personnel. Phrased in econometric terms, an internally valid small experiment might correctly measure a causal effect, holding constant the market or policy environment, but general equilibrium effects mean that these other factors are not, in fact, held constant when the program is implemented broadly.

Treatment vs. eligibility effects. Another potential threat to external validity arises because, in economics and social programs more generally, participation in an actual (nonexperimental) program is usually voluntary. Thus, an experimental study that measures the effect of the program on randomly selected members of the population will not, in general, provide an unbiased estimator of the program effect when the recipients of the actual implemented program are permitted to decide whether or not to participate. A job training program might be quite effective for the few who choose to take it, yet be relatively ineffective for a randomly selected member of the population. One way to address this issue is to design the experiment so that it mimics as closely as possible the real-world program that would be implemented. For example, if the real-world job training program is made available to individuals meeting certain income cutoffs, then the experimental protocol could adopt a similar rule: the randomly selected treatment group would be given the "treatment" of eligibility for the program, whereas the control group would not be made eligible. In this case, the differences estimator would estimate the effect of eligibility for the program, which is different than the job training treatment effect for a randomly selected member of the eligible population.

11.3 Regression Estimators of Causal Effects Using Experimental Data

In an ideal randomized controlled experiment with a binary treatment, the causal effect can be estimated by the differences estimator, that is, by the OLS estimator of β_1 in Equation (11.1). If treatment is randomly received, then the differences estimator is unbiased; however, it is not necessarily efficient. Moreover, if some of the problems with actual experiments discussed in Section 11.2 are present, then X_i and u_i are correlated, so $\hat{\beta}_1$ is biased.

This section presents some additional regression-based methods for analyzing experimental data. The aim is to obtain a more efficient estimator than the differences estimator when the treatment is randomly received, and to obtain an unbiased, or at least consistent, estimator of the causal effect when certain threats to internal validity are present. This section concludes with a discussion of how to test for randomization.

The Differences Estimator with Additional Regressors

Often data are available on other characteristics of the subjects that are relevant to determining the experimental outcome. Because earnings depend on prior education, for example, earnings in an experimental job training program evaluation will depend on prior education as well as on the job training program itself. In a medical drug test, the health outcome could depend on patient characteristics, such as age, weight, gender, and preexisting medical conditions, in addition to the drug treatment itself. Let $W_{1i}, \ldots, W_{ri}$ denote variables measuring r individual characteristics for the ith person in the sample, where these individual characteristics are not affected by the treatment (entering the job training program does not change your prior education). If these individual characteristics are a factor in determining the outcome Y_i in addition to the treatment X_i, then these variables implicitly are in the error term in Equation (11.1). Therefore, Equation (11.1) can be modified so that these characteristics enter the regression explicitly; assuming that these characteristics enter linearly, this leads to the multiple regression model

$$Y_i = \beta_0 + \beta_1 X_i + \beta_2 W_{1i} + \cdots + \beta_{1+r} W_{ri} + u_i,\ i = 1, \ldots, n. \quad (11.2)$$

The OLS estimator of β_1 in Equation (11.2) is the **differences estimator with additional regressors**.

Consistency of the differences estimator with additional regressors.   If the four least squares assumptions for multiple regression hold (Key Concept 5.4), then the OLS estimators of all the coefficients in Equation (11.2) are unbiased, consistent, and form a valid basis for statistical inference.

In some applications, the first least squares assumption, that $E(u_i | X_i, W_{1i}, \ldots, W_{ri}) = 0$, is not compelling. For example, if one of the W regressors is prior education, this could be correlated with the individual's unobserved ability, which enters u_i. The differences estimator with additional regressors is consistent, however, under a weaker assumption than the usual conditional mean zero assumption, specifically, under an assumption, stated mathematically in Appendix 11.3, called **conditional mean independence**. In brief, conditional mean independence requires that the conditional expectation of u_i given X_i and the W variables does not depend on X_i, although it can depend on the W variables.

There are two relevant cases in which, despite correlation between the W variables and u_i, conditional mean independence holds and the differences estimator with additional regressors is consistent (even though the OLS estimators of the coefficients on the W variables in general are not). The first case is when treatment is randomly assigned: X_i is uncorrelated with all individual characteristics, either included in the regression (a W variable) or excluded (in the error term), so X_i cannot "pick up" the effect of any individual characteristics, included or not. The second case is when X_i is *conditionally* randomly assigned, given W_i: X_i is randomly assigned, but the probability of being in the treatment group depends on W_i. Suppose, for example, that participants in a job training program are divided into two groups, those who graduated from high school and those who did not. Among graduates, 30% are randomly assigned to the treatment group, but among nongraduates, 70% are randomly assigned to the treatment group. Because each graduate has the same chance of being assigned to the treatment group, the mean of u_i is the same for graduates in the treatment and control groups. Similarly, the mean of u_i is the same for nongraduates in the treatment and control groups. The mean of u_i will, however, generally differ for graduates and nongraduates (graduation is correlated with the omitted variables ability and motivation). In this case, X_i is conditionally random (X_i is assigned randomly, given graduation status W_i). If X_i is conditionally random then, as discussed further in Appendix 11.3, conditional mean independence holds and the differences estimator with additional regressors is consistent.

It is important that the W_i regressors in Equation (11.2) not be experimental outcomes; otherwise, W_i is endogenous. For example, suppose that Y_i is earnings after the job training program, W_i indicates getting a job after the program, and X_i indicates treatment. If future employment status is included in the regression, then the coefficient on X_i no longer is the effect of the program; rather, it is the partial effect of the program, holding constant future employment. Moreover, future employment could be correlated with X_i (the program leads to getting a job) and with the error term (more able trainees receive a job). We therefore restrict attention in Equation (11.2) to W variables that measure pretreatment characteristics, which are not influenced by the experimental treatment.

Reasons for using the differences estimator with additional regressors.
There are three reasons for using this estimator.

1. *Efficiency*. If the treatment is randomly assigned, the OLS estimator of β_1 in the multiple regression model (Equation (11.2)) is more efficient (has a smaller variance) than the OLS estimator in the single regressor model (Equation (11.1)). The reason for this is that including the additional determinants of Y in Equation (11.2) reduces the variance of the error term (see Exercise 16.7).

2. *Check for randomization*. If the treatment is not randomly assigned, and in particular is assigned in a way that is related to the W's, then the differences estimator (Equation (11.1)) is inconsistent and in general has a different probability limit than the differences estimator with additional regressors (Equation (11.2)). Thus, a large discrepancy between the two OLS estimates suggests that X_i was not in fact randomly assigned.

3. *Adjust for "conditional" randomization*. As previously discussed, the probability of being assigned to the treatment group can differ from one group of subjects to another, that is, it can depend on pretreatment characteristics W_i. If so, including these W variables controls for the probability that the participant is assigned to the treatment group.

In practice, the second and third of these reasons can be related. If the check for randomization in #2 indicates that the treatment was not randomly assigned, it might be possible to adjust for this nonrandom assignment by using the differences estimator with regression controls. Whether this is in fact possible, however, depends on the details of the nonrandom assignment. If the assignment probability depends only on the observable variables W, then Equation (11.2) adjusts for this nonrandom assignment, but if the assignment probability depends on unobserved variables as well, then the adjustment made by including the W regressors is incomplete.

The Differences-in-Differences Estimator

Experimental data are often panel data, that is, observations on the same subjects before and after the experiment. With panel data, the causal effect can be estimated using the "differences-in-differences" estimator, which is the average change in Y in the treatment group over the course of the experiment, minus the average change in Y in the control group over the same time. This differences-in-differences estimator can be computed using a regression, which can be augmented with additional regressors measuring subject characteristics.

The differences-in-differences estimator. Let $\overline{Y}^{treatment, before}$ be the sample average of Y for those in the treatment group before the experiment, and let $\overline{Y}^{treatment, after}$ be the sample average for the treatment group after the experiment. Let $\overline{Y}^{control, before}$ and $\overline{Y}^{control, after}$ be the corresponding pretreatment and posttreatment sample averages for the control group. The average change in Y over the course of the experiment for those in the treatment group is $\overline{Y}^{treatment, after} - \overline{Y}^{treatment, before}$, and the average change in Y over this period for those in the control group is $\overline{Y}^{control, after} - \overline{Y}^{control, before}$. The **differences-in-differences estimator** is the average change in Y for those in the treatment group, minus the average change in Y for those in the control group:

$$
\begin{aligned}
\hat{\beta}_1^{diffs\text{-}in\text{-}diffs} &= \left(\overline{Y}^{treatment, after} - \overline{Y}^{treatment, before}\right) - \left(\overline{Y}^{control, after} - \overline{Y}^{control, before}\right) \\
&= \Delta\overline{Y}^{treatment} - \Delta\overline{Y}^{control},
\end{aligned}
\tag{11.3}
$$

where $\Delta\overline{Y}^{treatment}$ is the average change in Y in the treatment group and $\Delta\overline{Y}^{control}$ is the average change in Y in the control group. If the treatment is randomly assigned, then $\hat{\beta}_1^{diffs\text{-}in\text{-}diffs}$ is an unbiased and consistent estimator of the causal effect.

The differences-in-differences estimator can be written in regression notation. Let ΔY_i be the change in the value of Y_i for the ith individual over the course of the experiment, that is, ΔY_i is the value of Y for the ith individual after the experiment is completed, minus the value of Y before it starts. Assuming that the binary treatment variable X_i is randomly assigned, the causal effect is the coefficient β_1 in the population regression

$$\Delta Y_i = \beta_0 + \beta_1 X_i + u_i. \tag{11.4}$$

The OLS estimator $\hat{\beta}_1$ is the difference in the group means of ΔY (Section 4.7), that is, $\hat{\beta}_1$ is the differences-in-differences estimator in Equation (11.3).

Reasons for using the differences-in-differences estimator. The differences-in-differences estimator has two potential advantages over the single-difference estimator of Equation (11.1).

1. *Efficiency*. If the treatment is randomly received, then the differences-in-differences estimator can be more efficient than the differences estimator. This will be the case if some of the unobserved determinants of Y_i are persistent over time for a given individual, as are gender and prior education in the job training program example. Whether the differences estimator or the differences-in-differences estimator is more efficient depends on whether these persistent individual-specific characteristics explain a large or small amount of the variance in Y_i (Exercise 11.4).

2. *Eliminate pretreatment differences in Y.* If treatment is correlated with the initial level of Y_i before the experiment but $E(u_i|X_i) = 0$ in Equation (11.4), then the differences estimator is biased but the differences-in-differences estimator is not. This is illustrated in Figure 11.1. In that figure, the sample average of Y for the treatment group is 40 before the experiment, whereas the pretreatment sample average of Y for the control group is 20. Over the course of the experiment, the sample average of Y increases in the control group to 30, whereas it increases to 80 for the treatment group. Thus, the mean difference of the post-treatment sample averages is $80 - 30 = 50$. However, some of this difference arises because the treatment and control groups had different pretreatment means: the treatment group started out ahead of the control group. The differences-in-differences estimator measures the gains of the treatment group, relative to the control group, which in this example is $(80 - 40) - (30 - 20) = 30$. More generally, by focusing on the change in Y over the course of the experiment, the differences-in-differences estimators removes the influence of initial values of Y that vary systematically between the treatment and control groups.

FIGURE 11.1   The Differences-in-Differences Estimator

The post-treatment difference between the treatment and control groups is $80 - 30 = 50$, but this overstates the treatment effect because before the treatment $\bar{Y}$ was higher for the treatment than the control group by $40 - 20 = 20$. The differences-in-differences estimator is the difference between the final and initial gaps, so that $\hat{\beta}_1^{diffs-in-diffs} = (80 - 30) - (40 - 20) = 50 - 20 = 30$. Equivalently, the differences-in-differences estimator is the average change for the treatment group minus the average change for the control group, that is, $\hat{\beta}_1^{diffs-in-diffs} = \Delta\bar{Y}^{treatment} - \Delta\bar{Y}^{control} = (80 - 40) - (30 - 20) = 30$.

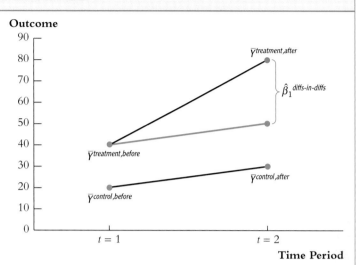

The differences-in-differences estimator with additional regressors.

The differences-in-differences estimator can be extended to include additional regressors $W_{1i}, \ldots, W_{ri}$, which measure individual characteristics prior to the experiment. For example, in a job training program evaluation in which Y is earnings, a W variable could be the prior education of the participant. These additional regressors can be incorporated using the multiple regression model

$$\Delta Y_i = \beta_0 + \beta_1 X_i + \beta_2 W_{1i} + \cdots + \beta_{1+r} W_{ri} + u_i, \quad i = 1, \ldots, n. \quad (11.5)$$

The OLS estimator of β_1 in Equation (11.5) is the **differences-in-differences estimator with additional regressors**. If X_i is randomly assigned, then the OLS estimator of $\hat{\beta}_1$ in Equation (11.5) is unbiased.

The reasons for including the additional W regressors in Equation (11.5) are the same three reasons as for including them in Equation (11.2), which only uses post-treatment data: if X_i is randomly assigned, including additional regressors can improve efficiency; by adding regressors it is possible to check for randomization; and adding regressors permits adjusting for conditional randomization, that is, randomization that depends on the observable W variables. As discussed in the context of Equation (11.2), it is important that the W variables not include variables that are themselves outcomes of the experiment.

The interpretation of the W variables in Equation (11.5) is different than in differences estimator with additional regressors (Equation (11.2)). In Equation (11.2), because only post-treatment outcomes were being compared, the W variables account for differences in the *level* of Y_i. In contrast, in Equation (11.5), the W variables account for differences in the *change* in Y_i over the course of the experiment. In the job training program example, the dependent variable in Equation (11.5) is the change in earnings over the time of the experiment, X_i indicates whether the participant was in the treatment group, and W_i might be prior education. Including prior education in this regression allows for the possibility that individuals with more education tend to have greater *changes* in earnings over the course of the experiment, regardless of whether they are in the treatment or control groups.

Extension of differences-in-differences to multiple time periods. In some experiments the individual is observed for multiple periods, not just two. In a job training program experiment, the individual's income and employment status might be observed monthly for a year or more. In this case, the population regression models in Equations (11.4) and (11.5), which are based on the change in the outcome between a single pretreatment observation and a single post-treatment observation, are not applicable. Such data can, however, be analyzed using the fixed effects regression model of Section 8.3; the details are provided in Appendix 11.2.

Estimation of Causal Effects for Different Groups

The causal effect can differ from one subject to the next, depending on individual characteristics. For example, the effect on cholesterol levels of a cholesterol-reducing drug could be greater for a patient with a high cholesterol level than for one whose cholesterol level is already low. Similarly, a job training program might be more effective for women than for men, and it might be more effective for motivated than for unmotivated subjects. More generally, the causal effect can depend on the value of one or more variables, which can either be observed (like gender) or unobserved (like motivation).

Causal effects that depend on the value of an observable variable, say W_i, can be estimated by interacting the treatment variable X_i with W_i in Equation (11.2) (differences estimator with additional regressors) or in Equation (11.5) (differences-in-differences estimator with additional regressors). For example, if W_i is binary, then the interactions specification permits estimation of the treatment effect for the two different groups corresponding to the two different values of W_i. More generally, the estimation of causal effects that depend on an observable regressor is an application of the interaction methods discussed in Section 6.3.

The topic of interpreting estimates of causal effects when the causal effect depends on the value of an unobservable variable is taken up in Section 11.7.

Estimation When There Is Partial Compliance

If there is partial compliance with the experimental protocol, then the treatment level X_i can be correlated with the unobserved individual characteristics u_i, and the OLS estimators discussed so far are inconsistent. For example, if only the most motivated trainees show up for the job training program, the job training program might appear to be effective—but only because the trainees are the hardest workers who would do well in the job market regardless of the training program.

As discussed in Chapter 10, instrumental variables regression provides a general solution to the problem of correlation between a regressor and the error term, assuming that there is an instrumental variable available. In an experiment with partial compliance, the *assigned* treatment level can serve as an instrumental variable for the *actual* treatment level.

Recall that a variable must satisfy the two conditions of instrument relevance and instrument exogeneity (Key Concept 10.3) to be a valid instrumental variable. As long as the protocol is partially followed, then the actual treatment level (X_i) is partially determined by the assigned treatment level (Z_i), so that the instrumental variable Z_i is relevant. If the assigned treatment level is determined randomly—that is, if the experiment has random assignment—and if the assignment itself has no effect on the outcome, other than through its influence on whether treatment is received, then Z_i is exogenous. That is, random assignment of Z_i implies that $E(u_i|Z_i) = 0$, where u_i is the error term in the differences specification in Equation (11.1) or in the differences-in-differences specification in Equation (11.4), depending upon which estimator is being used. Thus, in an experiment with partial compliance and randomly assigned treatment, the original random assignment is a valid instrumental variable.

Testing for Randomization

It is possible to test for randomization by checking whether the randomized variable actually depends on any observable individual characteristics.

Testing for random receipt of treatment. If the treatment is randomly received, then X_i will be uncorrelated with the observable individual characteristics. Thus, the hypothesis that treatment is randomly received can be tested by testing the hypothesis that the coefficients on $W_{1i}, \ldots, W_{ri}$ are zero in a regression of X_i on $W_{1i}, \ldots, W_{ri}$. In the job training program example, regressing receipt of job training (X_i) on gender, race, and prior education (W's), and computing the F-statistic testing whether the coefficients on the W's are zero provides a test of the null hypothesis that treatment was randomly received, against the alternative hypothesis that receipt of treatment depends on gender, race, or prior education.[1]

Testing for random assignment. If the treatment is randomly assigned, then the assignment Z_i will be uncorrelated with the observable individual characteristics. Thus, the hypothesis that treatment is randomly assigned can be tested by regressing Z_i on $W_{1i}, \ldots, W_{ri}$ and testing the null hypothesis that all the slope coefficients are zero.

11.4 Experimental Estimates of the Effect of Class Size Reductions

In this section we return to a question addressed in Part II: what is the effect on test scores of reducing class size in the early grades? In the late 1980s, Tennessee conducted a large, multimillion dollar randomized controlled experiment to ascertain whether class size reduction was an effective way to improve elementary education. The results of this experiment have strongly influenced our understanding of the effect of class size reductions.

Experimental Design

The Tennessee class size reduction experiment, known as Project STAR (Student-Teacher Achievement Ratio), was a four-year experiment designed to evaluate the effect on learning of small class sizes. Funded by the Tennessee state legislature, the experiment cost approximately $12 million over four years. The study compared three different class arrangements for kindergarten through third grade: a regular class size, with 22–25 students per class, a single teacher, and no aides; a small class size, with 13–17 students per class and no aide; and a regular-sized class plus a teacher's aide.

Each school participating in the experiment had at least one class of each type, and students entering kindergarten in a participating school were randomly

---

[1]In this example, X_i is binary so, as discussed in Chapter 9, the regression of X_i on $W_{1i}, \ldots, W_{ri}$ is a linear probability model and heteroskedasticity-robust standard errors are essential. Another way to test the hypothesis that $E(X_i|W_{1i}, \ldots, W_{ri})$ does not depend on $W_{1i}, \ldots, W_{ri}$ when X_i is binary is to use a probit or logit model (see Section 9.2).

assigned to one of these three groups at the beginning of the 1985–1986 academic year. Teachers were also assigned randomly to one of the three types of classes.

According to the original experimental protocol, students would stay in their initially assigned class arrangement for the four years of the experiment (kindergarten through third grade). However, because of parent complaints, students initially assigned to a regular class (with or without an aide) were randomly reassigned at the beginning of first grade to regular classes with an aide or to regular classes without an aide; students initially assigned to a small class remained in a small class. Students entering school in first grade (kindergarten was optional), in the second year of the experiment, were randomly assigned to one of the three groups. Each year, students in the experiment were given standardized tests (the Stanford Achievement Test) in reading and math.

The project paid for the additional teachers and aides necessary to achieve the target class sizes. During the first year of the study, approximately 6,400 students participated in 108 small classes, 101 regular classes, and 99 regular classes with aides. Over all four years of the study, a total of approximately 11,600 students at 80 schools participated in the study.

Deviations from the experimental design.   The experimental protocol specified that the students should not switch between class groups, other than through the re-randomization at the beginning of first grade. However, approximately 10% of the students switched in subsequent years for reasons including incompatible children and behavioral problems. These switches represent a departure from the randomization scheme and, depending on the true nature of the switches, have the potential to introduce bias into the results. Switches made purely to avoid personality conflicts might be sufficiently unrelated to the experiment that they would not introduce bias. If, however, the switches arose because the parents most concerned with their children's education pressured the school into switching a child into a small class, then this failure to follow the experimental protocol could bias the results towards overstating the effectiveness of small classes. Another deviation from the experimental protocol was that the class sizes changed over time because students switched between classes and moved in and out of the school district.

Analysis of the STAR Data

Because there are two treatment groups—small class and regular class with aide—the regression version of the differences estimator needs to be modified to handle the two treatment groups and the control group. This is done by introducing two binary variables, one indicating whether the student is in a small class and another indicating whether the student is in a regular sized class with an aide. This leads to the population regression model

$$Y_i = \beta_0 + \beta_1 SmallClass_i + \beta_2 RegAide_i + u_i, \tag{11.6}$$

where $SmallClass_i = 1$ if the ith student is in a small class and equals zero otherwise, $RegAide_i = 1$ if the ith student is in a regular class with an aide and equals zero otherwise, and Y_i is a test score. The effect on the test score of a small class, relative to a regular class, is β_1, and the effect of a regular class with an aide, relative to a regular class, is β_2. The differences estimator for the experiment can be computed by estimating β_1 and β_2 in Equation (11.6) by OLS.

Table 11.1 presents the differences estimates of the effect on test scores of being in a small class or in a regular sized class with an aide. The dependent variable Y_i in the regressions in Table 11.1 is the student's total score on the combined math and reading portions of the Stanford Achievement Test. According to the estimates in Table 11.1, for students in kindergarten, the effect of being in a small class is an increase of 13.9 points on the test, relative to being in a regular class; the estimated effect of being in a regular class with an aide is 0.31 points on the test. For each grade, the null hypothesis that small classes provide no improvement is rejected at the 1% (two-sided) significance level. However, it is not possible to reject the null hypothesis that having an aide in a regular class provides no improvement, relative to not having an aide, except in first grade. The estimated magnitudes of the improvements in small classes are broadly similar in grades K, 2, and 3, although the estimate is larger for first grade.

The differences estimates in Table 11.1 suggest that reducing class size has an effect on test performance, but adding an aide to a regular sized class has a much smaller effect, possibly zero. As discussed in Section 11.3, augmenting the regressions in Table 11.1 with additional regressors (the W regressors in Equation (11.2)) can provide more efficient estimates of the causal effects. Moreover, if the treatment received is not random because of failures to follow the treatment protocol, then the estimates of the experimental effects based on regressions with additional regressors could differ from the difference estimates reported in Table 11.1. For these two reasons, estimates of the experimental effects in which additional regressors are included in Equation (11.6) are reported for kindergarten in Table 11.2; the first column of Table 11.2 repeats the results of the first column (for kindergarten) from Table 11.1, and the remaining three columns include additional regressors that measure teacher, school, and student characteristics.

The main conclusion from Table 11.2 is that the multiple regression estimates of the causal effects of the two treatments (small class and regular sized class with

TABLE 11.1   Project STAR: Differences Estimates of Effect on Standardized Test Scores of Class Size Treatment Group

Regressor	Grade			
	K	**1**	**2**	**3**
Small class	13.90**	29.78**	19.39**	15.59**
	(2.45)	(2.83)	(2.71)	(2.40)
Regular size with aide	0.31	11.96**	3.48	−0.29
	(2.27)	(2.65)	(2.54)	(2.27)
Intercept	918.04**	1,039.39**	1,157.81**	1,228.51**
	(1.63)	(1.78)	(1.82)	(1.68)
Number of observations	5,786	6,379	6,049	5,967

The regressions were estimated using the Project STAR Public Access Data Set described in Appendix 11.1. The dependent variable is the student's combined score on the math and reading portions of the Stanford Achievement Test. Standard errors are given in parentheses under the coefficients. **The individual coefficient is statistically significant at the 1% significance level using a two-sided test.

aide) in the final three columns of Table 11.2 are similar to the differences estimate reported in the first column. The fact that adding these observable regressors does not change the estimated causal effects of the different treatments makes it more plausible that the random assignment to the smaller classes also does not depend on unobserved variables. As expected, these additional regressors increase the $\overline{R}^2$ of the regression, and the standard error of the estimated class size effect decreases from 2.45 in column (1) to 2.16 in column (4).

Because teachers were randomly assigned to class types within a school, the experiment also provides an opportunity to estimate the effect on test scores of teacher experience. Teachers were not, however, randomly assigned across participating schools, and some schools had more experienced teachers than others. Thus teacher experience could be correlated with the error term, as it would be if the more experienced teachers work at schools with more resources and with higher average test scores. Accordingly, to estimate the effect of teacher experience on test scores, we need to control for the other characteristics of the school, which is accomplished using a complete set of indicator variables for each school ("school effects"), that is, indicator variables denoting the school the student attended. Because teachers are randomly assigned within a school, the conditional mean of u_i given the school does not depend on the treatment; in the terminology of Appendix 11.3, because of random assignment within a school, the conditional mean independence assumption holds, where the additional W regressors are the

TABLE 11.2   Project STAR: Differences Estimates with Additional Regressors for Kindergarten

Regressor	(1)	(2)	(3)	(4)
Small class	13.90**	14.00**	15.93**	15.89**
	(2.45)	(2.45)	(2.24)	(2.16)
Regular size with aide	0.31	−0.60	1.22	1.79
	(2.27)	(2.25)	(2.04)	(1.96)
Teacher's years of experience		1.47**	0.74**	0.66**
		(0.17)	(0.17)	(0.17)
Boy				−12.09**
				(1.67)
Free lunch eligible				−34.70**
				(1.99)
Black				−25.43**
				(3.50)
Race other than black or white				−8.50
				(12.52)
Intercept	918.04**	904.72**		
	(1.63)	(2.22)		
School indicator variables?	no	no	yes	yes
$\overline{R}^2$	0.01	0.02	0.22	0.28
Number of observations	5,786	5,766	5,766	5,748

The regressions were estimated using the Project STAR Public Access Data Set described in Appendix 11.1. The dependent variable is the combined test score on the math and reading portions of the Stanford Achievement Test. The number of observations differ in the different regressions because of some missing data. Standard errors are given in parentheses under coefficients. The individual coefficient is statistically significant at the *5% level or **1% significance level using a two-sided test.

school effects. When school effects are included, the estimate of the effect of experience drops in half, from 1.47 in column (2) to 0.74 in column (3). Even so, the estimate in column (3) remains statistically significant and moderately large; ten years of experience corresponds to a predicted increase in test scores of 7.4 points.

It is tempting to interpret some of the other coefficients in Table 11.2. For example, kindergarten boys perform worse than girls on these standardized tests. But these individual student characteristics are *not* randomly assigned (the gender of the student taking the test is not randomly assigned!), so these additional regressors could be correlated with omitted variables. For example, if race or eligibility for a free lunch are correlated with reduced learning opportunities outside school (which is omitted from the Table 11.2 regressions), then their estimated coefficients would reflect these omitted influences. As discussed in Section 11.2, if the treatment is randomly assigned then the estimator of its coefficient is consistent, whether or not the other regressors are correlated with the error term, but if the additional regressors are correlated with the error term then their coefficient estimators have omitted variable bias.

Interpreting the estimated effects of class size.   Are the estimated effects of class size reported in Tables 11.1 and 11.2 large or small in a practical sense? There are two ways to answer this: first, by translating the estimated changes in raw test scores into units of standard deviations of test scores, so that the estimates in Table 11.1 are comparable across grades; and second, by comparing the estimated class size effect to the other coefficients in Table 11.2.

Because the distribution of test scores is not the same for each grade, the estimated effects in Table 11.1 are not directly comparable across grades. We faced this problem in Section 7.3, when we wanted to compare the effect on test scores of a reduction in the student-teacher ratio estimated using data from California to the estimate based on data from Massachusetts. Because the two tests differed, the coefficients could not be compared directly. The solution in Section 7.3 was to translate the estimated effects into units of standard deviations of the test, so that a unit decrease in the student-teacher ratio corresponds to a change of an estimated fraction of a standard deviation of test scores. We adopt this approach here so that the estimated effects in Table 11.1 can be compared across grades. For example, the standard deviation of test scores for children in kindergarten is 73.7, so the effect of being in a small class in kindergarten, based on the estimate in Table 11.1, is $13.9/73.7 = 0.19$, with a standard error of $2.45/73.7 = 0.03$. The estimated effects of class size from Table 11.1, converted into units of the standard deviation of test scores across students, are summarized in Table 11.3. Expressed in standard deviation units, the estimated effect of being in a small class is similar for grades K, 2, and 3, and is approximately one-fifth of a standard deviation of test scores. Similarly, the result of being in a regular sized class with an aide is approximately zero for grades K, 2, and 3. The estimated treatment effects are larger for first grade; however, the estimated difference between the small class and the regular sized class with an aide is 0.20 for first grade, the same as the other grades. Thus, one interpretation of the first-grade results is that the students in the control group—the regular sized class without an aide—happened to do poorly on the test that year for some unusual reason, perhaps simply random sampling variation.

Another way to gauge the magnitude of the estimated effect of being in a small class is to compare the estimated treatment effects to the other coefficients

TABLE 11.3   Estimated Class Size Effects in Units of Standard Deviations of the Test Score Across Students

Treatment Group	Grade			
	K	**1**	**2**	**3**
Small class	0.19** (0.03)	0.33** (0.03)	0.23** (0.03)	0.21** (0.03)
Regular size with aide	0.00 (0.03)	0.13** (0.03)	0.04 (0.03)	0.00 (0.03)
Sample standard deviation of test scores (s_Y)	73.70	91.30	84.10	73.30

The estimates and standard errors in the first two rows are the estimated effects in Table 11.1, divided by the sample standard deviation of the Stanford Achievement Test for that grade (the final row in this table), computed using data on the students in the experiment. Standard errors are given in parentheses under coefficients. **The individual coefficient is statistically significant at the 1% significance level using a two-sided test.

in Table 11.2. In kindergarten, the estimated effect of being in a small class is 13.9 points on the test (first row of Table 11.2). Holding constant race, teacher's years of experience, eligibility for free lunch, and the treatment group, boys score lower on the standardized test than girls by approximately 12 points according to the estimates in column (4) of Table 11.2. Thus, the estimated effect of being in a small class is somewhat larger than the performance gap between girls and boys. As another comparison, the estimated coefficient on the teacher's years of experience in column (4) is 0.66, so having a teacher with 20 years of experience is estimated to improve test performance by 13 points. Thus, the estimated effect of being in a small class is approximately the same as the effect of having a 20-year veteran as a teacher, relative to having a new teacher. These comparisons suggest that the estimated effect of being in a small class is substantial.

Additional results.   Econometricians, statisticians, and specialists in elementary education have studied various aspects of this experiment, and we briefly summarize some of those findings here. One of these findings is that the effect of a small class is concentrated in the earliest grades. This can be seen in Table 11.3; except for the anomalous first-grade results, the test score gap between regular and small classes reported in Table 11.3 is essentially constant across grades (0.19 standard deviation units in kindergarten, 0.23 in second grade, and 0.21 in third grade). Because the children initially assigned to a small class stayed in that small class, this means that staying in a small class did not result in additional gains;

rather, the gains made upon initial assignment were retained in the higher grades, but the gap between the treatment and control groups did not increase. Another finding is that, as indicated in the second row of Table 11.3, this experiment shows little benefit of having an aide in a regular-sized classroom. One potential concern about interpreting the results of the experiment is the failure to follow the treatment protocol for some students (some students switched from the small classes). If initial placement in a kindergarten classroom is random and has no direct effect on test scores, then initial placement can be used as an instrumental variable that partially, but not entirely, influences placement. This strategy was pursued by Krueger (1999), who used two stage least squares (TSLS) to estimate the effect on test scores of class size using initial classroom placement as the instrumental variable; he found that the TSLS and OLS estimates were similar, leading him to conclude that deviations from the experimental protocol did not introduce substantial bias into the OLS estimates.[2]

Comparison of the Observational and Experimental Estimates of Class Size Effects

Part II presented multiple regression estimates of the class size effect based on observational data for California and Massachusetts school districts. In those data, class size was *not* randomly assigned, but instead was determined by local school officials trying to balance educational objectives against budgetary realities. How do those observational estimates compare with the experimental estimates from Project STAR?

To compare the California and Massachusetts estimates to those in Table 11.3, it is necessary to evaluate the same class size reduction and to express the predicted effect in units of standard deviations of test scores. Over the four years of the STAR experiment, the small classes had, on average, approximately 7.5 fewer students than the large classes, so we use the observational estimates to predict the effect on test scores of a reduction of 7.5 students per class. Based on the OLS estimates for the linear specifications summarized in the first column of Table 7.3, the California estimates predict an increase of 5.5 points on the test for a 7.5 student reduction in the student-teacher ratio ($0.73 \times 7.5 \cong 5.5$ points). The standard deviation of the test across students in California is approximately 38 points,

[2]For further reading about Project STAR, see Mosteller (1995), Mosteller, Light, and Sachs (1996), and Krueger (1999). Ehrenberg, Brewer, Gamoran, and Willms (2001a, 2001b) discuss Project STAR and place it in the context of the policy debate on class size and related research on the topic. For some criticisms of Project STAR, see Hanushek (1999a), and for a critical view of the relationship between class size and performance more generally, see Hanushek (1999b).

so the estimated effect of the reduction of 7.5 students, expressed in units of standard deviations across students, is $5.5/38 \cong 0.14$ standard deviations.[3] The standard error of the estimated slope coefficient for California is 0.26 (Table 7.3), so the standard error of the estimated effect of a 7.5 student reduction in standard deviation units is $0.26 \times 7.5/38 \cong 0.05$. Thus, based on the California data, the estimated effect of reducing classes by 7.5 students, expressed in units of standard deviations of test scores across students, is 0.14 standard deviations, with a standard error of 0.05. These calculations and similar calculations for Massachusetts, are summarized in Table 11.4, along with the STAR estimates for kindergarten taken from column (1) of Table 11.2.

The estimated effects from the California and Massachusetts observational studies are somewhat smaller than the STAR estimates. One reason that estimates from different studies differ, however, is random sampling variability, so it makes sense to compare confidence intervals for the estimated effects from the three studies. Based on the STAR data for kindergarten, the 95% confidence interval for the effect of being in a small class (reported in the final column of Table 11.4) is 0.13 to 0.25. The comparable 95% confidence interval based on the California observational data is 0.04 to 0.24, and for Massachusetts it is 0.02 to 0.22. Thus, the 95% confidence intervals from the California and Massachusetts studies contain most of the 95% confidence interval from the STAR kindergarten data. Viewed in this way, the three studies give generally similar ranges of estimates.

There are many reasons why the experimental and observational estimates might differ. One reason is that, as discussed in Section 7.3, there are remaining threats to the internal validity of the observational studies. For example, because children move in and out of districts, the district student-teacher ratio might not reflect the student-teacher ratio actually experienced by the students, so the coefficient on the student-teacher ratio in the Massachusetts and California studies could be biased towards zero because of errors-in-variables bias. Other reasons concern external validity. The district average student-teacher ratio used in the observational studies is not the same thing as the actual number of children in the class, the STAR experimental variable. Project STAR was in a southern state in the 1980s, potentially different than California and Massachusetts in 1998, and the grades being compared differ (K–3 in STAR, fourth grade in Massachusetts,

---

[3]In Table 7.3, the estimated effects are presented in terms of the standard deviation of test scores across *districts*; in Table 11.3, the estimated effects are in terms of the standard deviation of test scores across *students*. The standard deviation across students is greater than the standard deviation across districts. For California, the standard deviation across students is 38, but the standard deviation across districts is 19.1.

TABLE 11.4   Estimated Effects of Reducing the Student-Teacher Ratio by 7.5 Based on the STAR Data and the California and Massachusetts Observational Data

Study	$\hat{\beta}_1$	Change in Student-Teacher Ratio	Standard Deviation of Test Scores Across Students	Estimated Effect	95% Confidence Interval
STAR (grade K)	−13.90** (2.45)	Small class vs. regular class	73.8	0.19** (0.03)	(0.13, 0.25)
California	−0.73** (0.26)	−7.5	38.0	0.14** (0.05)	(0.04, 0.24)
Massachusetts	−0.64* (0.27)	−7.5	39.0	0.12* (0.05)	(0.02, 0.22)

The estimated coefficient $\hat{\beta}_1$ for the STAR study is taken from column (1) of Table 11.2. The estimated coefficients for the California and Massachusetts studies are taken from the first column of Table 7.3. The estimated effect is the effect of being in a small class versus a regular class (for STAR) or the effect of reducing the student-teacher ratio by 7.5 (for the California and Massachusetts studies). The 95% confidence interval for the reduction in the student-teacher ratio is this estimated effect ±1.96 standard errors. Standard errors are given in parentheses under estimated effects. The estimated effects are statistically significantly different from zero at the *5% level or **1% significance level using a two-sided test.

fifth grade in California). In light of all these reasons to expect different estimates, the findings of the three studies are remarkably similar. The fact that the observational studies are similar to the Project STAR estimates suggests that the remaining threats to the internal validity of the observational estimates are minor.

11.5 Quasi-Experiments

True randomized controlled experiments can be expensive—the STAR experiment cost $12 million—and they often raise ethical concerns. In medicine, it would be unethical to determine the effect on longevity of smoking by randomly assigning subjects to a smoking treatment group and a nonsmoking control group; in economics, it would be unethical to estimate the demand elasticity for cigarettes among teenagers by selling subsidized cigarettes to randomly selected high school students. For cost, ethical, and practical reasons, true randomized controlled experiments are rare in economics.

Nevertheless, the statistical insights and methods of randomized controlled experiments can carry over to nonexperimental settings. In a **quasi-experiment**, also called a **natural experiment**, randomness is introduced by variations in individual circumstances that make it appear *as if* the treatment is randomly assigned. These variations in individual circumstances might arise because of vagaries in legal institutions, location, timing of policy or program implementation, natural randomness such as birth dates, rainfall, or other factors that are unrelated to the causal effect under study.

There are two types of quasi-experiments. In the first, whether or not an individual (or, more generally, an entity) receives treatment is viewed as if it is randomly determined. In this case, the causal effect can be estimated by OLS using the treatment, X_i, as a regressor.

In the second type of quasi-experiment, the "as if" random variation is only a partial determinant of treatment. Section 11.3 discusses how, in an experiment, random assignment can be used as an instrumental variable when it influences the treatment actually received. Similarly, in a quasi-experiment, "as if" random variation sometimes provides an instrumental variable (Z_i) that influences the treatment actually received (X_i). Accordingly, the causal effect is estimated by instrumental variables regression, where the "as if" random source of variation provides the instrumental variable.

Examples

We illustrate the two types of quasi-experiments by examples. The first example is a quasi-experiment in which the treatment is "as if" randomly determined. The second and third examples illustrate quasi-experiments in which the "as if" random variation influences, but does not entirely determine, the level of the treatment.

Example #1: Labor market effects of immigration.   Does immigration reduce wages? Economic theory suggests that if the supply of labor increases because of an influx of immigrants, the "price" of labor—the wage—should fall. However, all else being equal, immigrants are attracted to cities with high labor demand, so the OLS estimator of the effect on wages of immigration will be biased. An ideal randomized controlled experiment for estimating the effect on wages of immigration would randomly assign different numbers of immigrants (different "treatments") to different labor markets ("subjects") and measure the effect on wages (the "outcome"). Such an experiment, however, faces severe practical, financial, and ethical problems.

The labor economist David Card (1990) therefore used a quasi-experiment in which a large number of Cuban immigrants entered the Miami, Florida, labor market in the "Mariel boatlift," which resulted from a temporary lifting of restrictions on emigration from Cuba in 1980. Half of the immigrants settled in Miami, in part because it had a large preexisting Cuban community. Card used the differences-in-differences estimator to estimate the causal effect of an increase in immigration by comparing the change in wages of low-skilled workers in Miami to the change in wages of similar workers in other comparable U.S. cities over the same period. He concluded that this influx of immigrants had a negligible effect on wages of less-skilled workers.

Example #2: Effects on civilian earnings of military service.   Does serving in the military improve your prospects on the labor market? The military provides training that future employers might find attractive. However, an OLS regression of individual civilian earnings against prior military service could produce a biased estimator of the effect on civilian earnings of military service because military service is determined, at least in part, by individual choices and characteristics. For example, the military accepts only applicants who meet minimum physical requirements, and a lack of success in the private sector labor market might make an individual more likely to sign up for the military.

To circumvent this selection bias, Joshua Angrist (1990) used a quasi-experimental design in which he examined labor market histories of those who served in the U.S. military during the Vietnam War. During this period, whether a young man was drafted into the military was determined in part by a national lottery system based on birthdays: men randomly assigned low lottery numbers were eligible to be drafted, while those with high numbers were not. Actual entry into the military was determined by complicated rules, including physical screening and certain exemptions, and some young men volunteered for service, so serving in the military was only partially influenced by whether you were draft-eligible. Thus, being draft-eligible serves as an instrumental variable that partially determines military service but is randomly assigned. In this case, there was true random assignment of draft eligibility via the lottery, but because this randomization was not done as part of an experiment to evaluate the effect of military service, this is a quasi-experiment. Angrist concluded that the long-term effect of military service was to reduce earnings of white, but not nonwhite, veterans.

Example #3: The effect of cardiac catheterization.   Section 10.5 described the study by McClellan, McNeil, and Newhouse (1994) in which they used the distance from a heart attack patient's home to a cardiac catheterization hospital, relative to the distance to a hospital lacking catheterization facilities, as an instrumental variable for actual treatment by cardiac catheterization. This study is a quasi-experiment with a variable that partially determines the treatment. The treatment itself, cardiac catheterization, is determined by personal characteristics of the patient and by the decision of the patient and doctor; however, it is also influenced by whether a nearby hospital is capable of performing this procedure. If the location of the patient is "as if" randomly assigned and has no direct effect on health outcomes, other than through its effect on the probability of catheterization, then the relative distance to a catheterization hospital is a valid instrumental variable.

Other examples.   The quasi-experiment research strategy has been applied in other areas as well. Garvey and Hanka (1999) used variation in U.S. state laws to examine the effect on corporate financial structure (for example, the use of debt by corporations) of anti-takeover laws. Meyer, Viscusi, and Durbin (1995) used large discrete changes in the generosity of unemployment insurance benefits in Kentucky and Michigan, which differentially affected workers with high but not low earnings, to estimate the effect on time out of work of a change in unemployment benefits. The surveys of Meyer (1995), Rosenzweig and Wolpin (2000), and Angrist and Krueger (2001) give other examples of quasi-experiments in the fields of economics and social policy.

Econometric Methods for Analyzing Quasi-Experiments

The econometric methods for analyzing quasi-experiments are for the most part the same as those laid out in Section 11.3 for analyzing true experiments. If the treatment level X is "as if" randomly determined, then the OLS estimator of the coefficient of X is an unbiased estimator of the causal effect. If the treatment level is only partially random but is influenced by a variable Z that is "as if" randomly assigned, then the causal effect can be estimated by instrumental variables regression using Z as an instrument.

Because quasi-experiments typically do not have true randomization, there can be systematic differences between the treatment and control groups. If so, it is important to include observable measures of pretreatment characteristics of the individual subjects in the regression (the W's in the regressions in Section 11.3). As discussed in Section 11.3, including W regressors that are endogenous (that are results of treatment), in general, results in an inconsistent estimator of the causal effect.

Data in quasi-experiments typically are collected for reasons other than the particular study, so panel data on the "subjects" of the quasi-experiment sometimes are unavailable (an exception is discussed in the box on the minimum wage). If so, one way to proceed is to use a series of cross sections collected over time, and to modify the methods of Section 11.3 for repeated cross-sectional data.

What Is the Effect on Employment of the Minimum Wage?

How much does an increase in the minimum wage reduce demand for low-skilled workers? Economic theory says that demand falls when the price rises, but precisely how much is an empirical question. Because prices and quantities are determined by supply and demand, the OLS estimator in a regression of employment against wages has simultaneous causality bias. Hypothetically, a randomized controlled experiment might randomly assign different minimum wages to different employers and then compare changes in employment (outcomes) in the treatment and control groups, but how could this hypothetical experiment be done in practice?

The labor economists David Card and Alan Krueger (1994) decided to conduct such an experiment, but to let "nature"—or, more precisely, geography—perform the randomization for them. In 1992, the minimum wage in New Jersey rose from $4.25 to $5.05 per hour, but the minimum wage in neighboring Pennsylvania stayed constant. In this experiment, the "treatment" of the minimum wage increase—being located in New Jersey or Pennsylvania—is viewed "as if" randomly assigned in the sense that being subject to the wage hike is assumed to be uncorrelated with the other determinants of employment changes over this period. Card and Krueger collected data on employment at fast food restaurants before and after the wage increase in the two states. When they computed the differences-in-differences estimator, they found a surprising result: there was no evidence that employment fell at New Jersey fast food restaurants, relative to those in Pennsylvania. In fact, some of their estimates actually suggest that employment *increased* in New Jersey restaurants after its minimum wage went up, relative to Pennsylvania!

This finding conflicts with basic microeconomic theory and has been quite controversial. Subsequent analysis, using a different source of employment data, suggests that there might have been a small drop in employment in New Jersey after the wage hike, but even so the estimated labor demand curve is very inelastic (Neumark and Wascher, 2000). Although the exact wage elasticity in this quasi-experiment is a matter of debate, the effect on employment of a hike in the minimum wage appears to be smaller than many economists had previously thought.

Differences in differences using repeated cross-sectional data.   A **repeated cross-sectional data** set is a collection of cross-sectional data sets, where each cross-sectional data set corresponds to a different time period. For example, the data set might contain observations on 400 individuals in the year 2001 and on 500 different individuals in 2002, for a total of 900 different individuals. One example of repeated cross-sectional data is political polling data, in which political preferences are measured by a series of surveys of randomly selected potential voters, where the surveys are taken at different dates and each survey has different respondents.

The premise of using repeated cross-sectional data is that, if the individuals (more generally, entities) are randomly drawn from the same population, then the individuals in the earlier cross section can be used as surrogates for the individuals in the treatment and control groups in the later cross section. For example, suppose that, because of an increase of funds that had nothing to do with the local labor market, a job training program was expanded in southern but not northern California. Suppose you have survey data on two randomly selected cross sections of adult Californians, with one survey taken before the training program expanded and one after. Then the "treatment group" would be southern Californians and the "control group" would be northern Californians. You do not have data on the southern Californians actually treated before the treatment (because you do not have panel data), but you do have data on southern Californians who are statistically similar to those who were treated. Thus you can use the cross-sectional data on southern Californians in the first period as a surrogate for the pretreatment observations on the treatment group, and the cross-sectional data on northern Californians as a surrogate for the pretreatment observations on the control group.

When there are two time periods, the regression model for repeated cross-sectional data is

$$Y_{it} = \beta_0 + \beta_1 X_{it} + \beta_2 G_i + \beta_3 D_t + \beta_4 W_{1it} + \cdots + \beta_{3+r} W_{rit} + u_{it}. \quad (11.7)$$

where X_{it} is the actual treatment of the ith individual (entity) in the cross section in period t ($t = 1, 2$), D_t is the binary indicator that equals zero in the first period and equals one in the second period, and G_i is a binary variable indicating whether the individual is in the treatment group (or in the surrogate treatment group, if the observation is in the pretreatment period). The ith individual receives treatment if he or she is in the treatment group in the second period, so in Equation (11.7), $X_{it} = G_i \times D_t$, that is, X_{it} is the interaction between G_i and D_t.

If the quasi-experiment makes X_{it} "as if" randomly received, then the causal effect can be estimated by the OLS estimator of β_1 in Equation (11.7). If there are more than two time periods, then Equation (11.7) is modified to contain $T - 1$ binary variables indicating the different time periods (see Appendix 11.2).

If the quasi-experiment makes the treatment X_{it} only partially randomly received, then in general X_{it} will be correlated with u_{it} and the OLS estimator is biased and inconsistent. In this case, the source of randomness in the quasi-experiment takes the form of the instrumental variable Z_{it} that partially influences the treatment level and is "as if" randomly assigned. As usual, for Z_{it} to be a valid instrumental variable it must be relevant (that is, it must be related to the actual treatment X_{it}) and exogenous.

11.6 Potential Problems with Quasi-Experiments

Like all empirical studies, quasi-experiments face threats to internal and external validity. A particularly important potential threat to internal validity is whether the "as if" randomization in fact can be treated reliably as true randomization.

Threats to Internal Validity

The threats to the internal validity of true randomized controlled experiments listed in Section 11.2 also apply to quasi-experiments, but with some modifications.

Failure of randomization.   Quasi-experiments rely on differences in individual circumstances—legal changes, sudden unrelated events, and so forth—to provide the "as if" randomization in the treatment level. If this "as if" randomization fails to produce a treatment level X (or an instrumental variable Z) that is random, then in general the OLS estimator is biased (or the instrumental variable estimator is not consistent).

As in a true experiment, one way to test for failure of randomization is to check for systematic differences between the treatment and control groups, for example by regressing X (or Z) on the individual characteristics (the W's) and testing the hypothesis that the coefficients on the W's are zero. If differences exist that are not readily explained by the nature of the quasi-experiment, then this is evidence that the quasi-experiment did not produce true randomization. Even if there is no relationship between X (or Z) and the W's, X (or Z) could be related to some of the unobserved factors in the error term u. Because these factors are unobserved, this cannot be tested, and the validity of the assumption of "as if" randomization must be evaluated using expert knowledge and judgment applied to the application at hand.

Failure to follow treatment protocol.   In a true experiment, failure to follow the treatment protocol arises when members of the treatment group fail to receive treatment and/or members of the control group actually receive treatment; in consequence, the OLS estimator of the causal effect has selection bias. The counterpart to this in a quasi-experiment is when the "as if" randomization influences, but does not determine, the treatment level. In this case, the instrumental variables estimator based on the quasi-experimental influence Z can be consistent even though the OLS estimator is not.

Attrition.   Attrition in a quasi-experiment is similar to attrition in a true experiment in the sense that if it arises because of personal choices or characteristics, then attrition can induce correlation between the treatment level and the error term. This results in sample selection bias, so the OLS estimator of the causal effect is biased and inconsistent.

Experimental effects.   An advantage of quasi-experiments is that, because they are not true experiments, there typically is no reason for individuals to think they are experimental subjects. Thus experimental effects such as the Hawthorne effect generally are not germane in quasi-experiments.

Instrument validity in quasi-experiments.   An important step in evaluating a study that uses instrumental variables regression is careful consideration of whether the instrument is in fact valid. This general statement remains true in quasi-experimental studies in which the instrument is "as if" randomly determined. As discussed in Chapter 10, instrument validity requires both instrument relevance and instrument exogeneity. Because instrument relevance can be checked using the statistical methods summarized in Key Concept 10.5, here we focus on the second, more judgmental requirement of instrument exogeneity.

Although it might seem that a randomly assigned instrumental variable is necessarily exogenous, this is not so. Consider the examples of Section 11.5. In Angrist's (1990) use of draft lottery numbers as an instrumental variable in studying the effect on civilian earnings of military service, the lottery number was in fact randomly assigned. But, as Angrist (1990) points out and discusses, if a low draft number results in behavior aimed at avoiding the draft, and that avoidance behavior subsequently affects civilian earnings, then a low lottery number (Z_i) could be related to unobserved factors that determine civilian earnings (u_i); that is, Z_i and u_i are correlated even though Z_i is randomly assigned. As a second example, McClellan, McNeil, and Newhouse's (1994) study of the effect on heart attack patients of cardiac catheterization treated the relative distance to a catheterization hospital as if it were randomly assigned. But, as the authors highlight and examine, if patients who live close to a catheterization hospital are healthier than those who live far way (perhaps because of better access to medical care generally), then the relative distance to a catheterization hospital would be correlated with omitted variables in the error term of the health outcome equation. In short, just because an instrument is randomly determined or "as if" randomly determined does not necessarily mean it is exogenous in the sense that $\text{corr}(Z_i, u_i) = 0$.

Thus, the case for exogeneity must be scrutinized closely even if the instrument arises from a quasi-experiment.

Threats to External Validity

Quasi-experimental studies use observational data, and the threats to the external validity of a study based on a quasi-experiment are generally similar to the threats discussed in Section 7.1 for conventional regression studies using observational data.

One important consideration is that the special events that create the "as if" randomness at the core of a quasi-experimental study can result in other special features that threaten external validity. For example, Card's (1990) study of labor market effects of immigration discussed in Section 11.5 used the "as if" randomness induced by the influx of Cuban immigrants in the Mariel boatlift. There were, however, special features of the Cuban immigrants, Miami, and its Cuban community that might make it difficult to generalize these findings to immigrants from other countries or to other destinations. Similarly, Angrist's (1990) study of the labor market effects of serving in the U.S. military during the Vietnam War presumably would not generalize to peacetime military service. As usual, whether a study generalizes to a specific population and setting of interest depends on the details of the study and must be assessed on a case-by-case basis.

11.7 Experimental and Quasi-Experimental Estimates in Heterogeneous Populations

The causal effect can depend on individual characteristics, that is, it can vary from one member of the population to the next. Section 11.3 discusses estimating causal effects for different groups using interactions when the source of the variation in the effect, such as gender, is observed. In this section, we consider the consequences of *unobserved* variation in the causal effect. We refer to this circumstance, in which there is unobserved variation in the causal effect within the population, as having a heterogeneous population. This section begins with a discussion of population heterogeneity, then turns to the interpretation of the OLS and IV estimators when there is a heterogeneous population. To keep things simple, this discussion focuses on the case of a binary treatment variable X_i (which may or may not be randomly assigned) with no additional regressors.

Population Heterogeneity: Whose Causal Effect?

If the causal effect is the same for every member of the population, then in this sense the population is homogenous and Equation (11.1), with its single causal effect β_1, applies to all members of the population. In reality, however, the population studied can be heterogeneous; specifically, the causal effect can vary from one individual to the next based on the individual's circumstances, background, and other characteristics. For example, the effect on employment prospects of a job training program that teaches resume-writing skills presumably is greater for workers who lack resume-writing skills than for those who already have those skills. Similarly, the effect of a medical procedure could depend on the eating, smoking, and drinking habits of the patient.

If the causal effect is different for different people, Equation (11.1) no longer applies. Instead, the ith individual now has his or her own causal effect, β_{1i}, the effect of the treatment on that person. Thus the population regression equation can be written

$$Y_i = \beta_0 + \beta_{1i}X_i + u_i. \tag{11.8}$$

For example, β_{1i} might be zero for a resume-writing training program if the ith individual already knows how to write a resume. Because β_{1i} varies from one individual to the next in the population and the individuals are selected from the population at random, we can think of β_{1i} as a random variable which, just like u_i, reflects unobserved variation across individuals (for example, variation in preexisting resume-writing skills).

As discussed in Section 11.1, the causal effect in a given population is the expected effect from an experiment in which members of the population are selected at random. When the population is heterogeneous, this causal effect is in fact the **average causal effect**, also called the **average treatment effect**, which is the population average of the individual causal effects. In terms of Equation (11.8), the average causal effect in the population is the population mean value of the causal effect $E(\beta_{1i})$, that is, the expected causal effect of a randomly selected member of the population.

What do the estimators of Section 11.3 estimate if there is population heterogeneity of the form in Equation (11.8)? We first consider the OLS estimator in the case that X_i is "as if" randomly determined; in this case, the OLS estimator is a consistent estimator of the average causal effect. This is generally not true for the IV estimator, however. Instead, if X_i is partially influenced by Z_i, then the IV estimator using the instrument Z estimates a weighted average of the causal effects, where those for whom the instrument is most influential receive the most weight.

OLS with Heterogeneous Causal Effects

Suppose that the treatment received, X_i, is randomly assigned with perfect compliance (in an experiment) or "as if" randomly assigned (in a quasi-experiment), so that $E(u_i | X_i) = 0$. Then it is reasonable to consider using the differences estimator, that is, the OLS estimator $\hat{\beta}_1$ obtained from a regression of Y_i on X_i.

We now show that if there is heterogeneity in the causal effect in the population and if X_i is randomly assigned, then the differences estimator is a consistent estimator of the average causal effect. The OLS estimator is $\hat{\beta}_1 = s_{XY}/s_X^2$ (Equation (4.8)). If the observations are i.i.d., the sample covariance and variance are consistent estimators of the population covariance and variance, so $\hat{\beta}_1 \xrightarrow{p} \sigma_{XY}/\sigma_X^2$. If X_i is randomly assigned, then X_i is distributed independently of other individual characteristics, both observed and unobserved, and in particular is distributed independently of β_{1i}. Accordingly, the OLS estimator $\hat{\beta}_1$ has the limit

$$\hat{\beta}_1 = \frac{s_{XY}}{s_X^2} \xrightarrow{p} \frac{\sigma_{XY}}{\sigma_X^2} = \frac{\mathrm{cov}(\beta_0 + \beta_{1i}X_i + u_i, X_i)}{\sigma_X^2} = \frac{\mathrm{cov}(\beta_{1i}X_i, X_i)}{\sigma_X^2} = E(\beta_{1i}), \quad (11.9)$$

where the third equality uses the facts about covariances in Key Concept 2.3 and $\mathrm{cov}(u_i, X_i) = 0$, which is implied by $E(u_i | X_i) = 0$ (Equation (2.25)), and the final equality follows from β_{1i} being distributed independently of X_i, which it is if X_i is randomly determined (Exercise 11.7). Thus, if X_i is randomly determined, $\hat{\beta}_1$ is a consistent estimator of the average causal effect $E(\beta_{1i})$.

IV Regression with Heterogeneous Causal Effects

Suppose that treatment is only partially randomly determined, that Z_i is a valid instrumental variable (relevant and exogenous), and that there is heterogeneity in the effect on X_i of Z_i. Specifically, suppose that X_i is related to Z_i by the linear model

$$X_i = \pi_0 + \pi_{i1}Z_i + v_i, \quad (11.10)$$

where the coefficient π_{1i} varies from one individual to the next. Equation (11.10) is the first stage equation of TSLS (Equation (10.2)) with the modification that the effect on X_i of a change in Z_i is allowed to vary from one individual to the next.

The TSLS estimator is $\hat{\beta}_1^{TSLS} = s_{ZY}/s_{ZX}$ (Equation (10.4)), the ratio of the sample covariance between Z and Y to the sample covariance between Z and X. If the observations are i.i.d., then these sample covariances are consistent estimators of the population covariances, so $\hat{\beta}_1^{TSLS} \xrightarrow{p} \sigma_{ZY}/\sigma_{ZX}$. Suppose that π_{1i} and β_{1i} are distributed independently of u_i, v_i, and Z_i; that $E(u_i|Z_i) = E(v_i|Z_i) = 0$; and that $E(\pi_{1i}) \neq 0$. It is shown in Appendix 11.4 that, under these assumptions,

$$\hat{\beta}_1^{TSLS} = \frac{s_{ZY}}{s_{ZX}} \xrightarrow{p} \frac{\sigma_{ZY}}{\sigma_{ZX}} = \frac{E(\beta_{1i}\pi_{1i})}{E(\pi_{1i})}. \tag{11.11}$$

That is, the TSLS estimator converges in probability to the ratio of the expected value of the product of β_{1i} and π_{1i} to the expected value of π_{1i}.

The final ratio in Equation (11.11) can be interpreted as a weighted average of the individual causal effects β_{1i}. The weights are π_{1i}, which measure the degree to which the instrument influences whether the ith individual receives treatment. Thus, the TSLS estimator is a consistent estimator of a weighted average of the individual causal effects, where the individuals who receive the most weight are those for whom the instrument is most influential.

To see this, consider two cases in which the TSLS estimator is a consistent estimator of the average causal effect and one in which it is not. First, suppose that all the individuals have the same causal effect, so $\beta_{1i} = \beta_1$ for all i. Then the final expression in Equation (11.11) simplifies to $E(\beta_{1i}\pi_{1i})/E(\pi_{1i}) = \beta_1 E(\pi_{1i})/E(\pi_{1i}) = \beta_1$, and the TSLS estimator is a consistent estimator of the causal effect β_1. That is, if the causal effect is the same for all individuals, then this causal effect is consistently estimated by TSLS, even if there is heterogeneity in the influence of the instrument on the probability of treatment.

Second, suppose that there are heterogeneous causal effects, but that the instrument affects each individual equally, so that $\pi_{1i} = \pi_1$. In this case, the final expression in Equation (11.11) simplifies to $E(\beta_{1i}\pi_{1i})/E(\pi_{1i}) = \pi_1 E(\beta_{1i})/\pi_1 = E(\beta_{1i})$, and the TSLS estimator is a consistent estimator of the average causal effect $E(\beta_{1i})$. Thus, if the instrument has the same influence on all individuals, the TSLS estimator is a consistent estimator of the average causal effect even if there is population heterogeneity in the treatment effect.

As a third example, suppose that Z_i has no influence on the treatment decision for half the population (for them, $\pi_{1i} = 0$) and that Z_i has the same, nonzero influence on the treatment decision for the other half (for them, π_{1i} is a nonzero constant). Then TSLS is a consistent estimator of the average treatment effect in the half of the population for which the instrument influences the treatment decision. For example, suppose that subjects in a job training program are given a random priority number Z, which influences (but does not determine) their ability to enroll. Some of the subjects already have the resume-writing skills taught in the program (for them, $\beta_{1i} = 0$), and they consider the training program a waste of time and never enroll whatever their priority number is (so $\pi_{1i} = 0$). However, for subjects who want the skills taught in the program (for whom $\beta_{1i} > 0$), the priority number has an effect. In this example, TSLS estimates the average causal effect for those subjects who would like to enroll in the program. The average causal effect among those who would like to enroll is greater than the average causal effect for the full population, which includes subjects for whom the program is effective and subjects for whom it is not.

In general, the final ratio in Equation (11.11) is a weighted average of the individual causal effects β_{1i}, weighted by the influence of the instrument on the treatment. If the effect of the instrument, π_{1i}, is independent of the causal effect β_{1i}, then $E(\beta_{1i}\pi_{1i}) = E(\beta_{1i})E(\pi_{1i})$, so $E(\beta_{1i}\pi_{1i})/E(\pi_{1i}) = E(\beta_{1i})$, and thus TSLS is a consistent estimator of the causal effect. In practice, however, the influence of the instrument can be related to the causal effect because an individual's decision to receive treatment (to participate in the program) can depend on how beneficial he or she thinks the treatment will be. Accordingly, the causal effects of individuals for whom the instrument is an important influence in determining whether they receive treatment are given more weight in the average in Equation (11.11) than are the causal effects of individuals for whom the instrument is not influential.

Implications.   This discussion has two implications. First, in the circumstances in which OLS would normally be consistent — that is, when $E(u_i | X_i) = 0$ — the OLS estimator continues to be consistent in the presence of heterogeneous causal effects in the population; however, because there is no single causal effect, the OLS estimator is properly interpreted as a consistent estimator of the average causal effect in the population being studied.

Second, if an individual's decision to receive treatment depends on the effectiveness of the treatment for that individual, then the TSLS estimator in general is not a consistent estimator of the average causal effect. Instead, TSLS estimates a weighted average of the causal effect, where the causal effects of the individuals who are most influenced by the instrument receive the greatest weight. This leads to a disconcerting situation in which two researchers, armed with different instrumental variables that are both valid in the sense that both are relevant and exogenous, would obtain different estimates of "the" causal effect, even in large samples. Although both estimators provide some insight into the distribution of the causal effects via their respective weighted averages of the form in Equation (11.11), neither estimator is in general a consistent estimator of the average causal effect.[4]

Example: The cardiac catheterization study.

Sections 10.5 and 11.5 discuss McClellan, McNeil, and Newhouse's (1991) study of the effect on mortality of cardiac catheterization of heart attack patients. The authors used instrumental variables regression, with the relative distance to a cardiac catheterization hospital as the instrumental variable. Based on their TSLS estimates, they found that cardiac catheterization had little or no effect on health outcomes. This result is surprising: medical procedures such as cardiac catheterization are subjected to rigorous clinical trials prior to approval for widespread use. Moreover, cardiac catheterization allows surgeons to perform medical interventions that would have required major surgery a decade earlier, making these interventions safer and, presumably, better for long-term patient health. How could this econometric study fail to find beneficial effects of cardiac catheterization?

One possible answer is that there is heterogeneity in the treatment effect of cardiac catheterization. For some patients, this is an effective intervention, but for others, perhaps those who are healthier, this procedure is less effective or, given the risks involved with any surgery, perhaps on net ineffective. Thus, the average causal effect in the population of heart attack patients could be, and presumably is, positive. The IV estimator, however, measures a marginal effect, not an average effect, where the marginal effect is the effect of the procedure on those patients for whom distance to the hospital is an important factor in whether they receive treatment. But those patients could be just the relatively healthy patients for whom, on the margin, cardiac catheterization is a relatively ineffective procedure. If so, McClellan, McNeil, and Newhouse's (1991) TSLS estimator measures the effect of the procedure for the marginal patient (for whom it is relatively ineffective), not for the average patient (for whom it might be effective).

---

[4]There are several good (but advanced) discussions of the effect of population heterogeneity on program evaluation estimators. These include the survey by Heckman, LaLonde, and Smith (1999, Section 7) and James Heckman's lecture delivered when he received the Nobel Prize in economics (Heckman, (2001, Section 7)). The latter reference and Angrist, Graddy, and Imbens (2000) provide detailed discussion of the random effects model (which treats β_{1i} as varying across individuals) and provide more general versions of the result in Equation (11.11).

11.8 Conclusion

In Chapter 1, we defined the causal effect in terms of the expected outcome of an ideal randomized controlled experiment. If a randomized controlled experiment is available or can be performed, it can provide compelling evidence on the causal effect under study, although even randomized controlled experiments are subject to potentially important threats to internal and external validity.

Despite their advantages, randomized controlled experiments in economics face severe hurdles, including ethical concerns and cost. The insights of experimental methods can, however, be applied to quasi-experiments, in which special circumstances make it seem "as if" randomization has occurred. In quasi-experiments, the causal effect can be estimated using a differences-in-differences estimator, possibly augmented with additional regressors; if the "as if" randomization only partly influences the treatment, then instrumental variables regression can be used instead. An important advantage of quasi-experiments is that the source of the "as if" randomness in the data is usually transparent and thus can be evaluated in a concrete way. An important threat confronting quasi-experiments is that sometimes the "as if" randomization is not really random, so the treatment (or the instrumental variable) is correlated with omitted variables and the resulting estimator of the causal effect is biased.

Quasi-experiments provide a bridge between observational data sets and true randomized controlled experiments. The econometric methods used in this chapter for analyzing quasi-experiments are those developed, in different contexts, in earlier chapters: OLS, panel data estimation methods, and instrumental variables regression. What differentiates quasi-experiments from the applications examined in Part II and earlier in Part III is the way in which these methods are interpreted and the data sets to which they are applied. Quasi-experiments provide econometricians with a way to think about how to acquire new data sets, how to think of instrumental variables, and how to evaluate the plausibility of the exogeneity assumptions that underlie OLS and instrumental variables estimation.[5]

---

[5]Shadish, Cook, and Campbell (2002) provide a comprehensive treatment of experiments and quasi-experiments in the social sciences and in psychology. Examples of experiments in economics include negative income tax experiments (for example, see **www.aspe.hhs.gov/hsp/sime–dime83**) and the Rand health insurance experiment (Newhouse (1983)). To learn more about quasi-experiments in economics, see Meyer (1995), Rosenzweig and Wolpin (2000), and Angrist and Krueger (2001).

Summary

1. The causal effect is defined in terms of an ideal randomized controlled experiment, and the causal effect can be estimated by the difference in the average outcomes for the treatment and control groups. Actual experiments with human subjects deviate from an ideal experiment for various practical reasons, especially the failure of people to comply with the experimental protocol.

2. If the *actual* treatment level X_i is random, then the treatment effect can be estimated by regressing the outcome on the treatment, optionally using additional pretreatment characteristics as regressors to improve efficiency. If the *assigned* treatment Z_i is random but the actual treatment X_i is partly determined by individual choice, then the causal effect can be estimated by instrumental variables regression using Z_i as an instrument.

3. In a quasi-experiment, variations in laws or circumstances or accidents of nature are treated "as if" they induce random assignment to treatment and control groups. If the actual treatment is "as if" random, then the causal effect can be estimated by regression (possibly with additional pretreatment characteristics as regressors); if the assigned treatment is "as if" random, then the causal effect can be estimated by instrumental variables regression.

4. A key threat to the internal validity of a quasi-experimental study is whether the "as if" randomization actually results in exogeneity. Because of behavioral responses, just because an instrument is generated by "as if" randomization does not mean it is necessarily exogenous in the sense required for a valid instrumental variable.

5. When the treatment effect varies from one individual to the next, the OLS estimator is a consistent estimator of the average causal effect if the actual treatment is randomly assigned or "as if" randomly assigned. However, the instrumental variables estimator is a weighted average of the individual treatment effects, where the individuals for whom the instrument is most influential receive the greatest weight.

Key Terms

program evaluation (374)

causal effect (376)

treatment effect (376)

differences estimator (376)

partial compliance (378)

attrition (378)

Hawthorne effect (379)

differences estimator with additional
    regressors (383)

conditional mean independence (383)

differences-in-differences estimator (385)

differences-in-differences estimator with
   additional regressors (387)

quasi-experiment (399)

natural experiment (399)

repeated cross-sectional data (403)

average causal effect (408)

average treatment effect (408)

Review the Concepts

11.1 A researcher studying the effects of a new fertilizer on crop yields plans to carry out an experiment in which different amounts of the fertilizer are applied to 100 different one-acre parcels of land. There will be four treatment levels. Treatment level one is no fertilizer; treatment level two is 50% of the manufacturer's recommended amount of fertilizer; treatment level three is 100%; and treatment level four is 150%. The researcher plans to apply treatment level one to the first 25 parcels of land, treatment level two to the second 25 parcels, and so forth. Can you suggest a better way to assign treatment levels? Why is your proposal better than the researcher's method?

11.2 A clinical trial is carried out for a new cholesterol-lowering drug. The drug is given to 500 patients and a placebo given to another 500 patients, using random assignment of the patients. How would you estimate the treatment effect of the drug? Suppose that you had data on the weight, age, and gender of each patient. Could you use these data to improve your estimate? Explain. Suppose that you had data on the cholesterol levels of each patient before they entered the experiment. Could you use these data to improve your estimate? Explain.

11.3 Researchers studying the STAR data report anecdotal evidence that school principals were pressured by some parents to place their children in the small classes. Suppose that some principals succumbed to this pressure and transferred some children into the small classes. How would this compromise the internal validity of the study? Suppose that you had data on the original random assignment of each student before the principal's intervention. How could you use this information to restore the internal validity of the study?

11.4 Explain whether experimental effects (like the Hawthorne effect) might be important in each of the experiments in the previous three questions.

11.5 Section 10.1 gives a hypothetical example in which some schools were damaged by an earthquake. Explain why this is an example of a quasi-experiment. How could you use the induced changes in class sizes to estimate the effect of class size on test scores?

Exercises

*11.1 Using the results in Table 11.1, calculate the following for each grade: an estimate of the small class treatment effect, relative to the regular class; its standard error; and its 95% confidence interval. (For this exercise, ignore the results for regular classes with aides.)

11.2 For the following calculations, use the results in column (4) of Table 11.2. Consider two classrooms, A and B, with identical values of the regressors in column (4) of Table 11.2, except that:

    a. Classroom A is a "small class" and classroom B is a "regular class." Construct a 95% confidence interval for the expected difference in average test scores.

    b. Classroom A has a teacher with five years of experience and classroom B has a teacher with 10 years of experience. Construct a 95% confidence interval for the expected difference in average test scores.

    c. Classroom A is a small class with a teacher with five years of experience and classroom B is a regular class with a teacher with 10 years of experience. Construct a 95% confidence interval for the expected difference in average test scores. (*Hint:* In STAR, the teachers were randomly assigned to the different types of classrooms.)

    d. Why is the intercept missing from column (4)?

11.3 Consider a study to evaluate the effect on college student grades of dorm room Internet connections. In a large dorm, half the rooms are randomly wired for high-speed Internet connections (the treatment group), and final course grades are collected for all residents. Which of the following pose threats to internal validity, and why?

    a. Midway through the year all the male athletes move into a fraternity and drop out of the study (their final grades are not observed).

    *b. Engineering students assigned to the control group put together a local area network so that they can share a private wireless Internet connection that they pay for jointly.

    c. The art majors in the treatment group never learn how to access their Internet accounts.

d. The economics majors in the treatment group provide access to their Internet connection to those in the control group, for a fee.

11.4 Suppose that there are panel data for $T = 2$ time periods for a randomized controlled experiment, where the first observation ($t = 1$) is taken before the experiment and the second observation ($t = 2$) is for the post-treatment period. Suppose that the treatment is binary, that is, $X_{it} = 1$ if the ith individual is in the treatment group and $t = 2$, and $X_{it} = 0$ otherwise. Further suppose that the treatment effect can be modeled using the specification

$$Y_{it} = \alpha_i + \beta_1 X_{it} + u_{it}, \tag{11.12}$$

where α_i are individual-specific effects (see Equation (8.10)) with a mean of zero and a variance of σ_α^2 and u_{it} is an error term, where u_{it} is homoskedastic, $\text{cov}(u_{i1}, u_{i2}) = 0$, and $\text{cov}(u_{it}, \alpha_i) = 0$ for all i. Let $\hat{\beta}_1^{differences}$ denote the differences estimator, that is, the OLS estimator in a regression of Y_{i2} on X_{i2} with an intercept, and let $\hat{\beta}_1^{diffs\text{-}in\text{-}diffs}$ denote the differences-in-differences estimator, that is, the estimator of β_1 based on the OLS regression of $\Delta Y_i = Y_{i2} - Y_{i1}$ against $\Delta X_i = X_{i2} - X_{i1}$ and an intercept.

*a. Show that $n\text{var}(\hat{\beta}_1^{differences}) \longrightarrow (\sigma_u^2 + \sigma_\alpha^2)/\text{var}(X_{i2})$. (*Hint:* Use the homoskedasticity-only formulas for the variance of the OLS estimator in Appendix 4.4.)

b. Show that $n\text{var}(\hat{\beta}_1^{diffs\text{-}in\text{-}diffs}) \longrightarrow 2\sigma_u^2/\text{var}(X_{i2})$. (*Hint:* Note that $\Delta X_i = X_{i2}$; why?)

c. Based on your answers to (a) and (b), when would you prefer the differences-in-differences estimator over the differences estimator, based purely on efficiency considerations?

11.5 Suppose you have panel data from an experiment with $T = 2$ periods (so $t = 1, 2$). Consider the panel data regression model with fixed individual and time effects and individual characteristics W_i that do not change over time, such as gender. Let the treatment be binary, so $X_{it} = 1$ for $t = 2$ for the individuals in the treatment group and let $X_{it} = 0$ otherwise. Consider the population regression model

$$Y_{it} = \alpha_i + \beta_1 X_{it} + \beta_2(D_t \times W_i) + \beta_0 D_t + v_{it}, \tag{11.13}$$

where α_i are individual fixed effects, D_t is the binary variable that equals 1 if $t = 2$ and equals 0 if $t = 1$, $D_t \times W_i$ is the product of D_t and W_i, and the α's and β's are unknown coefficients. Let $\Delta Y_i = Y_{i2} - Y_{i1}$. Derive Equation (11.5) (in the case of a single W regressor, so $r = 1$) from Equation(11.13).

11.6 Suppose you have the same data as in Exercise 11.5 (panel data with two periods, n observations), but ignore the W regressor. Consider the alternative regression model

$$Y_{it} = \beta_0 + \beta_1 X_{it} + \beta_2 G_i + \beta_3 D_t + u_{it},\qquad(11.14)$$

where $G_i = 1$ if the individual is in the treatment group and $G_i = 0$ if the individual is in the control group. Show that the OLS estimator of β_1 in Equation (11.14) is the differences-in-differences estimator in Equation (11.3). (*Hint:* See Section 6.3).

11.7 Derive the final equality in Equation (11.9). (*Hint:* Use the definition of the covariance and the fact that, because the actual treatment X_i is random, β_{1i} and X_i are independently distributed.)

APPENDIX

11.1 The Project STAR Data Set

The Project STAR public access data set contains data on test scores, treatment groups, and student and teacher characteristics for the four years of the experiment, from academic year 1985–86 to academic year 1988–89. The test score data analyzed in this chapter are the sum of the scores on the math and reading portions of the Stanford Achievement Test. The binary variable "Boy" in Table 11.2 indicates whether the student is a boy (= 1) or girl (= 0); the binary variables "Black" and "Race other than black or white" indicate the student's race. The binary variable "Free lunch eligible" indicates whether the student is eligible for a free lunch during that school year. The teacher's years of experience are the total years of experience of the teacher whom the student had in the grade for which the test data apply. The data set also indicates which school the student attended in a given year, making it possible to construct binary school-specific indicator variables.

Extension of the Differences-in-Differences Estimator to Multiple Time Periods[6]

When there are more than two time periods, the causal effect can be estimated using the fixed effects regression model of Chapter 8.

First consider the case that there are no additional "W" regressors. Then the population regression model is the combined time and individual fixed effects regression model (Equation (8.18)):

$$Y_{it} = \beta_0 + \beta_1 X_{it} + \gamma_2 D2_i + \cdots + \gamma_n Dn_i + \delta_2 B2_t + \cdots + \delta_T BT_t + v_{it}, \quad (11.15)$$

where $i = 1, \ldots, n$ denotes the individual, $t = 1, \ldots, T$ denotes the time period of measurement, $X_{it} = 1$ if the ith individual has received the treatment by date t and $= 0$ otherwise, $D2_i$ is a binary variable indicating the ith individual (that is, $D2_i = 1$ for $i = 2$ and 0 otherwise), $B2_t$ is a binary variable indicating the second time period and the other binary variables are defined similarly, v_{it} is an error term, and $\beta_0, \beta_1, \gamma_2, \ldots, \gamma_n, \delta_2, \ldots, \delta_T$ are unknown coefficients. Including the individual effects (the binary variables indicating each individual) controls for unobserved individual characteristics that affect Y. Including the time effects (the binary variables indicating the time periods) controls for differences from one period to the next that affect the outcome regardless of whether the individual is in the treatment or control group, for example, an economic recession that occurs during the course of a job training program experiment. When $T = 2$, the time and fixed effects regression model in Equation (11.15) simplifies to the differences-in-differences regression model in Equation (11.4). Methods for estimating β_1 in Equation (11.15) are discussed in Section 8.4.

Additional regressors (W) that measure pretreatment characteristics, or characteristics that do not change over time, can be incorporated into the fixed effects regression framework. As discussed in the context of Equation (11.5), in the differences-in-differences specification with additional regressors the W regressors affect the *change* in Y from one period to the next, not its *level*. An individual's prior education, for example, is an observable factor that might influence the change in earnings whether or not he or she is in the job training program. Thus, to extend Equation (11.5) to multiple periods, the W regressors are interacted with the time effect binary variables.

---

[6]This appendix draws on material in Sections 8.3 and 8.4.

For convenience, suppose there is a single W regressor; then the multiperiod extension of Equation (11.5) is

$$
\begin{aligned}
Y_{it} = \beta_0 + \beta_1 X_{it} + \beta_2(B2_t \times W_i) + \ \cdots \ + \beta_T(BT_t \times W_i) + \\
\gamma_2 D2_i + \ \cdots \ + \gamma_n Dn_i + \delta_2 B2_t + \ \cdots \ + \delta_T BT_t + v_{it},
\end{aligned}
\tag{11.16}
$$

where the regressor $B2_t \times W_i$ is the interaction between the binary variable $B2_t$ and W_i (etc.). When there are only two time periods, the population regression model with individual fixed effects, time effects, the W regressors, and the W's interacted with the single time binary variable $B2_t$ is the same as the population regression model in Equation (11.5) (Exercise 11.5).

Panel data with multiple time periods also can be used to trace out causal effects over time, thereby asking, for example, whether the effect on income of a job training program persists or wears off over time. The methods for doing this are discussed in Chapter 13 in the context of estimating causal effects using time series data.

APPENDIX 11.3 | Conditional Mean Independence

This appendix discusses the conditional mean independence assumption mentioned in Section 11.3 and its role in the estimation of a common treatment effect β_1. This discussion focuses on the differences estimator with additional regressors ($\hat{\beta}_1$ in Equation (11.2)) but the ideas generalize to the differences-in-differences estimator with additional regressors.

The **conditional mean independence** assumption is that the conditional mean of the error term u_i in Equation (11.2) can depend on the pretreatment characteristics $W_{1i}, \ldots, W_{ri}$, but not on X_i, specifically,

$$
E(u_i | X_i, W_{1i}, \ldots, W_{ri}) = \gamma_0 + \gamma_1 W_{1i} + \ \cdots \ + \gamma_r W_{ri}.
\tag{11.17}
$$

Under the conditional mean independence assumption, the unobserved characteristics in u_i can be correlated with the observed pretreatment characteristics (the W's), but given the W's, the conditional mean of u_i does not depend on the treatment.

The assumption of linearity in Equation (11.17) is not restrictive if W_i is a complete set of binary indicator variables. If a W variable is continuous, then the linear conditional expectation in Equation (11.17) can be interpreted as a nonlinear conditional expectation with suitable redefinition of the W's. As discussed in Section 6.2, for example, the additional terms on the right hand side of Equation (11.17) can be polynomial functions of an original continuous W.

It is useful to consider three cases in which Equation (11.17) holds. First, if the first least squares assumption of Key Concept 5.4 holds, then $E(u_i | X_i, W_{1i}, \ldots, W_{ri}) = 0$ so Equation (11.17) is satisfied and the conditional expectation equals zero.

Second, Equation (11.17) holds if the treatment X_i is randomly assigned, and thus is distributed independently of all individual characteristics, whether observed and included in the regression (the W variables) or unobserved and in the error term. If X_i is distributed independently of u_i and W_i, then the conditional distribution of u_i given W_i and X_i does not depend on X_i, so in particular the mean of that conditional distribution does not depend on X_i (even though it might depend on W_i). In the job training program example, if treatment is assigned randomly then it will not pick up the effect of prior education whether education is an included regressor or an omitted part of the error term.

In the third case, the treatment X_i is assigned randomly, *conditional on* W_i. In this case, the mean of u_i does not depend on X_i because, given W_i, treatment is randomly assigned. If, conditional on W_i, u_i and X_i are independent, then the conditional distribution of u_i given W_i does not depend on X_i, so its conditional mean does not depend on X_i even though it might depend on W_i. If W_i is a set of indicator variables, conditional mean independence means that X_i is randomly assigned within each group, or "block," defined by the indicator variables, but that the assignment probability can vary from one block to the next. Random assignment within blocks of individuals is sometimes called **block randomization**.

Under the conditional mean assumption, β_1 is the treatment effect. To see this, compute the conditional expectation of both sides of Equation (11.2):

$$
\begin{aligned}
E(Y_i | X_i, W_{1i}, \ldots, W_{ri}) &= \beta_0 + \beta_1 X_i + \beta_2 W_{1i} + \cdots + \beta_{r+1} W_{ri} + \\
&\quad E(u_i | X_i, W_{1i}, \ldots, W_{ri}) \\
&= \beta_0 + \beta_1 X_i + \beta_2 W_{1i} + \cdots + \beta_{r+1} W_{ri} + \gamma_0 + \gamma_1 W_{1i} + \cdots + \gamma_r W_{ri},
\end{aligned} \tag{11.18}
$$

where the second equality follows from the conditional mean independence assumption (Equation (11.17)). Evaluating the conditional expectation in Equation (11.18) at $X_i = 1$ (treatment group) and at $X_i = 0$ (control group) and subtracting yields

$$
E(Y_i | X_i = 1, W_{1i}, \ldots, W_{ri}) - E(Y_i | X_i = 0, W_{1i}, \ldots, W_{ri}) = \beta_1. \tag{11.19}
$$

The left-hand side of Equation (11.19) is the causal effect defined by an experiment where individuals with given W characteristics are randomly assigned to treatment and control groups, and the causal effect is the expected value of the outcome. Because this causal effect does not depend on W, it is also the causal effect for a randomly selected member of the population.

When Equation (11.17) holds (along with the second through fourth least squares assumptions in Key Concept 5.4), the differences estimator with additional regressors is consistent. Intuitively, by including W_i as a regressor, the differences estimator controls for the fact that the treatment probability can depend on W_i. The mathematical argument that $\hat{\beta}_1$ is consistent under the conditional mean independence assumption involves matrix algebra and is left to Exercise 16.9.

Conditional mean independence also provides a framework for interpreting regressions with observational data in which some coefficients (on "control" variables) do not have a causal interpretation but other coefficients do, as in Tables 5.2, 6.2, and 7.2.

APPENDIX 11.4 | IV Estimation When the Causal Effect Varies Across Individuals

This appendix derives the probability limit of the TSLS estimator in Equation (11.11) when there is population heterogeneity in the treatment effect and in the influence of the instrument on the receipt of treatment. Specifically, it is assumed that the IV regression assumptions in Key Concept 10.4 hold, except that Equations (11.8) and (11.10) hold with heterogeneous effects. Further assume that π_{1i} and β_{1i} are distributed independently of u_i, v_i, and Z_i; that $E(u_i|Z_i) = E(v_i|Z_i) = 0$; and that $E(\pi_{1i}) \neq 0$.

Because (X_i, Y_i, Z_i), $i = 1, \ldots, n$ are i.i.d. with four moments, the law of large numbers in Key Concept 2.6 applies and

$$\hat{\beta}_1^{TSLS} = s_{ZY}/s_{ZX} \xrightarrow{p} \sigma_{ZY}/\sigma_{ZX} \tag{11.20}$$

(Appendix 3.3 and Exercise 15.2). The task thus is to obtain expressions for σ_{ZY} and σ_{ZX} in terms of the moments of π_{1i}, and β_{1i}. Now $\sigma_{ZX} = E[(Z_i - \mu_Z)(X_i - \mu_X)] = E[(Z_i - \mu_Z)X_i]$. Substituting Equation (11.10) into this expression for σ_{ZX} yields,

$$\begin{aligned} \sigma_{ZX} &= E[(Z_i - \mu_Z)(\pi_0 + \pi_{1i}Z_i + v_i)] \\ &= \pi_0 \times 0 + E[\pi_{1i}Z_i(Z_i - \mu_Z)] + \text{cov}(Z_i, v_i) \\ &= \sigma_Z^2 E(\pi_{1i}), \end{aligned} \tag{11.21}$$

where the second equality obtains because $\mathrm{cov}(Z_i, v_i) = 0$ (which follows from the assumption $E(v_i | Z_i) = 0$; see Equation (2.25)) and because $E[\pi_{1i} Z_i (Z_i - \mu_Z)] = E\{E[\pi_{1i} Z_i (Z_i - \mu_Z)] | Z_i\} = E(\pi_{1i}) E[Z_i(Z_i - \mu_Z)] = \sigma_Z^2 E(\pi_{1i})$ (using the law of iterated expectations in Equation (2.18) and the assumption that π_{1i} is independent of Z_i).

Next consider σ_{ZY}. Substituting Equation (11.10) into Equation (11.8) yields $Y_i = \beta_0 + \beta_{1i}(\pi_0 + \pi_{1i} Z_i + v_i) + u_i$, so

$$
\begin{aligned}
\sigma_{ZY} &= E[(Z_i - \mu_Z) Y_i] &\text{(11.22)}\\
&= E[(Z_i - \mu_Z)(\beta_0 + \beta_{1i}\pi_0 + \beta_{1i}\pi_{1i} Z_i + \beta_{1i} v_i + u_i)]\\
&= \beta_0 \times 0 + \pi_0 \mathrm{cov}(Z_i, \beta_{1i}) + E[\beta_{1i}\pi_{1i} Z_i (Z_i - \mu_Z)] + E[\beta_{1i} v_i (Z_i - \mu_Z)] + \mathrm{cov}(Z_i, u_i).
\end{aligned}
$$

Because β_{1i} and Z_i are independently distributed, $\mathrm{cov}(Z_i, \beta_{1i}) = 0$; because β_{1i} is distributed independently of v_i and Z_i and $E(v_i | Z_i) = 0$, $E[\beta_{1i} v_i (Z_i - \mu_Z)] = E(\beta_{1i}) E[v_i(Z_i - \mu_Z)] = 0$; because $E(u_i | Z_i) = 0$, $\mathrm{cov}(Z_i, u_i) = 0$; and because β_{1i} and π_{1i} are distributed independently of Z_i, $E[\beta_{1i}\pi_{1i} Z_i (Z_i - \mu_Z)] = \sigma_Z^2 E(\beta_{1i}\pi_{1i})$. Thus, the final expression in Equation (11.22) yields

$$
\sigma_{ZY} = \sigma_Z^2 E(\beta_{1i}\pi_{1i}). \tag{11.23}
$$

Substituting Equations (11.21) and (11.23) into Equation (11.20) yields $\hat{\beta}_1^{TSLS} \xrightarrow{p} \sigma_Z^2 E(\beta_{1i}\pi_{1i}) / \sigma_Z^2 E(\pi_{1i}) = E(\beta_{1i}\pi_{1i})/E(\pi_{1i})$, which is the result stated in Equation (11.11).

PART FOUR | Regression Analysis of Economic Time Series Data

CHAPTER 12

Introduction to Time Series Regression and Forecasting

Time series data—data collected for a single entity at multiple points in time—can be used to answer quantitative questions for which cross-sectional data are inadequate. One such question is, what is the causal effect on a variable of interest, Y, of a change in another variable, X, over time? In other words, what is the *dynamic* causal effect on Y of a change in X? For example, what is the effect on traffic fatalities of a law requiring passengers to wear seatbelts, both initially and subsequently as drivers adjust to the law? Another such question is, what is your best forecast of the value of some variable at a future date? For example, what is your best forecast of next month's rate of inflation, interest rates, or stock prices? Both of these questions—one about dynamic causal effects, the other about economic forecasting—can be answered using time series data. But time series data pose special challenges, and overcoming those challenges requires some new techniques.

Chapters 12–14 introduce techniques for the econometric analysis of time series data and apply these techniques to the problems of forecasting and estimating dynamic causal effects. Chapter 12 introduces the basic concepts and tools of regression with time series data and applies them to economic forecasting. In Chapter 13, the concepts and tools developed in Chapter 12 are applied to the problem of estimating dynamic causal effects using time series data. Chapter 14 takes up some more advanced topics in time series analysis, including forecasting multiple time series and modeling changes in volatility over time.

The empirical problem studied in this chapter is forecasting the rate of inflation, that is, the percentage increase in overall prices. While in a sense forecasting is just an application of regression analysis, forecasting is quite different from the estimation of causal effects, the focus of this book until now. As discussed in Section 12.1, models that are useful for forecasting need not have a causal interpretation: if you see pedestrians carrying umbrellas you might forecast rain, even though carrying an umbrella does not *cause* it to rain. Section 12.2 introduces some basic concepts of time series analysis and presents some examples of economic time series data. Section 12.3 presents time series regression models in which the regressors are past values of the dependent variable; these "autoregressive" models use the history of inflation to forecast its future. Often, forecasts based on autoregressions can be improved by adding additional predictor variables and their past values, or "lags," as regressors, and these so-called autoregressive distributed lag models are introduced in Section 12.4. For example, we find that inflation forecasts made using lagged values of the rate of unemployment in addition to lagged inflation—that is, forecasts based on an empirical Phillips curve—improve upon the autoregressive inflation forecasts. A practical issue is deciding how many past values to include in autoregressions and autoregressive distributed lag models, and Section 12.5 describes methods for making this decision.

The assumption that the future will be like the past is an important one in time series regression, sufficiently so that it is given its own name, "stationarity." Time series variables can fail to be stationary in various ways, but two are especially relevant for regression analysis of economic time series data: (1) the series can have persistent, long-run movements, that is, the series can have trends; and (2) the population regression can be unstable over time, that is, the population regression can have breaks. These departures from stationarity jeopardize forecasts and inferences based on time series regression. Fortunately, there are statistical procedures for detecting trends and breaks and, once detected, for adjusting the model specification. These procedures are presented in Sections 12.6 and 12.7.

12.1 Using Regression Models for Forecasting

Chapter 4 began by considering the problem of a school superintendent who wants to know how much test scores would increase if she reduces class sizes in her school district; that is, the superintendent wants to know the causal effect on test scores of a change in class size. Accordingly, Parts II and III focused on using regression analysis to estimate causal effects using observational data.

Now consider a different problem, that of a parent moving to a metropolitan area and choosing a town within that area in part based on the local school system. The parent would like to know how the different school districts perform on standardized tests. Suppose, however, that test score data are unavailable (perhaps they are confidential) but data on class sizes are. The parent thus must guess at how well the different districts perform on standardized tests based on a limited amount of information. That is, the parent's problem is to forecast average test scores in a given district based on information related to test scores, such as class size.

The superintendent's problem and the parent's problem are conceptually very different. Multiple regression is a powerful tool for both, but because the problems are different, the criteria used to assess the suitability of a particular regression model is different as well. To obtain the credible estimates of causal effects desired by the superintendent, we must worry about the issues raised in Chapter 7: omitted variable bias, selection, simultaneous causality, and so forth. In contrast, to obtain the reliable forecast desired by the parent, it is important that the estimated regression have good explanatory power, that its coefficients be estimated precisely, and that it is stable in the sense that the regression estimated on one set of data can be reliably used to make forecasts using other data.

For example, recall the regression of test scores on the student-teacher ratio (STR) from Chapter 4:

$$TestScore = 698.9 - 2.28 \times STR. \tag{12.1}$$

We concluded that this regression is not useful for the superintendent: the OLS estimator of the slope is biased because of omitted variables such as the composition of the student body and their other learning opportunities outside school. The superintendent cannot change the district's average income or the fraction of non-English speakers, both of which affect test scores. Because these variables are also correlated with class size, there is omitted variable bias. Thus the regression of test scores on the student-teacher ratio yields a biased estimator of the effect on test scores of a change in the student-teacher ratio, and Equation (12.1) does not answer the superintendent's question.

Nevertheless, Equation (12.1) could be useful to the parent trying to choose a district. To be sure, class size is not the only determinant of test performance, but from the parent's perspective what matters is whether it is a reliable predictor of test performance. The parent interested in forecasting test scores does not care whether the coefficient in Equation (12.1) estimates the causal effect on test scores of class size. Rather, the parent simply wants the regression to explain much of the variation in test scores across districts and to be stable, that is, to apply to the districts to which the parent is considering moving. Although omitted variable bias makes Equation (12.1) useless for answering the causal question, it still can be useful for forecasting.

The applications in this chapter are different than the test score/class size prediction problem because this chapter focuses on using time series data to forecast future events. Yet time series forecasting is similar conceptually to the parent's problem: the task is to use the known values of some variables (current and past values of the rate of price inflation instead of class size) to forecast the value of another variable (future inflation instead of test scores). As in the parent's problem, regression models can produce reliable forecasts, even if their coefficients have no causal interpretation. In Chapter 13, we return to problems like that faced by the school superintendent and discuss the estimation of causal effects using time series variables.

12.2 Introduction to Time Series Data and Serial Correlation

This section introduces some basic concepts and terminology that arise in time series econometrics. A good place to start any analysis of time series data is by plotting the data, so that is where we begin.

The Rates of Inflation and Unemployment in the United States

Figure 12.1a plots the U.S. rate of inflation—the annual percentage change in prices in the United States, as measured by the Consumer Price Index (CPI)—from 1960 to 1999 (the data are described in Appendix 12.1). The inflation rate

FIGURE 12.1   Inflation and Unemployment in the United States, 1960–1999

(a) U.S. CPI Inflation Rate

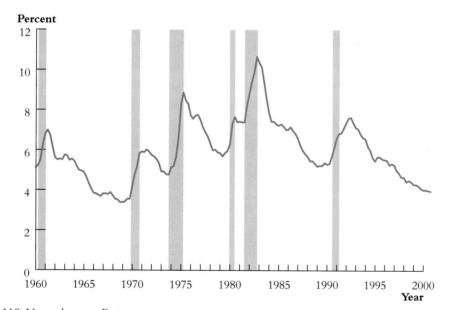

(b) U.S. Unemployment Rate

Price inflation in the United States (Figure 12.1a) drifted upwards from 1960 until 1980, and then fell sharply during the early 1980s. The unemployment rate in the United States (Figure 12.1b) rises during recessions (the shaded episodes) and falls during expansions.

was low in the 1960s, rose through the 1970s to a postwar peak of 15.5% in the first quarter of 1980 (that is, January, February, and March 1980), and then fell to less than 3% by the end of the 1990s. As can be seen in Figure 12.1a, the inflation rate also can fluctuate by one percentage point or more from one quarter to the next.

The U.S. unemployment rate—the fraction of the labor force out of work, as measured in the Current Population Survey (see Appendix 3.1)—is plotted in Figure 12.1b. Changes in the unemployment rate are mainly associated with the business cycle in the United States. For example, the unemployment rate increased during the recessions of 1960–61, 1970, 1974–75, the twin recessions of 1980 and 1981–82, and the recession of 1990–91, episodes denoted by shading in Figure 12.1b.

Lags, First Differences, Logarithms, and Growth Rates

The observation on the time series variable Y made at date t is denoted Y_t, and the total number of observations is denoted T. The interval between observations, that is, the period of time between observation t and observation $t + 1$, is some unit of time such as weeks, months, quarters (three-month units), or years. For example, the inflation data studied in this chapter are quarterly, so the unit of time (a "period") is a quarter of a year.

Special terminology and notation are used to indicate future and past values of Y. The value of Y in the previous period is called its **first lagged value** or, more simply, its **first lag,** and is denoted Y_{t-1}. Its jth **lagged value** (or simply its jth **lag**) is its value j periods ago, which is Y_{t-j}. Similarly Y_{t+1} denotes the value of Y one period into the future.

The change in the value of Y between period $t - 1$ and period t is $Y_t - Y_{t-1}$; this change is called the **first difference** in the variable Y_t. In time series data, "Δ" is used to represent the first difference, so that $\Delta Y_t = Y_t - Y_{t-1}$.

Economic time series are often analyzed after computing their logarithms or the changes in their logarithms. One reason for this is that many economic series, such as gross domestic product (GDP), exhibit growth that is approximately exponential, that is, over the long run the series tends to grow by a certain percentage per year on average; if so, the logarithm of the series grows approximately linearly. Another reason is that the standard deviation of many economic time series is approximately proportional to its level, that is, the standard deviation is well expressed as a percentage of the level of the series; if so, then the standard deviation of the logarithm of the series is approximately constant. In either case, it is useful to transform the series so that changes in the transformed series are

Lags, First Differences, Logarithms, and Growth Rates

- The first lag of a time series Y_t is Y_{t-1}; its jth lag is Y_{t-j}.
- The first difference of a series, ΔY_t, is its change between periods $t-1$ and t, that is, $\Delta Y_t = Y_t - Y_{t-1}$.
- The first difference of the logarithm of Y_t is $\Delta \ln(Y_t) = \ln(Y_t) - \ln(Y_{t-1})$.
- The percentage change of a time series Y_t between periods $t-1$ and t is approximately $100\Delta \ln(Y_t)$, where the approximation is most accurate when the percentage change is small.

proportional (or percentage) changes in the original series, and this is achieved by taking the logarithm of the series.[1]

Lags, first differences, and growth rates are summarized in Key Concept 12.1.

Lags, changes, and percentage changes are illustrated using the U.S. inflation rate in Table 12.1. The first column shows the date, or period, where the first quarter of 1999 is denoted 1999:I, the second quarter of 1999 is denoted 1999:II, and so forth. The second column shows the value of the CPI in that quarter, and the third column shows the rate of inflation. For example, from the first to the second quarter of 1999, the index increased from 164.9 to 166.0, a percentage increase of $100 \times (166.03 - 164.87)/164.87 = 0.704\%$. This is the percentage increase from one quarter to the next. It is conventional to report rates of inflation (and other growth rates in macroeconomic time series) on an annual basis, which is the percentage increase in prices that would occur over a year, if the series were to continue to increase at the same rate. Because there are four quarters a year, the annualized rate of inflation in 1999:II is $0.704 \times 4 = 2.82$, or 2.8% per year after rounding.

This percentage change can also be computed using the differences-of-logarithms approximation in Key Concept 12.1. The difference in the logarithm of the CPI from 1999:I to 1999:II is $\ln(166.03) - \ln(164.87) = 0.00701$, yielding

---

[1]Recall from Section 6.2 that the change of the logarithm of a variable is approximately equal to the proportional change of that variable; that is, $\ln(X + a) - \ln(X) \cong a/X$, where the approximation works best when a/X is small. Now, replace X with Y_{t-1}, a with ΔY_t, and note that $Y_t = Y_{t-1} + \Delta Y_t$. This means that the proportional change in the series Y_t between periods $t-1$ and t is approximately $\ln(Y_t) - \ln(Y_{t-1}) = \ln(Y_{t-1} + \Delta Y_t) - \ln(Y_{t-1}) \cong \Delta Y_t/Y_{t-1}$. The expression $\ln(Y_t) - \ln(Y_{t-1})$ is the first difference of $\ln(Y_t)$, $\Delta \ln(Y_t)$. Thus $\Delta \ln(Y_t) \cong \Delta Y_t/Y_{t-1}$. The percentage change is 100 times the fractional change, so the percentage change in the series Y_t is approximately $100\Delta \ln(Y_t)$.

TABLE 12.1 Inflation in the United States in 1999 and the First Quarter of 2000

Quarter	U.S. CPI	Rate of Inflation at an Annual Rate (Inf_t)	First Lag (Inf_{t-1})	Change in Inflation (ΔInf_t)
1999:I	164.87	1.6	2.0	−0.4
1999:II	166.03	2.8	1.6	1.2
1999:III	167.20	2.8	2.8	0.0
1999:IV	168.53	3.2	2.8	0.4
2000:I	170.27	4.1	3.2	0.9

The annualized rate of inflation is the percentage change in the CPI from the previous quarter to the current quarter, times four. The first lag of inflation is its value in the previous quarter, and the change in inflation is the current inflation rate minus its first lag. All entries are rounded to the nearest decimal.

the approximate quarterly percentage difference $100 \times 0.00701 = 0.701\%$. On an annualized basis, this is $0.701 \times 4 = 2.80$, or 2.8% after rounding, the same as obtained by directly computing the percentage growth. These calculations can be summarized as

$$\text{annualized rate of inflation} = Inf_t \cong 400[\ln(CPI_t) - \ln(CPI_{t-1})] = 400\Delta\ln(CPI_t), \quad (12.2)$$

where CPI_t is the value of the Consumer Price Index at date t. The factor of 400 arises from converting fractional change to percentages (multiplying by 100) and converting quarterly percentage change to an equivalent annual rate (multiplying by 4).

The final two columns of Table 12.1 illustrate lags and changes. The first lag of inflation in 1999:II is 1.6%, the inflation rate in 1999:I. The change in the rate of inflation from 1999:I to 1999:II was $2.8\% - 1.6\% = 1.2\%$.

Autocorrelation

In time series data, the value of Y in one period typically is correlated with its value in the next period. The correlation of a series with its own lagged values is called **autocorrelation** or **serial correlation**. The first autocorrelation (or **autocorrelation coefficient**) is the correlation between Y_t and Y_{t-1}, that is, the correlation between values of Y at two adjacent dates. The second autocorrelation is the correlation between Y_t and Y_{t-2}, and the jth autocorrelation is the

Autocorrelation (Serial Correlation) and Autocovariance

The jth autocovariance of a series Y_t is the covariance between Y_t and its jth lag, Y_{t-j}, and the jth autocorrelation coefficient is the correlation between Y_t and Y_{t-j}. That is,

$$j^{\text{th}} \text{ autocovariance} = \text{cov}(Y_t, Y_{t-j}) \tag{12.3}$$

$$j^{\text{th}} \text{ autocorrelation} = \rho_j = \text{corr}(Y_t, Y_{t-j}) = \frac{\text{cov}(Y_t, Y_{t-j})}{\sqrt{\text{var}(Y_t)\text{var}(Y_{t-j})}}. \tag{12.4}$$

The jth autocorrelation coefficient is sometimes called the jth serial correlation coefficient.

Key Concept 12.2

correlation between Y_t and Y_{t-j}. Similarly, the **j^{th} autocovariance** is the covariance between Y_t and Y_{t-j}. Autocorrelation and autocovariance are summarized in Key Concept 12.2.

The jth population autocovariances and autocorrelations in Key Concept 12.2 can be estimated by the jth sample autocovariances and autocorrelations, $\widehat{\text{cov}(Y_t, Y_{t-j})}$ and $\hat{\rho}_j$:

$$\widehat{\text{cov}(Y_t, Y_{t-j})} = \frac{1}{T-j-1} \sum_{t=j+1}^{T} (Y_t - \overline{Y}_{j+1,T})(Y_{t-j} - \overline{Y}_{1,T-j}) \tag{12.5}$$

$$\hat{\rho}_j = \frac{\widehat{\text{cov}(Y_t, Y_{t-j})}}{\widehat{\text{var}(Y_t)}}, \tag{12.6}$$

where $\overline{Y}_{j+1,T}$ denotes the sample average of Y_t computed over the observations $t = j + 1, \ldots, T$ and where $\widehat{\text{var}(Y_t)}$ is the sample variance of Y. (Equation (12.6) uses the assumption that $\text{var}(Y_t)$ and $\text{var}(Y_{t-j})$ are the same, an implication of the assumption that Y is stationary, which is discussed in Section 12.4.)

The first four sample autocorrelations of the inflation rate and of the change in the inflation rate are listed in Table 12.2. These entries show that inflation is strongly positively autocorrelated: the first autocorrelation is 0.85. The sample autocorrelation declines as the lag increases, but it remains large even at a lag of four quarters. The change in inflation is negatively autocorrelated: an increase in

TABLE 12.2 First Four Sample Autocorrelations of the U.S. Inflation Rate and Its Change, 1960:I–1999:IV

| | Autocorrelation of: | |
Lag	Inflation Rate (Inf_t)	Change of Inflation Rate (ΔInf_t)
1	0.85	−0.24
2	0.77	−0.27
3	0.77	0.32
4	0.68	−0.06

the rate of inflation in one quarter tends to be associated with a decrease in the next quarter.

At first, it might seem contradictory that the level of inflation is strongly positively correlated but its change is negatively correlated. These two autocorrelations, however, measure different things. The strong positive autocorrelation in inflation reflects the long-term trends in inflation evident in Figure 12.1: inflation was low in the first quarter of 1965 and again in the second; it was high in the first quarter of 1981 and again in the second. In contrast, the negative autocorrelation of the change of inflation means that, on average, an increase in inflation in one quarter is associated with a decrease in inflation in the next.

Other Examples of Economic Time Series

Economic time series differ greatly. Four examples of economic time series are plotted in Figure 12.2: the U.S. Federal Funds interest rate; the rate of exchange between the dollar and the British pound; the logarithm of real Japanese gross domestic product; and the daily return on the Standard and Poor's 500 (S&P 500) stock market index.

The U.S. Federal Funds rate (Figure 12.2a) is the interest rate that banks pay to each other to borrow funds overnight. This rate is important because it is controlled by the Federal Reserve and is the Fed's primary monetary policy instrument. If you compare the plots of the Federal Funds rate and the rates of unemployment and inflation in Figure 12.1, you will see that sharp increases in the Federal Funds rate often have been associated with subsequent recessions.

The dollar/pound exchange rate (Figure 12.2b) is the price of a British pound (£) in U.S. dollars. Before 1972, the developed economies ran a system of fixed exchange rates—called the "Bretton Woods" system—under which governments worked to keep exchange rates from fluctuating. In 1972, inflationary pressures

---

FIGURE 12.2   Four Economic Time Series

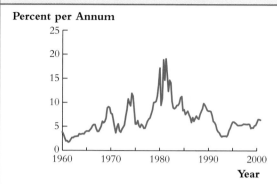

(a) Federal Funds Interest Rate

(b) U.S. Dollar/British Pound Exchange Rate

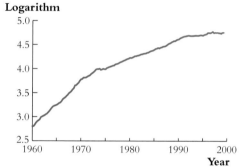

(c) Logarithm of Real GDP in Japan

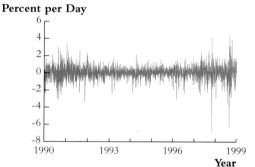

(d) Percentage Changes in Daily Values of the NYSE Composite Stock Index

The four time series have markedly different patterns. The Federal Funds Rate (Figure 12.2a) has a pattern similar to price inflation. The exchange rate between the U.S. dollar and the British pound (Figure 12.2b) shows a discrete change after the 1972 collapse of the Bretton Woods system of fixed exchange rates. The logarithm of real GDP in Japan (Figure 12.2c) shows relatively smooth growth, although the growth rate decreases in the 1970s and again in the 1990s. The daily returns on the NYSE stock price index (Figure 12.2d) are essentially unpredictable, but its variance changes: this series shows "volatility clustering."

---

led to the breakdown of this system; thereafter, the major currencies were allowed to "float", that is, their values were determined by the supply and demand for currencies in the market for foreign exchange. Prior to 1972, the exchange rate was approximately constant, with the exception of a single devaluation in 1968 in which the official value of the pound, relative to the dollar, was decreased to $2.40. Since 1972 the exchange rate has fluctuated over a very wide range.

Real quarterly Japanese GDP (Figure 12.2c) is the total value of goods and services produced in Japan during a quarter, adjusted for inflation. GDP is the broadest measure of total economic activity. The logarithm of the series is plotted in Figure 12.2c, and changes in this series can be interpreted as (decimal) growth rates. During the 1960s and early 1970s, Japanese real GDP grew quickly, but this growth slowed in the late 1970s and 1980s. Growth slowed further during the 1990s, averaging only 1.5% per year from 1990–1999.

The daily return on the NYSE index of stock prices (Figure 12.2d) is the percentage change from one trading day to the next of the NYSE Composite market index, a broad index of the share prices of all firms traded on the New York Stock Exchange. Figure 12.2d plots these daily returns for January 2, 1990, to December 31, 1998 (a total of 1,771 observations). Unlike the other series in Figure 12.2, there is very little serial correlation in these daily returns: if there were, then you could predict these returns using past daily returns and make money by buying when you expect the market to rise and selling when you expect it to fall. Although the return itself is essentially unpredictable, inspection of Figure 12.2d reveals patterns in the volatility of returns. For example, the standard deviation of returns was relatively large in 1991 and 1998, and relatively small in 1995. This "volatility clustering" is found in many financial time series, and econometric models for modeling this special type of heteroskedasticity are taken up in Section 14.5.

12.3 Autoregressions

What will the rate of price inflation—the percentage increase in overall prices—be next year? Wall Street investors rely on forecasts of inflation when deciding how much to pay for bonds. Economists at central banks, like the U.S. Federal Reserve Bank, use inflation forecasts when they set monetary policy. Firms use inflation forecasts when they forecast sales of their product, and local governments use inflation forecasts when they develop their budget for the upcoming year. In this section, we consider forecasts made using an **autoregression**, a regression model that relates a time series variable to its past values.

The First Order Autoregressive Model

If you want to predict the future of a time series, a good place to start is in the immediate past. For example, if you want to forecast the change in inflation from this quarter to the next, you might see whether inflation rose or fell last quarter. A systematic way to forecast the change in inflation, ΔInf_t, using the previous quarter's change, ΔInf_{t-1}, is to estimate an OLS regression of ΔInf_t on ΔInf_{t-1}. Estimated using data from 1962–1999, this regression is

$$\widehat{\Delta Inf_t} = 0.02 - 0.211\Delta Inf_{t-1}, \qquad (12.7)$$
$$(0.14) \quad (0.106)$$

where, as usual, standard errors are given in parentheses under the estimated coefficients, and $\widehat{\Delta Inf_t}$ is the predicted value of ΔInf_t based on the estimated regression line. The model in Equation (12.7) is called a first order autoregression: an autoregression because it is a regression of the series onto its own lag, ΔInf_{t-1}, and first order because only one lag is used as a regressor. The coefficient in Equation (12.7) is negative, so an increase in the inflation rate in one quarter is associated with a decline in the inflation rate in the next quarter.

A first order autoregression is abbreviated by AR(1), where the "1" indicates that it is first order. The population AR(1) model for the series Y_t is

$$Y_t = \beta_0 + \beta_1 Y_{t-1} + u_t, \qquad (12.8)$$

where u_t is an error term.

Forecasts and forecast errors.   Suppose you have historical data on Y and you want to forecast its future value. If Y_t follows the AR(1) model in Equation (12.8) and if β_0 and β_1 are known, then the forecast of Y_t based on Y_{t-1} is $\beta_0 + \beta_1 Y_{t-1}$.

In practice, β_0 and β_1 are unknown, so forecasts must be based on estimates of β_0 and β_1. We will use the OLS estimators $\hat{\beta}_0$ and $\hat{\beta}_1$, which are constructed using historical data. In general, $\hat{Y}_{t|t-1}$ will denote the forecast of Y_t based on information through period $t-1$ using a model estimated with data through period $t-1$. Accordingly, the forecast based on the AR(1) model in Equation (12.8) is

$$\hat{Y}_{t|t-1} = \hat{\beta}_0 + \hat{\beta}_1 Y_{t-1} \qquad (12.9)$$

where $\hat{\beta}_0$ and $\hat{\beta}_1$ are estimated using historical data through time $t-1$.

The **forecast error** is the mistake made by the forecast; this is the difference between the value of Y_t that actually occurred and its forecasted value based on Y_{t-1}:

$$\text{forecast error} = Y_t - \hat{Y}_{t|t-1}. \qquad (12.10)$$

Forecasts vs. predicted values.   The forecast is *not* an OLS predicted value, and the forecast error is *not* an OLS residual. OLS predicted values are calculated for the observations in the sample used to estimate the regression. In contrast, the forecast is made for some date beyond the data set used to estimate the regression, so the data on the actual value of the forecasted dependent variable are not in the sample used to estimate the regression. Similarly, the OLS residual is the difference between the actual value of Y and its predicted value for observations in the sample, whereas the forecast error is the difference between the future value of Y, which is not contained in the estimation sample, and the forecast of that future value. Said differently, forecasts and forecast errors pertain to "out-of-sample" observations, whereas predicted values and residuals pertain to "in-sample" observations.

Root mean squared forecast error.   The **root mean squared forecast error (RMSFE)** is a measure of the size of the forecast error, that is, of the magnitude of a typical mistake made using a forecasting model. The RMSFE is the square root of the mean squared forecast error:

$$RMSFE = \sqrt{E[(Y_t - \hat{Y}_{t|t-1})^2]}. \tag{12.11}$$

The RMSFE has two sources of error: the error arising because future values of u_t are unknown, and the error in estimating the coefficients β_0 and β_1. If the first source of error is much larger than the second, as it can be if the sample size is large, then the RMSFE is approximately $\sqrt{var(u_t)}$, the standard deviation of the error u_t in the population autoregression (Equation (12.8)). The standard deviation of u_t is in turn estimated by the standard error of the regression (*SER*, see Section 5.10). Thus, if uncertainty arising from estimating the regression coefficients is small enough to be ignored, the RMSFE can be estimated by the standard error of the regression. Estimation of the RMSFE including both sources of forecast error is taken up in Section 12.4.

Application to inflation.   What is the forecast of inflation in the first quarter of 2000 (2000:I) that a forecaster would have made in 1999:IV, based on the estimated AR(1) model in Equation (12.7) (which was estimated using data through 1999:IV)? From Table 12.1, the inflation rate in 1999:IV was 3.2% (so $Inf_{1999:IV} = 3.2\%$), an increase of 0.4 percentage points from 1999:III (so $\Delta Inf_{1999:IV} = 0.4$). Plugging these values into Equation (12.7), the forecast of the change in inflation from 1999:IV to 2000:I is $\widehat{\Delta Inf}_{2000:I} = 0.02 - 0.211 \times \Delta Inf_{1999:IV} = 0.02 - 0.211 \times 0.4 =$

$-0.06 \cong -0.1$ (rounded to the nearest tenth). The predicted rate of inflation is the past rate of inflation plus its predicted change:

$$\widehat{Inf}_{t|t-1} = Inf_{t-1} + \widehat{\Delta Inf}_{t|t-1}. \tag{12.12}$$

Because $Inf_{1999:IV} = 3.2\%$ and the predicted change in the inflation rate from 1999:IV to 2000:I is -0.1, the predicted rate of inflation in 2000:I is $\widehat{Inf}_{2000:I} = Inf_{1999:IV} + \widehat{\Delta Inf}_{2000:I} = 3.2\% - 0.1\% = 3.1\%$. Thus, the AR(1) model forecasts that inflation will drop slightly from 3.2% in 1999:IV to 3.1% in 2000:I.

How accurate was this AR(1) forecast? From Table 12.1, the actual value of inflation in 2000:I was 4.1%, so the AR(1) forecast is low by a full percentage point; that is, the forecast error is 1.0%. The $\overline{R}^2$ of the AR(1) model in Equation (12.7) is only 0.04, so the lagged change of inflation explains a very small fraction of the variation in inflation in the sample used to fit the autoregression. This low $\overline{R}^2$ is consistent with the poor forecast of inflation in 2000:I produced using Equation (12.7). More generally, the low $\overline{R}^2$ suggests that this AR(1) model will forecast only a small amount of the variation in the change of inflation.

The standard error of the regression in Equation (12.7) is 1.67; ignoring uncertainty arising from estimation of the coefficients, our estimate of the RMSFE for forecasts based on Equation (12.7) therefore is 1.67 percentage points.

The pth Order Autoregressive Model

The AR(1) model uses Y_{t-1} to forecast Y_t, but doing so ignores potentially useful information in the more distant past. One way to incorporate this information is to include additional lags in the AR(1) model; this yields the pth order autoregressive, or AR(p), model.

The **p^{th} order autoregressive model** (the **AR(p)** model) represents Y_t as a linear function of p of its lagged values; that is, in the AR(p) model, the regressors are Y_{t-1}, Y_{t-2}, . . . , Y_{t-p}, plus an intercept. The number of lags, p, included in an AR(p) model is called the order, or lag length, of the autoregression.

For example, an AR(4) model of the change in inflation uses four lags of the change in inflation as regressors. Estimated by OLS over the period 1962–1999, the AR(4) model is

$$\widehat{\Delta Inf}_t = 0.02 - 0.21\Delta Inf_{t-1} - 0.32\Delta Inf_{t-2} + 0.19\Delta Inf_{t-3} - 0.04\Delta Inf_{t-4}. \tag{12.13}$$
$$\phantom{\widehat{\Delta Inf}_t = }(0.12)\ (0.10)\qquad (0.09)\qquad (0.09)\qquad (0.10)$$

The coefficients on the final three additional lags in Equation (12.13) are jointly significantly different from zero at the 5% significance level: the F-statistic is 6.43

Autoregressions

Key Concept 12.3

The pth order autoregressive model (the AR(p) model) represents Y_t as a linear function of p of its lagged values:

$$Y_t = \beta_0 + \beta_1 Y_{t-1} + \beta_2 Y_{t-2} + \cdots + \beta_p Y_{t-p} + u_t, \qquad (12.14)$$

where $E(u_t|Y_{t-1}, Y_{t-2}, \dots) = 0$. The number of lags p is called the order, or the lag length, of the autoregression.

(p-value < 0.001). This is reflected in an improvement in the $\overline{R}^2$ from 0.04 for the AR(1) model in Equation (12.7) to 0.21 for the AR(4). Similarly, the SER of the AR(4) model in Equation (12.13) is 1.53, an improvement over the SER of the AR(1) model, which is 1.67.

The AR(p) model is summarized in Key Concept 12.3.

Properties of the forecast and error term in the AR(p) model.   The assumption that the conditional expectation of u_t is zero given past values of Y_t (that is, $E(u_t | Y_{t-1}, Y_{t-2}, \dots) = 0$) has two important implications.

The first implication is that the best forecast of Y_t based on its entire history depends on only the most recent p past values. Specifically, let $Y_{t|t-1} = E(Y_t | Y_{t-1}, Y_{t-2}, \dots)$ denote the conditional mean of Y_t given its entire history. Then $Y_{t|t-1}$ has the smallest RMSFE of any forecast based on the history of Y (Exercise 12.5). If Y_t follows an AR(p), then its conditional mean is

$$Y_{t|t-1} = \beta_0 + \beta_1 Y_{t-1} + \beta_2 Y_{t-2} + \cdots + \beta_p Y_{t-p}, \qquad (12.15)$$

which follows from the AR(p) model in Equation (12.14) and the assumption that $E(u_t|Y_{t-1}, Y_{t-2}, \dots) = 0$. In practice, the coefficients $\beta_0, \beta_1, \dots, \beta_p$ are unknown, so actual forecasts from an AR(p) use Equation (12.15) with estimated coefficients.

The second implication is that the errors u_t are serially uncorrelated, a result that follows from Equation (2.25) (Exercise 12.5).

Application to inflation.   What is the forecast of inflation in 2000:I using data through 1999:IV, based on the AR(4) model of inflation in Equation (12.13)? To compute this forecast, substitute the values of the change of inflation in each of the four quarters of 1999 into Equation (12.13): $\widehat{\Delta Inf}_{2000:I \mid 1999:IV} = 0.02 - 0.21\Delta Inf_{1999:IV} - 0.32\Delta Inf_{1999:III} + 0.19\Delta Inf_{1999:II} - 0.04\Delta Inf_{1999:I} = 0.02 - 0.21 \times 0.4 - 0.32 \times 0.0 + 0.19 \times 1.1 - 0.04 \times (-0.4) \cong 0.2$, where the 1999 values for the change of inflation are taken from the final column of Table 12.1.

The corresponding forecast of inflation in 2000:I is the value of inflation in 1999:IV, plus the forecasted change, that is, $3.2\% + 0.2\% = 3.4\%$. The forecast error is the actual value, 4.1%, minus the forecast, or $4.1\% - 3.4\% = 0.7\%$, slightly smaller than the AR(1) forecast error of 1.0%.

12.4 Time Series Regression with Additional Predictors and the Autoregressive Distributed Lag Model

Economic theory often suggests other variables that could help to forecast the variable of interest. These other variables, or predictors, can be added to an autoregression to produce a time series regression model with multiple predictors. When other variables and their lags are added to an autoregression, the result is an autoregressive distributed lag model.

Forecasting Changes in the Inflation Rate Using Past Unemployment Rates

A high value of the unemployment rate tends to be associated with a future decline in the rate of inflation. This negative relationship, known as the short-run Phillips curve, is evident in the scatterplot of Figure 12.3, in which year-to-year changes in the rate of price inflation are plotted against the rate of unemployment in the previous year. For example, in 1982 the unemployment rate averaged 9.7%, and during the next year the rate of inflation fell by 2.9%. Overall, the correlation in Figure 12.3 is -0.40.

The scatterplot in Figure 12.3 suggests that past values of the unemployment rate might contain information about the future course of inflation that is not already contained in past changes of inflation. This conjecture is readily checked by augmenting the AR(4) model in Equation (12.13) to include the first lag of the unemployment rate:

$$
\widehat{\Delta Inf}_t = 1.42 - 0.26\Delta Inf_{t-1} - 0.40\Delta Inf_{t-2} + 0.11\Delta Inf_{t-3} - 0.09\Delta Inf_{t-4} - 0.23 Unemp_{t-1}.
$$
$$
\quad\;\; (0.55) \;\; (0.09) \qquad\;\; (0.10) \qquad\quad (0.08) \qquad\quad (0.10) \qquad\quad (0.10)
$$

(12.16)

In 1982, the U.S. unemployment rate was 9.7% and the rate of inflation in 1983 fell by 2.9% (the large dot). In general, high values of the unemployment rate in year *t* tend to be followed by decreases in the rate of price inflation in the next year, year *t* + 1, with a correlation of −0.40.

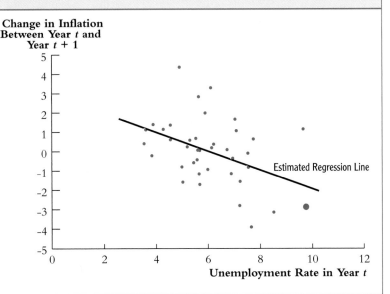

The *t*-statistic on $Unemp_{t-1}$ is −2.33, so this term is significant at the 5% level. The $\overline{R}^2$ of this regression is 0.22, a small improvement over the AR(4) $\overline{R}^2$ of 0.21.

The forecast of the change of inflation in 2000:I is obtained by substituting the 1999 values of the change of inflation into Equation (12.16), along with the value of the unemployment rate in 1999:IV (which is 4.1%); the resulting forecast is $\widehat{\Delta Inf}_{2000:I \mid 1999:IV} = 0.5$. Thus the forecast of inflation in 2000:I is 3.2% + 0.5% = 3.7%, and the forecast error is 0.4%. This forecast is closer to actual 2000:I inflation than was the AR(4) forecast.

If one lag of the unemployment rate is helpful for forecasting inflation, several lags might be even more helpful; adding three more lags of the unemployment rate yields

$$\widehat{\Delta Inf_t} = 1.32 - 0.36\Delta Inf_{t-1} - 0.34\Delta Inf_{t-2} + 0.07\Delta Inf_{t-3} - 0.03\Delta Inf_{t-4}$$
$$\quad (0.47)\ (0.09) \qquad (0.10) \qquad (0.08) \qquad (0.09)$$

$$- 2.68Unemp_{t-1} + 3.43Unemp_{t-2} - 1.04Unemp_{t-3} + 0.07Unemp_{t-4}.$$
$$\quad (0.47) \qquad (0.89) \qquad (0.89) \qquad (0.44)$$

$$(12.17)$$

The *F*-statistic testing the joint significance of the second through fourth lags of the unemployment rate is 4.93 (*p*-value = 0.003), so they are jointly significant.

The $\overline{R}^2$ of the regression in Equation (12.17) is 0.35, a solid improvement over 0.22 for Equation (12.16). The F-statistic on all the unemployment coefficients is 8.51 (p-value < 0.001), indicating that this model represents a statistically significant improvement over the AR(4) model of Section 12.3 (Equation (12.13)). The standard error of the regression in Equation (12.17) is 1.37, a substantial improvement over the SER of 1.53 for the AR(4).

The forecasted change in inflation from 1999:IV to 2000:I using Equation (12.17) is computed by substituting the values of the variables into the equation. The unemployment rate was 4.3% in 1999:I and 1999:II, 4.2% in 1999:III, and 4.1% in 1999:IV. The forecast of the change in inflation from 1999:IV to 2000:I, based on Equation (12.17), is

$$
\begin{aligned}
\widehat{\Delta Inf}_{2000:I\,|\,1999:IV} &= 1.32 - 0.36 \times 0.4 - 0.34 \times 0.0 + 0.07 \times 1.1 - 0.03 \\
&\quad \times (-0.4) - 2.68 \times 4.1 + 3.43 \times 4.2 - 1.04 \times 4.3 + 0.07 \times 4.3 = 0.5
\end{aligned}
\tag{12.18}
$$

Thus the forecast of inflation in 2000:I is 3.2% + 0.5% = 3.7%. The forecast error is small, 0.4. Adding multiple lags of the unemployment rate appears to improve inflation forecasts beyond those of an AR(4).

The autoregressive distributed lag model.   The models in Equations (12.16) and (12.17) are **autoregressive distributed lag (ADL)** models: "autoregressive" because lagged values of the dependent variable are included as regressors, as in an autoregression, and "distributed lag" because the regression also includes multiple lags (a "distributed lag") of an additional predictor. In general, an autoregressive distributed lag model with p lags of the dependent variable Y_t and q lags of an additional predictor X_t is called an **ADL(p,q)** model. In this notation, the model in Equation (12.16) is an ADL(4,1) model and the model in Equation (12.17) is an ADL(4,4) model.

The autoregressive distributed lag model is summarized in Key Concept 12.4. With all these regressors, the notation in Equation (12.19) is somewhat cumbersome, and alternative optional notation, based on the so-called lag operator, is presented in Appendix 12.3.

The assumption that the errors in the ADL model have a conditional mean of zero given all past values of Y and X, that is, that $E(u_t\,|\,Y_{t-1}, Y_{t-2}, \ldots, X_{t-1}, X_{t-2}, \ldots) = 0$, implies that no additional lags of either Y or X belong in the ADL model. In other words, the lag lengths p and q are the true lag lengths and the coefficients on additional lags are zero.

The ADL model contains lags of the dependent variable (the autoregressive component) and a distributed lag of a single additional predictor, X. In general,

The Autoregressive Distributed Lag Model

Key Concept 12.4

The autoregressive distributed lag model with p lags of Y_t and q lags of X_t, denoted **ADL(p,q)**, is

$$Y_t = \beta_0 + \beta_1 Y_{t-1} + \beta_2 Y_{t-2} + \cdots + \beta_p Y_{t-p} + \delta_1 X_{t-1} + \delta_2 X_{t-2} + \cdots + \delta_q X_{t-q} + u_t. \tag{12.19}$$

where $\beta_0, \beta_1, \ldots, \beta_p, \delta_1, \ldots, \delta_q$ are unknown coefficients and u_t is the error term with $E(u_t | Y_{t-1}, Y_{t-2}, \ldots, X_{t-1}, X_{t-2}, \ldots) = 0$.

however, forecasts can be improved by using multiple predictors. But before turning to the general time series regression model with multiple predictors, we first introduce the concept of stationarity, which will be used in that discussion.

Stationarity

Regression analysis of time series data necessarily uses data from the past to quantify historical relationships. If the future is like the past, then these historical relationships can be used to forecast the future. But if the future differs fundamentally from the past, then those historical relationships might not be reliable guides to the future.

In the context of time series regression, the idea that historical relationships can be generalized to the future is formalized by the concept of **stationarity**. The precise definition of stationarity, given in Key Concept 12.5, is that the distribution of the time series variable does not change over time.

Time Series Regression with Multiple Predictors

The general time series regression model with multiple predictors extends the ADL model to include multiple predictors and their lags. The model is summarized in Key Concept 12.6. The presence of multiple predictors and their lags leads to double subscripting of the regression coefficients and regressors.

The time series regression model assumptions. The assumptions in Key Concept 12.6 modify the four least squares assumptions of the multiple regression model for cross-sectional data (Key Concept 5.4) for time series data.

Stationarity

A time series Y_t is **stationary** if its probability distribution does not change over time, that is, if the joint distribution of $(Y_{s+1}, Y_{s+2}, \ldots, Y_{s+T})$ does not depend on s; otherwise, Y_t is said to be **nonstationary**. A pair of time series, X_t and Y_t, are said to be **jointly stationary** if the joint distribution of $(X_{s+1}, Y_{s+1}, X_{s+2}, Y_{s+2}, \ldots, X_{s+T}, Y_{s+T})$ does not depend on s. Stationarity requires the future to be like the past, at least in a probabilistic sense.

Key Concept 12.5

The first assumption is that u_t has conditional mean zero, given all the regressors *and* the additional lags of the regressors beyond the lags included in the regression. This assumption extends the assumption used in the AR and ADL models and implies that the best forecast of Y_t using all past values of Y and the X's is given by the regression in Equation (12.20).

The second least squares assumption for cross-sectional data (Key Concept 5.4) is that $(X_{1i}, \ldots, X_{ki}, Y_i)$, $i = 1, \ldots, n$, are independently and identically distributed (i.i.d.). The second assumption for time series regression replaces the i.i.d. assumption by a more appropriate one with two parts. Part (a) is that the data are drawn from a stationary distribution, so that the distribution of the data today is the same as its distribution in the past. This assumption is a time series version of the "identically distributed" part of the i.i.d. assumption: the cross-sectional requirement of each draw being identically distributed is replaced by the time series requirement that the joint distribution of the variables, *including lags*, does not change over time. In practice, many economic time series appear to be nonstationary, which means that this assumption can fail to hold in applications. If the time series variables are nonstationary, then one or more problems can arise in time series regression: the forecast can be biased, the forecast can be inefficient (there can be alternative forecasts based on the same data with lower variance), or conventional OLS-based statistical inferences (for example performing a hypothesis test by comparing the OLS t-statistic to ± 1.96) can be misleading. Precisely which of these problems occurs, and its remedy, depends on the source of the nonstationarity. In Sections 12.6 and 12.7, we study the problems posed by, tests for, and solutions to two empirically important types of nonstationarity in economic time series, trends and breaks. For now, however, we simply assume that the series are jointly stationary and accordingly focus on regression with stationary variables.

Time Series Regression with Multiple Predictors

Key Concept 12.6

The general time series regression model allows for k additional predictors, where q_1 lags of the first predictor are included, q_2 lags of the second predictor are included, and so forth:

$$Y_t = \beta_0 + \beta_1 Y_{t-1} + \beta_2 Y_{t-2} + \cdots + \beta_p Y_{t-p} + \delta_{11} X_{1t-1} + \delta_{12} X_{1t-2} + \cdots + \delta_{1q_1} X_{1t-q_1} +$$
$$\cdots + \delta_{k1} X_{kt-1} + \delta_{k2} X_{kt-2} + \cdots + \delta_{kq_k} X_{kt-q_k} + u_t, \qquad (12.20)$$

where

1. $E(u_t | Y_{t-1}, Y_{t-2}, \ldots, X_{1t-1}, X_{1t-2}, \ldots, X_{kt-1}, X_{kt-2}, \ldots) = 0$;
2. (a) The random variables $(Y_t, X_{1t}, \ldots, X_{kt})$ have a stationary distribution, and (b) $(Y_t, X_{1t}, \ldots, X_{kt})$ and $(Y_{t-j}, X_{1t-j}, \ldots, X_{kt-j})$ become independent as j gets large;
3. $X_{1t}, \ldots, X_{kt}$ and Y_t have nonzero, finite fourth moments; and
4. There is no perfect multicollinearity.

Part (b) of the second assumption requires that the random variables become independently distributed when the amount of time separating them becomes large. This replaces the cross-sectional requirement that the variables be independently distributed from one observation to the next with the time series requirement that they be independently distributed when they are separated by long periods of time. This assumption is sometimes referred to as **weak dependence**, and it ensures that in large samples there is sufficient randomness in the data for the law of large numbers and the central limit theorem to hold. We do not provide a precise mathematical statement of the weak dependence condition, rather, the reader is referred to Hayashi (2000, Chapter 2).

The third assumption, which is the same as the third least squares assumption for cross-sectional data, is that all the variables have nonzero finite fourth moments. This is the same as for cross-sectional data, is that the regressors are not perfectly multicollinear.

Statistical inference and the Granger causality test. Under the assumptions of Key Concept 12.6, inference on the regression coefficients using OLS proceeds in the same way as it usually does using cross-sectional data.

Granger Causality Tests (Tests of Predictive Content)

The Granger causality statistic is the *F*-statistic testing the hypothesis that the coefficients on all the values of one of the variables in Equation (12.20) (for example, the coefficients on X_{1t-1}, X_{1t-2}, ..., X_{1t-q_1}) are zero. This null hypothesis implies that these regressors have no predictive content for Y_t beyond that contained in the other regressors, and the test of this null hypothesis is called the Granger causality test.

Key Concept 12.7

One useful application of the *F*-statistic in time series forecasting is to test whether the lags of one of the included regressors has useful predictive content, above and beyond the other regressors in the model. The claim that a variable has no predictive content corresponds to the null hypothesis that the coefficients on all lags of that variable are zero. The *F*-statistic testing this null hypothesis is called the **Granger causality statistic**, and the associated test is called a **Granger causality test** (Granger (1969)). This test is summarized in Key Concept 12.7.

Granger causality has little to do with causality in the sense that it is used elsewhere in this book. In Chapter 1, causality was defined in terms of an ideal randomized controlled experiment, in which different values of *X* are applied experimentally and we observe the subsequent effect on *Y*. In contrast, Granger causality means that if *X* Granger-causes *Y*, then *X* is a useful predictor of *Y*, given the other variables in the regression. While "Granger predictability" is a more accurate term than "Granger causality," the latter has become part of the jargon of econometrics.

As an example, consider the relationship between the change in the inflation rate and its past values and past values of the unemployment rate. Based on the OLS estimates in Equation (12.17), the *F*-statistic testing the null hypothesis that the coefficients on all four lags of the unemployment rate are zero is 8.51 ($p < 0.001$): in the jargon of Key Concept 12.7, we can conclude (at the 1% significance level) that the unemployment rate Granger-causes changes in the inflation rate. This *does not* necessarily mean that a change in the unemployment rate will cause—in the sense of Chapter 1—a subsequent change in the inflation rate. It *does* mean that the past values of the unemployment rate appear to contain information that is useful for forecasting changes in the inflation rate, beyond that contained in past values of the inflation rate.

Forecast Uncertainty and Forecast Intervals

In any estimation problem, it is good practice to report a measure of the uncertainty of that estimate, and forecasting is no exception. One measure of the uncertainty of a forecast is its root mean square forecast error. Under the additional assumption that the errors u_t are normally distributed, the RMSFE can be used to construct a forecast interval, that is, an interval that contains the future value of the variable with a certain probability.

Forecast uncertainty. The forecast error consists of two components: uncertainty arising from estimation of the regression coefficients, and uncertainty associated with the future unknown value of u_t. For regression with few coefficients and many observations, the uncertainty arising from future u_t can be much larger than the uncertainty associated with estimation of the parameters. In general, however, both sources of uncertainty are important, so we now develop an expression for the RMSFE that incorporates these two sources of uncertainty.

To keep the notation simple, consider forecasts of Y_{T+1} based on an ADL(1,1) model with a single predictor, that is, $Y_t = \beta_0 + \beta_1 Y_{t-1} + \delta_1 X_{t-1} + u_t$, and suppose that u_t is homoskedastic. The forecast is $\hat{Y}_{T+1|T} = \hat{\beta}_0 + \hat{\beta}_1 Y_T + \hat{\delta}_1 X_T$, and the forecast error is

$$Y_{T+1} - \hat{Y}_{T+1|T} = u_{T+1} - [(\hat{\beta}_0 - \beta_0) + (\hat{\beta}_1 - \beta_1)Y_T + (\hat{\delta}_1 - \delta_1)X_T]. \quad (12.21)$$

Because u_{T+1} has conditional mean zero and is homoskedastic, u_{T+1} has variance σ_u^2 and is uncorrelated with the final expression in brackets in Equation (12.21). Thus the mean squared forecast error (MSFE) is

$$\begin{aligned} \text{MSFE} &= E[(Y_{T+1} - \hat{Y}_{T+1|T})^2] \\ &= \sigma_u^2 + \text{var}[(\hat{\beta}_0 - \beta_0) + (\hat{\beta}_1 - \beta_1)Y_T + (\hat{\delta}_1 - \delta_1)X_T], \end{aligned} \quad (12.22)$$

and the RMSFE is the square root of the MSFE.

Estimation of the MSFE entails estimation of the two parts in Equation (12.22). The first term, σ_u^2, can be estimated by the square of the standard error of the regression, as discussed in Section 12.3. The second term requires estimating the variance of a weighted average of the regression coefficients, and methods for doing so were discussed in Section 6.1 (see the discussion following Equation (6.7)).

An alternative method for estimating the MSFE is to use the variance of pseudo out–of–sample forecasts, a procedure discussed in Section 12.7.

Forecast intervals.   A forecast interval is like a confidence interval, except that it pertains to a forecast. That is, a 95% **forecast interval** is an interval that contains the future value of the series in 95% of repeated applications.

One important difference between a forecast interval and a confidence interval is that the usual formula for a 95% confidence interval (the estimator ± 1.96 standard errors) is justified by the central limit theorem and therefore holds for a wide range of distributions of the error term. In contrast, because the forecast error in Equation (12.21) includes the future value of the error u_{T+1}, to compute a forecast interval requires either estimating the distribution of the error term or making some assumption about that distribution.

In practice, it is convenient to assume that u_{T+1} is normally distributed. If so, Equation (12.21) and the central limit theorem applied to $\hat{\beta}_0$, $\hat{\beta}_1$, and $\hat{\delta}_1$ imply that the forecast error is the sum of two independent, normally distributed terms, so that the forecast error is itself normally distributed with variance equaling the MSFE. It follows that a 95% confidence interval is given by $\hat{Y}_{T+1|T} \pm 1.96 \, SE(Y_{T+1} - \hat{Y}_{T+1|T})$, where $SE(Y_{T+1} - \hat{Y}_{T+1|T})$ is an estimator of the RMSFE.

This discussion has focused on the case that the error term, u_{T+1}, is homoskedastic. If instead u_{T+1} is heteroskedastic, then one needs to develop a model of the heteroskedasticity so that the term σ_u^2 in Equation (12.22) can be estimated, given the most recent values of Y and X, and methods for modeling this conditional heteroskedasticity are presented in Section 14.5.

Because of uncertainty about future events—that is, uncertainty about u_{T+1}—95% forecast intervals can be so wide that they have limited use in decision making. Professional forecasters therefore often report forecast intervals that are tighter than 95%, for example, one standard error forecast intervals (which are 68% forecast intervals if the errors are normally distributed). Alternatively, some forecasters report multiple forecast intervals, as is done by the economists at the Bank of England when they publish their inflation forecasts (see the River of Blood box on the following page).

12.5 Lag Length Selection Using Information Criteria

The estimated inflation regressions in Sections 12.3 and 12.4 have either one or four lags of the predictors. One lag makes some sense, but why four? More generally, how many lags should be included in a time series regression? This section discusses statistical methods for choosing the number of lags, first in an autoregression, then in a time series regression model with multiple predictors.

The River of Blood

As part of its efforts to inform the public about monetary policy decisions, the Bank of England regularly publishes forecasts of inflation. These forecasts combine output from econometric models maintained by professional econometricians at the bank with the expert judgment of the members of the bank's senior staff and Monetary Policy Committee. The forecasts are presented as a set of forecast intervals designed to reflect what these economists consider to be the range of probable paths that inflation might take. In its *Inflation Report*, the bank prints these ranges in red, with the darkest red reserved for the central band. Although the bank prosaically refers to this as the "fan chart," the press has called these spreading shades of red the "river of blood."

The river of blood for February 2001 is shown in Figure 12.4 (in this figure the blood is green, not red, so you will need to use your imagination). This chart shows that, as of February 2001, the bank's economists expected inflation to remain essentially unchanged over the next year at approximately 2%, but then to increase. There is considerable uncertainty about this forecast, however. In their written discussion, they cited in particular the possibility of a further slowdown in the United States—which in

(Continued)

FIGURE 12.4 **The River of Blood**

The Bank of England's fan chart for February 2001 shows forecast ranges for inflation.

fact became the recession of 2001—that could lead to lower inflation in the United Kingdom As it happened, their forecast was a good one: in the fourth quarter of 2001, the rate of inflation was 2.0%.

The Bank of England has been a pioneer in the movement towards greater openness by central banks, and other central banks now also publish inflation forecasts. The decisions made by monetary policymakers are difficult ones and affect the lives—and wallets—of many of their fellow citizens. In a democracy in the information age, reasoned the economists at the Bank of England, it is particularly important for citizens to understand the bank's economic outlook and the reasoning behind its difficult decisions.

To see the river of blood in its original red hue, visit the Bank of England's Web site at **www.bankofengland.co.uk/inflationreport**.

Determining the Order of an Autoregression

In practice, choosing the order p of an autoregression requires balancing the benefit of including more lags against the cost of additional estimation uncertainty. On the one hand, if the order of an estimated autoregression is too low, you will omit potentially valuable information contained in the more distant lagged values. On the other hand, if it is too high, you will be estimating more coefficients than necessary, which in turn introduces additional estimation error into your forecasts.

The F-statistic approach.   One approach to choosing p is to start with a model with many lags and to perform hypothesis tests on the final lag. For example, you might start by estimating an AR(6) and test whether the coefficient on the sixth lag is significant at the 5% level; if not, drop it and estimate an AR(5), test the coefficient on the fifth lag, and so forth. The drawback of this method is that it will produce too large a model, at least some of the time: even if the true AR order is five, so the sixth coefficient is zero, a 5% test using the t-statistic will incorrectly reject this null hypothesis 5% of the time just by chance. Thus, when the true value of p is five, this method will estimate p to be six 5% of the time.

The BIC.   A way around this problem is to estimate p by minimizing an "information criterion." One such information criterion is the **Bayes information criterion (BIC)**, also called the **Schwarz information criterion (SIC)**, which is

$$\text{BIC}(p) = \ln\left(\frac{SSR(p)}{T}\right) + (p + 1)\frac{\ln T}{T}, \tag{12.23}$$

where $SSR(p)$ is the sum of squared residuals of the estimated $AR(p)$. The BIC estimator of p, $\hat{p}$, is the value that minimizes $BIC(p)$ among the possible choices $p = 0, 1, \ldots, p_{max}$, where p_{max} is the largest value of p considered.

The formula for the BIC might look a bit mysterious at first, but it has an intuitive appeal. Consider the first term in Equation (12.23). Because the regression coefficients are estimated by OLS, the sum of squared residuals necessarily decreases (or at least does not increase) when you add a lag. In contrast, the second term is the number of estimated regression coefficients (the number of lags, p, plus one for the intercept) times the factor $(\ln T)/T$. This second term increases when you add a lag. The BIC trades off these two forces so that the number of lags that minimizes the BIC is a consistent estimator of the true lag length. The mathematics of this argument is given in Appendix 12.5.

As an example, consider estimating the AR order for an autoregression of the change in the inflation rate. The various steps in the calculation of the BIC are carried out in Table 12.3 for autoregressions of maximum order six ($p_{max} = 6$). For example, for the AR(1) model in Equation (12.7), $SSR(1)/T = 2.726$, so $\ln(SSR(1)/T) = 1.003$. Because $T = 152$ (38 years, four quarters per year), $\ln(T)/T = 0.033$ and $(p + 1)\ln(T)/T = 2 \times 0.033 = 0.066$. Thus $BIC(1) = 1.003 + 0.066 = 1.069$.

The BIC is smallest when $p = 3$ in Table 12.3. Thus the BIC estimate of the lag length is 3. As can be seen in Table 12.3, as the number of lags increases the

TABLE 12.3 **The Bayes Information Criterion (BIC) and the R^2 for Autoregressive Models of U.S. Inflation, 1962–1999**

p	$SSR(p)/T$	$\ln(SSR(p)/T)$	$(p + 1)\ln(T)/T$	$BIC(p)$	R^2
0	2.853	1.048	0.033	1.081	0.000
1	2.726	1.003	0.066	1.069	0.045
2	2.361	0.859	0.099	0.958	0.173
3	2.264	0.817	0.132	0.949	0.206
4	2.261	0.816	0.165	0.981	0.207
5	2.260	0.815	0.198	1.013	0.208
6	2.257	0.814	0.231	1.045	0.209

R^2 increases and the SSR decreases. The increase in the R^2 is large from one to two lags, smaller from two to three, and quite small from three to four. The BIC helps decide precisely how large the increase in the R^2 must be to justify including the additional lag.

The AIC. The BIC is not the only information criterion; another is the **Akaike information criterion,** or **AIC**:

$$\text{AIC}(p) = \ln\left(\frac{SSR(p)}{T}\right) + (p+1)\frac{2}{T}. \tag{12.24}$$

The difference between the AIC and the BIC is that the term "$\ln T$" in the BIC is replaced by "2" in the AIC, so the second term in the AIC is smaller. For example, for the 152 observations used to estimate the inflation autoregressions, $\ln T = \ln(152) = 5.02$, so that the second term for the BIC is more than twice as large as the term in AIC. Thus a smaller decrease in the SSR is needed in the AIC to justify including another lag. As a matter of theory, the second term in the AIC is not large enough to ensure that the correct lag length is chosen, even in large samples, so the AIC estimator of p is not consistent. As is discussed in Appendix 12.5, in large samples the AIC will overestimate p with nonzero probability.

Despite this theoretical blemish, the AIC is widely used in practice. If you are concerned that the BIC might yield a model with too few lags, the AIC provides a reasonable alternative.

A note on calculating information criteria. How well two estimated regressions fit the data is best assessed when they are estimated using the same data sets. Because the BIC and AIC are formal methods for making this comparison, the autoregressions under consideration should be estimated using the same observations. For example, in Table 12.3 all the regressions were estimated using data from 1962:I–1999:IV, for a total of 152 observations. Because the autoregressions involve lags of the change of inflation, this means that earlier values of the change of inflation (values before 1962:I) were used as regressors for the preliminary observations. Said differently, the regressions examined in Table 12.3 each include observations on ΔInf_t, ΔInf_{t-1}, . . . , ΔInf_{t-p} for $t = $ 1962:I, . . . , 1999:IV, corresponding to 152 observations on the dependent variable and regressors, so $T = $ 152 in Equations (12.23) and (12.24).

Lag Length Selection in Time Series Regression with Multiple Predictors

The tradeoff involved with lag length choice in the general time series regression model with multiple predictors (Equation (12.20)) is similar to that in an autoregression: using too few lags can decrease forecast accuracy because valuable information is lost, but adding lags increases estimation uncertainty. The choice of lags must balance the benefit of using additional information against the cost of estimating the additional coefficients.

The F-statistic approach.   As in the univariate autoregression, one way to determine the number of lags to include is to use F-statistics to test joint hypotheses that sets of coefficients equal zero. For example, in the discussion of Equation (12.17), we tested the hypothesis that the coefficients on the second through fourth lag of the unemployment rate equal zero against the alternative that they are nonzero; this hypothesis was rejected at the 1% significance level, lending support to the longer-lag specification. If the number of models being compared is small, then this F-statistic method is easy to use. In general, however, the F-statistic method can produce models that are too large, in the sense that the true lag order is overestimated.

Information criteria.   As in an autoregression, the BIC and AIC can be used to estimate the number of lags and variables in the time series regression model with multiple predictors. If the regression model has K coefficients (including the intercept), the BIC is

$$\text{BIC}(K) = \ln\left(\frac{SSR(K)}{T}\right) + K\frac{\ln T}{T}. \tag{12.25}$$

The AIC is defined in the same way, but with 2 replacing $\ln T$ in Equation (12.25). For each candidate model, the BIC (or AIC) can be evaluated, and the model with the lowest value of the BIC (or AIC) is the preferred model, based on the information criterion.

There are two important practical considerations when using an information criterion to estimate the lag lengths. First, as is the case for the autoregression, all the candidate models must be estimated over the same sample; in the notation of Equation (12.25), the number of observations used to estimate the model, T, must be the same for all models. Second, when there are multiple predictors, this approach is computationally demanding because it requires computing many different models (many combinations of the lag parameters). In practice, a convenient shortcut is to require all the regressors to have the same number of lags, that is, to require that $p = q_1 = \cdots = q_k$, so that only $p_{max} + 1$ models need to be compared (corresponding to $p = 0, 1, \ldots, p_{max}$).

12.6 Nonstationarity I: Trends

In Key Concept 12.6, it was assumed that the dependent variable and the regressors are stationary. If this is not the case, that is, if the dependent variable and/or regressors are nonstationary, then conventional hypothesis tests, confidence intervals, and forecasts can be unreliable. The precise problem created by nonstationarity, and the solution to that problem, depends on the nature of that nonstationarity.

In this and the next section, we examine two of the most important types of nonstationarity in economic time series data: trends and breaks. In each section, we first describe the nature of the nonstationarity, then discuss the consequences for time series regression if this type of nonstationarity is present but is ignored. We next present tests for nonstationarity and discuss remedies for, or solutions to, the problems caused by that particular type of nonstationarity. We begin by discussing trends.

What Is a Trend?

A **trend** is a persistent long-term movement of a variable over time. A time series variable fluctuates around its trend.

Inspection of Figure 12.1a suggests that the U.S. inflation rate has a trend consisting of a general upward tendency through 1982 and a downward tendency thereafter. The series in Figures 12.2a, b, and c also have trends, but their trends are quite different. The trend in the U.S. Federal Funds interest rate is similar to the trend in the U.S. inflation rate. The \$/£ exchange rate clearly had a prolonged downward trend after the collapse of the fixed exchange rate system in 1972. The logarithm of Japanese real GDP has a complicated trend: fast growth at first, then moderate growth, and finally slow growth.

Deterministic and stochastic trends.   There are two types of trends seen in time series data, deterministic and stochastic. A **deterministic trend** is a nonrandom function of time. For example, a deterministic trend might be linear in time; if inflation had a deterministic linear trend so that it increased by 0.1 percentage point per quarter, this trend could be written as $0.1t$, where t is measured in quarters. In contrast, a **stochastic trend** is random and varies over time. For example, a stochastic trend in inflation might exhibit a prolonged period of increase followed by a prolonged period of decrease, like the inflation trend in Figure 12.1.

Like many econometricians, we think it is more appropriate to model economic time series as having stochastic rather than deterministic trends. Economics is complicated stuff. It is hard to reconcile the predictability implied by a deterministic trend with the complications and surprises faced year after year by workers, businesses, and governments. For example, although U.S. inflation rose through the 1970s, it was neither destined to rise forever nor destined to fall again. Rather, the slow rise of inflation is now understood to have occurred because of bad luck and bad monetary policy, and its taming was in large part a consequence of tough decisions made by the Board of Governors of the Federal Reserve. Similarly, the $/£ exchange rate trended down from 1972 to 1985 and subsequently drifted up, but these movements too were the consequences of complex economic forces; because these forces change unpredictably, these trends are usefully thought of as having a large unpredictable, or random, component.

For these reasons, our treatment of trends in economic time series focuses on stochastic rather than deterministic trends, and when we refer to "trends" in time series data we mean stochastic trends unless we explicitly say otherwise. This section presents the simplest model of a stochastic trend, the random walk model; other models of trends are discussed in Section 14.3.

The random walk model of a trend.   The simplest model of a variable with a stochastic trend is the random walk. A time series Y_t is said to follow a **random walk** if the change in Y_t is i.i.d., that is, if

$$Y_t = Y_{t-1} + u_t, \tag{12.26}$$

where u_t is i.i.d. We will, however, use the term "random walk" more generally to refer to a time series that follows Equation (12.26), where u_t has conditional mean zero, that is, $E(u_t | Y_{t-1}, Y_{t-2}, \ldots) = 0$.

The basic idea of a random walk is that the value of the series tomorrow is its value today, plus an unpredictable change: because the path followed by Y_t consists of random "steps" u_t, that path is a "random walk." The conditional mean of Y_t based on data through time $t - 1$ is Y_{t-1}; that is, because $E(u_t | Y_{t-1}, Y_{t-2}, \ldots) = 0$, $E(Y_t | Y_{t-1}, Y_{t-2}, \ldots) = Y_{t-1}$. In other words, if Y_t follows a random walk, then the best forecast of tomorrow's value is its value today.

Some series, such as the logarithm of Japanese GDP in Figure 12.2c, have an obvious upward tendency, in which case the best forecast of the series must include an adjustment for the tendency of the series to increase. This adjustment leads to an extension of the random walk model to include a tendency to move, or "drift" in one direction or the other. This extension is referred to as a **random walk with drift**:

$$Y_t = \beta_0 + Y_{t-1} + u_t, \tag{12.27}$$

where $E(u_t | Y_{t-1}, Y_{t-2}, \ldots) = 0$ and β_0 is the "drift" in the random walk. If β_0 is positive, then Y_t increases on average. In the random walk with drift model, the best forecast of the series tomorrow is the value of the series today, plus the drift β_0.

The random walk model (with drift as appropriate) is simple yet versatile, and it is the primary model for trends used in this book.

A random walk is nonstationary.   If Y_t follows a random walk, then it is not stationary: the variance of a random walk increases over time so the distribution of Y_t changes over time. One way to see this is to recognize that, because u_t is serially uncorrelated in Equation (12.26), $\text{var}(Y_t) = \text{var}(Y_{t-1}) + \text{var}(u_t)$; for Y_t to be stationary, $\text{var}(Y_t)$ cannot depend on time, so in particular $\text{var}(Y_t) = \text{var}(Y_{t-1})$ must hold, but this can only happen if $\text{var}(u_t) = 0$. Another way to see this is to imagine that Y_t starts out at zero, that is, $Y_0 = 0$. Then $Y_1 = u_1$, $Y_2 = u_1 + u_2$, and so forth, so that $Y_t = u_1 + u_2 + \cdots + u_t$. Because u_t is serially uncorrelated, $\text{var}(Y_t) = \text{var}(u_1 + u_2 + \cdots + u_t) = t\sigma_u^2$. Thus the variance of Y_t depends on t; in fact, it increases as t increases. Because the variance of Y_t depends on t, its distribution depends on t, that is, it is nonstationary.

Because the variance of a random walk increases without bound, its *population* autocorrelations are not defined (the first autocovariance and variance are infinite and the ratio of the two is not well defined). However, a feature of a random walk is that its *sample* autocorrelations tend to be very close to one, in fact, the jth sample autocorrelation of a random walk converges to one in probability.

Stochastic trends, autoregressive models, and a unit root.   The random walk model is a special case of the AR(1) model (Equation (12.8)) in which $\beta_1 = 1$. In other words, if Y_t follows an AR(1) with $\beta_1 = 1$, then Y_t contains a stochastic trend and is nonstationary. If, however, $|\beta_1| < 1$ and u_t is stationary, then the joint distribution of Y_t and its lags does not depend on t (a result shown in Appendix 12.2) so Y_t is stationary as long as u_t is stationary.

The analogous condition for an AR(p) to be stationary is more complicated than the condition $|\beta_1| < 1$ for an AR(1). Its formal statement involves the roots of the polynomial, $1 - \beta_1 z - \beta_2 z^2 - \beta_3 z^3 - \cdots - \beta_p z^p$. (The roots of this polynomial are the solutions to the equation $1 - \beta_1 z - \beta_2 z^2 - \beta_3 z^3 - \cdots - \beta_p z^p = 0$.) For an AR($p$) to be stationary, the roots of this polynomial must all be greater than one in absolute value. In the special case of an AR(1), the root is the value of z that solves $1 - \beta_1 z = 0$, so its root is $z = 1/\beta_1$. Thus the statement that the root be greater than one in absolute value is equivalent to $|\beta_1| < 1$.

If an AR(p) has a root that equals one, the series is said to have a **unit autoregressive root** or, more simply, a **unit root**. If Y_t has a unit root, then it contains a stochastic trend. If Y_t is stationary (and thus does not have a unit root), it does not contain a stochastic trend. For this reason, we will use the terms "stochastic trend" and "unit root" interchangeably.

Problems Caused by Stochastic Trends

If a regressor has a stochastic trend (has a unit root), then the OLS estimator of its coefficient and its OLS t-statistic can have nonstandard (that is, nonnormal) distributions, even in large samples. We discuss three specific aspects of this problem: first, the estimator of the autoregressive coefficient in an AR(1) is biased towards zero if its true value is one; second, t-statistics on regressors with a stochastic trends can have a nonnormal distribution, even in large samples; and third, an extreme example of the risks posed by stochastic trends is that two series that are independent will, with high probability, misleadingly appear to be related if they both have stochastic trends, a situation known as spurious regression.

Problem #1: Autoregressive coefficients that are biased towards zero.
Suppose that Y_t follows the random walk in Equation (12.26) but this is unknown to the econometrician, who instead estimates the AR(1) model in Equation (12.8). Because Y_t is nonstationary, the least squares assumptions for time series regression in Key Concept 12.6 do not hold, so as a general matter we cannot rely on estimators and test statistics having their usual large-sample normal distributions. In fact, in this example the OLS estimator of the autoregressive coefficient, $\hat{\beta}_1$, is consistent, but it has a nonnormal distribution, even in large samples: the asymptotic distribution of $\hat{\beta}_1$ is shifted towards zero. The expected value of $\hat{\beta}_1$ is approximately $E(\hat{\beta}_1) = 1 - 5.3/T$. This results in a large bias in sample sizes typically encountered in economic applications. For example, 20 years of quarterly data contain 80 observations, in which case the expected value of $\hat{\beta}_1$ is $E(\hat{\beta}_1) = 1 - 5.3/80 = 0.934$. Moreover, this distribution has a long left tail: the 5% percentile of $\hat{\beta}_1$ is approximately $1 - 14.1/T$ which, for $T = 80$, corresponds to 0.824, so that 5% of the time $\hat{\beta}_1 < 0.824$.

One implication of this bias towards zero is that, if Y_t follows a random walk, then forecasts based on the AR(1) model can perform substantially worse than those based on the random walk model, which imposes the true value $\beta_1 = 1$. This conclusion also applies to higher order autoregressions, in which there are forecasting gains from imposing a unit root (that is, from estimating the autoregression in first differences instead of in levels) when in fact the series contains a unit root.

Problem #2: Nonnormal distributions of t-statistics. If a regressor has a stochastic trend, then its usual OLS t-statistic can have a nonnormal distribution under the null hypothesis, even in large samples. This nonnormal distribution means that conventional confidence intervals are not valid and hypothesis tests cannot be conducted as usual. In general, the distribution of this t-statistic is not readily tabulated because the distribution depends on the relationship between the regressor in question and the other regressors. One important case in which it *is* possible to tabulate this distribution is in the context of an autoregression with a unit root, and we return to this special case when we take up the problem of testing whether a time series contains a stochastic trend.

Problem #3: Spurious regression. Stochastic trends can lead two time series to appear related when they are not, a problem called **spurious regression**.

For example, U.S. inflation was steadily rising from the mid–1960s through the early 1980s, and at the same time Japanese GDP was steadily rising. These two trends conspire to produce a regression that appears to be "significant" using conventional measures. Estimated by OLS using data from 1965 through 1981, this regression is

$$\widehat{U.S.Inflation}_t = -2.84 + 0.18 Japanese \ GDP_t, \ \overline{R}^2 = 0.56. \quad (12.28)$$
$$(0.08) \quad (0.02)$$

The t-statistic on the slope coefficient exceeds 9, which by our usual standards indicates a strong positive relationship between the two series, and the $\overline{R}^2$ is high. However, running this regression using data from 1982 through 1999 yields

$$\widehat{U.S.Inflation}_t = 6.25 - 0.03 Japanese \ GDP_t, \ \overline{R}^2 = 0.07. \quad (12.29)$$
$$(1.37) \quad (0.01)$$

The regressions in Equation (12.28) and (12.29) could hardly be more different. Interpreted literally, Equation (12.28) indicates a strong positive relationship, while Equation (12.29) indicates a weak negative relationship.

The source of these conflicting results is that both series have stochastic trends. These trends happened to align from 1965 through 1981, but did not align from 1982 through 1999. There is, in fact, no compelling economic or political reason to think that the trends in these two series are related. In short, these regressions are spurious.

The regressions in Equations (12.28) and (12.29) illustrate empirically the theoretical point that OLS can be misleading when the series contain stochastic trends (see Exercise 12.6 for a computer simulation that demonstrates this result). One special case in which certain regression-based methods *are* reliable is when the trend component of the two series is the same, that is, when the series contain a *common* stochastic trend; if so, the series are said to be cointegrated. Econometric methods for detecting and analyzing cointegrated economic time series are discussed in Section 14.4.

Detecting Stochastic Trends: Testing for a Unit AR Root

Trends in time series data can be detected by informal and formal methods. The informal methods involve inspecting a time series plot of the data and computing the autocorrelation coefficients, as we did in Section 12.2. Because the first autocorrelation coefficient will be near one if the series has a stochastic trend, at least in large samples, a small first autocorrelation coefficient combined with a time series plot that has no apparent trend suggests that the series does not have a trend. If doubt remains, however, there are formal statistical procedures that can be used to test the hypothesis that there is a stochastic trend in the series against the alternative that there is no trend.

In this section, we use the Dickey-Fuller test (named after its inventors David Dickey and Wayne Fuller (1979)) to test for a stochastic trend. Although the Dickey-Fuller test is not the only test for a stochastic trend (another test is discussed in Section 14.3), it is the most commonly used test in practice and is one of the most reliable.

The Dickey-Fuller test in the AR(1) model.   The starting point for the **Dickey-Fuller test** is the autoregressive model. As discussed earlier, the random walk in Equation (12.27) is a special case of the AR(1) model with $\beta_1 = 1$. If $\beta_1 = 1$, Y_t is nonstationary and contains a (stochastic) trend. Thus, within the AR(1) model, the hypothesis that Y_t has a trend can be tested by testing

$$H_0: \beta_1 = 1 \text{ vs. } H_1: \beta_1 < 1 \text{ in } Y_t = \beta_0 + \beta_1 Y_{t-1} + u_t. \quad (12.30)$$

If $\beta_1 = 1$, the AR(1) has an autoregressive root of one, so the null hypothesis in Equation (12.30) is that the AR(1) has a unit root, and the alternative is that it is stationary.

This test is most easily implemented by estimating a modified version of Equation (12.30) obtained by subtracting Y_{t-1} from both sides. Let $\delta = \beta_1 - 1$; then Equation (12.30) becomes

$$H_0: \delta = 0 \text{ vs. } H_1: \delta < 0 \text{ in } \Delta Y_t = \beta_0 + \delta Y_{t-1} + u_t. \tag{12.31}$$

The OLS t-statistic testing $\delta = 0$ in Equation (12.31) is called the **Dickey-Fuller statistic**. The formulation in Equation (12.31) is convenient because regression software automatically prints out the t-statistic testing $\delta = 0$. Note that the Dickey-Fuller test is one-sided, because the relevant alternative is that Y_t is stationary so $\beta_1 < 1$ or, equivalently, $\delta < 0$. The Dickey-Fuller statistic is computed using "nonrobust" standard errors, that is, the "homoskedasticity-only" standard errors presented in Appendix 4.4 (Equation (4.62) for the case of a single regressor and in Section 16.4 for the multiple regression model).[2]

The Dickey-Fuller test in the AR(p) model.   The Dickey-Fuller statistic presented in the context of Equation (12.31) applies only to an AR(1). As discussed in Section 12.3, for some series the AR(1) model does not capture all the serial correlation in Y_t, in which case a higher order autoregression is more appropriate.

The extension of the Dickey-Fuller test to the AR(p) model is summarized in Key Concept 12.8. Under the null hypothesis, $\delta = 0$ and ΔY_t is a stationary AR(p). Under the alternative hypothesis, $\delta < 0$ so that Y_t is stationary. Because the regression used to compute this version of the Dickey-Fuller statistic is augmented by lags of ΔY_t, the resulting t-statistic is referred to as the **augmented Dickey-Fuller (ADF) statistic**.

In general the lag length p is unknown, but it can be estimated using an information criterion applied to regressions of the form (12.32) for various values of p. Studies of the ADF statistic suggest that it is better to have too many lags than too few, so it is recommended to use the AIC instead of the BIC to estimate p for the ADF statistic.[3]

---

[2]Under the null hypothesis of a unit root the usual "nonrobust" standard errors produce a t-statistic that is in fact robust to heteroskedasticity, a surprising and special result.

[3]See Stock (1994) for a review of simulation studies of the finite-sample properties of the Dickey-Fuller and other unit root test statistics.

Key Concept 12.8

The Augmented Dickey-Fuller Test for a Unit Autoregressive Root

The augmented Dickey–Fuller (ADF) test for a unit autoregressive root tests the null hypothesis H_0: $\delta = 0$ against the one-sided alternative H_1: $\delta < 0$ in the regression

$$\Delta Y_t = \beta_0 + \delta Y_{t-1} + \gamma_1 \Delta Y_{t-1} + \gamma_2 \Delta Y_{t-2} + \cdots + \gamma_p \Delta Y_{t-p} + u_t. \quad (12.32)$$

Under the null hypothesis, Y_t has a stochastic trend; under the alternative hypothesis, Y_t is stationary. The ADF statistic is the OLS t-statistic testing $\delta = 0$ in Equation (12.32).

If instead the alternative hypothesis is that Y_t is stationary around a deterministic linear time trend, then this trend, "t" (the observation number), must be added as an additional regressor, in which case the Dickey-Fuller regression becomes

$$\Delta Y_t = \beta_0 + \alpha t + \delta Y_{t-1} + \gamma_1 \Delta Y_{t-1} + \gamma_2 \Delta Y_{t-2} + \cdots + \gamma_p \Delta Y_{t-p} + u_t, \quad (12.33)$$

where α is an unknown coefficient and the ADF statistic is the OLS t-statistic testing $\delta = 0$ in Equation (12.33).

The lag length p can be estimated using the BIC or AIC. The ADF statistic does *not* have a normal distribution, even in large samples. Critical values for the one-sided ADF test depend on whether the test is based on Equation (12.32) or (12.33) and are given in Table 12.4.

Testing against the alternative of stationarity around a linear deterministic time trend. The discussion so far has considered the null hypothesis that the series has a unit root and the alternative hypothesis that it is stationary. This alternative hypothesis of stationarity is appropriate for series, like the rate of inflation, that do not exhibit long-term growth. But other economic time series, like Japanese GDP (Figure 12.2c), exhibit long-run growth, and for such series the alternative of stationarity without a trend is inappropriate. Instead, a commonly used alternative is that the series are stationary around a deterministic time trend, that is, a trend that is a deterministic function of time.

One specific formulation of this alternative hypothesis is that the time trend is linear, that is, the trend is a linear function of t; thus, the null hypothesis is that the series has a unit root and the alternative is that it does not have a unit root but does have a deterministic time trend. The Dickey-Fuller regression must be modified to test the null hypothesis of a unit root against the alternative that it is stationary around a linear time trend. As summarized in Equation (12.33) in Key Concept 12.8, this is accomplished by adding a time trend (the regressor $X_t = t$) to the regression.

A linear time trend is not the only way to specify a deterministic time trend; for example, the deterministic time trend could be quadratic, or it could be linear but have breaks (that is, be linear with slopes that differ in two parts of the sample). The use of alternatives like these with nonlinear deterministic trends should be motivated by economic theory. For a discussion of unit root tests against stationarity around nonlinear deterministic trends, see Maddala and Kim (1998, Chapter 13).

Critical values for the ADF statistic. Under the null hypothesis of a unit root, the ADF statistic does *not* have a normal distribution, even in large samples. Because its distribution is nonstandard, the usual critical values from the normal distribution cannot be used when using the ADF statistic to test for a unit root; a special set of critical values, based on the distribution of the ADF statistic under the null hypothesis, must be used instead.

The critical values for the ADF test are given in Table 12.4. Because the alternative hypothesis of stationarity implies that $\delta < 0$ in Equations (12.32) and (12.33), the ADF test is one-sided. For example, if the regression does not include a time trend, then the hypothesis of a unit root is rejected at the 5% significance level if the ADF statistic is less than -2.86. If a time trend is included in the regression, the critical value is instead -3.41.

The critical values in Table 12.4 are substantially larger (more negative) than the one-sided critical values of -1.28 (at the 10% level) and -1.645 (at the 5% level) from the standard normal distribution. The nonstandard distribution of the ADF statistic is an example of how OLS t-statistics for regressors with stochastic trends can have nonnormal distributions. Why the large-sample distribution of the ADF statistic is nonstandard is discussed further in Section 14.3.

TABLE 12.4 Large-Sample Critical Values of the Augmented Dickey-Fuller Statistic			
Deterministic Regressors	**10%**	**5%**	**1%**
Intercept only	−2.57	−2.86	−3.43
Intercept and time trend	−3.12	−3.41	−3.96

Does U.S. inflation have a stochastic trend?   The null hypothesis that inflation has a stochastic trend can be tested against the alternative that it is stationary by performing the ADF test for a unit autoregressive root. The ADF regression with four lags of Inf_t is

$$(12.34)$$

$$\widehat{\Delta Inf_t} = 0.53 - 0.11 Inf_{t-1} - 0.14\Delta Inf_{t-1} - 0.25\Delta Inf_{t-2} + 0.24\Delta Inf_{t-3} + 0.01\Delta Inf_{t-4}$$
$$\quad\ (0.23)\ \ (0.04)\qquad (0.08)\qquad\quad (0.08)\qquad\quad (0.08)\qquad\quad (0.08)$$

The ADF t-statistic is the t-statistic testing the hypothesis that the coefficient on Inf_{t-1} is zero; this is $t = -2.60$. From Table 12.4, the 5% critical value is -2.86. Because the ADF statistic of -2.60 is less negative than -2.86, the test does not reject at the 5% significance level. Based on the regression in Equation (12.34), we therefore cannot reject (at the 5% significance level) the null hypothesis that inflation has a unit autoregressive root, that is, that inflation contains a stochastic trend, against the alternative that it is stationary.

The ADF regression in Equation (12.34) includes four lags of ΔInf_t to compute the ADF statistic. When the number of lags is estimated using the AIC, where $0 \le p \le 6$, the AIC estimator of the lag length is, however, three. When three lags are used (that is, when ΔInf_{t-1}, ΔInf_{t-2}, and ΔInf_{t-3} are included as regressors), the ADF statistic is -2.65, which is less negative than -2.86. Thus, when the number of lags in the ADF regression is chosen by AIC, the hypothesis that inflation contains a stochastic trend is not rejected at the 5% significance level.

These tests were performed at the 5% significance level. At the 10% significance level, however, the tests reject the null hypothesis of a unit root: the ADF statistics of -2.60 (four lags) and -2.65 (three lags) are slightly more negative than the 10% critical value of -2.57. Thus the ADF statistics paint a rather ambiguous picture, and the forecaster must make an informed judgment about whether or not to model inflation as having a stochastic trend. Clearly, inflation in Figure 12.1a exhibits long-run swings, consistent with the stochastic trend model. Moreover, in practice, many forecasters treat U.S. inflation as having a stochastic trend, and we follow that strategy here.

Avoiding the Problems Caused by Stochastic Trends

The most reliable way to handle a trend in a series is to transform the series so that it does not have the trend. If the series has a stochastic trend, that is, if the series has a unit root, then the first difference of the series does not have a trend.

For example, if Y_t follows a random walk so $Y_t = \beta_0 + Y_{t-1} + u_t$, then $\Delta Y_t = \beta_0 + u_t$ is stationary. Thus using first differences eliminates random walk trends in a series.

In practice, you can rarely be sure whether a series has a stochastic trend or not. Recall that, as a general point, failure to reject the null hypothesis does not necessarily mean that the null hypothesis is true; rather, it simply means that you have insufficient evidence to conclude that it is false. Thus, failure to reject the null hypothesis of a unit root using the ADF test does not mean that the series actually *has* a unit root. For example, in an AR(1) the true coefficient β_1 might be very close to one, say 0.98, in which case the ADF test would have low power, that is, a low probability of correctly rejecting the null hypothesis in samples the size of our inflation series. Even though failure to reject the null hypothesis of a unit root does not mean the series has a unit root, it still can be reasonable to approximate the true autoregressive root as equaling one and therefore to use differences of the series rather than its levels.[4]

12.7 Nonstationarity II: Breaks

A second type of nonstationarity arises when the population regression function changes over the course of the sample. In economics, this can occur for a variety of reasons, such as changes in economic policy, changes in the structure of the economy, or an invention that changes a specific industry. If such changes, or "breaks," occur, then a regression model that neglects those changes can provide a misleading basis for inference and forecasting.

This section presents two strategies for checking for breaks in a time series regression function over time. The first strategy looks for potential breaks from the perspective of hypothesis testing, and entails testing for changes in the regression coefficients using F-statistics. The second strategy looks for potential breaks from the perspective of forecasting: you pretend that your sample ends sooner than it actually does and evaluate the forecasts you would have made had this been so. Breaks are detected when the forecasting performance is substantially poorer than expected.

What Is a Break?

Breaks can arise either from a discrete change in the population regression coefficients at a distinct date or from a gradual evolution of the coefficients over a longer period of time.

---

[4]For additional discussion of stochastic trends in economic time series variables and of the problems they pose for regression analysis, see Stock and Watson (1988).

One source of discrete breaks in macroeconomic data is a major change in macroeconomic policy. For example, the breakdown of the Bretton Woods system of fixed exchange rates in 1972 produced the break in the time series behavior of the $/£ exchange rate that is evident in Figure 12.2b. Prior to 1972, the exchange rate was essentially constant, with the exception of a single devaluation in 1968 in which the official value of the pound, relative to the dollar, was decreased. In contrast, since 1972 the exchange rate has fluctuated over a very wide range.

Breaks also can occur more slowly as the population regression evolves over time. For example, such changes can arise because of slow evolution of economic policy and ongoing changes in the structure of the economy. The methods for detecting breaks described in this section can detect both types of breaks, distinct changes and slow evolution.

Problems caused by breaks.   If a break occurs in the population regression function during the sample, then the OLS regression estimates over the full sample will estimate a relationship that holds "on average," in the sense that the estimate combines the two different periods. Depending on the location and the size of the break, the "average" regression function can be quite different than the true regression function at the end of the sample, and this leads to poor forecasts.

Testing for Breaks

One way to detect breaks is to test for discrete changes, or breaks, in the regression coefficients. How this is done depends on whether the date of the suspected break (the **break date**) is known or not.

Testing for a break at a known date.   In some applications you might suspect that there is a break at a known date. For example, if you are studying international trade relationships using data from the 1970s, you might hypothesize that there is a break in the population regression function of interest in 1972 when the Bretton Woods system of fixed exchange rates was abandoned in favor of floating exchange rates.

If the date of the hypothesized break in the coefficients is known, then the null hypothesis of no break can be tested using a binary variable interaction regression of the type discussed in Chapter 6 (Key Concept 6.4). To keep things simple, consider an ADL(1,1) model, so there is an intercept, a single lag of Y_t, and a single lag of X_t. Let τ denote the hypothesized break date and let $D_t(\tau)$ be a binary variable that equals zero before the break date and one after, so $D_t(\tau) = 0$

if $t \le \tau$ and $D_t(\tau) = 1$ if $t > \tau$. Then the regression including the binary break indicator and all interaction terms is

$$Y_t = \beta_0 + \beta_1 Y_{t-1} + \delta_1 X_{t-1} + \gamma_0 D_t(\tau) + \gamma_1 [D_t(\tau) \times Y_{t-1}] + \gamma_2 [D_t(\tau) \times X_{t-1}] + u_t. \tag{12.35}$$

If there is not a break, then the population regression function is the same over both parts of the sample so the terms involving the break binary variable $D_t(\tau)$ do not enter Equation (12.35). That is, under the null hypothesis of no break, $\gamma_0 = \gamma_1 = \gamma_2 = 0$. Under the alternative hypothesis that there is a break, then the population regression function is different before and after the break date τ, in which case at least one of the γ's is nonzero. Thus the hypothesis of a break can be tested using the F-statistic that tests the hypothesis that $\gamma_0 = \gamma_1 = \gamma_2 = 0$ against the hypothesis that at least one of the γ's is nonzero. This is often called a Chow test for a break at a known break date, named for its inventor, Gregory Chow (1960).

If there are multiple predictors or more lags, then this test can be extended by constructing binary variable interaction variables for all the regressors and testing the hypothesis that all the coefficients on terms involving $D_t(\tau)$ are zero.

This approach can be modified to check for a break in a subset of the coefficients by including only the binary variable interactions for that subset of regressors of interest.

Testing for a break at an unknown break date   Often the date of a possible break is unknown or known only within a range. Suppose, for example, you suspect that a break occurred sometime between two dates, τ_0 and τ_1. The Chow test can be modified to handle this by testing for breaks at all possible dates τ in between τ_0 and τ_1, then using the largest of the resulting F-statistics to test for a break at an unknown date. This modified Chow test is variously called the **Quandt likelihood ratio (QLR) statistic** (Quandt, 1960) (the term we shall use) or, more obscurely, the **sup-Wald statistic**.

Because the QLR statistic is the largest of many F-statistics, its distribution is not the same as an individual F-statistic. Instead, the critical values for the QLR statistic must be obtained from a special distribution. Like the F-statistic, this distribution depends on the number of restrictions being tested, q, that is, the number of coefficients (including the intercept) that are being allowed to break, or change, under the alternative hypothesis. The distribution of the QLR statistic also depends on τ_0 / T and τ_1 / T, that is, on the endpoints, τ_0 and τ_1, of the subsample over which the F-statistics are computed, expressed as a fraction of the total sample size.

For the large-sample approximation to the distribution of the QLR statistic to be a good one, the subsample endpoints, τ_0 and τ_1, cannot be too close to the end of the sample. For this reason, in practice the QLR statistic is computed over a "trimmed" range, or subset, of the sample. A common choice is to use 15% trimming, that is, to set for $\tau_0 = 0.15T$ and $\tau_1 = 0.85T$ (rounded to the nearest integer). With 15% trimming, the F-statistic is computed for break dates in the central 70% of the sample.

The critical values for the QLR statistic, computed with 15% trimming, are given in Table 12.5. Comparing these critical values with those of the $F_{q,\infty}$ distribution (Appendix Table 4) shows that the critical values for the QLR statistics are larger. This reflects the fact that the QLR statistic looks at the largest of many individual F-statistics. By examining F-statistics at many possible break dates, the QLR statistic has many opportunities to reject, leading to QLR critical values that are larger than the individual F-statistic critical values.

Like the Chow test, the QLR test can be used to focus on the possibility that there are breaks in only some of the regression coefficients. This is done by first computing the Chow tests at different break dates using binary variable interactions only for the variables with the suspect coefficients, then computing the maximum of those Chow tests over the range $\tau_0 \leq \tau \leq \tau_1$. The critical values for this version of the QLR test are also taken from Table 12.5, where the number of restrictions (q) is the number of restrictions tested by the constituent F-tests.

If there is a discrete break at a date within the range tested, then the QLR statistic will reject with high probability in large samples. Moreover, the date at which the constituent F-statistic is at its maximum, $\hat{\tau}$, is an estimate of the break date τ. This estimate is a good one in the sense that, under certain technical conditions, $\hat{\tau}/T \xrightarrow{p} \tau/T$, that is, the fraction of the way through the sample at which the break occurs is estimated consistently.

The QLR statistic also rejects with high probability in large samples when there are multiple discrete breaks or when the break comes in the form of a slow evolution of the regression function. This means that the QLR statistic detects forms of instability other than a single discrete break. As a result, if the QLR statistic rejects, it can mean that there is a single discrete break, that there are multiple discrete breaks, or that there is slow evolution of the regression function.

The QLR statistic is summarized in Key Concept 12.9.

Warning: You probably don't know the break date even if you think you do. Sometimes an expert might believe that he or she knows the date of a possible break, so that the Chow test can be used instead of the QLR test. But if this knowledge is based on the expert's knowledge of the series being analyzed, then

TABLE 12.5 Critical Values of the QLR Statistic with 15% Trimming			
Number of Restrictions (q)	**10%**	**5%**	**1%**
1	7.12	8.68	12.16
2	5.00	5.86	7.78
3	4.09	4.71	6.02
4	3.59	4.09	5.12
5	3.26	3.66	4.53
6	3.02	3.37	4.12
7	2.84	3.15	3.82
8	2.69	2.98	3.57
9	2.58	2.84	3.38
10	2.48	2.71	3.23
11	2.40	2.62	3.09
12	2.33	2.54	2.97
13	2.27	2.46	2.87
14	2.21	2.40	2.78
15	2.16	2.34	2.71
16	2.12	2.29	2.64
17	2.08	2.25	2.58
18	2.05	2.20	2.53
19	2.01	2.17	2.48
20	1.99	2.13	2.43

These critical values apply when $\tau_0 = 0.15T$ and $\tau_1 = 0.85T$ (rounded to the nearest integer), so that the F-statistic is computed for all potential break dates in the central 70% of the sample. The number of restrictions q is the number of restrictions tested by each individual F-statistic. This table was kindly provided to us by Donald Andrews, and supercedes Table 1 in Andrews (1993).

in fact this date was estimated using the data, albeit in an informal way. Preliminary estimation of the break date means that the usual F critical values cannot be used for the Chow test for a break at that date. Thus it remains appropriate to use the QLR statistic in this circumstance.

The QLR Test for Coefficient Stability

Key Concept 12.9

Let $F(\tau)$ denote the F-statistic testing the hypothesis of a break in the regression coefficients at date τ; in the regression in Equation (12.35), for example, this is the F-statistic testing the null hypothesis that $\gamma_0 = \gamma_1 = \gamma_2 = 0$. The QLR (or Sup-Wald) test is the largest of statistics in the range $\tau_0 \le \tau \le \tau_1$:

$$\text{QLR} = \max[F(\tau_0), F(\tau_0 + 1), \ldots, F(\tau_1)]. \qquad (12.36)$$

1. Like the F-statistic, the QLR statistic can be used to test for a break in all or just some of the regression coefficients.

2. In large samples, the distribution of the QLR statistic under the null hypothesis depends on the number of restrictions being tested, q, and on the endpoints τ_0 and τ_1 as a fraction of T. Critical values are given in Table 12.5 for 15% trimming ($\tau_0 = 0.15T$ and $\tau_1 = 0.85T$, rounded to the nearest integer).

3. The QLR test can detect a single discrete break, multiple discrete breaks, and/or slow evolution of the regression function.

4. If there is a distinct break in the regression function, the date at which the largest Chow statistic occurs is an estimator of the break date.

Application: Has the Phillips curve been stable?   The QLR test provides a way to check whether the Phillips curve has been stable from 1962 to 1999. Specifically, we focus on whether there have been changes in the coefficients on the lagged values of the unemployment rate and the intercept in the ADL(4,4) specification in Equation (12.17) containing four lags each of ΔInf_t and $Unemp_t$.

The Chow F-statistics testing the hypothesis that the intercept and the coefficients on $Unemp_{t-1}, \ldots, Unemp_{t-4}$ in Equation (12.17) are constant against the alternative that they break at a given date are plotted in Figure 12.5 for breaks in the central 70% of the sample. For example, the F-statistic testing for a break in 1980:I is 2.26, the value plotted at that date in the figure. Each F-statistic tests five restrictions (no change in the intercept and in the four coefficients on lags of the unemployment rate), so $q = 5$. The largest of these F-statistics is 3.53, which occurs in 1982:II; this is the QLR statistic. Comparing 3.53 to the critical values for $q = 5$ in Table 12.5 indicates that the hypothesis that these coefficients are stable is rejected at the 10% significance level (the critical value is 3.26), but not 5% significance level (the critical value is 3.66). Thus there is some evidence that at

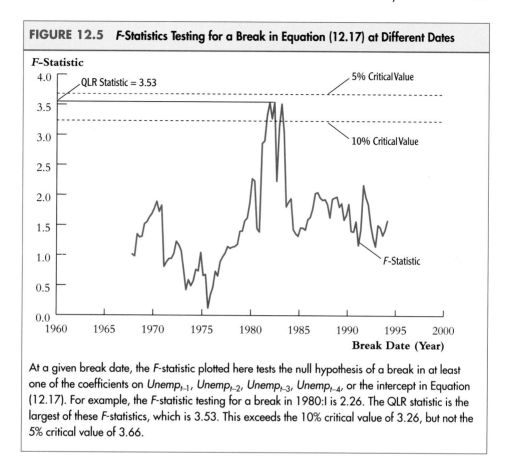

FIGURE 12.5 *F-Statistics Testing for a Break in Equation (12.17) at Different Dates*

F-Statistic

QLR Statistic = 3.53

5% Critical Value

10% Critical Value

F-Statistic

Break Date (Year)

At a given break date, the *F*-statistic plotted here tests the null hypothesis of a break in at least one of the coefficients on $Unemp_{t-1}$, $Unemp_{t-2}$, $Unemp_{t-3}$, $Unemp_{t-4}$, or the intercept in Equation (12.17). For example, the *F*-statistic testing for a break in 1980:I is 2.26. The QLR statistic is the largest of these *F*-statistics, which is 3.53. This exceeds the 10% critical value of 3.26, but not the 5% critical value of 3.66.

least one of these five coefficients has changed over the sample, but the evidence is not especially strong.

Pseudo Out-of-Sample Forecasting

The ultimate test of a forecasting model is its out-of-sample performance, that is, its forecasting performance in "real time," after the model has been estimated. **Pseudo out-of-sample forecasting** is a method for simulating the real-time performance of a forecasting model. The idea of pseudo out-of-sample forecasting is simple: pick a date near the end of the sample, estimate your forecasting model using data up to that date, then use that estimated model to make a forecast. Performing this exercise for multiple dates near the end of your sample yields a series of pseudo forecasts and thus pseudo forecast errors. The pseudo forecast errors can then be examined to see if they are representative of what you would expect if the forecasting relationship were stationary.

Key Concept 12.10

Pseudo Out-of-Sample Forecasts

Pseudo out-of-sample forecasts are computed using the following steps:

1. Choose a number of observations, P, for which you will generate pseudo out-of-sample forecasts; for example, P might be 10% or 15% of the sample size. Let $s = T - P$.

2. Estimate the forecasting regression using the shortened data set for $t = 1, \ldots, s$.

3. Compute the forecast for the first period beyond this shortened sample, $s + 1$; call this $\tilde{Y}_{s+1|s}$.

4. Compute the forecast error, $\tilde{u}_{s+1} = Y_{s+1} - \tilde{Y}_{s+1|s}$.

5. Repeat steps 2–4 for the remaining dates, $s = T - P + 1$ to $T - 1$ (re-estimate the regression at each date). The pseudo out-of-sample forecasts are $\{\tilde{Y}_{s+1|s}, s = T - P, \ldots, T - 1\}$ and the pseudo out-of-sample forecast errors are $\{\tilde{u}_{s+1}, s = T - P, \ldots, T - 1\}$.

The reason this is called "pseudo" out-of-sample forecasting is that it is not true out-of-sample forecasting. True out-of-sample forecasting occurs in real time, that is, you make your forecast without the benefit of knowing the future values of the series. In pseudo out-of-sample forecasting, you simulate real time forecasting using your model, but you have the "future" data against which to assess those simulated, or pseudo, forecasts. Pseudo out-of-sample forecasting mimics the forecasting process that would occur in real time, but without having to wait for new data to arrive.

Pseudo out-of-sample forecasting gives a forecaster a sense of how well the model has been forecasting at the end of the sample. This can provide valuable information, either bolstering confidence that the model has been forecasting well or suggesting that the model has gone off track in the recent past. The methodology of pseudo out-of-sample forecasting is summarized in Key Concept 12.10.

Other uses of pseudo out-of-sample forecasting. A second use of pseudo out-of-sample forecasting is to estimate the RMSFE. Because the pseudo out-of-sample forecasts are computed using only data prior to the forecast date, the pseudo out-of-sample forecast errors reflect both the uncertainty associated with future values of the error term and the uncertainty arising because the regression coefficients were estimated; that is, the pseudo out-of-sample forecast errors include both sources of error in Equation (12.21). Thus the sample standard deviation of the pseudo out-of-sample forecast errors is an estimator of the RMSFE. As discussed in Section 12.4, this estimator of the RMSFE can be used to quantify forecast uncertainty and to construct forecast intervals.

A third use of pseudo out-of-sample forecasting is to compare two or more candidate forecasting models. Two models that appear to fit the data equally well can perform quite differently in a pseudo out-of-sample forecasting exercise. When the models are different, for example, when they include different predictors, pseudo out-of-sample forecasting provides a convenient way to compare the two models that focuses on their potential to provide reliable forecasts.

Application: Did the Phillips curve change during the 1990s?   If the coefficients of the Phillips curve changed during the 1990s, then pseudo out-of-sample forecasts computed over that period should deteriorate. The pseudo out-of-sample forecasts of inflation for the period 1994:I to 1999:IV, computed using the four-lag Phillips curve, are plotted in Figure 12.6 along with the actual values of inflation. For example, the forecast of inflation for 1994:I was computed by regressing ΔInf_t on $\Delta Inf_{t-1}, \ldots, \Delta Inf_{t-4}, Unemp_{t-1}, \ldots, Unemp_{t-4}$ with an intercept using the data through 1993:IV, then computing the forecast $\widehat{\Delta Inf}_{t1994:I \mid 1993:IV}$ using these estimated coefficients and the data through 1993:IV. The inflation forecast for 1994:I is then $\widehat{Inf}_{1994:I \mid 1993:IV} = Inf_{1993:IV} + \widehat{\Delta Inf}_{t1994:I \mid 1993:IV}$. This entire procedure was repeated using data through 1994:I to compute the forecast $\widehat{Inf}_{1994:II \mid 1994:I}$. Doing this for all 24 quarters from 1994:I–1999:IV creates 24 pseudo out-of-sample forecasts, which are plotted in Figure 12.6. The pseudo out-of-sample forecast errors are the differences between actual inflation and its pseudo out-of-sample forecast, that is, the differences between the two lines in Figure 12.6. For example, in the third quarter of 1997, the inflation rate rose by 0.9 percentage points, but the pseudo out-of-sample forecast of $\Delta Inf_{1997:III}$ was 1.9 percentage points, so the pseudo out-of-sample forecast error was $\Delta Inf_{1997:III} - \widehat{\Delta Inf}_{1997:III \mid 1997:II} = 0.9 - 1.9 = -1.0$ percentage points. In other words, a forecaster using the ADL(4,4) model of the Phillips curve, estimated through 1997:II, would have forecasted that inflation would increase by 1.9 percentage points in 1997:III, whereas in reality it only increased by 0.9 percentage points.

How do the mean and standard deviation of the pseudo out-of-sample forecast errors compare with the in-sample fit of the model? The standard error of the regression of the four-lag Phillips curve fit using data through 1993:IV is 1.47, so based on the in-sample fit we would expect the out-of-sample forecast errors to have mean zero and root mean square forecast error of 1.47. In fact, the aver-

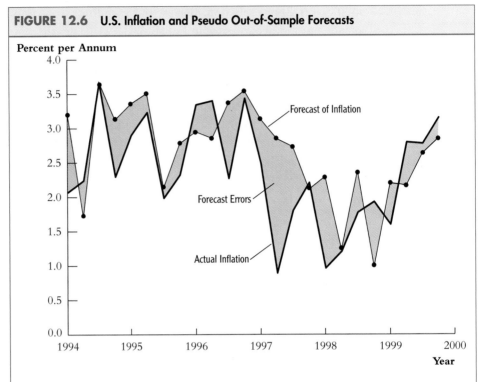

FIGURE 12.6 U.S. Inflation and Pseudo Out-of-Sample Forecasts

The pseudo out-of-sample forecasts made using a four-lag Phillips curve of the form in Equation (12.17) generally track actual inflation, but on average the forecasts are higher than actual inflation. This upward bias in the forecasts may have been caused by a decline in the natural rate of unemployment, which would appear as a shift in the intercept of the Phillips curve.

age forecast error is −0.37 and the sample RMSFE is 0.75. Thus the RMSFE of the pseudo out-of-sample forecasts is *less* than predicted by the in-sample fit of the regression. However, the average forecast error is negative rather than zero, that is, on average the forecasts predicted larger increases in inflation (and thus higher inflation) than actually occurred. In fact, the *t*-statistic testing the hypothesis that the mean out-of-sample forecast error is zero is $t = -2.71$, so the hypothesis that the mean is zero is rejected at the 1% significance level. This suggests that the forecasts were biased over this period, systematically forecasting higher inflation than actually occurred. The finding that the pseudo out-of-sample forecasts are biased is reflected in Figure 12.6: forecasted inflation typically exceeds actual inflation so the average forecast error is negative.

These biased forecasts suggest that the Phillips curve regression was unstable towards the end of this sample, and that this instability led to forecasts of the change in inflation that were systematically too high. Before using this model for real-time forecasting, it would be important to try to identify the source of this shift and to incorporate it into a modified version of the Phillips curve model.

Taken together, this bias in the pseudo out-of-sample forecasts and the rejection of stability by the QLR statistic (at the 10% level) suggest that the four-lag Phillips curve has been unstable. This instability was a matter of considerable interest during the 1990s and early 2000s because economic forecasters recognized that, as seen in Figure 12.6, inflation forecasts based on the Phillips curve were too high. Some macroeconomists think that the source of this instability was a decline in the natural rate of unemployment during the 1990s, which would translate into a negative shift in the intercept in the regressions examined here. Other macroeconomists think that this breakdown is more complete, however, and that the entire concept of the Phillips curve—a link between the pressures of excess demand and overall price inflation—is just an antiquated feature of the pre-information age economy. If you are interested in reading more on this debate, see the symposium on the Phillips curve in the Winter 1997 issue of the *Journal of Economic Perspectives.*

Avoiding the Problems Caused by Breaks

The best way to adjust for a break in the population regression function depends on the source of that break. If a distinct break occurs at a specific date, this break will be detected with high probability by the QLR statistic, and the break date can be estimated. Thus the regression function can be estimated using a binary variable indicating the two subsamples associated with this break, interacted with the other regressors as needed. If all the coefficients break, then this regression takes the form of Equation (12.35), where τ is replaced by the estimated break date, $\hat{\tau}$, while if only some of the coefficients break, then only the relevant interaction terms appear in the regression. If there is in fact a distinct break, then inference on the regression coefficients can proceed as usual, for example using the usual normal critical values for hypothesis tests based on *t*-statistics. In addition, forecasts can be produced using the estimated regression function that applies to the end of the sample.

If the break is not distinct but rather arises from a slow, ongoing change in the parameters, the remedy is more difficult, and goes beyond the scope of this book.[5]

---

[5]For additional discussion of estimation and testing in the presence of discrete breaks, see Hansen (2001). For an advanced discussion of estimation and forecasting when there are slowly evolving coefficients, see Hamilton (1994, Chapter 13).

12.8 Conclusion

In time series data, a variable generally is correlated from one observation, or date, to the next. A consequence of this correlation is that linear regression can be used to forecast future values of a time series based on its current and past values. The starting point for time series regression is an autoregression, in which the regressors are lagged values of the dependent variable. If additional predictors are available, then their lags can be added to the regression.

This chapter has considered several technical issues that arise when estimating and using regressions with time series data. One such issue is determining the number of lags to include in the regressions. As discussed in Section 12.5, if the number of lags is chosen to minimize the BIC, then the estimated lag length is consistent for the true lag length.

Another of these issues concerns whether or not the series being analyzed are stationary. If the series are stationary, then the usual methods of statistical inference (such as comparing t-statistics to normal critical values) can be used, and, because the population regression function is stable over time, regressions estimated using historical data can be used reliably for forecasting. If, however, the series are nonstationary, then things become more complicated, where the specific complication depends on the nature of the nonstationarity. For example, if the series is nonstationary because it has a stochastic trend, then the OLS estimator and t-statistic can have nonstandard (nonnormal) distributions, even in large samples, and forecast performance can be improved by specifying the regression in first differences. A test for detecting this type of nonstationarity—the augmented Dickey-Fuller test for a unit root—was introduced in Section 12.6. Alternatively, if the population regression function has a break, then neglecting this break results in estimating an average version of the population regression function that in turn can lead to biased and/or imprecise forecasts. Procedures for detecting a break in the population regression function were introduced in Section 12.7.

In this chapter, the methods of time series regression were applied to economic forecasting, and the coefficients in these forecasting models were not given a causal interpretation. You do not need a causal relationship to forecast, and ignoring causal interpretations liberates the quest for good forecasts. In some applications, however, the task is not to develop a forecasting model but rather to estimate causal relationships among time series variables, that is, to estimate the *dynamic* causal effect on Y *over time* of a change in X. Under the right conditions, the methods of this chapter, or closely related methods, can be used to estimate dynamic causal effects, and that is the topic of the next chapter.

Summary

1. Regression models used for forecasting need not have a causal interpretation.
2. A time series variable generally is correlated with one or more of its lagged values; that is, it is serially correlated.
3. An autoregression of order p is a linear multiple regression model in which the regressors are the first p lags of the dependent variable. The coefficients of an $AR(p)$ can be estimated by OLS, and the estimated regression function can be used for forecasting. The lag order p can be estimated using an information criterion such as the BIC.
4. Adding other variables and their lags to an autoregression can improve forecasting performance. Under the least squares assumptions for time series regression (Key Concept 12.6), the OLS estimators have normal distributions in large samples and statistical inference proceeds the same way as for cross-sectional data.
5. Forecast intervals are one way to quantify forecast uncertainty. If the errors are normally distributed, an approximate 68% forecast interval can be constructed as the forecast ± an estimate of the root mean squared forecast error.
6. A series that contains a stochastic trend is nonstationary, violating the second least squares assumption in Key Concept 12.6. The OLS estimator and t-statistic for the coefficient of a regressor with a stochastic trend can have a nonstandard distribution, potentially leading to biased estimators, inefficient forecasts, and misleading inferences. The ADF statistic can be used to test for a stochastic trend. A random walk stochastic trend can be eliminated by using first differences of the series.
7. If the population regression function changes over time, then OLS estimates neglecting this instability are unreliable for statistical inference or forecasting. The QLR statistic can be used to test for a break and, if a discrete break is found, the regression function can be re-estimated in a way that allows for the break.
8. Pseudo out-of-sample forecasts can be used to assess model stability towards the end of the sample, to estimate the root mean squared forecast error, and to compare different forecasting models.

Key Terms

first lag (432)

j^{th} lag (432)

first difference (432)

autocorrelation (434)

serial correlation (434)

autocorrelation coefficient (434)

j^{th} autocovariance (435)

autoregression (438)

forecast error (439)

root mean squared forecast error (440)

AR(p) (441)

autoregressive distributed lag model (445)

ADL(p,q) (445)

stationarity (446)

weak dependence (448)

Granger causality test (449)

forecast interval (451)

BIC (453)

AIC (455)

trend (457)

deterministic trend (457)

stochastic trend (457)

random walk (458)

random walk with drift (459)

unit root (460)

spurious regression (461)

Dickey-Fuller statistic (463)

augmented Dickey-Fuller (ADF) statistic (463)

break date (468)

Quandt likelihood ratio (QLR) statistic (469)

pseudo out-of-sample forecast (473)

Review the Concepts

12.1 Look at the plot of the logarithm of real GDP for Japan in Figure 12.2c. Does this time series appear to be stationary? Explain. Suppose that you calculated the first difference of this series. Would it appear to be stationary? Explain.

12.2 Many financial economists believe that the random walk model is a good description of the logarithm of stock prices. It implies that the percentage changes in stock prices are unforecastable. A financial analyst claims to have a new model that predicts better than the random walk model. Explain how you would examine the analyst's claim that his model is superior.

12.3 A researcher estimates an AR(1) with an intercept and finds that the OLS estimate of β_1 is 0.95, with a standard error of 0.02. Does a 95% confidence interval include $\beta_1 = 1$? Explain.

12.4 Suppose that you suspected that the intercept in Equation (12.17) changed in 1992:I. How would you modify the equation to incorporate this change? How would you test for a change in the intercept? How would you test for a change in the intercept if you did not know the date of the change?

Exercises

*12.1 Suppose that Y_t follows the stationary AR(1) model $Y_t = 2.5 + 0.7Y_{t-1} + u_t$, where u_t is i.i.d. with $E(u_t) = 0$ and $\text{var}(u_t) = 9$.

   a. Compute the mean and variance of Y_t.

   b. Compute the first two autocovariances of Y_t.

   c. Compute the first two autocorrelations of Y_t.

   d. Suppose that $Y_T = 102.3$. Compute $Y_{T+1|T} = E(Y_{T+1} | Y_T, Y_{T-1}, \ldots)$.

12.2 The index of industrial production (IP_t) is a monthly time series that measures the quantity of industrial commodities produced in a given month. This problem uses data on this index for the United States. All regressions are estimated over the sample period 1960:1 to 2000:12 (that is, January 1960 through December 2000). Let $Y_t = 1200 \times \ln(IP_t/IP_{t-1})$.

   a. The forecaster states that Y_t shows the monthly percentage change in IP, measured in percentage points per annum. Is this correct? Why?

   b. Suppose a forecaster estimates the following AR(4) model for Y_t:

   $$\hat{Y}_t = 1.377 + 0.318Y_{t-1} + 0.123Y_{t-2} + 0.068Y_{t-3} + 0.001Y_{t-4}.$$
   $$\quad\;\, (0.062)\;\;\; (0.078) \qquad (0.055) \qquad (0.068) \qquad (0.056)$$

   Use this AR(4) to forecast the value of Y_t in January 2001 using the following values of IP for August 2000 through December 2000:

Date	2000:7	2000:8	2000:9	2000:10	2000:11	2000:12
IP	147.595	148.650	148.973	148.660	148.206	147.300

   c. Worried about potential seasonal fluctuations in production, the forecaster adds Y_{t-12} to the autoregression. The estimated coefficient on Y_{t-12} is -0.054 with a standard error of 0.053. Is this coefficient statistically significant?

   d. Worried about a potential break, she computes a QLR test (with 15% trimming) on the constant and AR coefficients in the AR(4) model. The resulting QLR statistic was 3.45. Is there evidence of a break? Explain.

   e. Worried that she might have included too few or too many lags in the model, the forecaster estimates AR(p) models for $p = 1, \ldots, 6$ over the same sample period. The sum of squared residuals from each of these estimated models is shown in the table. Use the BIC to estimate the number of lags that should be included in the autoregression. Do the results differ if you use the AIC?

AR Order	1	2	3	4	5	6
SSR	29175	28538	28393	28391	28378	28317

*12.3 Using the same data as in Exercise 12.2, a researcher tests for a stochastic trend in $\ln(IP_t)$ using the following regression:

$$\widehat{\Delta\ln(IP_t)} = 0.061 + 0.00004t - 0.018\ln(IP_{t-1}) + 0.333\Delta\ln(IP_{t-1}) + 0.162\Delta\ln(IP_{t-2})$$
$$(0.024)\ (0.00001)\ (0.007)\qquad\qquad (0.075)\qquad\qquad\qquad (0.055)$$

where the standard errors shown in parentheses are computed using the homoskedasticity-only formula and the regressor "t" is a linear time trend.

a. Use the ADF statistic to test for a stochastic trend (unit root) in $\ln(IP)$.

b. Do these results support the specification used in Exercise 12.2? Explain.

12.4 The forecaster in Exercise 12.2 augments her $AR(4)$ model for IP growth to include 4 lagged values of ΔR_t where R_t is the interest rate on 3-month U.S. Treasury bills (measured in percentage points at an annual rate).

a. The Granger-causality F-statistic on the four lags of ΔR_t is 2.35. Do interest rates help to predict IP growth? Explain.

b. The researcher also regresses ΔR_t on a constant, four lags of ΔR_t and four lags of IP growth. The resulting Granger-causality F-statistic on the four lags of IP growth is 2.87. Does IP growth help to predict interest rates? Explain.

12.5 Prove the following results about conditional means, forecasts, and forecast errors:

a. Let W be a random variable with mean μ_W and variance σ_W^2 and let c be a constant. Show that $E[(W-c)^2] = \sigma_W^2 + (\mu_W - c)^2$.

b. Consider the problem of forecasting Y_t using data on $Y_{t-1}, Y_{t-2}, \ldots$. Let f_{t-1} denote some forecast of Y_t, where the subscript $t-1$ on f_{t-1} indicates that the forecast is a function of data through date $t-1$. Let $E[(Y_t - f_{t-1})^2 | Y_{t-1}, Y_{t-2}, \ldots]$ be the conditional mean squared error of the forecast f_{t-1}, conditional on Y observed through date $t-1$. Show that the conditional mean squared forecast error is minimized when $f_{t-1} = Y_{t|t-1}$, where $Y_{t|t-1} = E(Y_t | Y_{t-1}, Y_{t-2}, \ldots)$. (*Hint:* Extend the result in part (a) to conditional expectations.)

c. Show that the errors u_t of an AR(p) (Equation (12.14) in Key Concept 12.3) are serially uncorrelated. (*Hint:* Use Equation (2.25).)

12.6 In this exercise you will conduct a Monte Carlo experiment that studies the phenomenon of spurious regression discussed in Section 12.6. In a Monte Carlo study, artificial data are generated using a computer, then these artificial data are used to calculate the statistics being studied. This makes it possible to compute the distribution of statistics for known models when mathematical expressions for those distributions are complicated (as they are here) or even unknown. In this exercise, you will generate data so that two series, Y_t and X_t, are independently distributed random walks. The specific steps are

i. Use your computer to generate a sequence of $T = 100$ i.i.d. standard normal random variables. Call these variables $e_1, e_2, \ldots, e_{100}$. Set $Y_1 = e_1$ and $Y_t = Y_{t-1} + e_t$ for $t = 2, 3, \ldots, 100$.

ii. Use your computer to generate a new sequence, $a_1, a_2, \ldots, a_{100}$, of $T = 100$ i.i.d. standard normal random variables. Set $X_1 = a_1$ and $X_t = X_{t-1} + a_t$ for $t = 2, 3, \ldots, 100$.

iii. Regress Y_t onto a constant and X_t. Compute the OLS estimator, the regression R^2, and the (homoskedastic-only) t-statistic testing the null hypothesis that β_1 (the coefficient on X_t) is zero.

Use this algorithm to answer the following questions:

a. Run the algorithm (i)–(iii) once. Use the t-statistic from (iii) to test the null hypothesis that $\beta_1 = 0$ using the usual 5% critical value of 1.96. What is the R^2 of your regression?

b. Repeat (a) 1,000 times, saving each value of R^2 and the t-statistic. Construct a histogram of the R^2 and t-statistic. What are the 5%, 50%, and 95% percentiles of the distributions of the R^2 and the t-statistic? In what fraction of your 1,000 simulated data sets does the t-statistic exceed 1.96 in absolute value?

c. Repeat (b) for different numbers of observations, for example $T = 50$ and $T = 200$. As the sample size increases, does the fraction of times that you reject the null hypothesis approach 5%, as it should because you have generated Y and X to be independently distributed? Does this fraction seem to approach some other limit as T gets large? What is that limit?

12.1 | Time Series Data Used in Chapter 12

Macroeconomic time series data for the United States are collected and published by various government agencies. The U.S. Consumer Price Index is measured using monthly surveys and is compiled by the Bureau of Labor Statistics (BLS). The unemployment rate is computed from the BLS's Current Population Survey (see Appendix 3.1). The quarterly data used here were computed by averaging the monthly values. The Federal Funds rate data are the monthly average of daily rates as reported by the Federal Reserve and the dollar-pound exchange rate data are the monthly average of daily rates; both are for the final month in the quarter. Japanese real GDP data were obtained from the OECD. The daily percentage change in the NYSE Composite Index was computed as $100\Delta\ln(NYSE_t)$, where $NYSE_t$ is the value of the index at the daily close of the New York Stock Exchange; because the stock exchange is not open on weekends and holidays, the time period of analysis is a business day. These and thousands of other economic time series are freely available on the websites maintained by various data collecting agencies.

12.2 | Stationarity in the AR(1) Model

This appendix shows that, if $|\beta_1| < 1$ and u_t is stationary, then Y_t is stationary. Recall from Key Concept 12.5 that the time series variable Y_t is stationary if the joint distribution of $(Y_{s+1}, \ldots, Y_{s+T})$ does not depend on s. To streamline the argument, we show this formally for $T = 2$ under the simplifying assumptions that $\beta_0 = 0$ and $\{u_t\}$ are i.i.d. $N(0, \sigma_u^2)$.

The first step is deriving an expression for Y_t in terms of the u_t's. Because $\beta_0 = 0$, Equation (12.8) implies that $Y_t = \beta_1 Y_{t-1} + u_t$. Substituting $Y_{t-1} = \beta_1 Y_{t-2} + u_{t-1}$ into this expression yields $Y_t = \beta_1(\beta_1 Y_{t-2} + u_{t-1}) + u_t = \beta_1^2 Y_{t-2} + \beta_1 u_{t-1} + u_t$. Continuing this substitution another step yields $Y_t = \beta_1^3 Y_{t-3} + \beta_1^2 u_{t-2} + \beta_1 u_{t-1} + u_t$, and continuing indefinitely yields

$$Y_t = u_t + \beta_1 u_{t-1} + \beta_1^2 u_{t-2} + \beta_1^3 u_{t-3} + \ldots = \sum_{i=0}^{\infty} \beta_1^i u_{t-i}. \tag{12.37}$$

Thus Y_t is a weighted average of current and past u_t's. Because the u_t's are normally distributed and because the weighted average of normal random variables is normal (Section 2.6), Y_{s+1} and Y_{s+2} have a bivariate normal distribution. Recall from Section 2.6 that the bivariate normal distribution is completely determined by the means of the two variables, their variances, and their covariance. Thus, to show that Y_s is stationary, we need to show that the means, variances, and covariance of (Y_{s+1}, Y_{s+2}) do not depend on s. An extension of the argument used below can be used to show that the distribution of $(Y_{s+1}, Y_{s+2}, \ldots, Y_{s+T})$ does not depend on s.

The means and variances of Y_{s+1} and Y_{s+2} can be computed using Equation (12.37), with the subscripts $s + 1$ or $s + 2$ replacing t. First, because $E(u_t) = 0$ for all t, $E(Y_t) = E(\sum_{i=0}^{\infty} \beta_1^i u_{t-i}) = \sum_{i=0}^{\infty} \beta_1^i E(u_{t-i}) = 0$, so the mean of Y_{s+1} and Y_{s+2} are both zero and in particular do not depend on s. Second, $\text{var}(Y_t) = \text{var}(\sum_{i=0}^{\infty} \beta_1^i u_{t-i}) = \sum_{i=0}^{\infty} (\beta_1^i)^2 \text{var}(u_{t-i}) = \sigma_u^2 \sum_{i=0}^{\infty} (\beta_1^i)^2 = \sigma_u^2/(1 - \beta_1^2)$, where the final equality follows from the fact that, if $|a| < 1$, $\sum_{i=0}^{\infty} a^i = 1/(1 - a)$; thus $\text{var}(Y_{s+1}) = \text{var}(Y_{s+2}) = \sigma_u^2/(1 - \beta_1^2)$, which does not depend on s as long as $|\beta_1| < 1$. Finally, because $Y_{s+2} = \beta_1 Y_{s+1} + u_{s+2}$, $\text{cov}(Y_{s+1}, Y_{s+2}) = E(Y_{s+1} Y_{s+2}) = E[Y_{s+1}(\beta_1 Y_{s+1} + u_{s+2})] = \beta_1 \text{var}(Y_{s+1}) + \text{cov}(Y_{s+1}, u_{s+2}) = \beta_1 \text{var}(Y_{s+1}) = \beta_1 \sigma_u^2/(1 - \beta_1^2)$. The covariance does not depend on s, so Y_{s+1} and Y_{s+2} have a joint probability distribution that does not depend on s, that is, their joint distribution is stationary. If $|\beta_1| \geq 1$, this calculation breaks down because the infinite sum in Equation (12.37) does not converge and the variance of Y_t is infinite. Thus Y_t is stationary if $|\beta_1| < 1$, but not if $\beta_1 = 1$.

The preceding argument was made under the assumptions that $\beta_0 = 0$ and u_t is normally distributed. If $\beta_0 \neq 0$, the argument is similar except that the means of Y_{s+1} and Y_{s+2} are $\beta_0/(1 - \beta_1)$ and Equation (12.37) must be modified for this nonzero mean. The assumption that u_t is i.i.d. normal can be replaced with the assumption that u_t is stationary with a finite variance because, by Equation (12.37), Y_t can still be expressed as a function of current and past u_t's, so the distribution of Y_t is stationary as long as the distribution of u_t is stationary and the infinite sum expression in Equation (12.37) is meaningful in the sense that it converges, which requires $|\beta_1| < 1$.

APPENDIX
12.3 | Lag Operator Notation

The notation in this and the next two chapters is streamlined considerably by adopting what is known as lag operator notation. Let L denote the **lag operator**, which has the property that it transforms a variable into its lag. That is, the lag operator L has the property, $LY_t = Y_{t-1}$. By applying the lag operator twice, one obtains the second lag: $L^2 Y_t = L(LY_t) = LY_{t-1} = Y_{t-2}$. More generally, by applying the lag operator j times, one obtains the jth lag. In summary, the lag operator has the property that

$$LY_t = Y_{t-1}, \; L^2 Y_t = Y_{t-2}, \; \text{and} \; L^j Y_t = Y_{t-j}. \tag{12.38}$$

The lag operator notation permits us to define the **lag polynomial**, which is a polynomial in the lag operator:

$$a(L) = a_0 + a_1 L + a_2 L^2 + \cdots + a_p L^p = \sum_{j=0}^{p} a_j L^j, \tag{12.39}$$

where $a_0, \ldots, a_p$ are the coefficients of the lag polynomial and $L^0 = 1$. The degree of the lag polynomial $a(L)$ in Equation (12.39) is p. Multiplying Y_t by $a(L)$ yields

$$a(L)Y_t = \left(\sum_{j=0}^{p} a_j L^j \right) Y_t = \sum_{j=0}^{p} a_j (L^j Y_t) = \sum_{j=0}^{p} a_j Y_{t-j} = a_0 Y_t + a_1 Y_{t-1} + \cdots + a_p Y_{t-p}. \tag{12.40}$$

The expression in Equation (12.40) implies that the $AR(p)$ model in Equation (12.14) can be written compactly as

$$a(L)Y_t = \beta_0 + u_t, \tag{12.41}$$

where $a_0 = 1$ and $a_j = -\beta_j$, for $j = 1, \ldots, p$. Similarly, an $ADL(p,q)$ model can be written

$$a(L)Y_t = \beta_0 + c(L)X_{t-1} + u_t, \tag{12.42}$$

where $a(L)$ is a lag polynomial of degree p (with $a_0 = 1$) and $c(L)$ is a lag polynomial of degree $q - 1$.

APPENDIX

12.4 | ARMA Models

The **autoregressive–moving average (ARMA) model** extends the autoregressive model by modeling u_t as serially correlated, specifically, as being a distributed lag (or "moving average") of another unobserved error term. That is, in the lag operator notation of

Appendix 12.3, let $u_t = b(\mathrm{L})e_t$, where e_t is a serially uncorrelated, unobserved random variable, and $b(\mathrm{L})$ is a lag polynomial of degree q with $b_0 = 1$. Then the ARMA(p,q) model is

$$a(\mathrm{L})Y_t = \beta_0 + b(\mathrm{L})e_t, \tag{12.43}$$

where $a(\mathrm{L})$ is a lag polynomial of degree p with $a_0 = 1$.

Both AR and ARMA models can be thought of as ways to approximate the autocovariances of Y_t. The reason for this is that any stationary time series Y_t with a finite variance can be written either as an AR or as a MA with a serially uncorrelated error term, although the AR or MA models might need to have an infinite order. The second of these results, that a stationary process can be written in moving average form, is known as the Wold decomposition theorem, and is one of the fundamental results underlying the theory of stationary time series analysis.

As a theoretical matter, the families of AR, MA, and ARMA models are equally rich, as long as the lag polynomials have a sufficiently high degree. Still, in some cases the autocovariances can be better approximated using an ARMA(p,q) model with small p and q than by a pure AR model with only a few lags. As a practical matter, however, the estimation of ARMA models is more difficult than the estimation of AR models, and ARMA models are more difficult to extend to additional regressors than are AR models.

APPENDIX 12.5 | Consistency of the BIC Lag Length Estimator

This appendix summarizes the argument that the BIC estimator of the lag length, $\hat{p}$, in an autoregression is correct in large samples, that is, $\Pr(\hat{p} = p) \longrightarrow 1$. This is not true for the AIC estimator, which can overestimate p even in large samples.

BIC

First consider the special case that the BIC is used to choose among autoregressions with zero, one, or two lags, when the true lag length is one. It is shown below that (i) $\Pr(\hat{p} = 0) \longrightarrow 0$, and (ii) $\Pr(\hat{p} = 2) \longrightarrow 0$, from which it follows that $\Pr(\hat{p} = 1) \longrightarrow 1$. The extension of this argument to the general case of searching over $0 \le p \le p_{max}$ entails showing that $\Pr(\hat{p} < p) \longrightarrow 0$ and $\Pr(\hat{p} > p) \longrightarrow 0$; the strategy for showing these is the same as used in (i) and (ii) below.

Proof of (i) and (ii)

Proof of (i).   To choose $\hat{p} = 0$ it must be the case that $\text{BIC}(0) < \text{BIC}(1)$; that is, $\text{BIC}(0) - \text{BIC}(1) < 0$. Now $\text{BIC}(0) - \text{BIC}(1) = [\ln(SSR(0)/T) + (\ln T)/T] - [\ln(SSR(1)/T) + 2(\ln T)/T] = \ln(SSR(0)/T) - \ln(SSR(1)/T) - (\ln T)/T$. Now $SSR(0)/T = [(T-1)/T]s_Y^2 \xrightarrow{p} \sigma_Y^2$, $SSR(1)/T \xrightarrow{p} \sigma_u^2$, and $(\ln T)/T \longrightarrow 0$; putting these pieces together, $\text{BIC}(0) - \text{BIC}(1) \xrightarrow{p} \ln\sigma_Y^2 - \ln\sigma_u^2 > 0$ because $\sigma_Y^2 > \sigma_u^2$. It follows that $\Pr[\text{BIC}(0) < \text{BIC}(1)] \longrightarrow 0$, so that $\Pr(\hat{p} = 0) \longrightarrow 0$.

Proof of (ii).   To choose $\hat{p} = 2$ it must be the case that $\text{BIC}(2) < \text{BIC}(1)$, or $\text{BIC}(2) - \text{BIC}(1) < 0$. Now $T[\text{BIC}(2) - \text{BIC}(1)] = T\{[\ln(SSR(2)/T) + 3(\ln T)/T] - [\ln(SSR(1)/T) + 2(\ln T)/T]\} = T\ln[SSR(2)/SSR(1)] + \ln T = -T\ln[1 + F/(T-2)] + \ln T$, where $F = [SSR(1) - SSR(2)]/[SSR(2)/(T-2)]$ is the "rule of thumb" F-statistic (Appendix 5.3) testing the null hypothesis that $\beta_2 = 0$ in the AR(2). If u_t is homoskedastic, F has a χ_1^2 asymptotic distribution; if not, it has some other asymptotic distribution. Thus $\Pr[\text{BIC}(2) - \text{BIC}(1) < 0] = \Pr[T(\text{BIC}(2) - \text{BIC}(1)) < 0] = \Pr\{-T\ln[1 + F/(T-2)] + (\ln T) < 0\} = \Pr\{T\ln[1 + F/(T-2)] > \ln T\}$. As T increases, $T\ln[1 + F/(T-2)] - F \longrightarrow 0$ (a consequence of the logarithmic approximation $\ln(1 + a) \cong a$, which becomes exact as $a \longrightarrow 0$). Thus $\Pr[\text{BIC}(2) - \text{BIC}(1) < 0] \longrightarrow \Pr(F > \ln T) \longrightarrow 0$, so that $\Pr(\hat{p} = 2) \longrightarrow 0$.

AIC

In the special case of an AR(1) when zero, one, or two lags are considered, (i) applies to the AIC where the term $\ln T$ is replaced by 2, so $\Pr(\hat{p} = 0) \longrightarrow 0$. All the steps in the proof of (ii) for the BIC also apply to the AIC, with the modification that $\ln T$ is replaced by 2; thus $\Pr(\text{AIC}(2) - \text{AIC}(1) < 0) \longrightarrow \Pr(F > 2) > 0$. If u_t is homoskedastic, $\Pr(F > 2) \longrightarrow \Pr(\chi_1^2 > 2) = 0.16$, so that $\Pr(\hat{p} = 2) \longrightarrow 0.16$. In general, when $\hat{p}$ is chosen using the AIC, $\Pr(\hat{p} < p) \longrightarrow 0$ but $\Pr(\hat{p} > p)$ tends to a positive number, so $\Pr(\hat{p} = p)$ does not tend to 1.

CHAPTER 13 | # Estimation of Dynamic Causal Effects

In the 1983 movie *Trading Places*, the characters played by Dan Aykroyd and Eddie Murphy used inside information on how well Florida oranges had fared the winter to make millions in the orange juice concentrate futures market, a market for contracts to buy or sell large quantities of orange juice concentrate at a specified price on a future date. In real life, traders in orange juice futures in fact do pay close attention to the weather in Florida: freezes in Florida kill Florida oranges, the source of almost all frozen orange juice concentrate made in the United States, so its supply falls and the price rises. But precisely how much does the price rise when the weather in Florida turns sour? Does the price rise all at once, or are there delays; if so, for how long? These are questions that real life traders in orange juice futures need to answer if they want to succeed.

This chapter takes up the problem of estimating the effect on Y now and in the future of a change in X, that is, the **dynamic causal effect** on Y of a change in X. What, for example, is the effect on the path of orange juice prices over time of a freezing spell in Florida? The starting point for modeling and estimating dynamic causal effects is the so-called distributed lag regression model, in which Y_t is expressed as a function of current and past values of X_t. Section 13.1 introduces the distributed lag model in the context of estimating the effect of cold weather in Florida on the price of orange juice concentrate over time. Section 13.2 takes a closer look at what, precisely, is meant by a dynamic causal effect.

One way to estimate dynamic causal effects is to estimate the coefficients of the distributed lag regression model using OLS. As discussed in Section 13.3, this estimator is consistent if the regression error has a conditional mean of zero given current and past values of X, a condition that (as in Chapter 10) is

489

referred to as exogeneity. Because the omitted determinants of Y_t are correlated over time—that is, because they are serially correlated—the error term in the distributed lag model can be serially correlated. This possibility in turn requires new, "heteroskedasticity- and autocorrelation-consistent" (HAC) formulas for standard errors, the topic of Section 13.4.

A second way to estimate dynamic causal effects, discussed in Section 13.5, is to model the serial correlation in the error term as an autoregression and then to use this autoregressive model to derive an autoregressive distributed lag (ADL) model. Alternatively, the coefficients of the original distributed lag model can be estimated by generalized least squares (GLS). Both the ADL and GLS methods, however, require a stronger version of exogeneity than we have used so far: *strict* exogeneity, under which the regression errors have a conditional mean of zero given past, present, *and future* values of X.

Section 13.6 provides a more complete analysis of the relationship between orange juice prices and the weather. In this application, the weather is beyond human control and thus is exogenous (although, as discussed in Section 13.6, economic theory suggests that it is not necessarily strictly exogenous). Because exogeneity is necessary for estimating dynamic causal effects, Section 13.7 examines this assumption in several applications taken from macroeconomics and finance.

This chapter builds on the material in Sections 12.1–12.4 but, with the exception of a subsection (that can be skipped) of the empirical analysis in Section 13.6, does not require the material in Sections 12.5–12.8.

13.1 An Initial Taste of the Orange Juice Data

Orlando, the center of Florida's orange growing region, is normally sunny and warm. But now and then there is a cold snap, and if temperatures drop below freezing for too long the trees drop many of their oranges and, if the freeze is severe, the trees freeze. Following a freeze, the supply of orange juice concentrate falls and its price rises. The timing of the price increases is rather complicated, however. Orange juice concentrate is a "durable," or storable, commodity; that is, it can be stored in its frozen state, albeit at some cost (to run the freezer). Thus the price of orange juice concentrate depends not only on current supply but also on expectations of future supply. A freeze today means that future supplies of concentrate will be low, but because concentrate currently in storage can be used to meet either current or future demand, the price of existing concentrate rises today. But precisely how much does the price of concentrate rise when there is a freeze? The answer to this question is of interest not just to orange juice traders but more generally to economists interested in studying the operations of modern commodity markets. To learn how the price of orange juice changes in response to weather conditions, we must analyze data on orange juice prices and the weather.

Monthly data on the price of frozen orange juice concentrate, its monthly percentage change, and temperatures in the orange growing region of Florida from January 1950 to December 2000 are plotted in Figure 13.1. The price, plotted in Figure 13.1a, is a measure of the average real price of frozen orange juice concentrate paid by wholesalers. This price was deflated by the overall producer price index for finished goods to eliminate the effects of overall price inflation. The percentage price change plotted in Figure 13.1b is the change in the price over the month. The temperature data plotted in Figure 13.1c are the number of "freezing degree days" at the Orlando, Florida, airport, calculated as the sum of the number of degrees Fahrenheit that the minimum temperature falls below freezing in a given day over all days in the month; for example, in November 1950 the airport temperature dropped below freezing twice, on the 25th ($31°$) and on the 29th ($29°$) for a total of four freezing degree days $((32 - 31) + (32 - 29) = 4)$. (The data are described in more detail in Appendix 13.1.) As you can see by comparing the panels in Figure 13.1, the price of orange juice concentrate has large swings, some of which appear to be associated with cold weather in Florida.

We begin our quantitative analysis of the relationship between orange juice price and the weather by using a regression to estimate the amount by which orange juice prices rise when the weather turns cold. The dependent variable is the percentage change in the price over that month ($\%ChgP_t$, where $\%ChgP_t = 100 \times \Delta\ln(P_t^{OJ})$ and P_t^{OJ} is the real price of orange juice). The regressor is the number of freezing degree days during that month (FDD_t). This regression is estimated using monthly data from January 1950 to December 2000 (as are all regressions in this chapter), for a total of $T = 612$ observations:

$$\widehat{\%ChgP_t} = -0.40 + 0.47FDD_t.$$
$$\phantom{\widehat{\%ChgP_t} = }(0.22)\ \ (0.13)$$

(13.1)

FIGURE 13.1   Orange Juice Prices and Florida Weather, 1950–2000

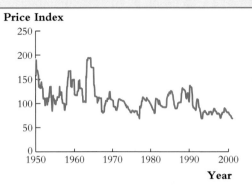

(a) Price Index for Frozen Concentrated Orange Juice

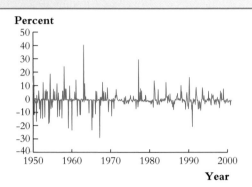

(b) Percent Change in the Price of
Frozen Concentrated Orange Juice

(c) Monthly Freezing Degree Days in Orlando, Florida

There have been large month-to-month changes in the price of frozen concentrated orange juice. Many of the large movements coincide with freezing weather in Orlando, home of the orange groves.

The standard errors reported in this section are not the usual OLS standard errors, but rather are heteroskedasticity- and autocorrelation-consistent (HAC) standard errors that are appropriate when the error term and regressors are autocorrelated. HAC standard errors are discussed in Section 13.4, and for now they are used without further explanation.

According to this regression, an additional freezing degree day during a month increases the price of orange juice concentrate over that month by 0.47%. In a month with four freezing degree days, such as November 1950, the price of orange juice concentrate is estimated to have increased by 1.88% (4 × 0.47% = 1.88%), relative to a month with no days below freezing.

Because the regression in Equation (13.1) includes only a contemporaneous measure of the weather, it does not capture any lingering effects of the cold snap on the orange juice price over the coming months. To capture these we need to consider the effect on prices of both contemporaneous and lagged values of *FDD*, which in turn can be done by augmenting the regression in Equation (13.1) with, for example, lagged values of *FDD* over the previous six months:

$$\widehat{\%ChgP_t} = -0.65 + 0.47FDD_t + 0.14FDD_{t-1} + 0.06FDD_{t-2}$$
$$\phantom{\widehat{\%ChgP_t} =} (0.23)\ \ (0.14) \qquad (0.08) \qquad\quad (0.06)$$
$$+\ 0.07FDD_{t-3} + 0.03FDD_{t-4} + 0.05FDD_{t-5} + 0.05FDD_{t-6}.$$
$$ (0.05) \qquad\quad (0.03) \qquad\quad (0.03) \qquad\quad (0.04)$$

(13.2)

Equation (13.2) is a distributed lag regression. The coefficient on FDD_t in Equation (13.2) estimates the percentage increase in prices over the course of the month in which the freeze occurs; an additional freezing degree day is estimated to increase prices that month by 0.47%. The coefficient on the first lag of FDD_t, FDD_{t-1}, estimates the percentage increase in prices arising from a freezing degree day in the preceding month, the coefficient on the second lag estimates the effect of a freezing degree day two months ago, and so forth. Equivalently, the coefficient on the first lag of *FDD* estimates the effect of a unit increase in *FDD* one month after the freeze occurs. Thus the estimated coefficients in Equation (13.2) are estimates of the effect of a unit increase in FDD_t on current and future values of *%ChgP*, that is, they are estimates of the dynamic effect of FDD_t on $\%ChgP_t$. For example, the four freezing degree days in November 1950 are estimated to have increased orange juice prices by 1.88% during November 1950, by an additional 0.56% (= 4 × 0.14) in December 1950, by an additional 0.24% (= 4 × 0.06) in January 1951, and so forth.

13.2 Dynamic Causal Effects

Before learning more about the tools for estimating dynamic causal effects, we should spend a moment thinking about what, precisely, is meant by a dynamic causal effect. Having a clear idea about what a dynamic causal effect is leads to a clearer understanding of the conditions under which it can be estimated.

Causal Effects and Time Series Data

Section 1.2 defined a causal effect as the outcome of an ideal randomized controlled experiment: when a horticulturalist randomly applies fertilizer to some tomato plots but not others and then measures the yield, the expected difference in yield between the fertilized and unfertilized plots is the effect on tomato yield of the fertilizer. This concept of an experiment, however, is one in which there are multiple subjects (multiple tomato plots or multiple people), so the data are either cross-sectional (the tomato yield at the end of the harvest) or panel data (individual incomes before and after an experimental job training program). By having multiple subjects, it is possible to have both treatment and control groups and thereby to estimate the causal effect of the treatment.

In time series applications, this definition of causal effects in terms of an ideal randomized controlled experiment needs to be modified. To be concrete, consider an important problem of macroeconomics: estinating the effect of an unanticipated change in the short-term interest rate on the current and future economic activity in a given country, as measured by GDP. Taken literally, the randomized controlled experiment of Section 1.2 would entail randomly assigning different economies to treatment and control groups. The central banks in the treatment group would apply the treatment of a random interest rate change, while those in the control group would apply no such random changes; for both groups, economic activity (for example, GDP) would be measured over the next few years. But what if we are interested in estimating this effect for a specific country, say the United States? Then this experiment would entail having different "copies" of the United States as subjects, and assigning some copies to the treatment and some to the control group. Obviously, this "parallel universes" experiment is infeasible.

Instead, in time series data it is useful to think of a randomized controlled experiment consisting of the same subject (e.g., the U.S. economy) being given different treatments (randomly chosen changes in interest rates) at different points in time (the 1970s, the 1980s, and so forth). In this framework, the single subject at different times plays the role of both treatment and control group: sometimes the Fed changes the interest rate while at other times it does not. Because data are collected over time, it is possible to measure the dynamic causal effect, that is, the time path of the effect on the outcome of interest of the treatment. For example, a surprise increase in the short-term interest rate of two percentage points, sustained for one quarter, might initially have a negligible effect on output; after two quarters GDP growth might slow, with the greatest slowdown after one and one-half years; then over the next two years, GDP growth might return to normal. This time path of causal effects is the dynamic causal effect on GDP growth of a surprise change in the interest rate.

As a second example, consider the causal effect on orange juice price changes of a freezing degree day. It is possible to imagine a variety of hypothetical experiments, each yielding a different causal effect. One experiment would be to change the weather in the Florida orange groves, holding constant weather else-where—for example, holding constant weather in the Texas grapefruit groves and in other citrus fruit regions. This experiment would measure a partial effect, hold-ing other weather constant. A second experiment might change the weather in all the regions, where the "treatment" is application of overall weather patterns. If weather is correlated across regions for competing crops, then these two dynamic causal effects differ. In this chapter, we consider the causal effect in the latter experiment, that is, the causal effect of applying general weather patterns. This corresponds to measuring the dynamic effect on prices of a change in Florida weather, *not* holding constant weather in other agricultural regions.

Dynamic effects and the distributed lag model.   Because dynamic effects necessarily occur over time, the econometric model used to estimate dynamic causal effects needs to incorporate lags. To do so, Y_t can be expressed as a distrib-uted lag of current and r past values of X_t:

$$Y_t = \beta_0 + \beta_1 X_t + \beta_2 X_{t-1} + \beta_3 X_{t-2} + \cdots + \beta_{r+1} X_{t-r} + u_t, \qquad (13.3)$$

where u_t is an error term that includes measurement error in Y_t and the effect of omitted determinants of Y_t. The model in Equation (13.3) is called the **distrib-uted lag model** relating X_t, and r of its lags, to Y_t.

As an illustration of Equation (13.3), consider a modified version of the tomato/fertilizer experiment: because fertilizer applied today might remain in the ground in future years, the horticulturalist wants to determine the effect on tomato yield *over time* of applying fertilizer. Accordingly, she designs a three-year experi-ment and randomly divides her plots into four groups: the first is fertilized in only the first year; the second is fertilized in only the second year; the third is fertilized in only the third year; and the fourth, the control group, is never fertilized. Toma-toes are grown annually in each plot, and the third-year harvest is weighed. The three treatment groups are denoted by the binary variables X_{t-2}, X_{t-1}, and X_t, where t represents the third year (the year in which the harvest is weighed), $X_{t-2} = 1$ if the plot is in the first group (fertilized two years earlier), $X_{t-1} = 1$ if the plot was fertilized one year earlier, and $X_t = 1$ if the plot was fertilized in the final year. In the context of Equation (13.3) (which applies to a single plot), the effect of being fertilized in the final year is β_1, the effect of being fertilized one year earlier is β_2, and the effect of being fertilized two years earlier is β_3. If the effect of fertilizer is greatest in the year it is applied, then β_1 would be larger than β_2 and β_3.

More generally, the coefficient on the contemporaneous value of X_t, β_1, is the contemporaneous or immediate effect of a unit change in X_t on Y_t. The coefficient on X_{t-1}, β_2, is the effect on Y_t of a unit change in X_{t-1} or, equivalently, the effect on Y_{t+1} of a unit change in X_t; that is, β_2 is the effect of a unit change in X on Y one period later. In general, the coefficient on X_{t-h} is the effect of a unit change in X on Y after h periods. The dynamic causal effect is the effect of a change in X_t on Y_t, Y_{t+1}, Y_{t+2}, and so forth, that is, it is the sequence of causal effects on current and future values of Y. Thus, in the context of the distributed lag model in Equation (13.3), the dynamic causal effect is the sequence of coefficients β_1, β_2, . . . , β_{r+1}.

Implications for empirical time series analysis. This formulation of dynamic causal effects in time series data as the expected outcome of an experiment in which different treatment levels are repeatedly applied to the same subject has two implications for empirical attempts to measure the dynamic causal effect with observational time series data. The first implication is that the dynamic causal effect should not change over the sample on which we have data. This in turn is implied by the data being jointly stationary (Key Concept 12.5). As discussed in Section 12.7, the hypothesis that a population regression function is stable over time can be tested using the QLR test for a break, in which case it is possible to estimate the dynamic causal effect in different subsamples. The second implication is that X must be uncorrelated with the error term, and it is to this implication that we now turn.

Two Types of Exogeneity

Section 10.1 defined an "exogenous" variable to be a variable that is uncorrelated with the regression error term and an "endogenous" variable to be a variable that is correlated with the error term. This terminology traces to models with multiple equations, in which an "endogenous" variable is determined within the model while an "exogenous" variable is determined outside the model. Loosely speaking, if we are to estimate dynamic causal effects using the distributed lag model in Equation (13.3), the regressors (the X's) must be uncorrelated with the error term. Thus, X must be exogenous. Because we are working with time series data, however, we need to refine the definitions of exogeneity. In fact, there are two different concepts of exogeneity that we use here.

The first concept of exogeneity is that the error term has a conditional mean of zero given current and all past values of X_t, that is, that $E(u_t | X_t, X_{t-1}, X_{t-2}, \ldots) = 0$. This modifies the standard conditional mean assumption for multiple regression with cross-sectional data (Assumption 1 in Key Concept 5.4), which requires only that u_t has a conditional mean of zero given the included regressors; that is, that $E(u_t | X_t, X_{t-1}, \ldots, X_{t-r}) = 0$. Including all lagged values of X_t in the conditional expectation implies that all the more distant causal effects—all the causal effects beyond lag r—are zero. Thus, under this assumption, the r distributed lag coefficients in Equation (13.3) constitute all of the nonzero dynamic causal effects. We can refer to this assumption—that $E(u_t | X_t, X_{t-1}, \ldots) = 0$—as **past and present exogeneity**, but because of the similarity of this definition and the definition of exogeneity in Chapter 10, we just use the term **exogeneity**.

The second concept of exogeneity is that the error term has mean zero, given all past, present, and *future* values of X_t, that is, that $E(u_t | \ldots, X_{t+2}, X_{t+1}, X_t, X_{t-1}, X_{t-2}, \ldots) = 0$. This is called **strict exogeneity**; for clarity, we also call it **past, present, and future exogeneity**. The reason for introducing the concept of strict exogeneity is that, when X is strictly exogenous, there are more efficient estimators of dynamic causal effects than the OLS estimators of the coefficients of the distributed lag regression in Equation (13.3).

The difference between exogeneity (past and present) and strict exogeneity (past, present, and future) is that strict exogeneity includes future values of X in the conditional expectation. Thus, strict exogeneity implies exogeneity, but not vice versa. One way to understand the difference between the two concepts is to consider the implications of these definitions for correlations between X and u. If X is (past and present) exogenous, then u_t is uncorrelated with current and past values of X_t. If X is strictly exogenous, then in addition u_t is uncorrelated with *future* values of X_t. For example, if a change in Y_t causes *future* values of X_t to change, then X_t is not strictly exogenous even though it might be (past and present) exogenous.

As an illustration, consider the hypothetical multiyear tomato/fertilizer experiment described following Equation (3.3). Because the fertilizer is randomly applied in the hypothetical experiment, it is exogenous. Because tomato yield today does not depend on the amount of fertilizer applied in the future, the fertilizer time series is also strictly exogenous.

As a second illustration, consider the orange juice price example, in which Y_t is the monthly percentage change in orange juice prices and X_t is the number of freezing degree days in that month. From the perspective of orange juice markets, we can think of the weather—the number of freezing degree days—as if it were randomly assigned, in the sense that the weather is outside human control. If the effect of FDD is linear and if it has no effect on prices after r months, then it follows that the weather is exogenous. But is the weather *strictly* exogenous? If the conditional mean of u_t given future FDD is nonzero, then FDD is not strictly exogenous. To answer this question requires thinking carefully about what, precisely, is contained in u_t. In particular, if OJ market participants use forecasts of FDD when they decide how much they will buy or sell at a given price, then

Key Concept 13.1

The Distributed Lag Model and Exogeneity

In the distributed lag model

$$Y_t = \beta_0 + \beta_1 X_t + \beta_2 X_{t-1} + \beta_3 X_{t-2} + \cdots + \beta_{r+1} X_{t-r} + u_t, \qquad (13.4)$$

there are two different types of exogeneity, that is, two different exogeneity conditions:

Past and present exogeneity (exogeneity):

$$E(u_t \mid X_t, X_{t-1}, X_{t-2}, \dots) = 0; \qquad (13.5)$$

Past, present, and future exogeneity (strict exogeneity):

$$E(u_t \mid \dots, X_{t+2}, X_{t+1}, X_t, X_{t-1}, X_{t-2}, \dots) = 0. \qquad (13.6)$$

If X is strictly exogenous it is exogenous, but exogeneity does not imply strict exogeneity.

OJ prices, and thus the error term u_t, could incorporate information about future *FDD* that would make u_t a useful predictor of *FDD*. This means that u_t will be correlated with future values of FDD_t. According to this logic, because u_t includes forecasts of future Florida weather, *FDD* would be (past and present) exogenous but not *strictly* exogenous. The difference between this and the tomato/fertilizer example is that, while tomato plants are unaffected by future fertilizing, OJ market participants *are* influenced by forecasts of future Florida weather. We return to the question of whether *FDD* is strictly exogenous when we analyze the orange juice price data in more detail in Section 13.6.

The two definitions of exogeneity are summarized in Key Concept 13.1.

13.3 Estimation of Dynamic Causal Effects with Exogenous Regressors

If X is exogenous, then its dynamic causal effect on Y can be estimated by OLS estimation of the distributed lag regression in Equation (13.4). This section summarizes the conditions under which these OLS estimators lead to valid statistical inferences and introduces dynamic multipliers and cumulative dynamic multipliers.

The Distributed Lag Model Assumptions

The four assumptions of the distributed lag regression model are similar to the four assumptions for the cross-sectional multiple regression model (Key Concept 5.4), modified for time series data.

The first assumption is that X is exogenous, which extends the zero conditional mean assumption for cross-sectional data to include all lagged values of X. As discussed in Section 13.2, this assumption implies that the r distributed lag coefficients in Equation (13.3) constitute all of the nonzero dynamic causal effects. In this sense, the population regression function summarizes the entire dynamic effect on Y of a change in X.

The second assumption has two parts: part (a) requires that the variables have a stationary distribution, and part (b) requires that they become independently distributed when the amount of time separating them becomes large. This assumption is the same as the corresponding assumption for the ADL model (the second assumption in Key Concept 12.6), and the discussion of this assumption in Section 12.4 applies here as well.

The third assumption is that the variables have more than eight nonzero, finite moments. This is stronger than the assumption of four finite moments that is used elsewhere in this book. As discussed in Section 13.4, this stronger assumption is used in the mathematics behind the HAC variance estimator.

The fourth assumption, which is the same as in the cross-sectional multiple regression model, is that there is no perfect multicollinearity.

The distributed lag regression model and assumptions are summarized in Key Concept 13.2.

Extension to additional X's.   The distributed lag model extends directly to multiple X's: the additional X's and their lags are simply included as regressors in the distributed lag regression, and the assumptions in Key Concept 13.2 are modified to include these additional regressors. Although the extension to multiple X's is conceptually straightforward, it complicates the notation, obscuring the main ideas of estimation and inference in the distributed lag model. For this reason, the case of multiple X's is not treated explicitly in this chapter but is left as a straightforward extension of the distributed lag model with a single X.

Autocorrelated u_t, Standard Errors, and Inference

In the distributed lag regression model, the error term u_t can be autocorrelated, that is, u_t can be correlated with its lagged values. This autocorrelation arises

The Distributed Lag Model Assumptions

Key Concept 13.2

The distributed lag model is given in Key Concept 13.1 (Equation (13.4)), where

1. X is exogenous, that is, $E(u_t | X_t, X_{t-1}, X_{t-2}, \dots) = 0$;
2. (a) The random variables Y_t and X_t have a stationary distribution, and
   (b) (Y_t, X_t) and $(Y_{t-j,} X_{t-j})$ become independent as j gets large;
3. Y_t and X_t have more than eight nonzero, finite moments; and
4. There is no perfect multicollinearity.

because, in time series data, the omitted factors included in u_t can themselves be serially correlated. For example, suppose that the demand for orange juice also depends on income, so that one factor that influences the price of orange juice is income, specifically, the aggregate income of potential orange juice consumers. Then aggregate income is an omitted variable in the distributed lag regression of orange juice price changes against freezing degree days. Aggregate income, however, is serially correlated: income tends to fall in recessions and rise in expansions. Thus, income is serially correlated, and, because it is part of the error term, u_t will be serially correlated. This example is typical: because omitted determinants of Y are themselves serially correlated, in general u_t in the distributed lag model will be correlated.

The autocorrelation of u_t does not affect the consistency of OLS, nor does it introduce bias. If, however, the errors are autocorrelated, then in general the usual OLS standard errors are inconsistent and a different formula must be used. Thus correlation of the errors is analogous to heteroskedasticity: the homoskedasticity-only standard errors are "wrong" when the errors are in fact heteroskedastic, in the sense that using homoskedasticity-only standard errors results in misleading statistical inferences when the errors are heteroskedastic. Similarly, when the errors are serially correlated, standard errors predicated upon i.i.d. errors are "wrong" in the sense that they result in misleading statistical inferences. The solution to this problem is to use heteroskedasticity- and autocorrelation-consistent (HAC) standard errors, the topic of Section 13.4.

Dynamic Multipliers and Cumulative Dynamic Multipliers

Another name for the dynamic causal effect is the dynamic multiplier. The cumulative dynamic multipliers are the cumulative causal effects, up to a given lag; thus the cumulative dynamic multipliers measure the cumulative effect on Y of a change in X.

Dynamic multipliers.   The effect of a unit change in X on Y after h periods, which is β_{h+1} in Equation (13.4), is called the h-period **dynamic multiplier**. Thus, the dynamic multipliers relating X to Y are the coefficients on X_t and its lags in Equation (13.4). For example, β_2 is the one-period dynamic multiplier, β_3 is the two-period dynamic multiplier, and so forth. In this terminology, the zero-period (or contemporaneous) dynamic multiplier, or **impact effect**, is β_1, the effect on Y of a change in X in the same period.

Because the dynamic multipliers are estimated by the OLS regression coefficients, their standard errors are the HAC standard errors of the OLS regression coefficients.

Cumulative dynamic multipliers.   The h-period **cumulative dynamic multiplier** is the cumulative effect of a unit change in X on Y over the next h periods. Thus, the cumulative dynamic multipliers are the cumulative sum of the dynamic multipliers. In terms of the coefficients of the distributed lag regression in Equation (13.4), the zero-period cumulative multiplier is β_1, the one-period cumulative multiplier is $\beta_1 + \beta_2$, and the h-period cumulative dynamic multiplier is $\beta_1 + \beta_2 + \cdots + \beta_{h+1}$. The sum of all the individual dynamic multipliers, $\beta_1 + \beta_2 + \cdots + \beta_{r+1}$, is the cumulative long-run effect on Y of a change in X, and is called the **long-run cumulative dynamic multiplier.**

For example, consider the regression in Equation (13.2). The immediate effect of an additional freezing degree day is that the price of orange juice concentrate rises by 0.47%. The cumulative effect of a price change over the next month is the sum of the impact effect and the dynamic effect one month ahead; thus the cumulative effect on prices is the initial increase of 0.47% plus the subsequent smaller increase of 0.14% for a total of 0.61%. Similarly, the cumulative dynamic multiplier over two months is 0.47% + 0.14% + 0.06% = 0.67%.

The cumulative dynamic multipliers can be estimated directly using a modification of the distributed lag regression in Equation (13.4). This modified regression is

$$Y_t = \delta_0 + \delta_1 \Delta X_t + \delta_2 \Delta X_{t-1} + \delta_3 \Delta X_{t-2} + \cdots + \delta_r \Delta X_{t-r+1} + \delta_{r+1} X_{t-r} + u_t. \quad (13.7)$$

The coefficients in Equation (13.7), $\delta_1, \delta_2, \ldots, \delta_{r+1}$ are in fact the cumulative dynamic multipliers. This can be shown by a bit of algebra (Exercise 13.5), which demonstrates that the population regressions in Equations (13.7) and (13.4) are equivalent, where $\delta_0 = \beta_0$, $\delta_1 = \beta_1$, $\delta_2 = \beta_1 + \beta_2$, $\delta_3 = \beta_1 + \beta_2 + \beta_3$, and so forth. The coefficient on X_{t-r}, δ_{r+1}, is the long-run cumulative dynamic multiplier, that is, $\delta_{r+1} = \beta_1 + \beta_2 + \beta_3 + \cdots + \beta_{r+1}$. Moreover, the OLS estimators of the coefficients in Equation (13.7) are the same as the corresponding cumulative sum of the OLS estimators in Equation (13.4). For example, $\hat{\delta}_2 = \hat{\beta}_1 + \hat{\beta}_2$. The main benefit of estimating the cumulative dynamic multipliers using the specification in Equation (13.7) is that, because the OLS estimators of the regression coefficients are estimators of the cumulative dynamic multipliers, the HAC standard errors of the coefficients in Equation (13.7) are the HAC standard errors of the cumulative dynamic multipliers.

13.4 Heteroskedasticity- and Autocorrelation-Consistent Standard Errors

If the error term u_t is autocorrelated, then OLS is consistent, but in general the usual OLS standard errors for cross-sectional data are not. This means that conventional statistical inferences—hypothesis tests and confidence intervals—based on the usual OLS standard errors will, in general, be misleading. For example, confidence intervals constructed as the OLS estimator ± 1.96 conventional standard errors need not contain the true value in 95% of repeated samples, even if the sample size is large. This section begins with a derivation of the correct formula for the variance of the OLS estimator with autocorrelated errors, then turns to heteroskedasticity and autocorrelation-consistent standard errors.

Distribution of the OLS Estimator with Autocorrelated Errors

To keep things simple, consider the OLS estimator $\hat{\beta}_1$ in the distributed lag regression model with no lags, that is, the linear regression model with a single regressor X_t:

$$Y_t = \beta_0 + \beta_1 X_t + u_t \tag{13.8}$$

where the assumptions of Key Concept 13.2 are satisfied. This section shows that the variance of $\hat{\beta}_1$ can be written as the product of two terms: the expression for $\text{var}(\hat{\beta}_1)$, applicable if u_t is not serially correlated, times a correction factor that arises from the autocorrelation in u_t or, more precisely, the autocorrelation in $(X_t - \mu_X)u_t$.

As shown in Appendix 4.3, the formula for the OLS estimator $\hat{\beta}_1$ in Key Concept 4.2 can be rewritten as

$$\hat{\beta}_1 = \beta_1 + \frac{\dfrac{1}{T}\sum_{t=1}^{T}(X_t - \overline{X})u_t}{\dfrac{1}{T}\sum_{t=1}^{T}(X_t - \overline{X})^2}, \tag{13.9}$$

where Equation (13.9) is Equation (4.51) with a change of notation so that i and n are replaced by t and T. Because $\overline{X} \xrightarrow{p} \mu_X$ and $\frac{1}{T}\sum_{t=1}^{T}(X_t - \overline{X})^2 \xrightarrow{p} \sigma_X^2$, in large samples $\hat{\beta}_1 - \beta_1$ is approximately given by

$$\hat{\beta}_1 - \beta_1 \cong \frac{\dfrac{1}{T}\sum_{t=1}^{T}(X_t - \mu_X)u_t}{\sigma_X^2} = \frac{\dfrac{1}{T}\sum_{t=1}^{T}v_t}{\sigma_X^2} = \frac{\overline{v}}{\sigma_X^2}, \tag{13.10}$$

where $v_t = (X_t - \mu_X)u_t$ and $\overline{v} = \frac{1}{T}\sum_{t=1}^{T}v_t$. Thus,

$$\text{var}(\hat{\beta}_1) = \text{var}\left(\frac{\overline{v}}{\sigma_X^2}\right) = \frac{\text{var}(\overline{v})}{(\sigma_X^2)^2}. \tag{13.11}$$

If v_t is i.i.d.—as assumed for cross-sectional data in Key Concept 4.3—then $\text{var}(\overline{v}) = \text{var}(v_t)/T$ and the formula for the variance of $\hat{\beta}_1$ from Key Concept 4.4 applies. If, however, u_t and X_t are not independently distributed over time, then in general v_t will be serially correlated, so the formula for the variance of $\overline{v}$ from Key Concept 4.4 does not apply. Instead, if v_t is serially correlated, the variance of $\overline{v}$ is given by

$$\begin{aligned}
\text{var}(\overline{v}) &= \text{var}[(v_1 + v_2 + \cdots + v_T)/T] \\
&= [\text{var}(v_1) + \text{cov}(v_1,v_2) + \cdots + \text{cov}(v_1,v_T) \\
&\quad + \text{cov}(v_2,v_1) + \text{var}(v_2) + \cdots + \text{var}(v_T)]/T^2 \\
&= [T\text{var}(v_t) + 2(T-1)\text{cov}(v_t,v_{t-1}) + 2(T-2)\text{cov}(v_t,v_{t-2}) \\
&\quad + \cdots + 2\text{cov}(v_t,v_{t-T+1})]/T^2 \\
&= \frac{\sigma_v^2}{T}f_T,
\end{aligned} \tag{13.12}$$

where

$$f_T = 1 + 2\sum_{j=1}^{T-1} \left(\frac{T-j}{T}\right)\rho_j, \tag{13.13}$$

where $\rho_j = \text{corr}(v_t, v_{t-j})$. In large samples, f_T tends to the limit, $f_T \longrightarrow f_\infty = 1 + 2\sum_{j=1}^{\infty}\rho_j$.

Combining the expressions in Equation (13.10) for $\hat{\beta}_1$ and Equation (13.12) for $\text{var}(\bar{v})$ gives the formula for the variance of $\hat{\beta}_1$ when v_t is autocorrelated:

$$\text{var}(\hat{\beta}_1) = \left[\frac{1}{T}\frac{\sigma_v^2}{(\sigma_X^2)^2}\right]f_T, \tag{13.14}$$

where f_T is given in Equation (13.13).

Equation (13.14) expresses the variance of $\hat{\beta}_1$ as the product of two terms. The first, in square brackets, is the formula for the variance of $\hat{\beta}_1$ given in Key Concept 4.4, which applies in the absence of serial correlation. The second is the factor f_T, which adjusts this formula for serial correlation. Because of this additional factor f_T in Equation (13.14), the OLS standard errors computed using the formula in Key Concept 4.4 are incorrect if the errors are serially correlated: more precisely, if $v_t = (X_t - \mu_X)u_t$ is serially correlated, the estimator of the variance is off by the factor f_T.

HAC Standard Errors

If the factor f_T, defined in Equation (13.13), was known, then the variance of $\hat{\beta}_1$ could be estimated by multiplying the usual cross-sectional estimator of the variance by f_T. This factor, however, depends on the unknown autocorrelations of v_t, so it must be estimated. The estimator of the variance of $\hat{\beta}_1$ that incorporates this adjustment is consistent whether or not there is heteroskedasticity and whether or not v_t is autocorrelated. Accordingly, this estimator is called the **heteroskedasticity- and autocorrelation-consistent (HAC)** estimator of the variance of $\hat{\beta}_1$, and the square root of the HAC variance estimator is the **HAC standard error** of $\hat{\beta}_1$.

The HAC variance formula. The heteroskedasticity- and autocorrelation-consistent estimator of the variance of $\hat{\beta}_1$ is

$$\tilde{\sigma}_{\hat{\beta}_1}^2 = \hat{\sigma}_{\hat{\beta}_1}^2 \hat{f}_T, \tag{13.15}$$

where $\hat{\sigma}_{\tilde{\beta}_1}^2$ is the estimator of the variance of $\hat{\beta}_1$ in the absence of serial correlation, given in Equation (4.19), and where $\hat{f}_T$ is an estimator of the factor f_T in Equation (13.13).

The task of constructing a consistent estimator $\hat{f}_T$ is challenging. To see why, consider two extremes. At one extreme, given the formula in Equation (13.13), it might seem natural to replace the population autocorrelations ρ_j with the sample autocorrelations $\hat{\rho}_j$ (defined in Equation (12.6)), yielding the estimator $1 + 2\sum_{j=1}^{T-1}\left(\frac{T-j}{T}\right)\hat{\rho}_j$. But this estimator contains so many estimated autocorrelations that it is inconsistent. Intuitively, because each of the estimated autocorrelations contains estimation error, by estimating so many autocorrelations the estimation error in this estimator of f_T remains large even in large samples. At the other extreme, one could imagine using only a few sample autocorrelations, for example only the first sample autocorrelation, and ignoring all the higher autocorrelations. Although this estimator eliminates the problem of estimating too many autocorrelations, it has a different problem: it is inconsistent because it ignores the additional autocorrelations that appear in Equation (13.13). In short, using too many sample autocorrelations makes the estimator have a large variance, but using too few autocorrelations ignores the autocorrelations at higher lags, so in either of these extreme cases the estimator is inconsistent.

Estimators of f_T used in practice strike a balance between these two extreme cases by choosing the number of autocorrelations to include in a way that depends on the sample size T. If the sample size is small, only a few autocorrelations are used, but if the sample size is large, more autocorrelations are included (but still far fewer than T). Specifically, let $\hat{f}_T$ be given by

$$\hat{f}_T = 1 + 2\sum_{j=1}^{m-1}\left(\frac{m-j}{m}\right)\tilde{\rho}_j, \tag{13.16}$$

where $\tilde{\rho}_j = \sum_{t=j+1}^{T}\hat{v}_t\hat{v}_{t-j}\Big/\sum_{t=1}^{T}\hat{v}_t^2$, where $\hat{v}_t = (X_t - \overline{X})\hat{u}_t$ (as in the definition of $\hat{\sigma}_{\tilde{\beta}_1}^2$). The parameter m in Equation (13.16) is called the **truncation parameter** of the HAC estimator because the sum of autocorrelations is shortened, or truncated, to include only $m-1$ autocorrelations instead of the $T-1$ autocorrelations appearing in the population formula in Equation (13.13).

For $\hat{f}_T$ to be consistent, m must be chosen so that it is large in large samples, although still much less than T. One guideline for choosing m in practice is to use the formula

$$m = 0.75T^{1/3}, \tag{13.17}$$

rounded to an integer. This formula, which is based on the assumption that there is a moderate amount of autocorrelation in v_t, gives a benchmark rule for determining m as a function of the number of observations in the regression.[1]

The value of the truncation parameter m resulting from Equation (13.17) can be modified using your knowledge of the series at hand. If there is a great deal of serial correlation in v_t, then you could increase m beyond the value from Equation (13.17). On the other hand if v_t has little serial correlation, you could decrease m. Because of the ambiguity associated with the choice of m, it is good practice to try one or two alternative values of m for at least one specification to make sure your results are not sensitive to m.

The HAC estimator in Equation (13.15), with $\hat{f}_T$ given in Equation (13.16), is called the **Newey-West variance estimator**, after the econometricians Whitney Newey and Kenneth West who proposed it. They showed that, when used along with a rule like that in Equation (13.17), under general assumptions this estimator is a consistent estimator of the variance of $\hat{\beta}_1$ (Newey and West, 1987). Their proofs (and those in Andrews (1991)) assume that v_t has more than four moments, which in turn is implied by X_t and u_t having more than eight moments, and this is the reason that the third assumption in Key Concept 13.2 is that X_t and u_t have more than eight moments.

Other HAC estimators.   The Newey-West variance estimator is not the only HAC estimator. For example, the weights $(m - j)/m$ in Equation (13.16) can be replaced by different weights. If different weights are used, then the rule for choosing the truncation parameter in Equation (13.17) no longer applies and a different rule, developed for those weights, should be used instead. Discussion of HAC estimators using other weights goes beyond the scope of this book. For more information on this topic, see Hayashi (2000, Section 6.6).

Extension to multiple regression.   All the issues discussed in this section generalize to the distributed lag regression model in Key Concept 13.1 with multiple lags and, more generally, to the multiple regression model with serially correlated errors. In particular, if the error term is serially correlated, then the usual OLS standard errors are an unreliable basis for inference and HAC standard errors should be used instead. If the HAC variance estimator used is the Newey-West estimator (the HAC variance estimator based on the weights $(m - j)/m$), then the

---

[1]Equation (13.17) gives the "best" choice of m if u_t and X_t are first order autoregressive processes with first autocorrelation coefficients 0.5, where "best" means the estimator that minimizes $E(\tilde{\sigma}^2_{\hat{\beta}_1} - \sigma^2_{\hat{\beta}_1})^2$. Equation (13.17) is based on a more general formula derived by Andrews (1991, Equation (5.3)).

HAC Standard Errors

The problem: The error term u_t in the distributed lag regression model in Key Concept 13.1 can be serially correlated. If so, the OLS coefficient estimators are consistent but in general the usual OLS standard errors are not, resulting in misleading hypothesis tests and confidence intervals.

The solution: Standard errors should be computed using a heteroskedasticity- and autocorrelation-consistent (HAC) estimator of the variance. The HAC estimator involves estimates of $m - 1$ autocovariances as well as the variance; in the case of a single regressor, the relevant formulas are given in Equations (13.15) and (13.16).

In practice, using HAC standard errors entails choosing the truncation parameter m. To do so, use the formula in Equation (13.17) as a benchmark, then increase or decrease m depending on whether your regressors and errors have high or low serial correlation.

truncation parameter m can be chosen according to the rule in Equation (13.17) whether there is a single regressor or multiple regressors. The formula for HAC standard errors in multiple regression is incorporated into modern regression software designed for use with time series data. Because this formula involves matrix algebra, we omit it here, and instead refer the reader to Hayashi (2000, Section 6.6) for the mathematical details.

HAC standard errors are summarized in Key Concept 13.3.

13.5 Estimation of Dynamic Causal Effects with Strictly Exogenous Regressors

When X_t is strictly exogenous, two alternative estimators of dynamic causal effects are available. The first such estimator involves estimating an autoregressive distributed lag (ADL) model instead of a distributed lag model, and calculating the dynamic multipliers from the estimated ADL coefficients. This method can entail estimating fewer coefficients than OLS estimation of the distributed lag model, thus potentially reducing estimation error. The second method is to estimate the coefficients of the distributed lag model, using **generalized least squares (GLS)** instead of OLS.

Although the same number of coefficients in the distributed lag model are estimated by GLS as by OLS, the GLS estimator has a smaller variance. To keep the exposition simple, these two estimation methods are initially laid out and discussed in the context of a distributed lag model with a single lag and AR(1) errors. The potential advantages of these two estimators are greatest, however, when many lags appear in the distributed lag model, so these estimators are then extended to the general distributed lag model with higher order autoregressive errors.

The Distributed Lag Model with AR(1) Errors

Suppose that the causal effect on Y of a change in X lasts for only two periods, that is, it has an initial impact effect β_1 and an effect in the next period of β_2, but no effect thereafter. Then the appropriate distributed lag regression model is the distributed lag model with only current and past values of X_{t-1}:

$$Y_t = \beta_0 + \beta_1 X_t + \beta_2 X_{t-1} + u_t. \tag{13.18}$$

As discussed in Section 13.2, in general the error term u_t in Equation (13.18) is serially correlated. One consequence of this serial correlation is that, if the distributed lag coefficients are estimated by OLS, then inference based on the usual OLS standard errors can be misleading. For this reason, Sections 13.3 and 13.4 emphasized the use of HAC standard errors when β_1 and β_2 in Equation (13.18) are estimated by OLS.

In this section, we take a different approach towards the serial correlation in u_t. This approach, which is possible if X_t is strictly exogenous, involves adopting an autoregressive model for the serial correlation in u_t, then using this AR model to derive some estimators that can be more efficient than the OLS estimator in the distributed lag model.

Specifically, suppose that u_t follows the AR(1) model

$$u_t = \phi_1 u_{t-1} + \tilde{u}_t, \tag{13.19}$$

where ϕ_1 is the autoregressive parameter, $\tilde{u}_t$ is serially uncorrelated, and where no intercept is needed because $E(u_t) = 0$. Equations (13.18) and (13.19) imply that the distributed lag model with a serially correlated error can be rewritten as an autoregressive distributed lag model with a serially uncorrelated error. To do so, lag each side of Equation (13.18) and subtract ϕ_1 times this lag from each side:

$$Y_t - \phi_1 Y_{t-1} = (\beta_0 + \beta_1 X_t + \beta_2 X_{t-1} + u_t) - \phi_1(\beta_0 + \beta_1 X_{t-1} + \beta_2 X_{t-2} + u_{t-1})$$
$$= \beta_0 + \beta_1 X_t + \beta_2 X_{t-1} - \phi_1 \beta_0 - \phi_1 \beta_1 X_{t-1} - \phi_1 \beta_2 X_{t-2} + \tilde{u}_t, \tag{13.20}$$

where the second equality uses $\tilde{u}_t = u_t - \phi_1 u_{t-1}$. Collecting terms in Equation (13.20), we have that

$$Y_t = \alpha_0 + \phi_1 Y_{t-1} + \delta_0 X_t + \delta_1 X_{t-1} + \delta_2 X_{t-2} + \tilde{u}_t \qquad (13.21)$$

where

$$\alpha_0 = \beta_0(1 - \phi_1), \ \delta_0 = \beta_1, \ \delta_1 = \beta_2 - \phi_1\beta_1, \ \text{and} \ \delta_2 = -\phi_1\beta_2, \qquad (13.22)$$

where β_0, β_1, and β_2 are the coefficients in Equation (13.18) and ϕ_1 is the auto-correlation coefficient in Equation (13.19).

Equation (13.21) is an ADL model that includes a contemporaneous value of X and two of its lags. We will refer to (13.21) as the ADL representation of the distributed lag model with autoregressive errors given in Equations (13.18) and (13.19).

The terms in Equation (13.20) can be reorganized differently to obtain an expression that is equivalent to Equations (13.21) and (13.22). Let $\tilde{Y}_t = Y_t - \phi_1 Y_{t-1}$ be the **quasi-difference** of Y_t ("quasi" because it is not the first difference, the difference between Y_t and Y_{t-1}; rather, it is the difference between Y_t and $\phi_1 Y_{t-1}$). Similarly, let $\tilde{X}_t = X_t - \phi_1 X_{t-1}$ be the quasi-difference of X_t. Then Equation (13.20) can be written

$$\tilde{Y}_t = \alpha_0 + \beta_1 \tilde{X}_t + \beta_2 \tilde{X}_{t-1} + \tilde{u}_t. \qquad (13.23)$$

We will refer to Equation (13.23) as the quasi-difference representation of the distributed lag model with autoregressive errors given in Equations (13.18) and (13.19).

The ADL model Equation (13.21) (with the parameter restrictions in Equation (13.22)) and the quasi-difference model in Equation (13.23) are equivalent. In both models, the error term, $\tilde{u}_t$, is serially uncorrelated. The two representations, however, suggest different estimation strategies. But before discussing those strategies, we turn to the assumptions under which they yield consistent estimators of the dynamic multipliers, β_1 and β_2.

The conditional mean zero assumption in the ADL(2,1) and quasi-differenced models. Because Equations (13.21) (with the restrictions in Equation (13.22)) and (13.23) are equivalent, the conditions for their estimation are the same, so for convenience we consider Equation (13.23).

The quasi-difference model in Equation (13.23) is a distributed lag model involving the quasi-differenced variables with a serially uncorrelated error.

Accordingly, the conditions for OLS estimation of the coefficients in Equation (13.23) are the least squares assumptions for the distributed lag model in Key Concept 13.2, expressed in terms of $\tilde{u}_t$ and $\tilde{X}_t$. The critical assumption here is the first assumption which, applied to Equation (13.23), is that $\tilde{X}_t$ is exogenous; that is,

$$E(\tilde{u}_t | \tilde{X}_t, \tilde{X}_{t-1}, \ldots) = 0, \tag{13.24}$$

where letting the conditional expectation depend on distant lags of $\tilde{X}_t$ ensures that no additional lags of $\tilde{X}_t$, other than those appearing in Equation (13.23), enter the population regression function.

Because $\tilde{X}_t = X_t - \phi_1 X_{t-1}$, so $X_t = \tilde{X}_t + \phi_1 X_{t-1}$, conditioning on $\tilde{X}_t$ and all of its lags is equivalent to conditioning on X_t and all of its lags. Thus, the conditional expectation condition in Equation (13.24) is equivalent to the condition that $E(\tilde{u}_t | X_t, X_{t-1}, \ldots) = 0$. Furthermore, because $\tilde{u}_t = u_t - \phi_1 u_{t-1}$, this condition in turn implies

$$\begin{aligned} 0 &= E(\tilde{u}_t | X_t, X_{t-1}, \ldots) \\ &= E(u_t - \phi_1 u_{t-1} | X_t, X_{t-1}, \ldots) \\ &= E(u_t | X_t, X_{t-1}, \ldots) - \phi_1 E(u_{t-1} | X_t, X_{t-1}, \ldots). \end{aligned} \tag{13.25}$$

For the equality in Equation (13.25) to hold for general values of ϕ_1, it must be the case that both $E(u_t | X_t, X_{t-1}, \ldots) = 0$ and $E(u_{t-1} | X_t, X_{t-1}, \ldots) = 0$. By shifting the time subscripts, the condition that $E(u_{t-1} | X_t, X_{t-1}, \ldots) = 0$ can be rewritten as

$$E(u_t | X_{t+1}, X_t, X_{t-1}, \ldots) = 0, \tag{13.26}$$

which (by the law of iterated expectations) implies that $E(u_t | X_t, X_{t-1}, \ldots) = 0$. In summary, having the zero conditional mean assumption in Equation (13.24) hold for general values of ϕ_1 is equivalent to having the condition in Equation (13.26) hold.

The condition in Equation (13.26) is implied by X_t being strictly exogenous, but it is *not* implied by X_t being (past and present) exogenous. Thus, the least squares assumptions for estimation of the distributed lag model in Equation (13.23) hold if X_t is strictly exogenous, but it is not enough that X_t be (past and present) exogenous.

Because the ADL representation (Equations (13.21) and (13.22)) is equivalent to the quasi-differenced representation (Equation (13.23)), the conditional mean assumption needed to estimate the coefficients of the quasi-differenced representation (that $E(u_t | X_{t+1}, X_t, X_{t-1}, \ldots) = 0$) is also the conditional mean assumption for consistent estimation of the coefficients of the ADL representation.

We now turn to the two estimation strategies suggested by these two representations, estimation of the ADL coefficients and estimation of the coefficients of the quasi-differenced model.

OLS Estimation of the ADL Model

The first strategy is to use OLS to estimate the coefficients in the ADL model in Equation (13.21). As the derivation leading to Equation (13.21) shows, including the lag of Y and the extra lag of X as regressors makes the error term serially uncorrelated (under the assumption that the error follows a first order autoregression). Thus the usual OLS standard errors can be used, that is, HAC standard errors are not needed when the ADL model coefficients in Equation (13.21) are estimated by OLS.

The estimated ADL coefficients are not themselves estimates of the dynamic multipliers, but the dynamic multipliers can be computed from the ADL coefficients. A general way to compute the dynamic multipliers is to express the estimated regression function as a function of current and past values of X_t, that is, to eliminate Y_t from the estimated regression function. To do so, repeatedly substitute expressions for lagged values of Y_t into the estimated regression function. Specifically, consider the estimated regression function

$$\hat{Y}_t = \hat{\phi}_1 Y_{t-1} + \hat{\delta}_0 X_t + \hat{\delta}_1 X_{t-1} + \hat{\delta}_2 X_{t-2}, \tag{13.27}$$

where the estimated intercept has been omitted because it does not enter any expression for the dynamic multipliers. Lagging both sides of Equation (13.27) yields $\hat{Y}_{t-1} = \hat{\phi}_1 Y_{t-2} + \hat{\delta}_0 X_{t-1} + \hat{\delta}_1 X_{t-2} + \hat{\delta}_2 X_{t-3}$, so replacing Y_{t-1} in Equation (13.27) by $\hat{Y}_{t-1}$ and collecting terms yields

$$\begin{aligned}
\hat{Y}_t &= \hat{\phi}_1 (\hat{\phi}_1 Y_{t-2} + \hat{\delta}_0 X_{t-1} + \hat{\delta}_1 X_{t-2} + \hat{\delta}_2 X_{t-3}) + \hat{\delta}_0 X_t + \hat{\delta}_1 X_{t-1} + \hat{\delta}_2 X_{t-2} \\
&= \hat{\delta}_0 X_t + (\hat{\delta}_1 + \hat{\phi}_1 \hat{\delta}_0) X_{t-1} + (\hat{\delta}_2 + \hat{\phi}_1 \hat{\delta}_1) X_{t-2} + \hat{\phi}_1 \hat{\delta}_2 X_{t-3} + \hat{\phi}_1^2 Y_{t-2}.
\end{aligned} \tag{13.28}$$

Repeating this process by repeatedly substituting expressions for Y_{t-2}, Y_{t-3}, and so forth yields

$$\begin{aligned}
\hat{Y}_t = \hat{\delta}_0 X_t &+ (\hat{\delta}_1 + \hat{\phi}_1 \hat{\delta}_0) X_{t-1} + (\hat{\delta}_2 + \hat{\phi}_1 \hat{\delta}_1 + \hat{\phi}_1^2 \hat{\delta}_0) X_{t-2} + \\
\hat{\phi}_1 (\hat{\delta}_2 &+ \hat{\phi}_1 \hat{\delta}_1 + \hat{\phi}_1^2 \hat{\delta}_0) X_{t-3} + \hat{\phi}_1^2 (\hat{\delta}_2 + \hat{\phi}_1 \hat{\delta}_1 + \hat{\phi}_1^2 \hat{\delta}_0) X_{t-4} + \cdots.
\end{aligned} \tag{13.29}$$

The coefficients in Equation (13.29) are the estimators of the dynamic multipliers, computed from the OLS estimators of the coefficients in the ADL model in Equation (13.21). If the restrictions on the coefficients in Equation (13.22) were to hold exactly for the *estimated* coefficients, then all the dynamic multipliers beyond the second (that is, the coefficients on X_{t-2}, X_{t-3}, and so forth) would all be zero.[2] However, under this estimation strategy those restrictions will not hold exactly, so the estimated multipliers beyond the second in Equation (13.29) will generally be nonzero.

GLS Estimation

The second strategy for estimating the dynamic multipliers when X_t is strictly exogenous is to use generalized least squares (GLS), which entails estimating Equation (13.23). To describe the GLS estimator, we initially assume that ϕ_1 is known; because in practice it is unknown, this estimator is infeasible, so it is called the infeasible GLS estimator. The infeasible GLS estimator, however, can be modified using an estimator of ϕ_1, which yields a feasible version of the GLS estimator.

Infeasible GLS.   Suppose that ϕ_1 were known; then the quasi-differenced variables $\tilde{X}_t$ and $\tilde{Y}_t$ could be computed directly. As discussed in the context of Equations (13.24) and (13.26), if X_t is strictly exogenous, then $E(\tilde{u}_t | \tilde{X}_t, \tilde{X}_{t-1}, \dots) = 0$. Thus, if X_t is strictly exogenous and if ϕ_1 is known, the coefficients α_0, β_1, and β_2 in Equation (13.23) can be estimated by the OLS regression of $\tilde{Y}_t$ on $\tilde{X}_t$ and $\tilde{X}_{t-1}$ (including an intercept). The resulting estimators of β_1 and β_2—that is, the OLS estimators of the slope coefficients in Equation (13.23) when ϕ_1 is known—are the **infeasible GLS estimators**. This estimator is infeasible because ϕ_1 is unknown, so $\tilde{X}_t$ and $\tilde{Y}_t$ cannot be computed and thus these OLS estimators cannot actually be computed.

Feasible GLS.   The **feasible GLS estimator** modifies the infeasible GLS estimator by using a preliminary estimator of ϕ_1, $\hat{\phi}_1$, to compute the estimated quasi-differences. Specifically, the feasible GLS estimators of β_1 and β_2 are the OLS estimators of β_1 and β_2 in Equation (13.23), computed by regressing $\hat{\tilde{Y}}_t$ on $\hat{\tilde{X}}_t$ and $\hat{\tilde{X}}_{t-1}$ (with an intercept), where $\hat{\tilde{X}}_t = X_t - \hat{\phi}_1 X_{t-1}$ and $\hat{\tilde{Y}}_t = Y_t - \hat{\phi}_1 Y_{t-1}$.

The preliminary estimator, $\hat{\phi}_1$, can be computed by first estimating the distributed lag regression in Equation (13.18) by OLS, then using OLS to estimate ϕ_1 in Equation (13.19) with the OLS residuals $\hat{u}_t$ replacing the unobserved regression errors u_t. This version of the GLS estimator is called the Cochrane-Orcutt (1949) estimator.

---

[2]Substitute the equalities in Equation (13.22) to show that, if those equalities hold, then $\delta_2 + \phi_1 \delta_1 + \phi_1^2 \delta_0 = 0$.

An extension of the Cochrane-Orcutt method is to continue this process iteratively: use the GLS estimator of β_1 and β_2 to compute revised estimators of u_t; use these new residuals to re-estimate ϕ_1; use this revised estimator of ϕ_1 to compute revised estimated quasi-differences; use these revised estimated quasi-differences to re-estimate β_1 and β_2; and continue this process until the estimators of β_1 and β_2 converge. This is referred to as the iterated Cochrane-Orcutt estimator.

A nonlinear least squares interpretation of the GLS estimator. An equivalent interpretation of the GLS estimator is that it estimates the ADL model in Equation (13.21), imposing the parameter restrictions in Equation (13.22). These restrictions are nonlinear functions of the original parameters β_0, β_1, β_2, and ϕ_1, so this estimation cannot be performed using OLS. Instead, the parameters can be estimated by nonlinear least squares (NLLS). As discussed in Section 9.3, NLLS minimizes the sum of squared mistakes made by the estimated regression function, recognizing that the regression function is a nonlinear function of the parameters being estimated. In general, NLLS estimation can require sophisticated algorithms for minimizing nonlinear functions of unknown parameters. In the special case at hand, however, those sophisticated algorithms are not needed; rather, the NLLS estimator can be computed using the algorithm described above for the iterated Cochrane-Orcutt estimator. Thus, the iterated Cochrane-Orcutt GLS estimator is in fact the NLLS estimator of the ADL coefficients, subject to the nonlinear constraints in Equation (13.22).

Efficiency of GLS. The virtue of the GLS estimator is that when X is strictly exogenous and the transformed errors $\tilde{u}_t$ are homoskedastic, it is efficient among linear estimators, at least in large samples. To see this, first consider the infeasible GLS estimator. If $\tilde{u}_t$ is homoskedastic, if ϕ_1 is known (so that $\tilde{X}_t$ and $\tilde{Y}_t$ can be treated as if they are observed), and if X_t is strictly exogenous, then the Gauss-Markov theorem implies that the OLS estimator of α_0, β_1, and β_2 in Equation (13.23) is efficient among all linear conditionally unbiased estimators; that is, the OLS estimator of the coefficients in Equation (13.23) is the best linear unbiased estimator, or BLUE (Section 4.9). Because the OLS estimator of Equation (13.23) is the infeasible GLS estimator, this means that the infeasible GLS estimator is BLUE. The feasible GLS estimator is similar to the infeasible GLS estimator, except that ϕ_1 is estimated. Because the estimator of ϕ_1 is consistent and its variance is inversely proportional to T, the feasible and infeasible GLS estimators have the same variances in large samples. In this sense, if X is strictly exogenous, then the feasible GLS estimator is BLUE in large samples. In particular, if X is strictly exogenous then GLS is more efficient than the OLS estimator of the distributed lag coefficients discussed in Section 13.3.

The Cochrane-Orcutt and iterated Cochrane-Orcutt estimators presented here are special cases of GLS estimation. In general, GLS estimation involves transforming the regression model so that the errors are homoskedastic and serially uncorrelated, then estimating the coefficients of the transformed regression model by OLS. In general, the GLS estimator is consistent and BLUE if X is strictly exogenous, but is not consistent if X is only (past and present) exogenous. The mathematics of GLS involve matrix algebra, so they are postponed to Section 16.6.

The Distributed Lag Model with Additional Lags and AR(p) Errors

The foregoing discussion of the distributed lag model in Equations (13.18) and (13.19), which has a single lag of X_t and an AR(1) error term, carries over to the general distributed lag model with multiple lags and an AR(p) error term.

The general distributed lag model with autoregressive errors.   The general distributed lag model with r lags and AR(p) error term is

$$Y_t = \beta_0 + \beta_1 X_t + \beta_2 X_{t-1} + \cdots + \beta_{r+1} X_{t-r} + u_t, \tag{13.30}$$

$$u_t = \phi_1 u_{t-1} + \phi_2 u_{t-2} + \cdots + \phi_p u_{t-p} + \tilde{u}_t, \tag{13.31}$$

where $\beta_1, \ldots, \beta_{r+1}$ are the dynamic multipliers and $\phi_1, \ldots, \phi_p$ are the autoregressive coefficients of the error term. Under the AR(p) model for the errors, $\tilde{u}_t$ is serially uncorrelated.

Algebra of the sort that led to the ADL model in Equation (13.21) shows that Equations (13.30) and (13.31) imply that Y_t can be written in ADL form:

$$Y_t = \alpha_0 + \phi_1 Y_{t-1} + \cdots + \phi_p Y_{t-p} + \delta_0 X_t + \delta_1 X_{t-1} + \cdots + \delta_q X_{t-q} + \tilde{u}_t, \tag{13.32}$$

where $q = r + p$ and $\delta_0, \ldots, \delta_q$ are functions of the β's and ϕ's in Equations (13.30) and (13.31). Equivalently, the model of Equations (13.30) and (13.31) can be written in quasi-difference form as

$$\tilde{Y}_t = \alpha_0 + \beta_1 \tilde{X}_t + \beta_2 \tilde{X}_{t-1} + \cdots + \beta_{r+1} \tilde{X}_{t-r} + \tilde{u}_t, \tag{13.33}$$

where $\tilde{Y}_t = Y_t - \phi_1 Y_{t-1} - \cdots - \phi_p Y_{t-p}$ and $\tilde{X}_t = X_t - \phi_1 X_{t-1} - \cdots - \phi_p X_{t-p}$.

Conditions for estimation of the ADL coefficients.   The foregoing discussion of the conditions for consistent estimation of the ADL coefficients in the

AR(1) case extends to the general model with AR(p) errors. The conditional mean zero assumption for Equation (13.33) is that

$$E(\widetilde{u}_t \,|\, \widetilde{X}_t, \widetilde{X}_{t-1}, \ldots) = 0. \tag{13.34}$$

Because $\widetilde{u}_t = u_t - \phi_1 u_{t-1} - \phi_2 u_{t-2} - \cdots - \phi_p u_{t-p}$ and $\widetilde{X}_t = X_t - \phi_1 X_{t-1} - \cdots - \phi_p X_{t-p}$, this condition is equivalent to

$$\tag{13.35}$$

$$E(u_t \,|\, X_t, X_{t-1}, \ldots) - \phi_1 E(u_{t-1} \,|\, X_t, X_{t-1}, \ldots) - \cdots - \phi_p E(u_{t-p} \,|\, X_t, X_{t-1}, \ldots) = 0.$$

For Equation (13.35) to hold for general values of $\phi_1, \ldots, \phi_p$, it must be the case that each of the conditional expectations in Equation (13.35) is zero; equivalently, it must be the case that

$$E(u_t \,|\, X_{t+p}, X_{t+p-1}, X_{t+p-2}, \ldots) = 0 \tag{13.36}$$

This condition is not implied by X_t being (past and present) exogenous, but it is implied by X_t being strictly exogenous. In fact, in the limit when p is infinite (so that the error term in the distributed lag model follows an infinite order autoregression), then the condition in Equation (13.36) becomes the condition in Key Concept 13.1 for strict exogeneity.

Estimation of the ADL model by OLS.   As in the distributed lag model with a single lag and an AR(1) error term, the dynamic multipliers can be estimated from the OLS estimators of the ADL coefficients in Equation (13.32). The general formulas are similar to, but more complicated than, those in Equation (13.29) and are best expressed using lag multiplier notation; these formulas are given in Appendix 13.2. In practice, modern regression software designed for time series regression analysis does these computations for you.

Estimation by GLS.   Alternatively, the dynamic multipliers can be estimated by (feasible) GLS. This entails OLS estimation of the coefficients of the quasi-differenced specification in Equation (13.33), using estimated quasi-differences. The estimated quasi-differences can be computed using preliminary estimators of the autoregressive coefficients $\phi_1, \ldots, \phi_p$, as in the AR(1) case. The GLS estimator is asymptotically BLUE, in the sense discussed above for the AR(1) case.

Key Concept 13.4

Estimation of Dynamic Multipliers Under Strict Exogeneity

The general distributed lag model with r lags and $AR(p)$ error term is

$$Y_t = \beta_0 + \beta_1 X_t + \beta_2 X_{t-1} + \cdots + \beta_{r+1} X_{t-r} + u_t \qquad (13.37)$$

$$u_t = \phi_1 u_{t-1} + \phi_2 u_{t-2} + \cdots + \phi_p u_{t-p} + \tilde{u}_t. \qquad (13.38)$$

If X_t is strictly exogenous, then the dynamic multipliers $\beta_1, \ldots, \beta_{r+1}$ can be estimated by first using OLS to estimate the coefficients of the ADL model

$$Y_t = \alpha_0 + \phi_1 Y_{t-1} + \cdots + \phi_p Y_{t-p} + \delta_0 X_t + \delta_1 X_{t-1} + \cdots + \delta_q X_{t-q} + \tilde{u}_t, \qquad (13.39)$$

where $q = r + p$, then computing the dynamic multipliers using regression software. Alternatively, the dynamic multipliers can be estimated by estimating the distributed lag coefficients in Equation (13.37) by GLS.

Estimation of dynamic multipliers under strict exogeneity is summarized in Key Concept 13.4.

Which to use: OLS or GLS?   The two estimation options, OLS estimation of the ADL coefficients and GLS estimation of the distributed lag coefficients, have advantages and disadvantages.

The advantage of the ADL approach is that it can reduce the number of parameters needed for estimating the dynamic multipliers, compared to OLS estimation of the distributed lag model. For example, the estimated ADL model in Equation (13.27) led to the infinitely long estimated distributed lag representation in Equation (13.29). To the extent that distributed lag model with only r lags is really an approximation to a longer-lagged distributed lag model, the ADL model thus can provide a simple way to estimate those many longer lags using only a few unknown parameters. Thus, in practice it might be possible to estimate the ADL model in Equation (13.39) with values of p and q much smaller than the value of r needed for OLS estimation of the distributed lag coefficients in Equation (13.37). In other words, the ADL specification can provide a compact, or parsimonious, summary of a long and complex distributed lag (see Appendix 13.2 for additional discussion).

The advantage of the GLS estimator is that, for a given lag length r in the distributed lag model, the GLS estimator of the distributed lag coefficients is more efficient than the OLS estimator, at least in large samples. In practice, then, the advantage of using the ADL approach arises because the ADL specification can permit estimating fewer parameters than are estimated by GLS.

13.6 Orange Juice Prices and Cold Weather

This section uses the tools of time series regression to squeeze additional insights from our data on Florida temperatures and orange juice prices. First, how long lasting is the effect of a freeze on the price? Second, has this dynamic effect been stable or has it changed over the 51 years spanned by the data and if so, how?

We begin this analysis by estimating the dynamic causal effects using the method of Section 13.3, that is, by OLS estimation of the coefficients of a distributed lag regression of the percentage change in prices ($\%ChgP_t$) on the number of freezing degree days in that month (FDD_t) and its lagged values. For the distributed lag estimator to be consistent, FDD must be (past and present) exogenous. As discussed in Section 13.2, this assumption is reasonable here. Humans cannot influence the weather, so treating the weather as if it were randomly assigned experimentally is appropriate. Because FDD is exogenous, we can estimate the dynamic causal effects by OLS estimation of the coefficients in the distributed lag model of Equation (13.4) in Key Concept 13.1.

As discussed in Sections 13.3 and 13.4, the error term can be serially correlated in distributed lag regressions, so it is important to use HAC standard errors, which adjust for this serial correlation. For the initial results, the truncation parameter for the Newey-West standard errors (m in the notation of Section 13.4) was chosen using the rule in Equation (13.17): because there are 612 monthly observations, according to that rule $m = 0.75\,T^{1/3} = 0.75 \times 612^{1/3} = 6.37$, but because m must be an integer this was rounded up to $m = 7$; the sensitivity of the standard errors to this choice of truncation parameter is investigated below.

The results of OLS estimation of the distributed lag regression of $\%ChgP_t$ on $FDD_t, FDD_{t-1}, \ldots, FDD_{t-18}$ are summarized in column (1) of Table 13.1. The coefficients of this regression (only some of which are reported in the table) are estimates of the dynamic causal effect on orange juice price changes (in percent) for the first 18 months following a unit increase in the number of freezing degree days in a month. For example, a single freezing degree day is estimated to increase prices by 0.50% over the month in which the freezing degree day occurs. The subsequent effect on price in later months of a freezing degree day is less: after one month the estimated effect is to increase the price by a further 0.17%, and after two months the estimated effect is to increase the price by an additional .07%. The R^2 from this regression is 0.12, indicating that much of the monthly variation in orange juice prices is not explained by current and past values of *FDD*.

Plots of dynamic multipliers can convey information more effectively than tables such as Table 13.1. The dynamic multipliers from column (1) of Table 13.1 are plotted in Figure 13.2a along with their 95% confidence intervals, computed as the estimated coefficient ±1.96 HAC standard errors. After the initial sharp price rise, subsequent price rises are less, although prices are estimated to rise slightly in each of the first six months after the freeze. As can be seen from Figure 13.2a, for months other than the first the dynamic multipliers are not statistically significantly different from zero at the 5% significance level, although they are estimated to be positive through the seventh month.

Column (2) of Table 13.1 contains the cumulative dynamic multipliers for this specification, that is, the cumulative sum of the dynamic multipliers reported in column (1). These dynamic multipliers are plotted in Figure 13.2b along with their 95% confidence intervals. After one month, the cumulative effect of the freezing degree day is to increase prices by 0.67%, after two months the price is estimated to have risen by 0.74%, and after six months the price is estimated to have risen by 0.90%. As can be seen in Figure 13.2b, these cumulative multipliers increase through the seventh month, because the individual dynamic multipliers are positive for the first seven months. In the eighth month, the dynamic multiplier is negative, so the price of orange juice begins to fall slowly from its peak. After 18 months, the cumulative increase in prices is only 0.37%, that is, the long-run cumulative dynamic multiplier is only 0.37%. This long-run cumulative dynamic multiplier is not statistically significantly different from zero at the 10% significance level ($t = 0.37/0.30 = 1.23$).

Sensitivity analysis.   As in any empirical analysis, it is important to check if these results are sensitive to changes in the details of the empirical analysis. We therefore examine three aspects of this analysis: sensitivity to the computation of the HAC standard errors; an alternative specification that investigates potential omitted variable bias; and an analysis of the stability over time of the estimated multipliers.

First, we investigate whether the standard errors reported in the second column of Table 13.1 are sensitive to different choices of the HAC truncation parameter *m*. In column (3), results are reported for $m = 14$, twice the value used in column (2). The regression specification is the same as in column (2), so the esti-

TABLE 13.1   The Dynamic Effect of a Freezing Degree Day (*FDD*) on the Price of Orange Juice: Selected Estimated Dynamic Multipliers and Cumulative Dynamic Multipliers

Lag number	(1) Dynamic Multipliers	(2) Cumulative Multipliers	(3) Cumulative Multipliers	(4) Cumulative Multipliers
0	0.50 (0.14)	0.50 (0.14)	0.50 (0.14)	0.51 (0.15)
1	0.17 (0.09)	0.67 (0.14)	0.67 (0.13)	0.70 (0.15)
2	0.07 (0.06)	0.74 (0.17)	0.74 (0.16)	0.76 (0.18)
3	0.07 (0.04)	0.81 (0.18)	0.81 (0.18)	0.84 (0.19)
4	0.02 (0.03)	0.84 (0.19)	0.84 (0.19)	0.87 (0.20)
5	0.03 (0.03)	0.87 (0.19)	0.87 (0.19)	0.89 (0.20)
6 ⋮	0.03 (0.05)	0.90 (0.20)	0.90 (0.21)	0.91 (0.21)
12 ⋮	−0.14 (0.08)	0.54 (0.27)	0.54 (0.28)	0.54 (0.28)
18	0.00 (0.02)	0.37 (0.30)	0.37 (0.31)	0.37 (0.30)
Monthly indicators?	No	No	No	Yes $F = 1.01$ ($p = 0.43$)
HAC standard error truncation parameter (m)	7	7	14	7

All regressions were estimated by OLS using monthly data (described in Appendix 13.1) from January 1950 to December 2000, for a total of $T = 612$ monthly observations. The dependent variable is the monthly percentage change in the price of orange juice (%*ChgP_t*). Regression (1) is the distributed lag regression with the monthly number of freezing degree days and eighteen of its lagged values, that is, $FDD_t, FDD_{t-1}, \ldots, FDD_{t-18}$, and the reported coefficients are the OLS estimates of the dynamic multipliers. The cumulative multipliers are the cumulative sum of estimated dynamic multipliers. All regressions include an intercept, which is not reported. Newey-West HAC standard errors, computed using the truncation number given in the final row, are reported in parentheses.

mated coefficients and dynamic multipliers are identical; only the standard errors differ but, as it happens, not by much. We conclude that the results are insensitive to changes in the HAC truncation parameter.

Second, we investigate a possible source of omitted variable bias. Freezes in Florida are not randomly assigned throughout the year, but rather occur in the

FIGURE 13.2 **The Dynamic Effect of a Freezing Degree Day (*FDD*) on the Price of Orange Juice**

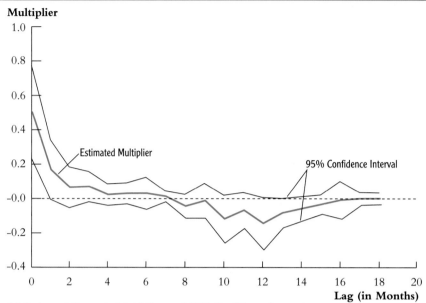

(a) Estimated Dynamic Multipliers and 95% Confidence Interval

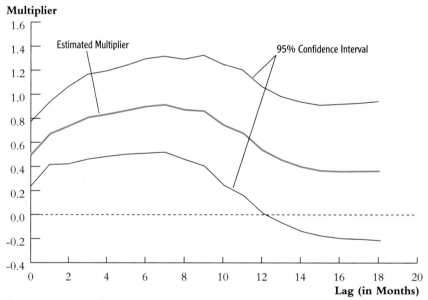

(b) Estimated Cumulative Dynamic Multipliers and 95% Confidence Interval

The estimated dynamic multipliers show that a freeze leads to an immediate increase in prices. Future price rises are much smaller than the initial impact. The cumulative multiplier shows that freezes have a persistent effect on the level of orange juice prices, with prices peaking seven months after the freeze.

winter (of course). If demand for orange juice is seasonal (is demand for orange juice greater in the winter than the summer?), then the seasonal patterns in orange juice demand could be correlated with *FDD*, resulting in omitted variable bias. The quantity of oranges sold for juice is endogenous: prices and quantities are simultaneously determined by the forces of supply and demand. Thus, as discussed in Section 7.2, including quantity would lead to simultaneity bias. Nevertheless, the seasonal component of demand can be captured by including seasonal variables as regressors. The specification in column (4) of Table 13.1 therefore includes eleven monthly binary variables, one indicating whether the month is January, one indicating February, and so forth (as usual one binary variable must be omitted to prevent perfect multicollinearity with the intercept). These monthly indicator variables are not jointly statistically significant at the 10% level ($p = .43$), and the estimated cumulative dynamic multipliers are essentially the same as for the specifications excluding the monthly indicators. In summary, seasonal fluctuations in demand are not an important source of omitted variable bias.

Have the dynamic multipliers been stable over time?[3]   To assess the stability of the dynamic multipliers, we need to check whether the distributed lag regression coefficients have been stable over time. Because we do not have a specific break date in mind, we test for instability in the regression coefficients using the Quandt Likelihood Ratio (QLR) statistic (Key Concept 12.9). The QLR statistic (with 15% trimming and HAC variance estimator), computed for the regression of column (1) with all coefficients interacted, has a value of 9.08, with $q = 20$ degrees of freedom (the coefficients on FDD_t, its 18 lags, and the intercept). The 1% critical value in Table 12.5 is 2.43, so the QLR statistic rejects at the 1% significance level. These QLR regressions have 40 regressors, a large number; recomputing them for six lags only (so there are 16 regressors and $q = 8$) also results in rejection at the 1% level. Thus, the hypothesis that the dynamic multipliers are stable is rejected at the 1% significance level.

One way to see how the dynamic multipliers have changed over time is to compute them for different parts of the sample. Figure 13.3 plots the estimated cumulative dynamic multipliers for the first third (1950–1966), middle third (1967–1983), and final third (1984–2000) of the sample, computed by running separate regressions on each subsample. These estimates show an interesting and noticeable pattern. In the 1950s and early 1960s, a freezing degree day had a large and persistent effect on the price. The magnitude of the effect on price of a freez-

---

[3]The discussion of stability in this subsection draws on material from Section 12.7 and can be skipped if that material has not been covered.

FIGURE 13.3 Estimated Cumulative Dynamic Multipliers from Different Sample Periods

The dynamic effect on orange juice prices of freezes changed significantly over the second half of the twentieth century. A freeze had a larger impact on prices during 1950 to 1966 than later, and the effect of a freeze was less persistent during 1984–2000 than earlier.

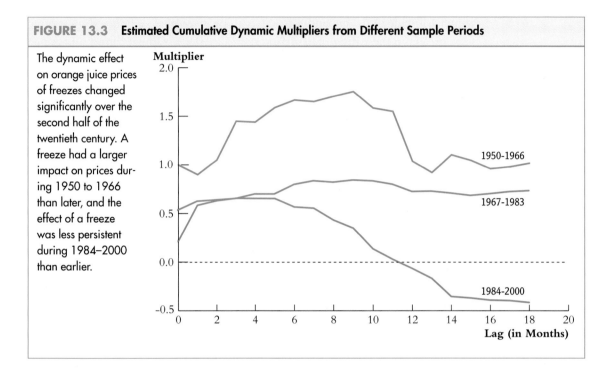

ing degree day diminished in the 1970s, although it remained highly persistent. In the late 1980s and 1990s, the short-run effect of a freezing degree day was the same as in the 1970s but it became much less persistent, and was essentially eliminated after a year. These estimates suggest that the dynamic causal effect on orange juice prices of a Florida freeze became smaller and less persistent over the second half of the twentieth century.

ADL and GLS estimates. As discussed in Section 13.5, if the error term in the distributed lag regression is serially correlated and *FDD* is strictly exogenous, it is possible to estimate the dynamic multipliers more efficiently than by OLS estimation of the distributed lag coefficients. Before using either the GLS estimator or the estimator based on the ADL model, however, we need to consider whether *FDD* is in fact strictly exogenous. True, humans cannot affect the weather, but does that mean that the weather is *strictly* exogenous? Does the error term u_t in the distributed lag regression have conditional mean zero, given past, present, and *future* values of *FDD*?

The error term in the population counterpart of the distributed lag regression in column (1) of Table 13.1 is the discrepancy between the price and its population prediction based on the past 18 months of weather. This discrepancy might arise for many reasons, one of which is that traders use forecasts of the weather in Orlando. For example, if an especially cold winter is forecasted, then traders would incorporate

NEWS FLASH: Commodity Traders Send Shivers Through Disney World

Although the weather at Disney World in Orlando, Florida, is usually pleasant, now and then a cold spell can settle in. If you are visiting Disney World on a winter evening, should you bring a warm coat? Some people might check the weather forecast on TV, but those in the know can do better: they can check that day's closing price on the New York orange juice futures market!

The financial economist Richard Roll undertook a detailed study of the relationship between orange juice prices and the weather. Roll (1984) examined the effect on prices of cold weather in Orlando, but he also studied the "effect" of changes in the price of an orange juice futures contract (a contract to buy frozen orange juice concentrate at a specified date in the future) on the weather. Roll used daily data from 1975 to 1981 on the prices of OJ futures contracts traded at the New York Cotton Exchange and on daily and overnight temperatures in Orlando. He found that a rise in the price of the futures contract during the trading day in New York predicted cold weather, in particular a freezing spell, in Orlando over the following night. In fact, the market was so

effective in predicting cold weather in Florida that a price rise during the trading day actually predicted forecast errors in the official U.S. government weather forecasts for that night.

Roll's study is also interesting for what he did *not* find: although his detailed weather data explained some of the variation in daily OJ futures prices, most of the daily movements in OJ prices remained unexplained. He therefore suggested that the OJ futures market exhibits "excess volatility," that is, more volatility than can be attributed to movements in fundamentals. Understanding why (and if) there is excess volatility in financial markets is now an important area of research in financial economics.

Roll's finding also illustrates the difference between forecasting and estimating dynamic causal effects. Price changes on the OJ futures market are a useful predictor of cold weather, but that does not mean that commodity traders are so powerful that they can *cause* the temperature to fall. Visitors to Disney World might shiver after an OJ futures contract price rise, but they are not shivering *because* of the price rise—unless, of course, they went short in the OJ futures market.

this into the price so the price would be above its predicted value based on the population regression; that is, the error term would be positive. If this forecast is accurate, then in fact future weather would turn out to be cold. Thus future freezing degree days would be positive ($X_{t+1} > 0$) when the current price is unusually high ($u_t > 0$), so that corr(X_{t+1}, u_t) is positive. Stated more simply, although orange juice traders cannot influence the weather, they can—and do—predict it (see the box). Consequently, the error term in the price/weather regression is correlated with future weather. In other words, *FDD* is exogenous, but if this reasoning is true, it is not strictly exogenous, and the GLS and ADL estimators will not be consistent estimators of the dynamic multipliers. These estimators therefore are not used in this application.

13.7 Is Exogeneity Plausible? Some Examples

As in regression with cross-sectional data, the interpretation of the coefficients in a distributed lag regression as causal dynamic effects hinges on the assumption that X is exogenous. If X_t or its lagged values are correlated with u_t, then the conditional mean of u_t will depend on X_t or its lags, in which case X is not (past and present) exogenous. Regressors can be correlated with the error term for several reasons, but with economic time series data a particularly important concern is that there could be simultaneous causality, which (as discussed in Section 10.1) results in endogenous regressors. In Section 13.6, we discussed the assumptions of exogeneity and strict exogeneity of freezing degree days in detail. In this section, we examine the assumption of exogeneity in four other economic applications.

U.S. Income and Australian Exports

The United States is an important source of demand for Australian exports. Precisely how sensitive Australian exports are to fluctuations in U.S. aggregate income could be investigated by regressing Australian exports to the United States against a measure of U.S. income. Strictly speaking, because the world economy is integrated, there is simultaneous causality in this relationship: a decline in Australian exports reduces Australian income, which reduces demand for imports from the United States, which reduces U.S. income. As a practical matter, however, this effect is very small because the Australian economy is much smaller than the U.S. economy. Thus, U.S. income plausibly can be treated as exogenous in this regression.

In contrast, in a regression of European Union exports to the United States against U.S. income the argument for treating U.S. income as exogenous is less convincing because demand by residents of the European Union for American exports constitutes a substantial fraction of the total demand for U.S. exports. Thus a decline in U.S. demand for EU exports would decrease EU income, which in turn would decrease demand for U.S. exports and thus decrease U.S.income. Because of these linkages through international trade, EU exports to the United States and U.S. income are simultaneously determined, so in this regression U.S. income arguably is not exogenous. This example illustrates a more general point that whether a variable is exogenous depends on the context: U.S. income is plausibly exogenous in a regression explaining Australian exports, but not in a regression explaining EU exports.

Oil Prices and Inflation

Ever since the oil price increases of the 1970s, macroeconomists have been interested in estimating the dynamic effect of an increase in the international price of crude oil on the U.S. rate of inflation. Because oil prices are set in world markets in large part by foreign oil-producing countries, initially one might think that oil prices are exogenous. But oil prices are not like the weather: members of OPEC set oil production levels strategically, taking many factors, including the state of the world economy, into account. To the extent that oil prices (or quantities) are set based on an assessment of current and future world economic conditions, including inflation in the United States, oil prices are endogenous.

Monetary Policy and Inflation

The central bankers in charge of monetary policy need to know the effect on inflation of monetary policy. Because the main tool of monetary policy is the short-term interest rate (the "short rate"), this means they need to know the dynamic causal effect on inflation of a change in the short rate. Although the short rate is determined by the central bank, it is not set by the central bankers at random (as it would be in an ideal randomized experiment) but rather is set endogenously: the central bank determines the short rate based on an assessment of the current and future state of the economy, especially including the current and future rates of inflation. The rate of inflation in turn depends on the interest rate (higher interest rates reduce aggregate demand), but the interest rate depends on the rate of inflation, its past, and its (expected) future value. Thus the short rate is endogenous and the causal dynamic effect of a change in the short rate on future inflation cannot be consistently estimated by an OLS regression of the rate of inflation on current and past interest rates.

The Phillips Curve

The Phillips curve investigated in Chapter 12 is a regression of the change in the rate of inflation against lagged changes in inflation and lags of the unemployment rate. Because lags of the unemployment rate happened in the past, one might initially think that there cannot be feedback from current rates of inflation to past values of the unemployment rate, so that past values of the unemployment rate can be treated as exogenous. But past values of the unemployment rate were not randomly assigned in an experiment; instead, the past unemployment rate was simultaneously determined with past values of inflation. Because inflation and the unemployment rate are simultaneously determined, the other factors that determine inflation contained in u_t are correlated with past values of the unemployment rate, that is, the unemployment rate is not exogenous. It follows that the unemployment rate is not strictly exogenous, so the dynamic multipliers computed using an empirical Phillips curve (for example, the ADL model in Equation (12.17)) are not consistent estimates of the dynamic causal effect on inflation of a change in the unemployment rate.

13.8 Conclusion

Time series data provide the opportunity to estimate the time path of the effect on Y of a change in X, that is, the dynamic causal effect on Y of a change in X. To estimate dynamic causal effects using a distributed lag regression, however, X must be exogenous, as it would be if it were set randomly in an ideal randomized experiment. If X is not just exogenous but is *strictly* exogenous, then the dynamic causal effects can be estimated using an autoregressive distributed lag model or by GLS.

In some applications, such as estimating the dynamic causal effect on the price of orange juice of freezing weather in Florida, a convincing case can be made that the regressor (freezing degree days) is exogenous; thus the dynamic causal effect can be estimated by OLS estimation of the distributed lag coefficients. Even in this application, however, economic theory suggests that the weather is not strictly exogenous, so the ADL or GLS methods are inappropriate. Moreover, in many relations of interest to econometricians, there is simultaneous causality, so the regressor in these specifications are not exogenous, strictly or otherwise. Ascertaining whether or not the regressor is exogenous (or strictly exogenous) ultimately requires combining economic theory, institutional knowledge, and expert judgment.

Summary

1. Dynamic causal effects in time series are defined in the context of a randomized experiment, where the same subject (entity) receives different randomly assigned treatments at different times. The coefficients in a distributed lag regression of Y on X and its lags can be interpreted as the dynamic causal effects when the time path of X is determined randomly and independently of other factors that influence Y.

2. The variable X is (past and present) exogenous if the conditional mean of the error u_t in the distributed lag regression of Y on current and past values of X does not depend on current and past values of X. If in addition the conditional mean of u_t does not depend on future values of X, then X is strictly exogenous.

3. If X is exogenous, then the OLS estimators of the coefficients in a distributed lag regression of Y on current and past values of X are consistent estimators of the dynamic causal effects. In general, the error u_t in this regression is serially correlated, so conventional standard errors are misleading and HAC standard errors must be used instead.

4. If X is strictly exogenous, then the dynamic multipliers can be estimated by OLS estimation of an ADL model or by GLS.

5. Exogeneity is a strong assumption that often fails to hold in economic time series data because of simultaneous causality, and the assumption of strict exogeneity is even stronger.

Key Terms

dynamic causal effect (489)

distributed lag model (495)

exogeneity (497)

strict exogeneity (497)

dynamic multiplier (501)

impact effect (501)

cumulative dynamic multiplier (501)

long-run cumulative dynamic multiplier (501)

heteroskedasticity- and autocorrelation-consistent (HAC) standard error (504)

truncation parameter (505)

Newey-West variance estimator (506)

generalized least squares (GLS) (507)

quasi-difference (509)

infeasible GLS estimator (512)

feasible GLS estimator (512)

Review the Concepts

13.1 In the 1970s a common practice was to estimate a distributed lag model relating changes in nominal gross domestic product (Y) to current and past changes in the money supply (X). Under what assumptions will this regression estimate the causal effects of money on nominal GDP? Are these assumptions likely to be satisfied in a modern economy like the United States?

13.2 Suppose that X is strictly exogenous. A researcher estimates an ADL(1,1) model, calculates the regression residual, and finds the residual to be highly serially correlated. Should the researcher estimate a new ADL model with additional lags, or simply use HAC standard errors for the ADL(1,1) estimated coefficients?

13.3 Suppose that a distributed lag regression is estimated, where the dependent variable is ΔY_t instead of Y_t. Explain how you would compute the dynamic multipliers of X_t on Y_t.

13.4 Suppose that you added FDD_{t+1} as an additional regressor in Equation (13.2). If FDD is strictly exogenous, would you expect the coefficient on FDD_{t+1} to be zero or nonzero? Would your answer change if FDD is exogenous but not strictly exogenous?

Exercises

*13.1 Increases in oil prices have been blamed for several recessions in developed countries. To quantify the effect of oil prices on real economic activity researchers have done regressions like those discussed in this chapter. Let GDP_t denote the value of quarterly gross domestic product in the United States, and let $Y_t = 100\ln(GDP_t / GDP_{t-1})$ be the quarterly percentage change in GDP. James Hamilton, an econometrician and macroeconomist, has suggested that oil prices adversely affect that economy only when they jump above their values in the recent past. Specifically, let O_t equal the greater of zero or the percentage point difference between oil prices at date t and their maximum value during the past year. A distributed lag regression relating Y_t and O_t, estimated over 1955:I–2000:IV, is

$$\hat{Y}_t = 1.0 - 0.055 O_t - 0.026 O_{t-1} - 0.031 O_{t-2} - 0.109 O_{t-3} - 0.128 O_{t-4}$$
$$\quad (0.1) \;\; (0.054) \quad\;\; (0.057) \qquad (0.048) \qquad (0.042) \qquad (0.053)$$

$$+ \; 0.008 O_{t-5} + 0.025 O_{t-6} - 0.019 O_{t-7} + 0.067 O_{t-8}.$$
$$\quad (0.025) \qquad\;\; (0.048) \qquad (0.039) \qquad (0.042)$$

a. Suppose that oil prices jump 25% above their previous peak value and stay at this new higher level (so that $O_t = 25$ and $O_{t+1} = O_{t+2} = \cdots = 0$). What is the predicted effect on output growth for each quarter over the next two years?

b. Construct a 95% confidence interval for your answers in (a).

c. What is the predicted cumulative change in GDP growth over eight quarters?

d. The HAC F-statistic testing whether the coefficients on O_t and its lags are zero is 3.49. Are the coefficients significantly different from zero?

13.2 Macroeconomists have also noticed that interest rates change following oil price jumps. Let R_t denote the interest rate on 3-month Treasury Bills (in percentage points at an annual rate). The distributed lag regression relating the change in R_t (ΔR_t) to O_t estimated over 1955:I–2000:IV is

$$\widehat{\Delta R_t} = 0.07 + 0.062O_t + 0.048O_{t-1} - 0.014O_{t-2} - 0.086O_{t-3} - 0.000O_{t-4}$$
$$\phantom{\widehat{\Delta R_t} =} (0.06) \ (0.045) \qquad (0.034) \qquad (0.028) \qquad (0.169) \qquad (0.058)$$

$$+ \ 0.023O_{t-5} - 0.010O_{t-6} - 0.100O_{t-7} - 0.014O_{t-8}.$$
$$ (0.065) \qquad (0.047) \qquad (0.038) \qquad (0.025)$$

a. Suppose that oil prices jump 25% above their previous peak value and stay at this new higher level (so that $O_t = 25$ and $O_{t+1} = O_{t+2} = \cdots = 0$). What is the predicted change in interest rates for each quarter over the next two years?

b. Construct 95% confidence intervals for your answers to (a).

c. What is the effect of this change in oil prices on the level of interest rates in period $t + 8$? How is your answer related to the cumulative multiplier?

d. The HAC F-statistic testing whether the coefficients on O_t and its lags are zero is 4.25. Are the coefficients significantly different from zero?

13.3 Consider two different randomized experiments. In experiment A, oil prices are set randomly and the Central Bank reacts according to its usual policy rules in response to economic conditions, including changes in the oil price. In experiment B, oil prices are set randomly and the Central Bank holds interest rates constant, and in particular does not respond to the oil price changes. In both, GDP growth is observed. Now suppose that oil prices are exogenous in the regression in Exercise 13.1. To which experiment, A or B, does the dynamic causal effect estimated in Exercise 13.1 correspond?

13.4 Suppose that oil prices are strictly exogenous. Discuss how you could improve upon the estimates of the dynamic multipliers in Exercise 13.1.

13.5 Derive Equation (13.7) from Equation (13.4) and show that $\delta_0 = \beta_0$, $\delta_1 = \beta_1$, $\delta_2 = \beta_1 + \beta_2$, $\delta_3 = \beta_1 + \beta_2 + \beta_3$ (etc.). (*Hint:* Note that $X_t = \Delta X_t + \Delta X_{t-1} + \cdots + \Delta X_{t-p+1} + X_{t-p}$.)

13.1 | The Orange Juice Data Set

The orange juice price data are the frozen orange juice component of processed foods and feeds group of the producer price index (PPI), collected by the U.S. Bureau of Labor Statistics (BLS series wpu02420301). The orange juice price series was divided by the overall PPI for finished goods to adjust for general price inflation. The freezing degree days series was constructed from daily minimum temperatures recorded at Orlando area airports, obtained from the National Oceanic and Atmospheric Administration (NOAA) of the U.S. Department of Commerce. The *FDD* series was constructed so that its timing, and the timing of the orange juice price data, were approximately aligned. Specifically, the frozen orange juice price data are collected by surveying a sample of producers in the middle of every month, although the exact date varies from month to month. Accordingly, the *FDD* series was constructed to be the number of freezing degree days from the 11th of one month to the 10th of the next month; that is, *FDD* is the maximum of zero and 32 minus the minimum daily temperature, summed over all days from the 11th to the 10th. Thus, $\%ChgP_t$ for February is the percentage change in real orange juice prices from mid-January to mid-February, and FDD_t for February is the number of freezing degree days from January 11 to February 10.

13.2 | The ADL Model and Generalized Least Squares in Lag Operator Notation

This appendix presents the distributed lag model in lag operator notation, derives the ADL and quasi-differenced representations of the distributed lag model, and discusses the conditions under which the ADL model can have fewer parameters than the original distributed lag model.

The Distributed Lag, ADL, and Quasi-Differenced Models, in Lag Operator Notation

As defined in Appendix 12.3, the lag operator, L, has the property that $L^j X_t = X_{t-j}$, and the distributed lag $\beta_1 X_t + \beta_2 X_{t-1} + \cdots + \beta_{r+1} X_{t-r}$ can be expressed as $\beta(L)X_t$, where $\beta(L) = \sum_{j=0}^{r} \beta_{j+1} L^j$, where $L^0 = 1$. Thus, the distributed lag model in Key Concept 13.1 (Equation (13.4)) can be written in lag operator notation as

$$Y_t = \beta_0 + \beta(L)X_t + u_t. \tag{13.40}$$

In addition, if the error term u_t follows an $AR(p)$, then it can be written as

$$\phi(L)u_t = \widetilde{u}_t, \tag{13.41}$$

where $\phi(L) = \sum_{j=0}^{p} \phi_j L^j$, where $\phi_0 = 1$ and $\widetilde{u}_t$ is serially uncorrelated (note that $\phi_1, \ldots, \phi_p$ as defined here are the negative of $\phi_1, \ldots, \phi_p$ in the notation of Equation (13.31)).

To derive the ADL model, premultiply each side of Equation (13.40) by $\phi(L)$, so that

$$\phi(L)Y_t = \phi(L)[\beta_0 + \beta(L)X_t + u_t] = \alpha_0 + \delta(L)X_t + \widetilde{u}_t, \tag{13.42}$$

where

$$\alpha_0 = \phi(1)\beta_0 \text{ and } \delta(L) = \phi(L)\beta(L), \text{ where } \phi(1) = \sum_{j=0}^{p} \phi_j. \tag{13.43}$$

To derive the quasi-differenced model, note that $\phi(L)\beta(L)X_t = \beta(L)\phi(L)X_t = \beta(L)\widetilde{X}_t$, where $\widetilde{X}_t = \phi(L)X_t$. Thus, rearranging Equation (13.42) yields

$$\widetilde{Y}_t = \alpha_0 + \beta(L)\widetilde{X}_t + \widetilde{u}_t, \tag{13.44}$$

where $\widetilde{Y}_t$ is the quasi-difference of Y_t, that is, $\widetilde{Y}_t = \phi(L)Y_t$.

The ADL and GLS Estimators

The OLS estimator of the ADL coefficients is obtained by OLS estimation of Equation (13.42). The original distributed lag coefficients are $\beta(L)$ which, in terms of the estimated coefficients, is $\beta(L) = \delta(L)/\phi(L)$; that is, the coefficients in $\beta(L)$ satisfy the restrictions implied by $\phi(L)\beta(L) = \delta(L)$. Thus, the estimator of the dynamic multipliers based on the OLS estimators of the coefficients of the ADL model, $\hat{\delta}(L)$ and $\hat{\phi}(L)$, is

$$\hat{\beta}^{ADL}(L) = \hat{\delta}(L)/\hat{\phi}(L). \tag{13.45}$$

The expressions for the coefficients in Equation (13.29) in the text are obtained as a special case of Equation (13.45) when $r = 1$ and $p = 1$.

The feasible GLS estimator is computed by obtaining a preliminary estimator of $\phi(L)$, computing estimated quasi-differences, estimating $\beta(L)$ in Equation (13.44) using these estimated quasi-differences, and (if desired) iterating until convergence. The iterated GLS estimator is the NLLS estimator computed by NLLS estimation of the ADL model in Equation (13.42), subject to the nonlinear restrictions on the parameters contained in Equation (13.43).

As stressed in the discussion surrounding Equation (13.36) in the text, it is not enough for X_t to be (past and present) exogenous to use either of these estimation methods, for exogeneity alone does not ensure that Equation (13.36) holds. If, however, X is strictly exogenous, then Equation (13.36) does hold and, assuming that Assumptions 2–4 of Key Concept 12.6 hold, these estimators are consistent and asymptotically normal. Moreover, the usual (cross-sectional heteroskedasticity-robust) OLS standard errors provide a valid basis for statistical inference.

Parameter reduction using the ADL model.   Suppose that the distributed lag polynomial $\beta(L)$ can be written as a ratio of lag polynomials, $\theta_1(L)/\theta_2(L)$, where $\theta_1(L)$ and $\theta_2(L)$ are both lag polynomials of a low degree. Then $\phi(L)\beta(L)$ in Equation (13.43) is $\phi(L)\beta(L)=\phi(L)\theta_1(L)/\theta_2(L) = [\phi(L)/\theta_2(L)]\theta_1(L)$. If it so happens that $\phi(L) = \theta_2(L)$, then $\delta(L) = \phi(L)\beta(L)= \theta_1(L)$. If the degree of $\theta_1(L)$ is low, then q, the number of lags of X_t in the ADL model, can be much less than r. Thus, under these assumptions, estimation of the ADL model entails estimating potentially many fewer parameters than the original distributed lag model. It is in this sense that the ADL model can achieve a more parsimonious parameterizations (that is, use fewer unknown parameters) than the distributed lag model.

As developed here, the assumption that $\phi(L)$ and $\theta_2(L)$ happen to be the same seems like a coincidence that would not occur in an application. However, the ADL model is able to capture a large number of shapes of dynamic multipliers with only a few coefficients. For this reason, unrestricted estimation of the ADL model presents an attractive way to approximate a long distributed lag (that is, many dynamic multipliers) whenever X is strictly exogenous.

CHAPTER 14

Additional Topics in Time Series Regression

T his chapter takes up some further topics in time series regression, starting with forecasting. Chapter 12 considered forecasting a single variable. In practice, however, you might want to forecast two or more variables such as the rate of inflation and the growth rate of the GDP. Section 14.1 introduces a model for forecasting multiple variables, vector autoregressions (VARs), in which lagged values of two or more variables are used to forecast future values of those variables. Chapter 12 also focused on making forecasts one period (e.g., one quarter) into the future, but making forecasts two, three, or more periods into the future also is important. Methods for making such forecasts are discussed in Section 14.2.

Sections 14.3 and 14.4 return to the topic of Section 12.6, stochastic trends. Section 14.3 introduces additional models of stochastic trends and an alternative test for a unit autoregressive root. Section 14.4 introduces the concept of cointegration, which arises when two variables share a common stochastic trend, that is, when each variable contains a stochastic trend, but a weighted difference of the two variables does not.

In some time series data, especially financial data, the variance changes over time: sometimes the series exhibits high volatility, while at other times the volatility is low, so that the data exhibit clusters of volatility. Section 14.5 discusses volatility clustering and introduces models in which the variance of the forecast error changes over time, that is, models in which the forecast error is conditionally heteroskedastic. Models of conditional heteroskedasticity have several applications. One application is computing forecast intervals, where the width of the interval changes over time to reflect periods of high or low uncertainty. Another application is to forecasting the uncertainty of returns on an asset, such as a stock, which in turn can be useful in assessing the risk of owning a stock.

14.1 Vector Autoregressions

Chapter 12 focused on forecasting the rate of inflation, but in reality economic forecasters are in the business of forecasting other key macroeconomic variables as well, such as the rate of unemployment, the growth rate of GDP, and interest rates. One approach is to develop a separate forecasting model for each variable using the methods of Section 12.4. Another approach, however, is to develop a single model that can forecast all the variables, which can help to make the forecasts mutually consistent. One way to forecast several variables with a single model is to use a vector autoregression (VAR). A VAR extends the univariate autoregression to multiple time series variables, that is, it extends the univariate autoregression to a "vector" of time series variables.

The VAR Model

A **vector autoregression**, or **VAR**, with two time series variables, Y_t and X_t, consists of two equations: in one, the dependent variable is Y_t; in the other, the dependent variable is X_t. The regressors in both equations are lagged values of both variables. More generally, a VAR with k time series variables consists of k equations, one for each of the variables, where the regressors in all equations are lagged values of all the variables. The coefficients of the VAR are estimated by estimating each of the equations by OLS.

VARs are summarized in Key Concept 14.1.

Inference in VARs. Under the VAR assumptions, the OLS estimators are consistent and have a joint normal distribution in large samples. Accordingly, statistical inference proceeds in the usual manner; for example, 95% confidence intervals on coefficients can be constructed as the estimated coefficient ±1.96 standard errors.

One new aspect of hypothesis testing arises in VARs because a VAR with k variables is a collection, or system, of k equations. Thus it is possible to test joint hypotheses that involve restrictions across multiple equations.

Vector Autoregressions

Key Concept 14.1

A vector autoregression (VAR) is a set of k time series regressions, in which the regressors are lagged values of all k series. A VAR extends the univariate autoregression to a list, or "vector," of time series variables. When the number of lags in each of the equations is the same and is equal to p, the system of equations is called a VAR(p).

In the case of two time series variables, Y_t and X_t, the VAR(p) consists of the two equations

$$Y_t = \beta_{10} + \beta_{11}Y_{t-1} + \cdots + \beta_{1p}Y_{t-p} + \gamma_{11}X_{t-1} + \cdots + \gamma_{1p}X_{t-p} + u_{1t} \quad (14.1)$$

$$X_t = \beta_{20} + \beta_{21}Y_{t-1} + \cdots + \beta_{2p}Y_{t-p} + \gamma_{21}X_{t-1} + \cdots + \gamma_{2p}X_{t-p} + u_{2t} \quad (14.2)$$

where the β's and the γ's are unknown coefficients and u_{1t} and u_{2t} are error terms.

The VAR assumptions are the time series regression assumptions of Key Concept 12.6, applied to each equation. The coefficients of a VAR are estimated by estimating each equation by OLS.

For example, in the two-variable VAR(p) in Equations (14.1) and (14.2), you could ask whether the correct lag length is p or $p - 1$; that is, you could ask whether the coefficients on Y_{t-p} and X_{t-p} are zero in these two equations. The null hypothesis that these coefficients are zero is

$$H_0: \beta_{1p} = 0, \beta_{2p} = 0, \gamma_{1p} = 0, \text{ and } \gamma_{2p} = 0. \quad (14.3)$$

The alternative hypothesis is that at least one of these four coefficients is nonzero. Thus the null hypothesis involves coefficients from *both* of the equations, two from each equation.

Because the estimated coefficients have a jointly normal distribution in large samples, it is possible to test restrictions on these coefficients by computing an F-statistic. The precise formula for this statistic is complicated because the notation must handle multiple equations, so we omit it. In practice, most modern software packages have automated procedures for testing hypotheses on coefficients in systems of multiple equations.

How many variables should be included in a VAR? The number of coefficients in each equation of a VAR is proportional to the number of variables in the VAR. For example, a VAR with five variables and four lags will have 21 coefficients (four lags each of five variables, plus the intercept) in each of the five equations, for a total of 105 coefficients! Estimating all these coefficients increases the amount of estimation error entering a forecast, which can result in a deterioration of the accuracy of the forecast.

The practical implication is that one needs to keep the number of variables in a VAR small and, especially, to make sure that the variables are plausibly related to each other so that they will be useful for forecasting each other. For example, we know from a combination of empirical evidence (such as that discussed in Chapter 12) and economic theory that the inflation rate, the unemployment rate, and the short-term interest rate are related to each other, suggesting that these variables could help to forecast each other in a VAR. Including an unrelated variable in a VAR, however, introduces estimation error without adding predictive content, thereby reducing forecast accuracy.

Determining lag lengths in VARs.[1] Lag lengths in a VAR can be determined using either *F*-tests or information criteria.

The information criterion for a system of equations extends the single-equation information criterion in Section 12.5. To define this information criterion we need to adopt matrix notation. Let Σ_u be the $k \times k$ covariance matrix of the VAR errors, and let $\hat{\Sigma}_u$ be the estimate of the covariance matrix where the i,j element of $\hat{\Sigma}_u$ is $\frac{1}{T}\sum_{t=1}^{T}\hat{u}_{it}\hat{u}_{jt}$, where $\hat{u}_{it}$ is the OLS residual from the ith equation and $\hat{u}_{jt}$ is the OLS residual from the jth equation. The BIC for the VAR is

$$\text{BIC}(p) = \ln[\det(\hat{\Sigma}_u)] + k(kp + 1)\frac{\ln T}{T}, \tag{14.4}$$

where $\det(\hat{\Sigma}_u)$ is the determinant of the matrix $\hat{\Sigma}_u$. The AIC is computed using Equation (14.4), modified by replacing the term "$\ln T$" by "2".

The expression for the BIC for the k equations in the VAR in Equation (14.4) extends the expression for a single equation given in Section 12.5. When there is a single equation, the first term simplifies to $\ln(SSR(p)/T)$. The second term in Equation (14.4) is the penalty for adding additional regressors; $k(kp + 1)$ is the total number of regression coefficients in the VAR (there are k equations, each of which has an intercept and p lags of each of the k time series variables).

---

[1]This section uses matrices and may be skipped for less mathematical treatments.

Lag length estimation in a VAR using the BIC proceeds analogously to the single equation case: among a set of candidate values of p, the estimated lag length $\hat{p}$ is the value of p that minimizes $\text{BIC}(p)$.

Using VARs for causal analysis.   The discussion so far has focused on using VARs for forecasting. Another use of VAR models is for analyzing causal relationships among economic time series variables; indeed, it was for this purpose that VARs were first introduced to economics by the econometrician and macroeconomist Christopher Sims (1980). The use of VARs for causal inference is known as structural VAR modeling, "structural" because in this application VARs are used to model the underlying structure of the economy. Structural VAR analysis uses the techniques introduced in this section in the context of forecasting, plus some additional tools. The biggest conceptual difference between using VARs for forecasting and using them for structural modeling, however, is that structural modeling requires very specific assumptions, derived from economic theory and institutional knowledge, of what is exogenous and what is not. The discussion of structural VARs is best undertaken in the context of estimation of systems of simultaneous equations, which goes beyond the scope of this book. For an introduction to using VARs for forecasting and policy analysis, see Stock and Watson (2001). For additional mathematical detail on structural VAR modeling, see Hamilton (1994) or Watson (1994).

A VAR Model of the Rates of Inflation and Unemployment

As an illustration, consider a two-variable VAR for the inflation rate, Inf_t, and the rate of unemployment, $Unemp_t$. As in Chapter 12, we treat the rate of inflation as having a stochastic trend, so that it is appropriate to transform it by computing its first difference, ΔInf_t.

A VAR for ΔInf_t and $Unemp_t$ consists of two equations, one in which ΔInf_t is the dependent variable and one in which $Unemp_t$ is the dependent variable. The regressors in both equations are lagged values of ΔInf_t and $Unemp_t$. In Section 12.4 (Equation (12.17)), we reported the following regression of ΔInf_t on four lags each of ΔInf_t and $Unemp_t$, estimated using quarterly U.S. data from 1962:I–1999:IV:

$$\widehat{\Delta Inf_t} = 1.32 - 0.36\Delta Inf_{t-1} - 0.34\Delta Inf_{t-2} + 0.07\Delta Inf_{t-3} - 0.03\Delta Inf_{t-4}$$
$$\quad\quad (0.47)\ \ (0.09)\quad\quad (0.10)\quad\quad (0.08)\quad\quad (0.09)$$

$$- 2.68 Unemp_{t-1} + 3.43 Unemp_{t-2} - 1.04 Unemp_{t-3} + 0.07 Unemp_{t-4}.$$
$$\quad (0.47)\quad\quad\quad (0.89)\quad\quad\quad (0.89)\quad\quad\quad (0.44)$$

(14.5)

The adjusted R^2 is $\overline{R}^2 = 0.35$.

This is in fact the first equation of a VAR(4) model of the change in inflation and the unemployment rate. The second equation has the same regressors, but the dependent variable is the unemployment rate:

$$\widehat{Unemp_t} = 0.12 + 0.043\Delta Inf_{t-1} + 0.000\Delta Inf_{t-2} + 0.021\Delta Inf_{t-3} + 0.021\Delta Inf_{t-4}$$
$$\quad (0.09)\ (0.020)\qquad\quad (0.015)\qquad\qquad (0.16)\qquad\qquad (0.15)$$
$$+\ 1.68 Unemp_{t-1} - 0.70 Unemp_{t-2} - 0.03 Unemp_{t-3} + 0.02 Unemp_{t-4}.$$
$$\quad (0.12)\qquad\qquad (0.20)\qquad\qquad (0.20)\qquad\qquad (0.09)$$

(14.6)

The adjusted R^2 is $\overline{R}^2 = 0.975$.

Equations (14.5) and (14.6), taken together, are a VAR(4) model of the change in the rate of inflation, ΔInf_t, and the unemployment rate, $Unemp_t$.

These VAR equations can be used to perform Granger causality tests. The F-statistic testing the null hypothesis that the coefficients on $Unemp_{t-1}$, $Unemp_{t-2}$, $Unemp_{t-3}$, and $Unemp_{t-4}$ are zero in the inflation equation (Equation (14.5)) is 8.51, which has a p-value less than 0.001. Thus, the null hypothesis is rejected, so we can conclude that the unemployment rate is a useful predictor of changes in inflation, given lags in inflation (that is, the unemployment rate Granger-causes changes in inflation). Similarly, the F-statistic testing the hypothesis that the coefficients on the four lags of ΔInf_t are zero in the unemployment equation (Equation (14.6)) is 2.41, which has a p-value of 0.051. Thus four lags of the change in the inflation rate Granger-cause the unemployment rate at the 10% significance level but not at the 5% significance level.

Forecasts of the rates of inflation and unemployment one period ahead are obtained exactly as discussed in Section 12.4. The forecast of the change of inflation from 1999:IV to 2000:I, based on Equation (14.5) and using data through 1999:IV, was computed in Section 12.4; this forecast is $\widehat{\Delta Inf}_{2000:I|1999:IV} = 0.5$ percentage points. A similar calculation using Equation (14.6) gives a forecast of the unemployment rate in 2000:I based on data through 1999:IV of $\widehat{Unemp}_{2000:I|1999:IV} = 4.1\%$, very close to its actual value, $Unemp_{2000:I} = 4.0\%$.

14.2 Multiperiod Forecasts

The discussion of forecasting so far has focused on making forecasts one period in advance. Often, however, forecasters are called upon to make forecasts further into the future. The forecasting regression models of Chapter 12 can produce such multiperiod forecasts, but some modifications are needed. This section discusses those modifications, first for univariate autoregressions and then for multivariate forecasting.

Multiperiod Forecasting: Univariate Autoregressions

We present two methods for making multiperiod forecasts from a univariate autoregression. The first is the "multiperiod regression method"; the second is the "iterated autoregression" method.

The multiperiod regression method: AR(1).   Suppose you want to use an autoregression to make a forecast two periods ahead. In the multiperiod regression method, each predictor is replaced by its lagged value, and the coefficients of this modified autoregression are estimated by OLS. If Y_t follows an AR(1), then in the one-step ahead regression Y_t is regressed onto a constant and Y_{t-1}. In the two-step ahead regression, however, Y_{t-1} is unavailable, so the two-step ahead regression entails regressing Y_t onto a constant and Y_{t-2}.

For example, consider forecasting the quarterly change in the inflation rate two quarters ahead using an AR(1) model for the change in inflation. The modified two-period ahead regression, estimated over the period 1962:I–1999:IV, is

$$\widehat{\Delta Inf}_{t|t-2} = 0.02 - 0.30\Delta Inf_{t-2}, \tag{14.7}$$
$$\quad\quad\quad\;\;(0.12)\;\;(0.09)$$

where $\widehat{\Delta Inf}_{t|t-2}$ is the predicted value of ΔInf_t based on values of the inflation rate through period $t-2$.

Equation (14.7) illustrates the key idea of the multiperiod regression method: no data from period $t-1$ appear as a regressor, so only values of inflation dated $t-2$ and earlier are used to forecast ΔInf_t. For example, according to Equation (14.7), the forecast of the change of inflation between the first and the second quarter of 2000, based on information through the fourth quarter of 1999, is $\widehat{\Delta Inf}_{2000:II|1999:IV} = 0.02 - 0.30\Delta Inf_{1999:IV}$. From Table 12.1 (p. 434), $\Delta Inf_{1999:IV} = 0.4$. Thus $\widehat{\Delta Inf}_{2000:II|1999:IV} = 0.02 - 0.30 \times 0.4 = -0.1$. That is, based on data through the fourth quarter of 1999, inflation is forecasted to decline by one tenth of a percentage point from the first to the second quarter of 2000.

To compute forecasts into the more distant future, the multiperiod regression method involves using more distant lags. For example, when Y_t follows an AR(1), the three-period ahead forecast is computed from a regression of Y_t onto a constant and Y_{t-3}.

The multiperiod regression method: AR(p). The multiperiod regression approach can be extended to higher order autoregressions by including additional lagged values in the regression. In general, in an AR(p), the modified two-step ahead regression would entail regressing Y_t onto a constant and Y_{t-2}, Y_{t-3}, ..., Y_{t-p-1}. Similarly, the three-step ahead regression would entail regressing Y_t onto a constant and Y_{t-3}, Y_{t-4}, ..., Y_{t-p-2}.

For example, the two-period ahead forecast from an AR(4) model for ΔInf_t is obtained using the regression of ΔInf_t onto ΔInf_{t-2}, ..., ΔInf_{t-5}:

$$\widehat{\Delta Inf}_{t|t-2} = 0.02 - 0.27\Delta Inf_{t-2} + 0.25\Delta Inf_{t-3} - 0.08\Delta Inf_{t-4} - 0.01\Delta Inf_{t-5}. \quad (14.8)$$
$$(0.10)\ (0.08) \qquad (0.09) \qquad (0.10) \qquad (0.08)$$

The values in Table 12.1 and the coefficients in Equation (14.8) can be used to forecast the change in inflation from 2000:I to 2000:II: $\widehat{\Delta Inf}_{2000:II|1999:IV} = 0.02 - 0.27\Delta Inf_{1999:IV} + 0.25\Delta Inf_{1999:III} - 0.08\Delta Inf_{1999:II} - 0.01\Delta Inf_{1999:I} = 0.02 - 0.27 \times 0.4 + 0.25 \times 0.0 - 0.08 \times 1.1 - 0.01 \times (-0.4) = -0.2$. That is, based on Equation (14.8), based on inflation data through the fourth quarter of 1999, inflation is forecasted to decline by 0.2 percentage points from the first to the second quarter of 2000.

To make forecasts three periods in advance using an AR(4), Equation (14.8) would be modified so that ΔInf_t is regressed onto ΔInf_{t-3}, ..., ΔInf_{t-6}. More generally, to make an h-period ahead forecast of Y_t using an AR(p), the variable of interest is regressed on its p lags, where the most recent date of the regressors is $t - h$.

Standard errors in multiperiod regressions. Because the dependent variable in a multiperiod regression occurs two or more periods into the future, the error term in a multiperiod regression is serially correlated. To see this, consider the two-period ahead inflation forecasts, and suppose there is a surprise jump in oil prices next quarter. Then today's two-period ahead forecast of inflation will be too low because it does not incorporate this unexpected event. Because the oil price rise was also unknown last quarter, the two-period ahead forecast made last quarter will also be too low: thus, the surprise oil price hike next quarter means that *both* last quarter's and this quarter's two-period ahead forecasts are too low. Because of such intervening events, the error term in a multiperiod regression is serially correlated.

As discussed in Section 13.4, if the error term is serially correlated, the usual OLS standard errors are incorrect or, more precisely, they are not a reliable basis for inference. Therefore heteroskedasticity- and autocorrelation-consistent (HAC) standard errors must be used with multiperiod regressions. The standard errors reported in this section for multiperiod regressions therefore are Newey-West HAC standard errors, where the truncation parameter m is set according to Equation (13.17); for these data (for which $T = 152$), Equation (13.17) yields $m = 4$. For longer forecast horizons the amount of overlap, and thus the degree of serial correlation in the error, increases: in general, the first $h - 1$ autocorrelation coefficients of the errors in an h-period ahead regression are nonzero. Thus, larger values of m than indicated by Equation (13.17) are appropriate for multiperiod regressions with long forecast horizons.

The iterated AR forecast method: AR(1).   The iterated AR forecast method uses the AR model to extend a one-period ahead forecast to two or more periods ahead. The two-period ahead forecast is computed in two steps. In the first step, the one-period ahead forecast is computed as in Section 12.3. In the second step, the two-period ahead forecast is computed using the one-period ahead forecast for the intervening period. Thus, the one-period ahead forecast is used as an intermediate step to make the two-period ahead forecast. For more distant horizons, this process is repeated or "iterated."

As an example, consider the first order autoregression for ΔInf_t (Equation (12.7)), which is

$$\widehat{\Delta Inf_t} = 0.02 - 0.21\Delta Inf_{t-1}. \qquad (14.9)$$
$$\hspace{1.2cm}(0.14)\ \ (0.11)$$

The first step in computing the two-quarter ahead forecast of $\Delta Inf_{2000:\text{II}}$ based on Equation (14.9) using data through 1999:IV is to compute the one-quarter ahead forecast of $\Delta Inf_{2000:\text{I}}$ based on data through 1999:IV: $\widehat{\Delta Inf}_{2000:\text{I}|1999:\text{IV}} = 0.02 - 0.21\Delta Inf_{1999:\text{IV}} = 0.02 - 0.21 \times 0.4 = -0.1$. In the second step, this forecast is substituted into Equation (14.9); that is, $\widehat{\Delta Inf}_{2000:\text{II}|1999:\text{IV}} = 0.02 - 0.21\widehat{\Delta Inf}_{2000:\text{I}|1999:\text{IV}} = 0.02 - 0.21 \times (-0.1) = 0.0$. Thus, based on information through the fourth quarter of 1999, this forecast is that the rate of inflation will not change between the first and second quarters of 2000.

The iterated AR forecast method: AR(p).   The iterated AR(1) strategy is extended to an AR(p) by replacing Y_{t-1} in the estimated AR(p) with its forecast made the previous period.

For example, consider the iterated two-step ahead forecast of inflation based on the AR(4) model from Section 12.3 (Equation (12.13)),

$$\widehat{\Delta Inf_t} = 0.02 - 0.21\Delta Inf_{t-1} - 0.32\Delta Inf_{t-2} + 0.19\Delta Inf_{t-3} - 0.04\Delta Inf_{t-4}. \quad (14.10)$$
$$\hspace{0.3cm}(0.12)\ \ (0.10)\hspace{1.2cm}(0.09)\hspace{1.3cm}(0.09)\hspace{1.3cm}(0.10)$$

Multiperiod Forecasting Using Univariate Autoregressions

Key Concept 14.2

The **multiperiod regression forecast** h periods into the future based on an $AR(p)$ is computed by estimating the multiperiod regression

$$Y_t = \delta_0 + \delta_1 Y_{t-h} + \cdots + \delta_p Y_{t-p-h+1} + u_t, \qquad (14.11)$$

then using the estimated coefficients to compute the forecast h periods in advance.

The **iterated AR forecast** is computed in steps: first compute the one-period ahead forecast, next use that to compute the two-period ahead forecast, and so forth. The two- and three-period ahead iterated forecasts based on an $AR(p)$ are

$$\hat{Y}_{t|t-2} = \hat{\beta}_0 + \hat{\beta}_1 \hat{Y}_{t-1|t-2} + \hat{\beta}_2 Y_{t-2} + \hat{\beta}_3 Y_{t-3} + \cdots + \hat{\beta}_p Y_{t-p} \qquad (14.12)$$

$$\hat{Y}_{t|t-3} = \hat{\beta}_0 + \hat{\beta}_1 \hat{Y}_{t-1|t-3} + \hat{\beta}_2 \hat{Y}_{t-2|t-3} + \hat{\beta}_3 Y_{t-3} + \cdots + \hat{\beta}_p Y_{t-p} \qquad (14.13)$$

where the $\hat{\beta}$'s are the OLS estimates of the $AR(p)$ coefficients. Continuing this process ("iterating") produces forecasts further into the future.

The iterated two-quarter ahead forecast is computed by replacing ΔInf_{t-1} in Equation (14.10) with the forecast $\widehat{\Delta Inf}_{t|t-1}$. In Section 12.3, we computed the forecast of $\Delta Inf_{2000:I}$ based on data through 1999:IV using this $AR(4)$ to be $\widehat{\Delta Inf}_{2000:I|1999:IV} = 0.2$. Thus, the two-quarter ahead iterated forecast based on the $AR(4)$ is $\widehat{\Delta Inf}_{2000:II|1999:IV} = 0.02 - 0.21 \widehat{\Delta Inf}_{2000:I|1999:IV} - 0.32 \Delta Inf_{1999:IV} + 0.19 \Delta Inf_{1999:III} - 0.04 \Delta Inf_{1999:II} = 0.02 - 0.21 \times 0.2 - 0.32 \times 0.4 + 0.19 \times 0.1 - 0.04 \times 1.1 = -0.2$. According to this iterated $AR(4)$ forecast, based on data through the fourth quarter of 1999, the rate of inflation will fall by 0.2 percentage points between the first and second quarters of 2000.

Both methods for multiperiod univariate forecasting are summarized in Key Concept 14.2.

Multiperiod Forecasting: Multivariate Forecasts

The same two methods for multiperiod forecasting from univariate models can be used in multivariate forecasting regressions.

The multiperiod regression method. In the general multiperiod regression method, all predictors are lagged h periods to produce the h-period ahead forecast.

For example, the forecast of ΔInf_t two quarters ahead using four lags each of ΔInf_t and $Unemp_t$ is computed by first estimating the regression

$$\widehat{\Delta Inf}_{t|t-2} = 0.27 - 0.28\Delta Inf_{t-2} + 0.15\Delta Inf_{t-3} - 0.21\Delta Inf_{t-4} - 0.06\Delta Inf_{t-5}$$
$$(0.40)\ (0.11)(0.10)(0.11)(0.08)$$

$$- 0.21\, Unemp_{t-2} + 0.79\, Unemp_{t-3} - 2.11\, Unemp_{t-4} + 1.49\, Unemp_{t-5}.$$
$$(0.46)(0.98)(1.12)(0.56)$$

$$(14.14)$$

The two-quarter ahead forecast is computed by substituting the values of $\Delta Inf_{1999:I}, \ldots, \Delta Inf_{1999:IV}, Unemp_{1999:I}, \ldots, Unemp_{1999:IV}$ into Equation (14.14); this yields $\widehat{\Delta Inf}_{2000:II|1999:IV} = 0.27 - 0.28\Delta Inf_{1999:IV} + 0.15\Delta Inf_{1999:III} - .21\Delta Inf_{1999:II} - 0.06\Delta Inf_{1999:I} - 0.21\, Unemp_{1999:IV} + 0.79\, Unemp_{1999:III} - 2.11\, Unemp_{1999:II} + 1.49\, Unemp_{1999:I} = 0.0.$

The three-quarter ahead forecast of ΔInf_t is computed by lagging all the regressors in Equation (14.14) by one additional quarter, estimating that regression, and computing the forecast, and so forth for forecasts farther into the future.

The iterated VAR forecast method. The iterated AR method extends to a VAR, with the modification that because the VAR has one or more additional predictors it is necessary to compute intermediate forecasts of all the predictors.

The two-period ahead **iterated VAR forecast** is computed in two steps. In the first step, the VAR is used to produce one-quarter ahead forecasts of all the variables in the VAR, as discussed in Section 14.1. In the second step, these forecasts take the place of the first lagged values in the VAR, that is, the two-period ahead forecast is based on the one-period ahead forecast, plus additional lags as specified in the VAR. Repeating this produces the iterated VAR forecast further into the future.

As an example, we compute the iterated VAR forecast of $\Delta Inf_{2000:II}$ based on data through 1999:IV based on the VAR(4) for ΔInf_t and $Unemp_t$ in Section 14.1 (Equations (14.5) and(14.6)). The first step is to compute the one-quarter ahead forecasts $\widehat{\Delta Inf}_{2000:I|1999:IV}$ and $\widehat{Unemp}_{2000:I|1999:IV}$ from that VAR. The forecast $\widehat{\Delta Inf}_{2000:I|1999:IV}$ based on Equation (14.5) was computed in Section 12.3 and is 0.5 percentage points (Equation (12.18)); a similar calculation based on Equation (14.6) shows that $\widehat{Unemp}_{2000:I|1999:IV} = 4.1\%$. In the second step, these forecasts are substituted into Equations (14.5) and (14.6) to produce the two-quarter ahead forecast. Accordingly,

$$
\begin{aligned}
\widehat{\Delta Inf}_{2000:II|1999:IV} &= 1.32 - 0.36\widehat{\Delta Inf}_{2000:I|1999:IV} - 0.34\Delta Inf_{1999:IV} \qquad (14.15)\\
&\quad + 0.07\Delta Inf_{1999:III} - 0.03\Delta Inf_{1999:II} - 2.68\widehat{Unemp}_{2000:I|1999:IV}\\
&\quad + 3.43Unemp_{1999:IV} - 1.04Unemp_{1999:III} + 0.07Unemp_{1999:II}\\
&= 1.32 - 0.36 \times 0.7 - 0.34 \times 0.4 + 0.07 \times 0.1 - 0.03 \times 1.1\\
&\quad - 2.68 \times 4.1 + 3.43 \times 4.1 - 1.04 \times 4.2 + 0.07 \times 4.3\\
&= -0.1.
\end{aligned}
$$

Thus, the iterated VAR(4) forecast, based on data through the fourth quarter of 1999, is that inflation will decline by 0.1 percentage points between the first and second quarters of 2000.

Multiperiod forecasts with multiple predictors are summarized in Key Concept 14.3.

Which Method Should You Use?

Each of the two methods has its advantages and disadvantages. If the autoregressive (or vector autoregressive) model provides a good approximation to the correlations in the data, then the iterated forecast method will tend to produce more precise forecasts. This is because the iterated forecasts use coefficient estimators in a one-period ahead regression, which have a smaller variance (are more efficient) than the estimators from the multiperiod regression.

On the other hand, if the AR or VAR is incorrectly specified and does not provide a good approximation to the correlations in the data, then extrapolating these forecasts by iterating can lead to biased forecasts. Accordingly, if the AR or VAR model is poor, the multiperiod regression forecasts can be more accurate.

Thus there is no easy answer as to whether one method is better than the other. If the difference between the two forecasts is large, this could be an indication that the one-period ahead model is incorrectly specified, and if so the multiperiod ahead forecast tends to be more accurate. Often, however, the differences between the two forecasts is small, as was the case in the inflation forecasts computed in this section, in which case the choice of which method to use can be based on which is most conveniently implemented in your software.

Multiperiod Forecasting with Multiple Predictors

Key Concept 14.3

The multiperiod regression forecast h periods into the future based on p lags each of Y_t and an additional predictor X_t is computed by first estimating the multiperiod regression

$$Y_t = \delta_0 + \delta_1 Y_{t-h} + \cdots + \delta_p Y_{t-p-h+1} + \delta_{p+1} X_{t-h} + \cdots + \delta_{2p} X_{t-p-h+1} + u_t, \tag{14.16}$$

then using the estimated coefficients to make the forecast h periods in advance.

The iterated VAR forecast is computed in steps: first compute the one-period ahead forecasts of all the variables in the VAR, next use those to compute the two-period ahead forecasts, and so forth. The two-period ahead iterated forecast of Y_t based on the two-variable VAR(p) in Key Concept 14.1 is

$$\begin{aligned}
\hat{Y}_{t|t-2} = {} & \hat{\beta}_{10} + \hat{\beta}_{11}\hat{Y}_{t-1|t-2} + \hat{\beta}_{12}Y_{t-2} + \hat{\beta}_{13}Y_{t-3} + \cdots + \hat{\beta}_{1p}Y_{t-p} \\
& + \hat{\gamma}_{11}\hat{X}_{t-1|t-2} + \hat{\gamma}_{12}X_{t-2} + \hat{\gamma}_{13}X_{t-3} + \cdots + \hat{\gamma}_{1p}X_{t-p},
\end{aligned} \tag{14.17}$$

where the coefficients in Equation (14.17) are the OLS estimates of the VAR coefficients. Iterating produces forecasts further into the future.

14.3 Orders of Integration and Another Unit Root Test

This section extends the treatment of stochastic trends in Section 12.6 by addressing two further topics. First, the trends of some time series are not well described by the random walk model, so we introduce an extension of that model and discuss its implications for regression modeling of such series. Second, we continue the discussion of testing for a unit root in time series data and, among other things, introduce a second test for a unit root.

Other Models of Trends and Orders of Integration

Recall that the random walk model for a trend, introduced in Section 12.6, specifies that the trend at date t equals the trend at date $t - 1$, plus a random error term. If Y_t follows a random walk with drift β_0, then

$$Y_t = \beta_0 + Y_{t-1} + u_t, \tag{14.18}$$

where u_t is serially uncorrelated. Also recall from Section 12.6 that, if a series has a random walk trend, then it has an autoregressive root that equals one.

Although the random walk model of a trend describes the long-run movements of many economic time series, some economic time series have trends that are smoother—that is, vary less from one period to the next—than is implied by Equation (14.18). A different model is needed to describe the trends of such series.

One model of a smooth trend makes the first difference of the trend follow a random walk; that is,

$$\Delta Y_t = \beta_0 + \Delta Y_{t-1} + u_t, \tag{14.19}$$

where u_t is serially uncorrelated. Thus, if Y_t follows Equation (14.19), ΔY_t follows a random walk, so $\Delta Y_t - \Delta Y_{t-1}$ is stationary. The difference of the first differences, $\Delta Y_t - \Delta Y_{t-1}$, is called the **second difference** of Y_t, and is denoted $\Delta^2 Y_t = \Delta Y_t - \Delta Y_{t-1}$. In this terminology, if Y_t follows Equation (14.19), then its second difference is stationary. If a series has a trend of the form in Equation (14.19), then the first difference of the series has an autoregressive root that equals one.

"Orders of integration" terminology.   Some additional terminology is useful for distinguishing between these two models of trends. A series that has a random walk trend is said to be **integrated of order one**, or **I(1)**. A series that has a trend of the form in Equation (14.19) is said to be **integrated of order two**, or **I(2).** A series that does not have a stochastic trend and is stationary is said to be **integrated of order zero**, or **I(0)**.

The **order of integration** in the $I(1)$ and $I(2)$ terminology is the number of times that the series needs to be differenced for it to be stationary: if Y_t is $I(1)$, then the first difference of Y_t, ΔY_t, is stationary, and if Y_t is $I(2)$, then the second difference of Y_t, $\Delta^2 Y_t$, is stationary. If Y_t is $I(0)$, then Y_t is stationary.

Orders of integration are summarized in Key Concept 14.4.

How to test whether a series is I(2) or I(1).   If Y_t is $I(2)$, then ΔY_t is $I(1)$, so that ΔY_t has an autoregressive root that equals one. If, however, Y_t is $I(1)$, then ΔY_t

Orders of Integration, Differencing, and Stationarity

Key
Concept
14.4

- If Y_t is integrated of order 1, that is, if Y_t is $I(1)$, then Y_t has a unit autoregressive root and its first difference, ΔY_t, is stationary.

- If Y_t is integrated of order 2, that is, if Y_t is $I(2)$, then ΔY_t has a unit autoregressive root and its second difference, $\Delta^2 Y_t$, is stationary.

- If Y_t is **integrated of order d** (is **$I(d)$**), then Y_t must be differenced d times to eliminate its stochastic trend, that is, $\Delta^d Y_t$ is stationary.

is stationary. Thus the null hypothesis that Y_t is $I(2)$ can be tested against the alternative hypothesis that Y_t is $I(1)$ by testing whether ΔY_t has a unit autoregressive root. If the hypothesis that ΔY_t has a unit autoregressive root is rejected, then the hypothesis that Y_t is $I(2)$ is rejected in favor of the alternative that Y_t is $I(1)$.

Examples of I(2) and I(1) series: The price level and the rate of inflation.
In Chapter 12, we concluded that the rate of inflation in the United States plausibly has a random walk stochastic trend, that is, that the rate of inflation is $I(1)$. If inflation is $I(1)$, then its stochastic trend is removed by first differencing, so ΔInf_t is stationary. Recall from Section 12.2 (Equation (12.2)) that quarterly inflation at an annual rate is the first difference of the logarithm of the price level, times 400; that is, $Inf_t = 400 \Delta p_t$, where $p_t = \ln(CPI_t)$. Thus treating the rate of inflation as $I(1)$ is equivalent to treating Δp_t as $I(1)$, but this in turn is equivalent to treating p_t as $I(2)$. Thus, we have all along been treating the logarithm of the price level as $I(2)$, even though we have not used that terminology.

The logarithm of the price level, p_t, and the rate of inflation are plotted in Figure 14.1. The long-run trend of the logarithm of the price level (Figure 14.1a) varies more smoothly than the long-run trend in the rate of inflation (Figure 14.1b). The smoothly varying trend in the logarithm of the price level is typical of $I(2)$ series.

The DF-GLS Test for a Unit Root

This section continues the discussion of Section 12.6 regarding testing for a unit autoregressive root. We first describe another test for a unit autoregressive root, the so-called DF-GLS test. Next, in an optional mathematical section, we discuss why unit root test statistics do not have normal distributions, even in large samples.

FIGURE 14.1   The Logarithm of the Price Level and the Inflation Rate in the United States, 1960–2000

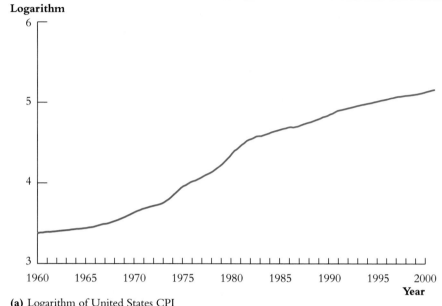

(a) Logarithm of United States CPI

(b) United States CPI Inflation

The trend in the logarithm of prices (Figure 14.1a) is much smoother than the trend in inflation (Figure 14.1b).

The DF-GLS test.   The ADF test was the first test developed for testing the null hypothesis of a unit root and is the most commonly used test in practice. Other tests subsequently have been proposed, however, many of which have higher power (Key Concept 3.5) than the ADF test. A test with higher power than the ADF test is more likely to reject the null hypothesis of a unit root against the stationary alternative when the alternative is true; thus, a more powerful test is better able to distinguish between a unit AR root and a root that is large but less than one.

This section discusses one such test, the so-called **DF-GLS test** developed by Elliott, Rothenberg, and Stock (1996). The test is introduced for the case that, under the null hypothesis, Y_t has a random walk trend, possibly with drift, and under the alternative Y_t is stationary around a linear time trend.

The DF-GLS test is computed in two steps. In the first step, the intercept and trend are estimated by generalized least squares (GLS; see Section 13.5). The GLS estimation is performed by computing three new variables, V_t, X_{1t}, and X_{2t}, where $V_1 = Y_1$ and $V_t = Y_t - \alpha^* Y_{t-1}$, $t = 2, \ldots, T$, $X_{11} = 1$ and $X_{1t} = 1 - \alpha^*$, $t = 2, \ldots, T$, and $X_{21} = 1$ and $X_{2t} = t - \alpha^*(t - 1)$, where α^* is computed using the formula, $\alpha^* = 1 - 13.5/T$. Then V_t is regressed against X_{1t} and X_{2t}; that is, OLS is used to estimate the coefficients of the population regression equation

$$V_t = \delta_0 X_{1t} + \delta_1 X_{2t} + e_t, \tag{14.20}$$

using the observations $t = 1, \ldots, T$, where e_t is the error term. Note that there is no intercept in the regression in Equation (14.20). The OLS estimators $\hat{\delta}_0$ and $\hat{\delta}_1$ are then used to compute a "detrended" version of Y_t, $Y_t^d = Y_t - (\hat{\delta}_0 + \hat{\delta}_1 t)$.

In the second step, the Dickey-Fuller test is used to test for a unit autoregressive root in Y_t^d, where the Dickey-Fuller regression does not include an intercept or a time trend. That is, ΔY_t^d is regressed against Y_{t-1}^d and $\Delta Y_{t-1}^d, \ldots, \Delta Y_{t-p}^d$, where the number of lags p is determined, as usual, either by expert knowledge or by using a data-based method such as the AIC or BIC as discussed in Section 12.5.

If the alternative hypothesis is that Y_t is stationary with a mean that might be nonzero but without a time trend, then the preceding steps are modified. Specifically, α^* is computed using the formula $\alpha^* = 1 - 7/T$, X_{2t} is omitted from the regression in Equation (14.20), and the series Y_t^d is computed as $Y_t^d = Y_t - \hat{\delta}_0$.

The GLS regression in the first step of the DF-GLS test makes this test more complicated than the conventional ADF test, but it is also what improves its ability to discriminate between the null hypothesis of a unit autoregressive root and the alternative that Y_t is stationary. This improvement can be substantial. For example, suppose that Y_t is in fact a stationary AR(1) with autoregressive coefficient $\beta_1 = 0.95$, that there are $T = 200$ observations, and the unit root tests are computed without a time trend (that is, t is excluded from the Dickey-Fuller regression, and X_{2t} is omitted from Equation (14.20)). Then the probability that the ADF test correctly rejects the null hypothesis at the 5% significance level is approximately 31% compared to 75% for the DF-GLS test.

Critical values for DF-GLS test. Because the coefficients on the deterministic terms are estimated differently in the ADF and DF-GLS tests, the tests have different critical values. The critical values for the DF-GLS test are given in Table 14.1. If the DF-GLS test statistic (the t-statistic on Y_{t-1}^d in the regression in the second step) is less than the critical value, then the null hypothesis that Y_t has a unit root is rejected. Like the critical values for the Dickey-Fuller test, the appropriate critical value depends on which version of the test is used, that is, on whether or not a time trend is included (whether or not X_{2t} is included in Equation (14.20)).

Application to Inflation. The DF-GLS statistic, computed for the rate of CPI inflation, Inf_t, over the period 1962:I to 1999:IV, is -1.98 when three lags of ΔY_t^d are included in the Dickey-Fuller regression in the second stage. This value is just less than the 5% critical value in Table 14.1, -1.95, so using the DF-GLS test with three lags leads to rejecting the null hypothesis of a unit root at the 5% significance level. The choice of three lags was based on the AIC (out of a maximum of six lags), which in this case happens to choose the same number of lags as the BIC.

Because the DF-GLS test is better able to discriminate between the unit root null hypothesis and the stationary alternative, one interpretation of this finding is that inflation is in fact stationary, but the Dickey-Fuller test implemented in Section 12.6 failed to detect this (at the 5% level). This conclusion, however, should be tempered by noting that whether the DF-GLS test rejects is, in this application, sensitive to the choice of lag length. If the test is based on four lags, it rejects at the

TABLE 14.1 Critical Values of the DF-GLS Test

Deterministic Regressors (Regressors in Equation (14.20))	10%	5%	1%
Intercept only (X_{1t} only)	-1.62	-1.95	-2.58
Intercept and time trend (X_{1t} and X_{2t})	-2.57	-2.89	-3.48

Source: Fuller (1976) and Elliott, Rothenberg, and Stock (1996, Table 1).

10% but not the 5% level, and if it is instead based on two lags it does not reject at the 10% level. The result is also sensitive to the choice of sample; if the statistic is instead computed over the period 1963:I to 1999:IV (that is, dropping just the first year), the test rejects at the 10% level but not at the 5% level. The overall picture therefore is rather ambiguous (as it is based on the ADF test, as discussed following Equation (12.34)) and requires the forecaster to make an informed judgment about whether it is better to model inflation as $I(1)$ or stationary.

Why Do Unit Root Tests Have Nonnormal Distributions?

In Section 12.6, it was stressed that the large-sample normal distribution upon which regression analysis relies so heavily does not apply if the regressors are nonstationary. Under the null hypothesis that the regression contains a unit root, the regressor Y_{t-1} in the Dickey-Fuller regression (and the regressor Y^d_{t-1} in the modified Dickey-Fuller regression in the second step of the DF-GLS test) is nonstationary. The nonnormal distribution of the unit root test statistics is a consequence of this nonstationarity.

To gain some mathematical insight into this nonnormality, consider the simplest possible Dickey-Fuller regression, in which ΔY_t is regressed against the single regressor Y_{t-1} and the intercept is excluded. In the notation of Key Concept 12.8, the OLS estimator in this regression is $\hat{\delta} = \sum_{t=1}^{T} Y_{t-1}\Delta Y_t / \sum_{t=1}^{T} Y^2_{t-1}$, so that

$$T\hat{\delta} = \frac{\frac{1}{T}\sum_{t=1}^{T}Y_{t-1}\Delta Y_t}{\frac{1}{T^2}\sum_{t=1}^{T}Y^2_{t-1}}. \tag{14.21}$$

Consider the numerator in Equation (14.21). Under the additional assumption that $Y_0 = 0$, a bit of algebra (Exercise 14.5) shows that

$$\frac{1}{T}\sum_{t=1}^{T}Y_{t-1}\Delta Y_t = \frac{1}{2}\left[(Y_T/\sqrt{T})^2 - \frac{1}{T}\sum_{t=1}^{T}(\Delta Y_t)^2\right]. \tag{14.22}$$

Under the null hypothesis, $\Delta Y_t = u_t$, which is serially uncorrelated and has a finite variance, so the second term in Equation (14.22) has the probability limit

$\frac{1}{T}\sum_{t=1}^{T}(\Delta Y_t)^2 \xrightarrow{p} \sigma_u^2$. Under the assumption that $Y_0 = 0$, the first term in Equation (14.22) can be written $Y_T/\sqrt{T} = \sqrt{\frac{1}{T}}\sum_{t=1}^{T}\Delta Y_t = \sqrt{\frac{1}{T}}\sum_{t=1}^{T}u_t$, which in turn obeys the central limit theorem; that is, $Y_T/\sqrt{T} \xrightarrow{d} N(0, \sigma_u^2)$. Thus $(Y_T/\sqrt{T})^2 - \frac{1}{T}\sum_{t=1}^{T}(\Delta Y_t)^2 \xrightarrow{d} \sigma_u^2(Z^2 - 1)$, where Z is a standard normal random variable. Recall, however, that the square of a standard normal distribution has a chi-squared distribution with one degree of freedom. It therefore follows from Equation (14.22) that, under the null hypothesis, the numerator in Equation (14.21) has the limiting distribution

$$\frac{1}{T}\sum_{t=1}^{T}Y_{t-1}\Delta Y_t \xrightarrow{d} \frac{\sigma_u^2}{2}(\chi_1^2 - 1). \tag{14.23}$$

The large-sample distribution in Equation (14.23) is different than the usual large-sample normal distribution when the regressor is stationary. Instead, the numerator of the OLS estimator of the coefficient on Y_t in this Dickey-Fuller regression has a distribution that is proportional to a chi-squared distribution with one degree of freedom, minus one.

This discussion has only considered the numerator of $T\hat{\delta}$. The denominator also behaves unusually under the null hypothesis: because Y_t follows a random walk under the null hypothesis, $\frac{1}{T}\sum_{t=1}^{T}Y_{t-1}^2$ does not converge in probability to a constant. Instead, the denominator in Equation (14.21) is a random variable, even in large samples: under the null hypothesis, $\frac{1}{T^2}\sum_{t=1}^{T}Y_{t-1}^2$ converges in distribution jointly with the numerator. The unusual distributions of the numerator and denominator in Equation (14.21) are the source of the nonstandard distribution of the Dickey-Fuller test statistic and the reason that the ADF statistic has its own special table of critical values.

14.4 Cointegration

Sometimes two or more series have the same stochastic trend in common. In this special case, referred to as cointegration, regression analysis can reveal long–run relationships among time series variables, but some new methods are needed.

Cointegration and Error Correction

Two or more time series with stochastic trends can move together so closely over the long run that they appear to have the same trend component, that is, they appear to have a **common trend**. For example, two interest rates on U.S.

FIGURE 14.2 **One-Year Interest Rate, Three-Month Interest Rate, and Interest Rate Spread**

One-year and three-month interest rates share a common stochastic trend. The spread, or the difference, between the two rates does not exhibit a trend. These two interest rates appear to be cointegrated.

---

government debt are plotted in Figure 14.2. One of the rates is the interest rate on 90-day U.S. Treasury bills, at an annual rate $(R90_t)$; the other is the interest rate on a one-year U.S. Treasury bond $(R1yr_t)$; these interest rates are discussed in Appendix 14.1. The interest rates exhibit the same long-run tendencies or trends: both were low in the 1960s, both rose through the 1970s to peaks in the early 1980s, then both fell through the 1990s. Moreover, the difference between the two series, $R1yr_t - R90_t$, which is called the "spread" between the two interest rates and is also plotted in Figure 14.2, does not appear to have a trend. That is, subtracting the 90-day interest rate from the one-year interest rate appears to eliminate the trends in both of the individual rates. Said differently, although the two interest rates differ, they appear to share a common stochastic trend: because the trend in each individual series is eliminated by subtracting one series from the other, the two series must have the same trend, that is, they must have a common stochastic trend.

Two or more series that have a common stochastic trend are said to be **cointegrated**. The formal definition of cointegration (due to Granger, 1983) is given in Key Concept 14.5. In this section, we introduce a test for whether cointegration is present, discuss estimation of the coefficients of regressions relating cointegrated variables, and illustrate the use of the cointegrating relationship for forecasting. The discussion initially focuses on the case that there are only two variables, X_t and Y_t.

Vector error correction model. Until now, we have eliminated the stochastic trend in an $I(1)$ variable Y_t by computing its first difference, ΔY_t; the problems created by stochastic trends were then avoided by using ΔY_t instead of Y_t in time series regressions. If X_t and Y_t are cointegrated, however, another way to eliminate the trend is to compute the difference $Y_t - \theta X_t$. Because the term $Y_t - \theta X_t$ is stationary, it too can be used in regression analysis.

In fact, if X_t and Y_t are cointegrated, the first differences of X_t and Y_t can be modeled using a VAR, augmented by including $Y_{t-1} - \theta X_{t-1}$ as an additional regressor:

$$\Delta Y_t = \beta_{10} + \beta_{11}\Delta Y_{t-1} + \cdots + \beta_{1p}\Delta Y_{t-p} + \gamma_{11}\Delta X_{t-1} + \cdots +$$
$$\gamma_{1p}\Delta X_{t-p} + \alpha_1(Y_{t-1} - \theta X_{t-1}) + u_{1t} \tag{14.24}$$

$$\Delta X_t = \beta_{20} + \beta_{21}\Delta Y_{t-1} + \cdots + \beta_{2p}\Delta Y_{t-p} + \gamma_{21}\Delta X_{t-1} + \cdots +$$
$$\gamma_{2p}\Delta X_{t-p} + \alpha_2(Y_{t-1} - \theta X_{t-1}) + u_{2t}. \tag{14.25}$$

The term $Y_t - \theta X_t$ is called the **error correction term**. The combined model in Equations (14.24) and (14.25) is called a **vector error correction model** (VECM). In a VECM, past values of $Y_t - \theta X_t$ help to predict future values of ΔY_t and/or ΔX_t.

How Can You Tell Whether Two Variables Are Cointegrated?

There are three ways to decide whether two variables can plausibly be modeled as cointegrated: use expert knowledge and economic theory, graph the series and see whether they appear to have a common stochastic trend, and perform statistical tests for cointegration. All three methods should be used in practice.

First, you must use your expert knowledge of these variables to decide whether cointegration is in fact plausible. For example, the two interest rates in Figure 14.2 are linked together by the so-called expectations theory of the term structure of interest rates. According to this theory, the interest rate on January 1

Cointegration

Suppose X_t and Y_t are integrated of order one. If, for some coefficient θ, $Y_t - \theta X_t$ is integrated of order zero, then X_t and Y_t are said to be **cointegrated**. The coefficient θ is called the **cointegrating coefficient**.

If X_t and Y_t are cointegrated, then they have the same, or common, stochastic trend. Computing the difference $Y_t - \theta X_t$ eliminates this common stochastic trend.

Key Concept 14.5

on the one-year Treasury bond is the average of the interest rate on a 90-day Treasury bill for the first quarter of the year and the expected interest rates on future 90-day Treasury bills issued in the second, third, and fourth quarters of the year; if not, then investors could expect to make money by holding either the one-year Treasury note or a sequence of four 90-day Treasury bills, and they would bid up prices until the expected returns are equalized. If the 90-day interest rate has a random walk stochastic trend, this theory implies that this stochastic trend is inherited by the one-year interest rate and that the difference between the two rates, that is, the spread, is stationary. Thus, the expectations theory of the term structure implies that, if the interest rates are $I(1)$, then they will be cointegrated with a cointegrating coefficient of $\theta = 1$ (Exercise 14.2).

Second, visual inspection of the series helps to identify cases in which cointegration is plausible. For example, the graph of the two interest rates in Figure 14.2 shows that each of the series appears to be $I(1)$ but that the spread appears to be $I(0)$, so that the two series appear to be cointegrated.

Third, the unit root testing procedures introduced so far can be extended to test for cointegration. The insight on which these tests are based is that if Y_t and X_t are cointegrated with cointegrating coefficient θ, then $Y_t - \theta X_t$ is stationary; otherwise, $Y_t - \theta X_t$ is nonstationary (is $I(1)$). The hypothesis that Y_t and X_t are not cointegrated (that is, that $Y_t - \theta X_t$ is $I(1)$) therefore can be tested by testing the null hypothesis that $Y_t - \theta X_t$ has a unit root; if this hypothesis is rejected, then Y_t and X_t can be modeled as cointegrated. The details of this test depend on whether the cointegrating coefficient θ is known.

Testing for cointegration when θ is known.   In some cases expert knowledge or economic theory suggests values of θ. When θ is known, the Dickey-Fuller and

DF-GLS unit root tests can be used to test for cointegration by first constructing the series $z_t = Y_t - \theta X_t$, then testing the null hypothesis that z_t has a unit autoregressive root.

Testing for cointegration when θ is unknown.   If the cointegrating coefficient θ is unknown then it must be estimated prior to testing for a unit root in the error correction term. This preliminary step makes it necessary to use different critical values for the subsequent unit root test.

Specifically, in the first step the cointegrating coefficient θ is estimated by OLS estimation of the regression

$$Y_t = \alpha + \theta X_t + z_t. \tag{14.26}$$

In the second step, a Dickey-Fuller t-test (with an intercept but no time trend) is used to test for a unit root in the residual from this regression, $\hat{z}_t$. This two-step procedure is called the Engle-Granger Augmented Dickey-Fuller test for cointegration, or **EG-ADF** (Engle and Granger, 1987).

Critical values of the EG-ADF statistic are given in Table 14.2.[2] The critical values in the first row apply when there is a single regressor in Equation (14.26), so that there are two cointegrated variables (X_t and Y_t). The subsequent rows apply to the case of multiple cointegrated variables, which is discussed at the end of this section.

Estimation of Cointegrating Coefficients

If X_t and Y_t are cointegrated, then the OLS estimator of the coefficient in the cointegrating regression in Equation (14.26) is consistent. However, in general the OLS estimator has a nonnormal distribution, and inferences based on its t-statistics can be misleading whether or not those t-statistics are computed using HAC standard errors. Because of these drawbacks of the OLS estimator of θ, econometricians have developed a number of other estimators of the cointegrating coefficient.

One such estimator of θ that is simple to use in practice is the so-called **dynamic OLS (DOLS)** estimator (Stock and Watson, 1993). The DOLS esti-

---

[2]The critical values in Table 14.2 are taken from Fuller (1976) and Phillips and Ouliaris (1990). Following a suggestion by Hansen (1992), the critical values in Table 14.2 are chosen so that they apply whether or not X_t and Y_t have drift components.

TABLE 14.2 Critical Values for the Engle-Granger ADF statistic			
Number of X's in Equation (14.26)	**10%**	**5%**	**1%**
1	−3.12	−3.41	−3.96
2	−3.52	−3.80	−4.36
3	−3.84	−4.16	−4.73
4	−4.20	−4.49	−5.07

mator is based on a modified version of Equation (14.26) that includes past, present, and future values of the change in X_t:

$$Y_t = \beta_0 + \theta X_t + \sum_{j=-p}^{p} \delta_j \Delta X_{t-j} + u_t. \tag{14.27}$$

Thus, in Equation (14.27), the regressors are X_t, ΔX_{t+p}, ..., ΔX_{t-p}. The DOLS estimator of θ is the OLS estimator of θ in the regression of Equation (14.27).

If X_t and Y_t are cointegrated, then the DOLS estimator is efficient in large samples. Moreover, statistical inferences about θ and the δ's in Equation (14.27) based on HAC standard errors are valid. For example, the t-statistic constructed using the DOLS estimator with HAC standard errors has a standard normal distribution in large samples.

One way to interpret Equation (14.27) is to recall from Section 13.3 that cumulative dynamic multipliers can be computed by modifying the distributed lag regression of Y_t on X_t and its lags. Specifically, in Equation (13.7), the cumulative dynamic multipliers were computed by regressing Y_t on ΔX_t, lags of ΔX_t, and X_{t-r}; the coefficient on X_{t-r} in that specification is the long-run cumulative dynamic multiplier. Similarly, if X_t were strictly exogenous, then in Equation (14.27), the coefficient on X_t, θ, would be the long-run cumulative multiplier, that is, the long-run effect on Y of a change in X. If X_t is not strictly exogenous, then the coefficients do not have this interpretation. Nevertheless, because X_t and Y_t have a common stochastic trend if they are cointegrated, the DOLS estimator is consistent even if X_t is endogenous.

The DOLS estimator is not the only efficient estimator of the cointegrating coefficient. The first such estimator was developed by Søren Johansen (Johansen, 1988). For a discussion of Johansen's method and of other ways to estimate the cointegrating coefficient, see Hamilton (1994, Chapter 20).

Even if economic theory does not suggest a specific value of the cointegrating coefficient, it is important to check whether the estimated cointegrating relationship makes sense in practice. Because cointegration tests can be misleading (they can improperly reject the null hypothesis of no cointegration more frequently than they should, and frequently they improperly fail to reject the null), it is especially important to rely on economic theory, institutional knowledge, and common sense when estimating and using cointegrating relationships.

Extension to Multiple Cointegrated Variables

The concepts, tests, and estimators discussed here extend to more than two variables. For example, if there are three variables, Y_t, X_{1t}, and X_{2t}, each of which is $I(1)$, then they are cointegrated with cointegrating coefficients θ_1 and θ_2 if $Y_t - \theta_1 X_{1t} - \theta_2 X_{2t}$ is stationary. When there are three or more variables, there can be multiple cointegrating relationships. For example, consider modeling the relationship among three interest rates: the three-month rate, the one-year rate, and the five-year rate $(R5yr)$. If they are $I(1)$, then the expectations theory of the term structure of interest rates suggests that they will all be cointegrated. One cointegrating relationship suggested by the theory is $R90_t - R1yr_t$, and a second relationship is $R90_t - R5yr_t$. (The relationship $R1yr_t - R5yr_t$ is also a cointegrating relationship, but it contains no additional information beyond that in the other relationships because it is perfectly multicollinear with the other two cointegrating relationships.)

The EG-ADF procedure for testing for a single cointegrating relationship among mulitple variables is the same as for the case of two variables, except that the regression in Equation (14.26) is modified so that both X_{1t} and X_{2t} are regressors; the critical values for the EG-ADF test are given in Table 14.2, where the appropriate row depends on the number of regressors in the first-stage OLS cointegrating regression. The DOLS estimator of a single cointegrating relationship among multiple X's involves including the level of each X along with leads and lags of the first difference of each X. Tests for multiple cointegrating relationships can be performed using the system methods, such as Johansen's (1988) method, and the DOLS estimator can be extended to multiple cointegrating relationships by estimating multiple equations, one for each cointegrating relationship. For additional discussion of cointegration methods for multiple variables, see Hamilton (1994).

A cautionary note. If two or more variables are cointegrated then the error correction term can help to forecast these variables and, possibly, other related variables. However, cointegration requires the variables to have the same stochastic trends. Trends in economic variables typically arise from complex interactions of disparate forces, and closely related series can have different trends for subtle reasons. If variables that are not cointegrated are incorrectly modeled using a VECM, then the error correction term will be $I(1)$; this introduces a trend into the forecast that can result in poor out-of-sample forecast performance. Thus forecasting using a VECM must be based on a combination of compelling theoretical arguments in favor of cointegration and careful empirical analysis.

Application to Interest Rates

As discussed above, the expectations theory of the term structure of interest rates implies that, if two interest rates of different maturities are $I(1)$, then they will be cointegrated with a cointegrating coefficient of $\theta = 1$, that is, the spread between the two rates will be stationary. Inspection of Figure 14.2 provides qualitative support for the hypothesis that the one-year and three-month interest rates are cointegrated. We first use unit root and cointegration test statistics to provide more formal evidence on this hypothesis, then estimate a vector error correction model for these two interest rates.

Unit root and cointegration tests. Various unit root and cointegration test statistics for these two series are reported in Table 14.3. The unit root test statistics in the first two rows examine the hypothesis that the two interest rates, the three-month rate ($R90$) and the one-year rate ($R1yr$), individually have a unit root. Two of the four statistics in the first two rows fail to reject this hypothesis at the 10% level, and three of the four fail to reject at the 5% level. The exception is the ADF statistic evaluated for the 90-day Treasury bill rate (-2.96), which rejects the unit root hypothesis at the 5% level. The ADF and DF-GLS statistics lead to

TABLE 14.3 Unit Root and Cointegration Test Statistics for Two Interest Rates

Series	ADF Statistic	DF-GLS Statistic
$R90$	-2.96^*	-1.88^+
$R1yr$	-2.22	-1.37
$R1yr - R90$	-6.31^{**}	-5.59^{**}
$R1yr - 1.046R90$	-6.97^{**}	—

$R90$ is the interest rate on 90-day U.S. Treasury bills, at an annual rate, and $R1yr$ is the interest rate on one-year U.S. Treasury bonds. Regressions were estimated using quarterly data over the period 1962:I–1999:IV. The number of lags in the unit root test statistic regressions were chosen by AIC (six lags maximum). Unit root test statistics are significant at the $^+$10%, *5%, or **1% significance level.

different conclusions for this variable (the ADF test rejects the unit root hypothesis at the 5% level while the DF–GLS test does not), which means that we must exercise some judgment in deciding whether these variables are plausibly modeled as $I(1)$. Taken together, these results suggest that the interest rates are plausibly modeled as $I(1)$.

The unit root statistics for the spread, $R1yr_t - R90_t$, test the further hypothesis that these variables are not cointegrated against the alternative that they are. The null hypothesis that the spread contains a unit root is rejected at the 1% level using both unit root tests. Thus we reject the hypothesis that the series are not cointegrated against the alternative that they are, with a cointegrating coefficient $\theta = 1$. Taken together, the evidence in the first three rows of Table 14.3 suggests that these variables plausibly can be modeled as cointegrated with $\theta = 1$.

Because in this application economic theory suggests a value for θ (the expectations theory of the term structure suggests that $\theta = 1$) and because the error correction term is $I(0)$ when this value is imposed (the spread is stationary), in principle it is not necessary to use the EG–ADF test, in which θ is estimated. Nevertheless, we compute the test as an illustration. The first step in the EG–ADF test is to estimate θ by the OLS regression of one variable on the other; the result is

$$\widehat{R1yr_t} = 0.361 + 1.046R90_t, \ \overline{R}^2 = 0.973. \tag{14.28}$$

The second step is computing the ADF statistic for the residual from this regression, $\hat{z}_t$. The result, given in the final row of Table 14.3, is less than the 1% critical value of -3.96 in Table 14.2, so the null hypothesis that $\hat{z}_t$ has a unit autoregressive root is rejected. This statistic also points towards treating the two interest rates as cointegrated. Note that no standard errors are presented in Equation (14.28) because, as previously discussed, the OLS estimator of the cointegrating coefficient has a nonnormal distribution and its t-statistic is not normally distributed, so presenting standard errors (HAC or otherwise) would be misleading.

A vector error correction model of the two interest rates. If Y_t and X_t are cointegrated, then forecasts of ΔY_t and ΔX_t can be improved by augmenting a VAR of ΔY_t and ΔX_t by the lagged value of the error correction term, that is, by computing forecasts using the VECM in Equations (14.24) and (14.25). If θ is known, then the unknown coefficients of the VECM can be estimated by OLS, including $z_{t-1} = Y_{t-1} - \theta X_{t-1}$ as an additional regressor. If θ is unknown, then the

VECM can be estimated using $\hat{z}_{t-1}$ as a regressor, where $\hat{z}_t = Y_t - \hat{\theta}X_t$, where $\hat{\theta}$ is an estimator of θ.

In the application to the two interest rates, theory suggests that $\theta = 1$, and the unit root tests supported modeling the two interest rates as cointegrated with a cointegrating coefficient of 1. We therefore specify the VECM using the theoretically suggested value of $\theta = 1$, that is, by adding the lagged value of the spread, $R1yr_{t-1} - R90_{t-1}$ to a VAR in $\Delta R1yr_t$ and $\Delta R90_t$. Specified with two lags of first differences, the resulting VECM is

$$\widehat{\Delta R90_t} = 0.14 - 0.24\Delta R90_{t-1} - 0.44\Delta R90_{t-2} - 0.01\Delta R1yr_{t-1}$$
$$\quad (0.17)\ \ (0.32) \qquad\quad (0.34) \qquad\qquad (0.39)$$

$$+ 0.15\Delta R1yr_{t-2} - 0.18(R1yr_{t-1} - R90_{t-1}) \qquad\qquad (14.29)$$
$$\quad (0.27) \qquad\qquad (0.27)$$

$$\widehat{\Delta R1yr_t} = 0.36 - 0.14\Delta R90_{t-1} - 0.33\Delta R90_{t-2} - 0.11\Delta R1yr_{t-1}$$
$$\quad (0.16)\ \ (0.30) \qquad\quad (0.29) \qquad\qquad (0.35)$$

$$+ 0.10\Delta R1yr_{t-2} - 0.52(R1yr_{t-1} - R90_{t-1}) \qquad\qquad (14.30)$$
$$\quad (0.25) \qquad\qquad (0.24)$$

In the first equation, none of the coefficients are individually significant at the 5% level and the coefficients on the lagged first differences of the interest rates are not jointly significant at the 5% level. In the second equation, the coefficients on the lagged first differences are not jointly significant, but the coefficient on the lagged spread (the error correction term), which is estimated to be $-.52$, has a t-statistic of -2.17, so it is statistically significant at the 5% level. Although lagged values of the first difference of the interest rates are not useful for predicting future interest rates, the lagged spread does help to predict the change in the one-year Treasury bond rate. When the one-year rate exceeds the 90-day rate, the one-year rate is forecasted to fall in the future.

14.5 Conditional Heteroskedasticity

The phenomenon that some times are tranquil while others are not—that is, that volatility comes in clusters—shows up in many economic time series. This section presents a pair of models for quantifying **volatility clustering** or, as it is also known, **conditional heteroskedasticity**.

Volatility Clustering

Section 12.7 had a curious empirical result: the root mean squared forecast error of the pseudo out-of-sample forecasts of inflation from 1996 to 1999, produced using the four-lag Phillips curve, was 0.75 percentage points, whereas the standard error of the OLS regression that produced those forecasts was 1.47. That is, the out-of-sample errors were half the size of the in-sample errors! A forecaster faced with this happy situation might be forgiven for crowing about this to his or her clients. Might it be, however, that forecasting is simply easier at some times than at others, and the late 1990s was just one of those easy times?

Visual inspection of the residuals from the four-lag Phillips curve (Equation (14.5)), plotted in Figure 14.3, suggest so: these residuals exhibit volatility clustering. In the late 1970s and early 1980s the absolute forecast errors often exceeded two percentage points. In the 1960s and 1990s, however, the absolute forecast errors typically are less than one percentage point.

Volatility clustering is evident in many financial time series. An example discussed in Section 12.2 is shown in Figure 12.2d, a plot of 1,771 daily returns on the NYSE Composite Index of stock prices from 1990 to 1998. The absolute

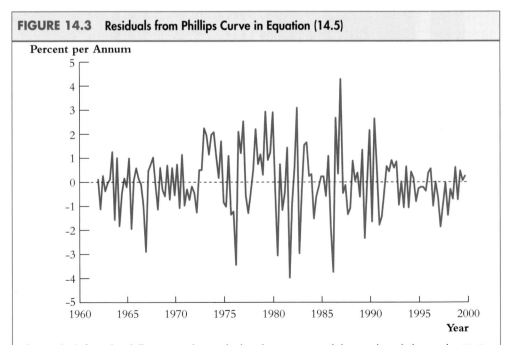

FIGURE 14.3   Residuals from Phillips Curve in Equation (14.5)

The residuals from the Phillips curve show volatility clustering. Variability is relatively low in the 1960s and 1990s and higher in the 1970s and 1980s.

daily percentage changes were, on average, larger in 1991 and 1998 than in 1994 and 1995. Within any given year, some months have greater volatility than others. Like the Phillips curve residuals, these percentage price changes have extended periods of high volatility and extended periods of relative tranquility.

Volatility clustering can be thought of as clustering of the variance of the error term over time: if the regression error has a small variance in one period, its variance tends to be small in the next period too. In other words, volatility clustering implies that the error exhibits time-varying heteroskedasticity.

Autoregressive Conditional Heteroskedasticity

Two models of volatility clustering are the autoregressive conditional heteroskedasticity (ARCH) model and its extension, the generalized ARCH (GARCH) model.

ARCH. Consider the ADL(1,1) regression

$$Y_t = \beta_0 + \beta_1 Y_{t-1} + \gamma_1 X_{t-1} + u_t. \tag{14.31}$$

In the **ARCH** model, developed by the econometrician Robert Engle (Engle, 1982), the error u_t is modeled as being normally distributed with mean zero and variance σ_t^2, where σ_t^2 depends on past squared values u_t. Specifically, the ARCH model of order p, denoted ARCH(p), is

$$\sigma_t^2 = \alpha_0 + \alpha_1 u_{t-1}^2 + \alpha_2 u_{t-2}^2 + \cdots + \alpha_p u_{t-p}^2, \tag{14.32}$$

where $\alpha_0, \alpha_1, \ldots, \alpha_p$ are unknown coefficients. If these coefficients are positive, then if recent squared errors are large the ARCH model predicts that the current squared error will be large in magnitude in the sense that its variance, σ_t^2, is large.

Although it is described here for the ADL(1,1) model in Equation (14.31), the ARCH model can be applied to the error variance of any time series regression model with an error that has a conditional mean of zero, including higher order ADL models, autoregressions, and time series regressions with multiple predictors.

GARCH. The generalized ARCH (**GARCH**) model, developed by the econometrician Timothy Bollerslev (1986), extends the ARCH model to let σ_t^2 depend on its own lags as well as lags of the squared error. The GARCH(p,q) model is

$$\sigma_t^2 = \alpha_0 + \alpha_1 u_{t-1}^2 + \cdots + \alpha_p u_{t-p}^2 + \phi_1 \sigma_{t-1}^2 \cdots + \phi_q \sigma_{t-q}^2, \tag{14.33}$$

where $\alpha_0, \alpha_1, \ldots, \alpha_p, \phi_1, \ldots, \phi_q$ are unknown coefficients.

The ARCH model is analogous to a distributed lag model, and the GARCH model is analogous to an ADL model. As discussed in Appendix 13.2, the ADL model (when appropriate) can provide a more parsimonious model of dynamic multipliers than the distributed lag model. Similarly, by incorporating lags of σ_t^2, the GARCH model can capture slowly changing variances with fewer parameters than the ARCH model.

An important application of ARCH and GARCH models is to measuring and forecasting the time-varying volatility of returns on financial assets, particularly assets observed at high sampling frequencies such as the daily stock returns in Figure 12.2d. In such applications the return itself is often modeled as unpredictable, so the regression in Equation (14.31) only includes the intercept.

Estimation and inference. ARCH and GARCH models are estimated by the method of maximum likelihood (Appendix 9.2). The estimators of the ARCH and GARCH coefficients are normally distributed in large samples, so in large samples t-statistics have standard normal distributions and confidence intervals for a coefficient can be constructed as its maximum likelihood estimate ±1.96 standard errors.

Application to Inflation Forecasts

The four-lag Phillips curve, estimated by OLS in Equation (14.5), was re-estimated using a GARCH(1,1) model for the error term over the same period, yielding

$$\widehat{\Delta Inf_t} = 1.29 - 0.41\Delta Inf_{t-1} - 0.31\Delta Inf_{t-2} + 0.02\Delta Inf_{t-3} - 0.03\Delta Inf_{t-4}$$
$$\quad\ (0.33)\ \ (0.10)\qquad (0.09)\qquad\ (0.11)\qquad\ \ (0.09)$$
$$- 2.50Unemp_{t-1} + 2.76Unemp_{t-2} + 0.15Unemp_{t-3} - 0.64Unemp_{t-4;}$$
$$\ \ (0.34)\qquad\qquad (0.71)\qquad\qquad (0.81)\qquad\qquad (0.40)$$

$$(14.34)$$

$$\hat\sigma_t^2 = 0.26 + 0.47u_{t-1}^2 + 0.45\sigma_{t-1}^2. \qquad (14.35)$$
$$\quad\ (0.14)\ \ (0.20)\qquad (0.17)$$

The two coefficients in the GARCH model (the coefficients on u_{t-1}^2 and σ_{t-1}^2) are both individually statistically significant at the 5% significance level, and the joint hypothesis that both coefficients are zero also can be rejected at the 5% significance level. Thus, we can reject the null hypothesis that the Phillips curve errors are homoskedastic against the alternative that they are conditionally heteroskedastic.

The ADL coefficients estimated by OLS (Equation (14.5)) and by maximum likelihood with the GARCH model (Equation (14.34)) are slightly different. If the two GARCH coefficients in Equation (14.35) were exactly zero, then the two sets of estimates would be identical. However, these coefficients are nonzero; because maximum likelihood estimation estimates the coefficients in Equations (14.34) and (14.35) simultaneously, the two sets of estimated ADL coefficients differ.

The predicted variances, $\hat{\sigma}_t^2$, can be computed using the coefficients in Equation (14.35) and the residuals from Equation (14.34). These residuals are plotted in Figure 14.4, along with bands of plus or minus one predicted standard deviation (that is, $\pm\hat{\sigma}_t$) based on the GARCH(1,1) model. These bands quantify the changing volatility of the Phillips curve residuals over time. During the early 1980s, these conditional standard deviation bands are wide, indicating considerable volatility in the Phillips curve regression error and thus considerable

FIGURE 14.4   **Residuals from the Phillips Curve in Equation (14.34) and GARCH(1,1) Bands**

The GARCH(1,1) bands, which are $\pm\hat{\sigma}_t$ computed using Equation (14.35), are narrow when the conditional variance is small and wide when it is large. The forecast interval is narrower at the beginning and end of the sample when $\hat{\sigma}_t$ is small.

uncertainty about the resulting inflation forecasts. In the late 1960s and late 1990s, however, these bands are tight.

With these conditional standard deviation bands in hand, we now can return to the question with which we started this section: was the late 1990s an unusually tranquil period for forecasting inflation? The estimated conditional variances suggest that it was. For example, the predicted standard deviation in 1993:IV is $\hat{\sigma}_{1993:IV} = 0.97$, well less than the OLS standard error of the regression in Equation (14.5), which was 1.47. The actual pseudo out-of-sample RMSFE of 0.75 is still less than the GARCH estimate of 0.97, but not by much.

14.6 Conclusion

This part of the book has covered some of the most frequently used tools and concepts of time series regression. Many other tools for analyzing economic time series have been developed for specific applications. If you are interested in learning more about economic forecasting, see the introductory textbooks by Enders (1995) and Diebold (2000). For an advanced, modern, and comprehensive treatment of econometrics with time series data, see Hamilton (1994).

Summary

1. Vector autoregressions model a "vector" of k time series variables as each depends on its own lags and the lags of the $k - 1$ other series. The forecasts of each of the time series produced by a VAR are mutually consistent, in the sense that they are based on the same information.

2. Forecasts two or more periods ahead can be computed either by iterating forward a one-step ahead model (an AR or a VAR) or by estimating a multiperiod ahead regression.

3. Two series that share a common stochastic trend are cointegrated; that is, Y_t and X_t are cointegrated if Y_t and X_t are $I(1)$ but $Y_t - \theta X_t$ is $I(0)$. If Y_t and X_t are cointegrated, the error correction term $Y_t - \theta X_t$ can help to predict ΔY_t and/or ΔX_t. A vector error correction model is a VAR model of ΔY_t and ΔX_t, augmented to include the lagged error correction term.

4. Volatility clustering—when the variance of a series is high in some periods and low in others—is common in economic time series, especially financial time series.

5. The ARCH model of volatility clustering expresses the conditional variance of the regression error as a function of recent squared regression errors. The GARCH model augments the ARCH model to include lagged conditional variances as well. Estimated ARCH and GARCH models produce forecast intervals with widths that depend on the volatility of the most recent regression residuals.

Key Terms

vector autoregression (VAR) (534)

multiperiod regression forecast (542)

iterated AR forecast (542)

iterated VAR forecast (543)

second difference (546)

$I(0)$, $I(1)$, and $I(2)$ (546)

order of integration (546)

integrated of order d $(I(d))$ (547)

DF-GLS test (549)

common trend (553)

error correction term (554)

vector error correction model (554)

cointegration (555)

cointegrating coefficient (555)

EG-ADF test (556)

DOLS estimator (557)

volatility clustering (561)

conditional heteroskedasticity (561)

ARCH (563)

GARCH (563)

Review the Concepts

14.1 A macroeconomist wants to construct forecasts for the following macroeconomic variables: GDP, consumption, investment, government purchases, exports, imports, short-term interest rates, long-term interest rates, and the rate of price inflation. He has quarterly time series for each of these variables from 1970–2001. Should he estimate a VAR for these variables and use this for forecasting? Why or why not? Can you suggest an alternative approach?

14.2 Suppose that Y_t follows a stationary AR(1) model with $\beta_0 = 0$ and $\beta_1 = 0.7$. If $Y_t = 5$, what is your forecast of Y_{t+2} (that is, what is $Y_{t+2|t}$)? What is $Y_{t+h|t}$ for $h = 30$? Does this forecast for $h = 30$ seem reasonable to you?

14.3 A version of the permanent income theory of consumption implies that the logarithm of real GDP (Y) and the logarithm of real consumption (C) are cointegrated with a cointegrating coefficient equal to 1. Explain how you would investigate this implication by (a) plotting the data, and (b) using a statistical test.

14.4 Consider the ARCH model, $\sigma_t^2 = 1.0 + 0.8u_{t-1}^2$. Explain why this will lead to volatility clustering. (*Hint:* What happens when u_{t-1}^2 is unusually large?)

14.5 The DF-GLS test for a unit root has higher power than the Dickey-Fuller test. Why should you use a more powerful test?

Exercises

14.1 Suppose that Y_t follows a stationary AR(1) model, $Y_t = \beta_0 + \beta_1 Y_{t-1} + u_t$.

    ***a.** Show that the h-period ahead forecast of Y_t is given by $Y_{t+h|t} = \mu_Y + \beta_1^h(Y_t - \mu_Y)$, where $\mu_Y = \beta_0/(1-\beta_1)$.

    b. Suppose that X_t is related to Y_t by $X_t = \sum_{i=0}^{\infty}\delta^i Y_{t+i|t}$, where $|\delta| < 1$. Show that $X_t = \dfrac{\mu_Y}{1-\delta} + \dfrac{Y_t - \mu_Y}{1-\beta_1\delta}$.

14.2 One version of the expectations theory of the term structure of interest rates holds that a long-term rate equals the average of the expected values of short-term interest rates into the future, plus a term premium that is $I(0)$. Specifically, let Rk_t denote a k-period interest rate, let $R1_t$ denote a one-period interest rate, and let e_t denote an $I(0)$ term premium. Then $Rk_t = \dfrac{1}{k}\sum_{i=1}^{k}R1_{t+i|t} + e_t$, where $R1_{t+i|t}$ is the forecast made at date t of the value of $R1$ at date $t + i$. Suppose that $R1_t$ follows a random walk, so that $R1_t = R1_{t-1} + u_t$.

    a. Show that $Rk_t = R1_t + e_t$.

    b. Show that Rk_t and $R1_t$ are cointegrated. What is the cointegrating coefficient?

    c. Now suppose that $\Delta R1_t = 0.5\Delta R1_{t-1} + u_t$. How does your answer to (b) change?

    d. Now suppose that $R1_t = 0.5R1_{t-1} + u_t$. How does your answer to (b) change?

14.3 Suppose that u_t follows the ARCH process, $\sigma_t^2 = 1.0 + 0.5u_{t-1}^2$.

    ***a.** Let $E(u_t^2) = \text{var}(u_t)$ be the unconditional variance of u_t. Show that $\text{var}(u_t) = 2$.

b. Suppose that the distribution of u_t conditional on lagged values of u_t is $N(0, \sigma_t^2)$. If $u_{t-1} = 0.2$, what is $\Pr(-3 \leq u_t \leq 3)$? If $u_{t-1} = 2.0$, what is $\Pr(-3 \leq u_t \leq 3)$?

14.4 Suppose that Y_t follows the $AR(p)$ model $Y_t = \beta_0 + \beta_1 Y_{t-1} + \cdots + \beta_p Y_{t-p} + u_t$, where $E(u_t | Y_{t-1}, Y_{t-2}, \cdots) = 0$. Let $Y_{t+h|t} = E(Y_{t+h} | Y_t, Y_{t-1}, \ldots)$. Show that $Y_{t+h|t} = \beta_0 + \beta_1 Y_{t-1+h|t} + \cdots + \beta_p Y_{t-p+h|t}$ for $h > p$.

14.5 Verify Equation (14.22). (*Hint:* use $\sum_{t=1}^{T} Y_t^2 = \sum_{t=1}^{T}(Y_{t-1} + \Delta Y_t)^2$ to show that $\sum_{t=1}^{T} Y_t^2 - \sum_{t=1}^{T} Y_{t-1}^2 = 2\sum_{t=1}^{T} Y_{t-1}\Delta Y_t + \sum_{t=1}^{T}\Delta Y_t^2$ and solve for $\sum_{t=1}^{T} Y_{t-1}\Delta Y_t$.)

APPENDIX

14.1 U.S. Financial Data Used in Chapter 14

The interest rates on three-month U.S. Treasury bills and on one-year U.S. Treasury bonds are the monthly average of their daily rates, converted to an annual basis, as reported by the U.S. Federal Reserve Bank. The quarterly data used in this chapter are the monthly average interest rates for the final month in the quarter.

PART FIVE

The Econometric Theory of Regression Analysis

CHAPTER 15

The Theory of Linear Regression with One Regressor

There are several good reasons for an applied econometrician to learn some econometric theory. Learning econometric theory turns your statistical software from a "black box" into a flexible toolkit from which you are able to select the right tool for a given job. Understanding econometric theory lets you appreciate why these tools work and what assumptions are required for each tool to work properly. Perhaps most importantly, knowing econometric theory helps you recognize when a tool will *not* work well in an application and when it is time for you to look for a different econometric approach.

This chapter provides an introduction to the econometric theory of linear regression with a single regressor. We address two questions. First, what are the characteristics of the sampling distributions of the OLS estimator and *t*-statistic and, in particular, under what circumstances are the statistical inferences (tests and confidence intervals) laid out in Chapter 4 reliable? Second, under what circumstances is OLS theoretically desirable, in the sense that its sampling distribution has a small variance?

The econometric methods described in Parts I–IV of this book rely extensively on asymptotic distribution theory, that is, the theory of the sampling distributions of estimators and test statistics when the sample size is large. The great virtue of the asymptotic approximations used throughout this book is that they hold quite generally, that is, they hold without restricting the errors to have a specific distribution or requiring them to be homoskedastic. But if the errors *do* have such special features—in particular if they are homoskedastic or, even more specially, homoskedastic and normally distributed—then the OLS estimator has some desirable theoretical properties. Although these stronger assumptions of homoskedasticity or normality can be unrealistic in applications, they are of theoretical interest because they allow us to explore further the performance of the OLS estimator and to reach a deeper understanding of OLS regression.

This chapter begins in Section 15.1 by summarizing the linear model with a single regressor, presented in Chapter 4, and by laying out the extended set of least squares assumptions that are used in this chapter. The first three of these extended least squares assumptions are the assumptions of Key Concept 4.3, and they are all that are needed for the asymptotic distribution theory. Accordingly, these three assumptions are used in Sections 15.2 and 15.3, which provide a mathematical exposition of the asymptotic results concerning the OLS estimator and t-statistic that are used in Chapter 4.

In general, the exact, or finite-sample, distributions of the OLS estimator and t-statistic are very complicated. In one special case, however, the exact distributions are relatively simple and closely mirror the asymptotic distributions. This occurs when the regression errors are homoskedastic and normally distributed, conditional on $X_1, \ldots, X_n$. The distributions of OLS statistics under these assumptions are presented in Section 15.4.

The remaining sections of this chapter turn to the theory of efficient estimation in the linear regression model. If, in addition to the least squares assumptions of Chapter 4, the errors are homoskedastic, then the OLS estimator is efficient in the sense that it has the smallest variance of all estimators that are linear functions of $Y_1, \ldots, Y_n$ and are conditionally unbiased, that is, unbiased conditional on $X_1, \ldots, X_n$. This result, known as the Gauss-Markov theorem, is presented in Section 15.5. The Gauss-Markov theorem is an example of a general approach in theoretical statistics and econometrics to choosing an estimator on the basis of statistical efficiency. Section 15.6 turns to efficient estimation when the errors are heteroskedastic. In this case, the Gauss-Markov theorem does not apply, but if the functional form of the heteroskedasticity is known, then an alternative estimator, weighted least squares (WLS), is efficient, at least in large samples.

This chapter is designed to supplement Chapter 4, not to replace it, and should be read after reading (at least) Chapter 4.

15.1 The Extended Least Squares Assumptions and the OLS Estimator

This section introduces a set of assumptions that extend and strengthen the three least squares assumptions of Chapter 4. These stronger assumptions are used in subsequent sections to derive stronger theoretical results about the OLS estimator than are possible under the weaker (but more realistic) assumptions of Chapter 4.

The Extended Least Squares Assumptions

The extended least squares assumptions #1, #2 and #3.   The first three extended least squares assumptions are the same three assumptions in Key Concept 4.3: that the conditional mean of u_i, given X_i, is zero; that (X_i, Y_i), $i = 1, \ldots, n$, are i.i.d. draws from their joint distribution; and that X_i and u_i have four moments.

Under these three assumptions, the OLS estimator is unbiased, consistent, and has an asymptotically normal sampling distribution. If these three assumptions hold, then the methods for inference introduced in Chapter 4—hypothesis testing using the t-statistic and construction of 95% confidence intervals as ± 1.96 standard errors—are justified when the sample size is large. To develop a theory of efficient estimation using OLS or to characterize the exact sampling distribution of the OLS estimator, however, requires stronger assumptions.

Extended least squares assumption #4.   The fourth extended least squares assumption is that u_i is homoskedastic, that is, $\text{var}(u_i | X_i) = \sigma_u^2$ where σ_u^2 is a constant. As seen in Section 15.5, if this additional assumption holds, then the OLS estimator is efficient among all linear estimators that are unbiased, conditional on $X_1, \ldots, X_n$.

Extended least squares assumption #5.   The fifth least squares assumption is that the conditional distribution of u_i, given X_i, is normal. As shown in Section 15.4, if this assumption holds, then it is possible to derive simple expressions for the exact sampling distribution of the OLS estimator and homoskedasticity-only t-statistic.

The fourth and fifth extended least squares assumptions are much more restrictive than the first three. Although it might be reasonable to assume that the first three assumptions hold in an application, the final two assumptions are less realistic. Even though these final two assumptions might not hold in practice, they are of theoretical interest because if one or both of them hold then the OLS estimator has additional properties beyond those discussed in Chapter 4. Thus, we

The Extended Least Squares Assumptions for Regression with a Single Regressor

The linear regression model with a single regressor is

$$Y_i = \beta_0 + \beta_1 X_i + u_i, \ i = 1, \ldots, n, \tag{15.1}$$

The extended least squares assumptions are

1. $E(u_i | X_i) = 0$ (conditional mean zero);
2. (X_i, Y_i), $i = 1, \ldots, n$ are independent and identically distributed (i.i.d.) draws from their joint distribution;
3. (X_i, u_i) have nonzero finite fourth moments;
4. $\text{var}(u_i | X_i) = \sigma_u^2$ (homoskedasticity); and
5. The conditional distribution of u_i given X_i is normal (normal errors).

can enhance our understanding of the OLS estimator, and more generally of the theory of estimation in the linear regression model, by exploring estimation under these stronger assumptions.

The five extended least squares assumptions for the single-regressor model are summarized in Key Concept 15.1.

The OLS Estimator

For easy reference, we restate the OLS estimators of β_0 and β_1 here:

$$\hat{\beta}_1 = \frac{\sum\limits_{i=1}^{n}(X_i - \overline{X})(Y_i - \overline{Y})}{\sum\limits_{i=1}^{n}(X_i - \overline{X})^2} \tag{15.2}$$

$$\hat{\beta}_0 = \overline{Y} - \hat{\beta}_1 \overline{X}. \tag{15.3}$$

Equations (15.2) and (15.3) are derived in Appendix 4.2.

15.2 Fundamentals of Asymptotic Distribution Theory

Asymptotic distribution theory is the theory of the distribution of statistics—estimators, test statistics, and confidence intervals—when the sample size is large. Formally, this theory involves characterizing the behavior of the sampling distribution of a statistic along a sequence of ever-larger samples. The theory is asymptotic in the sense that it characterizes the behavior of the statistic in the limit as $n \longrightarrow \infty$.

Even though sample sizes are, of course, never infinite, asymptotic distribution theory plays a central role in econometrics and statistics for two reasons. First, if the number of observations used in an empirical application is sufficiently large, then the asymptotic limit can provide a high-quality approximation to the finite sample distribution. Second, asymptotic sampling distributions typically are much simpler, and thus easier to use in practice, than exact finite-sample distributions. Taken together, these two reasons mean that reliable and straightforward methods for statistical inference—tests using t-statistics and 95% confidence intervals calculated as ± 1.96 standard errors—can be based on approximate sampling distributions derived from asymptotic theory.

The two cornerstones of asymptotic distribution theory are the law of large numbers and the central limit theorem, both introduced in Section 2.6. We begin this section by continuing the discussion of the law of large numbers and the central limit theorem, including a proof of the law of large numbers. We then introduce two more tools, Slutsky's theorem and the continuous mapping theorem, that extend the usefulness of the law of large numbers and the central limit theorem. As an illustration, these tools are then used to prove that the distribution of the t-statistic based on $\overline{Y}$ testing the hypothesis $E(Y) = \mu_0$ has a standard normal distribution under the null hypothesis.

Convergence in Probability and the Law of Large Numbers

The concepts of convergence in probability and the law of large numbers were introduced in Section 2.6. Here we provide a precise mathematical definition of convergence in probability, followed by a statement and proof of the law of large numbers.

Consistency and convergence in probability.   Let $S_1, S_2, \ldots, S_n, \ldots$ be a sequence of random variables. For example, S_n could be the sample average $\overline{Y}$ of a sample of n observations of the random variable Y. The sequence of random variables $\{S_n\}$ is said to **converge in probability** to a limit, μ (that is, $S_n \xrightarrow{p} \mu$), if the probability that S_n is within $\pm\delta$ of μ tends to one as $n \longrightarrow \infty$, as long as the constant δ is positive. That is

$$S_n \xrightarrow{p} \mu \text{ if and only if } \Pr[\,|\,S_n - \mu\,| \geq \delta\,] \longrightarrow 0 \qquad (15.4)$$

as $n \longrightarrow \infty$ for every $\delta > 0$. If $S_n \xrightarrow{p} \mu$, then S_n is said to be a **consistent estimator** of μ.

The law of large numbers.   The law of large numbers says that, under certain conditions on $Y_1, \ldots, Y_n$, the sample average $\overline{Y}$ converges in probability to the population mean. Probability theorists have developed many versions of the law of large numbers, corresponding to various conditions on $Y_1, \ldots, Y_n$. The version of the law of large numbers used in this book is that $Y_1, \ldots, Y_n$ are i.i.d. draws from a distribution with finite variance. This law of large numbers (also stated in Key Concept 2.6) is

$$\text{if } Y_1, \ldots, Y_n \text{ are i.i.d., } E(Y_i) = \mu_Y, \text{ and var}(Y_i) < \infty, \text{ then } \overline{Y} \xrightarrow{p} \mu_Y. \quad (15.5)$$

The idea of the law of large numbers can be seen in Figure 2.6: as the sample size increases, the sampling distribution of $\overline{Y}$ concentrates around the population mean, μ_Y. One feature of the sampling distribution is that the variance of $\overline{Y}$ decreases as the sample size increases; another feature is that the probability that $\overline{Y}$ falls outside $\pm\delta$ of μ_Y vanishes as n increases. These two features of the sampling distribution are in fact linked, and the proof of the law of large numbers exploits this link.

Proof of the law of large numbers.   The link between the variance of $\overline{Y}$ and the probability that $\overline{Y}$ is within $\pm\delta$ of μ_Y is provided by Chebychev's inequality, which is stated and proven in Appendix 15.2 (see Equation (15.47)). Written in terms of $\overline{Y}$, Chebychev's inequality is

$$\Pr(|\overline{Y} - \mu_Y| \geq \delta) \leq \text{var}(\overline{Y})/\delta^2, \qquad (15.6)$$

for any positive constant δ. Because $Y_1, \ldots, Y_n$ are i.i.d. with variance σ_Y^2, $\text{var}(\overline{Y}) = \sigma_Y^2/n$; thus, for any $\delta > 0$, $\text{var}(\overline{Y})/\delta^2 = \sigma_Y^2/(\delta^2 n) \longrightarrow 0$. It follows from Equation (15.6) that $\Pr(|\overline{Y} - \mu_Y| \geq \delta) \longrightarrow 0$ for every $\delta > 0$, proving the law of large numbers.

Some examples.   Consistency is a fundamental concept in asymptotic distribution theory, so we present some examples of consistent and inconsistent estimators of the population mean, μ_Y. Suppose that Y_i, $i = 1, \ldots, n$ are i.i.d. with variance σ_Y^2 that is positive and finite. Consider the following three estimators of μ_Y: (a) $m_a = Y_1$; (b) $m_b = \left(\dfrac{1-a^n}{1-a}\right)^{-1}\sum_{i=1}^{n} a^{i-1}Y_i$, where $0 < a < 1$; and (c) $m_c = \overline{Y} + 1/n$. Are these estimators consistent?

The first estimator, m_a, is just the first observation, so $E(m_a) = E(Y_1) = \mu_Y$ and m_a is unbiased. However, m_a is not consistent: $\Pr(|m_a - \mu_Y| \geq \delta) = \Pr(|Y_1 - \mu_Y| \geq \delta)$, which must be positive for sufficiently small δ (because $\sigma_Y^2 > 0$), so $\Pr(|m_a - \mu_Y| \geq \delta)$ does not tend to zero as $n \longrightarrow \infty$, so m_a is not consistent. This inconsistency should not be surprising: because m_a only uses the information in one observation, its distribution cannot concentrate around μ_Y as the sample size increases.

The second estimator, m_b, is unbiased but is not consistent. It is unbiased because

$$E(m_b) = E\left[\left(\frac{1-a^n}{1-a}\right)^{-1}\sum_{i=1}^{n} a^{i-1}Y_i\right] = \left(\frac{1-a^n}{1-a}\right)^{-1}\sum_{i=1}^{n} a^{i-1}\mu_Y = \mu_Y,$$

$$\text{since } \sum_{i=1}^{n} a^{i-1} = (1-a^n)\sum_{i=0}^{\infty} a^i = (1-a^n)/(1-a).$$

The variance of m_b is

$$\text{var}(m_b) = \left(\frac{1-a^n}{1-a}\right)^{-2}\sum_{i=1}^{n} a^{2(i-1)}\sigma_Y^2 = \sigma_Y^2\frac{(1-a^{2n})(1-a)^2}{(1-a^2)(1-a^n)^2} = \sigma_Y^2\frac{(1+a^n)(1-a)}{(1-a^n)(1+a)},$$

which has the limit $\text{var}(m_b) \longrightarrow \sigma_Y^2(1-a)/(1+a)$ as $n \longrightarrow \infty$. Thus, the variance of this estimator does not tend to zero, the distribution does not concentrate around μ_Y, and the estimator, although unbiased, is not consistent. This is perhaps surprising, because all the observations enter this estimator. But most of the observations receive very small weight (the weight of the ith observation is proportional to a^{i-1} which approaches zero as i becomes large), and for this reason there is an insufficient amount of cancellation of sampling errors for the estimator to be consistent.

The third estimator, m_c, is biased but consistent. Its bias is $1/n$: $E(m_c) = E(\overline{Y} + 1/n) = \mu_Y + 1/n$. But the bias tends to zero as the sample size increases and m_c is consistent: $\Pr(|m_c - \mu_Y| \geq \delta) = \Pr(|\overline{Y} + 1/n - \mu_Y| \geq \delta) = \Pr(|(\overline{Y} - \mu_Y) + 1/n| \geq \delta)$. Now $|(\overline{Y} - \mu_Y) + 1/n| \leq |\overline{Y} - \mu_Y| + 1/n$, so if $|(\overline{Y} - \mu_Y) + 1/n| \geq \delta$, it must be the case that $|\overline{Y} - \mu_Y| + 1/n \geq \delta$; thus, $\Pr(|(\overline{Y} - \mu_Y) + 1/n| \geq \delta) \leq \Pr(|\overline{Y} - \mu_Y| + 1/n \geq \delta)$. But $\Pr(|\overline{Y} - \mu_Y| + 1/n \geq \delta) = \Pr(|\overline{Y} - \mu_Y| \geq \delta - 1/n) \leq \sigma_{\overline{Y}}^2/[n(\delta - 1/n)^2]$ $\longrightarrow 0$, where the final inequality follows from Chebychev's inequality (Equation (15.6), with δ replaced by $\delta - 1/n$ for $n > 1/\delta$). It follows that m_c is consistent. This example illustrates the general point that an estimator can be biased in finite samples but, if that bias vanishes as the sample size gets large, the estimator can still be consistent (Exercise 15.10).

The Central Limit Theorem and Convergence in Distribution

If the distributions of a sequence of random variables converge to a limit as $n \longrightarrow \infty$, then the sequence of random variables is said to converge in distribution. The central limit theorem says that, under general conditions, the standardized sample average converges in distribution to a normal random variable.

Convergence in distribution.   Let $F_1, F_2, \ldots, F_n, \ldots$ be a sequence of cumulative distribution functions corresponding to a sequence of random variables, $S_1,$ $S_2, \ldots, S_n, \ldots$ For example, S_n might be the standardized sample average, $(\overline{Y} - \mu_Y)/\sigma_{\overline{Y}}$. Then the sequence of random variables S_n is said to **converge in distribution** to S (denoted $S_n \overset{d}{\longrightarrow} S$) if the distribution functions $\{F_n\}$ converge to F, the distribution of S. That is,

$$S_n \overset{d}{\longrightarrow} S \text{ if and only if } \lim_{n\to\infty} F_n(t) = F(t), \tag{15.7}$$

where the limit holds at all points t at which the limiting distribution F is continuous. The distribution F is called the **asymptotic distribution** of S_n.

It is useful to contrast the concepts of convergence in probability ($\overset{p}{\longrightarrow}$) and convergence in distribution ($\overset{d}{\longrightarrow}$). If $S_n \overset{p}{\longrightarrow} \mu$, then S_n becomes close to μ with high probability as n increases. In contrast, if $S_n \overset{d}{\longrightarrow} S$, then the *distribution* of S_n becomes close to the *distribution* of S as n increases.

The central limit theorem.   We now restate the central limit theorem using the concept of convergence in distribution. The central limit theorem in Key Concept 2.7 states that if $Y_1, \ldots, Y_n$ are i.i.d. and $0 < \sigma_Y^2 < \infty$, then the asymptotic distribution of $(\overline{Y} - \mu_Y)/\sigma_{\overline{Y}}$ is $N(0, 1)$. Because $\sigma_{\overline{Y}} = \sigma_Y/\sqrt{n}$, $(\overline{Y} - \mu_Y)/\sigma_{\overline{Y}} = \sqrt{n}(\overline{Y} - \mu_Y)/\sigma_Y$. Thus, the central limit theorem can be restated as $\sqrt{n}(\overline{Y} - \mu_Y) \overset{d}{\longrightarrow} \sigma_Y Z$, where Z is a standard normal random variable. This means that the distribution of $\sqrt{n}\,(\overline{Y} - \mu_Y)$ converges to $N(0, \sigma_{\overline{Y}}^2)$ as $n \longrightarrow \infty$. Conventional shorthand for this limit is

$$\sqrt{n}\,(\overline{Y} - \mu_Y) \xrightarrow{d} N(0, \sigma_{\overline{Y}}^2). \tag{15.8}$$

That is, if $Y_1, \ldots, Y_n$ are i.i.d. and $0 < \sigma_Y^2 < \infty$, then the distribution of $\sqrt{n}\,(\overline{Y} - \mu_Y)$ converges to a normal distribution with mean zero and variance σ_Y^2.

Extensions to time series data.   The law of large numbers and central limit theorem stated in Section 2.6 apply to i.i.d. observations. As discussed in Chapter 12, the i.i.d. assumption is inappropriate for time series data, and these theorems need to be extended before they can be applied to time series observations. Those extensions are technical in nature, in the sense that the conclusion is the same—versions of the law of large numbers and the central limit theorem apply to time series data—but the conditions under which they apply are different. This is discussed briefly in Section 12.4, but a mathematical treatment of asymptotic distribution theory for time series variables is beyond the scope of this book and interested readers are referred to Hayashi (2000, Chapter 2).

Slutsky's Theorem and the Continuous Mapping Theorem

Slutsky's theorem combines consistency and convergence in distribution. Suppose that $a_n \xrightarrow{p} a$, where a is a constant, and $S_n \xrightarrow{d} S$. Then

$$a_n + S_n \xrightarrow{d} a + S, \ a_n S_n \xrightarrow{d} aS, \text{ and, if } a \neq 0, \ S_n/a_n \xrightarrow{d} S/a. \tag{15.9}$$

These three results are together called Slutsky's theorem.

The **continuous mapping theorem** concerns the asymptotic properties of a continuous function, g, of a sequence of random variables, S_n. The theorem has two parts. The first is that if S_n converges in probability to the constant a, then $g(S_n)$ converges in probability to $g(a)$; the second is that if S_n converges in distribution to S, then $g(S_n)$ converges in distribution to $g(S)$. That is, if g is a continuous function, then

$$
\begin{aligned}
&\text{(i) if } S_n \xrightarrow{p} a \text{ then } g(S_n) \xrightarrow{p} g(a), \text{ and}\\
&\text{(ii) if } S_n \xrightarrow{d} S \text{ then } g(S_n) \xrightarrow{d} g(S).
\end{aligned}
\tag{15.10}
$$

As an example of (i), if $s_Y^2 \xrightarrow{p} \sigma_Y^2$, then $\sqrt{s_Y^2} = s_Y \xrightarrow{p} \sigma_Y$. As an example of (ii), suppose $S_n \xrightarrow{d} Z$, where Z is a standard normal random variable, and let $g(S_n) = S_n^2$. Because g is continuous, the continuous mapping theorem applies and $g(S_n) \xrightarrow{d} g(Z)$, that is, $S_n^2 \xrightarrow{d} Z^2$. In other words, the distribution of S_n^2 converges to the distribution of a squared standard normal random variable, which in turn has a χ_1^2 distribution; that is, $S_n^2 \xrightarrow{d} \chi_1^2$.

Application to the *t*-Statistic Based on the Sample Mean

We now use the central limit theorem, the law of large numbers and Slutsky's theorem to prove that, under the null hypothesis, the *t*-statistic based on $\overline{Y}$ has a standard normal distribution when $Y_1, \ldots, Y_n$ are i.i.d. and $0 < E(Y_i^4) < \infty$.

The *t*-statistic for testing the null hypothesis that $E(Y_i) = \mu_0$ based on the sample average $\overline{Y}$ is given in Equation (2.50) and can be written

$$t = \frac{\overline{Y} - \mu_0}{s_Y / \sqrt{n}} = \left(\frac{\sqrt{n} \, (\overline{Y} - \mu_0)}{\sigma_Y} \right) \div \left(\frac{s_Y}{\sigma_Y} \right), \tag{15.11}$$

where the second equality uses the trick of dividing both the numerator and denominator by σ_Y.

Because $Y_1, \ldots, Y_n$ have two moments (which is implied by their having four moments; see Exercise 15.5), and because $Y_1, \ldots, Y_n$ are i.i.d., the first term in parentheses after the final equality in Equation (15.11) obeys the central limit theorem: under the null hypothesis, $\sqrt{n}(\overline{Y} - \mu_0)/\sigma_Y \xrightarrow{d} N(0, 1)$. In addition, $s_Y^2 \xrightarrow{p} \sigma_Y^2$ (as proven in Appendix 3.3) so $s_Y^2/\sigma_Y^2 \xrightarrow{p} 1$ and the ratio in the second term in Equation (15.11) tends to one (Exercise 15.4). Thus the expression after the final equality in Equation (15.11) has the form of the final expression in Equation (15.9), where (in the notation of Equation (15.9)) $S_n = \sqrt{n}(\overline{Y} - \mu_0)/\sigma_Y \xrightarrow{d} N(0, 1)$ and $a_n = s_Y/\sigma_Y \xrightarrow{p} 1$. It follows by applying Slutsky's theorem that $t \xrightarrow{d} N(0, 1)$.

15.3 Asymptotic Distribution of the OLS Estimator and *t*-Statistic

Recall from Chapter 4 that, under the assumptions of Key Concept 4.3 (the first three assumptions of Key Concept 15.1), the OLS estimator $\hat{\beta}_1$ is consistent and $\sqrt{n}(\hat{\beta}_1 - \beta_1)$ has an asymptotic normal distribution. Moreover, the *t*-statistic testing the null hypothesis $\beta_1 = \beta_{1,0}$ has an asymptotic standard normal distribution under the null hypothesis. This section summarizes these results and provides additional details of their proofs.

Consistency and Asymptotic Normality of the OLS Estimators

The large-sample distribution of $\hat{\beta}_1$, originally stated in Key Concept 4.4, is

$$\sqrt{n}(\hat{\beta}_1 - \beta_1) \xrightarrow{d} N(0, \frac{\text{var}(v_i)}{[\text{var}(X_i)]^2}), \tag{15.12}$$

where $v_i = (X_i - \mu_X)u_i$. The proof of this result was sketched in Appendix 4.3, but that proof omitted some details and involved an approximation that was not formally shown. The missing steps in that proof are left as Exercise 15.3.

An implication of Equation (15.12) is that $\hat{\beta}_1$ is consistent (Exercise 15.4).

Consistency of Heteroskedasticity-Robust Standard Errors

Under the first three least squares assumptions, the heteroskedasticity-robust standard error for $\hat{\beta}_1$ forms the basis for valid statistical inferences. Specifically,

$$\frac{\hat{\sigma}^2_{\hat{\beta}_1}}{\sigma^2_{\hat{\beta}_1}} \xrightarrow{p} 1, \tag{15.13}$$

where $\sigma^2_{\hat{\beta}_1} = \text{var}(v_i)/\{n[\text{var}(X_i)]^2\}$ and $\hat{\sigma}^2_{\hat{\beta}_1}$ is square of the heteroskedasticity-robust standard error defined in Equation (4.19); that is,

$$\hat{\sigma}^2_{\hat{\beta}_1} = \frac{1}{n-2} \frac{\frac{1}{n}\sum_{i=1}^{n}(X_i - \overline{X})^2\hat{u}_i^2}{\left[\frac{1}{n}\sum_{i=1}^{n}(X_i - \overline{X})^2\right]^2}. \tag{15.14}$$

To show the result in Equation (15.13), first use the definitions of $\sigma^2_{\hat{\beta}_1}$ and $\hat{\sigma}^2_{\hat{\beta}_1}$ to rewrite the ratio in Equation (15.13) as

$$\frac{\hat{\sigma}^2_{\hat{\beta}_1}}{\sigma^2_{\hat{\beta}_1}} = \left[\frac{n}{n-2}\right] \left[\frac{\frac{1}{n}\sum_{i=1}^{n}(X_i - \overline{X})^2\hat{u}_i^2}{\text{var}(v_i)}\right] \div \left[\frac{\frac{1}{n}\sum_{i=1}^{n}(X_i - \overline{X})^2}{\text{var}(X_i)}\right]^2. \tag{15.15}$$

We need to show that each of the three terms in brackets on the right-hand side of Equation (15.15) converge in probability to one. Clearly the first term converges to one, and by the consistency of the sample variance (Appendix 3.3) the final term converges in probability to one. Thus, all that remains is to show that the second term converges in probability to one, that is, that $\frac{1}{n}\sum_{i=1}^{n}(X_i - \overline{X})^2\hat{u}_i^2 \xrightarrow{p} \text{var}(v_i)$.

The proof that $\frac{1}{n}\sum_{i=1}^{n}(X_i - \overline{X})^2\hat{u}_i^2 \xrightarrow{p} \text{var}(v_i)$ proceeds in two steps. The first shows that $\frac{1}{n}\sum_{i=1}^{n}v_i^2 \xrightarrow{p} \text{var}(v_i)$; the second shows that $\frac{1}{n}\sum_{i=1}^{n}(X_i - \overline{X})^2\hat{u}_i^2 - \frac{1}{n}\sum_{i=1}^{n}v_i^2 \xrightarrow{p} 0$.

For the moment, suppose that X_i and u_i have eight moments (that is, $E(X_i^8) < \infty$ and $E(u_i^8) < \infty$)—a stronger assumption than the four moments required by the third least squares assumption. To show the first step, we must show that $\frac{1}{n}\sum_{i=1}^{n}v_i^2$ obeys the law of large numbers in Equation (15.5). To do so, v_i^2 must be i.i.d. (which it is by the second least squares assumption) and $\text{var}(v_i^2)$ must be finite. To show that $\text{var}(v_i^2) < \infty$, apply the Cauchy-Schwarz inequality (Appendix 15.2): $\text{var}(v_i^2) \le E(v_i^4) = E[(X_i - \mu_X)^4 u_i^4] \le \{E[(X_i - \mu_X)^8]E(u_i^8)\}^{1/2}$. Thus, if X_i and u_i have eight moments, then v_i^2 has a finite variance and thus satisfies the law of large numbers in Equation (15.5).

The second step is to prove that $\frac{1}{n}\sum_{i=1}^{n}(X_i - \overline{X})^2\hat{u}_i^2 - \frac{1}{n}\sum_{i=1}^{n}v_i^2 \xrightarrow{p} 0$. Because $v_i = (X_i - \mu_X)u_i$, this second step is the same as showing that

$$\frac{1}{n}\sum_{i=1}^{n}[(X_i - \overline{X})^2\hat{u}_i^2 - (X_i - \mu_X)^2u_i^2] \xrightarrow{p} 0. \tag{15.16}$$

Showing this result entails setting $\hat{u}_i = u_i - (\hat{\beta}_0 - \beta_0) - (\hat{\beta}_1 - \beta_1)X_i$, expanding the term in Equation (15.16) in brackets, repeatedly applying the Cauchy-Schwarz inequality, and using the consistency of $\hat{\beta}_0$ and $\hat{\beta}_1$. The details of the algebra are left as Exercise 15.9.

The preceding argument supposes that X_i and u_i have eight moments. This is not necessary, however, and the result $\frac{1}{n}\sum_{i=1}^{n}(X_i - \overline{X})^2\hat{u}_i^2 \xrightarrow{p} \text{var}(v_i)$ can be proven under the weaker assumption that X_i and u_i have four moments, as stated in the third least squares assumption. That proof, however, is beyond the scope of this textbook; see Hayashi (2000, Section 2.5) for details.

Asymptotic Normality of the Heteroskedasticity-Robust *t*-Statistic

We now show that, under the null hypothesis, the heteroskedasticity-robust OLS *t*-statistic testing the hypothesis $\beta_1 = \beta_{1,0}$ has an asymptotic standard normal distribution if least squares assumptions 1–3 hold.

The *t*-statistic constructed using the heteroskedasticity–robust standard error $SE(\hat{\beta}_1) = \hat{\sigma}_{\hat{\beta}_1}$ (defined in Equation (15.14)) is

$$t = \frac{\hat{\beta}_1 - \beta_{1,0}}{\hat{\sigma}_{\hat{\beta}_1}} = \left[\frac{\sqrt{n}(\hat{\beta}_1 - \beta_{1,0})}{\sqrt{n\sigma_{\hat{\beta}_1}^2}}\right] \div \sqrt{\frac{\hat{\sigma}_{\hat{\beta}_1}^2}{\sigma_{\hat{\beta}_1}^2}}. \tag{15.17}$$

It follows from Equation (15.12) that the term in brackets after the second equality in Equation (15.17) converges in distribution to a standard normal random variable. In addition, because the heteroskedasticity-robust standard error is consistent (Equation (15.13)), $\sqrt{\hat{\sigma}^2_{\tilde{\beta}_1}/\sigma^2_{\tilde{\beta}_1}} \xrightarrow{p} 1$ (Exercise 15.4). It follows from Slutsky's theorem that $t \xrightarrow{d} N(0, 1)$.

15.4 Exact Sampling Distributions When the Errors Are Normally Distributed

In small samples, the distribution of the OLS estimator and t-statistic depends on the distribution of the regression error and typically is complicated. If, however, the regression errors are homoskedastic and normally distributed, then these distributions are simple. Specifically if all five extended least squares assumptions in Key Concept 15.1 hold, then the OLS estimator has a normal sampling distribution, conditional on $X_1, \ldots, X_n$. Moreover, the t-statistic has a Student t distribution. We present these results here for $\hat{\beta}_1$.

Distribution of $\hat{\beta}_1$ with Normal Errors

If the regressors are nonrandom and the errors are i.i.d normally distributed, then the distribution of $\hat{\beta}_1$, conditional on $X_1, \ldots, X_n$ is $N(\beta_1, \sigma^2_{\hat{\beta}_{1|X}})$, where

$$\sigma^2_{\hat{\beta}_{1|X}} = \frac{\sigma^2_u}{\displaystyle\sum_{i=1}^{n}(X_i - \overline{X})^2}. \tag{15.18}$$

The derivation of the normal distribution $N(\beta_1, \sigma^2_{\hat{\beta}_{1|X}})$, conditional on $X_1, \ldots, X_n$, entails (i) establishing that the distribution is normal; (ii) showing that $E(\hat{\beta}_1 | X_1, \ldots, X_n) = \beta_1$; and (iii) verifying Equation (15.18).

To show (i), note that conditional on $X_1, \ldots, X_n$, $\hat{\beta}_1 - \beta_1$ is a weighted average of $u_1, \ldots, u_n$:

$$\hat{\beta}_1 = \beta_1 + \frac{\dfrac{1}{n}\displaystyle\sum_{i=1}^{n}(X_i - \overline{X})u_i}{\dfrac{1}{n}\displaystyle\sum_{i=1}^{n}(X_i - \overline{X})^2}. \tag{15.19}$$

(This equation was derived in Appendix 4.3 (Equation (4.51)) and is restated here for convenience.) By assumption, $u_1, \ldots, u_n$ are i.i.d. and normally distributed, conditional on $X_1, \ldots, X_n$. Because weighted averages of normally distributed variables are themselves normally distributed, it follows that $\hat{\beta}_1$ is normally distributed, conditional on $X_1, \ldots, X_n$.

To show (ii), take conditional expectations of both sides of Equation (15.19): $E[(\hat{\beta}_1 - \beta_1) | X_1, \ldots, X_n] = E[\sum_{i=1}^{n}(X_i - \overline{X})u_i / \sum_{i=1}^{n}(X_i - \overline{X})^2 | X_1, \ldots, X_n] = \sum_{i=1}^{n}(X_i - \overline{X}) E(u_i | X_1, \ldots, X_n) / \sum_{i=1}^{n}(X_i - \overline{X})^2 = 0$ where the final equality follows because $E(u_i | X_1, X_2, \ldots, X_n) = E(u_i | X_i) = 0$. Thus $\hat{\beta}_1$ is conditionally unbiased, that is,

$$E(\hat{\beta}_1 | X_1, \ldots, X_n) = \beta_1. \tag{15.20}$$

To show (iii), use the fact that the errors are independently distributed, conditional on $X_1, \ldots, X_n$, to calculate the conditional variance of $\hat{\beta}_1$ using Equation (15.19):

$$\text{var}(\hat{\beta}_1 | X_1, \ldots, X_n) = \text{var}\left(\frac{\sum_{i=1}^{n}(X_i - \overline{X})u_i}{\sum_{i=1}^{n}(X_i - \overline{X})^2} \Big| X_1, \ldots, X_n\right)$$

$$= \frac{\sum_{i=1}^{n}(X_i - \overline{X})^2 \text{var}(u_i | X_1, \ldots, X_n)}{\left[\sum_{i=1}^{n}(X_i - \overline{X})^2\right]^2} \tag{15.21}$$

$$= \frac{\sum_{i=1}^{n}(X_i - \overline{X})^2 \sigma_u^2}{\left[\sum_{i=1}^{n}(X_i - \overline{X})^2\right]^2}.$$

Canceling the term in the numerator in the final expression in Equation (15.21) yields the formula for the conditional variance in Equation (15.18).

Distribution of the Homoskedasticity-only *t*-Statistic

The homoskedasticity–only *t*-statistic testing the null hypothesis $\beta_1 = \beta_{1,0}$ is

$$t = \frac{\hat{\beta}_1 - \beta_{1,0}}{SE(\hat{\beta}_1)}, \tag{15.22}$$

where $SE(\hat{\beta}_1)$ is computed using the homoskedasticity-only standard error of $\hat{\beta}_1$. Substituting the formula for $SE(\hat{\beta}_1)$ (Equation (4.58) of Appendix 4.4) into Equation (15.22) and rearranging yields

$$t = \frac{\hat{\beta}_1 - \beta_{1,0}}{\sqrt{s_{\hat{u}}^2 / \sum_{i=1}^{n}(X_i - \overline{X})^2}} = \frac{\hat{\beta}_1 - \beta_{1,0}}{\sqrt{\sigma_u^2 / \sum_{i=1}^{n}(X_i - \overline{X})^2}} \div \sqrt{\frac{s_{\hat{u}}^2}{\sigma_u^2}}$$

$$= \frac{(\hat{\beta}_1 - \beta_{1,0}) / \sigma_{\hat{\beta}_{1|X}}}{\sqrt{W/(n-2)}},$$

(15.23)

where $s_{\hat{u}}^2 = \frac{1}{n-2}\sum_{i=1}^{n}\hat{u}_i^2$ and $W = \sum_{i=1}^{n}\hat{u}_i^2/\sigma_u^2$. Under the null hypothesis, $\hat{\beta}_1$ has a $N(\beta_{1,0}, \sigma_{\hat{\beta}_{1|X}}^2)$ distribution conditional on $X_1, \ldots, X_n$, so the distribution of the numerator in the final expression in Equation (15.23) is $N(0,1)$. It is shown in Section 16.4 that W has a chi-squared distribution with $n-2$ degrees of freedom and moreover W is distributed independently of the standardized OLS estimator in the numerator of Equation (15.23). It follows from the definition of the Student t distribution (Appendix 15.1) that, under the five extended least squares assumptions, the homoskedasticity-only t-statistic has a Student t distribution with $n-2$ degrees of freedom.

Where does the degrees of freedom adjustment fit in? The degrees of freedom adjustment in $s_{\hat{u}}^2$ ensures that $s_{\hat{u}}^2$ is an unbiased estimator of σ_u^2 and that the t-statistic has a Student t distribution when the errors are normally distributed.

Because $W = \sum_{i=1}^{n}\hat{u}_i^2/\sigma_u^2$ is a chi-squared random variable with $n-2$ degrees of freedom, its mean is $E(W) = n-2$. Thus, $E[W/(n-2)] = (n-2)/(n-2) = 1$. Rearranging the definition of W, we have that $E\left(\frac{1}{n-2}\sum_{i=1}^{n}\hat{u}_i^2\right) = \sigma_u^2$. Thus, the degrees of freedom correction makes $s_{\hat{u}}^2$ an unbiased estimator of σ_u^2. Also, by dividing by $n-2$ rather than n, the term in the denominator of the final expression of Equation (15.23) matches the definition of a random variable with a Student t distribution given in Appendix 15.1. That is, by using the degrees of freedom adjustment to calculate the standard error, the t-statistic has the Student t distribution when the errors are normally distributed.

15.5 Efficiency of the OLS Estimator with Homoskedastic Errors

Why should you use OLS to estimate β_0 and β_1? In Chapter 4, we said that one reason to use the OLS estimator is that, by and large, everybody else does—that way, you will be "speaking the same language" as other empirical researchers. Although sensible, this argument is not compelling on a theoretical level. In theory, the choice of one estimator over another should be guided by general principles or by applying some agreed-upon criteria. As discussed in Section 3.1, two criteria commonly used to choose estimators are that the estimator be unbiased and that it have a variance that is as small as possible.

In this section, we show that, by these two criteria, the OLS estimator is, under certain conditions, the best estimator possible. Specifically, the Gauss-Markov theorem says that when the regression errors are homoskedastic, the OLS estimator has the smallest variance, conditional on $X_1, \ldots, X_n$, of all estimators that are linear in $Y_1, \ldots, Y_n$ and that are conditionally unbiased (that is, unbiased conditional on $X_1, \ldots, X_n$). Said differently, the OLS estimator is the **b**est **l**inear conditionally **u**nbiased **e**stimator (is **BLUE**). This result provides an important theoretical reason to use the OLS estimator.

We begin by stating the Gauss-Markov conditions, which are the conditions under which the Gauss-Markov theorem holds. We then define the class of linear unbiased estimators, show that OLS is in that class, and turn to the Gauss-Markov theorem itself.

The Gauss-Markov Conditions

There are three Gauss-Markov conditions. The first is that u_i has a conditional mean of zero, given all observations on the regressors, $X_1, \ldots, X_n$. The second is that u_i is homoskedastic, and the third is that the error terms are uncorrelated across observations, conditional on $X_1, \ldots, X_n$. That is, the three **Gauss-Markov conditions** are

i. $E(u_i | X_1, \ldots, X_n) = 0$

ii. $\text{var}(u_i | X_1, \ldots, X_n) = \sigma_u^2, 0 < \sigma_u^2 < \infty$ for $i = 1, \ldots, n$, and   (15.24)

iii. $E(u_i u_j | X_1, \ldots, X_n) = 0, i = 1, \ldots, n, j = 1, \ldots, n, i \neq j$.

The Gauss-Markov conditions are implied by the first four least squares assumptions in Key Concept 15.1. Because the observations are i.i.d. (assumption 2),

$E(u_i | X_1, \ldots, X_n) = E(u_i | X_i)$, and by assumption 1, $E(u_i | X_i) = 0$; thus condition (i) holds. Similarly, by assumption 2, $\text{var}(u_i | X_1, \ldots, X_n) = \text{var}(u_i | X_i)$, and by assumption 4 (homoskedasticity), $\text{var}(u_i | X_i) = \sigma_u^2$, which is constant. Assumption 3 (nonzero finite fourth moments) ensures that $0 < \sigma_u^2 < \infty$, so condition (ii) holds. To show that condition (iii) is implied by the first four least squares assumptions, note that $E(u_i u_j | X_1, \ldots, X_n) = E(u_i u_j | X_i, X_j)$ because (X_i, Y_i) are i.i.d. by assumption 2. Assumption 2 also implies that $E(u_i u_j | X_i, X_j) = E(u_i | X_i) E(u_j | X_j)$ for $i \neq j$ (Exercise 15.7); because $E(u_i | X_i) = 0$ for all i, it follows that $E(u_i u_j | X_1, \ldots, X_n) = 0$ for all $i \neq j$, so condition (iii) holds. Thus, the least squares assumptions 1–4 in Key Concept 15.1 imply the Gauss-Markov conditions in Equation (15.24).

Linear Conditionally Unbiased Estimators

The class of linear conditionally unbiased estimators consists of all estimators of β_1 that are linear functions of $Y_1, \ldots, Y_n$ and that are unbiased, conditional on $X_1, \ldots, X_n$. The OLS estimator is a linear conditionally unbiased estimator.

The class of linear conditionally unbiased estimators   Estimators that are linear in $Y_1, \ldots, Y_n$ are weighted averages of $Y_1, \ldots, Y_n$. That is, if $\tilde{\beta}_1$ is a linear estimator, then it can be written as

$$\tilde{\beta}_1 = \sum_{i=1}^{n} a_i Y_i, \quad (\tilde{\beta}_1 \text{ is linear}) \tag{15.25}$$

where $a_1, \ldots, a_n$ are weights that can depend on $X_1, \ldots, X_n$ and on nonrandom constants but *not* on $Y_1, \ldots, Y_n$.

The estimator $\tilde{\beta}_1$ is conditionally unbiased if the mean of its conditional sampling distribution, given $X_1, \ldots, X_n$, is β_1. That is, the estimator $\tilde{\beta}_1$ is conditionally unbiased if

$$E(\tilde{\beta}_1 | X_1, \ldots, X_n) = \beta_1. \quad (\tilde{\beta}_1 \text{ is conditionally unbiased}) \tag{15.26}$$

The estimator $\tilde{\beta}_1$ is a linear conditionally unbiased estimator if it can be written in the form of Equation (15.25) (it is linear) and if Equation (15.26) holds (it is conditionally unbiased).

The OLS estimator $\hat{\beta}_1$ Is a linear conditionally unbiased estimator.   To show that $\hat{\beta}_1$ is linear, first note that, because $\sum_{i=1}^{n}(X_i - \overline{X}) = 0$ (by the definition of $\overline{X}$),

$$\sum_{i=1}^{n}(X_i - \overline{X})(Y_i - \overline{Y}) = \sum_{i=1}^{n}(X_i - \overline{X})Y_i - \overline{Y}\sum_{i=1}^{n}(X_i - \overline{X}) = \sum_{i=1}^{n}(X_i - \overline{X})Y_i.$$ Substituting this result into the formula for $\hat{\beta}_1$ in Equation (15.2) yields

$$\hat{\beta}_1 = \frac{\sum_{i=1}^{n}(X_i - \overline{X})Y_i}{\sum_{i=1}^{n}(X_i - \overline{X})^2} = \sum_{i=1}^{n}\hat{a}_i Y_i, \text{ where } \hat{a}_i = \frac{(X_i - \overline{X})}{\sum_{j=1}^{n}(X_j - \overline{X})^2}. \qquad (15.27)$$

Because the weights $\hat{a}_i$, $i = 1, \ldots, n$ in Equation (15.27) depend on $X_1, \ldots, X_n$ but not on $Y_1, \ldots, Y_n$, the OLS estimator $\hat{\beta}_1$ is a linear estimator.

Under the Gauss-Markov conditions, $\hat{\beta}_1$ is conditionally unbiased, and the variance of the conditional distribution of $\hat{\beta}_1$, given $X_1, \ldots, X_n$, is

$$\text{var}(\hat{\beta}_1 | X_1, \ldots, X_n) = \sigma_{\hat{\beta}_{1|X}}^2 = \frac{\sigma_u^2}{\sum_{i=1}^{n}(X_i - \overline{X})^2}. \qquad (15.28)$$

The result that $\hat{\beta}_1$ is conditionally unbiased was previously shown in Equation (15.20), and the variance formula in Equation (15.28) was previously derived as Equation (15.18). Equations (15.18) and (15.20) were derived under all five least squares assumptions in Key Concept 15.1, including normally distributed errors. However, by working through the derivations, you can verify that the results in Equations (15.18) and (15.20) hold under the weaker Gauss-Markov conditions and in particular do not require the errors to be normally distributed.

The Gauss-Markov Theorem

The **Gauss-Markov theorem** says that, under the Gauss-Markov conditions in Equation (15.24), the OLS estimator $\hat{\beta}_1$ has the smallest conditional variance, given $X_1, \ldots, X_n$, of all linear conditionally unbiased estimators of β_1; that is, the OLS estimator is BLUE. The Gauss-Markov theorem is stated in Key Concept 15.2 and proven in Appendix 15.3.

The sample average is the efficient linear estimator of E(Y).   An implication of the Gauss-Markov theorem is that the sample average, $\overline{Y}$, is the most efficient linear estimator of $E(Y_i)$ when $Y_1, \ldots, Y_n$ are i.i.d. To see this, consider the case of regression without an "X," so that the only regressor is the constant regressor $X_{0i} = 1$. Then the OLS estimator $\hat{\beta}_0 = \overline{Y}$. It follows that, under the Gauss-Markov assumptions, $\overline{Y}$ is BLUE. Note that the Gauss-Markov requirement that the error be homoskedastic is irrelevant in this case because there is no regressor, so it follows that $\overline{Y}$ is BLUE if $Y_1, \ldots, Y_n$ are i.i.d. This result was stated previously in Key Concept 3.3.

The Gauss-Markov Theorem for $\hat{\beta}_1$

Suppose that the Gauss-Markov conditions in Equation (15.24) hold. Then the OLS estimator $\hat{\beta}_1$ is BLUE, that is, $\text{var}(\hat{\beta}_1 | X_1, \ldots, X_n) \leq \text{var}(\widetilde{\beta}_1 | X_1, \ldots, X_n)$ for all linear conditionally unbiased estimators $\widetilde{\beta}_1$.

The Gauss-Markov theorem when X is nonrandom.   With a minor change in interpretation, the Gauss-Markov theorem also applies to nonrandom regressors, that is, to regressors that do not change their values over repeated samples. Specifically, if the second least squares assumption is replaced by the assumption that $X_1, \ldots, X_n$ are nonrandom and $u_1, \ldots, u_n$ are i.i.d., then the foregoing statement and proof of the Gauss-Markov theorem apply directly, except that all the "conditional on $X_1, \ldots, X_n$" statements are unnecessary because $X_1, \ldots, X_n$ take on the same values from one sample to the next.

15.6 Weighted Least Squares

If the errors are heteroskedastic, so that $\text{var}(u_i | X_i)$ is a function of X_i and the fourth least squares assumption in Key Concept 15.1 does not hold, then the Gauss-Markov theorem does not apply and the OLS estimator is not BLUE. This section presents an alternative estimation method, **weighted least squares (WLS)**, that can be used when there is heteroskedasticity.

WLS requires knowing quite a bit about the conditional variance function, $\text{var}(u_i | X_i)$. We consider two cases. In the first case, $\text{var}(u_i | X_i)$ is known up to a factor of proportionality, and WLS is BLUE. In the second case, the functional form of the $\text{var}(u_i | X_i)$ is known, but this functional form has some unknown parameters that must be estimated. Under some additional conditions, the asymptotic distribution of WLS in the second case is the same as if the parameters of the conditional variance function were in fact known, and in this sense the WLS estimator is asymptotically BLUE. The section concludes with a discussion of the practical advantages and disadvantages of handling heteroskedasticity using WLS or, alternatively, heteroskedasticity-robust standard errors.

WLS with Known Heteroskedasticity

Suppose that the conditional variance $\text{var}(u_i | X_i)$ is known up to a factor of proportionality, that is,

$$\text{var}(u_i | X_i) = \lambda h(X_i), \tag{15.29}$$

and λ is a constant and h is a known function. In this case, the WLS estimator is the estimator obtained by first dividing the dependent variable and regressor by the square root of h, then regressing this modified dependent variable on the modified regressor using OLS. Specifically, divide both sides of the single-variable regressor model by $\sqrt{h(X_i)}$ to obtain

$$\tilde{Y}_i = \beta_0 \tilde{X}_{0i} + \beta_1 \tilde{X}_{1i} + \tilde{u}_i, \tag{15.30}$$

where $\tilde{Y}_i = Y_i / \sqrt{h(X_i)}$, $\tilde{X}_{0i} = 1 / \sqrt{h(X_i)}$, $\tilde{X}_{1i} = X_i / \sqrt{h(X_i)}$, and $\tilde{u}_i = u_i / \sqrt{h(X_i)}$.

The **WLS estimator** is the OLS estimator of β_1 in Equation (15.30), that is, it is the estimator obtained by the OLS regression of $\tilde{Y}_i$ on $\tilde{X}_{0i}$ and $\tilde{X}_{1i}$, where the coefficient on $\tilde{X}_{0i}$ takes the place of the intercept in the unweighted regression.

Under the first three least squares assumptions in Key Concept 15.1 plus the known heteroskedasticity assumption in Equation (15.29), WLS is BLUE. The reason that the WLS estimator is BLUE is that weighting the variables has made the error term $\tilde{u}_i$ in the weighted regression homoskedastic. That is,

$$\text{var}(\tilde{u}_i | X_i) = \text{var}\left(\frac{u_i}{\sqrt{h(X_i)}} | X_i\right) = \frac{\text{var}(u_i | X_i)}{h(X_i)} = \frac{\lambda h(X_i)}{h(X_i)} = \lambda, \tag{15.31}$$

so the conditional variance of $\tilde{u}_i$, $\text{var}(\tilde{u}_i | X_i)$, is constant. Thus the first four least squares assumptions apply to Equation (15.30). Strictly speaking, the Gauss-Markov theorem of Section 15.2 was proven for Equation (15.1), which includes the intercept β_0, so it does not apply to Equation (15.30), in which the intercept is replaced by $\beta_0 \tilde{X}_{0i}$. However, the extension of the Gauss-Markov theorem for multiple regression (Section 16.5) does apply to estimation of β_1 in the weighted population regression, Equation (15.30). Accordingly, the OLS estimator of β_1 in Equation (15.30)—that is, the WLS estimators of β_1—is BLUE.

In practice, the function h typically is unknown, so neither the weighted variables in Equation (15.30) nor the WLS estimator can be computed. For this reason, the WLS estimator described here is sometimes called the **infeasible WLS** estimator. To implement WLS in practice, the function h must be estimated, the topic to which we now turn.

WLS with Heteroskedasticity of Known Functional Form

If the heteroskedasticity has a known functional form, then the heteroskedasticity function h can be estimated and the WLS estimator can be calculated using this estimated function.

Example #1: The variance of u is quadratic in X. Suppose that the conditional variance is known to be the quadratic function

$$\text{var}(u_i | X_i) = \theta_0 + \theta_1 X_i^2, \tag{15.32}$$

where θ_0 and θ_1 are unknown parameters, $\theta_0 > 0$, and $\theta_1 \geq 0$.

Because θ_0 and θ_1 are unknown, it is not possible to construct the weighted variables $\widetilde{Y}_i$, $\widetilde{X}_{0i}$, and $\widetilde{X}_{1i}$. It is, however, possible to estimate θ_0 and θ_1, and to use those estimates to compute estimates of $\text{var}(u_i | X_i)$. Let $\hat{\theta}_0$ and $\hat{\theta}_1$ be estimators of θ_0 and θ_1, and let $\widehat{\text{var}}(u_i | X_i) = \hat{\theta}_0 + \hat{\theta}_1 X_i^2$. Define the weighted regressors $\hat{\widetilde{Y}}_i = Y_i / \sqrt{\widehat{\text{var}}(u_i | X_i)}$, $\hat{\widetilde{X}}_{0i} = 1 / \sqrt{\widehat{\text{var}}(u_i | X_i)}$, and $\hat{\widetilde{X}}_{1i} = X_{1i} / \sqrt{\widehat{\text{var}}(u_i | X_i)}$. The WLS estimator is the OLS estimator of the coefficients in the regression of $\hat{\widetilde{Y}}_i$ on $\hat{\widetilde{X}}_{0i}$ and $\hat{\widetilde{X}}_{1i}$ (where $\beta_0 \hat{\widetilde{X}}_{0i}$ takes the place of the intercept β_0).

Implementation of this estimator requires estimating the conditional variance function, that is, estimating θ_0 and θ_1 in Equation (15.32). One way to estimate θ_0 and θ_1 consistently is to regress $\hat{u}_i^2$ on X_i^2 using OLS, where $\hat{u}_i^2$ is the square of the ith OLS residual.

Suppose that the conditional variance has the form in Equation (15.32) and that $\hat{\theta}_0$ and $\hat{\theta}_1$ are consistent estimators of θ_0 and θ_1. Under Assumptions 1–3 of Key Concept 15.1, plus additional moment conditions that arise because θ_0 and θ_1 are estimated, the asymptotic distribution of the WLS estimator is the same as if θ_0 and θ_1 were known. Thus the WLS estimator with θ_0 and θ_1 estimated has the same asymptotic distribution as the infeasible WLS estimator, and is in this sense asymptotically BLUE.

Because this method of WLS can be implemented by estimating unknown parameters of the conditional variance function, this method is sometimes called **feasible WLS** or **estimated WLS**.

Example #2: The variance depends on a third variable.   WLS also can be used when the conditional variance depends on a third variable, W_i, which does not appear in the regression function. Specifically, suppose that data are collected on three variables, Y_i, X_i, and W_i, $i = 1, \ldots, n$; the population regression function depends on X_i but not W_i; and the conditional variance depends on W_i, but not X_i. That is, the population regression function is $E(Y_i|X_i,W_i) = \beta_0 + \beta_1 X_i$ and the conditional variance is $\text{var}(u_i|X_i,W_i) = \lambda h(W_i)$, where λ is a constant and h is a function that must be estimated.

For example, suppose that a researcher is interested in modeling the relationship between the unemployment rate in a state and a state economic policy variable (X_i). The measured unemployment rate (Y_i), however, is a survey-based estimate of the true unemployment rate (Y_i^*). Thus Y_i measures Y_i^* with error, where the source of the error is conventional random survey error, so $Y_i = Y_i^* + v_i$, where v_i is the measurement error arising from the survey. In this example, it is plausible that the survey sample size, W_i, is not itself a determinant of the true state unemployment rate. Thus the population regression function does not depend on W_i, that is, $E(Y_i^*|X_i,W_i) = \beta_0 + \beta_1 X_i$. We therefore have the two equations

$$Y_i^* = \beta_0 + \beta_1 X_i + u_i^*, \text{ and} \tag{15.33}$$

$$Y_i = Y_i^* + v_i, \tag{15.34}$$

where Equation (15.33) models the relationship between the state economic policy variable and the true state unemployment rate and Equation (15.34) represents the relationship between the measured unemployment rate Y_i and the true unemployment rate Y_i^*.

The model in Equations (15.33) and (15.34) can lead to a population regression in which the conditional variance of the error depends on W_i but not on X_i. The error term u_i^* in Equation (15.33) represents other factors omitted from this regression, while the error term v_i in Equation (15.34) represents measurement error arising from the unemployment rate survey. If u_i^* is homoskedastic, then $\text{var}(u_i^*|X_i,W_i) = \sigma_{u^*}^2$ is constant. The survey error variance, however, depends inversely on the survey sample size W_i, that is, $\text{var}(v_i|X_i,W_i) = a/W_i$, where a is a constant. Because v_i is random survey error, it is safely assumed to be uncorrelated with u_i^*, so $\text{var}(u_i^* + v_i \mid X_i, W_i) = \sigma_{u^*}^2 + a/W_i$. Thus, substituting Equation (15.33) into Equation (15.34) leads to the regression model with heteroskedasticity

$$Y_i = \beta_0 + \beta_1 X_i + u_i, \tag{15.35}$$

$$\text{var}(u_i \mid X_i, W_i) = \theta_0 + \theta_1(1/W_i) \tag{15.36}$$

where $u_i = u_i^* + v_i$, $\theta_0 = \sigma_{u^*}^2$, and $\theta_1 = a$, and $E(u_i \mid X_i, W_i) = 0$.

If θ_0 and θ_1 were known, then the conditional variance function in Equation (15.36) could be used to estimate β_0 and β_1 by WLS. In this example, θ_0 and θ_1 are unknown, but they can be estimated by regressing the squared OLS residual (from OLS estimation of Equation (15.35)) on $1/W_i$. Then the estimated conditional variance function can be used to construct the weights in feasible WLS.

It should be stressed that it is critical that $E(u_i \mid X_i, W_i) = 0$; if not, the weighted errors will have nonzero conditional mean and WLS will be inconsistent. Said differently, if W_i is in fact a determinant of Y_i, then Equation (15.35) should be a multiple regression equation that includes both X_i and W_i. If W_i and X_i are uncorrelated, if W_i is a determinant of Y_i, and if W_i is excluded from the regression, then OLS is unbiased but WLS is inconsistent.

General method of feasible WLS.   In general, feasible WLS proceeds in four steps:

1. Regress Y_i on X_i by OLS, and obtain the OLS residuals $\hat{u}_i$, $i = 1, \ldots, n$.

2. Estimate a model of the conditional variance function $\text{var}(u_i \mid X_i)$. For example, if the conditional variance function has the form in Equation (15.32), this entails regressing $\hat{u}_i^2$ on X_i^2. In general, this step entails estimating a function for the conditional variance, $\text{var}(u_i \mid X_i)$.

3. Use the estimated function to compute predicted values of the conditional variance function, $\widehat{\text{var}}(u_i \mid X_i)$.

4. Weight the dependent variable and regressor (including the intercept) by the inverse of the square root of the estimated conditional variance function.

5. Estimate the coefficients of the weighted regression by OLS; the resulting estimators are the WLS estimators.

Regression software packages typically include optional weighted least squares commands that automate the fourth and fifth of these steps.

Heteroskedasticity-Robust Standard Errors or WLS?

There are two ways to handle heteroskedasticity: estimating β_0 and β_1 by WLS, or estimating β_0 and β_1 by OLS and using heteroskedasticity-robust standard errors. Deciding which approach to use in practice requires weighing the advantages and disadvantages of each.

The advantage of WLS is that it is more efficient than the OLS estimator of the coefficients in the original regressors, at least asymptotically. The disadvantage of WLS is that it requires knowing the conditional variance function and estimating its parameters. If the conditional variance function has the quadratic form in Equation (15.32), this is easily done. In practice, however, the functional form of the conditional variance function is rarely known. Moreover, if the functional form is incorrect, then the standard errors computed by WLS regression routines are invalid in the sense that they lead to incorrect statistical inferences (tests have the wrong size).

The advantage of using heteroskedasticity-robust standard errors is that they produce asymptotically valid inferences even if you do not know the form of the conditional variance function. An additional advantage is that heteroskedasticity-robust standard errors are readily computed as an option in modern regression packages, so that no additional effort is needed to safeguard against this threat. The disadvantage of heteroskedasticity-robust standard errors is that the OLS estimator will have a larger variance than the WLS estimator (based on the true conditional variance function), at least asymptotically.

In practice, the functional form of $\text{var}(u_i | X_i)$ is rarely if ever known, which poses a problem for using WLS in real-world applications. This problem is difficult enough with a single regressor, but in applications with multiple regressors it is even more difficult to know the functional form of the conditional variance. For this reason, practical use of WLS confronts imposing challenges. In contrast, in modern statistical packages it is simple to use heteroskedasticity-robust standard errors, and the resulting inferences are reliable under very general assumptions; in particular, heteroskedasticity-robust standard errors can be used without needing to specify a functional form for the conditional variance. For these reasons, it is our opinion that, despite the theoretical appeal of WLS, heteroskedasticity-robust standard errors provide a better way to handle potential heteroskedasticity in most applications.

Summary

1. The asymptotic normality of the OLS estimator, combined with the consistency of heteroskedasticity-robust standard errors, implies that, if the first three least squares assumptions in Key Concept 15.1 hold, then the heteroskedasticity-robust t-statistic has an asymptotic standard normal distribution under the null hypothesis.

2. If the regression errors are i.i.d. and normally distributed, conditional on the regressors, then $\hat{\beta}_1$ has an exact normal sampling distribution, conditional on the regressors. In addition, the homoskedasticity-only t-statistic has an exact Student t_{n-2} sampling distribution under the null hypothesis.

3. If, in addition to the first three assumptions in Key Concept 15.1, the regression errors are homoskedastic, then the OLS estimator $\hat{\beta}_1$ is efficient (has the smallest variance) among all linear conditionally unbiased estimators of β_1. That is, the OLS estimator is the best linear conditionally unbiased estimator (OLS is BLUE).

4. The weighted least squares (WLS) estimator is OLS applied to a weighted regression, where all variables are weighted by the square root of the inverse of the conditional variance, $\text{var}(u_i | X_i)$, or its estimate. Although the WLS estimator is asymptotically more efficient than OLS, to implement WLS you must know the functional form of the conditional variance function, which usually is a tall order.

Key Terms

convergence in probability (578)
consistent estimator (578)
convergence in distribution (580)
asymptotic distribution (580)
Slutsky's theorem (581)
continuous mapping theorem (581)
BLUE (588)
Gauss-Markov conditions (588)

Gauss-Markov theorem (590)
weighted least squares (WLS) (591)
WLS estimator (592)
infeasible WLS (593)
feasible WLS (593)
normal p.d.f. (601)
bivariate normal p.d.f. (602)

Review the Concepts

15.1 Suppose that assumption 4 in Key Concept 15.1 is true, but you construct a 95% confidence interval for β_1 using the heteroskedastic-robust standard error in a large sample. Would this confidence interval be valid asymptotically, in the sense that it contained the true value of β_1 in 95% of all repeated samples for large n? Suppose instead that assumption 4 in Key Concept 15.1 is false, but you construct a 95% confidence interval for β_1 using the homoskedasticity-only standard error formula in a large sample. Would this confidence interval be valid asymptotically?

15.2 Suppose that A_n is a random variable that converges in probability to 3. Suppose that B_n is a random variable that converges in distribution to a standard normal. What is the asymptotic distribution of A_nB_n? Use this asymptotic distribution to compute an approximate value of $\Pr(A_nB_n < 2)$.

15.3 Suppose that Y and X are related by the regression $Y = 1.0 + 2.0X + u$. A researcher has observations on Y and X, where $0 \le X \le 20$, where the conditional variance is $\text{var}(u_i|X_i = x) = 1$ for $0 \le x \le 10$ and $\text{var}(u_i|X_i = x) = 16$ for $10 < x \le 20$. Draw a hypothetical scatterplot of the observations (X_i, Y_i), $i = 1, \ldots, n$. Does WLS put more weight on observations with $x \le 10$ or $x > 10$? Why?

15.4 Instead of using WLS, the researcher in the previous problem decides to compute the OLS estimator using only the observations for which $x \le 10$, then using only the observations for which $x > 10$, then average the two OLS of estimators. Is this better than WLS?

Exercises

15.1 Consider the regression model without an intercept term, $Y_i = \beta_1X_i + u_i$ (so the true value of the intercept, β_0, is zero).

 a. Derive the least squares estimator of β_1 for the restricted regression model $Y_i = \beta_1X_i + u_i$. This is called the restricted least squares estimator ($\hat{\beta}_1^{RLS}$) of β_1 because it is estimated under a restriction, which in this case is $\beta_0 = 0$.

 b. Derive the asymptotic distribution of $\hat{\beta}_1^{RLS}$ under assumptions 1–3 of Key Concept 15.1.

 c. Show that $\hat{\beta}_1^{RLS}$ is linear (Equation (15.25)) and, under assumptions 1 and 2 of Key Concept 15.1, conditionally unbiased (Equation (15.26)).

 d. Derive the conditional variance of $\hat{\beta}_1^{RLS}$ under the Gauss-Markov conditions.

 e. Compare the conditional variance of $\hat{\beta}_1^{RLS}$ in (d) to the conditional variance of the OLS estimator $\hat{\beta}_1$ (from the regression including an intercept) under the Gauss-Markov conditions. Which estimator is more efficient? Use the formulas for the variances to explain why.

f. Derive the exact sampling distribution of $\hat{\beta}_1^{RLS}$ under assumptions 1–5 of Key Concept 15.1.

g. Now consider the estimator $\tilde{\beta}_1 = \sum_{i=1}^{n} Y_i / \sum_{i=1}^{n} X_i$. Derive an expression for $\text{var}(\tilde{\beta}_1 | X_1, \ldots, X_n) - \text{var}(\hat{\beta}_1^{RLS} | X_1, \ldots, X_n)$ under the Gauss-Markov conditions, and use this expression to show that $\text{var}(\tilde{\beta}_1 | X_1, \ldots, X_n) \geq \text{var}(\hat{\beta}_1^{RLS} | X_1, \ldots, X_n)$.

*15.2 Suppose that (X_i, Y_i) are i.i.d. with finite fourth moments. Prove that the sample covariance is a consistent estimator of the population covariance, that is, $s_{XY} \xrightarrow{p} \sigma_{XY}$, where s_{XY} is defined in Equation (3.22). (*Hint:* Use the strategy of Appendix 3.3 and the Cauchy-Schwartz inequality.)

15.3 This exercise fills in the details of the derivation of the asymptotic distribution of $\hat{\beta}_1$ given in Appendix 4.3.

a. Use Equation (15.19) to derive the expression

$$\sqrt{n}(\hat{\beta}_1 - \beta_1) = \frac{\sqrt{\frac{1}{n}\sum_{i=1}^{n} v_i}}{\frac{1}{n}\sum_{i=1}^{n}(X_i - \overline{X})^2} - \frac{(\overline{X} - \mu_X)\sqrt{\frac{1}{n}\sum_{i=1}^{n} u_i}}{\frac{1}{n}\sum_{i=1}^{n}(X_i - \overline{X})^2}, \tag{15.37}$$

where $v_i = (X_i - \mu_X)u_i$.

b. Use the central limit theorem, the law of large numbers, and Slutsky's theorem to show that the final term in Equation (15.37) converges in probability to zero.

c. Use the Cauchy-Schwarz inequality and the third least squares assumption in Key Concept 15.1 to prove that $\text{var}(v_i) < \infty$. Does the term $\sqrt{\frac{1}{n}\sum_{i=1}^{n} v_i / \sigma_v}$ satisfy the central limit theorem?

d. Apply the central limit theorem and Slutsky's theorem to obtain the result in Equation (15.12).

*15.4 Show the following results:

a. Show that $\sqrt{n}(\hat{\beta}_1 - \beta_1) \xrightarrow{d} N(0, a^2)$, where a^2 is a constant, implies that $\hat{\beta}_1$ is consistent. (*Hint:* Use Slutsky's theorem.)

b. Show that $s_u^2 / \sigma_u^2 \xrightarrow{p} 1$ implies that $s_u / \sigma_u \xrightarrow{p} 1$.

15.5 Suppose that W is a random variable with $E(W^4) < \infty$. Show that $E(W^2) < \infty$.

15.6 Show that if $\hat{\beta}_1$ is conditionally unbiased then it is unbiased; that is, show that if $E(\hat{\beta}_1 | X_1, \ldots, X_n) = \beta_1$, then $E(\hat{\beta}_1) = \beta_1$.

15.7 Suppose that X and u are continuous random variables and $X_i, u_i, i = 1, \ldots, n$ are i.i.d.

    a. Show that the joint probability density function (p.d.f.) of u_i, u_j, X_i, X_j can be written as $f(u_i, X_i)f(u_j, X_j)$ for $i \neq j$ where $f(u_i, X_i)$ is the joint p.d.f. of u_i and X_i.

    b. Show that $E(u_i u_j | X_i, X_j) = E(u_i | X_i)E(u_j | X_j)$ for $i \neq j$.

    c. Show that $E(u_i | X_1, \ldots, X_n) = E(u_i | X_i)$.

    d. Show that $E(u_i u_j | X_1, X_2, \ldots, X_n) = E(u_i | X_i)E(u_j | X_j)$ for $i \neq j$.

15.8 Consider the regression model in Key Concept 15.1 and suppose that assumptions 1, 2, 3, and 5 hold. Suppose that assumption 4 is replaced by the assumption that $\text{var}(u_i | X_i) = \theta_0 + \theta_1 | X_i |$, where $| X_i |$ is the absolute value of X_i, $\theta_0 > 0$, and $\theta_1 \geq 0$.

    a. Is the OLS estimator of β_1 BLUE?

    b. Suppose that θ_0 and θ_1 are known. What is the BLUE estimator of β_1?

    c. Derive the exact sampling distribution of the OLS estimator, $\hat{\beta}_1$, conditional on $X_1, \ldots, X_n$.

    d. Derive the exact sampling distribution of the WLS estimator (treating θ_0 and θ_1 as known) of β_1, conditional on $X_1, \ldots, X_n$.

15.9 Prove Equation (15.16) under assumptions 1 and 2 of Key Concept 15.1 plus the assumption that X_i and u_i have eight moments.

*15.10 Let $\hat{\theta}$ be an estimator of the parameter θ, where $\hat{\theta}$ might be biased. Show that if $E[(\hat{\theta} - \theta)^2] \longrightarrow 0$ as $n \longrightarrow \infty$ (that is, the mean squared error of $\hat{\theta}$ tends to zero), then $\hat{\theta} \xrightarrow{p} \theta$. (*Hint*: Use (15.48) with $W = \hat{\theta} - \theta$.)

APPENDIX

15.1

The Normal and Related Distributions and Moments of Continuous Random Variables

This appendix defines and discusses the normal and F distributions. The definitions of the chi-squared and Student t distributions, given in Section 2.4, are restated here for convenient reference. We begin by presenting definitions of probabilities and moments involving continuous random variables.

Probabilities and Moments of Continuous Random Variables

As discussed in Section 2.1, if Y is a continuous random variable then its probability is summarized by its probability density function (p.d.f.). The probability that Y falls between two values is the area under its p.d.f. between those two values. As in the discrete case, the expected value of Y is its probability-weighted average value, where now the weights are given by the p.d.f.. Because Y is continuous, however, the mathematical expressions for its probabilities and expected values involve integrals rather than the summations that are appropriate for discrete random variables.

Let f_Y denote the probability density function of Y. Because probabilities cannot be negative, $f_Y(y) \geq 0$ for all y. The probability that Y falls between a and b (where $a < b$) is,

$$\Pr(a \leq Y \leq b) = \int_a^b f_Y(y)dy. \tag{15.38}$$

Because Y must take on some value on the real line, $\Pr(-\infty \leq Y \leq \infty) = 1$, which implies that $\int_{-\infty}^{\infty} f_Y(y)dy = 1$.

Expected values and moments of continuous random variables, like those of discrete random variables, are probability-weighted averages of their values, except that summations (for example, the summation in Equation (2.4)) are replaced by integrals. Accordingly, the expected value of Y is,

$$E(Y) = \mu_Y = \int y f_Y(y)dy, \tag{15.39}$$

where the range of integration is the set of values for which f_Y is nonzero. The variance is the expected value of $(Y - \mu_Y)^2$, and the rth moment of a random variable is the expected value of Y^r. Thus,

$$\text{var}(Y) = E(Y - \mu_Y)^2 = \int (y-\mu_Y)^2 f_Y(y)dy, \text{ and} \tag{15.40}$$

$$E(Y^r) = \int y^r f_Y(y)dy. \tag{15.41}$$

The Normal Distribution

The normal distribution for a single variable.   The probability density function of a normally distributed random variable (the **normal p.d.f.**) is

$$f_Y(y) = \frac{1}{\sigma_Y \sqrt{2\pi}} \exp\left[-\frac{1}{2}\left(\frac{y - \mu_Y}{\sigma_Y}\right)^2\right], \tag{15.42}$$

where $\exp(x)$ is the exponential function of x. The factor $1/(\sigma_Y \sqrt{2\pi})$ in Equation (15.42) ensures that $\Pr(-\infty \leq Y \leq \infty) = \int_{-\infty}^{\infty} f_Y(y)dy = 1$.

When $\mu_Y = 0$ and $\sigma_Y^2 = 1$, the normal distribution is called the standard normal distribution. The standard normal p.d.f. is denoted by ϕ and the standard normal c.d.f. is denoted by Φ. Thus the standard normal density is $\phi(y) = \frac{1}{\sqrt{2\pi}} \exp\left(-\frac{y^2}{2}\right)$ and $\Phi(y) = \int_{-\infty}^{y} \phi(s) ds$.

The bivariate normal distribution. The **bivariate normal p.d.f.** for the two random variables X and Y is

$$g_{X,Y}(x,y) = \frac{1}{2\pi\sigma_X\sigma_Y\sqrt{1-\rho_{XY}^2}} \tag{15.43}$$

$$\times \exp\left\{\frac{1}{-2(1-\rho_{XY}^2)}\left[\left(\frac{x-\mu_X}{\sigma_X}\right)^2 - 2\rho_{XY}\left(\frac{x-\mu_X}{\sigma_X}\right)\left(\frac{y-\mu_Y}{\sigma_Y}\right) + \left(\frac{y-\mu_Y}{\sigma_Y}\right)^2\right]\right\}$$

where ρ_{XY} is the correlation between X and Y.

When X and Y are uncorrelated ($\rho_{XY} = 0$), $g_{X,Y}(x,y) = f_X(x)f_Y(y)$, where f is the normal density given in Equation (15.42). This proves that if X and Y are jointly normally distributed and are uncorrelated, then they are independently distributed. This is a special feature of the normal distribution that is typically not true for other distributions.

The multivariate normal distribution extends the bivariate normal distribution to handle more than two random variables. This distribution is most conveniently stated using matrices and is presented in Appendix 16.1.

The conditional normal distribution. Suppose that X and Y are jointly normally distributed. Then the conditional distribution of Y given X is normal, with mean $\mu_{Y|X} = \mu_Y + (\sigma_{XY}/\sigma_X^2)(X - \mu_X)$ and variance $\sigma_{Y|X}^2 = (1 - \rho_{XY}^2)\sigma_Y^2$. The mean of this conditional distribution, conditional on $X = x$, is a linear function of x, and the variance does not depend on x.

Related Distributions

The chi-squared distribution. Let $Z_1, Z_2, \ldots, Z_n$ be n i.i.d standard normal random variables. The random variable

$$W = \sum_{i=1}^{n} Z_i^2 \tag{15.44}$$

has a chi-squared distribution with n degrees of freedom. This distribution is denoted χ_n^2. Because $E(Z_i^2) = 1$, $E(W) = n$.

The Student t distribution. Let Z have a standard normal distribution, let W have a χ_m^2 distribution, and let Z and W be independently distributed. Then the random variable

$$t = \frac{Z}{\sqrt{W/m}} \tag{15.45}$$

has a Student t distribution with m degrees of freedom, denoted t_m. The t_∞ distribution is the standard normal distribution.

The F distribution.   Let W_1 and W_2 be independent random variables with chi-squared distributions with respective degrees of freedom n_1 and n_2. Then the random variable

$$F = \frac{W_1 / n_1}{W_2 / n_2} \qquad (15.46)$$

has an F distribution with (n_1, n_2) degrees of freedom. This distribution is denoted F_{n_1, n_2}.

The F distribution depends on the numerator degrees of freedom n_1 and the denominator degrees of freedom n_2. As number of degrees of freedom in the denominator gets large, the F_{n_1, n_2} distribution is well approximated by a $\chi^2_{n_1}$ distribution, divided by n_1. In the limit, the $F_{n_1, \infty}$ distribution is the same as the $\chi^2_{n_1}$ distribution, divided by n_1, that is, it is the same as the $\chi^2_{n_1}/n_1$ distribution.

APPENDIX
15.2 | Two Inequalities

This appendix states and proves Chebychev's inequality and the Cauchy-Schwarz inequality.

Chebychev's Inequality

Chebychev's inequality uses the variance of the random variable V to bound the probability that V is farther than $\pm\delta$ from its mean, where δ is a positive constant:

$$\Pr(|V - \mu_V| \geq \delta) \leq \operatorname{var}(V)/\delta^2 \qquad \text{(Chebychev's inequality)}. \qquad (15.47)$$

To prove Equation (15.47), let $W = V - \mu_V$, let f be the p.d.f. of W, and let δ be any positive number. Now,

$$
\begin{aligned}
E(W^2) &= \int_{-\infty}^{\infty} w^2 f(w) dw \\
&= \int_{-\infty}^{-\delta} w^2 f(w) dw + \int_{-\delta}^{\delta} w^2 f(w) dw + \int_{\delta}^{\infty} w^2 f(w) dw \\
&\geq \int_{-\infty}^{-\delta} w^2 f(w) dw + \int_{\delta}^{\infty} w^2 f(w) dw \qquad (15.48) \\
&\geq \delta^2 \left[\int_{-\infty}^{-\delta} f(w) dw + \int_{\delta}^{\infty} f(w) dw \right] \\
&= \delta^2 \Pr(|W| \geq \delta)
\end{aligned}
$$

where the first equality is the definition of $E(W^2)$, the second equality holds because the ranges of integration divides up the real line, the first inequality holds because the term that was dropped is nonnegative, the second inequality holds because $w^2 \geq \delta^2$ over the range of integration, and the final equality holds by the definition of $\Pr(|W| \geq \delta)$. Substituting $W = V - \mu_V$ into the final expression, noting that $E(W^2) = E[(V - \mu_V)^2] = \text{var}(V)$, and rearranging yields the inequality (15.47). If V is discrete, this proof applies with summations replacing integrals.

The Cauchy-Schwarz Inequality

The Cauchy-Schwarz inequality is an extension of the correlation inequality, $|\rho_{XY}| \leq 1$, to incorporate nonzero means. The Cauchy-Schwarz inequality is

$$|E(XY)| \leq \sqrt{E(X^2)E(Y^2)} \text{ (Cauchy-Schwarz inequality).} \qquad (15.49)$$

The proof of Equation (15.49) is similar to the proof of the correlation inequality in Appendix 2.1. Let $W = Y + bX$, where b is a constant. Then $E(W^2) = E(Y^2) + 2bE(XY) + b^2E(X^2)$. Now let $b = -E(XY)/E(X^2)$, so that (after simplification) the expression becomes $E(W^2) = E(Y^2) - [E(XY)]^2/E(X^2)$. Because $E(W^2) \geq 0$ (since $W^2 \geq 0$), it must be the case that $[E(XY)]^2 \leq E(X^2)E(Y^2)$, and the Cauchy-Schwarz inequality follows by taking the square root.

APPENDIX

15.3 | Proof of the Gauss-Markov Theorem

We start by deriving some facts that hold for all linear unbiased estimators, that is, for all estimators $\widetilde{\beta}_1$ satisfying Equations (15.25) and (15.26). Substituting $Y_i = \beta_0 + \beta_1 X_i + u_i$ into $\widetilde{\beta}_1 = \sum_{i=1}^{n} a_i Y_i$ and collecting terms, we have that

$$\widetilde{\beta}_1 = \beta_0 \left(\sum_{i=1}^{n} a_i \right) + \beta_1 \left(\sum_{i=1}^{n} a_i X_i \right) + \sum_{i=1}^{n} a_i u_i. \qquad (15.50)$$

By the first Gauss-Markov condition, $E(\sum_{i=1}^{n} a_i u_i | X_1, \ldots, X_n) = \sum_{i=1}^{n} a_i E(u_i | X_1, \ldots, X_n) = 0$; thus, taking conditional expectations of both sides of Equation (15.50) yields $E(\widetilde{\beta}_1 | X_1, \ldots, X_n) = \beta_0 \left(\sum_{i=1}^{n} a_i \right) + \beta_1 \left(\sum_{i=1}^{n} a_i X_i \right)$. Because $\widetilde{\beta}_1$ is conditionally unbiased by assumption, it must be that

$\beta_0 \left(\sum_{i=1}^{n} a_i\right) + \beta_1 \left(\sum_{i=1}^{n} a_i X_i\right) = \beta_1$, but for this equality to hold for all values of β_0 and β_1 it must be the case that, for $\tilde{\beta}_1$ to be conditionally unbiased,

$$\sum_{i=1}^{n} a_i = 0 \text{ and } \sum_{i=1}^{n} a_i X_i = 1. \tag{15.51}$$

Under the Gauss-Markov conditions, the variance of $\tilde{\beta}_1$, conditional on $X_1, \ldots, X_n$, has a simple form. Substituting Equation (15.51) into Equation (15.50) yields $\tilde{\beta}_1 - \beta_1 = \sum_{i=1}^{n} a_i u_i$. Thus, $\text{var}(\tilde{\beta}_1 | X_1, \ldots, X_n) = \text{var}(\sum_{i=1}^{n} a_i u_i | X_1, \ldots, X_n) = \sum_{i=1}^{n}\sum_{j=1}^{n} a_i a_j \text{cov}(u_i, u_j | X_1, \ldots, X_n)$; applying the second and third Gauss-Markov conditions, the cross terms in the double summation vanish and the expression for the conditional variance simplifies to

$$\text{var}(\tilde{\beta}_1 | X_1, \ldots, X_n) = \sigma_u^2 \sum_{i=1}^{n} a_i^2. \tag{15.52}$$

Note that Equations (15.51) and (15.52) apply to $\hat{\beta}_1$ with weights $a_i = \hat{a}_i$, given in Equation (15.27).

We now show that the two restrictions in Equation (15.51) and the expression for the conditional variance in Equation (15.52) imply that the conditional variance of $\tilde{\beta}_1$ exceeds the conditional variance of $\hat{\beta}_1$ unless $\tilde{\beta}_1 = \hat{\beta}_1$. Let $a_i = \hat{a}_i + d_i$ so $\sum_{i=1}^{n} a_i^2 = \sum_{i=1}^{n}(\hat{a}_i + d_i)^2 = \sum_{i=1}^{n} \hat{a}_i^2 + 2\sum_{i=1}^{n} \hat{a}_i d_i + \sum_{i=1}^{n} d_i^2$.

Using the definition of $\hat{a}_i$, we have that

$$\sum_{i=1}^{n} \hat{a}_i d_i = \sum_{i=1}^{n}(X_i - \overline{X}) d_i / \sum_{j=1}^{n}(X_j - \overline{X})^2 = \left(\sum_{i=1}^{n} d_i X_i - \overline{X}\sum_{i=1}^{n} d_i\right) / \sum_{j=1}^{n}(X_j - \overline{X})^2 =$$
$$\left[\left(\sum_{i=1}^{n} a_i X_i - \sum_{i=1}^{n} \hat{a}_i X_i\right) - \overline{X}\left(\sum_{i=1}^{n} a_i - \sum_{i=1}^{n} \hat{a}_i\right)\right] / \sum_{j=1}^{n}(X_j - \overline{X})^2 = 0,$$

where the final equality follows from Equation (15.51) (which holds for both a_i and $\hat{a}_i$). Thus $\sigma_u^2 \sum_{i=1}^{n} a_i^2 = \sigma_u^2 \sum_{i=1}^{n} \hat{a}_i + \sigma_u^2 \sum_{i=1}^{n} d_i^2 = \text{var}(\hat{\beta}_1 | X_1, \ldots, X_n) + \sigma_u^2 \sum_{i=1}^{n} d_i^2$; substituting this result into Equation (15.51) yields

$$\text{var}(\tilde{\beta}_1 | X_1, \ldots, X_n) - \text{var}(\hat{\beta}_1 | X_1, \ldots, X_n) = \sigma_u^2 \sum_{i=1}^{n} d_i^2. \tag{15.53}$$

Thus $\tilde{\beta}_1$ has a greater conditional variance than $\hat{\beta}_1$ if d_i is nonzero for any $i = 1, \ldots, n$. But if $d_i = 0$ for all i, then $a_i = \hat{a}_i$ and $\tilde{\beta}_1 = \hat{\beta}_1$, which proves that OLS is BLUE.

CHAPTER 16

The Theory of Multiple Regression

This chapter provides an introduction to the theory of multiple regression analysis. The chapter has three objectives. The first is to present the multiple regression model in matrix form, which leads to compact formulas for the OLS estimator and test statistics. The second objective is to characterize the sampling distribution of the OLS estimator, both in large samples (using asymptotic theory) and in small samples (if the errors are homoskedastic and normally distributed). The third objective is to study the theory of efficient estimation of the coefficients of the multiple regression model and to describe generalized least squares (GLS), a method for estimating the regression coefficients efficiently when the errors are heteroskedastic and/or correlated across observations.

The chapter begins by laying out the multiple regression model and the OLS estimator in matrix form in Section 16.1. This section also presents the extended least squares assumptions for the multiple regression model. The first four of these assumptions are the same as the least squares assumptions of Key Concept 5.4, and underlie the asymptotic distributions used to justify the procedures described in Chapter 5. The remaining two extended least squares assumptions are stronger and permit us to explore in more detail the theoretical properties of the OLS estimator in the multiple regression model.

The next three sections examine the sampling distribution of the OLS estimator and test statistics. Section 16.2 presents the asymptotic distributions of the OLS estimator and t-statistic under the least squares assumptions of Key Concept 5.4. Section 16.3 unifies and generalizes the tests of hypotheses involving multiple coefficients presented in Sections 5.7 and 5.8, and provides the asymptotic distribution of the resulting F-statistic. In Section 16.4, we examine the exact sampling distributions of the OLS estimator and test statistics in the special case that the errors are homoskedastic and normally distributed. Although the assumption of homoskedastic normal errors is implausible in most econometric applications, the exact sampling distributions are of theoretical interest, and p-values computed using these distributions often appear in the output of regression software.

The final two sections turn to the theory of efficient estimation of the coefficients of the multiple regression model. Section 16.5 generalizes the Gauss-Markov theorem to multiple regression. Section 16.6 develops the method of generalized least squares (GLS).

Mathematical prerequisite.   The treatment of the linear model in this chapter uses matrix notation and the basic tools of linear algebra, and assumes that the reader has taken an introductory course in linear algebra. Appendix 16.1 reviews vectors, matrices, and the matrix operations used in this chapter. In addition, multivariate calculus is used in Section 16.1 to derive the OLS estimator.

16.1 The Linear Multiple Regression Model and OLS Estimator in Matrix Form

The linear multiple regression model and the OLS estimator can each be represented compactly using matrix notation.

The Multiple Regression Model in Matrix Notation

The population multiple regression model (Key Concept 5.2) is

$$Y_i = \beta_0 + \beta_1 X_{1i} + \beta_2 X_{2i} + \cdots + \beta_k X_{ki} + u_i, \, i = 1, \ldots, n. \qquad (16.1)$$

To write this in matrix form, define the following vectors and matrices:

$$\boldsymbol{Y} = \begin{pmatrix} Y_1 \\ Y_2 \\ \vdots \\ Y_n \end{pmatrix}, \boldsymbol{U} = \begin{pmatrix} u_1 \\ u_2 \\ \vdots \\ u_n \end{pmatrix}, \boldsymbol{X} = \begin{pmatrix} 1 & X_{11} & \cdots & X_{k1} \\ 1 & X_{12} & \cdots & X_{k2} \\ \vdots & \vdots & \ddots & \vdots \\ 1 & X_{1n} & \cdots & X_{kn} \end{pmatrix} = \begin{pmatrix} \boldsymbol{X}_1' \\ \boldsymbol{X}_2' \\ \vdots \\ \boldsymbol{X}_n' \end{pmatrix},$$

$$\text{and } \boldsymbol{\beta} = \begin{pmatrix} \beta_0 \\ \beta_1 \\ \vdots \\ \beta_k \end{pmatrix}, \tag{16.2}$$

so that $\boldsymbol{Y}$ is $n \times 1$, $\boldsymbol{X}$ is $n \times (k + 1)$, $\boldsymbol{U}$ is $n \times 1$, and $\boldsymbol{\beta}$ is $(k + 1) \times 1$. Throughout we denote matrices and vectors by bold type. In this notation,

- $\boldsymbol{Y}$ is the $n \times 1$ dimensional vector of n observations on the dependent variable.
- $\boldsymbol{X}$ is the $n \times (k + 1)$ dimensional matrix of n observations on the $k + 1$ regressors (including the "constant" regressor for the intercept).
- The $(k + 1) \times 1$ dimensional column vector $\boldsymbol{X}_i$ is the ith observation on the $k + 1$ regressors, that is, $\boldsymbol{X}_i' = (1 \ X_{1i} \cdots X_{ki})$, where $\boldsymbol{X}_i'$ denotes the transpose of $\boldsymbol{X}_i$.
- $\boldsymbol{U}$ is the $n \times 1$ dimensional vector of the n error terms.
- $\boldsymbol{\beta}$ is the $(k + 1) \times 1$ dimensional vector of the $k + 1$ unknown regression coefficients.

The multiple regression model in Equation (16.1) for the ith observation, written using the vectors $\boldsymbol{\beta}$ and $\boldsymbol{X}_i$, is

$$Y_i = \boldsymbol{X}_i'\boldsymbol{\beta} + u_i, \ i = 1, \ldots, n. \tag{16.3}$$

In Equation (16.3), the first regressor is the "constant" regressor that always equals 1, and its coefficient is the intercept. Thus the intercept does not appear separately in Equation (16.3), rather, it is the first element of the coefficient vector $\boldsymbol{\beta}$.

Stacking all n observations in Equation (16.3) yields the multiple regression model in matrix form:

$$\boldsymbol{Y} = \boldsymbol{X}\boldsymbol{\beta} + \boldsymbol{U}. \tag{16.4}$$

The Extended Least Squares Assumptions in the Multiple Regression Model

The linear regression model with multiple regressors is

$$Y_i = \mathbf{X}_i'\boldsymbol{\beta} + u_i, \ i = 1, \ldots, n. \tag{16.5}$$

The extended least squares assumptions are

1. $E(u_i|\mathbf{X}_i) = 0$ (u_i has conditional mean zero);
2. $(\mathbf{X}_i, Y_i)$, $i = 1, \ldots, n$ are independently and identically distributed (i.i.d.) draws from their joint distribution;
3. $\mathbf{X}_i$ and u_i have nonzero finite fourth moments;
4. $\mathbf{X}$ has full column rank (there is no perfect multicollinearity);
5. $\mathrm{var}(u_i|\mathbf{X}_i) = \sigma_u^2$ (homoskedasticity);
6. the conditional distribution of u_i given $\mathbf{X}_i$ is normal (normal errors).

Key Concept 16.1

The Extended Least Squares Assumptions

The extended least squares assumptions for the multiple regressor model are the four least squares assumptions for the multiple regression model in Key Concept 5.4, plus the two additional assumptions of homoskedasticity and normally distributed errors. The assumption of homoskedasticity is used when we study the efficiency of the OLS estimator, and the assumption of normality is used when we study the exact sampling distribution of the OLS estimator and test statistics.

The extended least squares assumptions are summarized in Key Concept 16.1.

Except for notational differences, the first three assumptions in Key Concept 16.1 are identical to the first three assumptions in Key Concept 5.4.

The fourth assumption in Key Concepts 5.4 and 16.1 might appear different, but in fact they are the same: they are simply different ways of saying that there cannot be perfect multicollinearity. Recall that perfect multicollinearity arises when one regressor can be written as a perfect linear combination of the others. In the matrix notation of Equation (16.2), perfect multicollinearity means that one column of $\mathbf{X}$ is a perfect linear combination of the other columns of $\mathbf{X}$, but if this is true then $\mathbf{X}$ does not have full column rank. Thus, saying that $\mathbf{X}$ has rank $k + 1$, that is, rank equal to the number of columns of $\mathbf{X}$, is just another way to say that the regressors are not perfectly multicollinear.

The fifth least squares assumption in Key Concept 16.1 is that the error term is homoskedastic, and the sixth assumption is that the conditional distribution of u_i, given X_i, is normal. These two assumptions are the same as the final two assumptions in Key Concept 15.1, except that they are now stated for multiple regressors.

Implications for the mean vector and covariance matrix of U.   The least squares assumptions in Key Concept 16.1 imply simple expressions for the mean vector and covariance matrix of the conditional distribution of U given the matrix of regressors X. (The mean vector and covariance matrix of a vector of random variables are defined in Appendix 16.2.) Specifically, the first and second assumptions in Key Concept 16.1 imply that that $E(u_i|X) = E(u_i|X_i) = 0$ and that $cov(u_i,u_j|X) = E(u_iu_j|X) = E(u_iu_j|X_i,X_j) = E(u_i|X_i)E(u_j|X_j) = 0$ for $i \neq j$ (Exercise 15.7). The first, second, and fifth assumptions imply that $E(u_i^2|X) = E(u_i^2|X_i) = \sigma_u^2$. Combining these results, we have that

$$\text{under assumptions 1 and 2, } E(U|X) = \mathbf{0}_n, \text{ and} \tag{16.6}$$

$$\text{under assumptions 1, 2, and 5, } E(UU'|X) = \sigma_u^2 I_n, \tag{16.7}$$

where $\mathbf{0}_n$ is the n-dimensional vector of zero's and I_n is the $n \times n$ identity matrix.

Similarly, the first, second, fifth, and sixth assumptions in Key Concept 16.1 imply that the conditional distribution of the n-dimensional random vector U, conditional on X, is the multivariate normal distribution (defined in Appendix 16.2). That is,

$$\begin{gathered}\text{under assumptions 1, 2, 5, and 6, the} \\ \text{conditional distribution of } U \text{ given } X \text{ is } N(\mathbf{0}_n, \sigma_u^2 I_n).\end{gathered} \tag{16.8}$$

The OLS Estimator

The OLS estimator minimizes the sum of squared prediction mistakes, $\sum_{i=1}^{n}(Y_i - b_0 - b_1X_{1i} - \cdots - b_kX_{ki})^2$ (Equation (5.8)). The formula for the OLS estimator is obtained by taking the derivative of the sum of squared prediction mistakes with respect to each element of the coefficient vector, setting these derivatives to zero, and solving for the estimator $\hat{\beta}$.

The derivative of the sum of squared prediction mistakes with respect to the jth regression coefficient, b_j, is

$$\begin{gathered}\frac{\partial}{\partial b_j}\sum_{i=1}^{n}(Y_i - b_0 - b_1X_{1i} - \cdots - b_kX_{ki})^2 = \\ -2\sum_{i=1}^{n}X_{ji}(Y_i - b_0 - b_1X_{1i} - \cdots - b_kX_{ki}).\end{gathered} \tag{16.9}$$

for $j = 0, \ldots, k$, where, for $j = 0$, $X_{0i} = 1$ for all i. The derivative on the right-hand side of Equation (16.9) is the jth element of the $k + 1$ dimensional vector, $-2X'(Y - Xb)$, where b is the $k + 1$ dimensional vector consisting of $b_0, \ldots, b_k$. There are $k + 1$ such derivatives, each corresponding to an element of b. Combined, these yield the system of $k + 1$ equations that constitute the first order conditions for the OLS estimator that, when set to zero, define the OLS estimator $\hat{\beta}$. That is, $\hat{\beta}$ solves the system of $k + 1$ equations

$$X'(Y - X\hat{\beta}) = 0_{k+1}, \tag{16.10}$$

or, equivalently, $X'Y = X'X\hat{\beta}$.

Solving the system of equations (16.10) yields the OLS estimator $\hat{\beta}$ in matrix form:

$$\hat{\beta} = (X'X)^{-1}X'Y, \tag{16.11}$$

where $(X'X)^{-1}$ is the inverse of the matrix $X'X$.

The role of "no perfect multicollinearity." The fourth least squares assumption in Key Concept 16.1 states that X has full column rank. In turn, this implies that the matrix $X'X$ has full rank, that is, that $X'X$ is nonsingular. Because $X'X$ is nonsingular, it is invertible. Thus, the assumption that there is no perfect multicollinearity ensures that $(X'X)^{-1}$ exists, so that Equation (16.10) has a unique solution and the formula in Equation (16.11) for the OLS estimator can actually be computed. Said differently, if X does *not* have full column rank, there is not a unique solution to Equation (16.10), and $X'X$ is singular. Therefore, $(X'X)^{-1}$ cannot be computed and, thus, $\hat{\beta}$ cannot be computed from Equation (16.11).

16.2 Asymptotic Distribution of the OLS Estimator and *t*-Statistic

If the sample size is large and the first four assumptions of Key Concept 16.1 are satisfied, then the OLS estimator has an asymptotic joint normal distribution, the heteroskedasticity-robust estimator of the covariance matrix is consistent, and the heteroskedasticity-robust OLS *t*-statistic has an asymptotic standard normal distribution. These results make use of the multivariate normal distribution (Appendix 16.2) and a multivariate extension of the central limit theorem.

The Multivariate Central Limit Theorem

The central limit theorem of Key Concept 2.7 applies to a one-dimensional random variable. To derive the *joint* asymptotic distribution of the elements of $\hat{\beta}$, we need a multivariate central limit theorem that applies to vector-valued random variables.

The multivariate central limit theorem extends the univariate central limit theorem to averages of observations on a vector-valued random variable, W, where W is m-dimensional. The difference between the central limit theorems for a scalar as opposed to a vector-valued random variable is the conditions on the variances. In the scalar case in Key Concept 2.7, the requirement is that the variance is both nonzero and finite. In the vector case, the requirement is that the covariance matrix is both positive definite and finite. If the vector valued random variable W has a finite positive definite covariance matrix, then $0 < \text{var}(c'W) < \infty$ for all nonzero m-dimensional vectors c (Exercise 16.3).

The multivariate central limit theorem that we will use is stated in Key Concept 16.2.

Asymptotic Normality of $\hat{\beta}$

In large samples, the OLS estimator has the multivariate normal asymptotic distribution

$$\sqrt{n}(\hat{\beta} - \beta) \xrightarrow{d} N(0_{k+1}, \Sigma_{\sqrt{n}(\hat{\beta}-\beta)}), \text{ where } \Sigma_{\sqrt{n}(\hat{\beta}-\beta)} = Q_X^{-1}\Sigma_V Q_X^{-1}, \quad (16.12)$$

where Q_X is the $(k+1) \times (k+1)$-dimensional matrix of second moments of the regressors, that is, $Q_X = E(X_i X_i')$, and Σ_V is the $(k+1) \times (k+1)$-dimensional covariance matrix of $V_i = X_i u_i$, that is, $\Sigma_V = E(V_i V_i')$. Note that the second least squares assumption in Key Concept 16.1 implies that V_i, $i = 1, \ldots, n$ are i.i.d.

Written in terms of $\hat{\beta}$ rather than $\sqrt{n}(\hat{\beta} - \beta)$, the normal approximation in Equation (16.12) is

$$\hat{\beta} \text{ is, in large samples, distributed } N(\beta, \Sigma_{\hat{\beta}}),$$
$$\text{where } \Sigma_{\hat{\beta}} = \Sigma_{\sqrt{n}(\hat{\beta}-\beta)}/n = Q_X^{-1}\Sigma_V Q_X^{-1}/n. \quad (16.13)$$

The covariance matrix $\Sigma_{\hat{\beta}}$ in Equation (16.13) is the covariance matrix of the approximate normal distribution of $\hat{\beta}$, whereas $\Sigma_{\sqrt{n}(\hat{\beta}-\beta)}$ in Equation (16.12) is the covariance matrix of the asymptotic normal distribution of $\sqrt{n}(\hat{\beta} - \beta)$. These two covariance matrices differ by a factor of n, depending on whether or not the OLS estimator is scaled by $\sqrt{n}$.

The Multivariate Central Limit Theorem

Suppose that $W_1, \ldots, W_n$ are i.i.d. m-dimensional random variables with mean vector $E(W_i) = \mu_W$ and covariance matrix $E[(W_i - \mu_W)(W_i - \mu_W)'] = \Sigma_W$, where Σ_W is positive definite and finite. Let $\overline{W} = \frac{1}{n}\sum_{i=1}^{n} W_i$. Then $\sqrt{n}(\overline{W} - \mu_W) \overset{d}{\longrightarrow} N(0_m, \Sigma_W)$.

Key Concept 16.2

Derivation of equation (16.12).   To derive Equation (16.12), first use Equations (16.4) and (16.11) to write $\hat{\beta} = (X'X)^{-1}X'Y = (X'X)^{-1}X'(X\beta + U)$, so that

$$\hat{\beta} = \beta + (X'X)^{-1}X'U. \tag{16.14}$$

Thus $\hat{\beta} - \beta = (X'X)^{-1}X'U$, so

$$\sqrt{n}(\hat{\beta} - \beta) = \left(\frac{X'X}{n}\right)^{-1}\left(\frac{X'U}{\sqrt{n}}\right). \tag{16.15}$$

The derivation of Equation (16.12) involves arguing first that the "denominator" matrix in Equation (16.15), $X'X/n$, is consistent, and second that the "numerator" matrix, $X'U/\sqrt{n}$, obeys the multivariate central limit theorem in Key Concept 16.2. The details are given in Appendix 16.3.

Heteroskedasticity-Robust Standard Errors

The heteroskedasticity-robust estimator of $\Sigma_{\sqrt{n}(\hat{\beta}-\beta)}$ is obtained by replacing the population moments in its definition (Equation (16.12)) by sample moments. Accordingly, the heteroskedasticity-robust estimator of the covariance matrix of $\sqrt{n}(\hat{\beta} - \beta)$ is

$$\Sigma_{\sqrt{n}(\hat{\beta}-\beta)} = \left(\frac{X'X}{n}\right)^{-1}\hat{\Sigma}_{\hat{v}}\left(\frac{X'X}{n}\right)^{-1}, \text{ where } \hat{\Sigma}_{\hat{v}} = \frac{1}{n-k-1}\sum_{i=1}^{n}X_i X_i' \hat{u}_i^2. \tag{16.16}$$

The estimator $\hat{\Sigma}_{\hat{v}}$ incorporates the same degrees-of-freedom adjustment that is in the *SER* for the multiple regression model (Section 5.10) to adjust for potential downward bias because of estimation of $k + 1$ regression coefficients.

The proof that $\hat{\Sigma}_{\sqrt{n}(\hat{\beta}-\beta)} \xrightarrow{p} \Sigma_{\sqrt{n}(\hat{\beta}-\beta)}$ is conceptually similar to the proof, presented in Section 15.3, of the consistency of heteroskedasticity-robust standard errors for the single-regressor model.

Heteroskedasticity-robust standard errors.   The heteroskedasticity-robust estimator of the covariance matrix of $\hat{\beta}$, $\Sigma_{\hat{\beta}}$ is

$$\hat{\Sigma}_{\hat{\beta}} = n^{-1}\hat{\Sigma}_{\sqrt{n}(\hat{\beta}-\beta)}. \tag{16.17}$$

The heteroskedasticity-robust standard error for the jth regression coefficient is the square root of the jth diagonal element of $\hat{\Sigma}_{\hat{\beta}}$. That is, the heteroskedasticity-robust standard error of the jth coefficient is

$$SE(\hat{\beta}_j) = \sqrt{(\hat{\Sigma}_{\hat{\beta}})_{jj}}, \tag{16.18}$$

where $(\hat{\Sigma}_{\hat{\beta}})_{jj}$ is the (j,j) element of $\hat{\Sigma}_{\hat{\beta}}$.

Confidence Intervals for Predicted Effects

Section 6.1 contains two methods for computing the standard error of predicted effects that involve changes in two or more regressors. There are compact matrix expressions for these standard errors and thus for confidence intervals for predicted effects.

Consider a change in the value of the regressors for the ith observation from some initial value, say $X_{i,0}$, to some new value, $X_{i,0} + d$, so that the change in X_i is $\Delta X_i = d$, where d is a $k + 1$ dimensional vector. This change in X can involve multiple regressors (that is, multiple elements of X_i). For example, if two of the regressors are the value of an independent variable and its square, then d is the difference between the subsequent and initial values of these two variables.

The expected effect of this change in X_i is $d'\beta$ and the estimator of this effect is $d'\hat{\beta}$. Because linear combinations of normally distributed random variables are themselves normally distributed, $\sqrt{n}(d'\hat{\beta} - d'\beta) = d'\sqrt{n}(\hat{\beta} - \beta) \xrightarrow{d} N(0, d'\Sigma_{\sqrt{n}(\hat{\beta}-\beta)}d)$. Thus the standard error of this predicted effect is $(d'\hat{\Sigma}_{\hat{\beta}}d)^{1/2}$. A 95% confidence interval for this predicted effect is

$$d'\hat{\beta} \pm 1.96\sqrt{d'\hat{\Sigma}_{\hat{\beta}}d}. \tag{16.19}$$

Asymptotic Distribution of the *t*-Statistic

The *t*-statistic testing the null hypothesis that $\beta_j = \beta_{j,0}$, constructed using the heteroskedasticity-robust standard error in Equation (16.18), is given in Key Concept 5.6. The argument that this *t*-statistic has an asymptotic standard normal distribution parallels the argument given in Section 15.3 for the single-regressor model.

16.3 Tests of Joint Hypotheses

Section 5.7 considers tests of joint hypotheses that involve multiple restrictions, where each restriction involves a single coefficient, and Section 5.8 considers tests of a single restriction involving two or more coefficients. The matrix setup of Section 16.1 permits a unified representation of these two types of hypotheses as linear restrictions on the coefficient vector, where each restriction can involve multiple coefficients. Under the first four least squares assumptions in Key Concept 16.1, the heteroskedasticity-robust OLS *F*-statistic testing these hypotheses has an $F_{q,\infty}$ asymptotic distribution under the null hypothesis.

Joint Hypotheses in Matrix Notation

Consider a joint hypothesis that is linear in the coefficients and imposes q restrictions, where $q \leq k + 1$. Each of these q restrictions can involve one or more of the regression coefficients. This joint null hypothesis can be written in matrix notation as

$$\mathbf{R\beta} = \mathbf{r}, \tag{16.20}$$

where $\mathbf{R}$ is a $q \times (k + 1)$ nonrandom matrix with full row rank and $\mathbf{r}$ is a nonrandom $q \times 1$ vector. The number of rows of $\mathbf{R}$ is q, which is the number of restrictions being imposed under the null hypothesis.

The null hypothesis in Equation (16.20) subsumes all the null hypotheses considered in Sections 5.7 and 5.8. For example, a joint hypothesis of the type considered in Section 5.7 is that $\beta_0 = 0$, $\beta_1 = 0$, . . . , $\beta_{q-1} = 0$. To write this joint hypothesis in the form of Equation (16.20), set $\mathbf{R} = [\mathbf{I}_q \ \mathbf{0}_{q\times(k+1-q)}]$ and $\mathbf{r} = \mathbf{0}_q$.

The formulation in Equation (16.20) also captures the restrictions of Section 5.8 involving multiple regression coefficients. For example, if $k = 2$, then the hypothesis that $\beta_1 + \beta_2 = 1$ can be written in the form of Equation (16.20) by setting $\mathbf{R} = [0 \ 1 \ 1]$, $\mathbf{r} = 1$, and $q = 1$.

Asymptotic Distribution of the *F*-statistic

The heteroskedasticity-robust *F*-statistic testing the joint hypothesis in Equation (16.20) is

$$F = (R\hat{\beta} - r)'[R\hat{\Sigma}_{\hat{\beta}}R']^{-1}(R\hat{\beta} - r)/q. \tag{16.21}$$

If the first four assumptions in Key Concept 16.1 hold, then under the null hypothesis

$$F \xrightarrow{d} F_{q,\infty}. \tag{16.22}$$

This result follows by combining the asymptotic normality of $\hat{\beta}$ with the consistency of the heteroskedasticity-robust estimator $\hat{\Sigma}_{\hat{\beta}}$ of the covariance matrix. Specifically, first note that Equation (16.12) and Equation (16.48) in Appendix 16.2 imply that, under the null hypothesis, $\sqrt{n}(R\hat{\beta} - r) = \sqrt{n}R(\hat{\beta} - \beta) \xrightarrow{d} N(0, R\Sigma_{\sqrt{n}(\hat{\beta}-\beta)}R')$. It follows from Equation (16.51) that, under the null hypothesis, $(R\hat{\beta} - r)'[R\hat{\Sigma}_{\hat{\beta}}R']^{-1}(R\hat{\beta} - r) = [\sqrt{n}R(\hat{\beta} - \beta)]'\ [R\Sigma_{\sqrt{n}(\hat{\beta}-\beta)}R']^{-1}\ [\sqrt{n}R(\hat{\beta} - \beta)] \xrightarrow{d} \chi_q^2$. However, because $\hat{\Sigma}_{\sqrt{n}(\hat{\beta}-\beta)} \xrightarrow{p} \Sigma_{\sqrt{n}(\hat{\beta}-\beta)}$, it follows from Slutsky's theorem that $[\sqrt{n}R(\hat{\beta} - \beta)]'[R\hat{\Sigma}_{\sqrt{n}(\hat{\beta}-\beta)}R']^{-1}\ [\sqrt{n}R(\hat{\beta} - \beta)] \xrightarrow{d} \chi_q^2$ or, equivalently (because $\hat{\Sigma}_{\hat{\beta}} = \hat{\Sigma}_{\sqrt{n}(\hat{\beta}-\beta)}/n$), that $F \xrightarrow{d} \chi_q^2/q$, which is in turn distributed $F_{q,\infty}$.

Confidence Sets for Multiple Coefficients

As discussed in Section 5.9, an asymptotically valid confidence set for two or more elements of β can be constructed as the set of values that, when taken as the null hypothesis, are not rejected by the *F*-statistic. In principal, this set could be computed by repeatedly evaluating the *F*-statistic for many values of β, but, as is the case with a confidence interval for a single coefficient, it is simpler to manipulate the formula for the test statistic to obtain an explicit formula for the confidence set.

Here is the procedure for constructing a confidence set for two or more of the elements of β. Let δ denote the q-dimensional vector consisting of the coefficients for which we wish to construct a confidence set. For example, if we are constructing a confidence set for the regression coefficients β_1 and β_2, then $q = 2$ and $\delta = (\beta_1\ \beta_2)'$. In general we can write $\delta = R\beta$, where the matrix R consists of zeros and ones (as discussed following Equation (16.20)). The *F*-statistic testing the hypothesis that $\delta = \delta_0$ is $F = (\hat{\delta} - \delta_0)'[R\hat{\Sigma}_{\hat{\beta}}R']^{-1}(\hat{\delta} - \delta_0)/q$, where $\hat{\delta} = R\hat{\beta}$. A 95% confidence set for δ is the set of values δ_0 that are not rejected by the *F*-statistic. That is, when $\delta = R\beta$, a 95% confidence set for δ is

$$\{\delta: (\hat{\delta} - \delta)'[R\hat{\Sigma}_{\hat{\beta}}R']^{-1}(\hat{\delta} - \delta)/q \leq c\}, \tag{16.23}$$

where c is the 95th percentile (the 5% critical value) of the $F_{q,\infty}$ distribution.

The set in Equation (16.23) consists of all the points contained inside the ellipse determined when the inequality in Equation (16.23) is an equality (this is an ellipsoid when $q > 2$). Thus, the confidence set for $\boldsymbol{\delta}$ can be computed by solving Equation (16.23) for the boundary ellipse.

16.4 Distribution of Regression Statistics with Normal Errors[1]

The distributions presented in Sections 16.2 and 16.3, which were justified by appealing to the law of large numbers and the central limit theorem, apply when the sample size is large. If, however, the errors are homoskedastic and normally distributed, conditional on $\boldsymbol{X}$, then the OLS estimator has a multivariate normal distribution, conditional on $\boldsymbol{X}$. In addition, the sampling distribution of the square of the standard error of the regression is proportional to the chi-squared distribution with $n - k - 1$ degrees of freedom, the homoskedasticity-only OLS t-statistic has a Student t distribution with $n - k - 1$ degrees of freedom, and the homoskedasticity-only F-statistic has a $F_{q,n-k-1}$ distribution. The arguments in this section employ some specialized matrix formulas for OLS regression statistics, which are presented first.

Matrix Representations of OLS Regression Statistics

The OLS predicted values, residuals, and sum of squared residuals have compact matrix representations. These representations make use of two matrices, $\boldsymbol{P_X}$ and $\boldsymbol{M_X}$.

The matrices P_X and M_X.   The algebra of OLS in the multivariate model relies on the two symmetric $n \times n$ matrices, $\boldsymbol{P_X}$ and $\boldsymbol{M_X}$:

$$\boldsymbol{P_X} = \boldsymbol{X}(\boldsymbol{X'X})^{-1}\boldsymbol{X'} \tag{16.24}$$

$$\boldsymbol{M_X} = \boldsymbol{I}_n - \boldsymbol{P_X}. \tag{16.25}$$

---

[1]This section can be skipped without compromising the subsequent material.

A matrix C is **idempotent** if C is square and $CC = C$. Because $P_X = P_X P_X$ and $M_X = M_X M_X$ (Exercise 16.5), and because P_X and M_X are symmetric, P_X and M_X are symmetric idempotent matrices.

The matrices P_X and M_X have some additional useful properties, which follow directly from the definitions in Equations (16.24) and (16.25):

$$P_X X = X \text{ and } M_X X = 0_{n \times (k+1)};$$
$$\text{rank}(P_X) = k + 1 \text{ and rank}(M_X) = n - k - 1. \tag{16.26}$$

where $\text{rank}(P_X)$ is the rank of P_X.

The matrices P_X and M_X can be used to decompose an n-dimensional vector Z into two parts: a part that is spanned by the columns of X, and a part orthogonal to the columns of X. In other words, $P_X Z$ is the projection of Z onto the space spanned by the columns of X, and $M_X Z$ is the part of Z orthogonal to the columns of X.

OLS predicted values and residuals.   The matrices P_X and M_X provide some simple expressions for OLS predicted values and residuals. The OLS predicted values, $\hat{Y} = X\hat{\beta}$, and the OLS residuals, $\hat{U} = Y - \hat{Y}$, can be expressed as (Exercise 16.5)

$$\hat{Y} = P_X Y \text{ and} \tag{16.27}$$

$$\hat{U} = M_X Y = M_X U. \tag{16.28}$$

The expressions in Equation (16.27) and (16.28) provide a simple proof that the OLS residuals and predicted values are orthogonal, that is, that Equation (4.58) holds: $\hat{Y}'\hat{U} = Y'P_X'M_X Y = 0$, where the second equality follows $P_X'M_X = 0_{n \times n}$ which in turn follows from $M_X X = 0_{n \times (k+1)}$ in Equation (16.26).

The standard error of the regression.   The *SER*, defined in Section 5.10, is $s_{\hat{u}}$, where

$$s_{\hat{u}}^2 = \frac{1}{n-k-1} \sum_{i=1}^{n} \hat{u}_i^2 = \frac{1}{n-k-1} \hat{U}'\hat{U} = \frac{1}{n-k-1} U'M_X U, \tag{16.29}$$

where the final equality follows because $\hat{U}'\hat{U} = (M_X U)'(M_X U) = U'M_X M_X U = U'M_X U$ (because M_X is symmetric and idempotent).

Distribution of $\hat{\beta}$ with Normal Errors

Because $\hat{\beta} = \beta + (X'X)^{-1}X'U$ (Equation (16.14)) and because the distribution of U conditional on X is, by assumption, $N(\mathbf{0}_n, \sigma_u^2 I_n)$ (Equation (16.8)), the conditional distribution of $\hat{\beta}$ given X is multivariate normal with mean β. The covariance matrix of $\hat{\beta}$, conditional on X, is $\Sigma_{\hat{\beta}|X} = E[(\hat{\beta} - \beta)(\hat{\beta} - \beta)'|X] = E[(X'X)^{-1}X'UU'X(X'X)^{-1}|X] = (X'X)^{-1}X'(I_n\sigma_u^2)X(X'X)^{-1} = \sigma_u^2(X'X)^{-1}$. Accordingly, under all six assumptions in Key Concept 16.1, the conditional distribution of $\hat{\beta}$ given X is

$$\hat{\beta} \text{ is distributed } N(\beta, \Sigma_{\hat{\beta}|X}), \text{ where } \Sigma_{\hat{\beta}|X} = \sigma_u^2(X'X)^{-1}. \qquad (16.30)$$

Distribution of $s_{\hat{u}}^2$

If all six assumptions in Key Concept 16.1 hold, then $s_{\hat{u}}^2$ has an exact sampling distribution that is proportional to a chi-squared distribution with $n - k - 1$ degrees of freedom:

$$s_{\hat{u}}^2 \text{ is distributed as } \chi_{n-k-1}^2 \text{ times } \sigma_u^2/(n - k - 1). \qquad (16.31)$$

The proof of Equation (16.31) starts with Equation (16.29). Because U is normally distributed conditional on X and because M_X is a symmetric idempotent matrix, the quadratic form $U'M_XU/\sigma_u^2$ has an exact chi-squared distribution with degrees of freedom equal to the rank of M_X (Equation (16.52) in Appendix 16.2). From Equation (16.26) the rank of M_X is $n - k - 1$. Thus $U'M_XU/\sigma_u^2$ has an exact χ_{n-k-1}^2 distribution, from which Equation (16.31) follows.

The degrees of freedom adjustment ensures that $s_{\hat{u}}^2$ is unbiased. The expectation of a random variable with a χ_{n-k-1}^2 distribution is $n - k - 1$; thus, $E(U'M_XU) = (n - k - 1)\sigma_u^2$, so $E(s_{\hat{u}}^2) = \sigma_u^2$.

Homoskedasticity-Only Standard Errors

The homoskedasticity-only estimator $\widetilde{\Sigma}_{\hat{\beta}}$ of the covariance matrix of $\hat{\beta}$, conditional on X, is obtained by substituting the sample variance $s_{\hat{u}}^2$ for the population variance σ_u^2 in the expression for $\Sigma_{\hat{\beta}|X}$ in Equation (16.30). Accordingly,

$$\widetilde{\Sigma}_{\hat{\beta}} = s_{\hat{u}}^2(X'X)^{-1}. \quad \text{(homoskedasticity-only)} \qquad (16.32)$$

The estimator of the variance of the normal conditional distribution of $\hat{\beta}_j$, given $\mathbf{X}$, is the (j,j) element of $\widetilde{\boldsymbol{\Sigma}}_{\hat{\boldsymbol{\beta}}}$. Thus the homoskedasticity-only standard error of $\hat{\beta}_j$ is the square root of the jth diagonal element of $\widetilde{\boldsymbol{\Sigma}}_{\hat{\boldsymbol{\beta}}}$. That is, the homoskedasticity-only standard error of $\hat{\beta}_j$ is

$$\widetilde{SE}(\hat{\beta}_j) = \sqrt{(\widetilde{\boldsymbol{\Sigma}}_{\hat{\boldsymbol{\beta}}})_{jj}} \text{ (homoskedasticity-only).} \tag{16.33}$$

Distribution of the *t*-Statistic

Let $\tilde{t}$ be the *t*-statistic testing the hypothesis $\beta_j = \beta_{j,0}$, constructed using the homoskedasticity-only standard error; that is, let

$$\tilde{t} = \frac{\hat{\beta}_j - \beta_{j,0}}{\sqrt{(\widetilde{\boldsymbol{\Sigma}}_{\hat{\boldsymbol{\beta}}})_{jj}}}. \tag{16.34}$$

Under all six of the extended least squares assumptions in Key Concept 16.1, the exact sampling distribution of $\tilde{t}$ is the Student t distribution with $n - k - 1$ degrees of freedom; that is,

$$\tilde{t} \text{ is distributed } t_{n-k-1}. \tag{16.35}$$

The proof of Equation (16.35) is given in Appendix 16.4.

Distribution of the *F*-statistic

If all six least squares assumptions in Key Concept 16.1 hold, then the *F*-statistic testing the hypothesis in Equation (16.20), constructed using the homoskedasticity-only estimator of the covariance matrix, has an exact $F_{q,n-k-1}$ distribution under the null hypothesis.

The homoskedasticity-only F-statistic. The homoskedasticity-only *F*-statistic is similar to the heteroskedasticity-robust *F*-statistic in Equation (16.21), except that the homoskedasticity-only estimator $\widetilde{\boldsymbol{\Sigma}}_{\hat{\boldsymbol{\beta}}}$ is used instead of the heteroskedasticity-robust estimator $\hat{\boldsymbol{\Sigma}}_{\hat{\boldsymbol{\beta}}}$. Substituting the expression $\widetilde{\boldsymbol{\Sigma}}_{\hat{\boldsymbol{\beta}}} = s_{\hat{u}}^2(\mathbf{X}'\mathbf{X})^{-1}$ into the expression for the *F*-statistic in Equation (16.21) yields the homoskedasticity-only *F*-statistic testing the null hypothesis in Equation (16.20):

$$\tilde{F} = \frac{(\mathbf{R}\hat{\boldsymbol{\beta}} - \mathbf{r})'[\mathbf{R}(\mathbf{X}'\mathbf{X})^{-1}\mathbf{R}']^{-1}(\mathbf{R}\hat{\boldsymbol{\beta}} - \mathbf{r})/q}{s_{\hat{u}}^2}. \tag{16.36}$$

If all six assumptions in Key Concept 16.1 hold, then under the null hypothesis

$$\widetilde{F} \text{ has a } F_{q,n-k-1} \text{ distribution.} \tag{16.37}$$

The proof of Equation (16.37) is given in Appendix 16.4.

The rule-of-thumb F-statistic formula.   The F-statistic in Equation (16.36) is called the Wald version of the F-statistic (named after the statistician Abraham Wald). Although the formula for the rule-of-thumb F-statistic given in Appendix 5.3 appears quite different than the formula for the Wald statistic in Equation (16.36), the rule-of-thumb F-statistic and the Wald F-statistic are two versions of the same statistic. That is, the two expressions are equivalent; for further discussion see Greene (1997, Chapter 7).

16.5 Efficiency of the OLS Estimator with Homoskedastic Errors

Under the Gauss-Markov conditions for multiple regression, the OLS estimator of β is efficient among all linear conditionally unbiased estimators, that is, the OLS estimator is BLUE.

The Gauss-Markov Conditions for Multiple Regression

The **Gauss-Markov conditions for multiple regression** are

$$\begin{aligned}
&\text{(i) } E(\boldsymbol{U}|\boldsymbol{X}) = \boldsymbol{0}_n, \\
&\text{(ii) } E(\boldsymbol{U}\boldsymbol{U}'|\boldsymbol{X}) = \sigma_u^2 \boldsymbol{I}_n, \text{ and} \\
&\text{(iii) } \boldsymbol{X} \text{ has full column rank.}
\end{aligned} \tag{16.38}$$

The Gauss-Markov conditions for multiple regression in turn are implied by the first five assumptions in Key Concept 16.1 (see Equations (16.6) and (16.7)). The conditions in Equation (16.38) generalize the Gauss-Markov conditions for a single regressor model to multiple regression. (By using matrix notation, the second and third Gauss-Markov conditions in Equation (15.24) are collected into the single condition (ii) in Equation (16.38).)

Linear Conditionally Unbiased Estimators

We start by describing the class of linear unbiased estimators and by showing that OLS is in that class.

The class of linear conditionally unbiased estimators. An estimator of $\boldsymbol{\beta}$ is said to be linear if it is a linear function of $Y_1, \ldots, Y_n$. Accordingly, the estimator $\tilde{\boldsymbol{\beta}}$ is linear in $\boldsymbol{Y}$ if it can be written in the form

$$\tilde{\boldsymbol{\beta}} = \boldsymbol{A}'\boldsymbol{Y}, \tag{16.39}$$

where $\boldsymbol{A}$ is a $n \times (k + 1)$ dimensional matrix of weights that may depend on $\boldsymbol{X}$ and on nonrandom constants, but not on $\boldsymbol{Y}$.

An estimator is conditionally unbiased if the mean of its conditional sampling distribution, given $\boldsymbol{X}$, is $\boldsymbol{\beta}$. That is, $\tilde{\boldsymbol{\beta}}$ is conditionally unbiased if $E(\tilde{\boldsymbol{\beta}} | \boldsymbol{X}) = \boldsymbol{\beta}$.

The OLS estimator is linear and conditionally unbiased. Comparison of Equations (16.11) and (16.39) shows that the OLS estimator is linear in $\boldsymbol{Y}$; specifically, $\hat{\boldsymbol{\beta}} = \hat{\boldsymbol{A}}'\boldsymbol{Y}$, where $\hat{\boldsymbol{A}} = \boldsymbol{X}(\boldsymbol{X}'\boldsymbol{X})^{-1}$. To show that $\hat{\boldsymbol{\beta}}$ is conditionally unbiased, recall from Equation (16.14) that $\hat{\boldsymbol{\beta}} = \boldsymbol{\beta} + (\boldsymbol{X}'\boldsymbol{X})^{-1}\boldsymbol{X}'\boldsymbol{U}$. Taking the conditional expectation of both sides of this expression yields $E(\hat{\boldsymbol{\beta}} | \boldsymbol{X}) = \boldsymbol{\beta} + E[(\boldsymbol{X}'\boldsymbol{X})^{-1}\boldsymbol{X}'\boldsymbol{U} | \boldsymbol{X}] = \boldsymbol{\beta} + (\boldsymbol{X}'\boldsymbol{X})^{-1}\boldsymbol{X}'E(\boldsymbol{U} | \boldsymbol{X}) = \boldsymbol{\beta}$, where the final equality follows because $E(\boldsymbol{U} | \boldsymbol{X}) = 0$ by the first Gauss-Markov condition.

The Gauss-Markov Theorem for Multiple Regression

The Gauss-Markov theorem for multiple regression provides conditions under which the OLS estimator is efficient among the class of linear conditionally unbiased estimators. A subtle point arises, however, because $\hat{\boldsymbol{\beta}}$ is a vector and its "variance" is a covariance matrix. When the "variance" of an estimator is a matrix, just what does it mean to say that one estimator has a smaller variance than another?

The Gauss-Markov theorem handles this problem by comparing the variance of a candidate estimator of a *linear combination* of the elements of $\boldsymbol{\beta}$ to the variance of the corresponding linear combination of $\hat{\boldsymbol{\beta}}$. Specifically, let $\boldsymbol{c}$ be a $k + 1$ dimensional vector, and consider the problem of estimating the linear combination $\boldsymbol{c}'\boldsymbol{\beta}$ using the candidate estimator $\boldsymbol{c}'\tilde{\boldsymbol{\beta}}$ (where $\tilde{\boldsymbol{\beta}}$ is a linear conditionally unbiased estimator) on the one hand and $\boldsymbol{c}'\hat{\boldsymbol{\beta}}$ on the other. Because $\boldsymbol{c}'\tilde{\boldsymbol{\beta}}$ and $\boldsymbol{c}'\hat{\boldsymbol{\beta}}$ are both scalars

Gauss-Markov Theorem for Multiple Regression

Suppose that the Gauss–Markov conditions for multiple regression in Equation (16.38) hold. Then the OLS estimator $\hat{\beta}$ is BLUE. That is, let $\tilde{\beta}$ be a linear conditionally unbiased estimator of β and let c be a nonrandom $k + 1$ dimensional vector. Then $\text{var}(c'\hat{\beta} | X) \leq \text{var}(c'\tilde{\beta} | X)$ for every nonzero vector c, where the inequality holds with equality for all c only if $\tilde{\beta} = \hat{\beta}$.

Key Concept 16.3

and are both linear conditionally unbiased estimators of $c'\beta$, it now makes sense to compare their variances.

The Gauss–Markov theorem for multiple regression says that the OLS estimator of $c'\beta$ is efficient, that is, the OLS estimator $c'\hat{\beta}$ has the smallest conditional variance of all linear conditionally unbiased estimators $c'\tilde{\beta}$. Remarkably, this is true no matter what the linear combination is. It is in this sense that the OLS estimator is BLUE in multiple regression.

The Gauss–Markov theorem is stated in Key Concept 16.3 and proven in Appendix 16.5.

16.6 Generalized Least Squares[2]

The assumption of i.i.d. sampling fits many applications. For example, suppose that Y_i and X_i correspond to information about individuals, such as their earnings, education, and personal characteristics, where the individuals are selected from a population by simple random sampling. In this case, because of the simple random sampling scheme, (X_i, Y_i) are necessarily i.i.d. Because (X_i, Y_i) and (X_j, Y_j) are independently distributed for $i \neq j$, u_i and u_j are independently distributed for $i \neq j$. This in turn implies that u_i and u_j are uncorrelated for $i \neq j$. In the context of the Gauss–Markov assumptions, the assumption that $E(UU' | X)$ is

---

[2]The GLS estimator was introduced in Section 13.5 in the context of distributed lag time series regression. This presentation here is a self-contained mathematical treatment of GLS that can be read independently of Section 13.5, but reading that section first will help to make these ideas more concrete.

diagonal therefore is appropriate if the data are collected in a way that makes the observations independently distributed.

Some sampling schemes encountered in econometrics do not, however, result in independent observations, and instead can lead to error terms u_i that are correlated from one observation to the next. The leading example is when the data are sampled over time for the same entity, that is, when the data are time series data. As discussed in Section 13.3, in regressions involving time series data, many omitted factors are correlated from one period to the next, and this can result in regression error terms (which represent those omitted factors) that are correlated from one period of observation to the next. In other words, the error term in one period will not, in general, be distributed independently of the error term in the next period. Instead, the error term in one period could be correlated with the error term in the next period.

The presence of correlated error terms creates two problems for inference based on OLS. First, *neither* the heteroskedasticity-robust nor the homoskedasticity-only standard errors produced by OLS provide a valid basis for inference. The solution to this problem is to use standard errors that are robust to both heteroskedasticity and correlation of the error terms across observations. This topic—heteroskedasticity- and autocorrelation-consistent (HAC) covariance matrix estimation—is the subject of Section 13.4 and we do not pursue it further here.

Second, if the error term is correlated across observations, then $E(UU'|X)$ is not diagonal, the second Gauss-Markov condition in Equation (16.38) does not hold, and OLS is not BLUE. In this section we study an estimator, **generalized least squares** (**GLS**), that is BLUE (at least asymptotically) when the conditional covariance matrix of the errors is no longer proportional to the identity matrix. A special case of GLS is weighted least squares, discussed in Section 15.5, in which the conditional covariance matrix is diagonal and the ith diagonal element is a function of X_i. Like WLS, GLS transforms the regression model so that the errors of the transformed model satisfy the Gauss-Markov conditions. The GLS estimator is the OLS estimator of the coefficients in the transformed model.

The GLS Assumptions

There are four assumptions under which GLS is valid. The first GLS assumption is that u_i has a mean of zero, conditional on $X_1, \ldots, X_n$; that is,

$$E(U|X) = 0_n. \tag{16.40}$$

This assumption is implied by the first two least squares assumption in Key Concept 16.1, that is, if $E(u_i | \boldsymbol{X}_i) = 0$ and $(\boldsymbol{X}_i, Y_i)$, $i = 1, \ldots , n$ are i.i.d, then $E(\boldsymbol{U} | \boldsymbol{X}) = \boldsymbol{0}_n$. In GLS, however, we will not want to maintain the i.i.d. assumption; after all, one purpose of GLS is to handle errors that are correlated across observations. We discuss the significance of the assumption in Equation (16.40) after introducing the GLS estimator.

The second GLS assumption is that the conditional covariance matrix of $\boldsymbol{U}$ given $\boldsymbol{X}$ is some function of $\boldsymbol{X}$:

$$E(\boldsymbol{U}\boldsymbol{U}' | \boldsymbol{X}) = \boldsymbol{\Omega}(\boldsymbol{X}), \tag{16.41}$$

where $\boldsymbol{\Omega}(\boldsymbol{X})$ is a $n \times n$ positive definite matrix-valued function of $\boldsymbol{X}$.

There are two main applications of GLS that are covered by this assumption. The first is independent sampling with heteroskedastic errors, in which case $\boldsymbol{\Omega}(\boldsymbol{X})$ is a diagonal matrix with diagonal element $\lambda h(\boldsymbol{X}_i)$, where λ is a constant and h is a function. In this case, discussed in Section 15.5, GLS is WLS.

The second application is to homoskedastic errors that are serially correlated. In practice, in this case a model is developed for the serial correlation. For example, one model is that the error term is correlated with only its neighbor, so that $\text{corr}(u_i, u_{i-1}) = \rho \neq 0$ but $\text{corr}(u_i, u_j) = 0$ if $|i - j| \geq 2$. In this case, $\boldsymbol{\Omega}(\boldsymbol{X})$ has σ_u^2 as its diagonal element, $\rho\sigma_u^2$ in the first off-diagonal, and zeros elsewhere. Thus, $\boldsymbol{\Omega}(\boldsymbol{X})$ does not depend on $\boldsymbol{X}$, $\boldsymbol{\Omega}_{ii} = \sigma_u^2$, $\boldsymbol{\Omega}_{ij} = \rho\sigma_u^2$ for $|i - j| = 1$, and $\boldsymbol{\Omega}_{ij} = 0$ for $|i - j| > 1$. Other models for serial correlation, including the first order autoregressive model, are discussed further in the context of GLS in Section 13.5 (also see Exercise 16.8).

One assumption that has appeared on all previous lists of least squares assumptions for cross-sectional data is that $\boldsymbol{X}_i$ and u_i have nonzero, finite fourth moments. In the case of GLS, the specific moment assumptions needed to prove asymptotic results depend on the nature of the function $\boldsymbol{\Omega}(\boldsymbol{X})$. The particular moment assumptions also depend on whether one is considering the GLS estimator, the GLS t- or F-statistics, and the moment requirements also depend on whether $\boldsymbol{\Omega}(\boldsymbol{X})$ is known or has estimated parameters. Because the assumptions are case- and model-specific, we do not present specific moment assumptions here, and the discussion of the large-sample properties of GLS assumes that such moment conditions apply for the relevant case at hand. For completeness, as the third GLS assumption, $\boldsymbol{X}_i$ and u_i are simply assumed to satisfy suitable moment conditions.

The fourth GLS assumption is that $\boldsymbol{X}$ has full column rank, that is, the regressors are not perfectly multicollinear.

The GLS assumptions are summarized in Key Concept 16.4.

The GLS Assumptions

Key Concept 16.4

In the linear regression model $Y = X\beta + U$, the GLS assumptions are:

1. $E(U|X) = 0_n$;
2. $E(UU'|X) = \Omega(X)$, where $\Omega(X)$ is a $n \times n$ positive definite matrix that can depend on X;
3. X_i and u_i satisfy suitable moment conditions;
4. X has full column rank (there is no perfect multicollinearity).

We consider GLS estimation in two cases. In the first case, $\Omega(X)$ is known. In the second case, the functional form of $\Omega(X)$ is known up to some parameters that can be estimated. To simplify notation, we refer to the function $\Omega(X)$ as the matrix Ω, so the dependence of Ω on X is implicit.

GLS When Ω Is Known

When Ω is known, the GLS estimator uses Ω to transform the regression model to one with errors that satisfy the Gauss-Markov conditions. Specifically, let F be a matrix square root of Ω^{-1}, that is, let F be a matrix that satisfies $F'F = \Omega^{-1}$ (such a matrix will always exist). A property of F is that $F\Omega F' = I_n$. Now premultiply both sides of Equation (16.4) by F to obtain

$$\widetilde{Y} = \widetilde{X}\beta + \widetilde{U}, \tag{16.42}$$

where $\widetilde{Y} = FY$, $\widetilde{X} = FX$, and $\widetilde{U} = FU$.

The key insight of GLS is that, under the four GLS assumptions, the Gauss-Markov assumptions hold for the transformed regression in Equation (16.42). That is, by transforming all the variables by the inverse of the matrix square root of Ω, the regression errors in the transformed regression have a conditional mean of zero and a covariance matrix that equals the identity matrix. To show this mathematically, first note that $E(\widetilde{U}|\widetilde{X}) = E(FU|FX) = FE(U|FX) = 0_n$ by the first GLS assumption (Equation (16.40)). In addition, $E(\widetilde{U}\widetilde{U}'|\widetilde{X}) = E[(FU)(FU)'|FX] = FE(UU'|FX)F' = F\Omega F' = I_n$, where the second equality follows because $(FU)' = U'F'$ and the final equality follows from the definition of F. It follows that the transformed regression model in Equation (16.42) satisfies the Gauss-Markov conditions in Key Concept 16.3.

The GLS estimator, $\hat{\beta}^{GLS}$, is the OLS estimator of β in Equation (16.42), that is, $\hat{\beta}^{GLS} = (\widetilde{X}'\widetilde{X})^{-1}(\widetilde{X}'\widetilde{Y})$. Because the transformed regression model satisfies the Gauss-Markov conditions, the GLS estimator is the best conditionally unbiased estimator that is linear in $\widetilde{Y}$. But because $\widetilde{Y} = FY$ and F is (here) assumed to be known, and because F is invertible (because Ω is positive definite), the class of estimators that are linear in $\widetilde{Y}$ is the same as the class of estimators that are linear in Y. Thus, the OLS estimator of β in Equation (16.42) is also the best conditionally unbiased estimator among estimators that are linear in Y. In other words, under the GLS assumptions, the GLS estimator is BLUE.

The GLS estimator can be expressed directly in terms of Ω, so that in principle there is no need to compute the square root matrix F. Because $\widetilde{X} = FX$ and $\widetilde{Y} = FY$, $\hat{\beta}^{GLS} = (X'F'FX)^{-1}(X'F'FY)$. But $F'F = \Omega^{-1}$, so

$$\hat{\beta}^{GLS} = (X'\Omega^{-1}X)^{-1}(X'\Omega^{-1}Y). \qquad (16.43)$$

In practice, Ω is typically unknown, so the GLS estimator in Equation (16.43) typically cannot be computed and thus is sometimes called the **infeasible GLS** estimator. If, however, Ω has a known functional form but the parameters of that function are unknown, then Ω can be estimated and a feasible version of the GLS estimator can be computed.

GLS When Ω Contains Unknown Parameters

If Ω is a known function of some parameters that in turn can be estimated, then these estimated parameters can be used to calculate an estimator of the covariance matrix Ω. For example, consider the time series application discussed following Equation (16.41), in which $\Omega(X)$ does not depend on X, $\Omega_{ii} = \sigma_u^2$, $\Omega_{ij} = \rho\sigma_u^2$ for $|i - j| = 1$, and $\Omega_{ij} = 0$ for $|i - j| > 1$. Then Ω has two unknown parameters, σ_u^2 and ρ. These parameters can be estimated using the residuals from a preliminary OLS regression; specifically, σ_u^2 can be estimated by $s_{\hat{u}}^2$ and ρ can be estimated by the sample correlation between all neighboring pairs of OLS residuals. These estimated parameters can in turn be used to compute an estimator of Ω, $\hat{\Omega}$.

In general, suppose that you have an estimator $\hat{\Omega}$ of Ω. Then the GLS estimator based on $\hat{\Omega}$ is

$$\hat{\beta}^{GLS} = (X'\hat{\Omega}^{-1}X)^{-1}(X'\hat{\Omega}^{-1}Y). \qquad (16.44)$$

The GLS estimator in Equation (16.44) is sometimes called the **feasible GLS** estimator because it can be computed if the covariance matrix contains some unknown parameters that can be estimated.

The Zero Conditional Mean Assumption and GLS

For the OLS estimator to be consistent, the first least squares assumption must hold, that is, $E(u_i|X_i)$ must be zero. In contrast, the first GLS assumption is that $E(u_i|X_1, \ldots, X_n) = 0$. In other words, the first OLS assumption is that the error for the ith observation has a conditional mean of zero, given the values of the regressors for that observation, whereas the first GLS assumption is that u_i has a conditional mean of zero, given the values of the regressors for *all* observations.

As discussed in Section 16.1, the assumptions that $E(u_i|X_i) = 0$ and that sampling is i.i.d. together imply that $E(u_i|X_1, \ldots, X_n) = 0$. Thus, when sampling is i.i.d., so that GLS is WLS, the first GLS assumption is implied by the first least squares assumption in Key Concept 16.1.

When sampling is not i.i.d., however, the first GLS assumption is not implied by the assumption that $E(u_i|X_i) = 0$; that is, the first GLS assumption is stronger. Although the distinction between these two conditions might seem slight, it can be very important in applications to time series data. This distinction is discussed in Section 13.5 in the context of whether the regressor is "past and present" exogenous or "strictly" exogenous; the assumption that $E(u_i|X_1, \ldots, X_n) = 0$ corresponds to strict exogeneity. Here, we discuss this distinction at a more general level using matrix notation. To do so, we focus on the case that U is homoskedastic, Ω is known, and Ω has nonzero off-diagonal elements.

The role of the first GLS assumption.   To see the source of the difference between these assumptions, it is useful to contrast the consistency arguments for GLS and OLS.

We first sketch the argument for the consistency of the GLS estimator in Equation (16.43). Substituting Equation (16.4) into Equation (16.43), we have $\hat{\beta}^{GLS} = \beta + (X'\Omega^{-1}X/n)^{-1}(X'\Omega^{-1}U/n)$. Under the first GLS assumption, $E(X'\Omega^{-1}U) = E[X'\Omega^{-1}E(U|X)] = 0_n$. If in addition the variance of $X'\Omega^{-1}U/n$ tends to zero and $X'\Omega^{-1}X/n \xrightarrow{p} \tilde{Q}$, where $\tilde{Q}$ is some invertible matrix, then $\hat{\beta}^{GLS} \xrightarrow{p} \beta$. Critically, when Ω has off-diagonal elements, the term $X'\Omega^{-1}U = \sum_{i=1}^{n}\sum_{j=1}^{n} X_i(\Omega^{-1})_{ij}u_j$ involves products of X_i and u_j for different i, j, where $(\Omega^{-1})_{ij}$ denotes the (i, j) element of Ω^{-1}. Thus for $X'\Omega^{-1}U$ to have a mean of zero, it is not enough that $E(u_i|X_i) = 0$; rather $E(u_i|X_j)$ must equal zero for all i, j pairs corresponding to nonzero values of $(\Omega^{-1})_{ij}$.

Depending on the covariance structure of the errors, only some or all the elements of $(\boldsymbol{\Omega}^{-1})_{ij}$ might be nonzero. For example, if u_i follows a first order autoregression (as discussed in Section 13.5), the only nonzero elements $(\boldsymbol{\Omega}^{-1})_{ij}$ are those for which $|i - j| \leq 1$. In general, however, all the elements of $\boldsymbol{\Omega}^{-1}$ can be nonzero, so in general for $\boldsymbol{X}'\boldsymbol{\Omega}^{-1}\boldsymbol{U}/n \xrightarrow{p} \boldsymbol{0}_{(k+1)\times 1}$ (and thus for $\hat{\boldsymbol{\beta}}^{GLS}$ to be consistent) we need that $E(\boldsymbol{U}|\boldsymbol{X}) = \boldsymbol{0}_n$, that is, the first GLS assumption must hold.

In contrast, recall the argument that the OLS estimator is consistent. Rewrite Equation (16.14) as $\hat{\boldsymbol{\beta}} = \boldsymbol{\beta} + (\boldsymbol{X}'\boldsymbol{X}/n)^{-1} \frac{1}{n}\sum_{i=1}^{n} \boldsymbol{X}_i u_i$. If $E(u_i|\boldsymbol{X}_i) = 0$, then the term $\frac{1}{n}\sum_{i=1}^{n} \boldsymbol{X}_i u_i$ has mean zero and, if this term has a variance that tends to zero, it converges in probability to zero. If in addition $\boldsymbol{X}'\boldsymbol{X}/n \xrightarrow{p} \boldsymbol{Q}_X$, then $\hat{\boldsymbol{\beta}} \xrightarrow{p} \boldsymbol{\beta}$.

Is the First GLS Assumption Restrictive?   The first GLS assumption requires that the errors for the ith observation be uncorrelated with the regressors for all other observations. This assumption can be dubious in some time series applications. This issue is discussed in Section 13.6 in the context of an empirical example, the relationship between the change in the price of a contract for future delivery of frozen orange concentrate and the weather in Florida. As explained there, the error term in the regression of price changes on the weather is plausibly uncorrelated with current and past values of the weather, so the first OLS assumption holds. However, this error term is plausibly correlated with future values of the weather, so the first GLS assumption does *not* hold.

This example illustrates a general phenomenon in economic time series data that arises when the value of a variable today is set in part based on expectations of the future: those future expectations typically imply that the error term today depends on a forecast of the regressor tomorrow, which in turn is correlated with the actual value of the regressor tomorrow. For this reason, the first GLS assumption is in fact much stronger than the first OLS assumption. Accordingly, in some applications with economic time series data the GLS estimator is not consistent even though the OLS estimator is.

Summary

1. The linear multiple regression model in matrix form is $\boldsymbol{Y} = \boldsymbol{X}\boldsymbol{\beta} + \boldsymbol{U}$, where $\boldsymbol{Y}$ is the $n \times 1$ vector of observations on the dependent variable, $\boldsymbol{X}$ is the $n \times (k + 1)$ matrix of n observations on the $k + 1$ regressors (including a constant), $\boldsymbol{\beta}$ is the $k + 1$ vector of unknown parameters, and $\boldsymbol{U}$ is the $n \times 1$ vector of error terms.

2. The OLS estimator is $\hat{\boldsymbol{\beta}} = (\boldsymbol{X}'\boldsymbol{X})^{-1}\boldsymbol{X}'\boldsymbol{Y}$. Under the first four least squares assumptions in Key Concept 16.1, $\hat{\boldsymbol{\beta}}$ is consistent and asymptotically normally distributed. If in addition the errors are homoskedastic, then the conditional variance of $\hat{\boldsymbol{\beta}}$ is $\text{var}(\hat{\boldsymbol{\beta}}\,|\,\boldsymbol{X}) = \sigma_u^2(\boldsymbol{X}'\boldsymbol{X})^{-1}$.

3. General linear restrictions on $\boldsymbol{\beta}$ can be written as the q equations $\boldsymbol{R}\boldsymbol{\beta} = \boldsymbol{r}$, and this formulation can be used to test joint hypotheses involving multiple coefficients or to construct confidence sets for elements of $\boldsymbol{\beta}$.

4. When the regression errors are i.i.d. and normally distributed, conditional on $\boldsymbol{X}$, $\hat{\boldsymbol{\beta}}$ has an exact normal distribution and the homoskedasticity-only t- and F-statistics respectively have exact t_{n-k-1} and $F_{q,n-k-1}$ distributions.

5. The Gauss-Markov theorem says that, if the errors are homoskedastic and conditionally uncorrelated across observations and if $E(u_i\,|\,\boldsymbol{X}) = 0$, the OLS estimator is efficient among linear conditionally unbiased estimators (OLS is BLUE).

6. If the error covariance matrix $\boldsymbol{\Omega}$ is not proportional to the identity matrix, and if $\boldsymbol{\Omega}$ is known or can be estimated, then the GLS estimator is asymptotically more efficient than OLS. However, GLS requires that, in general, u_i be uncorrelated with *all* observations on the regressors, not just with $\boldsymbol{X}_i$ as is required by OLS, an assumption that must be evaluated carefully in applications.

Key Terms

Review the Concepts

16.1 A researcher studying the relationship between earnings and gender for a group of workers specifies the regression model, $Y_i = \beta_0 + X_{1i}\beta_1 + X_{2i}\beta_2 + u_i$, where X_{1i} is a binary variable that equals one if the ith person is a female and X_{2i} is a binary variable that equals one if the ith person is a male. Write the model in the matrix form of Equation (16.2) for a hypothetical set of $n = 5$ observations. Show that the columns of $\boldsymbol{X}$ are linearly dependent, so that $\boldsymbol{X}$ does not have full rank. Explain how you would respecifiy the model to eliminate the perfect multicollinearity.

16.2 You are analyzing a linear regression model with 500 observations and one regressor. Explain how you would construct a confidence interval for β_1 if:

   a. Assumptions 1–4 in Key Concept 16.1 are true, but you think assumption 5 or 6 might not be true.

   b. Assumptions 1–5 are true, but you think assumption 6 might not be true (give two ways to construct the confidence interval);

   c. Assumptions 1–6 are true.

16.3 Suppose that assumptions 1–5 in Key Concept 16.1 are true, but that assumption 6 is not. Does the result in Equation (16.31) hold? Explain.

16.4 Can you compute the BLUE estimator of β if Equation (16.41) holds and you do not know $\boldsymbol{\Omega}$? What if you know $\boldsymbol{\Omega}$?

16.5 Construct an example of a regression model that satisfies the assumption $E(u_i | X_i) = 0$, but for which $E(\boldsymbol{U} | \boldsymbol{X}) \neq \boldsymbol{0}_n$.

Exercises

*16.1 Consider the population regression of test scores against income and the square of income in Equation (6.1).

   a. Write the regression in Equation (6.1) in the matrix form of Equation (16.4). Define $\boldsymbol{Y}$, $\boldsymbol{X}$, $\boldsymbol{U}$ and β.

   b. Explain how to test the null hypothesis that the relationship between test scores and income is linear against the alternative that it is quadratic. Write the null hypothesis in the form of Equation (16.20). What are $\boldsymbol{R}$, $\boldsymbol{r}$, and q?

16.2 Suppose a sample of $n = 20$ households has the sample means and sample covariances below for a dependent variable and two regressors:

		Sample covariances		
	Sample means	Y	X_1	X_2
$\boldsymbol{Y}$	6.39	0.26	0.22	0.32
$\boldsymbol{X}_1$	7.24		0.80	0.28
$\boldsymbol{X}_2$	4.00			2.40

   a. Calculate the OLS estimates of β_0, β_1, and β_2. Calculate $s_{\hat{u}}^2$. Calculate the R^2 of the regression.

b. Suppose that all six assumptions in Key Concept 16.1 hold. Test the hypothesis that $\beta_1 = 0$ at the 5% significance level.

16.3 Let W be an $m \times 1$ vector with covariance matrix Σ_W, where Σ_W is finite and positive definite. Let c be a nonrandom $m \times 1$ vector, and let $Q = c'W$.

a. Show that $\text{var}(Q) = c'\Sigma_W c$.

b. Suppose that $c \neq 0_m$. Show that $0 < \text{var}(Q) < \infty$.

16.4 Consider the regression model from Chapter 4, $Y_i = \beta_0 + \beta_1 X_i + u_i$, and assume that the assumptions in Key Concept 4.3 hold.

a. Write the model in the matrix form given in Equations (16.2) and (16.4).

b. Show that assumptions 1–4 in Key Concept 16.1 are satisfied.

c. Use the general formula for $\hat{\beta}$ in Equation (16.11) to derive the expressions for $\hat{\beta}_0$ and $\hat{\beta}_1$ given in Key Concept 4.2.

d. Show that the (1,1) element of $\Sigma_{\hat{\beta}}$ in Equation (16.13) is equal to the expression for $\sigma_{\hat{\beta}_0}^2$ given in Key Concept 4.4.

16.5 Let P_X and M_X be as defined in Equation (16.24) and (16.25).

a. Prove that $P_X M_X = 0_{n \times n}$ and that P_X and M_X are idempotent.

b. Derive Equations (16.27) and (16.28).

*16.6 Consider the regression model in matrix form, $Y = X\beta + W\gamma + u$, where X is an $n \times k_1$ matrix of regressors and W is an $n \times k_2$ matrix of regressors. Then the OLS estimator $\hat{\beta}$ can be expressed

$$\hat{\beta} = (X'M_W X)^{-1}(X'M_W Y). \tag{16.45}$$

Now let $\hat{\beta}_1^{BV}$ be the "binary variable" fixed effects estimator computed by estimating Equation (8.11) by OLS, and let $\hat{\beta}_1^{DM}$ be the "de-meaning" fixed effects estimator computed by estimating Equation (8.14) by OLS, in which the entity-specific sample means have been subtracted from X and Y. Use Equation (16.45) to prove that $\hat{\beta}_1^{BV} = \hat{\beta}_1^{DM}$. (*Hint:* Write (8.11) using a full set of fixed effects, $D1_i$, $D2_i$, ..., Dn_i and no constant term. Include all of the fixed effects in W. Write out the matrix $M_W X$.)

16.7 Consider the regression model, $Y_i = \beta_1 X_i + \beta_2 W_i + u_i$, where for simplicity the intercept is omitted and all variables are assumed to have a mean of zero. Suppose X_i is distributed independently of (W_i, u_i) but W_i and u_i might be correlated, and let $\hat{\beta}_1$ and $\hat{\beta}_2$ be the OLS estimators for this model. Show that

a. Whether or not W_i and u_i are correlated, $\hat{\beta}_1 \xrightarrow{p} \beta_1$.

b. If W_i and u_i are correlated, $\hat{\beta}_2$ is inconsistent.

c. Let $\hat{\beta}_1^r$ be the OLS estimator from the regression of Y on X (the restricted regression that excludes W). Provide conditions under which $\hat{\beta}_1$ has a smaller asymptotic variance than $\hat{\beta}_1^r$, allowing for the possibility that W_i and u_i are correlated.

16.8 Consider the regression model $Y_i = \beta_0 + \beta_1 X_i + u_i$, where $u_1 = \tilde{u}_1$ and $u_i = 0.5 u_{i-1} + \tilde{u}_i$ for $i = 2, 3, \ldots, n$. Suppose that $\tilde{u}_i$ are i.i.d. with mean zero and variance one and are distributed independently of X_j for all i and j.

*a. Derive an expression for $E(\boldsymbol{UU'}) = \boldsymbol{\Omega}$.

b. Explain how to estimate the model by GLS without explicitly inverting the matrix $\boldsymbol{\Omega}$. (*Hint*: Transform the model so that the regression errors are $\tilde{u}_1, \tilde{u}_2, \ldots, \tilde{u}_n$.)

16.9 This exercise shows that the OLS estimator of a subset of the regression coefficients is consistent under the conditional mean independence assumption stated in Appendix 11.3. Consider the multiple regression model in matrix form $\boldsymbol{Y} = \boldsymbol{X\beta} + \boldsymbol{W\gamma} + \boldsymbol{u}$, where $\boldsymbol{X}$ and $\boldsymbol{W}$ are, respectively, $n \times k_1$ and $n \times k_2$ matrices of regressors. Let $\boldsymbol{X}_i'$ and $\boldsymbol{W}_i'$ denote the ith rows of $\boldsymbol{X}$ and $\boldsymbol{W}$ (as in Equation (16.3)). Assume that (i) $E(u_i | \boldsymbol{X}_i, \boldsymbol{W}_i) = \boldsymbol{W}_i'\boldsymbol{\delta}$, where $\boldsymbol{\delta}$ is a $k_2 \times 1$ vector of unknown parameters; (ii) $(\boldsymbol{X}_i, \boldsymbol{W}_i, Y_i)$ are i.i.d.; (iii) $(\boldsymbol{X}_i, \boldsymbol{W}_i, u_i)$ have four finite, nonzero moments; and (iv) there is no perfect multicollinearity. These are assumptions $1 - 4$ of Key Concept 16.1, with the conditional mean independence assumption (i) replacing the usual conditional mean zero assumption.

a. Use Equation (16.45) to write $\hat{\boldsymbol{\beta}} - \boldsymbol{\beta} = (n^{-1}\boldsymbol{X'M_WX})^{-1}(n^{-1}\boldsymbol{X'M_WU})$.

b. Show that $n^{-1}\boldsymbol{X'M_WX} \xrightarrow{p} \boldsymbol{\Sigma_{XX}} - \boldsymbol{\Sigma_{XW}}\boldsymbol{\Sigma_{WW}^{-1}}\boldsymbol{\Sigma_{WX}}$, where $\boldsymbol{\Sigma_{XX}} = E(\boldsymbol{X}_i\boldsymbol{X}_i')$, $\boldsymbol{\Sigma_{XW}} = E(\boldsymbol{X}_i\boldsymbol{W}_i')$, etc. (The matrix $\boldsymbol{A}_n \xrightarrow{p} \boldsymbol{A}$ if $\boldsymbol{A}_{n,ij} \xrightarrow{p} \boldsymbol{A}_{ij}$ for all i, j, where $\boldsymbol{A}_{n,ij}$ and $\boldsymbol{A}_{ij}$ are the (i, j) elements of $\boldsymbol{A}_n$ and $\boldsymbol{A}$.)

c. Show that assumptions (i) and (ii) imply that $E(\boldsymbol{U}|\boldsymbol{X}, \boldsymbol{W}) = \boldsymbol{W\delta}$.

d. Use (c) and the law of iterated expectations to show that $n^{-1}\boldsymbol{X'M_WU} \xrightarrow{p} \boldsymbol{0}_{k_1 \times 1}$.

e. Use (a) $-$ (d) to conclude that, under conditions (i) $-$ (iv), $\hat{\boldsymbol{\beta}} \xrightarrow{p} \boldsymbol{\beta}$.

16.1 Summary of Matrix Algebra

This appendix summarizes vectors, matrices, and the elements of matrix algebra used in Chapter 16. The purpose of this appendix is to review some elementary concepts and definitions from a course in linear algebra, not to replace such a course.

Definitions of Vectors and Matrices

A **vector** is a collection of n numbers or elements, collected either in a column (a **column vector**) or in a row (a **row vector**). The n-dimensional column vector b and the n-dimensional row vector c are

$$b = \begin{bmatrix} b_1 \\ b_2 \\ \vdots \\ b_n \end{bmatrix} \text{ and } c = \begin{bmatrix} c_1 & c_2 & \cdots & c_n \end{bmatrix},$$

where b_1 is the first element of b and in general b_i is the ith element of b.

Throughout, a boldface symbol denotes a vector or matrix.

A **matrix** is a collection, or array, of numbers or elements in which the elements are laid out in columns and rows. The dimension of a matrix is $n \times m$, where n is the number of rows and m is the number of columns. The $n \times m$ matrix A is

$$A = \begin{bmatrix} a_{11} & a_{12} & \cdots & a_{1m} \\ a_{21} & a_{22} & \cdots & a_{2m} \\ \vdots & \vdots & & \vdots \\ a_{n1} & a_{n2} & \cdots & a_{nm} \end{bmatrix},$$

where a_{ij} is the (i, j) element of A, that is, a_{ij} is the element that appears in the ith row and j^{th} column. An $n \times m$ matrix consists of n row vectors or, alternatively, of m column vectors.

To distinguish one-dimensional numbers from vectors and matrices, a one-dimensional number is called a **scalar**.

Types of Matrices

Square, symmetric, and diagonal matrices. A matrix is said to be **square** if the number of rows equals the number of columns. A square matrix is said to be **symmetric** if its (i, j) element equals its (j, i) element. A **diagonal** matrix is a square matrix in which all the off-diagonal elements equal zero, that is, if the square matrix A is diagonal, then $a_{ij} = 0$ for $i \neq j$.

Special matrices. An important matrix is the **identity matrix**, I_n, which is an $n \times n$ diagonal matrix with ones on the diagonal. The **null matrix** $0_{n \times m}$ is the $n \times m$ matrix with all elements equal to zero.

The transpose. The **transpose** of a matrix switches the rows and the columns. That is, the transpose of a matrix turns the $n \times m$ matrix A into the $m \times n$ matrix, which is denoted by A', where the (i,j) element of A becomes the (j,i) element of A'; said differently, the transpose of the matrix A turns the rows of A into the columns of A'. If a_{ij} is the (i,j) element of A, then A' (the transpose of A) is

$$A' = \begin{bmatrix} a_{11} & a_{21} & \cdots & a_{n1} \\ a_{12} & a_{22} & \cdots & a_{n2} \\ \vdots & \vdots & & \vdots \\ a_{1m} & a_{2m} & \cdots & a_{nm} \end{bmatrix}.$$

The transpose of a vector is a special case of the transpose of a matrix. Thus the transpose of a vector turns a column vector into a row vector; that is, if b is an $n \times 1$ column vector, then its transpose is the $1 \times n$ row vector

$$b' = [b_1 \quad b_2 \quad \cdots \quad b_n].$$

The transpose of a row vector is a column vector.

Elements of Matrix Algebra
Addition and Multiplication

Matrix addition. Two matrices A and B that have the same dimensions (are both $n \times m$) can be added together. The sum of two matrices is the sum of their elements: That is, if $C = A + B$, then $c_{ij} = a_{ij} + b_{ij}$. A special case of matrix addition is vector addition: if a and b are both $n \times 1$ column vectors, then their sum $c = a + b$ is the element-wise sum, that is, $c_i = a_i + b_i$.

Vector and matrix multiplication. Let a and b be two $n \times 1$ column vectors. Then the product of the transpose of a (which is itself a row vector) with b is $a'b = \sum_{i=1}^{n} a_i b_i$. Applying this definition with $b = a$ yields $a'a = \sum_{i=1}^{n} a_i^2$.

Similarly, the matrices A and B can be multiplied together if they are conformable, that is, if the number of columns of A equals the number of rows of B. Specifically, suppose A has dimension $n \times m$ and B has dimension $m \times r$. Then the product of A and B is an $n \times r$ matrix, C; that is, $C = AB$, where the (i,j) element of C is $c_{ij} = \sum_{k=1}^{m} a_{ik} b_{kj}$. Said differently, the (i,j) element of AB is the product of multiplying the row vector that is the ith row of A with the column vector that is the jth column of B.

The product of a scalar d with the matrix A has the (i, j) element da_{ij}, that is, each element of A is multiplied by the scalar d.

Some useful properties of matrix addition and multiplication. Let A and B be matrices. Then:

    a. $A + B = B + A$;

    b. $(A + B) + C = A + (B + C)$;

    c. $(A + B)' = A' + B'$;

    d. If A is $n \times m$, then $AI_m = A$ and $I_n A = A$;

    e. $A(BC) = (AB)C$;

    f. $(A + B)C = AC + BC$;

    g. $(AB)' = B'A'$.

In general, matrix multiplication does not commute, that is, in general $AB \neq BA$, although there are some special cases in which matrix multiplication commutes, for example if A and B are both $n \times n$ diagonal matrices, then $AB = BA$.

Matrix Inverse, Matrix Square Roots, and Related Topics

The matrix inverse. Let A be a square matrix. Assuming it exists, the **inverse** of the matrix A is defined as the matrix for which $A^{-1}A = I_n$. If in fact the inverse matrix A^{-1} exists, then A is said to be **invertible** or **nonsingular**. If both A and B are invertible, then $(AB)^{-1} = B^{-1}A^{-1}$.

Positive definite and positive semidefinite matrices. Let V be an $n \times n$ square matrix. Then V is **positive definite** if $c'Vc > 0$ for all nonzero $n \times 1$ vectors c. Similarly, V is **positive semidefinite** if $c'Vc \geq 0$ for all nonzero $n \times 1$ vectors c. If V is positive definite then it is invertible.

Linear independence. The $n \times 1$ vectors a_1 and a_2 are **linearly independent** if there do not exist nonzero scalars c_1 and c_2 such that $c_1 a_1 + c_2 a_2 = 0_{n \times 1}$. More generally, the set of k vectors, $a_1, a_2, \ldots, a_k$ are linearly independent if there do not exist nonzero scalars $c_1, c_2, \ldots, c_k$ such that $c_1 a_1 + c_2 a_2 + \cdots + c_k a_k = 0_{n \times 1}$.

The rank of a matrix. The **rank** of the $n \times m$ matrix A is the number of linearly independent columns of A. The rank of A is denoted rank(A). If the rank of A equals the number of columns of A, then A is said to have full column rank. If the $n \times m$ matrix A has full column rank, then there does not exist a nonzero $m \times 1$ vector c such that $Ac = 0_{n \times 1}$. If A is $n \times n$ with rank(A) $= n$, then A is nonsingular. If the $n \times m$ matrix A has full column rank, then $A'A$ is nonsingular.

The matrix square root. Let V be an $n \times n$ square symmetric positive definite matrix. The matrix square root of V is defined to be an $n \times n$ matrix F such that $F'F = V$. The matrix square root of a positive definite matrix will always exist, but it is not unique. The matrix square root has the property that $FV^{-1}F' = I_n$. In addition, the matrix square root of a positive definite matrix is invertible, so that $F'^{-1}VF^{-1} = I_n$.

APPENDIX

16.2 | Multivariate Distributions

This appendix collects various definitions and facts about distributions of vectors of random variables. We start by defining the mean and covariance matrix of the n-dimensional random variable V. Next we present the multivariate normal distribution, and then summarize some facts about the distributions of linear and quadratic functions of jointly normally distributed random variables.

The Mean Vector and Covariance Matrix

The first and second moments of an $m \times 1$ vector of random variables, $V = (V_1\ V_2\ \cdots\ V_m)'$ are summarized by its mean vector and covariance matrix.

Because V is a vector, the vector of its means, that is, its **mean vector**, is $E(V) = \mu_V$. The ith element of the mean vector is the mean of the ith element of V.

The **covariance matrix** of V is the matrix consisting of the variance $\text{var}(V_i)$, $i = 1, \ldots, n$ along the diagonal and the (i,j) off-diagonal elements $\text{cov}(V_i, V_j)$. In matrix form, the covariance matrix Σ_V is

$$\Sigma_V = E[(V - \mu_V)(V - \mu_V)'] = \begin{pmatrix} \text{var}(V_1) & \cdots & \text{cov}(V_1, V_m) \\ \vdots & \ddots & \vdots \\ \text{cov}(V_m, V_1) & \cdots & \text{var}(V_m) \end{pmatrix}. \qquad (16.46)$$

The Multivariate Normal Distribution

The $m \times 1$ vector random variable V has a multivariate normal distribution with mean vector μ_V and covariance matrix Σ_V if it has the joint probability density function

$$f(V) = \frac{1}{\sqrt{(2\pi)^m \det(\Sigma_V)}} \exp\left[-\frac{1}{2}(V - \mu_V)' \Sigma_V^{-1}(V - \mu_V)\right], \qquad (16.47)$$

where $\det(\Sigma_V)$ is the determinant of the matrix Σ_V. The multivariate normal distribution is denoted $N(\mu_V, \Sigma_V)$.

An important fact about the multivariate normal distribution is that if two jointly normally distributed random variables are uncorrelated (equivalently, have a zero covariance matrix), then they are independently distributed. That is, let V_1 and V_2 be jointly normally distributed random variables with respective dimensions $m_1 \times 1$ and $m_2 \times 1$. Then if $\text{cov}(V_1, V_2) = E[(V_1 - \mu_{V_1})(V_2 - \mu_{V_2})'] = 0_{m_1 \times m_2}$, V_1 and V_2 are independent.

If $\{V_i\}$ are i.i.d. $N(0, \sigma_v^2)$, then $\Sigma_V = \sigma_v^2 I_m$, and the multivariate normal distribution simplifies to the product of m univariate normal densities.

Distributions of Linear Combinations and Quadratic Forms of Normal Random Variables

Linear combinations of multivariate normal random variables are themselves normally distributed, and certain quadratic forms of multivariate normal random variables have a chi-squared distribution. Let V be an $m \times 1$ random variable distributed $N(\mu_V, \Sigma_V)$, let A and B be nonrandom $a \times m$ and $b \times m$ matrices, and let d be a nonrandom $a \times 1$ vector. Then

$$d + AV \text{ is distributed } N(d + A\mu_V, A\Sigma_V A'); \tag{16.48}$$

$$\text{cov}(AV, BV) = A\Sigma_V B'; \tag{16.49}$$

$$\text{If } A\Sigma_V B' = 0_{a \times b}, \text{ then } AV \text{ and } BV \text{ are independently distributed}; \tag{16.50}$$

$$V' \Sigma_V^{-1} V \text{ is distributed } \chi_m^2. \tag{16.51}$$

Another useful result concerns quadratic forms involving idempotent matrices. The matrix C is idempotent if C is square and $CC = C$. Let V be an m-dimensional multivariate normal random variable with distribution $N(0, \sigma_v^2 I_m)$. If C is symmetric and idempotent, then

$$V'CV/\sigma_v^2 \text{ has a } \chi_r^2 \text{ distribution, where } r = \text{rank}(C). \tag{16.52}$$

APPENDIX

16.3 | Derivation of the Asymptotic Distribution of $\hat{\beta}$

This appendix provides the derivation of the asymptotic normal distribution of $\sqrt{n}(\hat{\beta} - \beta)$ given in Equation (16.12). An implication of this result is that $\hat{\beta} \xrightarrow{p} \beta$.

First consider the "denominator" matrix $X'X/n = \frac{1}{n}\sum_{i=1}^{n} X_i X_i'$ in Equation (16.15). The (j,l) element of this matrix is $\frac{1}{n}\sum_{i=1}^{n} X_{ji}X_{li}$. By the second assumption in Key Concept 16.1, X_i is i.i.d., so $X_{ji}X_{li}$ is i.i.d. By the third assumption in Key Concept 16.1, each element of X_i has four moments, so, by the Cauchy-Schwarz inequality (Appendix 15.2), $X_{ji}X_{li}$ has two moments. Because $X_{ji}X_{li}$ is i.i.d. with two moments, $\frac{1}{n}\sum_{i=1}^{n} X_{ji}X_{li}$ obeys the law of large numbers, so $\frac{1}{n}\sum_{i=1}^{n} X_{ji}X_{li} \xrightarrow{p} E(X_{ji}X_{li})$. This is true for all the elements of $X'X/n$, so $X'X/n \xrightarrow{p} E(X_i X_i') = Q_X$.

Next consider the "numerator" matrix in Equation (16.15), $X'U/\sqrt{n} = \sqrt{\frac{1}{n}}\sum_{i=1}^{n} V_i$, where $V_i = X_i u_i$. By the first assumption in Key Concept 16.1 and the law of iterated expectations, $E(V_i) = E[X_i E(u_i|X_i)] = 0_{k+1}$. By the second least squares assumption, V_i is i.i.d. Let c be a finite $k + 1$ dimensional vector. By the Cauchy-Schwarz inequality $E[(c'V_i)^2] = E[(c'X_i u_i)^2] = E[(c'X_i)^2(u_i)^2] \leq \sqrt{E[(c'X_i)^4]E(u_i^4)}$, which is finite by the third least squares assumption. This is true for every such vector c, so $E(V_i V_i') = \Sigma_V$ is finite and, we assume, positive definite. Thus the multivariate central limit theorem of Key Concept 16.2 applies to $\sqrt{\frac{1}{n}\sum_{i=1}^{n}}V_i = \frac{1}{\sqrt{n}}X'U$, that is,

$$\frac{1}{\sqrt{n}}X'U \xrightarrow{d} N(0_{k+1}, \Sigma_V). \tag{16.53}$$

The result in Equation (16.12) follows from Equations (16.15) and (16.53), the consistency of $X'X/n$, the fourth least squares assumption (which ensures that $(X'X)^{-1}$ exists), and Slutsky's theorem.

APPENDIX
16.4

Derivations of Exact Distributions of OLS Test Statistics with Normal Errors

This appendix presents the proofs of the distributions under the null hypothesis of the homoskedasticity-only t-statistic in Equation (16.35) and the homoskedasticity-only F-statistic in Equation (16.37), assuming that all six assumptions in Key Concept 16.1 hold.

Proof of Equation (16.35)

If (i) Z has a standard normal distribution, (ii) W has a χ^2_m distribution, and (iii) Z and W are independently distributed, then the random variable $Z/\sqrt{W/m}$ has the t-distribution with m degrees of freedom (Appendix 15.1). To put $\tilde{t}$ in this form, notice that $\tilde{\Sigma}_{\hat{\beta}} = (s_{\hat{u}}^2/\sigma_u^2)\Sigma_{\hat{\beta}|X}$. Then rewrite Equation (16.34) as

$$\tilde{t} = \frac{(\hat{\beta}_j - \beta_{j,0})/\sqrt{(\Sigma_{\hat{\beta}|X})_{jj}}}{\sqrt{W/(n-k-1)}}, \tag{16.54}$$

where $W = (n-k-1)(s_{\hat{u}}^2/\sigma_u^2)$, and let $Z = (\hat{\beta}_j - \beta_{j,0})/\sqrt{(\Sigma_{\hat{\beta}|X})_{jj}}$ and $m = n-k-1$. With these definitions, $\tilde{t} = Z/\sqrt{W/m}$. Thus, to prove the result in Equation (16.35) we must show (i)–(iii) for these definitions of Z, W, and m.

    i.   An implication of Equation (16.30) is that, under the null hypothesis, $Z = (\hat{\beta}_j - \beta_{j,0})/\sqrt{(\Sigma_{\hat{\beta}|X})_{jj}}$ has an exact standard normal distribution, which shows (i).

    ii. From Equation (16.31), W is distributed as χ^2_{n-k-1}, which shows (ii).

    iii. To show (iii), it must be shown that $\hat{\beta}_j$ and $s_{\hat{u}}^2$ are independently distributed.

From Equations (16.14) and (16.29), $\hat{\beta} - \beta = (X'X)^{-1}X'U$ and $s_{\hat{u}}^2 = (M_X U)'(M_X U)/(n-k-1)$. Thus $\hat{\beta} - \beta$ and $s_{\hat{u}}^2$ are independent if $(X'X)^{-1}X'U$ and

$M_X U$ are independent. Both $(X'X)^{-1}X'U$ and $M_X U$ are linear combinations of U, which has an $N(\mathbf{0}_{n\times 1}, \sigma_u^2 I_n)$ distribution, conditional on X. But because $M_X X(X'X)^{-1} = \mathbf{0}_{n\times(k+1)}$ (Equation (16.26)), it follows that $(X'X)^{-1}X'U$ and $M_X U$ are independently distributed (Equation (16.50)). Consequently, under all six assumptions in Key Concept 16.1,

$$\hat{\boldsymbol{\beta}} \text{ and } s_{\hat{u}}^2 \text{ are independently distributed,} \tag{16.55}$$

which shows (iii) and thus proves Equation (16.35).

Proof of Equation (16.37)

The F_{n_1, n_2} distribution is the distribution of $(W_1/n_1) / (W_2/n_2)$, where (i) W_1 is distributed $\chi_{n_1}^2$; (ii) W_2 is distributed $\chi_{n_2}^2$; and (iii) W_1 and W_2 are independently distributed (Appendix 15.1). To express $\widetilde{F}$ in this form, let $W_1 = (R\hat{\boldsymbol{\beta}} - r)'[R(X'X)^{-1}R'\sigma_u^2]^{-1}(R\hat{\boldsymbol{\beta}} - r)$ and $W_2 = (n - k - 1)s_{\hat{u}}^2/\sigma_u^2$. Substitution of these definitions into Equation (16.36) shows that $\widetilde{F} = (W_1/q)/[W_2/(n - k - 1)]$. Thus, by the definition of the F distribution, $\widetilde{F}$ has a $F_{q, n-k-1}$ distribution if (i)–(iii) hold with $n_1 = q$ and $n_2 = n - k - 1$.

    i.   Under the null hypothesis, $R\hat{\boldsymbol{\beta}} - r = R(\hat{\boldsymbol{\beta}} - \boldsymbol{\beta})$. Because $\hat{\boldsymbol{\beta}}$ has the conditional normal distribution in Equation (16.30) and because R is a nonrandom matrix, $R(\hat{\boldsymbol{\beta}} - \boldsymbol{\beta})$ is distributed $N(\mathbf{0}_{q\times 1}, R(X'X)^{-1}R'\sigma_u^2)$, conditional on X. Thus, by Equation (16.51) in Appendix 16.2, $(R\hat{\boldsymbol{\beta}} - r)'[R(X'X)^{-1}R'\sigma_u^2]^{-1}(R\hat{\boldsymbol{\beta}} - r)$ is distributed χ_q^2, proving (i).

   ii.   Requirement (ii) is shown in Equation (16.31).

  iii.   It has already been shown that $\hat{\boldsymbol{\beta}} - \boldsymbol{\beta}$ and $s_{\hat{u}}^2$ are independently distributed (Equation (16.55)). It follows that $R\hat{\boldsymbol{\beta}} - r$ and $s_{\hat{u}}^2$ are independently distributed, which in turn implies that W_1 and W_2 are independently distributed, proving (iii) and completing the proof.

Proof of the Gauss-Markov Theorem for Multiple Regression

This appendix proves the Gauss-Markov theorem (Key Concept 16.3) for the multiple regression model. Let $\widetilde{\boldsymbol{\beta}}$ be a linear conditionally unbiased estimator of $\boldsymbol{\beta}$, so that $\widetilde{\boldsymbol{\beta}} = A'Y$

and $E(\tilde{\beta}|X) = \beta$, where A is a $n \times (k + 1)$ matrix that can depend on X and nonrandom constants. We show that $\text{var}(c'\hat{\beta}) \leq \text{var}(c'\tilde{\beta})$ for all $k + 1$ dimensional vectors c, where the inequality holds with equality only if $\tilde{\beta} = \hat{\beta}$.

Because $\tilde{\beta}$ is linear, it can be written as $\tilde{\beta} = A'Y = A'(X\beta + U) = (A'X)\beta + A'U$. By the first Gauss-Markov condition, $E(U|X) = \mathbf{0}_{n\times1}$, so $E(\tilde{\beta}|X) = (A'X)\beta$, but because $\tilde{\beta}$ is conditionally unbiased $E(\tilde{\beta}|X) = \beta = (A'X)\beta$, which implies that $A'X = I_{k+1}$. Thus $\tilde{\beta} = \beta + A'U$, so $\text{var}(\tilde{\beta}|X) = \text{var}(A'U|X) = E(A'UU'A|X) = A'E(UU'|X)A = \sigma_u^2 A'A$, where the third equality follows because A can depend on X but not U and the final equality follows from second Gauss-Markov condition. That is, if $\tilde{\beta}$ is linear and unbiased, then under the Gauss-Markov conditions

$$A'X = I_{k+1} \text{ and } \text{var}(\tilde{\beta}|X) = \sigma_u^2 A'A. \tag{16.56}$$

The results in Equation (16.56) also apply to $\hat{\beta}$ with $A = \hat{A} = X(X'X)^{-1}$, where $(X'X)^{-1}$ exists by the third Gauss-Markov condition.

Now let $A = \hat{A} + D$, so that D is the difference between the weight matrices A and $\hat{A}$. Note that $\hat{A}'A = (X'X)^{-1}X'A = (X'X)^{-1}$ (by Equation (16.56)) and $\hat{A}'\hat{A} = (X'X)^{-1}X'X(X'X)^{-1} = (X'X)^{-1}$, so $\hat{A}'D = \hat{A}'(A - \hat{A}) = \hat{A}'A - \hat{A}'\hat{A} = \mathbf{0}_{(k+1)\times(k+1)}$. Substituting $A = \hat{A} + D$ into the formula for the conditional variance in Equation (16.56) yields

$$\begin{aligned}\text{var}(\tilde{\beta}|X) &= \sigma_u^2(\hat{A} + D)'(\hat{A} + D) \\ &= \sigma_u^2[\hat{A}'\hat{A} + \hat{A}'D + D'\hat{A} + D'D] \\ &= \sigma_u^2(X'X)^{-1} + \sigma_u^2 D'D,\end{aligned} \tag{16.57}$$

where the final equality uses the facts $\hat{A}'\hat{A} = (X'X)^{-1}$ and $\hat{A}'D' = \mathbf{0}_{(k+1)\times(k+1)}$.

Because $\text{var}(\hat{\beta}|X) = \sigma_u^2(X'X)^{-1}$, Equations (16.56) and (16.57) imply that $\text{var}(\tilde{\beta}|X) - \text{var}(\hat{\beta}|X) = \sigma_u^2 D'D$. The difference between the variances of the two estimators of the linear combination $c'\beta$ thus is

$$\text{var}(c'\tilde{\beta}|X) - \text{var}(c'\hat{\beta}|X) = \sigma_u^2\, c'D'D\, c \geq 0. \tag{16.58}$$

The inequality in Equation (16.58) holds for all linear combinations $c'\beta$, and the inequality holds with equality for all nonzero c only if $D = \mathbf{0}_{n\times(k+1)}$; that is, if $A = \hat{A}$ or, equivalently, $\tilde{\beta} = \hat{\beta}$. Thus $c'\hat{\beta}$ has the smallest variance of all linear conditionally unbiased estimators of $c'\beta$, that is, the OLS estimator is BLUE.

Appendix

TABLE 1   The Cumulative Standard Normal Distribution Function, $\Phi(z) = \Pr(Z \le z)$

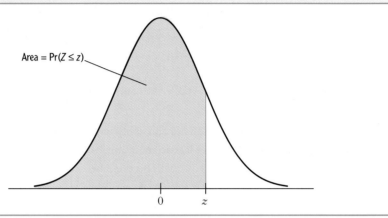

Area = $\Pr(Z \le z)$

0   z

| z | \multicolumn{10}{c}{Second Decimal Value of z} |
	0	1	2	3	4	5	6	7	8	9
−2.9	0.0019	0.0018	0.0018	0.0017	0.0016	0.0016	0.0015	0.0015	0.0014	0.0014
−2.8	0.0026	0.0025	0.0024	0.0023	0.0023	0.0022	0.0021	0.0021	0.0020	0.0019
−2.7	0.0035	0.0034	0.0033	0.0032	0.0031	0.0030	0.0029	0.0028	0.0027	0.0026
−2.6	0.0047	0.0045	0.0044	0.0043	0.0041	0.0040	0.0039	0.0038	0.0037	0.0036
−2.5	0.0062	0.0060	0.0059	0.0057	0.0055	0.0054	0.0052	0.0051	0.0049	0.0048
−2.4	0.0082	0.0080	0.0078	0.0075	0.0073	0.0071	0.0069	0.0068	0.0066	0.0064
−2.3	0.0107	0.0104	0.0102	0.0099	0.0096	0.0094	0.0091	0.0089	0.0087	0.0084
−2.2	0.0139	0.0136	0.0132	0.0129	0.0125	0.0122	0.0119	0.0116	0.0113	0.0110
−2.1	0.0179	0.0174	0.0170	0.0166	0.0162	0.0158	0.0154	0.0150	0.0146	0.0143
−2.0	0.0228	0.0222	0.0217	0.0212	0.0207	0.0202	0.0197	0.0192	0.0188	0.0183
−1.9	0.0287	0.0281	0.0274	0.0268	0.0262	0.0256	0.0250	0.0244	0.0239	0.0233
−1.8	0.0359	0.0351	0.0344	0.0336	0.0329	0.0322	0.0314	0.0307	0.0301	0.0294
−1.7	0.0446	0.0436	0.0427	0.0418	0.0409	0.0401	0.0392	0.0384	0.0375	0.0367
−1.6	0.0548	0.0537	0.0526	0.0516	0.0505	0.0495	0.0485	0.0475	0.0465	0.0455
−1.5	0.0668	0.0655	0.0643	0.0630	0.0618	0.0606	0.0594	0.0582	0.0571	0.0559
−1.4	0.0808	0.0793	0.0778	0.0764	0.0749	0.0735	0.0721	0.0708	0.0694	0.0681
−1.3	0.0968	0.0951	0.0934	0.0918	0.0901	0.0885	0.0869	0.0853	0.0838	0.0823
−1.2	0.1151	0.1131	0.1112	0.1093	0.1075	0.1056	0.1038	0.1020	0.1003	0.0985
−1.1	0.1357	0.1335	0.1314	0.1292	0.1271	0.1251	0.1230	0.1210	0.1190	0.1170
−1.0	0.1587	0.1562	0.1539	0.1515	0.1492	0.1469	0.1446	0.1423	0.1401	0.1379
−0.9	0.1841	0.1814	0.1788	0.1762	0.1736	0.1711	0.1685	0.1660	0.1635	0.1611

TABLE 1 *(continued)*

z	\multicolumn{10}{c}{Second Decimal Value of z}
	0	1	2	3	4	5	6	7	8	9
−0.8	0.2119	0.2090	0.2061	0.2033	0.2005	0.1977	0.1949	0.1922	0.1894	0.1867
−0.7	0.2420	0.2389	0.2358	0.2327	0.2296	0.2266	0.2236	0.2206	0.2177	0.2148
−0.6	0.2743	0.2709	0.2676	0.2643	0.2611	0.2578	0.2546	0.2514	0.2483	0.2451
−0.5	0.3085	0.3050	0.3015	0.2981	0.2946	0.2912	0.2877	0.2843	0.2810	0.2776
−0.4	0.3446	0.3409	0.3372	0.3336	0.3300	0.3264	0.3228	0.3192	0.3156	0.3121
−0.3	0.3821	0.3783	0.3745	0.3707	0.3669	0.3632	0.3594	0.3557	0.3520	0.3483
−0.2	0.4207	0.4168	0.4129	0.4090	0.4052	0.4013	0.3974	0.3936	0.3897	0.3859
−0.1	0.4602	0.4562	0.4522	0.4483	0.4443	0.4404	0.4364	0.4325	0.4286	0.4247
−0.0	0.5000	0.4960	0.4920	0.4880	0.4840	0.4801	0.4761	0.4721	0.4681	0.4641
0.0	0.5000	0.5040	0.5080	0.5120	0.5160	0.5199	0.5239	0.5279	0.5319	0.5359
0.1	0.5398	0.5438	0.5478	0.5517	0.5557	0.5596	0.5636	0.5675	0.5714	0.5753
0.2	0.5793	0.5832	0.5871	0.5910	0.5948	0.5987	0.6026	0.6064	0.6103	0.6141
0.3	0.6179	0.6217	0.6255	0.6293	0.6331	0.6368	0.6406	0.6443	0.6480	0.6517
0.4	0.6554	0.6591	0.6628	0.6664	0.6700	0.6736	0.6772	0.6808	0.6844	0.6879
0.5	0.6915	0.6950	0.6985	0.7019	0.7054	0.7088	0.7123	0.7157	0.7190	0.7224
0.6	0.7257	0.7291	0.7324	0.7357	0.7389	0.7422	0.7454	0.7486	0.7517	0.7549
0.7	0.7580	0.7611	0.7642	0.7673	0.7704	0.7734	0.7764	0.7794	0.7823	0.7852
0.8	0.7881	0.7910	0.7939	0.7967	0.7995	0.8023	0.8051	0.8078	0.8106	0.8133
0.9	0.8159	0.8186	0.8212	0.8238	0.8264	0.8289	0.8315	0.8340	0.8365	0.8389
1.0	0.8413	0.8438	0.8461	0.8485	0.8508	0.8531	0.8554	0.8577	0.8599	0.8621
1.1	0.8643	0.8665	0.8686	0.8708	0.8729	0.8749	0.8770	0.8790	0.8810	0.8830
1.2	0.8849	0.8869	0.8888	0.8907	0.8925	0.8944	0.8962	0.8980	0.8997	0.9015
1.3	0.9032	0.9049	0.9066	0.9082	0.9099	0.9115	0.9131	0.9147	0.9162	0.9177
1.4	0.9192	0.9207	0.9222	0.9236	0.9251	0.9265	0.9279	0.9292	0.9306	0.9319
1.5	0.9332	0.9345	0.9357	0.9370	0.9382	0.9394	0.9406	0.9418	0.9429	0.9441
1.6	0.9452	0.9463	0.9474	0.9484	0.9495	0.9505	0.9515	0.9525	0.9535	0.9545
1.7	0.9554	0.9564	0.9573	0.9582	0.9591	0.9599	0.9608	0.9616	0.9625	0.9633
1.8	0.9641	0.9649	0.9656	0.9664	0.9671	0.9678	0.9686	0.9693	0.9699	0.9706
1.9	0.9713	0.9719	0.9726	0.9732	0.9738	0.9744	0.9750	0.9756	0.9761	0.9767
2.0	0.9772	0.9778	0.9783	0.9788	0.9793	0.9798	0.9803	0.9808	0.9812	0.9817
2.1	0.9821	0.9826	0.9830	0.9834	0.9838	0.9842	0.9846	0.9850	0.9854	0.9857
2.2	0.9861	0.9864	0.9868	0.9871	0.9875	0.9878	0.9881	0.9884	0.9887	0.9890
2.3	0.9893	0.9896	0.9898	0.9901	0.9904	0.9906	0.9909	0.9911	0.9913	0.9916
2.4	0.9918	0.9920	0.9922	0.9925	0.9927	0.9929	0.9931	0.9932	0.9934	0.9936
2.5	0.9938	0.9940	0.9941	0.9943	0.9945	0.9946	0.9948	0.9949	0.9951	0.9952
2.6	0.9953	0.9955	0.9956	0.9957	0.9959	0.9960	0.9961	0.9962	0.9963	0.9964
2.7	0.9965	0.9966	0.9967	0.9968	0.9969	0.9970	0.9971	0.9972	0.9973	0.9974
2.8	0.9974	0.9975	0.9976	0.9977	0.9977	0.9978	0.9979	0.9979	0.9980	0.9981
2.9	0.9981	0.9982	0.9982	0.9983	0.9984	0.9984	0.9985	0.9985	0.9986	0.9986

This table can be used to calculate $\Pr(Z \leq z)$ where Z is a standard normal variable. For example, when $z = 1.17$, this probability is 0.8790, which is the table entry for the row labeled 1.1 and the column labeled 7.

TABLE 2   Critical Values for 2-Sided and 1-Sided Tests Using the Student *t* Distribution

Degrees of Freedom	20% (2-Sided) 10% (1-Sided)	10% (2-Sided) 5% (1-Sided)	5% (2-Sided) 2.5% (1-Sided)	2% (2-Sided) 1% (1-Sided)	1% (2-Sided) 0.5% (1-Sided)
1	3.08	6.31	12.71	31.82	63.66
2	1.89	2.92	4.30	6.96	9.92
3	1.64	2.35	3.18	4.54	5.84
4	1.53	2.13	2.78	3.75	4.60
5	1.48	2.02	2.57	3.36	4.03
6	1.44	1.94	2.45	3.14	3.71
7	1.41	1.89	2.36	3.00	3.50
8	1.40	1.86	2.31	2.90	3.36
9	1.38	1.83	2.26	2.82	3.25
10	1.37	1.81	2.23	2.76	3.17
11	1.36	1.80	2.20	2.72	3.11
12	1.36	1.78	2.18	2.68	3.05
13	1.35	1.77	2.16	2.65	3.01
14	1.35	1.76	2.14	2.62	2.98
15	1.34	1.75	2.13	2.60	2.95
16	1.34	1.75	2.12	2.58	2.92
17	1.33	1.74	2.11	2.57	2.90
18	1.33	1.73	2.10	2.55	2.88
19	1.33	1.73	2.09	2.54	2.86
20	1.33	1.72	2.09	2.53	2.85
21	1.32	1.72	2.08	2.52	2.83
22	1.32	1.72	2.07	2.51	2.82
23	1.32	1.71	2.07	2.50	2.81
24	1.32	1.71	2.06	2.49	2.80
25	1.32	1.71	2.06	2.49	2.79
26	1.32	1.71	2.06	2.48	2.78
27	1.31	1.70	2.05	2.47	2.77
28	1.31	1.70	2.05	2.47	2.76
29	1.31	1.70	2.05	2.46	2.76
30	1.31	1.70	2.04	2.46	2.75
60	1.30	1.67	2.00	2.39	2.66
90	1.29	1.66	1.99	2.37	2.63
120	1.29	1.66	1.98	2.36	2.62
∞	**1.28**	**1.64**	**1.96**	**2.33**	**2.58**

Values are shown for the critical values for 2-sided (≠) and 1-sided (>) alternative hypotheses. The critical value for the 1-sided (<) test is the negative of the 1-sided (>) critical value shown in the table. For example, 2.13 is the critical value for a 2-sided test with a significance level of 5% using the Student *t* distribution with 15 degrees of freedom.

TABLE 3 Critical Values for the χ^2 Distribution

Degrees of Freedom	Significance Level		
	10%	5%	1%
1	2.71	3.84	6.63
2	4.61	5.99	9.21
3	6.25	7.81	11.34
4	7.78	9.49	13.28
5	9.24	11.07	15.09
6	10.64	12.59	16.81
7	12.02	14.07	18.48
8	13.36	15.51	20.09
9	14.68	16.92	21.67
10	15.99	18.31	23.21
11	17.28	19.68	24.72
12	18.55	21.03	26.22
13	19.81	22.36	27.69
14	21.06	23.68	29.14
15	22.31	25.00	30.58
16	23.54	26.30	32.00
17	24.77	27.59	33.41
18	25.99	28.87	34.81
19	27.20	30.14	36.19
20	28.41	31.41	37.57
21	29.62	32.67	38.93
22	30.81	33.92	40.29
23	32.01	35.17	41.64
24	33.20	36.41	42.98
25	34.38	37.65	44.31
26	35.56	38.89	45.64
27	36.74	40.11	46.96
28	37.92	41.34	48.28
29	39.09	42.56	49.59
30	40.26	43.77	50.89

This table contains the 90th, 95th, and 99th percentiles of the χ^2 distribution. These serve as critical values for tests with significance levels of 10%, 5%, and 1%.

TABLE 4   Critical Values for the $F_{m,\infty}$ Distribution

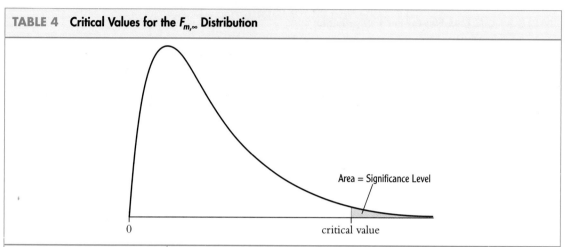

Area = Significance Level

critical value

Degrees of Freedom	Significance Level		
	10%	5%	1%
1	2.71	3.84	6.63
2	2.30	3.00	4.61
3	2.08	2.60	3.78
4	1.94	2.37	3.32
5	1.85	2.21	3.02
6	1.77	2.10	2.80
7	1.72	2.01	2.64
8	1.67	1.94	2.51
9	1.63	1.88	2.41
10	1.60	1.83	2.32
11	1.57	1.79	2.25
12	1.55	1.75	2.18
13	1.52	1.72	2.13
14	1.50	1.69	2.08
15	1.49	1.67	2.04
16	1.47	1.64	2.00
17	1.46	1.62	1.97
18	1.44	1.60	1.93
19	1.43	1.59	1.90
20	1.42	1.57	1.88
21	1.41	1.56	1.85
22	1.40	1.54	1.83
23	1.39	1.53	1.81
24	1.38	1.52	1.79
25	1.38	1.51	1.77
26	1.37	1.50	1.76
27	1.36	1.49	1.74
28	1.35	1.48	1.72
29	1.35	1.47	1.71
30	1.34	1.46	1.70

This table contains the 90th, 95th, and 99th percentiles of the $F_{m,\infty}$ distribution. These serve as critical values for tests with significance levels of 10%, 5%, and 1%.

TABLE 5A Critical Values for the F_{n_1, n_2} Distribution—10% Significance Level

Denominator Degrees of Freedom (n_2)	Numerator Degrees of Freedom (n_1)									
	1	2	3	4	5	6	7	8	9	10
1	39.86	49.50	53.59	55.83	57.24	58.20	58.90	59.44	59.86	60.20
2	8.53	9.00	9.16	9.24	9.29	9.33	9.35	9.37	9.38	9.39
3	5.54	5.46	5.39	5.34	5.31	5.28	5.27	5.25	5.24	5.23
4	4.54	4.32	4.19	4.11	4.05	4.01	3.98	3.95	3.94	3.92
5	4.06	3.78	3.62	3.52	3.45	3.40	3.37	3.34	3.32	3.30
6	3.78	3.46	3.29	3.18	3.11	3.05	3.01	2.98	2.96	2.94
7	3.59	3.26	3.07	2.96	2.88	2.83	2.78	2.75	2.72	2.70
8	3.46	3.11	2.92	2.81	2.73	2.67	2.62	2.59	2.56	2.54
9	3.36	3.01	2.81	2.69	2.61	2.55	2.51	2.47	2.44	2.42
10	3.29	2.92	2.73	2.61	2.52	2.46	2.41	2.38	2.35	2.32
11	3.23	2.86	2.66	2.54	2.45	2.39	2.34	2.30	2.27	2.25
12	3.18	2.81	2.61	2.48	2.39	2.33	2.28	2.24	2.21	2.19
13	3.14	2.76	2.56	2.43	2.35	2.28	2.23	2.20	2.16	2.14
14	3.10	2.73	2.52	2.39	2.31	2.24	2.19	2.15	2.12	2.10
15	3.07	2.70	2.49	2.36	2.27	2.21	2.16	2.12	2.09	2.06
16	3.05	2.67	2.46	2.33	2.24	2.18	2.13	2.09	2.06	2.03
17	3.03	2.64	2.44	2.31	2.22	2.15	2.10	2.06	2.03	2.00
18	3.01	2.62	2.42	2.29	2.20	2.13	2.08	2.04	2.00	1.98
19	2.99	2.61	2.40	2.27	2.18	2.11	2.06	2.02	1.98	1.96
20	2.97	2.59	2.38	2.25	2.16	2.09	2.04	2.00	1.96	1.94
21	2.96	2.57	2.36	2.23	2.14	2.08	2.02	1.98	1.95	1.92
22	2.95	2.56	2.35	2.22	2.13	2.06	2.01	1.97	1.93	1.90
23	2.94	2.55	2.34	2.21	2.11	2.05	1.99	1.95	1.92	1.89
24	2.93	2.54	2.33	2.19	2.10	2.04	1.98	1.94	1.91	1.88
25	2.92	2.53	2.32	2.18	2.09	2.02	1.97	1.93	1.89	1.87
26	2.91	2.52	2.31	2.17	2.08	2.01	1.96	1.92	1.88	1.86
27	2.90	2.51	2.30	2.17	2.07	2.00	1.95	1.91	1.87	1.85
28	2.89	2.50	2.29	2.16	2.06	2.00	1.94	1.90	1.87	1.84
29	2.89	2.50	2.28	2.15	2.06	1.99	1.93	1.89	1.86	1.83
30	2.88	2.49	2.28	2.14	2.05	1.98	1.93	1.88	1.85	1.82
60	2.79	2.39	2.18	2.04	1.95	1.87	1.82	1.77	1.74	1.71
90	2.76	2.36	2.15	2.01	1.91	1.84	1.78	1.74	1.70	1.67
120	2.75	2.35	2.13	1.99	1.90	1.82	1.77	1.72	1.68	1.65

This table contains the 90th percentile of the F_{n_1, n_2} distribution, which serves as the critical values for a test with a 10% significance level.

TABLE 5B   Critical Values for the F_{n_1, n_2} Distribution—5% Significance Level

Denominator Degrees of Freedom (n_2)	Numerator Degrees of Freedom (n_1)									
	1	2	3	4	5	6	7	8	9	10
1	161.40	199.50	215.70	224.60	230.20	234.00	236.80	238.90	240.50	241.90
2	18.51	19.00	19.16	19.25	19.30	19.33	19.35	19.37	19.39	19.40
3	10.13	9.55	9.28	9.12	9.01	8.94	8.89	8.85	8.81	8.79
4	7.71	6.94	6.59	6.39	6.26	6.16	6.09	6.04	6.00	5.96
5	6.61	5.79	5.41	5.19	5.05	4.95	4.88	4.82	4.77	4.74
6	5.99	5.14	4.76	4.53	4.39	4.28	4.21	4.15	4.10	4.06
7	5.59	4.74	4.35	4.12	3.97	3.87	3.79	3.73	3.68	3.64
8	5.32	4.46	4.07	3.84	3.69	3.58	3.50	3.44	3.39	3.35
9	5.12	4.26	3.86	3.63	3.48	3.37	3.29	3.23	3.18	3.14
10	4.96	4.10	3.71	3.48	3.33	3.22	3.14	3.07	3.02	2.98
11	4.84	3.98	3.59	3.36	3.20	3.09	3.01	2.95	2.90	2.85
12	4.75	3.89	3.49	3.26	3.11	3.00	2.91	2.85	2.80	2.75
13	4.67	3.81	3.41	3.18	3.03	2.92	2.83	2.77	2.71	2.67
14	4.60	3.74	3.34	3.11	2.96	2.85	2.76	2.70	2.65	2.60
15	4.54	3.68	3.29	3.06	2.90	2.79	2.71	2.64	2.59	2.54
16	4.49	3.63	3.24	3.01	2.85	2.74	2.66	2.59	2.54	2.49
17	4.45	3.59	3.20	2.96	2.81	2.70	2.61	2.55	2.49	2.45
18	4.41	3.55	3.16	2.93	2.77	2.66	2.58	2.51	2.46	2.41
19	4.38	3.52	3.13	2.90	2.74	2.63	2.54	2.48	2.42	2.38
20	4.35	3.49	3.10	2.87	2.71	2.60	2.51	2.45	2.39	2.35
21	4.32	3.47	3.07	2.84	2.68	2.57	2.49	2.42	2.37	2.32
22	4.30	3.44	3.05	2.82	2.66	2.55	2.46	2.40	2.34	2.30
23	4.28	3.42	3.03	2.80	2.64	2.53	2.44	2.37	2.32	2.27
24	4.26	3.40	3.01	2.78	2.62	2.51	2.42	2.36	2.30	2.25
25	4.24	3.39	2.99	2.76	2.60	2.49	2.40	2.34	2.28	2.24
26	4.23	3.37	2.98	2.74	2.59	2.47	2.39	2.32	2.27	2.22
27	4.21	3.35	2.96	2.73	2.57	2.46	2.37	2.31	2.25	2.20
28	4.20	3.34	2.95	2.71	2.56	2.45	2.36	2.29	2.24	2.19
29	4.18	3.33	2.93	2.70	2.55	2.43	2.35	2.28	2.22	2.18
30	4.17	3.32	2.92	2.69	2.53	2.42	2.33	2.27	2.21	2.16
60	4.00	3.15	2.76	2.53	2.37	2.25	2.17	2.10	2.04	1.99
90	3.95	3.10	2.71	2.47	2.32	2.20	2.11	2.04	1.99	1.94
120	3.92	3.07	2.68	2.45	2.29	2.18	2.09	2.02	1.96	1.91

This table contains the 95th percentile of the F_{n_1, n_2} distribution, which serves as the critical values for a test with a 5% significance level.

TABLE 5C Critical Values for the F_{n_1,n_2} Distribution—1% Significance Level

Denominator Degrees of Freedom (n_2)	Numerator Degrees of Freedom (n_1)									
	1	2	3	4	5	6	7	8	9	10
1	4052.00	4999.00	5403.00	5624.00	5763.00	5859.00	5928.00	5981.00	6022.00	6055.00
2	98.50	99.00	99.17	99.25	99.30	99.33	99.36	99.37	99.39	99.40
3	34.12	30.82	29.46	28.71	28.24	27.91	27.67	27.49	27.35	27.23
4	21.20	18.00	16.69	15.98	15.52	15.21	14.98	14.80	14.66	14.55
5	16.26	13.27	12.06	11.39	10.97	10.67	10.46	10.29	10.16	10.05
6	13.75	10.92	9.78	9.15	8.75	8.47	8.26	8.10	7.98	7.87
7	12.25	9.55	8.45	7.85	7.46	7.19	6.99	6.84	6.72	6.62
8	11.26	8.65	7.59	7.01	6.63	6.37	6.18	6.03	5.91	5.81
9	10.56	8.02	6.99	6.42	6.06	5.80	5.61	5.47	5.35	5.26
10	10.04	7.56	6.55	5.99	5.64	5.39	5.20	5.06	4.94	4.85
11	9.65	7.21	6.22	5.67	5.32	5.07	4.89	4.74	4.63	4.54
12	9.33	6.93	5.95	5.41	5.06	4.82	4.64	4.50	4.39	4.30
13	9.07	6.70	5.74	5.21	4.86	4.62	4.44	4.30	4.19	4.10
14	8.86	6.51	5.56	5.04	4.69	4.46	4.28	4.14	4.03	3.94
15	8.68	6.36	5.42	4.89	4.56	4.32	4.14	4.00	3.89	3.80
16	8.53	6.23	5.29	4.77	4.44	4.20	4.03	3.89	3.78	3.69
17	8.40	6.11	5.18	4.67	4.34	4.10	3.93	3.79	3.68	3.59
18	8.29	6.01	5.09	4.58	4.25	4.01	3.84	3.71	3.60	3.51
19	8.18	5.93	5.01	4.50	4.17	3.94	3.77	3.63	3.52	3.43
20	8.10	5.85	4.94	4.43	4.10	3.87	3.70	3.56	3.46	3.37
21	8.02	5.78	4.87	4.37	4.04	3.81	3.64	3.51	3.40	3.31
22	7.95	5.72	4.82	4.31	3.99	3.76	3.59	3.45	3.35	3.26
23	7.88	5.66	4.76	4.26	3.94	3.71	3.54	3.41	3.30	3.21
24	7.82	5.61	4.72	4.22	3.90	3.67	3.50	3.36	3.26	3.17
25	7.77	5.57	4.68	4.18	3.85	3.63	3.46	3.32	3.22	3.13
26	7.72	5.53	4.64	4.14	3.82	3.59	3.42	3.29	3.18	3.09
27	7.68	5.49	4.60	4.11	3.78	3.56	3.39	3.26	3.15	3.06
28	7.64	5.45	4.57	4.07	3.75	3.53	3.36	3.23	3.12	3.03
29	7.60	5.42	4.54	4.04	3.73	3.50	3.33	3.20	3.09	3.00
30	7.56	5.39	4.51	4.02	3.70	3.47	3.30	3.17	3.07	2.98
60	7.08	4.98	4.13	3.65	3.34	3.12	2.95	2.82	2.72	2.63
90	6.93	4.85	4.01	3.53	3.23	3.01	2.84	2.72	2.61	2.52
120	6.85	4.79	3.95	3.48	3.17	2.96	2.79	2.66	2.56	2.47

This table contains the 99th percentile of the F_{n_1,n_2} distribution, which serves as the critical values for a test with a 1% significance level.

References

Andrews, Donald W. K. 1991. "Heteroskedasticity and Autocorrelation Consistent Covariance Matrix Estimation." *Econometrica* 59 (3): 817–858.

Andrews, Donald W. K. 1993. "Tests for Parameter Instability and Structural Change with Unknown Change Point." *Econometrica* 61(4): 821–856.

Angrist, Joshua D. 1990. "Lifetime Earnings and the Vietnam Era Draft Lottery: Evidence from Social Security Administrative Records." *American Economic Review* 80(3): 313–336.

Angrist, Joshua D., Kathryn Graddy, and Guido Imbens. 2000. "The Interpretation of Instrumental Variables Estimators in Simultaneous Equations Models with an Application to the Demand for Fish." *Review of Economic Studies* 67(232): 499–527.

Angrist, Joshua and Alan Krueger. 1991. "Does Compulsory School Attendance Affect Schooling and Earnings?" *Quarterly Journal of Economics* 106(4): 979–1014.

Angrist, Joshua D. and Alan B. Krueger. 2001. "Instrumental Variables and the Search for Identification: From Supply and Demand to Natural Experiments." *Journal of Economic Perspectives* 15(4), Fall: 69–85.

Barendregt, Jan J. 1997. "The Health Care Costs of Smoking." *The New England Journal of Medicine* 337(15): 1052–1057.

Bergstrom, Theodore A. 2001. "Free Labor for Costly Journals?" *Journal of Economic Perspectives* 15(4), Fall: 183–198.

Bollersev, Timothy. 1986. "Generalized Autoregressive Conditional Heteroskedasticity." *Journal of Econometrics* 31(3): 307–327.

Bound, John, David A. Jaeger, and Regina M. Baker. 1995. "Problems with Instrumental Variables Estimation When the Correlation Between the Instrument and the Endogenous Explanatory Variable Is Weak." *Journal of the American Statistical Association* 90(430): 443–450.

Card, David. 1990. "The Impact of the Mariel Boatlift on the Miami Labor Market." *Industrial and Labor Relations Review* 43(2): 245–257.

Card, David and Alan B. Krueger. 1994. "Minimum Wages and Employment: A Case Study of the Fast Food Industry." *American Economic Review* 84(4): 772–793.

Chaloupka, Frank J. and Kenneth E. Warner. 2000. "The Economics of Smoking." Chap. 29 in *The Handbook of Health Economics*, edited by Joseph P. Newhouse and Anthony J. Cuyler. New York: North Holland, 2000.

Chow, Gregory. 1960. "Tests of Equality Between Sets of Coefficients in Two Linear Regressions." *Econometrica* 28(3): 591–605.

Cochrane, D. and Guy Orcutt. 1949. "Application of Least Squares Regression to Relationships Containing Autocorrelated Error Terms." *Journal of the American Statistical Association* 44(245): 32–61.

Cook, Philip J. and Michael J. Moore. 2000. "Alcohol." Chap. 30 in *The Handbook of Health Economics*, edited by Joseph P. Newhouse and Anthony J. Cuyler. New York: North Holland, 2000.

Cooper, Harris and Larry. V. Hedges. 1994. *The Handbook of Research Synthesis*. New York: Russell Sage Foundation.

Dickey, David A., and Wayne A. Fuller. 1979. "Distribution of the Estimators for Autoregressive Time Series With a Unit Root." *Journal of the American Statistical Association* 74(366): 427–431.

Diebold, Francis X. 1997. *Elements of Forecasting* (second edition). Cincinnati, OH: South-Western.

Ehrenberg, Ronald G., Dominic J. Brewer, Adam Gamoran, and J. Douglas Willms. 2001a. "Class Size and Student Achievement." *Psychological Science in the Public Interest* 2(1): 1–30.

Ehrenberg, Ronald G., Dominic J. Brewer, Adam Gamoran, and J. Douglas Willms. 2001b. "Does Class Size Matter?" *Scientific American* 285(5): 80–85.

Eicker, F. 1967. "Limit Theorems for Regressions with Unequal and Dependent Errors," *Proceedings of the Fifth Berkeley Symposium on Mathematical Statistics and Probability*, 1, 59–82. Berkeley: University of California Press.

Elliott, Graham, Thomas J. Rothenberg, and James H. Stock. 1996. "Efficient Tests for an Autoregressive Unit Root." *Econometrica* 64(4): 813–836.

Enders, Walter. 1995. *Applied Econometric Time Series*. New York: Wiley.

Engle, Robert F. 1982. "Autoregressive Conditional Heteroskedasticity with Estimates of the Variance of United Kingdom Inflation." *Econometrica* 50(4): 987–1007.

Engle, Robert F. and Clive W. J. Granger. 1987. "Cointegration and Error Correction: Representation, Estimation and Testing." *Econometrica* 55(2): 251–276.

Fuller, Wayne A. 1976. *Introduction to Statistical Time Series*. New York: Wiley.

Garvey, Gerald T. and Gordon Hanka. 1999. "Capital Structure and Corporate Control: The Effect of Antitakeover Statutes on Firm Leverage." *The Journal of Finance*, 54(2): 519–546.

Gillespie, Richard. 1991. *Manufacturing Knowledge: A History of the Hawthorne Experiments*. New York: Cambridge University Press.

Goering, John and Ron Wienk, eds. 1996. *Mortgage Lending, Racial Discrimination, and Federal Policy*. Washington, D.C.: Urban Institute Press.

Granger, Clive W. J. 1969. "Investigating Causal Relations by Econometric Models and Cross-Spectral Methods." *Econometrica* 37(3): 424–438.

Granger, Clive W. J. and A. A. Weiss. 1983. "Time Series Analysis of Error-Correction Models." In *Studies in Econometrics: Time Series and Multivariate Statistics,* edited by S. Karlin, T. Amemiya, and L. A. Goodman, 255–278. New York: Academic Press.

Greene, William H. 2000. *Econometric Analysis* (fourth edition). Upper Saddle River, NJ: Prentice Hall.

Gruber, Jonathan. 2001. "Tobacco at the Crossroads: The Past and Future of Smoking Regulation in the United States." *The Journal of Economic Perspectives* 15(2): 193–212.

Hamilton, James D. 1994. *Time Series Analysis.* Princeton, NJ: Princeton University Press.

Hansen, Bruce. 1992. "Efficient Estimation and Testing of Cointegrating Vectors in the Presence of Deterministic Trends." *Journal of Econometrics* 53(1-3): 86–121.

Hansen, Bruce. 2001. "The New Econometrics of Structural Change: Dating Breaks in U.S. Labor Productivity." *The Journal of Economic Perspectives* 15(4), Fall: 117–128.

Hanushek, Eric. 1999a. "Some Findings from an Independent Investigation of the Tennessee STAR Experiment and from Other Investigations of Class Size Effects." *Educational Evaluation and Policy Analysis* 21:143–164.

Hanushek, Eric. 1999b. "The Evidence on Class Size." Chap. 7 in *Earning and Learning: How Schools Matter*, edited by S. Mayer and P. Peterson. Washington, D.C.: Brookings Institution Press.

Hayashi, Fumio. 2000. *Econometrics.* Princeton, NJ: Princeton University Press.

Heckman, James J. 2001. "Micro Data, Heterogeneity, and the Evaluation of Public Policy: Nobel Lecture." *Journal of Political Economy* 109(4): 673–748.

Heckman, James J., Robert J. LaLonde, and Jeffrey A. Smith. 1999. "The Economics and Econometrics of Active Labor Market Programs." Chap. 31 in *Handbook of Labor Economics*, edited by Orley Ashenfelter and David Card. Amsterdam: Elsevier.

Hedges, Larry V. and Ingram Olkin. 1985. *Statistical Methods for Meta-analysis.* San Diego: Academic Press.

Hetland, Lois. 2000. "Listening to Music Enhances Spatial-Temporal Reasoning: Evidence for the 'Mozart Effect.'" *Journal of Aesthetic Education* 34(3-4): 179–238.

Hoxby, Caroline M. 2000. "The Effects of Class Size on Student Achievement: New Evidence from Population Variation." *The Quarterly Journal of Economics* 115(4): 1239–1285.

Huber, P. J. 1967. "The Behavior of Maximum Likelihood Estimates Under Nonstandard Conditions," *Proceedings of the Fifth Berkeley Symposium on Mathematical Statistics and Probability*, 1, 221–233. Berkeley: University of California Press.

Johansen, Søren. 1988. "Statistical Analysis of Cointegrating Vectors." *Journal of Economic Dynamics and Control* 12: 231–254.

Jones, Stephen R. G. 1992. "Was There a Hawthorne Effect?" *American Journal of Sociology* 98(3): 451–468.

Krueger, Alan B. 1999. "Experimental Estimates of Education Production Functions." *The Quarterly Journal of Economics* 14(2): 497–562.

Ladd, Helen. 1998. "Evidence on Discrimination in Mortgage Lending." *Journal of Economic Perspectives* 12(2), Spring: 41–62.

Levitt, Steven D. 1996. "The Effect of Prison Population Size on Crime Rates: Evidence from Prison Overcrowding Litigation." *The Quarterly Journal of Economics* 111(2): 319–351.

Levitt, Steven D. and Jack Porter. 2001. "How Dangerous Are Drinking Drivers?" *Journal of Political Economy* 109(6): 1198–1237.

Maddala, G. S. 1983. *Limited-Dependent and Qualitative Variables in Econometrics*. Cambridge: Cambridge University Press.

Maddala, G. S. and In-Moo Kim. 1998. *Unit Roots, Cointegration, and Structural Change*. Cambridge: Cambridge University Press.

Manning, Willard G., et al. 1989. "The Taxes of Sin: Do Smokers and Drinkers Pay Their Way?" *Journal of the American Medical Association* 261(11): 1604–1609.

McClellan, Mark, Barbara J. McNeil, and Joseph P. Newhouse. 1994. "Does More Intensive Treatment of Acute Myocardial Infarction in the Elderly Reduce Mortality?" *Journal of the American Medical Association* 272(11): 859–866.

Meyer, Bruce D. 1995. "Natural and Quasi-Experiments in Economics." *Journal of Business and Economic Statistics* 13(2): 151–161.

Meyer, Bruce D., W. Kip Viscusi, and David L. Durbin. 1995. "Workers' Compensation and Injury Duration: Evidence from a Natural Experiment." *American Economic Review* 85(3): 322–340.

Mosteller, Frederick. 1995. "The Tennessee Study of Class Size in the Early School Grades." *The Future of Children: Critical Issues for Children and Youths* 5(2), Summer/Fall: 113–127.

Mosteller, Frederick, Richard Light, and Jason Sachs. 1996. "Sustained Inquiry in Education: Lessons from Skill Grouping and Class Size." *Harvard Educational Review* 66(4), Winter: 631–676.

Munnell, Alicia H., Geoffrey M. B. Tootell, Lynne E. Browne, and James McEneaney. 1996. "Mortgage Lending in Boston: Interpreting HMDA Data." *American Economic Review* 86(1): 25–53.

Neumark, David and William Wascher. 2000. "Minimum Wages and Employment: A Case Study of the Fast-Food Industry in New Jersey and Pennsylvania: Comment." *American Economic Review* 90(5): 1362–1396.

Newey, Whitney and Kenneth West. 1987. "A Simple Positive Semi-Definite, Heteroskedastic and Autocorrelation Consistent Covariance Matrix." *Econometrica* 55(3): 703–708.

Newhouse, Joseph P. et. al. 1993. *Free for All? Lessons from the Rand Health Insurance Experiment*. Cambridge: Harvard University Press.

Phillips, Peter C. B. and Sam Ouliaris. 1990. "Asymptotic Properties of Residual Based Tests for Cointegration." *Econometrica* 58(1): 165–194.

Quandt, Richard. 1960. "Tests of the Hypothesis That a Linear Regression System Obeys Two Separate Regimes." *Journal of the American Statistical Association* 55(290): 324-330.

Rauscher, Frances, Gordon L. Shaw, and Katherine N. Ky. 1993. "Music and Spatial Task Performance." *Nature* 365, no. 6447, 611.

Roll, Richard. 1984. "Orange Juice and Weather." *American Economic Review* 74(5): 861–880.

Rosenzweig, Mark R. and Kenneth I. Wolpin. 2000. "Natural 'Natural Experiments' in Economics." *Journal of Economic Literature* 38(4): 827–874.

Ruhm, Christopher J. 1996. "Alcohol Policies and Highway Vehicle Fatalities." *Journal of Health Economics* 15(4): 435–454.

Ruud, Paul. 2000. *An Introduction to Classical Econometric Theory*. New York: Oxford University Press.

Shadish, William R., Thomas D. Cook, and Donald T. Campbell. 2002. *Experimental and Quasi-Experimental Designs for Generalized Causal Inference*. Boston: Houghton Mifflin.

Sims, Christopher A. 1980. "Macroeconomics and Reality." *Econometrica* 48(1): 1–48.

Stock, James H. and Mark W. Watson. 1988. "Variable Trends in Economic Time Series." *Journal of Economic Perspectives* 2(3): 147–174.

Stock, James H. and Mark W. Watson. 1993. "A Simple Estimator of Cointegrating Vectors in Higher-Order Integrated Systems." *Econometrica* 61(4): 783–820.

Stock, James H. 1994. "Unit Roots, Structural Breaks, and Trends." Chap. 46 in *Handbook of Econometrics*, volume IV, edited by Robert Engle and Daniel McFadden. Amsterdam: Elsevier.

Stock, James H. and Mark W. Watson. 2001. "Vector Autoregressions." *Journal of Economic Perspectives* 15(4), Fall: 101–115.

Tobin, James. 1958. "Estimation of Relationships for Limited Dependent Variables." *Econometrica* 26(1): 24–36.

Watson, Mark W. 1994. "Vector Autoregressions and Cointegration." Chap. 47 in *Handbook of Econometrics*, volume IV, edited by Robert Engle and Daniel McFadden. Amsterdam: Elsevier.

White, Halbert. 1980. "A Heteroskedasticity-Consistent Covariance Matrix Estimator and a Direct Test for Heteroskedasticity," *Econometrica*, 48, 827–838

Winner, Ellen and Monica Cooper. 2000. "Mute Those Claims: No Evidence (Yet) for a Causal Link between Arts Study and Academic Achievement." *Journal of Aesthetic Education* 34(3-4): 11–76.

Wright, Philip G. 1928. *The Tariff on Animal and Vegetable Oils*. New York: Macmillan.

Answers to the "Review the Concepts" Questions

Chapter 1

1.1. The experiment that you design should have one or more treatment groups and a control group; for example, one "treatment" could be studying for four hours, and the control would be not studying (no treatment). Students would be randomly assigned to the treatment and control groups, and the causal effect of hours of study on midterm performance is estimated by comparing the average midterm grades for each of the treatment groups to that of the control group. The largest impediment is to ensure that the students in the different treatment groups spend the correct number of hours studying. How can you make sure that the students in the control group do not study at all, since that might jeopardize their grade? How can you make sure that all students in the treatment group actually study for four hours?

1.2. This experiment needs the same ingredients as the experiment in the previous question: treatment and control groups, random assignment, and a procedure for analyzing the resulting experimental data. Here there are two treatment levels: not wearing a seatbelt (the control group) and wearing a seatbelt (the treated group). These treatments should be applied over a specified period of time, such as the next year. The effect of seat belt use on traffic fatalities could be estimated as the difference between fatality rates in the control and treatment group. One impediment to this study is ensuring that participants follow the treatment (do or do not wear a seat belt). More importantly, this study raises serious ethical concerns because it instructs participants to engage in known unsafe behavior (not wearing a seatbelt).

1.3. a. You will need to specify the treatment(s) and randomization method, as in Questions 1.1 and 1.2.

   b. One such cross sectional data set would consist of a number of different firms with the observations collected at the same point in time. For example, the data set might contain data on training levels and average labor productivity for 100 different firms during 2002.

Chapter four introduces linear regression as a way to estimate causal effects using cross sectional data.

c. The time series data would consist of observations for a single firm collected at different points in time. For example, the data set might contain data on training levels and average labor productivity for the firm for each year between 1960 and 2002. Chapter 13 discusses how linear regression can be used to estimate causal effects using time series data.

d. Panel data would consist of observations from different firms, each observed at different points in time. For example, the data might consist of training levels and average labor productivity for 100 different firms, with data on each firm in 1980, 1990, and 2000. Chapter 8 discusses how linear regression can be used to estimate causal effects using panel data.

Chapter 2

2.1. These outcomes are random because they are not known with certainty until they actually occur. You do not know with certainty the gender of the next person you will meet, the time that it will take to commute to school, and so forth.

2.2. If X and Y are independent, then $\Pr(Y \leq y \mid X = x) = \Pr(Y \leq y)$ for all values of y and x. That is, independence means that the conditional and marginal distributions of Y are identical so that learning the value of X does not change the probability distribution of Y: knowing the value of X says nothing about the probability that Y will take on different values.

2.3. Although there is no apparent causal link between rainfall and the number of children born, rainfall could tell you something about the number of children born. Knowing the amount of rainfall tells you something about the season, and births are seasonal. Thus, knowing rainfall tells you something about the month, which tell you something about the number of children born. Thus, rainfall and the number of children born are not independently distributed.

2.4. The average weight of four randomly selected students is unlikely to be exactly 145 lbs. Different groups of four students will have different sample average weights, sometimes greater than 145 lbs and sometimes less. Because the four students were selected at random, their sample average weight is also random.

2.5. All of the distributions will have a normal shape and will be centered at one, the mean of Y. However they will have different "spreads" because they have different variances. The variance of $\overline{Y}$ is $4/n$, so the variance shrinks as n gets larger. In your plots, the spread of the normal when $n = 2$ should be wider than when $n = 10$, which should be wider that when $n = 100$. As n gets very large, the variance approaches zero, and the normal distribution collapses around the mean of Y. That is, the distribution of $\overline{Y}$ becomes highly concentrated around μ_Y as n grows large (the probability that $\overline{Y}$ is close to μ_Y tends to one), which is just what the law of large numbers says.

2.6. The normal approximation does not look good when $n = 5$, but looks good for $n = 25$ and $n = 100$. Thus $\Pr(\overline{Y} \leq 0.1)$ is approximately equal to the value computed by the normal approximation when n is 25 or 100, but is not well approximated by the normal distribution when $n = 5$.

Chapter 3

3.1. The population mean is the average in the population. The sample average $\overline{Y}$ is the average of a sample drawn from the population.

3.2. An estimator is a procedure for computing an educated guess of the value of a population parameter, such as the population mean. An estimate is the number that the estimator produces in a given sample. $\overline{Y}$ is an example of an estimator. It gives a procedure (add up all of the values of Y in the sample and divide by n) for computing an educated guess of the value of the population mean. If a sample of size $n = 4$ produces values of Y of 100, 104, 123, and 96, then the estimate computed using the estimator $\overline{Y}$ is 105.75.

3.3. In all cases the mean of $\overline{Y}$ is 10. The variance of $\overline{Y}$ is $var(Y)/n$, which yields $var(\overline{Y}) = 1.6$ when $n = 10$, $var(\overline{Y}) = 0.16$ when $n = 100$, and $var(\overline{Y}) = 0.016$ when $n = 1000$. Since $var(\overline{Y})$ converges to zero as n increases, then, with probability approaching one, $\overline{Y}$ will be close to 10 as n increases. This is what the law of large numbers says.

3.4. The central limit theorem plays a key role when hypotheses are tested using the sample mean. Since the sample mean is approximately normally distributed when the sample size is large, critical values for hypothesis tests and p-values for test statistics can be computed using the normal distribution. Normal critical values are also used in the construction of confidence intervals.

3.5. These are described in Section 3.2.

3.6. A confidence interval contains all values of the parameter (for example, the mean) that cannot be rejected when used as a null hypothesis. Thus, it summarizes the results from a very large number of hypothesis tests.

3.7. The plot for (a) is upward sloping, and the points lie exactly on a line. The plot for (b) is downward sloping, and the points lie exactly on a line. The plot for (c) should show a positive relation, and the points should be close to, but not exactly on an upward sloping line. The plot for (d) shows a generally negative relation between the variables, and the points are scattered around a downward sloping line. The plot for (e) has no apparent linear relation between the variables.

Chapter 4

4.1. β_1 is the value of the slope in the population regression. This value is unknown. $\hat{\beta}_1$ (an estimator) gives a formula for estimating the unknown value of β_1 from a sample. Similarly, u_i is the value of the regression error for the ith observation; u_i is the difference between Y_i and the population regression line $\beta_0 + \beta_1 X_i$. Because the values of β_0 and β_1 are unknown, the value of u_i is unknown. In contrast, $\hat{u}_i$ is the difference between Y_i and $\hat{\beta}_0 + \hat{\beta}_1 X_i$; thus, $\hat{u}_i$ is an estimator of u_i. Finally, $E(Y|X) = \beta_0 + \beta_1 X$ is unknown because the values of β_0 and β_1 are unknown; an estimator for this is the OLS predicted value, $\hat{\beta}_0 + \hat{\beta}_1 X$.

4.2. The p-value for a two-sided test of H_0: $\mu = 0$ using an i.i.d. set of observations Y_i, $i = 1, \ldots, n$ can be constructed in three steps: (1) compute the sample mean and the standard error $SE(\overline{Y})$; (2) compute the t-statistic for this sample $t^{act} = \overline{Y}^{act}/SE(\overline{Y})$; (3) using the standard normal table, compute the p-value = $\Pr(|Z|>|t^{act}|) = 2\Phi(-|t^{act}|)$. A similar three-step procedure is used to construct the p-value for a two-sided test of H_0: $\beta_1 = 0$: (1) compute the OLS estimate of the regression slope and the standard error $SE(\hat{\beta}_1)$; (2) compute the t-statistic for this sample $t^{act} = \hat{\beta}_1^{act}/SE(\hat{\beta}_1)$; (3) using the standard normal table, compute the p-value = $\Pr(|Z| > |t^{act}|) = 2\Phi(-|t^{act}|)$.

4.3. The wage gender gap for 1992 can be estimated using the regression in Equation (4.41) and the data summarized in the 1992 row of Table 3.1. The dependent variable is the hourly earnings of the ith person in the sample. The independent variable is a binary variable that equals one if the person is a male and equals zero if the person is a female. The wage gender gap in the population is the population coefficient β_1 in the regression, which can be estimated using $\hat{\beta}_1$. The wage gender gap for the other years can be estimated in a similar fashion.

4.4. The value of the R^2 indicates how dispersed the points are around the estimated regression line. When $R^2 = 0.9$, the scatter of points should lie very close to the regression line. When $R^2 = 0.5$ the points should be more dispersed about the line. The R^2 does not indicate whether the line has a positive or a negative slope.

Chapter 5

5.1. It is likely that $\hat{\beta}_1$ will be biased because of omitted variables. Schools in more affluent districts are likely to spend more on all educational inputs and thus would have smaller class sizes, more books in the library, and more computers. These other inputs may lead to higher average test scores. Thus, $\hat{\beta}_1$ will be biased upward because the number of computers per student is positively correlated with omitted variables that have a positive effect on average test scores.

5.2. If X_1 increases by 3 units and X_2 is unchanged, then Y is expected to change by $3\beta_1$ units. If X_2 decreases by 5 units and X_1 is unchanged, then Y is expected to change by $-5\beta_2$ units. If X_1 increases by 3 units and X_2 decreases by 5 units, then Y is expected to change by $3\beta_1 - 5\beta_2$ units.

5.3. The regression cannot determine the effect of a change in one of the regressors assuming no change in the other regressors, because if the value of one of the perfectly multicollinear regressors is held constant, then so is the value of the other. That is, there is no independent variation in one multicollinear regressor. Two examples of perfectly multicollinear regressors are (1) a person's weight measured in pounds and the same person's weight measured in kilograms, and (2) the fraction of students who are male and the constant term, when the data come from all-male schools.

5.4. The null hypothesis that $\beta_1 = 0$ can be tested using the t-statistic for β_1 as described in Key Concept 5.6. Similarly, the null hypothesis that $\beta_2 = 0$ can be tested using the t-statistic for β_2. The null hypothesis that $\beta_1 = 0$ and $\beta_2 = 0$ can be tested using the F-statistic from Section 5.7. The F-statistic is necessary to test a joint hypothesis because the test will be based on both $\hat{\beta}_1$ and $\hat{\beta}_2$, and this means that the testing procedure must use properties of their joint distribution.

5.5. Here is one example. Using data from several years of her econometrics class, a professor regresses students' scores on the final exam (Y) on their score from the midterm exam (X). This regression will have a high R^2, because people who do well on the midterm tend to do well on the final. However, this regression produces a biased estimate of the causal effect of midterm scores on the final. Students who do well on the midterm tend to be students who attend class regularly, study hard, and have an aptitude for the subject. The variables are correlated with the midterm score but are determinants of the final exam score, so omitting them leads to omitted variable bias.

Chapter 6

6.1. The regression function will look like the quadratic regression in Figure 6.3 or the logarithmic function in Figure 6.4. The first of these is specified as the regression of Y onto X and X^2, and the second as the regression of Y onto $\ln(X)$. There are many economic relations with this shape. For example, this shape might represent the decreasing marginal productivity of labor in a production function.

6.2. Taking logarithms of both sides of the equation yields $\ln(Q) = \beta_0 + \beta_1 \ln(K) + \beta_2 \ln(L) + \beta_3 \ln(M) + u$, where $\beta_0 = \ln(\lambda)$. The production function parameters can be estimated by regressing the logarithm of production on the logarithms of capital, labor, and raw materials.

6.3. A 2% increase in GDP means that $\ln(GDP)$ increases by 0.02. The implied change in $\ln(m)$ is $1.0 \times 0.02 = 0.02$, which corresponds to a 2% increase in m. With R measured in percentage points, the increase in R is from 4.0 to 5.0 or 1.0 percentage point. This leads to a change of $\ln(m)$ of $-0.02 \times 1.0 = -0.02$ which corresponds to a 2% fall in m.

6.4. You want to compare the fit of your linear regression to the fit of a nonlinear regression. Your answer will depend on the nonlinear regression that you choose for the comparison. You might test your linear regression against a quadratic regression by adding X^2 to the linear regression. If the coefficient on X^2 is significantly different from zero, then you can reject the null hypothesis that the relationship is linear in favor of the alternative that it is quadratic.

6.5. Augmenting the equation in Question 6.2 with an interaction term yields: $\ln(Q) = \beta_0 + \beta_1 \ln(K) + \beta_2 \ln(L) + \beta_3 \ln(M) + \beta_4 [\ln(K) \times \ln(L)] + u$. The partial effect of $\ln(L)$ on $\ln(Q)$ is now $\beta_2 + \beta_4 \ln(K)$.

Chapter 7

7.1. See Key Concept 7.1 and the paragraph that immediately follows the Key Concept box.

7.2. Including an additional variable that belongs in the regression will eliminate or reduce omitted variable bias. However including an additional variable that does not belong in the regression will, in general, reduce the precision (increase the variance) of the estimator of the other coefficients.

7.3. It is important to distinguish between measurement error in Y or measurement error in X. If Y is measured with error, then the measurement error becomes part of the regression error term, u. If the assumptions of Key Concept 5.4 continue to hold, this will not affect the internal validity of OLS regression, although by making the variance of the regression error term larger, it increases the variance of the OLS estimator. If X is measured with error, however, this can result in correlation between the regressor and regression error, leading to inconsistency of the OLS estimator. As suggested by Equation (7.2), as this inconsistency becomes more severe, the larger is the measurement error (that is, the larger is σ_w^2 in Equation (7.2)).

7.4. Schools with higher-achieving students could be more likely to volunteer to take the test, so that the schools volunteering to take the test are not representative of the population of schools, and sample selection bias will result. For example, if all schools with a low student-teacher ratio take the test, but only the best-performing schools with a high student-teacher ratio do, the estimated class size effect will be biased.

7.5. Cities with high crime rates may decide that they need more police protection and spend more on police, but if police do their job then more police spending reduces crime. Thus, there are causal links from crime rates to police spending **and** from police spending to crime rates, leading to simultaneous causality bias.

7.6. If the regression has homoskedastic errors then the homoskedastic and heteroskedastic standard errors generally are similar, because both are consistent. However, if the errors are heteroskedastic, the homoskedastic standard errors are inconsistent, while the heteroskedastic standard errors are consistent. Thus, different values for the two standard errors constitutes evidence of heteroskedasticity, and this suggests that the heteroskedastic standard errors should be used.

Chapter 8

8.1. Panel data (also called longitudinal data) refers to data for n different entities observed at T different time periods. One of the subscripts, i, identifies the entity, and the other subscript, t, identifies the time period.

8.2. A person's ability or motivation might affect both education and earnings. More able individuals tend to complete more years of schooling, and, for a given level of education, they tend to have higher earnings. The same is true for highly motivated people. The state of the macroeconomy is a time-specific variable that affects both earnings and education. During recessions, unemployment is high, earnings are low, and enrollment in colleges increases. Person-specific and time-specific fixed effects can be included in the regression to control for person-specific and time-specific variables.

8.3. When person-specific fixed effects are included in a regression, they capture all features of the individual that do not vary over the sample period. Since gender does not vary over the sample period, its effect on earnings cannot be determined separately from the person-specific fixed effect. Similarly, time fixed effects capture all features of the time period that do not vary across individuals. The national unemployment rate is the same for all individuals in the sample at a given point in time, and thus its effect on earnings cannot be determined separately from the time-specific fixed effect.

Chapter 9

9.1. Because Y is binary, its predicted value is the probability that $Y = 1$. A probability must be between zero and one, so the value of 1.3 is nonsensical.

9.2. The results in column (1) are for the linear probability model. The coefficients in a linear probability model show the effect of a unit change in X on the probability that $Y = 1$. The results in columns (2) and (3) are for the logit and probit models. These coefficients are difficult to interpret. To compute the effect of a change in X on the probability that $Y = 1$ for logit and probit models, use the procedures outlined in Key Concept 9.2.

9.3. She should use a logit or probit. These models are preferred to the linear probability model because they constrain the regression's predicted values to be between zero and one. Usually, probit and logit regressions give similar results, and she should use the method that is easier to implement with her software.

9.4. OLS cannot be used because the regression function is not a linear function of the regression coefficients (the coefficients appear inside the nonlinear functions Φ or F). The maximum likelihood estimator is efficient and can handle regression functions that are nonlinear in the parameters.

Chapter 10

10.1. An increase in the regression error, u, shifts out the demand curve leading to an increase in both price and quantity. Thus $\ln(P^{butter})$ is positively correlated with the regression error. Because of this positive correlation, the OLS estimator of β_1 is inconsistent and is likely to be larger than the true value of β_1.

10.2. The number of trees per capita in the state is exogenous because it is plausibly uncorrelated with the error in the demand function. However, it probably is also uncorrelated with $\ln(P^{cigarettes})$, so it is not relevant. A valid instrument must be exogenous and relevant, so the number of trees per capita in the state is not a valid instrument.

10.3. The number of lawyers is arguably correlated with the incarceration rate, so it is relevant (although this should be checked using the methods in Section 10.3). However, states with higher than expected crime rates (with positive regression errors) are likely to have more lawyers (criminals must be defended and prosecuted), so the number of lawyers will be positively correlated with the regression error. This means that the number of lawyers is not exogenous. A valid instrument must be exogenous and relevant, so the number of lawyers is not a valid instrument.

10.4. If the difference in distance is a valid instrument then it must be correlated with X, which in this case is a binary variable indicating whether the patient received cardiac catheterization. Instrument relevance can be checked using the procedure outlined in Section 10.3. Checking instrument exogeneity is more difficult. If there are more instruments than endogenous regressors, then joint exogeneity of the instruments can be tested using the J-test outlined in Key Concept 10.6. However, if the number of instruments is equal to the number of endogenous regressors, then it is impossible to test for exogeneity statistically. In the McClellan, McNeil, and Newhouse study (1994) there is one endogenous regressor (treatment) and one instrument (difference in distance), so the J-test cannot be used. Expert judgment is required to assess the exogeneity.

Chapter 11

11.1. It would be better to assign the treatment level randomly to each parcel. The research plan outlined in the problem may be flawed because the different groups of parcels might differ systematically. For example, the first 25 parcels of land might have poorer drainage than the other parcels and this would lead to lower crop yields. The treatment assignment outlined in the problem would place these 25 parcels in the control group, thereby overestimating the effect of the fertilizer on crop yields. This problem is avoided with random assignment of treatments.

11.2. The treatment effect could be estimated as the difference in average cholesterol levels for the treated group and the untreated (control) group. Data on the weight, age, and gender of each patient could be used to improve the estimate using the differences estimator with additional regressors shown in Equation (11.2). This regression may produce a more accurate estimate because it controls for these additional factors that may affect cholesterol. If you had data on the cholesterol levels of each patient before they entered the experiment, then the differences-in-differences estimator could be used. This estimator controls for individual-specific determinants of cholesterol levels that are constant over the sample period, such as the person's genetic predisposition to high cholesterol.

11.3. If the students who were transferred to small classes differed systematically from the other students, then internal validity is compromised. For example, if the transferred students tended to have higher incomes and more learning opportunities outside of school, then they would tend to perform better on standardized tests. The experiment would incorrectly attribute this performance to the smaller class size. Information on original random assignment could be used as an instrument in a regression like Equation (11.6) to restore internal validity. The original random assignment is a valid instrument because it is exogenous (uncorrelated with the regression error) and is relevant (correlated with the actual assignment).

11.4. The Hawthorne effect is unlikely to be a problem in the fertilizer example, unless (for example) workers cultivated the different parcels of land more or less intensively depending on the treatment. Patients in the cholesterol study might be more diligent taking their medication than patients not in an experiment, making the cholesterol experiment double-blind, so that neither the doctor nor the patient know whether the patient is receiving the treatment or the placebo, would reduce experimental effects. Experimental effects may be important in experiments like STAR, if the teachers feel that the experiment provides them with an opportunity to prove that small class sizes are best.

11.5. The earthquake introduced randomness in class sizes that make it appear *as if* the treatment is randomly assigned. The discussion in Section 10.1 describes how instrumental variable regression can use the induced changes in class sizes to estimate the effect of class size on test scores.

Chapter 12

12.1. It does not appear stationary. The most striking characteristic of the series is that it has an upward trend. That is, observations at the end of the sample are systematically larger than observations at the beginning. This suggests that the mean of the series is not constant, which would imply that it is not stationary. The first difference of the series may look stationary, because first differencing eliminates the large trend. However, the level of the first difference series is the slope of the plot in Figure 12.2c. Looking carefully at the figure, the slope is steeper in 1960–1975 than in 1976–2000. Thus, there may have been a small change in the mean of the first difference series. If there was a change in the population mean of the first difference series, then it too is nonstationary.

12.2. One way to do this is to construct pseudo out-of-sample forecasts for the random walk model and the financial analyst's model. If the analyst's model is better, then it should have a lower RMSFE in the pseudo out-of-sample period. Even if the analyst's model outperformed the random walk in the pseudo out-of-sample period, you might still be wary of his claim. If he had access to the pseudo out-of-sample data, then his model may have been constructed to fit these data very well, so it still could produce poor *true* out-of-sample forecasters. Thus, a better test of the analyst's claim is to use his model and the random walk to forecast future stock returns and compare true out-of-sample performance.

12.3. Yes. The usual 95% confidence interval is $\hat{\beta}_1 \pm 1.96SE(\hat{\beta}_1)$, which in this case produces the interval 0.91–0.99. This interval does not contain 1.0. However, this method for constructing a confidence interval is based on the central limit theorem and the large-sample normal distribution of $\hat{\beta}_1$. When $\beta_1 = 1.0$, the normal approximation is not appropriate and this method for computing the confidence interval is not valid. Instead, we need to use the general method for constructing a confidence interval outlined in Sections 3.3 and 4.6. To find out whether 1.0 is in the 95% confidence interval we need to test the null hypothesis $\beta_1 = 1$ at the 5% level. If we do not reject this null, then 1.0 is in the confidence interval. The value of the t-statistic for this null is -2.50. From Table 12.4, the 5% critical value is -2.86, so the null hypothesis is not rejected. Thus $\beta_1 = 1.0$ is in the 95% confidence interval.

12.4. You would add a binary variable, say D_t, that equals zero for dates prior to 1992:1 and equals one for dates 1992:1 and beyond. If the coefficient on D_t is significantly different from zero in the regression (as judged by its t-statistic), then this would be evidence of an intercept break in 1992:1. If the date of the break is unknown, then you would need to carry out this test for many possible break dates using the QLR procedure summarized in Key Concept 12.8.

Chapter 13

13.1. As discussed in Key Concept 13.2, causal effects can be estimated by a distributed lag model when the regressors are exogenous. In this context, exogeneity means that current and lagged values of the money supply are uncorrelated with the regression error. This assumption is unlikely to be satisfied. For example, aggregate supply disturbances (oil price shocks, changes in productivity) have important effects on GDP. The Federal Reserve and the banking system also respond to these factors, thus changing the money supply. Thus the money supply is endogenous and is correlated with the regression error (which includes these omitted variables). Because the money supply is not exogenous, the distributed lag regression model cannot be used to estimate the dynamic causal effect of money on GDP.

13.2. The serially correlated error term could arise from including too few lags of X. Adding more lags will eliminate the serial correlation in the error term and produce a consistent estimator.

13.3. Cumulating the dynamic multipliers for ΔY_t yields the dynamic multipliers for Y_t. Said differently, the dynamic multipliers for Y_t are the cumulative multipliers from the ΔY_t regression.

13.4. The regression function that includes FDD_{t+1} can be written as $E(\%ChgP_t \mid FDD_{t+1}, FDD_t, FDD_{t-1}, \ldots) = \beta_0 + \beta_1 FDD_t + \beta_2 FDD_{t-1} + \beta_3 FDD_{t-2} + \cdots + \beta_7 FDD_{t-6} + E(u_t \mid FDD_{t+1}, FDD_t, FDD_{t-1}, \ldots)$. When FDD is strictly exogenous, then $E(u_t \mid FDD_{t+1}, FDD_t, FDD_{t-1}, \ldots) = 0$, so that FDD_{t+1} does not enter the regression. When FDD_t is exogenous, but not strictly exogenous, then it may be the case that $E(u_t \,|\, FDD_{t+1}, FDD_t,$ $FDD_{t-1}, \ldots) \neq 0$, so that FDD_{t+1} will enter the regression.

Chapter 14

14.1. The macroeconomist wants to construct forecasts for nine variables. If four lags of each variable are used in a VAR, then each VAR equation will include 37 regression coefficients (the constant term and four coefficients for each of the nine variables). The sample period includes 128 quarterly observations. When 37 coefficients are estimated using 128 observations, the estimated coefficients are likely to be imprecise, leading to inaccurate forecasts. One alternative is to use a univariate autoregression for each variable. The advantage of this approach is that relatively few parameters need to be estimated, so that the coefficients will be precisely estimated by OLS. The disadvantage is that the forecasts are constructed using only lags of the variable being forecast, and lags of the other variables might also contain additional useful forecasting information. A compromise is to use a set of time series regressions with additional predictors. For example, a GDP forecasting regression might be specified using lags of GDP, consumption, and long-term interest rates, but excluding the other variables. The short-term interest rate forecasting regression might be specified using lags of short-term rates, long-term rates, GDP, and inflation. The idea is to include the most important predictors in each of the regression equations, but leave out the variables that are not very important.

14.2. The forecast of Y_{t+2} is $Y_{t+2|t} = 0.7^2 \times 5 = 2.45$. The forecast of Y_{t+30} is $Y_{t+30|t} = 0.7^{30} \times 5 = .0001$. The result is reasonable. Because the process is moderately serially correlated ($\beta_1 = 0.7$), then Y_{t+30} is only weakly related to Y_t. This means that the forecast of Y_{t+30} should be very close to μ_Y, the mean of Y. Since the process is stationary and $\beta_0 = 0$, then $\mu_Y = 0$. Thus, as expected $Y_{t+30|t}$ is very close to zero.

14.3. If Y and C are cointegrated, then the error correction term $Y - C$ is stationary. A plot of the series $Y - C$ should appear stationary. Cointegration can be tested by carrying out a Dickey-Fuller or DF–GLS unit root test for the series $Y - C$. This is an example of a test for cointegration with a known cointegrating coefficient.

14.4. When u_{t-1}^2 is unusually large, then σ_t^2 will be large. Since σ_t^2 is the conditional variance of u_t, then u_t^2 is likely to be large. This will lead a large value of σ_{t+1}^2 and so forth.

14.5. A more powerful test is more likely to reject the null hypothesis when the null hypothesis is false. This improves your ability to distinguish between a unit AR root and a root less than one.

Chapter 15

15.1. If Assumption #4 in Key Concept 15.1 is true, in large samples a 95% confidence interval constructed using the heteroskedastic-robust standard error will contain the true value of β_1 with a probability of 95%. If #4 in Key Concept 15.1 is false, the homoskedasticity-only variance estimator is inconsistent. Thus, in general, in large samples a 95% confidence interval constructed using the homoskedasticity-only standard error will not contain the true value of β_1 with a probability of 95% if the errors are heteroskedastic, so the confidence interval will not be valid asymptotically.

15.2. From Slutsky's theorem, $A_n B_n$ has an asymptotic $N(0,9)$ distribution. Thus, $\Pr(A_n B_n < 2)$ is approximately equal to $\Pr(Z < (2/3))$, where Z is a standard normal random variable. Evaluating this probability yields $\Pr(Z < (2/3)) = 0.75$.

15.3. For values of $X_i \leq 10$, the points should lie very close to the regression line because the variance of u_i is small. When $X_i > 10$, the points should be much further from the regression line because the variance of u_i is large. Since the points with $X_i \leq 10$ are much closer to the regression line, WLS gives them more weight.

15.4. The Gauss-Markov theorem implies that the averaged estimator cannot be better than WLS. To see this, note that the averaged estimator is a linear function of $Y_1, \ldots, Y_n$ (the OLS estimators are linear functions as is their average) and is unbiased (the OLS estimators are unbiased as is their average). The Gauss Markov theorem implies the WLS is the best linear conditionally unbiased estimator. Thus, the averaged estimator cannot be better than WLS.

Chapter 16

16.1. Each entry of the first column of X is 1. The entries in the second and third columns are zeros and ones. The first column of the matrix X is the sum of the second and third column, thus the columns are linearly dependent, and X does not have full rank. The regression can be respecified by eliminating either X_{1i} or X_{2i}.

16.2.

    a. Estimate the regression coefficients by OLS and compute hetero-skedasticity-robust standard errors. Construct the confidence interval as $\hat{\beta}_1 \pm 1.96 SE(\hat{\beta}_1)$.

    b. Estimate the regression coefficients by OLS and compute heteroskedasticity-robust standard errors. Construct the confidence interval as $\hat{\beta}_1 \pm 1.96 SE(\hat{\beta}_1)$. Alternatively compute the homoskedasticity-only standard error $\widetilde{SE}(\hat{\beta}_1)$ and form the confidence interval as $\hat{\beta}_1 \pm 1.96 \widetilde{SE}(\hat{\beta}_1)$.

    c. The confidence intervals could be constructed as in (b). These use the large-sample normal approximation. Under Assumptions 1–6, the exact distribution can be used to form the confidence interval $\hat{\beta}_1 \pm t_{n-k-1,.975}\widetilde{SE}(\hat{\beta}_1)$, where $t_{n-k-1,.975}$ is the 97.5 percentile of the t distribution with $n - k - 1$ degrees of freedom. Here $n = 500$ and $k = 1$. An extended version of Appendix Table 2 shows $t_{498,.975} = 1.9648$.

16.3. No, this result requires normally distributed errors.

16.4. The BLUE estimator is the GLS estimator. You must know Ω to compute the exact GLS estimator. However, if Ω is a known function of some parameters that in turn can be consistently estimated, then estimators for these parameters can be used to construct an estimator of the covariance matrix Ω. This estimator can then be used to construct a feasible version of the GLS estimator. This estimator is approximately equal to the BLUE estimator when the sample size is large.

16.5. There are many examples. Here is one. Suppose that $X_i = Y_{i-1}$ and u_i is i.i.d. with mean 0 and variance σ^2. (That is, the regression model is an AR(1) model from Chapter 12.) In this case X_i depends on u_j for $j < i$ but does not depend on u_j for $j \geq i$. This implies $E(u_i|X_i) = 0$. However, $E(u_{i-1}|X_i) \neq 0$, and this implies $E(U|X) \neq 0_n$.

Glossary

Acceptance region: The set of values of a test statistic for which the null hypothesis is accepted (is not rejected).

Adjusted R^2 ($\overline{R}^2$): A modified version of R^2 that does not necessarily increase when a new regressor is added to the regression.

ADL(p, q): See *autoregressive distributed lag model.*

AIC: See *information criterion.*

Akaike information criterion: See *information criterion.*

Alternative hypothesis: The hypothesis that is assumed to be true if the null hypothesis is false. The alternative hypothesis is often denoted H_1.

AR(p): See *autoregression.*

ARCH: See *autoregressive conditional heteroskedasticity.*

Asymptotic distribution: The approximate sampling distribution of a random variable computed using a large sample. For example, the asymptotic distribution of the sample average is normal.

Asymptotic normal distribution: A normal distribution that approximates the sampling distribution of a statistic computed using a large sample.

Attrition: The loss of subjects from a study after assignment to the treatment or control group.

Augmented Dickey-Fuller (ADF) test: A regression-based test for a unit root in an AR(p) model.

Autocorrelation: The correlation between a time series variable and its lagged value. The jth autocorrelation of Y is the correlation between Y_t and Y_{t-j}.

Autocovariance: The covariance between a time series variable and its lagged value. The jth autocovariance of Y is the covariance between Y_t and Y_{t-j}.

Autoregression: A linear regression model that relates a time series variable to its past (that is, lagged) values. An autoregression with p lagged values as regressors is denoted AR(p).

Autoregressive conditional heteroskedasticity (ARCH): A time series model of conditional heteroskedasticity.

Autoregressive distributed lag model: A linear regression model in which the time series variable Y_t is expressed as a function of lags of Y_t and of another variable, X_t.

The model is denoted $ADL(p,q)$, where p denotes the number of lags of Y_t and q denotes the number of lags of X_t.

Average causal effect: The population average of the individual causal effects in a heterogeneous population. Also called the average treatment effect.

Balanced panel: A panel data set with no missing observations, that is, in which the variables are observed for each entity and each time period.

Base specification: A baseline or benchmark regression specification that includes a set of regressors chosen using a combination of expert judgment, economic theory, and knowledge of how the data were collected.

Bayes information criterion: See *information criterion*.

Bernoulli distribution: The probability distribution of a Bernoulli random variable.

Bernoulli random variable: A random variable that takes on two values, zero and one.

Best linear unbiased estimator: An estimator that has the smallest variance of any estimator that is a linear function of the sample values Y and is unbiased. Under the Gauss-Markov conditions, the OLS estimator is the best linear unbiased estimator of the regression coefficients.

Bias: The expected value of the difference between an estimator and the parameter that it is estimating. If $\hat{\mu}_Y$ is an estimator of μ_Y, then the bias of $\hat{\mu}_Y$ is $E(\hat{\mu}_Y) - \mu_Y$.

BIC: See *information criterion*.

Binary variable: A variable that is either zero or one. A binary variable is used to indicate a binary outcome. For example, X is a binary (or indicator, or dummy) variable for a person's gender if $X = 1$ if the person is female and $X = 0$ if the person is male.

Bivariate normal distribution: A generalization of the normal distribution to describe the joint distribution of two random variables.

BLUE: See *best linear unbiased estimator*.

Break date: The date of a discrete change in population time series regression coefficient(s).

Causal effect: The expected effect of a given intervention or treatment as measured in an ideal randomized controlled experiment.

Central limit theorem: A result in mathematical statistics that says that, under general conditions, the sampling distribution of the standardized sample average is well approximated by a standard normal distribution when the sample size is large.

Chi-squared distribution: The distribution of the sum of m squared independent standard normal random variables. The parameter m is called the degrees of the freedom of the chi-squared distribution.

Chow test: A test for a break in a time series regression at a known break date.

Coefficient of determination: See R^2.

Cointegration: When two or more time series variables share a common stochastic trend.

Common trend: A trend shared by two or more time series.

Conditional distribution: The probability distribution of one random variable given that another random variable takes on a particular value.

Conditional expectation: The expected value of one random value given that another random variable takes on a particular value.

Conditional heteroskedasticity: The variance, usually of an error term, depends on other variables.

Conditional mean: The mean of a conditional distribution; see *conditional expectation*.

Conditional mean independence: The conditional expectation of the regression error u_i, given the regressors, depends on some but not all of the regressors.

Conditional variance: The variance of a conditional distribution.

Confidence interval (or confidence set): An interval (or set) that contains the true value of a population parameter with a prespecified probability when computed over repeated samples.

Confidence level: The prespecified probability that a confidence interval (or set) contains the true value of the parameter.

Consistency: Means that an estimator is consistent. See *consistent estimator*.

Consistent estimator: An estimator that converges in probability to the parameter that it is estimating.

Continuous random variable: A random variable that can take on a continuum of values.

Control group: The group that does not receive the treatment or intervention in an experiment.

Control variable: Another term for a regressor; more specifically, a regressor that controls for one of the factors that determine the dependent variable.

Convergence in distribution: When a sequence of distributions converges to a limit; a precise definition is given in Section 15.2.

Convergence in probability: When a sequence of random variables converges to a specific value, for example, when the sample average becomes close to the population mean as the sample size increases; see Key Concept 2.6 and Section 15.2.

Correlation: A unit-free measure of the extent to which two random variables move, or vary, together. The correlation (or correlation coefficient) between X and Y is $\sigma_{XY}/\sigma_X\sigma_Y$ and is denoted $\text{corr}(X,Y)$.

Correlation coefficient: See *correlation*.

Covariance: A measure of the extent to which two random variables move together. The covariance between X and Y is the expected value $E[(X - \mu_X)(Y - \mu_Y)]$, and is denoted by $\text{cov}(X, Y)$ or by σ_{XY}.

Covariance matrix: A matrix composed of the variances and covariances of a vector of random variables.

Critical value: The value of a test statistic for which the test just rejects the null hypothesis at the given significance level.

Cross-sectional data: Data collected for different entities in a single time period.

Cubic regression model: A nonlinear regression function that includes X, X^2, and X^3 as regressors.

Cumulative distribution function (c.d.f.): See *cumulative probability distribution*.

Cumulative dynamic multiplier: The cumulative effect of a unit change in the time series variable X on Y. The h-period cumulative dynamic multiplier is the effect of a unit change in X_t on $Y_t + Y_{t+1} + \cdots + Y_{t+h}$.

Cumulative probability distribution: A function showing the probability that a random variable is less than or equal to a given number.

Dependent variable: The variable to be explained in a regression or other statistical model; the variable appearing on the left-hand side in a regression.

Deterministic trend: A persistent long-term movement of a variable over time that can be represented as a nonrandom function of time.

Dickey-Fuller test: A method for testing for a unit root in a first order autoregression (AR(1)).

Differences estimator: An estimator of the causal effect constructed as the difference in the sample average outcomes between the treatment and control groups.

Differences-in-differences estimator: The average change in Y for those in the treatment group, minus the average change in Y for those in the control group.

Discrete random variable: A random variable that takes on discrete values.

Distributed lag model: A regression model in which the regressors are current and lagged values of X.

Dummy variable: See *binary variable*.

Dynamic causal effect: The causal effect of one variable on current and future values of another variable.

Dynamic multiplier: The h-period dynamic multiplier is the effect of a unit change in the time series variable X_t on Y_{t+h}.

Endogenous variable: A variable that is correlated with the error term.

Errors-in-variables bias: The bias in an estimator of a regression coefficient that arises from measurement errors in the regressors.

Error term: The difference between Y and the population regression function, denoted by u in this textbook.

Estimate: The numerical value of an estimator computed from data in a specific sample.

Estimator: A function of a sample of data to be drawn randomly from a population. An estimator is a procedure for using sample data to compute an educated guess of the value of a population parameter, such as the population mean.

Exact distribution: The exact probability distribution of a random variable.

Exact identification: When the number of instrumental variables equals the number of endogenous regressors.

Exogenous variable: A variable that is uncorrelated with the regression error term.

Expected value: The long-run average value of a random variable over many repeated trials or occurrences. It is the probability-weighted average of all the possible values that the random variable can take on. The expected value of Y is denoted $E(Y)$ and is also called the expectation of Y.

Experimental data: Data obtained from an experiment designed to evaluate a treatment or policy or to investigate a causal effect.

Experimental effect: When experimental subjects change their behavior because they are part of an experiment.

Explained sum of squares (ESS): The sum of squared deviations of the predicted values of Y_i, $\hat{Y}_i$, from their average; see Equation (4.35).

Explanatory variable: See *regressor*.

External validity: Inferences and conclusions from a statistical study are externally valid if they can be generalized from the population and the setting studied to other populations and settings.

F-statistic: A statistic used to a test joint hypothesis concerning more than one of the regression coefficients.

$F_{m,\infty}$ distribution: The distribution of a random variable with a chi-squared distribution with m degrees of freedom, divided by m.

Feasible GLS: A version of the generalized least squares (GLS) estimator that uses an estimator of the conditional covariance between the regression errors at different observations.

Feasible WLS: A version of the weighted least squares (WLS) estimator that uses an estimator of the conditional variance of the regression errors.

First difference: The first difference of a time series variable Y_t is $Y_t - Y_{t-1}$, denoted ΔY_t.

First-stage regression: The regression of an included endogenous variable on the included exogenous variables, if any, and the instrumental variable(s) in two stage least squares.

Fitted values: See *predicted values*.

Fixed effects: Binary variables indicating the entity or time period in a panel data regression.

Fixed effects regression model: A panel data regression that includes entity fixed effects.

Forecast error: The difference between the value of the variable that actually occurs and its forecasted value.

Forecast interval: An interval that contains the future value of a time series variable with a prespecified probability.

Functional form misspecification: When the form of the estimated regression function does not match the form of the population regression function, for example, when a linear specification is used but the true population regression function is quadratic.

GARCH: See *generalized autoregressive conditional heteroskedasticity*.

Gauss-Markov theorem: Mathematical result stating that, under certain conditions, the OLS estimator is the best linear unbiased estimator of the regression coefficients.

Generalized autoregressive conditional heteroskedasticity: A time series model for conditional heteroskedasticity.

Generalized least squares (GLS): A generalization of OLS that is appropriate when the regression errors have a known form of heteroskedasticity (in which case GLS is also referred to as weighted least squares, WLS) or a known form of serial correlation.

Granger causality test: A procedure for testing whether current and lagged values of one time series help predict future values of another time series.

HAC standard errors: See *heteroskedasticity- and autocorrelation-consistent (HAC) standard errors*.

Hawthorne effect: See *experimental effect*.

Heteroskedasticity: The situation in which variance of the regression error term u_i, conditional on the regressors, is not constant.

Heteroskedasticity- and autocorrelation-consistent (HAC) standard errors: Standard errors for OLS estimators that are consistent whether or not the regression errors are heteroskedastic and autocorrelated.

Heteroskedasticity-robust standard error: Standard errors for the OLS estimator that are appropriate whether the error term is homoskedastic or heteroskedastic.

Heteroskedasticity-robust *t*-statistic: A *t*-statistic constructed using a heteroskedasticity-robust standard error.

Homoskedasticity: The variance of the error term u_i, conditional on the regressors, is constant.

Homoskedasticity-only standard errors: Standard errors for the OLS estimator that are appropriate only when the error term is homoskedastic.

Hypothesis test: A procedure for using sample evidence to help determine if a specific hypothesis about a population is true or false.

$I(0)$, $I(1)$, and $I(2)$: See *order of integration*.

Identically distributed: When two or more random variables have the same distribution.

Impact effect: The contemporaneous, or immediate, effect of a unit change in the time series variable X_t on Y_t.

Imperfect multicollinearity: The condition in which two or more of the regressors are highly correlated.

Included endogenous variables: Regressors that are correlated with the error term (usually in the context of instrumental variable regression).

Included exogenous variables: Regressors that are uncorrelated with the error term (usually in the context of instrumental variable regression).

Independence: When knowing the value of one random variable provides no information about the value of another random variable. Two random variables are independent if their joint distribution is the product of their marginal distributions.

Indicator variable: See *binary variable*.

Information criterion: A statistic used to estimate the number of lagged variables to include in an autoregression or a distributed lag model. Leading examples are the Akaike information criterion (AIC) and the Bayes information criterion (BIC).

Instrument: See *instrumental variable*.

Instrumental variable: A variable that is correlated with an endogenous regressor (instrument relevance) and is uncorrelated with the regression error (instrument exogeneity).

Instrumental variables (IV) regression: A way to obtain a consistent estimator of the unknown coefficients of the population regression function when the regressor, X, is correlated with the error term, u.

Interaction term: A regressor that is formed as the product of two other regressors, such as $X_{1i} \times X_{2i}$.

Intercept: The value of β_0 in the linear regression model.

Internal validity: When inferences about causal effects in a statistical study are valid for the population being studied.

Joint hypothesis: A hypothesis consisting of two or more individual hypotheses, that is, involving more than one restriction on the parameters of a model.

Joint probability distribution: The probability distribution determining the probabilities of outcomes involving two or more random variables.

Lags: The value of a time series variable in a previous time period. The jth lag of Y_t is Y_{t-j}.

Law of iterated expectations: A result in probability theory that says that the expected value of Y is the expected value of its conditional expectation given X, that is, $E(Y) = E[E(Y|X)]$.

Law of large numbers: According to this result from probability theory, under general conditions the sample average will be close to the population mean with very high probability when the sample size is large.

Least squares assumptions: The assumptions for the linear regression model listed in Key Concept 4.3 (single variable regression) and Key Concept 5.4 (multiple regression model).

Least squares estimator: An estimator formed by minimizing the sum of squared residuals.

Limited dependent variable: A dependent variable that can take on only a limited set of values. For example, the variable might be a 0–1 binary variable or arise from one of the models described in Appendix 9.3.

Linear-log model: A nonlinear regression function in which the dependent variable is Y and the independent variable is $\ln(X)$.

Linear regression function: A regression function with a constant slope.

Linear probability model: A regression model in which Y is a binary variable.

Logarithm: A mathematical function defined for a positive argument; its slope is always positive but tends to zero. The natural logarithm is the inverse of the exponential function, that is, $X = \ln(e^X)$.

Logit regression: A nonlinear regression model for a binary dependent variable in which the population regression function is modeled using the cumulative logistic distribution function.

Log-linear model: A nonlinear regression function in which the dependent variable is $\ln(Y)$ and the independent variable is X.

Log-log model: A nonlinear regression function in which the dependent variable is $\ln(Y)$ and the independent variable is $\ln(X)$.

Longitudinal data: See *panel data*.

Long-run cumulative dynamic multiplier: The cumulative long-run effect on the time series variable Y of a change in X.

Marginal probability distribution: Another name for the probability distribution of a random variable Y, which distinguishes the distribution of Y alone (the marginal distribution) from the joint distribution of Y and another random variable.

Maximum likelihood estimator (MLE): An estimator of unknown parameters that is obtained by maximizing the likelihood function; see Appendix 9.2.

Mean: The expected value of a random variable. The mean of Y is denoted μ_Y.

Moments of a distribution: The expected value of a random variable raised to different powers. The rth moment of the random variable Y is $E(Y^r)$.

Multicollinearity: See *perfect multicollinearity* and *imperfect multicollinearity*.

Multiple regression model: An extension of the single variable regression model that allows Y to depend on k regressors.

Natural experiment: See *quasi-experiment*.

Natural logarithm: See *logarithm*.

95% confidence set: A confidence set with a 95% confidence level; see *confidence interval*.

Nonlinear least squares: The analog of OLS that applies when the regression function is a nonlinear function of the unknown parameters.

Nonlinear regression function: A regression function with a slope that is not constant.

Nonstationary: When the joint distribution of a time series variable and its lags changes over time.

Normal distribution: A commonly used bell-shaped distribution of a continuous random variable.

Null hypothesis: The hypothesis being tested in a hypothesis test, often denoted by H_0.

Observational data: Data based on observing, or measuring, actual behavior outside an experimental setting.

Observation number: The unique identifier assigned to each entity in a data set.

OLS estimator. See *ordinary least squares estimator*.

OLS regression line: The regression line with population coefficients replaced by the OLS estimators.

OLS residual: The difference between Y_i and the OLS regression line, denoted by $\hat{u}_i$ in this textbook.

Omitted variables bias: The bias in an estimator that arises because a variable that is a determinant of Y and is correlated with a regressor has been omitted from the regression.

One-sided alternative hypothesis: The parameter of interest is on one side of the value given by the null hypothesis.

Order of integration: The number of times that a time series variable must be differenced to make it stationary. A time series variable that is integrated of order p must be differenced p times and is denoted $I(p)$.

Ordinary least squares estimator: The estimator of the regression intercept and slope(s) that minimizes the sum of squared residuals.

Overidentification: When the number of instrumental variables exceeds the number of included endogenous regressors.

p-value: The probability of drawing a statistic at least as adverse to the null hypothesis as the one actually computed, assuming the null hypothesis is correct. Also called the marginal significance probability, the p-value is the smallest significance level at which the null hypothesis can be rejected.

Panel data: Data for multiple entities where each entity is observed in two or more time periods.

Parameter: A constant that determines a characteristic of a probability distribution or population regression function.

Partial compliance: Occurs when some participants fail to follow the treatment protocol in a randomized experiment.

Partial effect: The effect on Y of changing one of the regressors, holding the other regressors constant.

Perfect multicollinearity: Occurs when one of the regressors is an exact linear function of the other regressors.

Polynomial regression model: A nonlinear regression function that includes X, X^2, ... and X^r as regressors, where r is an integer.

Population: The group of entities—such as people, companies, or school districts—being studied.

Population coefficients: See *population intercept and slope*.

Population intercept and slope: The true, or population, values of β_0 (the intercept) and β_1 (the slope) in a single variable regression. In a multiple regression, there are multiple slope coefficients ($\beta_1, \beta_2, \ldots, \beta_k$), one for each regressor.

Population multiple regression model: The multiple regression model in Key Concept 5.2.

Population regression line: In a single variable regression, the population regression line is $\beta_0 + \beta_1 X_i$, and in a multiple regression it is $\beta_0 + \beta_1 X_{1i} + \beta_2 X_{2i} + \cdots + \beta_k X_{ki}$.

Power: The probability that a test correctly rejects the null hypothesis when the alternative is true.

Predicted value: The value of Y_i that is predicted by the OLS regression line, denoted by $\hat{Y}_i$ in this textbook.

Price elasticity: The percentage change in the quantity demanded resulting from a one percent increase in price.

Probability: The proportion of the time that an outcome (or event) will occur in the long run.

Probability density function (p.d.f.): For a continuous random variable, the area under the probability density function between any two points is the probability that the random variable falls between those two points.

Probability distribution: For a discrete random variable, a list of all the values that a random variable can take on and the probability associated with each of these values.

Probit regression: A nonlinear regression model for a binary dependent variable in which the population regression function is modeled using the cumulative standard normal distribution function.

Program evaluation: The field of study concerned with estimating the effect of a program, policy, or some other intervention or "treatment."

Pseudo out-of-sample forecast: A forecast computed over part of the sample using a procedure that is *as if* these sample data have not yet been realized.

Quadratic regression model: A nonlinear regression function that includes X and X^2 as regressors.

Quasi-experiment: A circumstance in which randomness is introduced by variations in individual circumstances that make it appear *as if* the treatment is randomly assigned.

R^2: In a regression, the fraction of the sample variance of the dependent variable that is explained by the regressors.

$\overline{R}^2$: See *adjusted R^2*.

Randomized controlled experiment: An experiment in which participants are randomly assigned to a control group, which receives no treatment, or to a treatment group, which receives a treatment.

Random walk: A time series process in which the value of the variable equals its value in the previous period, plus an unpredictable error term.

Random walk with drift: A generalization of the random walk in which the change in the variable has a nonzero mean but is otherwise unpredictable.

Regressand: See *dependent variable*.

Regression specification: A description of a regression that includes the set of regressors and any nonlinear transformation that has been applied.

Regressor: A variable appearing on the right-hand side of a regression; an independent variable in a regression.

Rejection region: The set of values of a test statistic for which the test rejects the null hypothesis.

Repeated cross-sectional data: A collection of cross-sectional data sets, where each cross-sectional data set corresponds to a different time period.

Restricted regression: A regression in which the coefficients are restricted to satisfy some condition. For example, when computing the rule-of-thumb F-statistic, this is the regression with coefficients restricted to satisfy the null hypothesis.

Root mean squared forecast error: The square root of the mean of the squared forecast error.

Rule-of-thumb F-statistic: The F-statistic computed using the sum of squared residuals in the restricted and unrestricted regression. The rule-of-thumb F-statistic is appropriate when the regression errors are homoskedastic.

Sample correlation: An estimator of the correlation between two random variables.

Sample covariance: An estimator of the covariance between two random variables.

Sample selection bias: The bias in an estimator of a regression coefficient that arises when a selection process influences the availability of data and that process is related to the dependent variable. This induces correlation between one or more regressors and the regression error.

Sample standard deviation: An estimator of the standard deviation of a random variable.

Sample variance: An estimator of the variance of a random variable.

Sampling distribution: The distribution of a statistic over all possible samples; the distribution arising from repeatedly evaluating the statistic using a series of randomly drawn samples from the same population.

Scatterplot: A plot of n observations on X_i and Y_i, in which each observation is represented by the point (X_i, Y_i).

Serial correlation: See *autocorrelation*.

Serially uncorrelated: A time series variable with all autocorrelations equal to zero.

Significance level: The prespecified rejection probability of a statistical hypothesis test when the null hypothesis is true.

Simple random sampling: When entities are chosen randomly from a population using a method that ensures that each entity is equally likely to be chosen.

Simultaneous causality bias: When, in addition to the causal link of interest from X to Y, there is a causal link from Y to X. Simultaneous causality makes X correlated with the error term in the population regression of interest.

Simultaneous equations bias: See *simultaneous causality bias.*

Size of a test: The probability that a test incorrectly rejects the null hypothesis when the null hypothesis is true.

Standard deviation: The square root of the variance. The standard deviation of the random variable Y, denoted σ_Y, has the units of Y and is a measure of the spread of the distribution of Y around its mean.

Standard error of an estimator: An estimator of the standard deviation of the estimator.

Standard error of the regression (*SER*): An estimator of the standard deviation of the regression error u.

Standard normal distribution: The normal distribution with mean equal to zero and variance equal to one, denoted $N(0, 1)$.

Standardizing a random variable: An operation accomplished by subtracting the mean and dividing by the standard deviation, which produces a random variable with a mean of zero and a standard deviation of one. The standardized value of Y is $(Y - \mu_Y)/\sigma_Y$.

Stationarity: When the joint distribution of a time series variable and its lagged values does not change over time.

Statistically insignificant: The null hypothesis (typically, that a regression coefficient is zero) cannot be rejected at a given significance level.

Statistically significant: The null hypothesis (typically, that a regression coefficient is zero) is rejected at a given significance level.

Stochastic trend: A persistent but random long-term movement of a variable over time.

Strict exogeneity: The requirement that the regression error has a mean of zero conditional on current, future, and past values of the regressor in a distributed lag model.

Student t distribution: The Student t distribution with m degrees of freedom is the distribution of the ratio of a standard normal random variable, divided by the square root of an independently distributed chi-squared random variable with m degrees of freedom divided by m. As m gets large, the Student t distribution converges to the standard normal distribution.

Sum of squared residuals (*SSR*): The sum of the squared OLS residuals.

***t*-distribution**: See *Student t distribution.*

***t*-ratio**: See *t-statistic.*

***t*-statistic**: A statistic used for hypothesis testing. See Key Concept 4.5.

Test for a difference in means: A procedure for testing whether two populations have the same mean.

Time and entity fixed effects regression model: A panel data regression that includes both entity fixed effects and time fixed effects.

Time effects: Binary variables indicating the time period in a panel data regression.

Time fixed effects: See *time effects*.

Time series data: Data for the same entity for multiple time periods.

Total sum of squares (*TSS*): The sum of squared deviations of Y_i, from its average, $\overline{Y}$.

Treatment effect: The causal effect in an experiment or a quasi-experiment; see *causal effect*.

Treatment group: The group that receives the treatment or intervention in an experiment.

TSLS: See *two stage least squares*.

Two-sided alternative hypothesis: When, under the alternative hypothesis, the parameter of interest is not equal to the value given by the null hypothesis.

Two stage least squares: An instrumental variable estimator, described in Key Concept 10.2.

Unbalanced panel: A panel data set in which some data are missing.

Unbiased estimator: An estimator with a bias that is equal to zero.

Uncorrelated: Two random variables are uncorrelated if their correlation is zero.

Underidentification: When the number of instrumental variables is less than the number of endogenous regressors.

Unit root: Refers to an autoregression with a largest root equal to one.

Unrestricted regression: When computing the rule-of-thumb F-statistic, this is the regression that applies under the alternative hypothesis, so the coefficients are not restricted to satisfy the null hypothesis.

VAR: See *vector autoregression*.

Variance: The expected value of the squared difference between a random variable and its mean; the variance of Y is denoted σ_Y^2.

Vector autoregression: A model of k time series variables consisting of k equations, one for each variable, in which the regressors in all equations are lagged values of all the variables.

Volatility clustering: When a time series variable exhibits some clustered periods of high variance and other clustered periods of low variance.

Weak instruments: Instrumental variables that have a low correlation with the endogenous regressor(s).

Weighted least squares (WLS): An alternative to OLS that can be used when the regression error is heteroskedastic and the form of the heteroskedasticity is known or can be estimated.

Index

Page numbers followed by italicized f and t refer to figures and tables, respectively.

Large-Sample Critical Values for the *t*-statistic from the Standard Normal Distibution

	Significance Level		
	10%	5%	1%
2-Sided Test (≠) Reject if $|t|$ is greater than	1.64	1.96	2.58
1-Sided Test (>) Reject if t is greater than	1.28	1.64	2.33
1-Sided Test (<) Reject if t is less than	−1.28	−1.64	−2.33